APPLIED SOCIAL RESEARCH

APPLIED SOCIAL RESEARCH

Tool for the Human Services

Second Edition

Duane R. Monette
Thomas J. Sullivan
Cornell R. DeJong
Northern Michigan University

Harcourt Brace Jovanovich College Publishers
Fort Worth   Philadelphia   San Diego
New York   Orlando   Austin   San Antonio
Toronto   Montreal   London   Sydney   Tokyo

TO MY MOTHER,
THANKS FOR EVERYTHING.
TO NANCY,
WHO ACCEPTED MY FLEETING PRESENCE.
TO SUSAN,
ACROSS THE MILES.

Publisher: Ted Buchholz
Acquisitions Editor: Christopher Klein
Project Editor: Mark Hobbs
Production Manager: Ken Dunaway
Design Supervisor: John Ritland
Cover Design: Nancy Turner
Text Design: Caliber Design Planning, Inc.

Library of Congress Cataloging-in-Publication Data

Monette, Duane R.
    Applied social research : tool for the human services / Duane R.
Monette, Thomas J. Sullivan, Cornell R. DeJong.—2nd ed.
        p.   cm.
    Bibliography: p.
    Includes index.
    1. Social service—Research—Methodology.   2. Human services—
Research—Methodology.   3. Social case work.   4. Social workers—
Professional ethics.   I. Sullivan, Thomas J., 1944–
II. DeJong, Cornell R.   III. Title.
HV11.M59   1989
361'.0072—dc20   89-15311
                                                       CIP

ISBN 0-03-026293-3

Printed in the United States of America
    2 3 4 016 10 9 8 7 6 5 4

Harcourt Brace Jovanovich, Inc.
The Dryden Press
Saunders College Publishing

Preface

The social science and human service fields have been changing in important ways over the past decade. The human services have sustained a growing emphasis on the integration of research methods and techniques into practice delivery. The social sciences have directed additional energy toward the application of research tools to help solve problems and assist practitioners with service delivery tasks. In preparing this second edition of *Applied Social Research,* we have attempted to reflect these changes by retaining and further developing our emphasis on the integration of social research and human service practice.

We have retained the interdisciplinary cooperative effort of the first edition, involving a research methodologist, a social psychologist, and a social worker. This enhances the effort to link research and practice. We conceive of social research and human service practice as allies bound by the common goals of advancing knowledge and creating a better world, goals that neither can achieve alone. We believe that researchers and practitioners have for too long gone their separate ways. Each group can learn from the other, and each has something of considerable value to offer the other. We are now at the point where we need to look for the many ways in which researchers and practitioners can merge their activities into a single enterprise. In this context the book has been useful to those in human service departments who integrate research into the students' practice education as well as to social scientists who emphasize the applied dimension of social science research methods.

The special theme of this book, then, is that there are many parallels and linkages between social research and human service practice. We outline these ideas in the first chapter and then carry this theme through the remainder of the book. This text is primarily an introduction to social research as it relates to the human services. As such, we have presented all of the topics of scientific research important for such an introduction.

But we have also offered a challenge. The challenge is for students to learn that social research has many parallels with human service practice. The challenge is also to recognize the ways in which the two can be linked—by incorporating research activities into practice settings and by shaping practice settings into research opportunities.

FEATURES

We have included a number of special features in this book that we feel will be helpful in developing an appreciation for social research and its importance to the human services. Some of these features are, as noted, new to the second edition.

Research in Practice: Each chapter includes boxed inserts entitled "Research in Practice," in which we discuss some special examples where research and practice have been linked. In this way, we emphasize the theme of the book and encourage students to consider the many ways in which this linkage can be achieved.

Computers in Research (New): Recognizing that computers have now become an integral part of both research and human service practice, we have included in many chapters boxed inserts that present some application of computers in research. These inserts require no previous experience with or knowledge of computers, and they are intended to inform students of the general capabilities of software rather than to train them to use particular types of software.

Content on Women and Minorities (New): In the second edition, we have given additional recognition to the need for human service workers to be knowledgeable of the special needs and problems of women and minorities. To this end, we have addressed in most chapters some special considerations in research methods as they apply to these groups.

Grant Proposals and Writing (New): We have added a chapter on writing grant proposals and research reports. To be knowledgeable about research, students should understand how this process works since it is integral to the tasks of securing funding and communicating research findings.

For Further Reading: Each chapter includes a brief, annotated list of books that students will find useful for pursuing chapter topics in greater depth. An important consideration in choosing readings was that they further the overall theme of the book.

Exercises for Class Discussion: Each chapter ends with a set of exercises in which we present the student with some problem or setting in human service practice and ask questions that call for students to consider the parallels and linkages between research and practice. These exercises can be used as a context for class discussion, or they can serve as out-of-class assignments. Either way, students should find them challenging and stimulating.

Appendix on Library Usage: We have included an appendix in which we discuss how to use the library, focusing specifically on the special needs of students in the human services. Although many college students will be familiar with the library by the time they take a research course, some may find they have a weakness in this area that can be strengthened by studying the appendix. Even those familiar with the library will find some new and useful information about library resources relevant to the human services.

Instructor's Manual: A manual of test items and suggested lecture and class discussion topics is available from your local Holt representative or by contacting the Sociology Editor: Holt, Rinehart and Winston, Inc., 301 Commerce Street, Suite 3700, Fort Worth, TX 76102

ACKNOWLEDGMENTS

This preface represents the end of a journey that has spanned a number of years. It affords us an opportunity to look back and reflect on the help we have received. A special note of gratitude must go to the many students who have passed through our courses over the years. Although they probably did not realize it at the time, they helped shape our own thoughts and skills as much as we tried to shape theirs. This book is much improved because they insisted on challenging our ideas.

Many people at Northern Michigan University contributed to our ability to complete this project. Richard D. Wright and Kenneth W. Kelley made available to us whatever resources they had at their disposal. Other colleagues—they know who they are—created an atmosphere that made this project not only possible but also highly rewarding. Two university librarians, Roberta Henderson and John Berens, also provided invaluable assistance.

For their many helpful suggestions and comments we also wish to thank the following reviewers: John Alessio, St. Cloud State University; John Bower, Bethel College; Gregg Carter, Bryant College; David Mitchell, University of North Carolina–Greensboro; Ron Ramke, High Point College; James Rosenthal, University of Oklahoma; Darrell Sabers, University of Arizona; Jane Strobino, Marywood College; Steven L. Vassar, Mankato State University.

We have had the pleasure of working with a number of talented editors at Holt, Rinehart and Winston. The most recent are Kris Olson and Chris Klein, who assisted us in shaping this second edition through their very helpful suggestions and criticisms and their knowledge of both the behavioral sciences and the human services.

There are many people to thank for their assistance, but, of course, we take final responsibility for whatever weaknesses this book contains—and rightly so, since we decided which advice to accept and which to ignore. But then, we should also take responsibility for whatever insight or passion we generate in the students who read this book. We hope at least a few of you come away from it with a new view of research and practice.

Finally, we have dedicated this book to those crucial people the readers will never see—the relatives, friends, companions, and lovers who put up with the fact that we have had a "mistress" these past few years in the form of a keyboard and monitor. They understood, with great patience, that the absences and the working weekends were unavoidable and important to us. To all of these people, we now put the question, "Are you free this weekend?"

DRM
TJS
CRDeJ

Contents

Research in Practice

Computers in Research

APPLIED
SOCIAL
RESEARCH

1

Research in the Human Services

This book is about the use of research in human services. The term **human services** refers to those professions whose primary goal is to enhance the relationship between people and societal institutions so that people may maximize their potential and alleviate distress. Among the human service professionals can be found social workers, psychologists, counselors, probation officers, and day-care providers. Others who are not normally considered human service professionals, such as teachers and nurses, contribute to the delivery of human services as a part of their respective tasks. For all of these groups, research is becoming increasingly essential to their delivery of human services. To illustrate how central research can be, consider the following actual case:

> Two months after giving birth to a baby boy, a young mother kills her infant son and disposes of the body by dumping it in the trash. Through a routine visit by a public health nurse, the tragedy is discovered. In the course of the investigation, it is learned that the mother had made threatening remarks about the child while still in the hospital. The local community is outraged. Why was the mother allowed to leave the hospital with the child? Why was there no police intervention? Where was the local community mental health agency? The various human service agencies of the community are called on to do something

to make sure that similar events will not happen again.

Do something. But what? The human service professionals charged with taking action can first of all turn to research studies on the nature of child abuse and the effectiveness of child abuse programs in other communities. Second, they can use research to ascertain just how much abuse actually occurs in their community. The community response will undoubtedly be different if this event is an isolated one. In addition, research can help identify factors that can predict which families are most at risk for some sort of family violence and assess the consequences of abuse in child development. Finally, once a plan is put into operation with the support of community funds, research can be conducted to assess whether the program is working properly.

Thus, there are numerous links between research and human service practice. Because research provides the means for understanding the problems with which professionals work and the means for evaluating change, practitioners in the human services are certain to encounter the need to understand, apply, and in some cases, conduct research in carrying out the goals of their professions (Reinherz, Grob, and Berkman, 1983). Some would go further and argue that the link between research and practice is even more intimate, namely, that there can be—and should be—a fruitful merger of the two. In fact, the notion that scientific research and human service practice are totally distinct enterprises is gradually disappearing (Barlow, Hayes, and Nelson, 1984). There are two reasons for this.

First, it is now recognized that there are strong parallels between the conduct of research and the conduct of practice, and practitioners can benefit by incorporating into practice some of the techniques used in research. Both research and practice, for example, are based on observation, but the observations of practitioners are often unstructured and intuitive. Thus, practitioners can benefit from some of the techniques, discussed in Chapters 7 and 9, that researchers use to make structured observations. A second reason for the changing views of research and practice is the realization that practice intervention, properly conducted, can provide scientifically valid knowledge about human behavior and the effectiveness of intervention. Practitioners, for example, can scientifically assess the effectiveness of their interventions if those interventions are organized in a manner, called "single-subject design" by researchers, that parallels the scientific experiment. We discuss single-subject designs in Chapter 11. Some illustrations of how the tasks of research have been incorporated into the very definition of the human services are provided in Research in Practice 1.1.

||||||||||||||||||||||||||||||||||||||||||||||||||||||||||||||||||||||||||||||||||||||||||||||||

RESEARCH IN PRACTICE 1.1
Practice Effectiveness: "Scientific Practice" as a Challenge to the Human Services

A few years ago, the Health Research Group, one of Ralph Nader's public citizen organizations, aimed a challenge in the direction of the human services (Adams and Orgel, 1975). The group suggested that people seeking help from human service professionals should demand a written contract, at the outset of the relationship, that specified the conditions of the therapy, the goals of the intervention, and even the site at which the therapy would take place. They also suggested that the contract specify the character of the practitioner–client relationship, especially regarding the empirical evidence showing what kind of relationship would enhance the achievement of the client's goals. Permeating these recommendations was a demand for a high degree of *accountability* on the part of the helping professions. In a sense, the group was suggesting that clients have a right to demand that practitioners justify their actions and recommendations on specific and demonstrable grounds. Though these demands for accountability are not new, they are becoming louder and broader in scope (*see* Sheafor, Horejsi, and Ho-

(Continued on next page)

rejsi, 1988). And they even come from clients themselves. Some practitioners believe that clients would be upset if systematic evaluation procedures were used in treatment. Yet, research indicates that clients are overwhelmingly in favor of the use of systematic data collection procedures to assess treatment rather than relying merely on the opinions of practitioners (Campbell, 1988).

These demands have motivated many human service professionals to begin defining the human services as a *scientific* discipline. Some have called it "scientific practice"; others use the term "data-guided practice" or "practice research" (Thomas, 1977; Bloom, 1978; Connaway and Gentry, 1988). In the field of community mental health, Abraham Jeger and Robert Slotnick (1982) have developed what they call a "behavioral–ecological" approach to the delivery of mental health services. It represents a coalescence of "behavioral" approaches that derive from psychology and "ecological" approaches found in such disciplines as anthropology and sociology. More important, they view research as an integral part of the delivery system:

> The behavioral–ecological approach emphasizes incorporation of an evaluation design into all intervention programs. As such, it represents a merging of research and service, in contrast to traditional mental health models that tend to separate research and clinical practice. . . . A major characteristic of such evaluation is that program participants are involved in all phases of the evaluation process [Jeger and Slotnick, 1982, p. 13].

On a similar note, Scott Briar (1979, pp. 132–133) challenges the social work profession to begin training "clinical scientists." By "clinical scientist," he means a direct service practitioner who

—uses practice methods that are known *empirically* to be effective
—continuously *evaluates* the outcome of practice
—participates in the *discovery, testing,* and *reporting* of effective practice techniques
—uses untested practice methods with great caution and only with adequate control and evaluation of the outcome
—*communicates* the results of evaluations to others.

In fact, the Council on Social Work Education (1987) now calls for social work education to impart an understanding and appreciation for the necessity of a scientific approach to knowledge building and practice, including the systematic evaluation of practice.

So the Jeger–Slotnick approach to the community mental health field and the Briar and CSWE approaches to the social services illustrate efforts to merge research and practice. The outcome, it is hoped, will be more effective, accountable, and creditable practitioners.

In each chapter, we will set aside separate space entitled "Research in Practice," where we will discuss particular instances where research and practice have been linked. In this fashion, students in the human services can gain a deeper understanding of the many ways in which this linkage might be achieved.

The purpose of this book is to introduce students in the human services to social research logic, methods, and design. We do this by emphasizing the parallels and linkages between research and practice. Because research and practice are intertwined, human service professionals need training in the techniques of social research as much as they need to know about group processes or theories of personality (Weinbach and Rubin, 1980). In some situations, human service providers will *consume social research* as they apply the findings of research to practice intervention. Therefore, they need to understand the logic of research and be able to assess research procedures critically to decide whether and in what fashion research findings can be introduced into practice. In other situations, human service workers may conduct social research as a part of their overall intervention strategy, so they need to know how to design and carry out scientifically valid research projects.

In this chapter, we discuss the goals of research in the human services and then illustrate five areas of human service activities in which research can make a contribution. Next, we draw some of the parallels between the steps in social research and the steps in the intervention process. Finally, we provide an overview of the plan of the book, including previews of later chapters.

Research in the Human Services

Goals of Research

The word "research" is applied to many activities: the student who browses in the library for a few hours; the social worker who, while visiting clients about other issues, makes a mental note of some of their social characteristics; the parole officer who routinely inquires, as a part of an intake interview, about a parolee's family life. All these people might claim to be doing "research." Yet the term, as it is commonly used in the social and behavioral sciences, has a considerably more precise meaning according to which none of these activities would be considered scientific research. This is not to say that these activities are unimportant. They may have a variety of uses. However, social research has very specific goals that can be achieved only through utilizing the proper procedures.

Social research *is the systematic examination (or reexamination) of empirical data, collected by someone first-hand, concerning the social or psychological forces operating in a situation.* There are three major elements in this definition. First, social research is *systematic.* That is, all aspects of the research process are carefully planned in advance, and nothing is done in a casual or haphazard fashion. The systematic nature of research is at the core of the scientific method, which will be discussed in more detail in Chapter 2. Second, social research involves the collection of *empirical data,* that is, information or facts about the world based on sensory experiences. As such, it should not be confused with philosophizing or speculating, which lack the empirical base of research. Third, social research studies *social and psychological* factors that affect human behavior. It is not concerned with biological, physiological, nutritional, or other such factors except to the extent that they affect, or are affected by, social and psychological factors.

Research in the human services generally focuses on one or more of the following goals: description, prediction, explanation, or evaluation. **Descriptive**

research has as its goal *description*, or the attempt to discover facts or describe reality. Descriptive research, for example, might deal with such questions as, What are people's attitudes toward welfare? How much child abuse is there? or, How many people avail themselves of the services of home health-care workers? Some descriptive research efforts are quite extensive. For example, the National Center for Health Statistics and the Centers for Disease Control collect voluminous amounts of data each year for purposes of describing the health status of Americans.

Predictive research focuses on *prediction*, or making projections about what will occur in the future or in other settings. Insurance companies, for example, make use of sophisticated actuarial schemes for predicting the risks involved in insuring people or property. Based on past descriptive research on deaths and injuries, they can project how long people with certain characteristics will live or the likelihood that they will suffer injuries. Such projections can also be made by the National Center for Health Statistics. For example, they can project that infants and children with particular social characteristics will have an increased likelihood of being undernourished or suffering from infectious or parasitic diseases. Armed with this information, one would find it possible to devise preventive health-care programs targeted at the high-risk groups.

Explanatory research involves *explanation*, or determining why or how something occurred. Explanatory research, for example, would go beyond describing rates of juvenile delinquency or even predicting who will engage in delinquent acts. Explanatory research would focus on *why* certain people become delinquents. Some explanatory research is

called **basic** (or **pure**) **research** in that its purpose is to advance our knowledge about human behavior with little concern for any immediate, practical benefits that might result. Many sociologists and psychologists conduct basic research. Explanatory research in the human services, however, is more likely to be **applied research**—research designed with a practical outcome in mind and with the assumption that some group or society as a whole will gain specific benefits from the research. Thus, explaining juvenile delinquency is important to social workers, probation officers, and the police because it can lead to programs intended to alleviate delinquency in a community. The goal of explanation may appear to be quite similar to that of prediction, but there is a difference: One can make predictions without an accompanying explanation. Insurance companies, for example, make actuarial predictions based on past statistical associations, often without knowing why those associations occurred.

Evaluation research focuses on *evaluation*, or the use of scientific research methods to plan intervention programs, to monitor the implementation of new programs and the operation of existing ones, and to determine how effectively programs or clinical practices achieve their goals. Evaluation research can also determine whether a program has unintended consequences that are either desirable or undesirable. In the past few decades, there has emerged a vast array of social programs—relating to poverty, child development, crime, alcoholism, delinquency, and the like—that attempt to ameliorate undesirable social conditions. As competition for funds for such programs has increased, especially in the past few years, program directors are commonly required to justify and defend their programs in terms of cost effectiveness. Thus, evaluation research is now often an integral part of human service programs.

Applications of Research

The focus of this book is on applied social research, especially the linkage of social research with the human services. Although we distinguished earlier between basic and applied research, the line between the two is vague and, in fact, even pure research can have applications in the human service field. In order to organize our thinking about the applications of research to the human services, we find it useful to think in terms of five focal areas in which this linkage occurs: understanding human functioning in social environments, needs assessment, assessment of client functioning, program evaluation, and practice effectiveness evaluation. We do not claim that this is the only way to divide up the human service field or that our list of areas is exhaustive. These five categories, however, will serve as a helpful aid as we analyze the links between research and practice. We will review each area briefly here. Then each ''Research in Practice'' in this and subsequent chapters will emphasize one of the focal areas.

Behavior and Social Environments Human service providers do many things: link people to resources they can use, enhance people's coping abilities, improve the operation of social systems, and participate in the development of social policy, to name a few. All these activities rest on an understanding of the people to whom services are provided and a comprehension of the social environment in which they function. Social research can provide much of this knowledge. An

agency providing services to pregnant teenagers, for example, can turn to research on adolescents in American society for a better understanding of the problems facing their clients. Studies of changing values among teenagers could help the agency assess the stigma their particular clients might face. Research on how families react to stress might aid in understanding how the families of pregnant teens might cope with the crisis they confront. In other words, there is a wide range of behavioral research, much of it basic research, that is only indirectly linked to practice but that can inform intervention. Human service providers need to be able to understand and assess this research in terms of whether it is sufficiently valid to incorporate into practice.

Although much research on human behavior is conducted by behavioral scientists, human service professionals themselves—therapists, social workers, nurses, and other practitioners—are increasingly doing research of this type.

Needs Assessment Social research can also be used to make an accurate assessment of the need for various forms of service and suggest alternative strategies for meeting those needs (Rossi and Freeman, 1985; McKillip, 1987). The purpose of this research is to determine whether a problem exists, to indicate the severity of the problem, and to estimate the number and characteristics of people adversely affected by the problem. Needs assessment research is often highly descriptive rather than focusing on explanation or prediction. One illustration of needs assessment research is a project that involved the cooperation of a mental health agency and a local university to collect data from a community about mental health needs and services (Witkin, 1984). Labeled a Community-Oriented Needs

Assessment (CONA), it was based on questionnaires mailed to key informants, interviews of a random sample of community residents, and profiles based on demographic statistics. From it, the mental health agency received community input into client needs, service delivery planning, and evaluation. The data were used to help plan and implement programs and to support requests for additional funds from government and other funding agencies.

Assessment of Client Functioning   In the provision of human services, it is often necessary to assess the level of functioning of clients. What kind of communication problems exist in a family? How capable is a teenage parent of dealing with the stresses of motherhood? How skilled is a person in negotiating a job interview? Though practitioners make such assessments often, there is a danger that they will be made unsystematically. In the past twenty years, there has been extensive development of systematic and, in some cases, quantitative assessment tools that can be used for both research and practice tasks. As one example, Ray McNair and associates at the University of Georgia developed two such instruments: Assessment of Adolescent Social Functioning (AASF) and Assessment of Child and Adolescent Functioning (ACAF) (McNair, 1981; McNair and McKinney, 1983). These instruments enable researchers and practitioners to assess, on a scale of 1 to 4, how well clients manage crises, solve problems, organize their family life, and cope with addiction. These assessments can be compared at different times to see if any change or improvement has occurred. Additional examples of such client assessment tools can be found in Sheafor, Horejsi, and Horejsi (1988).

Program Evaluation   In the past few decades, we have seen the burgeoning of many large, ambitious, and expensive programs intended to cope with social problems and provide services to individuals. Along with the growth of these programs has emerged an increasing concern over their results: Do they achieve their intended goals? These programs are costly, and some evaluation is needed to assess whether resources are being used effectively. Equally important, a program that fails to achieve its goals leaves a problem unsolved or a service undelivered. *Program evaluation* is the use of scientific research techniques to assess the results of a program and evaluate whether the program as currently designed achieves its stated goals (Rutman, 1984). For example, one such evaluation project was part of an attempt in New York to replace foster care with a new method of providing services to children of families in need (Jones, 1976). The innovation was a response to a dramatic increase in the number of children in foster care and rapidly rising costs per child of providing that care. A program was developed around the idea that rather than using foster care, the family unit could be preserved by providing intensive services such as family casework, homemaker services, and vocational and referral services. In order to assess whether the program was effective, authorities provided some families with the intensive family services while other, comparable families were served as usual by the child welfare system (which, in most cases, meant foster care). The effectiveness of the program was then determined by comparing the two groups after one year in terms of the cost of providing services to each group, the amount of services provided, and the level of functioning of parents and children. The results of the program indicated that it was a success by all criteria.

It is crucial that human service providers understand when program evaluation is called for and when it is possible to conduct an effective evaluation. In addition, many practitioners will likely find themselves participating in programs that will include evaluation as one of their goals.

Practice Effectiveness Evaluation

Whereas program evaluation focuses on the assessment of entire programs, the concern of human service professionals is often considerably more specific; namely, "Is what I am doing right now with this particular client working?" For this reason, practitioners have often been disenchanted with the utility of evaluation research as a direct aid to helping clients. However, in recent years there have been major advances in the capacity of research to answer professionals' questions about the efficacy of intervention efforts on specific clients.

One form of such research is called *single-subject design,* where clinicians devise a way to measure the occurrence of a problem and monitor the behavior of a client for a baseline period. Then intervention begins, and the behavior is again monitored. Comparison between the baseline and intervention periods permits the practitioner to make more accurate assessments of progress than the informal assessment on which human service professionals have traditionally relied. The procedures can be quite elaborate, but even a beginning staff member can readily apply the basic model. For example, an undergraduate student recently submitted a paper that described her work with a young mother who was trying to reduce the thumb-sucking behavior of her six-year-old daughter. Adapting

a measurement scheme reported in a professional journal, the student designed a monitoring system involving observation of the child by means of a small piece of litmus paper taped to the child's thumb. Through this procedure it was possible to determine how much time the child actually spent thumb-sucking and to specify the conditions under which the behavior occurred. A behavior modification procedure was implemented, and the amount of thumb-sucking declined dramatically. (Single-subject research will be discussed at length in Chapter 11.) Through such careful monitoring of behavior and measuring of intervention effects, it is possible for the individual human service worker not only to enhance his or her own effectiveness but also to contribute to the development of an intervention technology that others can successfully apply.

There are obvious similarities between program evaluation and practice effectiveness research. Both, for example, are concerned with the effectiveness of certain practices. The difference, however, is in the scope of the efforts. Program evaluation focuses on complete programs whereas practice effectiveness research emphasizes the assessment of some particular aspect of a practice situation in a way that will not necessarily affect the entire program.

Special Issues in Human Service Research

The human services devote special attention to the problems of minority groups, whether their minority status be a function of race, ethnicity, sex, or something else. The reason for this special attention is twofold: First, minorities tend to suffer disproportionately from the problems that human service workers attempt to alleviate; second, there are many social conditions that affect minorities very negatively and limit their opportunities and achievements. Because of the position of minorities in American society, conducting research that produces accurate and complete data on them can be a challenge. In fact, there are circumstances in which the standard research methods used in human service research result in misleading and, in some cases, outright false conclusions regarding a minority.

This problem is sufficiently important to modern human service research that we will devote special attention to it throughout the book. In each chapter where it is relevant, we will point to particular ways in which problems or biases in research on minorities can occur. We will also discuss strategies for overcoming these problems and biases. The goal is to create a sensitivity to the fact that research methods can have built-in biases when focused on particular minority groups and that care must be exercised to detect and avoid this.

Parallels Between Research and Practice

Although scientific research is different in many respects from human service practice, there are important parallels between the two. In fact, researchers and practitioners use many of the same strategies in approaching their problems. After reviewing the steps in conducting research, we will point out parallels that can be found in practice.

Steps in Conducting Research

Although each research project is unique in some fashion, there are some general

steps through which virtually every project proceeds. The research process can be divided into five identifiable stages: problem formulation, research design development, data collection, data analysis, and drawing conclusions.

Problem Formulation The first step in conducting social research is to decide on the problem that will be researched. When first encountering the issue of problem formulation, students commonly question its importance. There are so many problems around that it would appear to be a simple matter to select one on which to conduct research. However, such a casual view of scientific problem formulation is erroneous. For example, some problems about which we might desire answers are not scientific questions at all, and no amount of research will answer them. Other problems, though possibly interesting and intriguing, might prove impractical from a methodological, ethical, or financial standpoint.

Another element of problem formulation is to shape a concern into a specific researchable question. Such global concerns as "the state of the modern family" are far too broad to be considered research problems. They need to be narrowed down to specific problems for which empirical data can be gathered, such as, What is the divorce rate? How does it compare with the divorce rate of past years? or, Do children raised in single-parent families exhibit poorer social development than children raised in two-parent families? As the initial step in research, developing a researchable problem is highly important. In Chapter 4, we outline the many issues involved in this process.

Research Design Development Having successfully established a researchable problem, we next must develop a **research design,** a detailed plan outlining how observations will be made. It is a plan followed by the researcher as the project is carried out. The research design may be either very formal, as when the research design is a part of a grant proposal, or quite informal if it is only for the researcher's own use. Regardless of its degree of formality, the research design will always address itself to certain key issues, such as who will be studied, how these people will be selected, and what information will be gathered from or about them. In fact, the research design spells out in considerable detail what will occur in the following stages of the research process. Chapters 7 to 11 describe the different kinds of research designs and issues that must be considered in their development.

Data Collection   A part of any research design is a description of what data will be collected and how this will be done. The data collected at this stage constitute the basic information from which conclusions will be drawn, so great care must be exercised. Two aspects of data collection, *pretests* and *pilot studies,* illustrate just how careful scientists are about this. The **pretest,** as the name implies, is a preliminary application of the data-gathering technique for the purpose of determining its adequacy. It would certainly be risky and unwise to jump prematurely into data gathering without first knowing that all the data collection procedures are sound. For example, if our study were a needs assessment of homemakers to determine how many would make use of occupational training services, we would choose a small group of homemakers and collect the same data from them that we plan to collect in the final project. It is, in a sense, a "trial run." And, unless we are

very good or very lucky, some modifications in the data collection technique will likely be required based on the results of the pretest. After these modifications are made, the technique is pretested again. Additional pretests are always desirable after any modifications in the data-gathering technique in order to assess whether the modifications handle the problems encountered in the previous pretest.

In some cases, it may even be necessary to do a **pilot study,** which is a small-scale "trial run" of all the procedures planned for use in the main study. In addition to administering the data-gathering instrument, a pilot study might also include such things as a test of the procedures for selecting the sample and an application of the statistical procedures to be used in the data analysis stage.

It is this kind of care in data collection that improves the validity of the data collected and bolsters our confidence in the conclusions drawn.

Data Analysis   As with data collection, data analysis is spelled out in the research design. Despite this preplanning, it can be the most challenging and interesting aspect of a research project. It is challenging because data in raw form can be quite unrevealing. Data analysis is what unlocks the information hidden in the raw data and transforms it into something useful and meaningful. It is interesting because it is during data analysis that one learns whether one's ideas are confirmed or refuted by empirical reality. During the course of data analysis, researchers often make use of statistical tools that can range from simple percentages to very complex statistical tests that require much training to understand and master. These statistics aid in communicating the findings of research to others. Once the special language and interpretations of statistics have been learned, one can be more effective at communicating research findings in a clear, concise manner than conventional English. In Chapter 14, we will review some of the basic data analysis and data manipulation techniques that are used in social research. We will see there that modern data analysis is typically done with computers, so a research design must specify data collection procedures that are compatible with computer equipment.

Drawing Conclusions The final step in conducting social research is to draw some conclusions from the data analysis. The form this takes depends in part on the goals of the research project. A descriptive study, for example, would simply present what was found, possibly in a summarized form to make it more easily understood. Predictive research and explanatory research, on the other hand, usually have hypotheses, or statements of what the researchers expect to find, stated before the data are collected. In this case, a major element of drawing conclusions is to assess how much support there is for the hypotheses. The support that data provide for hypotheses can range from strong to weak to none, and researchers have an obligation to those who might use their research to represent accurately the strength of their findings. Finally, in evaluation research, drawing conclusions would normally involve making a judgment about the adequacy and effectiveness of programs and changes that might improve conditions.

It is not uncommon for research to discover some things that do not relate directly to any specific hypothesis or things that are completely unanticipated. When drawing conclusions, the researchers should make note of the implications of any such findings that are of sufficient importance to warrant mention. When complete, the conclusions should clearly indicate what has been learned by conducting the research and the impact of this new knowledge.

Steps in Practice Intervention

With these five steps in conducting social research clearly in mind, consider the following phases of practice intervention and how they parallel the steps in research (see Figure 1.1).

Problem Assessment In much the same way that social researchers must decide on the problem that will be researched, practitioners must specify the precise problem with which they are con-

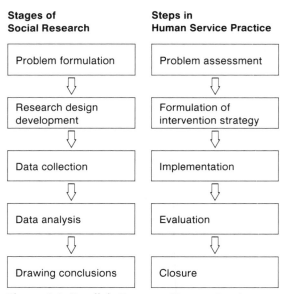

Figure 1.1 Parallels Between Human Service Practice and Social Research

cerned, what factors might contribute to the problem, and which aspects of the problem will be given priority. In problem formulation, researchers make judgments concerning the feasibility of researching a particular phenomenon. Likewise, in problem assessment, practitioners must decide which behavioral systems are involved in a problem —individual, group, or societal—and whether effective intervention is possible.

Formulation of Intervention Strategy

Just as researchers develop a research design, practitioners develop a strategy for intervention that will be effective in alleviating the problem specified in the assessment stage. Whereas researchers choose among a variety of research methods, practitioners choose among numerous intervention strategies, such as crisis intervention, behavior modification, or vocational training. Just as researchers may use more than one research technique over the course of a research project, so practitioners often use more than one intervention strategy in attacking a problem.

Implementation Following the development of the research design, researchers proceed to put it into practice. In similar fashion, practitioners implement the intervention strategies outlined in the preceding stage. Researchers' activities are normally limited to data collection, and they do not attempt to change the people they are studying. Practitioners, on the other hand, may collect data as a part of the implementation stage, but they are primarily concerned with the effectiveness of the intervention strategy in creating some change in clients or the systems in which they interact.

Evaluation Once researchers have collected their data, they analyze it in order to determine what their study has found. Similarly, practitioners evaluate the effectiveness of the intervention strategy implemented at the preceding stage. Were the goals of the plan achieved? What were the costs of the strategy? Were there any undesirable side effects of the changes brought about by the intervention? Which aspects of the intervention process seemed to be most important in producing the change that resulted?

Closure The final stage of the research process is to draw conclusions. The final stage for practitioners is also to bring some closure to the intervention effort. The extent to which the intervention has been effective must be determined and also the degree to which the goals of the intervention cannot be, and possibly never will be, achieved. Researchers may make suggestions for future research that might be helpful in further clarifying the relationships found in the study. Likewise, practitioners might suggest other sources of help that the client could use to cope with problems still unresolved by the intervention. In other words, for both researchers and practitioners, the conclusion is a time to look both back over what has been accomplished and forward to directions and alternatives for the future.

By this point, you should be gaining an appreciation for the parallels and linkages between social research and human service practice. The parallels involve the similarities between the activities of researchers and those of practitioners. The linkages involve the contributions that research can make to practice endeavors, and vice versa. In fact, as pointed out in Research in Practice 1.2, there are ways

||||||||||||||||||||||||||||||||||||||||||||||||||||||||||||||||||||||||||||||||||||||||||||||||||||||||||||||||||

RESEARCH IN PRACTICE 1.2
Practice Effectiveness: The Social Agency as a Research Machine

A central point of this first chapter has been the importance of research skills for human service workers. To document this, one study of social workers in agencies found that 73 percent had participated in a program evaluation, 66 percent had conducted a needs assessment, 36 percent had written a research grant proposal, and 35 percent had conducted a research project (Gentry, Connaway, and Morelock, 1984). In fact, the reciprocal relationship between practice and research is so central that suggestions have been made to reorganize human service delivery in such a way that it can make an even more valuable contribution to research. Along these lines, William Reid, a researcher and clinical practice theorist in social work, has suggested that social agencies can become "research machines" (Reid, 1978). Social agencies collect considerable amounts of data, in the form of case records, that are often a part of a computerized information system. These data are collected as a part of the everyday service delivery tasks of the agency, but they can also serve as data for research into many questions important to the agency.

If agencies are viewed not only as service delivery systems but also as "research machines," some reorganization could enhance their research potential. Reid suggests the following changes:

1. Build research questions into the routine collection of case information rather than simply attempt to devise problems from the data.
2. Devote special care and consideration to the selection and development of recording formats. Many data in agency records are ambiguous and haphazard, but with attention, this problem can be reduced.
3. Structure practice in such a way that goals and targets are clear and the intervention is well specified. This contributes to the utility of case records for research.
4. Rely on multiple data sources. Reid suggests, in addition to using the impressions of human service workers, also using client questionnaires, direct observation of client behavior, and other methods to supplement the primary case record approach.

The extent to which the research potential of social agencies is realized in the future depends on human service professionals with a knowledge of, and interest in, research and a commitment to scientifically based practice. Both improved practice and increased knowledge of human behavior and the social environment can be fruits of the same endeavor. As you learn more about research in the human services, you will begin to grasp numerous ways in which Reid's suggestions can be applied.

in which these parallels and linkages can be made even more explicit and direct.

The Plan of the Book

This first chapter has discussed the extent to which research is fundamental to the delivery of human services. The remainder of the book discusses how research is applied to the human services. Chapters 2 to 6 present some of the important issues that underlie research, including the role of hypotheses and theories and ethical problems that researchers are likely to confront. We will also address the issue of how to formulate a research problem and select a scientifically sound sample on which observations will be made.

With Chapter 7, we begin the first of five chapters on specific research techniques. Chapter 7 covers *survey research*, which is a very widely used data collection technique based on obtaining people's responses to questions. In Chapter 8, we discuss the use of *available data* in research. Though not as common as surveys, available data can be useful to human service researchers. The records kept by prisons, hospitals, or social service agencies, for example, would fall into the category of available data that could be used for research. Chapter 9 presents *observational methods*, which involve the observation of people's behavior. This is also a common research technique in the human services because human service practitioners typically make observations of clients in the course of intervention. In Chapter 10, we discuss *experiments*, which are research techniques designed to assess the effect of one factor on another. Although human service providers may only occasionally conduct conventional experiments, they are often in a position to

carry out single-subject research, the topic of Chapter 11. *Single-subject research* involves assessing the impact of some factor on the feelings or actions of a client, and it derives its basic logic from the experimental designs discussed in Chapter 10.

The remaining four chapters focus on issues that override the specific research methods used in a particular study. *Evaluation research*, discussed in Chapter 12, refers to assessing how well a particular program or practice achieves its goals. This has become an increasingly important element in the human services, and evaluation researchers often use some or all of the five research techniques discussed in the preceding five chapters. In Chapter 13, we analyze how to develop *scales*, which are a type of measuring device in which a single composite score is derived from a number of other scores that measure something of interest. Chapter 14 offers an introduction to *data analysis*, or what to do with numerical data once they are collected. Chapter 15 is an introduction to the *grant-seeking process*, or how to find financial support for research, including how to write grant proposals and research reports.

Computers have now become an important tool in the research process. In fact, as one recent assessment concluded, "The entire research process . . . can now be directed and/or accomplished with available microcomputer software. . . ." (Carpenter, 1987: 529). In recognition of this, we have included, beginning with this chapter, an insert in most chapters titled "Computers in Research." Each one describes a particular research use of the computer that is relevant to the topic of the chapter.

The book ends with three appendices. The first is a guide to using the library for

||||||||||||||||||||||||||||||||||||||||||||||||||||||||||||||||||||||||||||||||||||||||||||||||||||||||||||||||||||||

COMPUTERS IN RESEARCH
The Case for Applications

The computer, more than any other single invention, stands as a symbol of technological progress in the late 20th century. This ubiquitous device has entered all areas of society, including the human services. A few decades ago, computer applications in the human services were limited to accounting and bureaucratic recordkeeping. In fact, the impersonality and quantification that computers seem to need were viewed as antithetical to the personal and qualitative approach of human service practitioners. By the 1990s, computers have become an integral part of virtually all human service activities (Parker et al., 1987; Nurius, Hooyman, and Nicoll, 1988).

The traditional use of computers in social research has been to assist in coding and analyzing data. In later chapters, we will describe computer software that can run statistical tests, assist in interviewing respondents, help select a sample to use in data collection, and accomplish a host of other activities related directly to research fundamentals. (The term *software* refers simply to programs that instruct the computer in what to do.) However, computers today have many uses beyond these traditional ones. They can assist in the literature review process through computerized data base searches available at most libraries; they help in report preparation as word processors; and graphic display programs have become essential in producing charts and figures to communicate the findings of research.

Computers are also rapidly entering use for human service practice tasks, and with creativity, these service-delivery applications can be harnessed to make applied research easier and more feasible. This service base also increases the possibilities for making use of research in practice. Our discussion of computer applications illustrates a central theme of this book: That there are important linkages between social research and human service practice, and the imaginative application of computer technology is yet another way of forging this linkage.

For example, practitioners can do assessments of clients with ready-made computer programs. Evaluative systems such as the Clinical Measurement Package described elsewhere in the text are being automated for ease in administration and scoring. Computer programs can provide clinicians with data to assist in diverse tasks from assessing marital interaction to making child-placement decisions.

Data base programs are being applied to client recordkeeping. This is especially useful in the cases of geriatric patients or the chronically ill where records may be long and complex. The computer has potential for developing treatment plans and saving time in record reviews.

Although the use of computers in

therapy is controversial, there are several situations, such as self-help therapies, bio-feedback, and patient education, in which computers have been used creatively. Clinical history-taking is another task to which the computer can readily be applied—specifically, for example, in the Diagnostic Interview Schedule of the National Institute of Mental Health. This program can be administered by computer or by an interviewer without clinical training. The data gathered through this process are then computer scored by standard diagnostic systems including the *Diagnostic and Statistical Manual of Mental Disorders*, Third Edition, published by the American Psychiatric Association in 1980. This system is being used to develop an extensive data base for studying mental health problems in the United States.

Throughout this text, we will be featuring a number of computer applications that can contribute to the research process. Our goal is not to teach the student *how* to use computer software since this depends on what kind of software and computers you have available at your school, home, or agency; instead, our purpose is to educate the reader regarding the range of computer uses in the field of social research today and to stimulate thinking about ways of using this technology to link practice with research. This will enable you, when confronted with a research problem, to search for the computer tools that can assist in solving the problem.

research in the human services. Effective use of library resources is an essential step in most research projects. The second appendix presents ways of generating and using tables of random numbers. Random numbers have a number of uses in research and will be discussed in several chapters. The third appendix presents codes of ethics regarding research from two professional organizations.

☰ Main Points

- The human services are those professions having the goal of enhancing the relations between people and societal institutions to enable people to maximize their potential and alleviate distress.

- Both research and practice are based on observation, but practice can benefit from adopting the techniques of scientific observation.

- Research has become a fundamental part of delivering human services.

- A knowledge of research is necessary for both consumers of social research and those who produce it.

- Social research is a systematic examination of empirical data concerning social or psychological forces.

- Social research seeks to achieve the goals of description, prediction, explanation, and evaluation.

• The numerous links between social research and human service practice include understanding human functioning in social environments, needs assessment, assessment of client functioning, program evaluation, and practice effectiveness evaluation.

• Conducting accurate and unbiased research on members of minority groups confronts social researchers with special problems that must be attended to.

• Research and practice follow similar, parallel paths in approaching a problem.

☰ Important Terms for Review

applied research
basic research
descriptive research
evaluation research
explanatory research
human services
pilot study
predictive research
pretest
pure research
research design
social research

☰ For Further Reading

Bailey, Kenneth D. *Methods of Social Research*, 3d ed. New York: The Free Press, 1987.
A comprehensive textbook in social research by a sociologist. Any standard research methods text, such as Bailey's, would be a helpful supplement to this book.

Barlow, D. H., S. C. Hayes, and R. O. Nelson. *The Scientist-Practitioner: Research and Accountability in Clinical and Educational Settings.* New York: Pergamon, 1984.
This is an excellent book on the linkage of research and practice. While it focuses on psychology, it will be of interest to any professional attempting to establish a scientist-practitioner model.

Fanshel, David. *Future of Social Work Research.* Washington, D.C.: National Association of Social Workers, Inc., 1980.
An excellent assessment of the ways in which research can be linked to social work practice.

Finsterbush, Kurt, and Annabelle Bender Motz. *Social Research for Policy Decisions.* Belmont, Calif.: Wadsworth, 1980.
An excellent, brief book about research as it might be used by decision makers attempting to influence public policy.

Gilbert, Neil, and Harry Specht, eds. *Handbook of the Human Services.* Englewood Cliffs, N.J.: Prentice-Hall, 1981.
Although this book focuses primarily on service delivery, it emphasizes the integration of research into both direct and indirect practice.

Kemeny, John G. *A Philosopher Looks at Science.* Princeton, N.J.: D. Van Nostrand, 1959.
A discussion of the philosophical underpinnings of science and scientific research. To truly understand research, you need some knowledge of the basic logic of science, a field generally referred to as the "philosophy of science."

McCain, Garvin, and Ervin M. Segal. *The Game of Science*, 5th ed. Pacific Grove, Calif.: Brooks/Cole, 1988.
This is an easy to read, yet fairly complete overview of the logic of science. It has served as a useful supplement for college students for many years.

Rothman, Jack. *Social R & D: Research and Development in the Human Services.* Englewood Cliffs, N.J.: Prentice-Hall, 1980.
An effort to apply research and development technologies commonly used in industrial settings to the problem-solving tasks confronted in the human services.

Stricker, George, and Robert H. Keisner, eds. *From Research to Clinical Practice: The Implications of Social and Developmen-*

tal Research for Psychotherapy. New York: Plenum, 1985.

An excellent book of readings on the ways that research can be of value in human service practice. A number of authors address the issue of the tensions that can emerge between researchers and practitioners.

Zimbalist, Sidney E. *Historic Themes and Landmarks in Social Welfare Research.* New York: Harper & Row, 1977.

A historical overview of how research has been used to enhance social work practice going back into the last century.

☰ Exercises for Class Discussion

Use the case illustration presented below to do the following exercises.

> While out of the office on a home call, a teacher's aid for the first grade at a rural school called the Intermediate School District office where you serve as a school social worker. In addition to identifying information, the secretary left you a message that contains the following details:
>
> "Janet has been absent from school for 8 days—illness, she says—and she is now back in school. Janet's mother and father are separating. The mother moved out; Janet, age 6, remained with the father. Now, the mother has returned, but the father moved out last week. Janet says that a 15-year-old girl is baby-sitting for her and her 2-year-old brother all the time. She hates the sitter. Her mother works at the A & P store and hasn't responded to attendance letters. Janet is really upset and isn't doing schoolwork. She bursts into tears at the mention of her family.
>
> Janet's regular teacher is out for maternity leave."
>
> The school district is asking you to look into Janet's situation.

1.1 We have emphasized the parallels between practice and research. With this in mind, do the following:

a. Make a list of some problems in this referral that call for human service intervention. What additional information would you need in order to formulate an intervention plan?

b. Make a list of research problems or questions that are suggested in this referral. How is this list similar to or different from your list of intervention problems?

1.2 Professional journals typically include a mixture of research articles, practice- and service-delivery descriptions, and policy issue discussions. Select recent issues of a major journal in your profession, such as *Social Work,* and identify those articles that qualify as research articles. Two or three students should independently review the same journal issue so that findings can be compared. What features distinguish a research article from other articles?

1.3 This chapter discusses several goals of research. For each of the research articles located for Exercise 1.2, determine whether it is primarily descriptive, predictive, explanatory, or evaluative. Explain why you classified each article as you did. If you are uncertain as to how an article should be classified, indicate why and state what additional information is needed to help you classify the study.

1.4 For each research study, state how it applies to human service practice in terms of the five focal areas discussed in the chapter.

2

The Logic
of Social Research

After dashing through the Looking-glass House in order to view its garden, Alice says:

> I should see the garden far better . . . if I could get to the top of that hill: and here's a path that leads straight to it—at least, no, it doesn't do *that* . . . but I suppose it will at last. But how curiously it twists! It's more like a corkscrew than a path! Well *this* turn goes to the hill, I suppose—no it doesn't! This goes straight back to the house! Well then, I'll try it the other way [Carroll, 1946, pp. 21–22].

Understanding the world—especially human behavior—sometimes bears a striking resemblance to Alice's convoluted and frustrating journey. People do what we least expect, without any apparent rhyme or reason. A prisoner on parole who appeared to be "making it on the outside" suddenly commits another offense and lands back in jail; a marriage of 25 years that seemed to be quite solid suddenly ends in divorce; a respected and successful business executive commits suicide. Human service providers, in particular, are familiar with experiences such as these, and the "path" to understanding seems to mirror Alice's "corkscrew."

Science, however, provides us with a method for mapping and understanding that corkscrew. In this chapter, we will discuss the basic logic underlying scientific research, beginning with an assessment of how science differs from other ways of gaining knowledge. Then we will analyze the importance of theories and their role in scientific research, drawing a parallel with the use of theories in human service practice. Following this, the role of concepts and hypotheses will be discussed, showing how hypotheses serve to link theory and research. Finally, we will analyze the nature of causality because research is, at its core, a search for cause-and-effect relationships among phenomena.

Sources of Knowledge

Human service practice is based on a knowledge of human behavior and the social environment. There are numerous ways of gaining such knowledge, but all sources of knowledge have their pitfalls. We have argued in Chapter 1 that practice knowledge should be grounded in scientific research. This does not mean that science is infallible, but science does have advantages as a source of knowledge that make it superior to other ways of gaining knowledge.

To see why this is the case, we will contrast science with three other common sources of knowledge: tradition, experience, and common sense. We will then discuss how science can improve professional practice.

Tradition

Traditional knowledge is knowledge based on custom, habit, and repetition. It is founded on a belief in the sanctity of ancient wisdom and the ways of our forebears. People familiar with the musical *Fiddler on the Roof* will recall how the delightful character Tevye, a dairyman in the village of Anatevka, sang the praises of tradition:

> Because of our traditions, we've kept our balance for many, many years. Here in Anatevka we have traditions for everything—how to eat, how to sleep, how to wear clothes. . . . You may ask, how did this tradition start? I'll tell you— I don't know! But it's a tradition. Because of our traditions, everyone knows who he is and what God expects him to do. Tradition. Without our traditions, our lives would be as shaky as—as a fiddler on the roof! [Stein, 1964, pp. 1, 6]

For Tevye and the villagers of Anatevka, it is unimportant where traditions come from. Traditions provide guidance; they offer "truth"; they are the final word. Tradition tells us that something is correct because it has always been done that way.

Traditional knowledge is widespread in all societies. Many people, for example, believe that the two-parent family is preferable to the single-parent family in that the former provides a more stable and effective socializing experience for children and reduces the likelihood of maladjustment. In some cases, these beliefs are grounded in religious traditions, whereas in other cases they are accepted because "everybody knows" how important two parents are to a child's development. In fact, some human service providers accept these beliefs about the traditional two-parent family despite the existence of considerable research suggesting that the two-parent family may *not* always be the best setting for adoptive children or those in need of foster care (Wollins, 1969; Shireman and Johnson, 1986). Human service providers can be affected in other ways by traditional beliefs. For example, the works of a Sigmund Freud or an Erik Erikson might be accepted without question, and emphasis might be placed on remaining true to their words rather than assessing the accuracy or utility of their ideas.

Tradition can be an important source of knowledge, especially in such areas as moral judgments or value decisions, but it does have some major disadvantages. First, it is extremely resistant to change, even in those cases where change might be necessary because of the surfacing of new information or developments. Second, traditional knowledge easily confuses knowledge (an understanding of what *is*) with values (a preference for what *ought* to be). For many people, the traditional emphasis on the two-parent family is actually based on a value regarding the preferred family form rather than a knowledge of the effect such a family has on child development.

Experience

Experience as a source of knowledge refers to firsthand, personal observations of events. **Experiential knowledge** is based on the assumption that truth and understanding can be achieved through personal experience and that eyewitnessing events will lead to an accurate comprehension of those events.

Experience is a common source of knowledge for human service workers who have numerous opportunities to make firsthand observations of emotionally disturbed children, the physically handicapped, foster children, and other service populations. From these contacts, practitioners can develop an understanding—not necessarily accurate—of what motivates their clients and what social or psychological processes have influenced them.

For example, a person working in a spouse-abuse shelter will have considerable contact with women who have been physically and psychologically abused by their husbands. Because of this, the person is likely to be sensitive to the harm that can come to women from their husbands. After seeing women who have been so abused, this worker may conclude that marital counseling with such spouses cannot work in a climate of violence and anger and may even be dangerous. In fact, social worker Liane Davis (1984) found that shelter workers were much less likely to recommend marital counseling than were family court judges. Family court judges did not have the powerful experience of seeing women when the effects of their abuse were most visible, and they have a mandate to maintain the integrity of the family. For them, marital counseling seems both a feasible and an appropriate way to keep the family intact. However, this does not mean that the recommendations of family court judges are better for the battered women since the judges are being influenced by the court mandate. So, the experiences of shelter workers and judges in different settings can lead them to perceive the problem differently and assess solutions differently.

This experiential knowledge about family dynamics and abuse may be reinforced by traditional knowledge about the importance of family life. Armed with this knowledge, a practitioner might shape an intervention effort that focuses on individual counseling or marital counseling.

However, experiential knowledge should be relied on only with great caution because it has some severe limitations that can lead to erroneous conclusions. First, human perceptions are notoriously unreliable. Perception is affected by many factors, including the cultural background and the mood of the observer, the conditions under which something is observed, and the nature of what is being observed. Even under the best conditions, some misperception is likely, and thus, knowledge based on experience is often inaccurate.

Second, human knowledge and understanding do not result from direct perception but rather from *inferences* made from those perceptions. The conclusion that marital counseling doesn't work is an inference—it is not directly observed. All that has been observed is that these women have been battered by their husbands. There is no observation of the effectiveness of any type of counseling. (Later in this chapter, we will discuss in more detail this problem of making inferences from observations when we address the issue of causality.)

Third, the very people in a position to experience something directly frequently have a vested interest in perceiving that thing in a certain way. A teacher, for example, observes that the students who do poorly are the ones who do not pay strict attention during class. However, this teacher has a vested interest in showing that his or her teaching techniques are not the reason for poor performance among his or her students. This teacher would probably be inclined to attribute his or her students' failings to their lack of effort and attentiveness rather than to his or her own inadequacies as a teacher.

Common Sense

The accumulation of knowledge from tradition and experience often blends together to form what people call **"common sense"**: practical judgments based on the experiences, wisdoms, and prejudices of a people. People with common sense are presumed to be able to make sound decisions even though they lack any specialized training and knowledge. Yet, is common sense a very accurate source of knowledge? Consider the following contradictory examples. Common sense tells us that people with similar interests and inclinations will likely associate with one another. And when we see a youngster who smokes marijuana associating with others who do the same, we may sagely comment that "birds of a feather flock together." Then, we see an athletic woman become involved with a bookish, cerebral man, and we say "opposites attract."

In other words, common sense often explains everything—even when those explanations conflict with one another. Not that common sense is unimportant or always useless. Common sense can be valuable and accurate, which is not surprising because people need sound information as a basis for interacting with others and functioning in society. However, common sense does not normally involve a rigorous and systematic attempt to distinguish reality from fiction. Rather, it tends to accept what "everyone knows" to be true and to reject contradictory information. Furthermore, common sense is often considered something people either have or don't have because it is not teachable. In fact, it is often contrasted with "book learning." This discourages people from critically assessing their commonsense knowledge and tempering it with knowledge acquired from other sources. For this reason, commonsense knowledge should be accepted and used cautiously. As a basis for human service practice, knowledge needs to be based on the rigorous and systematic methods used in scientific research. Common sense or a vague feeling of "helping" is not enough.

Science

Winston Churchill, prime minister of Britain during World War II, is reported to have said that democracy is an imperfect form of government but that it is far superior to all other forms of government. Many scientists have a similar view of science: They realize that it is imperfect and limited, but they also recognize that it is far superior to other sources of knowledge for gaining an understanding of the world. **Science** is a method of obtaining objective knowledge about the world through systematic observation. (The term "science" is also sometimes used to refer to the accumulated body of knowledge that results from scientific inquiry.) Science has five distinguishing characteristics that, taken together, set it apart from the other sources of knowledge.

First, science is *empirical*, which means simply that science is based on direct observation of the world. Science is not, as some people mistakenly believe, founded in theorizing, philosophizing, or speculating. Though scientists at times do all these things, they must eventually observe the world to see whether their theories or speculations agree with the facts. Because of this, the topics that can be subjected to scientific scrutiny are limited since any issue that cannot be resolved through observation is not within the scope of science. For example, the questions of whether or not God exists or which values should underlie a human service profession are not scientific issues because there is no possible way to determine their truth or falsity through observation. These are matters of faith or preference, not of science.

Second, science is *systematic*, meaning that the procedures used by scientists are organized, methodical, public, and recognized by other scientists. One dimension of the systematic nature of science is that scientists report in detail all the procedures used in coming to a conclusion. This enables other scientists to assess whether inferences and conclusions drawn are warranted given the observations that were made. A second dimension of the systematic nature of science is *replication*—repeating studies numerous times to determine if the same results will be obtained. Scientists are very cautious about drawing hard-and-fast conclusions from a single observation or investigation. In fact, quite at variance with experiential knowledge, scientists assume that a single, direct observation is as likely to be incorrect as correct. Only repeated observations can reduce the chance of error and misinterpretation.

Third, science is *the search for causes*. Scientists assume that there is order in the universe, that there are ascertainable reasons for the occurrence of all events, and that scientists can discover the orderly nature of the world. If we assume there is no order, no pattern, then there would be no need to search for it. We could write off events as due to chance or the intervention of some benevolent or malevolent otherworldly force that we can never understand.

Fourth, science is *provisional*, which means that scientific conclusions are al-

ways accepted as tentative and subject to question and possible refutation. There are no ultimate, untouchable, irrevocable truths in science. There are no scientists whose work is held in such esteem that it cannot be criticized or rejected. As philosopher Jacob Bronowski (1978, pp. 121–122) puts it: "Science is not a finished enterprise. . . . The truth is [not] a thing, that you could find . . . the way you could find your hat or your umbrella." Science is a process of continuous movement toward a more accurate picture of the world, and scientists fully realize that we may never achieve the ultimate and final picture.

Finally, science is *objective*, which means that scientists attempt to remove their biases and values from their scientific research. This doesn't mean that scientists are devoid of values. Quite the contrary, they can be as passionate, concerned, and involved as any other group of citizens. They realize, however, that their values and biases can and probably will lead to erroneous scientific conclusions. To avoid this, science incorporates mechanisms to reduce the likelihood of biased observations becoming an accepted part of the body of scientific knowledge. For example, publicizing all research procedures enables others to assess whether the research was conducted in a way that justifies the conclusions reached. Furthermore, such detailed reporting permits replication, so that other researchers, with different values, can see if they come to the same conclusions regarding a set of observations.

Despite these checks, of course, values and biases will still be found in research. The very decision of what topics to investigate, for example, is often shaped by the researcher's values. One person studies family violence because a close friend was the victim of spouse abuse, and another person studies factors contributing to job satisfaction because of a personal belief that work is central to a person's identity. Values and biases also enter research through the interpretation of observations. For personal reasons, one researcher may want desperately to show that the criminal justice system rehabilitates (or does not rehabilitate). This may well influence how he or she goes about conducting research and interpreting the results. There are even a few cases, most common in biomedical research, of outright falsification of data to show a certain conclusion. The point is that values and biases commonly intrude on scientific research, but the overall scientific enterprise is organized to reduce their impact on the body of scientific knowledge.

The scientific method, then, with the characteristics given earlier, is viewed by scientists as preferable to other ways of gaining knowledge because it is more likely to lead to accurate knowledge of the world. To return to our earlier examples on family violence, adoption, and other matters, science views all knowledge regarding the family as provisional and open to question. And there has been a number of scientific investigations of the role of the family in these matters (see Wollins, 1969; Datesman and Scarpitti, 1975; Dougherty, 1978; Gove and Crutchfield, 1982; Rankin, 1983; Peterson and Zill, 1986; and Shireman and Johnson, 1986).

Child adjustment and development in intact families and single-parent families have been observed; comparisons have been made between children receiving group care and those in more traditional family settings; comparisons have been made between the family environments of delinquents, including delinquents who have not been brought before a juvenile court, and nondelinquents.

The conclusion from these various studies is that the traditional, intact family does not seem to play the indispensable role that much commonsense knowledge would accord it. Or at least, the role of single-parent and two-parent families is more complicated than was once thought. For example, adoption by a single parent is not detrimental when compared with two-parent adoptive settings, and some children in need of foster care do quite well in group settings rather than a family. Divorce can have some negative consequences for children: Youngsters who experience divorce are more prone to delinquency and more likely to show a decline in school performance. However, these behavior problems undoubtedly are a reaction to the feelings of anger and loss surrounding the divorce rather than a response to the one-parent living arrangement. Finally, children in one-parent families may actually have some advantages over their counterparts with both parents present. Single parents sometimes give their children more responsibility and a greater role in family decision making. As a result, these youngsters become more independent and resourceful, and the parent turns to them for some of the adult support previously sought from their spouse (McCoy, 1982; Amato, 1987).

In this fashion, then, scientific knowledge overcomes many of the weaknesses of traditional, experiential, and commonsense knowledge. In particular, it enables us to accumulate accurate information despite the personal biases of individual researchers or practitioners. These positive attributes of science do not mean, however, that science is perfect. Scientists make errors. But, as Jacob

Bronowski (1978, p. 122) so aptly put it, "Science is essentially a self-correcting activity." If proper scientific procedures are followed, today's errors will be corrected by researchers in the future, whose errors in turn will be corrected by yet further research.

Scientific Practice

We saw in Chapter 1 that there are parallels between the steps in the research process and the steps in practice intervention. Likewise, human service practice has characteristics, or at least it *should* have characteristics, that parallel those of science that were just described (Barlow, Hayes, and Nelson, 1984; Jayaratne and Levy, 1979). First of all, practice, like science, should be *empirical,* stressing problem assessment involving direct observation of client problems, actual counts of behaviors, and independent observations from multiple data sources. Such data are less subject to distortion and bias than self-reports, speculations, and philosophizing. Second, practice, like research, should be *systematic.* To the extent that practice procedures are well organized, clearly specified, and made public, they can be replicated and tested by others. In this manner, ineffective procedures can be eliminated, and promising ones can be refined and improved. One of the recurring criticisms of many human service interventions is that the intervention itself is not well specified. Consequently, research evaluating the intervention cannot clearly indicate what did or did not work. Practice models also involve *causality* in terms of specifying a clear link between cause and effect or explicating why some proposed intervention should work with the particular problem that

has been identified. Again, a criticism of human service demonstration projects in the past has been that many of them have consisted of a conglomeration of intervention efforts without a clearly articulated linkage between cause and effect.

Practice theory, like science, should be *provisional.* All practice models and techniques should be viewed as fair game for criticism and refutation. It is through such a process of testing and challenging existing practices that healthy growth can occur in practice methodology. Finally, human service professionals must deal with the problem of professional *objectivity.* The determination of the utility and effectiveness of practice procedures needs to be done under objective conditions. And just as the researcher must attempt to safeguard against the intrusion of personal values into the conduct of research, so practitioners must guard against the intrusion of personal values into practice. This issue of values and objectivity is a particularly difficult one for human service practitioners who often approach problems with a strong set of values, both personal and professional. Individually, practitioners may have strong feelings about such matters as abortion, alcohol use, or prison inmates. Many practitioners have religious values that may clash with those of groups with whom they work. Furthermore, some human service providers are conventional and middle class, which may influence what they see as successful social functioning. In addition to these personal values, human service practice is often heavily imbued with professional values: "It is impossible to structure an effective change effort in which an implicit or explicit imposition of values is totally absent" (Pincus and Minahan, 1973, p. 37). In fact, there are therapeutic approaches, such as those of Carl Rogers, Albert Ellis, and Hobart Mowrer, that may include as one of their goals the acceptance of new and more realistic values on the part of the client. In addition, many human services emphasize the value of alleviating deprivation and distress and of helping people achieve their aspirations (Gordon, 1979).

As a means of controlling the imposition of practitioner values on clients, the human services emphasize the importance of client self-determination, the notion that individuals have the right to make choices about their lives freely. This can confront practitioners with a dilemma: What if self-determination leads to client choices that run counter to the practitioner's personal or professional values? For example, should practitioners work in a child welfare agency that does abortion referrals if they are morally opposed to this procedure? But the issue need not be this dramatic and is often more subtle. Mental health has often been equated with a middle-class lifestyle. "Appropriate" behavior for women has been defined in terms of a male-dominated society, with one consequence being that there are now feminist therapists who target their services to clients with a feminist orientation.

So even though professional practice in the human services is clearly oriented toward the fulfillment of certain values, practicing in the profession requires that the worker establish checks on the intrusion of values into practice, much as the researcher does in the conduct of research. In later chapters, we will discuss research techniques that are less subject than others to biases in observation and measurement. Application of these principles in practice can also help restrict the unwanted intrusion of personal values into service delivery. Another way to control the influence of values is to do research on the role of values in practice and to design agency procedures that help provide services objectively. For example, Vannicelli and Hamilton (1984) conducted a study on sex-role values and bias among alcohol treatment personnel. Their results showed that clinicians viewed female clients as having poorer prognoses than males. Furthermore, presenting problems were perceived to be more important if they were "sex appropriate" than if they were not. So the clinicians viewed "typically" female problems in a male client as the least important. Armed with this knowledge, an agency can design procedures that will control the extent to which such biases might affect the equitable delivery of services to alcoholics.

As in research, the influence of values in the actual conduct of practice cannot be totally eliminated, but by relying on a practice approach that is empirically based, that employs procedures that have been supported by research, and that incorporates rigorous evaluation procedures, it is possible to sensitize professionals to the impact of their value positions and thus enhance the objectivity of service delivery. Research in Practice 2.1 offers an illustration of how this can be accomplished.

Theories in Research and Practice

"Theory" is a word that is misunderstood by many people. To the neophyte, theories are often associated with the abstract, the impractical, or the unreal. In actuality, nothing could be farther from the truth. In both research and practice settings, theories play a critical role in our understanding of reality and our ability to cope with problems. In fact, people

RESEARCH IN PRACTICE 2.1
Needs Assessment: Interviewing the Children of Lesbians

The extraordinary power and tenacity of stereotypes regarding homosexuals and lesbians is illustrated by the incredibly negative epithets in wide use in our society: fag, lesie, queer, butch, dyke, and the like. In part deriving from the Judeo-Christian values that pervade our culture, homosexuality is viewed by many as bizarre, evil, or a sign of psychological disturbance. In recent decades, a more accepting attitude toward homosexuality has emerged—at least in terms of reducing social and economic discrimination based on sexual preference. There remains, however, at least one bastion of heterosexuality: the family. In the view of most people, the family should be a heterosexual couple (or single parent) and children. In fact, it was not until 1973 that a lesbian mother was awarded custody of her children after a divorce. The belief is still quite strong that a lesbian is unfit to be a mother and that children will be harmed if raised by a lesbian mother or lesbian couple. It is still rare today for a homosexual to be allowed to adopt.

Human service practitioners often deal with clients or situations that involve value-laden controversies such as this. The difficult problem is how to serve clients within the context of one's own personal and professional values. In some cases, it is possible to use scientific research to assess whether personal or professional values are *unreasonably* influencing the services provided to clients. This was illustrated by a project at a child outreach program in a Massachusetts mental health center. Karen Lewis (1980), director of the program, saw several children in therapy whose mothers had recently made their lesbianism publicly known. In attempting to develop a knowledge base from which to establish a treatment strategy, she found very little literature on the children of lesbians. What she did find focused on the legal issues of whether lesbians should be permitted custody of their children or on what professionals *believed,* partly based on their own personal values, would be best for the children. No one had bothered to ask the clients—the children—about feelings, attitudes, and consequences of being raised by lesbian mothers.

Professional values dictate that intervention be based on what is in the best interests of the client. In determining what is best for the client, Lewis might have relied on traditional knowledge (for example, religious teachings or personal values regarding homosexuality, the family, and child-rearing) or experiential knowledge (her contact with the few children of lesbian mothers who sought her services). Instead, she turned to scientific observation. She contacted lesbian mothers through a number of sources such as local gay newspapers. She eventually interviewed 21 children from 8 fami-

(Continued on next page)

lies. The interviews were conducted with as many of the children in each family as possible, and the mothers were not present. The interviews were not considered therapy sessions—the goal was to gain information about the adjustment problems of the children rather than to confront and solve those problems. Lewis is careful to point out that her sample is not representative of all children with lesbian mothers. These were for the most part upper-middle-class, educated women who were willing to make their sexual preference public. What was learned from these children does not necessarily apply to all children of lesbian mothers.

Lewis found that these children had considerable adjustment problems that needed to be confronted. She further realized that her conclusions were not consistent with what one would expect from much traditional and experiential knowledge or personal values regarding children of homosexuals.

> The children unanimously agreed that the breakup of their parents' marriage was far more upsetting than the subsequent disclosure about their mother. . . . A heterosexual mother in remarrying confronts the same problems regarding the children's adjustment as a lesbian mother with a lover. . . . One striking point . . . was the children's desire to accept their mother's new life-style. Almost without exception, the children were proud of their mother for challenging society's rules and for standing up for what she believed. Problems between the mother and children seemed secondary to the children's respect for the difficult step she had taken [Lewis, 1980, pp. 199–203].

The work of Lewis illustrates the manner in which an objective science can work with a profession based on values to further the goals of the profession. Science cannot inform human service workers regarding what their personal values ought to be, but it can point to practice situations in which personal values seem to be unreasonably intruding on intervention decisions. Personal values might suggest that children should not live with a lesbian mother, but Lewis's data suggest that such living arrangements may not be all that detrimental to the children. Without such research, there is a greater danger that decisions based on personal values will parade as "what is in the client's best interest." So research can serve a watchdog function on the unwarranted intrusion of values into practice decisions.

commonly use theories in their daily lives without recognizing it. First, then, we need to understand what theories are.

What Is a Theory?

A **theory** is a set of interrelated propositions or statements, organized into a deductive system, that offers an explanation of some phenomenon (Homans, 1964, p. 951). There are three key elements in this definition that are important to understanding theories. First, theories are made up of **propositions,** which are statements about the relationship between some elements in the theory. For example, a proposition from the differential association theory of crime is that "a person becomes criminal because of an excess of definitions favorable to the violation of the law over definitions unfavorable to the violation of the law." Elements in this proposition include "criminal" and "definitions favorable to the violation of the law" (Sutherland, 1939). Behavior modification theory also contains numerous propositions, including "behavior change can occur through a reorganization of the environmental cues that reward and punish behavior." The elements in this proposition include "behavior change," "environmental cues," and "reward and punish behavior."

A second important part of our definition of theory is that theories are *deductive* systems, meaning they move from general, abstract propositions to particular, testable statements. For a set of propositions to constitute a theory, it must be possible to deduce from them further relationships between the elements. Differential association theory is again illustrative. As just noted, this theory relates definitions favorable to the violation of the law with the greater likelihood of criminal behavior. This means that the theory is meant to apply to *all* specific types of crimes, such as robbery, larceny, or auto theft. So it would be logical to deduce from the theory that greater exposure to definitions favorable to the violation of the law would be associated with higher incidences of robbery, larceny, or auto theft. Theories are abstract because they have this deductive power: The broader and more abstract the propositions and their related concepts are, the more numerous are the specific relationships that can be deduced from them.

The third key aspect of theories is that they provide *explanations* for the phenomena they address. Indeed, the ultimate purpose of a theory is to explain *why* something occurred. In differential association theory, the phenomenon to be explained is criminal behavior, and the explanation is that criminality is learned through much the same process as noncriminal behavior. It is the content of what is learned—definitions favorable to violation of the law—that makes the difference. Thus, differential association provides an explanation for the development of criminal behavior.

In comprehending theories and the role they play, it is helpful to realize that we all use "theories" in our everyday lives although we may not call them theories or be consciously aware of using them. Nonetheless, we base our decisions and behavior on our past experience and what we have learned from others. From these experiences, we generalize that certain physical, psychological, and social processes are operative and will continue to be important in the future with predictable consequences. This is our "commonsense theory" about how the world operates and forms the basis for our decisions. For example, most people have certain general notions—personal theories—about what causes poverty. Some personal theories emphasize poverty as an individual problem: People are poor because of their individual characteristics, such as laziness, low intelligence, poor education, or lack of marketable skills. Others' theories of poverty emphasize the structural features of the American economy that dictate that even in times of economic expansion some people will be left impoverished through no fault of their own. Which of these theories people identify with most closely will determine, in part, how they react to poor people and what public policy provisions toward poverty they support. Advocates of the individualistic theory might be hostile toward the poor and programs to aid them, seeing the poor as undeserving people suffering only from their own shortcomings. Supporters of the structural theory may view the poor as victims and tend to be more benevolent toward them.

Personal theories, like these concerning poverty, may be extreme and misleading because they are based on casual observations, personal experience, or other information lacking the rigorous concern for accuracy of scientific investigations. Unlike commonsense theories, theories in research and practice are precise, detailed, and explicit. It is, however, important to recognize that a theory is always tentative in nature. That is, any theory is best viewed as a *possible* explanation for the phenomenon under investigation. By conducting research, scientists gather evidence that either supports or fails to support a theoretical explanation or practice intervention. It is important to note that no theory stands or falls on the basis of one trial. Theories are tested over a long period of time by many investigations. Only with the accumulation of research outcomes can we begin to have confidence concerning the validity of a theory.

The Functions of Theories

We have all heard the refrain "It's only a theory" or "That's your theory." Such phrases are often used in the context of deflating an argument that someone has put forth. Actually, these comments, though often intended in a disparaging sense, convey some truth regarding theories. In particular, they point out that theories are often *untested* (but testable) assertions about reality and that theories are not the end product of scientific in-

vestigation but rather are a part of the process of science. Theories are used for particular purposes in both research and practice settings. In fact, the same theories are often used in both research and practice because both researchers and practitioners turn to theories for similar reasons. We can identify two major functions of theories in research and practice.

Guide for Research and Practice   Theories serve to guide and direct research and practice. They focus attention on certain phenomena as being relevant to the issues of concern. If we were to dispense with theories altogether, as some would suggest, then what would we study? What data would be collected? What intervention strategy would be adopted? Theories aid us in finding answers to these questions.

Imagine that a counseling center is concerned with attacking the problem of teenage alcohol consumption in a particular high school and that the staff decides to study the problem. Where to begin? What variables are important? As a first step, it is essential to fall back on some theory related to these issues. We might, for example, use the theory of differential association, which posits that alcohol consumption results from attitudes and patterns of behavior that are learned in association with others, particularly peer groups. In order to test this theory, we could determine whether alcohol consumption is more common when it is viewed as an acceptable form of behavior among peers. We are then in a position to collect data on attitudes toward alcohol and patterns of alcohol consumption in peer groups. If the theory is confirmed, then it supports the idea that effective intervention will need to focus on attitudes toward alcohol consumption in peer groups.

We could have selected quite a different theory regarding alcohol consumption. For example, some theories propose that there is an inherited predisposition toward alcoholism. Other theories suggest that alcoholism results from a nutritional deficiency that is satiated by alcohol consumption. We do not presume to suggest which of these is the more accurate theory—future research will, one hopes, settle that issue. The same thing occurs in practice intervention. If a practitioner used crisis intervention theory to deal with the disruption caused by an alcoholic parent, the theory would direct attention to such factors as family coping strengths and emotional adaptation. Community organization practice theory, on the other hand, would focus on community resources available to recovering alcoholics and community services for families of alcoholics. The point is that the theories used by researchers and practitioners serve to guide their approaches and focus their attention on particular phenomena.

Integration of Multiple Observations

Theories serve to integrate and explain the many observations made in diverse settings by researchers and practitioners. They tell us *why* something happened, and they enable us to link the outcomes of numerous studies and interventions made in a variety of settings. As long as the findings of these efforts remain individual and isolated, they are not particularly valuable to science. Recall that a single observation is viewed with considerable skepticism. Single research findings may be in error, they may be passed over and forgotten, or their broader implications may be missed entirely. Theo-

ries enable us to organize these dispersed findings into a larger explanatory scheme. For example, someone investigating problem pregnancies among teenagers might observe that the groups of teenagers among whom such pregnancies are common tend to view parenthood out of wedlock in a positive fashion. A familiarity with differential association theory would suggest that the social learning processes important in teenage drinking may also be relevant in problem pregnancies among teenagers. If this is the case, then practitioners working in one area may be able to borrow strategies for intervention from the other area. Thus, theories integrate the findings from independent research endeavors and provide implications for intervention strategies.

Theories, then, play an important part in both research and practice. But one point needs to be reiterated: The utility of theories must be based on their *demonstrated* effectiveness. Theories should never be allowed to become "sacred cows" whose use is based on tradition or custom. Human service providers today can choose from among a bewildering array of intervention theories, from crisis intervention to long-term psychotherapy, from individual behavior modification to community organization. A major consideration in such theory selection should be the extent to which a theory is supported by empirical evidence: Has the intervention been shown to produce the desired results? (Siporin, 1975; Fischer, 1978; Hepworth and Larsen, 1982.) In scientific research, this is called the **verification** of theories. Researchers approach the problem of verification by developing and testing hypotheses, which is our next topic. This process of verification is diagrammed in Figure 2.1,

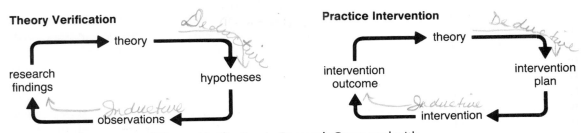

Figure 2.1 The Process of Theory Verification in Research Compared with Practice Intervention

which also shows a parallel process as it occurs in human service practice.

Concepts and Hypotheses

Defining Concepts

An important part of theories are **concepts:** mental constructs or images developed to symbolize ideas, persons, things, or events. Concepts are the "elements" of theories discussed earlier; they are the building blocks that are interrelated in propositions that form the explanatory statements of a theory. Some of the concepts in behavior modification theory, for example, are reinforcement, conditioning, learning, and behavior change.

Concepts are similar in function to the words we use in everyday communication. The word "automobile," for example, is the agreed-on symbol for a particular object that is used as a mode of transportation. The symbol or word is not the object itself but rather something that stands for or represents that object. Scientific concepts, like words in everyday language, are also symbols that can refer to an extremely broad range of referents. They may refer to something fairly concrete like leadership or something highly abstract like reinforcement or cohesion.

Despite the similarities between sci-entific concepts and ordinary words, there are some differences that are critical to the scientific endeavor. In particular, concepts used in scientific research must be defined very carefully. With the words we use for everyday communication, we can get along quite well with only a general idea of how these words are defined. In fact, it is doubtful if most people could give a dictionary-perfect definition of even the most commonly used words. Such imprecision in the use of scientific concepts, however, is totally inadequate. Scientists, widely scattered both geographically and temporally, carry on research that tests various aspects of theories. For these disconnected research projects to produce information of maximum utility, all the bits of knowledge need to be integrated into an explanatory scheme—a theory. This accumulation of knowledge is severely hampered—in fact, becomes practically impossible—if these isolated scientists use different definitions of the same concepts. For example, many studies of the relationship between reinforcement and learning have been conducted. If the results of different studies are to be comparable, the concepts of reinforcement and learning should be defined in the same way. Learning, for instance, can be defined in *behavioral* terms as the performance of a new behavior or in *cognitive* terms as the understanding of how a particular behavior might be performed. When defined in these different ways, the concept refers to something quite different in the world, and results from two investigations using the different definitions would not be directly comparable. It may be, for example, that behavioral learning occurs under quite different conditions than does cognitive learning.

Scientific analysis involves two types of definitions of concepts—each functioning at a different level of analysis and serving a different purpose. At the theoretical or abstract level, concepts are given **nominal definitions:** verbal definitions in which scientists agree that one set of words or symbols will be used to stand for another set of words or symbols. Nominal definitions are directly analogous to the dictionary definitions of ordinary words in which a phrase is designed to give meaning to the word or concept being defined (Cohen and Nagel, 1934). For example, a nominal definition of "poverty" might be a deficiency in resources to the extent that people are not able to maintain a life-style considered minimally acceptable in a particular society (Sullivan and Thompson, 1988, p. 144).

An important step in moving from the abstract level of theory to the concrete level of research is to give concepts **operational definitions:** definitions that indicate the precise procedures, or operations, to be followed in measuring a concept. For example, one of the most widely used operational definitions of poverty was developed by Mollie Orshansky (1965) for the Social Security Administration. Her measure, still used by the government as a basis for policy decisions, is based on what it costs to purchase a low budget, nutritious diet for a family. If we use United States Depart-

ment of Agriculture figures, the poverty line is determined by taking into account the cost of food, the size of the family, the age and sex of the head of the household, and other factors. This operational definition of poverty actually yields a series of income cutoffs below which families are defined as poor. This is a precise definition that lists the exact operations (in this case, mathematical operations) to follow in defining poverty. Anyone using this definition will be measuring the same thing in the same way.

The process of moving from nominal to operational definitions can be complex because concepts are very general and abstract, and there is often controversy over exactly what they refer to. Some concepts that have been a part of the literature for decades have yet to be operationalized in a way that is fully satisfactory. For example, "alcoholism" has proved extremely difficult to operationalize, especially establishing where alcoholism begins and social drinking leaves off. Owing to substantial individual and cultural differences, simple measures relying on amount and frequency of consumption are inadequate. Researchers have been forced to operationalize alcoholism on the basis of symptoms, such as family or work problems, morning drinking, poor eating, and recurrent blackouts. Whereas symptom-based measures of alcoholism avoid the errors inherent in consumption measures, substantial controversy remains concerning which symptoms are the best indicators, how many symptoms must be evident, and how serious they must be before the label of alcoholic may be meaningfully applied.

Even the concept of poverty, which may seem straightforward and easy to operationalize, has proven controversial. There is, of course, the issue of where to set the income cutoffs. Orshansky's cutoffs are based on the assumption that the average American family spends one-third of its income on food, and some critics have argued that this results in poverty thresholds that are too low. Furthermore, Orshansky's definition sets a fixed income level as the poverty level, and thus it is unaffected by changing levels of affluence within society as a whole. Some have argued for a "relative" definition of poverty that defines as poor those who earn one-third or one-half of the median family income (Bell, 1987). With such a definition, the poverty thresholds would automatically rise if the affluence of society as a whole increased. So, it should be evident that operationalizing concepts can be difficult, complex, and sometimes controversial. The process of moving from the nominal to the operational level is called *measurement,* and it is treated extensively in Chapter 5.

Developing Hypotheses

A common strategy in scientific investigations is to move from a general theory to a specific, researchable problem. A part of this strategy is to develop **hypotheses,** which are testable statements of presumed relationships between two or more concepts. Hypotheses state what we expect to find rather than what has already been determined to exist. A major purpose of developing hypotheses in research is to test the accuracy of a theory (see Fig. 2.1). The concepts and propositions of which theories are composed are usually too broad and too abstract to be directly tested. Such concepts as "reinforcement" or "learning," for example, need to be specified empirically through operational definitions before they are amenable to testing. Once operationally defined, these concepts are generally referred to as **variables,** or things that are

capable of taking on more than one value. If hypotheses are supported, then this supplies evidence for the accuracy of the theory on which they are based.

In the construction of hypotheses, the relationship between variables is stated in one of two possible directions: a positive relationship or a negative (also called inverse) relationship. In a *positive relationship,* the values of the variables change in the *same* direction, both increasing or both decreasing. For example, we might hypothesize that the acceptance of the use of alcohol among an adolescent's peers will lead to increased likelihood that the adolescent will consume alcohol. In other words, as acceptance of the use of alcohol by one's peers increases, so does the adolescent's own use of alcohol. In a *negative* or *inverse relationship,* the values of variables change in opposite directions. We might hypothesize, for example, that, among adolescents, reduced parental supervision will lead to an increase in the likelihood of substance abuse. In this case, as the value of one variable (parental supervision) declines, the value of the other (substance abuse) is predicted to increase.

There are a number of useful guidelines to keep in mind for developing hypotheses:

1. It is a *deductive* process in which testable statements are derived from abstract theories. Although it is possible to generate hypotheses without deducing them from theories, hypotheses are always linked to theories because the theories explain why things happen.

2. The *independent variable* is stated first in the hypothesis, followed by the *dependent variable.* The **independent variable** is the presumed active or causal variable. It is the one believed

to be producing changes in the dependent variable. The **dependent variable** is the passive variable or the one that is affected. In the examples given earlier, peer acceptance of alcohol and parental supervision are the independent variables, and alcohol use and substance abuse are the dependent variables.

3. The independent and dependent variables need to be clearly specified. Great confusion can arise if the precise variables that a hypothesis contains are not made clear.

4. Hypotheses should be so stated that they can be verified or refuted. Otherwise, they are not hypotheses. Hypotheses, after all, are statements about which we can gather empirical evidence to determine whether they are correct or false. One common pitfall in this regard is to make statements that involve judgments or values rather than issues of empirical observation. For example, we might "hypothesize" that investigations should be increased to reduce the incidence of welfare fraud. On the surface, this statement might appear to be a hypothesis because it relates investigations and welfare fraud in a negative direction. But note that, as stated, it is not a testable hypothesis. The problem is the evaluative "should be." What should or should not be social policy has no place in hypotheses. However, the statement can be modified so that it qualifies as a testable hypothesis: Increased levels of investigation tend to reduce the incidence of welfare fraud. The hypothesis is now making an empirical assertion that can be checked against fact.

5. Developing hypotheses from theories is a *creative process* that depends in part on the insight of the investigator. Because hypotheses link theories to particular concrete settings, it often takes insight on the part of the researcher to make such connections. In addition, researchers at times combine two or more theories to develop hypotheses that neither theory alone is capable of generating.

Concepts and Operational Definitions Among Minority Populations

When conducting research on minority populations, there is considerable opportunity for bias to enter if concepts and operational definitions are not carefully developed. This has been a chronic problem with research on crime. For example, many people believe that nonwhites commit crimes at a higher rate than we would expect given their numbers in the population. Although this is partly true, it greatly oversimplifies a complex reality, and it reflects how crime is typically operationalized. Official crime statistics from the Federal Bureau of Investigation (1987) are an important source of data on crime. The FBI operationalizes some crimes as "offenses cleared by arrest" and others as "offenses known to the police." In other words, an occurrence is not considered a crime until it is "known to the police" or "cleared by arrest." These official crime statistics show that nonwhites commit more crimes than do whites. However, this is in part a function of how the official statistics operationalize the concept of crime. We know that nonwhites are more likely to be arrested for a given offense, suggesting that it may be arrest that is more common among them rather than the actual commission of crimes. Nonwhites are also more likely to commit highly visible crimes, like armed robbery or assault, that are more frequently reported to the police and result in an arrest. Whites, on the other hand, commit more "hidden" crimes, like embezzlement or fraud, that are less likely to come to the attention of the police. Recent research suggests that there may be no class difference in the amount of "hidden" crimes that are committed (Elliott and Huizinga, 1983). There are other ways to operationalize crime, such as through victimization studies (asking people if they have been a victim of a crime) and self-reports (having people anonymously report their own involvement in crime). Studies based on these operational definitions tend to show much smaller differences between white and nonwhite crime rates.

Another area where poorly constructed operational definitions have produced misleading conclusions is in the area of spouse abuse (Lockhart, 1985). Most studies have found rates of spouse abuse to be considerably higher among blacks than among whites. Typically, these studies have used one of the following as an operational definition of the occurrence of wife abuse: a homicide involving a domestic killing, a battered woman seeking care in an emergency room or social service setting, a wife abuse claim handled by a domestic court, or a domestic dispute call to a police department. We know, however, that blacks are over-represented among people who come to the attention of the police, emergency room personnel, or social service workers. Because they are generally over-represented among these populations, they will appear to have higher rates of abuse than will whites. These problems can be avoided by selecting a sample of people from a community and having them answer questions about the amount of conflict and violence that occurs in their family. This avoids the bi-

ased effect of looking only at certain locales.

The Committee on the Status of Women in Sociology (1986) has pointed to yet another area where operational definitions have led to inaccurate results: studies of work and social contribution. Work is often operationalized in terms of paid employment, but this leaves many types of work, such as community service or home-based work, out of consideration. With such an operational definition, if an employee of a carpet-cleaning firm shampoos the carpets in a home for a fee, that would be counted as "work," but if a woman does the same activity on her own time in her own home, it would not be classified as "work." Such an operationalization of work would tend to underestimate the extent of productive activity engaged in by women since women are less likely than men to have paid employment.

So in developing operational definitions, care must be taken to assess whether they might lead to a distorted view of minorities. In some cases, this calls for careful consideration of what a concept is intended to mean. For example, is the focus of the research on "paid employment" or is it on "social contribution"? In other cases, it calls for careful assessment of whether a definition will lead to an inaccurate over- or under-representation of minorities.

Deduction Versus Induction

A comment should be made at this point about two forms of reasoning that are central to the scientific process: *deduction* and *induction*. We mentioned earlier that theories are deductive systems. This means that hypotheses can be logically derived from the propositions that make up a theory. So, **deductive reasoning** involves deducing or inferring a conclusion from some premises or propositions. If the propositions—or the theory—are correct, then hypotheses logically derived from them will also be correct. In Figure 2.1, deduction involves moving from the level of theory to that of hypotheses or an intervention plan. Deductive reasoning is central to the scientific process.

However, it is inductive reasoning that enables us to assess the validity of the hypotheses and the theory. **Inductive reasoning** involves inferring something about a whole group or class of objects from our knowledge of one or a few members of that group or class. We test one or a few hypotheses derived from a theory and then infer something about the validity of the theory as a whole. Thus, inductive reasoning carries us from observations or interventions in Figure 2.1 to some assessment regarding the validity of the theory. The logic of scientific analysis involves an interplay between deduction—deriving testable hypotheses—and induction—assessing theories based on tests of hypotheses derived from the theories.

There are times when inductive research is conducted without benefit of prior deductive reasoning. This occurs in descriptive or exploratory research where there is no preexisting theory from which to deduce hypotheses. In the absence of theory, we begin by making observations and then developing some theoretical propositions that would be plausible given those observations. Practitioners, for example, may observe that clients with problem pregnancies tend to come from families with low socioeconomic status. Based on the assumption that the parent–child bond is weaker in low socio-

economic families and that such parents, therefore, have less control over their children, the practitioners could inductively conclude that a weak parent–child bond leads to an increased risk of unwanted pregnancy. In other words, the observations are used to infer a proposition regarding the causes of unwanted pregnancies. Inductive research of this sort can serve as a foundation for building a theory, and the theory in turn can serve as a source of testable hypotheses through deductive reasoning. Thus, induction and deduction are each key links in the chain of scientific reasoning, and they parallel the reasoning process that is found in practice intervention.

Research in Practice 2.2 offers an illustration of a research project that highlights many of the issues discussed in the previous two sections regarding the use of theories and hypotheses in research and the importance of inductive and deductive reasoning.

Cause-and-Effect Relationships

One of the more important, yet difficult, tasks in scientific research is the search for causes—the reasons *why* particular forms of behavior occur. Why do child abuse and spouse abuse occur? Why do some juveniles become delinquent whereas others present no behavior problems? Why do some people exhibit symptoms of mental illness whereas others appear psychologically stable? Discovering causal relationships is a difficult task because causality cannot be directly observed. Rather, it must be inferred from the observation of other factors. Because of this, the philosopher John Kemeny has labeled causality "the mysterious force" (1959, p. 49). We cannot see it, feel it, or

RESEARCH IN PRACTICE 2.2
Practice Effectiveness: Social Theory and Burnout Among Social Workers

A SOCIAL WORKER: I began to despise everyone and could not conceal my contempt.

A PSYCHIATRIC NURSE: Sometimes you can't help but feel "Damn it, they want to be there, and they're fuckers, so let them stay there." You really put them down. . . .

A SOCIAL WORKER: I find myself caring less and possessing an extremely negative attitude.—Quoted in Maslach, 1979, p. 217

These are hardly the caring, empathic reactions one would expect from a human service worker. Yet these and similar negative attitudes toward clients are expressed at some point by many social workers, nurses, psychologists, and others. This problem—often referred to as "burnout"—is of considerable concern to human service professionals because it can impair their ability to deal with client problems. *Burnout* refers to a service worker's emotional disengagement from clients, dissatisfaction with his or her job, feelings of worthlessness, and physical and interpersonal problems (Harrison, 1980). At first glance, it would seem plausible to assume that burnout is a reaction among workers who tend to overidentify and overempathize with their clients. Yet this would be an intuitive rather than a the-

oretical approach. Recall that scientific theories serve to guide research by focusing our attention on variables that might play a role in some social phenomenon. The implicit "theory" underlying the preceding explanation is that an overload of empathy and caring will bring about a coping response of disengagement and hostility. This is certainly a plausible theory and could be subjected to empirical test.

When social work researcher W. David Harrison (1980) approached these issues, however, he utilized a different theoretical approach. He turned to *role theory*, which views human behavior as resulting from conformity to expectations that are associated with particular roles. One of the tenets of role theory is that role expectations should be clear, unambiguous, and achievable. Furthermore, the various expectations associated with a role should not conflict with one another. Much previous research suggests that situations where role expectations are conflicting, incompatible, or unclear lead to personal stress and dissatisfaction. *Role strain* refers to a felt difficulty in performing a role. There are two types of role strain: role conflict and role ambiguity. *Role conflict* refers to a situation in which there are conflicting and incompatible demands placed on a person in a role. *Role ambiguity* refers to a lack of clarity in terms of what is expected of a person in a particular role.

Harrison's research focused on child protective service (CPS) workers, and he found both role conflict and role ambiguity to be commonplace. Role conflict occurs because CPS workers must perform the role of advocate and enabler for the client while at the same time they represent the authority of law, often with involuntary clients. The expectations associated with the advocate-enabler role clash with those associated with the legal-representative role. Role ambiguity enters the picture for the CPS workers in terms of the lack of clarity regarding the ultimate goal of child protective services. The final step in Harrison's theoretical analysis was to hypothesize that role ambiguity and role conflict would be inversely related to job satisfaction and, therefore, positively related to burnout.

Thus, the theoretical considerations of role theory do not point to excessive empathy or identification as the culprits in burnout among human service workers. Rather, it has to do with the role structure that surrounds them. Harrison proceeded to collect data that would serve as a test of his hypotheses. He found that, though role conflict was important in some dimensions of CPS workers' jobs, the real problem seemed to be role ambiguity:

> It appears that workers need to be fairly clear about what is expected of them in fulfilling their role in order for them to feel good about their work. When ambiguous messages about a job well done are sent or received, little in the way of . . . satisfaction and competence is to be expected [Harrison, 1980, p. 41].

This investigation illustrates the importance of grounding research in theory. It is theory that suggests which variables might be important and how they might relate to one another. It also shows how hypotheses can be developed through deductive reasoning. Once confirmed, Harrison's hypotheses provided support, through inductive reasoning, for the role theory interpretation of burnout in the human services. Harrison's analysis is certainly not the final word on burnout, however. Other theories would lead to different, but testable, hypotheses that could be compared with Harrison's findings. Based on this slow, methodical accumulation of knowledge, we should eventually establish a solid foundation from which to develop programs to alleviate the problem of burnout among human service workers.

hear it; but we often assume it is there and many scientists search it out with hopefulness and tenacity. It is also a controversial task because some philosophers, like Bertrand Russell (1953), have argued for excluding the notion of causality from scientific investigation altogether. These people would opt for restricting ourselves to description and the analysis of "associations" without the implication that there is a "mysterious force" called causality that lurks behind the scene and orchestrates the actions of people and things. This controversy is a long-standing one, and we will not presume to resolve it here. Nonetheless, it is important to understand the criteria that need to be satisfied if one wants to infer that one event caused another.

By **causality,** we mean that some independent variable (X) is the factor, or one of several factors, whose change produces variation in a dependent variable (Y). As noted, causality can only be *inferred.* We can observe the relationships among things in the world, and from that we infer or deduce that changes in one factor are causing changes in another. However, it is always an inference. To infer the existence of a causal relationship, one must demonstrate the following:

1. There must be a statistical association between the independent and dependent variables.
2. The independent variable must occur prior in time to the dependent variable.
3. The relationship between independent and dependent variables must not be spurious; that is, it must not disappear when the effects of other variables are taken into account.

We will consider each requirement of causal inference in the context of an issue that is much in the news today: the campaign to reduce cigarette smoking. Over the years, there have been reports in the media about the negative impact of cigarette smoking on people's health. Some have argued that making these reports public as a part of a health campaign can have the desirable effect of motivating people to quit. In Table 2.1, we present hypothetical data seeming to show a link between reading such reports about smoking and actually quitting smoking: Fifty percent of those who read the reports quit smoking as compared with only 27 percent of those who do not read the reports. Finding such a statistical relationship satisfies the first criterion for establishing a causal relationship.

The second requirement, that the independent variable occur prior in time to the dependent, is often not as easy to establish. A major factor in this is the nature of the study one is conducting. Some research techniques, such as the experiment or participant observation, are inherently *longitudinal,* which means that the researcher is in a position to trace the development of behavior as it unfolds over time. In these cases, establishing the time sequence of events is generally simple. Questions of temporal order are more difficult to resolve when dealing with

TABLE 2.1   Effectiveness of Reading Media Reports on Smoking Cessation

		Person Reads Report	
		Yes	No
Person Quits Smoking	Yes	200 (50%)	135 (27%)
	No	200 (50%)	365 (73%)
	Totals	400 (100%)	500 (100%)

cross-sectional data, such as surveys, in which measurements of the independent and dependent variables occur at the same time. This is especially true if the question of temporal sequence is not addressed until after the data have been collected. It is sometimes possible to sort out the time sequence of variables in survey data by asking additional questions. However, if the necessary information is not gathered at the time of the survey, it may be impossible to establish the appropriate time order of the variables. This is a major reason why it is important to consider carefully issues of data analysis when originally developing a research design.

The data in our illustration may suffer from this problem. One interpretation of the data is that reading reports is the independent variable which has an influence on whether people quit smoking, the dependent variable. For this interpretation to be correct, the reports would have to have been publicized before the people quit smoking. If the respondents were not asked when they quit smoking, it would be impossible to say whether they quit smoking before or after reading the reports. Obviously, if they quit smoking before reading the reports, then such health campaigns could not have caused their quitting. In our example, without knowing the temporal sequence, one could argue logically for either factor being the cause of the other. Obviously, the health campaign could cause people to quit smoking if they become frightened by learning the dire consequences of their habit. However, it could also be that those who quit smoking are happy with and proud of their victory and enjoy reading reports on what could have happened to them had they not quit smoking. In this second scenario, quitting smoking would be the independent variable which in-creases the likelihood that people will read reports about the health threat of smoking, the dependent variable.

The final criterion necessary for inferring causality is that the relationship between the independent and dependent variables not be *spurious* or disappear when the effects of other variables are considered. (The logic of causal and spurious relationships is compared in Figure 2.2). This is often the most difficult of the three criteria to satisfy. In fact, one is never *totally* sure that some other variable—one you have not even considered—might not confound an apparent causal relationship. All that can be accomplished is to rule out as many extraneous variables as we can to the point where it is unlikely that a variable exists that could render a given relationship spurious or noncausal.

Considerable effort is expended during the design stage of research to control as many potentially troublesome extraneous variables as possible. Experiments, for example, are particularly good for avoiding spurious relationships owing to the high degree of control the experimental situation affords the researcher. Surveys, on the other hand, provide far less control, such that several variables

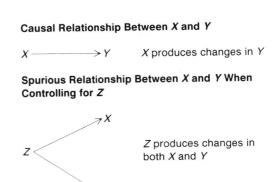

Figure 2.2 Causal and Spurious Relationships

Causal Relationship

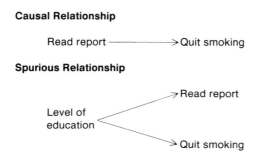

Figure 2.3 Causal and Spurious Relationships Between Reading a Report and Quitting Smoking

capable of producing spuriousness will typically have to be considered during data analysis. Several statistical techniques exist to control extraneous variables when the data are analyzed.

Returning to our example of smoking cessation, suppose we had solved the time sequence problem and, thus, had satisfied the first two requirements for establishing a causal relationship. We would now begin to consider variables that might render the relationship spurious. One variable that might do this is the level of education of the people studied. (The logic of this is outlined in Figure 2.3.) There is considerable research linking education with health behavior: Generally, people with higher levels of education engage in more health-promoting activities such as quitting smoking or exercising. How do we determine whether the link between report reading and smoking cessation is spurious? We introduce the level of education as a control variable, which is illustrated with our hypothetical data in Table 2.2. We have divided the respondents in Table 2.1 into those with at least a high school education and those with less than a high school education. First, we can see that education is related to health behavior: Sixty percent of the better educated group

have quit smoking compared with only 19 percent of the less educated group. However, we are really interested in what happens to the link between report reading and smoking cessation. Careful inspection of Table 2.2 will show that the relationship largely disappears: *Within each educational group,* the same percent of people quit smoking among those who read the report as among those who did not. So, it is educational level, not whether one has read the report, that influences a person's likelihood of quitting smoking. Furthermore, in our hypothetical example, educational level also influences whether one reads the report: Sev-

TABLE 2.2 Effectiveness of Reading Media Reports on Smoking Cessation, Controlling for Education

Less Than High School Education

		Person Reads Report		
		Yes	No	Totals
Person Quits Smoking	Yes	20 (20%)	75 (19%)	95 (19%)
	No	80 (80%)	325 (81%)	405 (81%)
	Totals	100 (100%)	400 (100%)	500

High-School Education or More

		Person Reads Report		
		Yes	No	Totals
Person Quits Smoking	Yes	180 (60%)	60 (60%)	240 (60%)
	No	120 (40%)	40 (40%)	160 (40%)
	Totals	300 (100%)	100 (100%)	400

enty-five percent of those with a high school education did so compared with only 20 percent of the others. So, in our example, the link between reading the report and quitting smoking is a spurious one; it occurs only because each of those two variables is affected by the same third variable.

If we had found the link between report reading and smoking cessation to be nonspurious when we controlled for education, could we conclude that the relationship was causal? The answer is no. We could not come to that conclusion—at least not yet. All that would have been shown was that the relationship remained when *one* alternative explanation was ruled out. Any other variables that could render the relationship spurious would also have to be investigated

and the relationship still hold before we could argue with any confidence that it was in fact causal. (More of the intricacies of this sort of analysis will be taken up in Chapter 14).

We said at the outset that establishing the existence of causal relationships is difficult. From the preceding discussion, the student should understand better why this is the case. Statistical relationships are easy to find but, on further investigation, all too frequently turn out to be spurious. The appropriate time sequence can also be problematic, especially with survey data. All in all, establishing causal relationships is a difficult task. Fortunately, it can also be challenging and exciting. Regardless of the outcome, knowledge is always gained.

||||||||||||||||||||||||||||||||||||||||||||||||||||||||||||||||||||||||||||||||||||||||||||||||||||||||||||||||

COMPUTERS IN RESEARCH
Using Agency Data Bases for Research: A Study of Leaving Welfare

A commonly held perception of welfare recipients is that, once on the rolls, they remain there for years as they develop a life-style of dependency. Is it true? If not, why does the perception persist? Creative research relying on a computerized data base from the state of Wisconsin known as the CRN (Computer Reporting Network) suggests some answers (Rank, 1985). It is also an excellent illustration of the point made in the first chapter regarding how social agencies can be organized such that they serve as "research machines."

In 1971, the Wisconsin Depart-

ment of Health and Social Services initiated a project designed to produce a computer-based information system to handle the administration of AFDC, food stamps, and Medicaid. The system is headquartered in Madison with remote terminals linking county social service offices in a statewide network. By 1981, more than 99 percent of all cases in the state's 72 counties had been loaded onto the system. Data enter the system when a county worker fills out an application form that determines eligibility for AFDC, Medicaid, and food stamps. The information is keyed into a terminal at the

(Continued on next page)

local office and sent to the centralized computer; within minutes a case determination sheet is printed out back at the county office while all the information on each case is saved on the central computer file. This system greatly reduces processing errors and speeds up benefit determination. While devised primarily to meet the data management demands of a complex welfare system, the CRN also provides an excellent source of data for research purposes, as illustrated by Mark Rank's (1985) study of how long people remain on welfare.

Rank used a 2-percent random sample of all cases in the CRN data base that were participating in welfare as of September 30, 1980. There were approximately 140,000 eligible cases on the CRN system, resulting in a sample of 2796. The cases were followed at six-month intervals through September 1983 by matching the Social Security number of the head of household for each case in the sample against the entire CRN file at the end of each interval. Any cases in the sample that no longer appeared on the active CRN file had left welfare in Wisconsin. While a study like this could have been done without computers, the collection and analysis of the data would have been far more costly and time consuming, probably prohibitively so.

The dependent variable in Rank's study was the length of time that people were on welfare. He had to decide on an operational definition of that concept based on the information available in the CRN. He used two operational definitions. First, he looked at recipients who entered welfare at the same time, referred to as a "case-

opening cohort." Second, he looked at a cross-section of recipients who were all on welfare on a given date, referred to as a "point-in-time cohort." With each method, he measured the average number of months until they left welfare ("exit time").

Contrary to popular belief, Rank found that most households who use welfare do so only briefly, typically for one to two years or less. Given this, why does the belief persist that welfare use equates with long-term dependency? At least part of the explanation may be found in the two different operational definitions described above: the case-opening cohort and the point-in-time definitions. When the study looked at a group of recipients who began using welfare at the same time (a case-opening cohort), the median exit time was 10.33 months. However, with a sample of people who happened to be on welfare at any given time (a point-in-time cohort), the median exit time was 20.58 months.—twice as long!

A little thought will show why these two different ways of measuring how long people stay on welfare come to strikingly different conclusions. To use a simplified example: Suppose 10 people get on welfare on January 1. A month later 5 people get off while a year later the other 5 are still on welfare. If we do a cohort study of those 10 people, our sample would consist of 5 people who got off welfare after a month and 5 who remained on for a year. However, if we did a point-in-time study at the end of the year, the sample would consist only of the 5 people who had been on welfare for a year. The latter sample would clearly show that people stay on welfare much longer than would the former sample. Now, reality is more complicated than this, with people getting on and off welfare constantly, but the impact is the same: Over time, any welfare caseload will tend to have a larger proportion of people who have been on welfare longer. People who get off welfare quickly will not show up in a point-in-time study that is done after they drop off welfare, while people who stay on welfare longer have a greater chance of showing up in such a study. Thus, point-in-time studies will tend to have proportionally more people who stay on longer than will cohort studies, and point-in-time studies will have a bias toward showing people to be on welfare longer. So, point-in-time studies will help to perpetuate the belief that people stay on welfare a long time. Likewise, people who stay on welfare a long time are more visible to workers in the system and to the public (for the same reason that they are more likely to show up in point-in-time samples), and this helps perpetuate beliefs about long-term welfare dependency. This comparison of point-in-time measures with cohort measures illustrates the care that must be taken in developing operational definitions that do not provide a biased view of reality.

Some people get off welfare much quicker than others. Using the case-opening cohort method, Rank found that single people and married couples were most likely to exit welfare (5.7- and 8.6-month exit times, respectively). Female-headed households and households headed by an elderly person remained on assistance much longer, for 22 months. So, if the media focuses on single welfare mothers, this will contribute to the myth that long-term dependency is common among welfare recipients.

In terms of policy implications, this study demonstrates that households participate in the welfare system very differently. Those groups with the least resources are most dependent on welfare and find it hardest to get off. Consequently, helping strategies for welfare recipients should be designed according to family type.

This study illustrates how information collected by human service agencies as a part of service delivery can be computerized and used in research that can further enhance effective service delivery. While this study focused on a statewide network, as personal computer technology advances, it is becoming feasible for small agencies to computerize their case record systems as well, making computer data-base research a potentially valuable tool for human service workers in a wide spectrum of settings.

|||||||||||||||||||||||||||||||||||||||||||||||||||||||||||||||||||||||||||||||||||||||||||||||||||||||||||||

☰ Main Points

• Science is one source of knowledge, along with tradition, experience, and common sense; but it is a superior source of objective and accurate knowledge about the world.

• The five key characteristics of science are that it is empirical, systematic, provisional, objective, and searches for the causes of events.

• These key characteristics are also central features of scientifically based practice.

• Theories are sets of interrelated propositions in deductive systems that explain phenomena.

• Theories perform two major functions: They guide research and practice, and they integrate observations from research.

• Concepts are mental constructs that symbolize ideas, persons, things, or events and form the basis for propositions and theories.

• Concepts are given both nominal definitions, which explain their meaning, and operational definitions, which indicate how they are measured. Care must be taken in developing operational definitions in research on minorities to ensure that such definitions do not lead to a distorted view of these populations.

• Hypotheses are statements that predict relationships between two or more variables and are tested through research.

• Causality means that some independent variable produces variation in a dependent variable.

• To demonstrate a causal relationship one must establish a statistical association between two variables, show that the independent variable occurs temporally first, and demonstrate that the relationship is not spurious.

• Computerized data bases developed by human service agencies as a part of their service delivery tasks can be an excellent source of data for social research, and this research can also enhance practice.

☰ Important Terms for Review

causality
common sense
concepts
deductive reasoning
dependent variable
experiential knowledge
hypotheses
independent variable
inductive reasoning
nominal definitions
operational definitions
propositions
science
theory
traditional knowledge
variables
verification

☰ For Further Reading

Babbie, Earl R. *Observing Ourselves: Essays in Social Research.* Belmont, Calif.: Wadsworth, 1986.
A thought-provoking anthology of essays concerning the fundamental issues in social science research including determinism, objectivity, and causation, along with several more.
Glaser, Barney G., and Anselm L. Strauss. *The Discovery of Grounded Theory.* New York: Aldine, 1967.
An excellent book about the virtues and procedures of developing theoretical propositions from data. This approach emphasizes qualitative research and induction.
Hoover, Kenneth R. *The Elements of Social Scientific Thinking,* 4th ed. New York: St. Martin's Press, 1988.
A brief and readable initiation into social science thinking and research. It is intended for those who use the results of research and those just getting into the field.
Kaplan, Abraham. *The Conduct of Inquiry.* New York: Harper & Row, 1963.

A very good discussion of the logic of scientific analysis in the behavioral sciences. It covers such topics as concepts, theories, and values.

Merton, Robert K. *Social Theory and Social Structure.* 2d ed. New York: Free Press, 1968.

A classic statement by a sociologist of the relationship between theory and research.

Phillips, D.C. *Philosophy, Science, and Social Inquiry: Contemporary Methodological Controversies in Social Science and Related Applied Fields of Research.* Elmsford, N.Y.: Pergamon Press, 1987.

An excellent philosophical analysis of issues in applied social research in areas such as social work and nursing. It addresses the issue of whether applied social research can or should emulate the positivist model found in the natural sciences.

Stinchcombe, Arthur L. *Constructing Social Theories.* New York: Harcourt Brace Jovanovich, 1968.

A technical book about social theories and their role in science and research.

Turner, Francis J., ed. *Social Work Treatment: Interlocking Theoretical Approaches.* 2d ed. New York: The Free Press, 1979.

A compendium of articles covering a wide range of human service practice theories. As emphasized in this chapter, these theoretical approaches can be used in both research and practice settings.

Wallace, Walter. *The Logic of Science in Sociology.* Chicago: Aldine-Atherton, 1971.

A readable book on the logic that underlies social research. The author clearly describes the process of verifying theories described in this chapter.

≡ Exercises for Class Discussion

2.1 There are many commonsense beliefs that relate to child development such as "spare the rod and spoil the child" or the belief that age-graded schools enhance learning. Through class discussion, develop a list of such "known" principles of child development. For each such principle, decide whether it is based on traditional knowledge, experiential knowledge, or a combination of these. How might you conduct systematic observations to determine the worth of these statements as scientific knowledge?

2.2 A mental health worker assigned to a large residential facility for senior citizens receives a request from staff members to "do something" about a new resident who is a 72-year-old woman. From the information provided, the woman has apparently been assigned to an eighth-floor room, but she refuses to take the elevator alone or if it is crowded. The woman becomes terrified of the enclosed space and will only use the stair unless she can ride with a staff member. The woman's husband died about six months ago, and she is now living alone for the first time.

a. Consider this case from the alternative theoretical positions of behavior modification versus traditional Freudian psychology. (You may substitute some other relevant theories of human behavior with which you are familiar.) What are some major theoretical concepts from each theory that apply to this case?

b. For the concepts that you identified in part **a,** use the illustrative case to develop an operational definition for each concept.

2.3 Using each theory from Exercise 2.2, construct a possible explanation for the woman's behavior. Now try to state your explanations in terms of testable hypotheses. Can you foresee any problems in assessing causality when testing these hypotheses? Compare the hypotheses you developed with those of other students in terms of the theory used, the concepts selected, and the variables identified. How are the concepts and variables that are derived from the same theory alike? How do they differ from those derived from the other theory?

2.4 We have made the point that the same theories can be useful to both practitioner and researcher. Using the hypotheses developed in Exercise 2.3, explain how they could be used either to help the worker change behavior or to conduct a study. How might the hypotheses need to be changed to be useful to both practice and research?

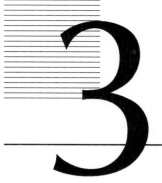

3

Ethical Issues in Social Research

The Minority Experience: The Need for Ethical Standards

Ethical Issues
  Informed Consent
  Confidentiality
  Privacy
  Physical or Mental Distress
  Sponsored Research
  Honest Disclosure of Results
  Scientific Advocacy
  Protecting Vulnerable Clients
  Withholding Treatment for Research Purposes

Codes of Ethics

Main Points

Important Terms for Review

For Further Reading

Exercises for Class Discussion

People are the subject matter of social research, and because people have rights and feelings, there are special considerations in social research that do not confront the chemist studying molecules or the physicist investigating gravity. Consider, for example, the area of substance-abuse control and treatment. In recent years, there has been substantial controversy over the use of drug testing to deal with the problem. Some employers have instituted random drug testing of their employees as a condition of gaining or remaining employed. Some college athletes are randomly tested, as are prison inmates. In the context of social research, drug testing of a population would be a useful method for assessing the effectiveness of drug interdiction programs or substance-abuse counseling programs. To be most effective, such testing should be required of all people affected by a program. So, if new security procedures to control the entrance of drugs into a prison are established, their effectiveness can be measured by random testing of a sample of inmates. Likewise, if a drug education program is established in a college, its effectiveness could be assessed by random testing of a sample of students at the college.

Would such involuntary drug testing of inmates or students be proper? This question can be answered only by referring to some cultural, professional, or personal values that help us decide what is right and proper behavior. There are three expressions of values with which most Americans and human service professionals would agree:

1. People have a right to privacy.
2. People have a right to self-determination.
3. One person should not do anything to intentionally harm another person.

Viewing drug testing in this context, some would argue that people's right to privacy precludes taking their bodily fluids against their will to find out something about them. Is such an invasion of the privacy of college students proper or acceptable? What about prison inmates? Involuntary testing of a whole population would also seem to violate people's self-determination: They have no choice about participating in the research. Finally, since a person who tests positive for drugs might be subject to criminal prosecution or stigmatization, it raises the question of whether the research could bring harm to the person.

These are complicated issues that we will grapple with in this chapter. We do not presume that our statement of values is the final word or that their application to particular cases is easy or straightforward. They do serve as a beginning, however, to the discussion of ethical issues in social research. **Ethics** is the study of what is proper and improper behavior, of moral duty and obligation (Reese and Fremouw, 1984). Moral principles can be grounded in philosophy, theology, or both. For social researchers, ethics involves the responsibilities that researchers bear toward those who participate in research, those who sponsor research, and those who are potential beneficiaries of research. It covers many specific issues. For example, is it ever permissible to harm people during the course of a research project? Should people who participate in a research project ever be deceived? Is it appropriate to suppress research findings that cast a sponsor's program in a negative light? Should researchers report to the police about crimes they uncover while conducting their research? The ethics of a given action depend on the standards used to assess the action, and those standards are grounded in human values. Because of this, there are few simple or final answers to ethical questions, and there are no scientific "tests" that can show us whether our actions are ethical. In fact, there is ongoing debate among scientists about ethical issues because such issues involve matters of judgment and assessment.

Our purpose in this chapter is to identify the basic ethical issues in social research and to suggest some strategies for making sure that ethical considerations are attended to in the conduct and use of research. We will begin by considering efforts to codify ethical standards in recent decades. Then we will review some of the core ethical dilemmas that researchers are likely to face. Finally, we will discuss some ethical matters of special concern to researchers in the human services.

The Minority Experience: The Need for Ethical Standards

Ethical issues do not exist in a vacuum but rather within the context of a partic-

ular society and its historical development. There have been two events in this century—one abroad and the other in the United States—that served as major catalysts for efforts to codify a set of ethical standards for research.

The first event occurred in Europe during World War II. It was the heinous series of experiments conducted by the Nazis on Jews and others in concentration camps (Beauchamp et al., 1982). Prior to this, there had been no codification of scientific ethics, and researchers were left largely to their own devices in deciding how to conduct their studies. The revelation of the German atrocities, exposed during the Nuremberg trials in 1945 and 1946, was to shock the sensibilities of the world and leave an indelible imprint on research ethics from that time forward. The cruelty of the experiments is almost inconceivable. Healthy people were infected with such serious diseases as spotted fever or malaria. Other people were used to test the effects of various poisons or had parts of their bodies frozen to test new treatments. Still others were purposely wounded to study new antibiotics and other treatments. Perhaps most evil of all were the excruciating decompression studies designed to test reactions to high altitude flight (Katz, 1972). These gruesome experiments brought home forcefully exactly how far people would go in using research to further their own ends. They also brought home the vulnerability of minorities to exploitation in research, especially when the resources and authority of powerful groups support the research of people with few ethical standards. Public outrage led to heightened concern for establishing codified standards for the ethical conduct of medical research on human subjects.

The second event that influenced the development of a codified set of ethical standards was an infamous study of syphilis conducted by the U.S. Public Health Service (PHS). The study began in 1932 with 425 black males with syphilis and 200 black males without syphilis. All were poor, semiliterate, and from Tuskegee, Alabama. The intent was to observe them over a span of years to find out how the disease progressed. When the study began, there was no cure for syphilis. Nevertheless, the men were led to believe they were being treated. Fifteen years later, penicillin was discovered to be an effective cure for this dreaded affliction. Despite this discovery, the PHS continued the syphilis study an additional 25 years, withholding treatment from all but those fortunate few who discovered its existence on their own and requested it. If syphilis is untreated, it can cause skin disorders and heart disease and can affect the central nervous system, including the brain. Ultimately, it can be fatal. Many of the afflicted participants in the Tuskegee study suffered serious physical disorders or died as a result of not receiving treatment for the disease (Jones, 1982).

Most Americans today—and especially those in the human services—would agree that the actions of the PHS were repugnant, racist, and unethical in the extreme. When the study began, however, and even when effective treatment for syphilis became available, the subordinate position of blacks and poor people in American society meant that they were often not accorded the same political, economic, and even medical rights as whites and the more affluent. It is unlikely that well-to-do whites would have been treated in the same arrogant fashion, and one would hope that no such debacle would be seriously contemplated today. Yet we should keep in mind that the PHS study continued into the

1970s—an era we like to consider a more enlightened one regarding human rights—and ended only when it received public notoriety. This further documents the extent to which minorities (and others) can be at risk of dangerous and inhumane treatment by researchers who are not governed by clear and enforceable ethical standards.

So, the highly immoral treatment of some minorities in research in this century, especially the Nazi and PHS episodes, brought home to people the need to codify standards for ethical conduct so that researchers would have guidelines available and research subjects would be afforded some protection. The first effort along these lines was the Nuremberg Code, developed in 1946 in direct response to the atrocities committed during World War II. The Nuremberg Code was limited to issues of ethics in medical research. In 1966, the United States Public Health Service established ethical regulations for medical research that emphasized the following: (1) Full disclosure of relevant information should be made to the participants, (2) the decision to participate must be completely voluntary, and (3) researchers should obtain documented, informed consent from participants (Reynolds, 1979; Gray, 1982). In 1974, the Department of Health, Education, and Welfare (DHEW, now the Department of Health and Human Services, or DHHS) decreed that the PHS guidelines would apply to social science research. Furthermore, DHEW recognized that codes of conduct alone would not ensure ethical research without some oversight procedures. To this end, DHEW required research institutions, such as universities, to establish institutional review boards, or IRBs, to review research proposals to ensure that the guidelines were followed. These DHHS regulations have been broadened so that they apply not only to those projects directly funded by that agency but also to any research carried on in organizations that obtain DHHS funding.

Reaction to the imposition of DHHS guidelines and the IRBs among social scientists has been somewhat hostile. A common feeling is that the risks to participants in most social science research are minimal and different from risks in medical research (Murray et al., 1980). Researchers see the major risk in social science research being a breach of confidentiality, not direct harm during the research process. Furthermore, researchers feel that the regulations obstruct important research, hinder response rates, and reduce the validity and generalizability of findings.

In response to these concerns, the Department of Health and Human Services, under a policy issued in July 1981, exempted the following research methodologies from IRB review: evaluation of teaching procedures or courses, educational testing, survey or interview techniques, observation of public behavior, and documentary research (Huber, 1981). The only exceptions are research dealing with "sensitive" behavior, such as drug and alcohol use, illegal behavior, or sexual conduct. In assessing social science research not exempt from IRB review, the IRBs have tended to subscribe to a risk/benefit doctrine (Smith, 1981). This means that questionable practices, such as deception or disguised observation, may be utilized if the purpose of the study is viewed as sufficiently important to justify them.

Although the DHHS regulations exempt much social science research from IRB review, many universities and other research institutions require that *all* research projects be reviewed in order to de-

termine whether they are legitimately exempt. Furthermore, it has become increasingly commonplace for private foundations to require IRB review as a prerequisite for funding (Ceci, Peters, and Plotkin, 1985). Although a project may be exempt from review, researchers are not exempt from ethical concerns. Whether one's research will be reviewed or not, one still has the responsibility of considering the impact of the research on those who participate and on those who might benefit from it. And, as we will see, the existence of ethical guidelines does not eliminate the controversy that surrounds ethical issues because guidelines need to be interpreted and applied to specific contexts. Much debate surrounds such interpretation and application.

The debate over the Nazi experiments is not over. Controversy over the issue persists in terms of whether the data from that research, some of which is valid and reliable, should be used today (Moe, 1984; Martin, 1986; Schafer, 1986). Some have argued that use of the data is justified if they are scientifically valid and no other source of such data exists. If they are used, it is argued, one should feel compelled to express horror and regret at the manner of their collection. On the other side, some argue that our collective outrage at the treatment of minorities by the Nazis should be so great that use of the data is repulsive. In this view, refusing to use the data is a symbolic denunciation of such atrocities while using the data might be interpreted as an acceptance of their methods or at least a willingness to let the importance of "the holocaust" diminish with the passage of time. Between these two extremes, some researchers argue that the data should be used only if there is some overriding need for them and the objective of using them is more important than our symbolic rejection of the manner in which they were collected. This continuing debate shows how long-lasting and deeply rooted ethical issues in research can be.

We will turn next to a consideration of the major ethical issues that should be assessed as a routine part of any research project.

Ethical Issues

There are basically seven major ethical issues in social science research: informed consent, confidentiality, privacy, physical or mental distress, problems in sponsored research, the disclosure of research results, and scientific advocacy. The unique situation that confronts the human service researcher raises two additional considerations: protecting vulnerable clients and withholding treatment for research purposes.

Informed Consent

Informed consent refers to telling potential research participants about all aspects of the research that might reasonably influence their decision to participate. Very often people are asked to sign a *consent form,* which describes the elements of the research that might influence a person's decision to participate (see Figure 3.1). General agreement exists today on the desirability of informed consent in behavioral science research, primarily because American cultural values place great emphasis on freedom and self-determination. Whether the issue be whom to marry, what career to pursue, or whether to participate in a research project, we value the right of individuals to assess information and weigh alterna-

tives before making their own judgments. To deceive potential research participants would be to deny them the ability to determine their own destiny.

Although there is consensus about the general principle of informed consent, there is heated debate regarding exactly how far researchers' obligations extend in this realm. At one extreme, researchers known as ethical "absolutists" would argue that people should be *fully* informed of all aspects of the research in which they might play a part (Erikson, 1967; Elms, 1982; Baumrind, 1985). Even when research is based on the public record, such as agency documents, or on observations of behavior in public, some absolutists would argue that people about whom observations have been made should be informed of the research. Otherwise, they do not have the full right to decide whether they will participate.

However, rigid adherence to the absolutist position would make social research much more difficult to conduct. First of all, it would rule out many practices that some researchers consider important or essential. Many experiments, for example, rely on some degree of deception, at least to the extent of not telling participants the true research hypotheses. The reason for this is that people might respond differently if they knew these hypotheses. However, all such studies would be unacceptable to the absolutists and could not be conducted. Disguised observation, in which people in public settings are not aware they are being observed, would also be disallowed by absolutists. No longer could researchers engage in such effective strategies as infiltrating organizations—unless, of course, they told all employees what they were doing. The net result

I, _____, in return for the opportunity of partici-
pating as a subject in a scientific research investigation and for other considerations, hereby authorize the
performance upon me of the following procedure:

_____

_____

_____

_____

_____

    This consent I give voluntarily as the nature and purpose of the experimental procedure, the known dan-

gers and the possible risks and complications have been fully explained to me by _____.

I understand the potential benefits of the investigation to be _____

_____

_____

as well as the above procedure(s) to be used which may involve the following risks or discomforts: _____

_____

_____

    I understand that, as a participant, my rights will not be jeopardized, that my privacy will be maintained
and that the data obtained in this study will be used in a manner to maintain confidentiality and personal rights.
    I knowingly assume the risks involved, and I am aware that I may withdraw my consent and discontinue
participation at any time without penalty to myself.
    I also am aware of the fact that in the event of physical injury or illness facilities and professional care
which are available will not be provided free of charge and that monetary compensation for such injuries or
illness will not be made.

Dated: _____   _____
                                         Signature

Dated: _____   _____
                                         Signature

Figure 3.1 Sample Content Form for Adult Human Subjects in Research

Source: Northern Michigan University Human Subjects Research Review
Committee, *Policies and Procedures,* December 20, 1982. Reprinted with
permission.

would be to make social science research highly conservative and very limited. It would become the study of people who volunteer to be studied, and we know that volunteers are different in many ways from people who do not volunteer. This would have the effect of seriously reducing the generalizability of research findings.

Second, the absolutist approach would call for obtaining informed consent in *all* research projects, and research has shown that obtaining *written* consent can reduce people's willingness to participate in research. One study found that formally requesting informed consent prior to conducting an interview reduced the rate of cooperation by 7 percent in comparison to cases where a formal request was not made (Singer, 1978). Because, as we will see in Chapter 7, any reduction in response rate reduces the generalizability of the findings, obtaining informed consent in survey research can have serious negative consequences in terms of the validity of the research.

The reason that written informed consent reduces people's willingness to participate is probably that it appears in the eyes of respondents to contradict the researcher's assurance of confidentiality. One minute people are being told that their answers will remain confidential, and the next they are asked to sign a consent form. Even though signing a consent form need not impede the maintenance of confidentiality, it is not surprising that respondents may not view it that way. Anything that undermines respondents' beliefs in the confidentiality of the answers will reduce response rates. It may also affect the quality of the data obtained because those who do give their consent may be less candid in their responses than they otherwise would have been. It is ironic that an attempt to enhance one aspect of ethical practice—informed consent—is potentially a threat to another aspect—confidentiality.

Because of these problems with the absolutist approach to informed consent, many researchers take a less extreme position. They argue, first of all, that people should be informed of factors that might reasonably be expected to influence their decision to participate, such as any harm that might occur or how much time and effort will be involved. However, they also use a "risk-benefit" approach: Questionable research strategies, such as deception, are appropriate if they are essential to conduct the research and will bring no harm to participants and if the outcome of the research is sufficiently important to warrant it. It is ironic, but one study found evidence that the use of deception in small groups research may be increasing, despite its status as a questionable practice (Adair, Dushenko, and Lindsey, 1985). Their review of major social psychology journals showed that the rate of use of deception increased from 14.3% in 1948 to 58.5% in 1979. Lively debate continues concerning the use of questionable practices and their routine approval by IRBs (see Baumrind, 1985).

A final issue regarding informed consent has to do with the possibility that a person might feel pressured to agree or might not understand precisely what he or she is agreeing to. After all, asking a person to participate in a study can involve social pressures not unlike those in other settings. We often feel pressured to help others when they ask our assistance, and some people find it difficult to say no to a face-to-face request. In addition, scientific researchers represent figures of some authority and status, and people are often disinclined to refuse their requests. In other cases, people may be momentarily confused about what is being asked of them. To get around these problems, a study involving institutionalized elderly people used a two-step consent procedure (Ratzan, 1981). In the first step, people were told what their participation would involve, what risks were entailed, and that several days later they would be asked whether they were willing to participate. This was meant to reduce any immediate pressures to agree and to enable people to talk it over with others and clarify any confusing issues. The second step, occurring a few days later, was when the actual consent was obtained. In this study, all those who were asked refused to participate. This was probably due to the fact that a part of the study involved having an indwelling butterfly needle inserted in a vein for eight days in order to take blood samples. However, some of the people may have agreed to participate had they been asked to sign a consent form during the first interview. Yet it is questionable whether consent obtained at that time would have been as "informed" and considered as it should be. The goal of obtaining informed consent is not to pressure people into participating in the research but rather to gain participation that is truly "informed."

Confidentiality

Another major ethical concern in scientific research is **confidentiality:** that particular information or responses not be publicly linked to any specific individual who participated in a study. Confidentiality was a major concern in the 1981 DHHS regulations. Participants in social research are commonly told that their responses will be confidential, and the overall record on this point has been very good. There have, however, been a few notable exceptions that serve to illustrate some of the ways in which confidentiality can be violated. Especially in observational and single-subject research, one must be careful to protect identities when presenting results. To do this, researchers make it a common practice in reporting research results to give the observational settings, as well as any individuals who are specifically referred to, fictitious names. This procedure works fairly well as long as researchers do not become so detailed in their descriptions of places, events, and people that the protection afforded by the fictitious names is undermined.

A now infamous example of this is *Small Town in Mass Society* by Arthur Vidich and Joseph Bensman. First published in 1958, this observational community study described the power relationships and local governmental operations in a small town the authors called "Springdale." The authors had assured everyone that confidentiality would be maintained. Even though no identities were, in fact, directly revealed, it was easy for the residents of the small community to recognize the people and events described in the highly detailed report. Because the study was very critical of some residents of Springdale, these people understandably became outraged. Local newspapers vociferously attacked the researchers for betraying the community. The townspeople even held a Fourth of July parade that featured a full manure spreader carrying mired effigies of the authors (Whyte, 1958). In order to avoid such breaches of confidentiality, one must balance one's enthusiasm for producing a highly detailed account against the ethical obligation to protect fully the identities of those observed.

Single-subject research requires particular caution in this regard. As we will see in Chapter 11, single-subject research involves observing the changes in feelings or behavior of a single person over time. Furthermore, the clients in these studies often suffer from some condition, such as a mental disorder, that might lead to stigmatization should others find out about it. Thus, great care must be taken to ensure that people's identities are not unintentionally revealed in the process of providing a description of the case. Researchers must often tread a fine line between providing sufficient case detail and minimizing the risk of identification of a client. Final reports should always be written with a sensitivity to this issue.

Confidentiality can also be threatened when third parties, such as the people sponsoring the research or the courts, seek to identify research participants. Intrusion by a sponsor is relatively easy to avoid. When establishing a research agreement with a sponsoring agency or organization, one should make it clear in the agreement that identities will not be revealed under any circumstances. If the sponsor objects, researchers should refuse to accept the agreement. We will have more to say about sponsors and ethics later.

A greater threat to confidentiality comes from the courts. Most communication that physicians, lawyers, and clergy have with their clients is protected from judicial subpoena. Social workers, in their clinical capacity, also are afforded such protection in many instances although the degree of protection varies with agency settings and jurisdictions. Social scientists, however, do not enjoy the protection of privileged communication (Reynolds, 1979). Thus, courts may subpoena research data that reveal participants' identities, and failure to comply with such a subpoena renders researchers open to contempt of court charges. Social science researchers have been

treated very inconsistently by the courts in this regard, and this leaves their exact status unclear. In civil cases, the courts have been reluctant to compel researchers to reveal information. In a civil suit in California, for example, the court refused to force a researcher to reveal the identities of respondents in confidential interviews (Smith, 1981). Researchers should be aware, however, that although this case does establish a precedent, courts in other states and the federal judiciary are not bound to follow it.

In criminal cases, the courts have generally held that the right of the public to be protected from criminal activity supersedes any assurance of confidentiality in research. In one case, for example, data from an experiment on the negative income tax were sought by a county prosecutor, a U.S. senator, and the General Accounting Office for purposes of identifying people who were perpetrating welfare fraud (Wolfgang, 1981). Although the researchers were able to avoid revealing identities in this case (described in more detail in Research in Practice 3.1), they had no legal grounds to do so, and future cases could turn out differently.

Concern with possible subpoena of their research data has led some researchers to adopt elaborate measures to protect the data. For example, it is common to establish computer files with the data identified only by numbers rather than by names. Often, it is unnecessary to retain name identification for research purposes, once the data have been collected. In such cases, the names should be destroyed. If name identification is required, say, because you want to interview the same people at a later time, the names should be stored in a separate computer file. This procedure reduces the possibility of unauthorized persons linking names with data. Where concern

RESEARCH IN PRACTICE 3.1
Program Evaluation: Confidentiality in Large-Scale Field Experiments

Researchers commonly offer confidentiality to those who participate in their investigations and follow procedures to prevent the disclosure of potentially damaging information about the participants. Yet confidentiality can be very difficult to maintain, especially in studies of controversial programs. Such difficulties are illustrated in the New Jersey Negative Income Tax Experiment funded by the U.S. Department of Health, Education, and Welfare (Kershaw and Small, 1972). Negative income tax programs provide people with a guaranteed minimum income by giving those below a specific income a subsidy payment, or "negative income tax," to bring them up to the minimum level. It is intended as a simpler, more equitable, and more dignified way of providing public assistance. The New Jersey experiment was designed to assess the feasibility of replacing conventional welfare programs with a negative income tax and whether the work incentive elements of that program were more likely than conventional assistance programs to encourage people to work. So the stakes in the experiment were high. If it were successful, it could mean a major improvement in the way public assistance is provided. It was a large-scale experiment: Each year over 5,000 hours of interviews were conducted, a total of $800,000 in assistance was distributed to participants, 10,000 Income Report forms were processed, and 30 million bits of data were added to computer files.

Because welfare is a volatile public issue, confidentiality was an especially important problem. First, confidentiality would protect participants from any unnecessary intrusions or possible risks or damage when the program was assessed by the public and politicians. Second, confidentiality would enhance the accuracy and completeness of the sensitive data that needed to be collected as a part of the assessment. Participants were formally promised the protection of confidentiality, and families were provided with brochures outlining the research policies used to ensure confidentiality. In addition, the staff was trained in procedures to maintain confidentiality and had to sign an agreement promising to treat all data as confidential.

Two major events occurred during the experiment that highlight the vulnerability of such good intentions. First, as a consequence of a major revision in New Jersey welfare laws, the possibility that families would be eligible for both the experimental payments and AFDC increased considerably. The local prosecutor in Trenton, New Jersey, subpoenaed the records of families who were thought to be receiving dual payments, a move that seriously threatened confidentiality. A major problem was avoided, however, when the researchers agreed to pay the County Welfare Department $20,000

(Continued on next page)

to cover the cost of estimated dual payments. There lingered, however, a threat of additional subpoenas from other counties. Though these never materialized, legal counsel for the project felt it would not be possible to resist such subpoenas if they were served. Thus, a major reservation about promises of confidentiality was raised.

A second threat to confidentiality in the New Jersey Experiment arose when the General Accounting Office (GAO) of the federal government demanded access to complete case records, including the names of those receiving assistance. The GAO was reacting to the publication of preliminary findings that were used in congressional debate over President Nixon's Family Assistance Plan. Staff members of the New Jersey Experiment, officials at the Office of Economic Opportunity, and GAO representatives were called to testify before the Senate Finance Committee. The New Jersey staffers had to convince the senators and the GAO that divulging the names of recipients was not necessary and would be detrimental to the experiment. In the end, representatives from GAO testified that the New Jersey staff were cooperative, and this

testimony played an important role in avoiding this breach of confidentiality.

The negative income tax experiment demonstrates just how vulnerable promises of confidentiality are. Though most research is not brought under the kind of public scrutiny that afflicted this study, the risk of intrusion by government officials armed with the power of subpoena can be serious for policy research in the human services because the profession commonly deals with services to help those whom many find undeserving or morally suspect. Some have suggested that such problems could be avoided by passage of a statute protecting the confidentiality of experimental data. The likelihood of extending the right of privileged communication to include researcher and research participant, however, is not great, and this means researchers must consider cautiously the extent to which confidentiality can be guaranteed to participants. One suggestion is to inform participants of the limitations on confidentiality. Another is to avoid procedures where possible that personally identify participants, or use ones that make the association of names and potentially damaging information impossible.

about possible court subpoena is great, researchers have even deposited the name identification files in secret, numbered deposit boxes in foreign banks (Wolfgang, 1981). Overtones of international intrigue notwithstanding, this procedure effectively thwarts U.S. courts from forcing third parties, such as U.S.

banks, to turn over the subpoenaed information. Though this protects the data, it does not protect the researcher from a possible contempt citation for failing to comply with the subpoena.

Despite the fact that intrusion by the courts is a real danger with research on some topics, the reality is that court involvement is extremely rare. Though there have been over 200 cases where courts have sought journalists' information, there are only a dozen or so cases where courts have sought research data (Reynolds, 1979; Smith, 1981). Thus, the odds of a researcher's becoming embroiled in such a situation are remote. Nonetheless, researchers have an obligation to inform potential subjects accurately of any possible threats to confidentiality that might arise, including what would be likely to happen should their data be subpoenaed by the courts. The lengths to which investigators will go to protect confidentiality indicate how important this ethical issue is. The bottom line is that no one should be threatened with harm to themselves or their reputation as a result of participating in a scientific study.

Privacy

The ethical issue of the right to privacy is related to confidentiality, but it also has some distinct elements. **Privacy** refers to the ability to control when and under what conditions others will have access to your beliefs, values, or behavior. Intrusions on our privacy have become endemic in modern society, and with the growth of social research in the past century the danger of even greater intrusion arises. Virtually any attempt to collect data from people raises the issue of privacy and confronts the investigator with the dilemma of whether threats to privacy are warranted by the research. An illustration will show the complexity of this issue.

The sociologist Laud Humphreys (1970), in an effort to understand a particular type of homosexuality, made observations of men having quick and impersonal sexual encounters in public restrooms. In order to gather his data without arousing suspicion, Humphreys played the role of the "watch queen," who keeps watch and warns participants of approaching police or "straight" males who might disrupt the activities. None of the men who went to the restrooms to engage in sex was aware that his behavior was being recorded by a researcher. Humphreys was heavily criticized for violating the privacy of these men engaging in highly stigmatized actions that, were they made public, might disrupt their family lives or threaten their jobs. Many sociologists believe that research on such sensitive topics is not merely a matter of confidentiality—that is, not letting people's identities become known. Rather, such data should not even be collected because these men were obviously trying to conceal their actions from prying eyes. Social science researchers, it is argued, should respect that privacy.

Humphreys defends his research on the grounds that the confidentiality of his subjects was maintained and the results of the study were of significant scientific value. In fact, there is probably no other way to study such sexual behavior. Humphreys discovered that the men who engage in this type of illicit sex are not unusual or deviant in the rest of their lives. In fact, they were, for the most part, normal, respectable citizens who had found a rather unusual sexual outlet. Humphreys believes that our greater understanding of what had been considered deviant sexual conduct justifies the threat to privacy these men experienced. In addition, the public setting in which they performed their acts, he argues, reduced their right to claim privacy.

As the Humphreys investigation shows, the right to privacy is often a difficult ethical issue to resolve. In fact, in some settings, people are fairly tolerant of invasions of privacy. A study of family interaction, for example, utilized video-tape cameras installed in apartments to record all interchanges between family members (Ashcraft and Scheflen, 1976). Even though the families consented to the taping, the investigators, sensitive to the issue of privacy, offered the families the opportunity to review the tapes and edit out anything they wished. The assumption was that, despite agreeing to participate, family members might do something on the spur of the moment that they would prefer not be made public. Surprisingly, not one family exercised the option to edit the tapes.

There are a number of ways that privacy can be ensured. One way, as illustrated in the preceding study, is to offer participants the opportunity to destroy any data they wish to remain private. A second—and very effective—means of ensuring privacy is to accord the participants **anonymity,** which means that *no one*, including the researcher, can link any data to a particular respondent. Most commonly, this is accomplished by not including any identifying names or numbers with the data collected or by destroying any such identifiers once the data have been put in a computer file.

Physical or Mental Distress

Researchers should avoid exposing participants to physical or mental distress or danger. If the potential for such distress exists in a research investigation, the participants should be fully informed about it, the potential research findings should be of sufficient importance that they warrant the risk, and there should be no possibility of achieving the results without the risk. People should never be exposed to situations that might cause serious or lasting harm.

Research in the human services would rarely involve physical danger, but there are research settings in which psychological distress may be an element. Some studies, for example, have asked people to view such things as pornographic pictures, victims of automobile accidents, and the emaciated inmates of Nazi concentration camps. Certainly, these stimuli can induce powerful emotions, in some cases emotions that the participants had not expected that they would experience. A strong emotional reaction, especially an unexpected one, can be very distressful. There have also been studies in which people have been given false feedback about themselves in order to see how they respond. People have been told, for example, that they failed an examination or that tests show that they have some negative personality characteristics. Any situation in which people might learn something about themselves of which they were unaware can be distressful. Even the minor deceptions that are a part of much research can be distressful to people who thought they could not be easily deceived.

Assuming that the scientific benefits warrant the risk of distress and the participants are fully informed, it is then the researcher's obligation to alleviate the impact of whatever distress does actually occur. This is most often accomplished through a *debriefing*, in which people's psychological and emotional reactions to the research are assessed (Holmes, 1976; Ring et al., 1970; Smith and Richardson, 1983). Clinician-researchers should be especially adept at this stage in using their human service training to cope with people's reactions. Because the distress is usually mild and transitory, it can normally be dissipated quickly and with no permanent impact.

Sponsored Research

Because much social research is conducted under the auspices of a third-party sponsor, certain ethical considerations arise from that relationship. When research is sponsored, some type of research agreement, essentially a contract, is developed. Researchers and sponsors alike should exercise great care in drafting this agreement. The potential for ethical problems to arise later is reduced when the research agreement clearly specifies the rights and obligations of the parties involved. Three areas are of particular concern in sponsored research (Tripodi, 1974). First, it is common for sponsors to want to retain control over the release of the data collected. The precise conditions of release should be specified in the research agreement to avoid conflicts. One limitation that should not be tolerated, however, is the conditional publication of results, that is, agreeing to publish results only if they turn out a certain way (usually so they support the preconceived notions of the sponsor). Such conditional publication violates the integrity of the research process and the autonomy of the researcher (Wolfgang, 1981). If the researcher agrees to some other type of limitation on release, however, it must be honored. To do otherwise would be a breach of the agreement and unethical.

The second major concern in sponsored research is the nature of the research project itself. The precise purpose and procedures of the study should be specified in the agreement. Ethical questions arise if the researcher heavily modifies the study to cover matters not in the agreement. Certainly the researcher should be able to use the data gathered for scientific purposes beyond the needs of the sponsor, but it is unethical to agree to do a study that a sponsor wants and then change it for personal reasons so that it no longer meets the expectations of the sponsor.

A third area of ethical concern in sponsored research relates to the issue of informed consent, namely, telling participants who the sponsor of the study is. Although there is controversy in this regard, some researchers take the stance that truly informed consent can be given only if one knows who is sponsoring the study and for what purpose. Some people might object, for example, to providing data that would help a company market a product better, a political party present a candidate better, or the government propagandize its citizens. In fact, studies show that people are less likely to participate in research they know to be sponsored by commercial organizations, which suggests that information about sponsorship can influence the decision of whether to participate (Bailey, 1987). So, each researcher must carefully consider whether to make the sponsorship of a research project explicit. At a minimum, it is certainly unethical ever to deceive people regarding the sponsorship of a study in order to gain their participation.

Honest Disclosure of Results

Research investigations will normally result in some disclosure of the results of the study—in the form of a report to a sponsoring agency, publication in a professional journal, or possibly a release to the media. The preeminent ethical obligation in this regard is not to disclose in-

accurate, deceptive, or fraudulent research results. To do so undermines the
very nature of the scientific process that,
as we have seen in Chapter 2, is based on
building future knowledge on the foundation of existing knowledge. If we cannot depend on the accuracy of existing
knowledge, then the scientific endeavor
is threatened. Furthermore, disclosing
fraudulent results reduces the credibility
of all research in the eyes of lay people.

Fortunately, the amount of fraudulent research in science is rather small,
but enough cases have come to light for it
to be considered a problem.

A recent example of a rather large-

scale fraud was one involving research on
the use of drugs to control the behavior of
severely retarded children. In 1988, a
psychologist was indicted on criminal
charges that he reported to the National
Institute of Mental Health about experiments that were never carried out or
about data that were falsified. The fraud
had come to light when another researcher grew suspicious. A large-scale
investigation culminated in the criminal
indictment. Since this case has important
implications, especially for the link between research and practice, it is discussed in more detail in Research in Practice 3.2.

RESEARCH IN PRACTICE 3.2
Program Evaluation: Vulnerable Clients at Risk

While science must be constantly vigi-
lant against the danger of fraud, no-
where is this more true than in applied
research, where client treatment programs may be founded on the basis of
research results. This hazard was
graphically illustrated in a recent case
of alleged fraudulent research on the
use of drugs to control the behavior of
an extremely vulnerable population:
severely retarded, hospitalized patients
(Greenberg, 1987a; 1987b). This case
is alarming not only because of the
questioned authenticity of the research
but also because it called into question,
as the drama of the case unfolded, the
adequacy of the institutionalized system of research safeguards for protecting society from fraudulent research.

According to reports, the National
Institute of Mental Health (NIMH) had

been supporting the work of Dr. Stephen E. Breuning, who is a widely published psychologist and is regarded as
an expert in the control and treatment
of the severely retarded. Based on his
research, Dr. Breuning advocated the
use of stimulants, such as dextroam-
phetamine, rather than neuroleptic
drugs, such as thorazine, to control
the behavior of the severely retarded.
Not only would the former more effectively control behavioral problems, he
claimed, but they would produce fewer
side effects. Dr. Breuning's research
and recommendations have been incorporated into many treatment programs. The NIMH report on Dr. Breuning's work stated, "There can be no
question that States (e.g., Connecticut)
have amended policies governing treatment practices in an effort to be con-

sistent with what Dr. Breuning reports as scientific findings in his public addresses" (quoted in Greenberg, 1987a).

The possibility that the research was fraudulent came to light through the alert assessment of a former colleague of Breuning who was involved in the study of the side effects of behavior-control drugs. Dr. Robert L. Sprague of the University of Illinois became suspicious because Breuning's results were simply too neat and without the variations in data typical of this kind of research. In 1983, Sprague contacted NIMH, informing them of his suspicions and urging them to investigate.

This request was the catalyst for a sequence of events that are as disturbing as the questioned research itself. Dr. Breuning was then working at the University of Pittsburgh, and NIMH reportedly asked the school to look into the charges. They did so, but the investigation stalled when Dr. Breuning suddenly resigned his position. Dr. Sprague continued to prod NIMH about the research, and finally, in early 1985, a panel of distinguished scientists was appointed to investigate the charges. The panel reported to NIMH in 1987 that Dr. Breuning had "knowingly, willfully and repeatedly engaged in misleading and deceptive practices in reporting results of research" (quoted in Greenberg, 1987a). However, the concern in this case is much deeper than the apparent discovery of fraud. Because of the applied nature of the research, the disconcerting question is, What about the patients confined in institutions where treatment is based on Breuning's research? Apparently, NIMH has no procedures for notifying institutions that this research was under investigation and that there were serious questions about applications based on it. In addition, NIMH may have been reluctant to contact institutions since the investigation report had not been finalized and Dr. Breuning was denying the charges against him. So, there is no way as yet to determine whether these patients suffered any harm or setbacks because of receiving treatments based on Dr. Breuning's recommendations or how many patients may have suffered.

Meanwhile, another disturbing event was the fact that Dr. Sprague, the researcher responsible for bringing the fraud to the attention of authorities in the first place, had his own NIMH grant cancelled. He had been receiving funding for 18 years in support of his work on drug side effects. One explanation of the sudden funding cutoff was that officials at NIMH were getting back at him for embarrassing them with his dogged pursuit of the Breuning affair. This has not been proved but is consistent with experiences of other "whistle-blowers."

Most recently, in an unprecedented move, the U.S. government indicted Dr. Breuning on charges of falsifying data for his 1982 NIMH grant. The U.S. attorney in Baltimore was quoted as saying, "Let this investigation send a clear message to doctors and researchers who play fast and loose with their research that they will have to deal with the criminal justice system in addition to their peer review panels" ("Leading Researcher Indicted . . . ," 1988). Dr. Breuning has denied the allegations,

(Continued on next page)

but if convicted, he could receive penalties of up to 10 years in prison plus substantial fines.

Regardless of the final outcome of this case, it highlights several disturbing issues in ethics, research, and human service practice. First, this research managed to pass through the filters of review panels and institutional procedures without being questioned. How well can the institutionalized research system protect against fraudulent work? Second, when unethical practices are discovered, who bears the responsibility for alerting practitioners and the public to potential harmful implications? In manufacturing, the government can require product recalls, but how do we protect the public from implementation of fraudulent research? Third, how do we safeguard those who detect potential fraud? In many cases, the people most likely to discover it are colleagues, assistants, students, and others close to the research. To the extent that these people perceive disclosure as risking unpleasant consequences for themselves, they will be reluctant to come forward. And finally, the slow, plodding nature of the bureaucratic process raises the question of what can be done to efficiently process cases while at the same time protecting the rights of individuals accused of fraud.

Fortunately, the occurrence of fraud in research is considered to be a relatively rare phenomenon. However, as the serious consequences of this case testify, it is imperative that human service practitioners continue to work to reduce fraud and to safeguard the service recipients who are vulnerable to abuse because of fraud.

We can hope that most cases of fraud are eventually discovered, as was this one. Two ways that fraud can be detected are through peer review and replication. There are, however, limitations to each of these, as illustrated by a recent case of fraud in medical research involving Dr. Robert Slutsky (Engler et al., 1987).

The prolific Dr. Slutsky had authored or co-authored 137 articles on cardiological and radiological research over a seven-year period. During an evaluation of his appointment as a researcher at a university, questions were raised about duplicate data in two of his papers. In the ensuing investigation, 12 articles were deemed fraudulent and 48 were considered questionable. In some cases, articles described experiments that had never been conducted. How is it that these articles eluded the net of peer review by respected medical journals? There seem to have been two problems. First, peer review of article submissions cannot detect plausible, internally consistent fabrications. Second, the sheer number of research articles submitted to publications for review requires a large number of qualified reviewers who understand both the methodology and the content of the article.

If peer review does not detect and deter fraud, then will replication solve the problem? It might, but the effectiveness of replication has been severely hobbled by the modern research system where research funds are not often appropriated for replication. Funding agencies prefer to fund research efforts delving into new areas. Furthermore, replication, where it does occur, tends to be reserved for projects that have produced unusual results. Fraudulent studies that enhance the prestige of researchers but that do not run counter to accepted findings in a field are not likely to arouse enough attention to warrant replication (Engler et al., 1987).

There are several ways of reducing the chances of fraud. One is to supervise novice researchers until they demonstrate good practices and ethical conduct as well as technical competency. Second, organizations need to guard against overly prolific researchers. Senior researchers and co-authors should not simply allow their names to be associated with research reports without carefully examining the work. Third, journals can reduce fraud by requiring more complete data to be submitted to reviewers, even if they cannot be included in the published article. When fraud is detected, the journals have a responsibility to make the fraud public so that others will not unsuspectingly base research or treatments on the fraudulent material. Fourth, professionals in the field can also help reduce fraud by considering it their ethical obligation to report suspected cases to appropriate authorities. Finally, organizations can reduce fraud by establishing standards and developing facilities to retain data from research projects. Although cases of documented fraud may be rare, the costs of even those few can be high. Thousands of people unwittingly learn untruths. Economic resources may be wasted by basing policy decisions on false information. Social programs may be established or rescinded based on fraudulent data.

Though not as unethical as purposeful deception, careless errors in research have the same effect of creating misinformation. Social researchers owe the scientific community carefully conducted research that is as free of error as possible. As with frauds, errors are discovered and corrected through replication. For example, a massive study of delinquency in Baltimore did not confirm many of the relationships that had been established in previous studies (Lander, 1954). Reanalysis of the Baltimore data found that the reason for the unusual results was an error made in the statistical analysis, which substantially distorted the original findings (Gordon, 1967). Scientists are human, and human beings make mistakes. But, as researchers, we must take extreme measures to keep mistakes to the absolute minimum. Fear of the embarrassment of being caught making a serious mistake is a powerful incentive for researchers to produce accurate work.

Beyond the problems of fraud and carelessness, researchers also have an obligation to report their results thoroughly. How much of the results can be published, we have seen, may be limited by a contract with a sponsoring agency, but researchers must then take care to ensure that what is disclosed does not give a distorted picture of the overall results. In addition, researchers should point out any limitations that might qualify the findings. As personally painful as it may be, it is unethical to overstate conclusions by covering up problems in a study. Furthermore, some research in the human services is highly newsworthy, and this can create special ethical dilemmas. For example, a study of crime, poverty, and other problems in an urban public housing project in St. Louis in the 1960s found itself under intense scrutiny by the press (Rainwater and Pittman, 1967). Journalists exerted considerable pressure on the researchers, before their study was complete, to release their findings about the housing project and its problems. Fearing that premature disclosure of results might be inadvertently inaccurate or deceptive, the researchers chose to say absolutely nothing: "Ethically, we did not want to be in a position of asserting findings before we were really sure of what we knew" (Rainwater and Pittman, 1967, p. 359).

Scientific Advocacy

Scientific knowledge rarely remains the exclusive domain of the scientific community. It typically finds its way into public life in the form of inventions, technological developments, or social policy. This raises potential ethical dilemmas in terms of the role of researchers in advocating particular uses of their research results. What responsibility, if any, do scientists have for overseeing the use to which their results are put? To what extent should scientists become advocates for applying knowledge in a particular way? Quite naturally, disagreements exist on how to resolve these issues. The controversy is compounded in the case of human service researchers because their research is normally initiated with some explicit clinical application in mind. The classic approach to these issues derives from the exhortations of the sociologist Max Weber that science should be "value-free" (Weber, 1946). Social scientists, according to Weber, should create knowledge, not apply it. They, therefore, have no special responsibility for the ultimate use to which that knowledge is put. Furthermore, according to Weber, they are under no obligation to advocate particular uses of scientific knowledge. Indeed, advocacy is frowned on as threatening objectivity, which is a central concern of science. So while remaining value-free is difficult, many argue that abandoning the effort would be disastrous in that it would prevent us from ac-

quiring an accurate body of knowledge about human social behavior and might threaten the researcher's credibility as a disinterested expert (Sibley, 1971; Gibbs, 1983; Gordon, 1988).

The opposite stance in this controversy was originally developed by Karl Marx (1964, orig. pub. 1848). Marx championed the cause of the poor and downtrodden, and he believed that social researchers should bring strong moral commitments to their work. They should strive to change unfair or immoral conditions. Following Marx, some researchers today feel that social research should be guided by personal and political values and should be directed toward alleviating social ills (Bodemann, 1978; Brunswick-Heinemann, 1981). Furthermore, scientists should advocate for uses of their research by others that would help accomplish those personal goals.

A compromise position on the value-free controversy was developed by sociologist Alvin Gouldner (1962). He pointed to the obvious, namely, that scientists have values just as do other human beings. Furthermore, he noted, those values can influence research in so many subtle ways that their effects can never be totally eliminated. Instead of denying or ignoring the existence or impact of these personal values, scientists need to be acutely aware of them and up front about them in their research findings. Being thus forewarned, consumers of their research are then better able to assess whether the findings have been influenced by personal bias. In addition, Gouldner argued that social scientists have not only the right but also the duty to promote the constructive use of scientific knowledge (Becker, 1967; Gouldner, 1962). Because decisions will be made by someone concerning the use of scientific knowledge, scientists themselves are best equipped to make those judgments. As

Gouldner states, technical competence would seem to provide a person with some warrant for making value judgments. People who take this position view the value-free stance as a potentially dangerous dereliction of a responsibility that accrues to scientists by virtue of their role in developing new knowledge and their expertise.

Clinician-researchers, in particular, may be attracted by this stance. Because their research is conducted, in part, to advance the practice goals of the profession, they would likely view it as one of their duties to ensure that any clinical application of the results be faithful to the outcome of the research. Thus, human service researchers are more likely than many other behavioral scientists to take a strong stand in favor of advocacy.

It is our view that there is nothing wrong with researchers openly pressing for the application of scientific knowledge in ways they see as desirable so long as their advocacy is tempered with respect for objectivity. The danger of advocacy is that scientists can come to feel so strongly about issues they promote that it might hamper the objective collection and analysis of data.

Protecting Vulnerable Clients

Human service clients, because they are often involuntary recipients of services, may find themselves vulnerable to pressures to cooperate in research projects conducted by the organizations providing them with services. Such clients are likely to be sought out as research subjects because they are often viewed as deviant in some ways and, therefore, interesting to study or because they may be easier than other groups to locate and keep track of during a research project.

Welfare recipients, children in day-care settings, patients in public mental hospitals, participants in job training programs, to name only a few, are likely candidates for participation in social research projects. In fact, it is common for operators of new or special programs to be required by their funding sources to do research on the effects of their programs as a requirement for receiving funds. Thus, people who obtain human services are likely to be solicited for research. Though such safeguards as codes of ethics and governmental regulations may serve as useful guides, special obligations fall on human service practitioners to safeguard their clients from unreasonable pressures to participate in research.

A crucial issue in this regard is the matter of voluntary and informed consent. Can clients actually give consent freely? For example, this has been a criticism of medical research on prisoners (Gettinger and Krajick, 1979; Krajick and Moriarty, 1979). Until recently, it was common for drug companies to operate test laboratories inside state prisons. Jackson State Prison in Michigan, for example, has had a large program operated by the Upjohn Corporation for many years. Inmate participation in such programs is, on the face of it, voluntary. But it is debatable just how free inmates actually are to give consent. Typically, such projects offer participants separate living quarters, greater privacy, some payment for participation, and other amenities not available to the general inmate population. Though such inducements may appear only as niceties to those unfamiliar with prison life, they can take on the character of essentials in the Spartan, degrading, and often dangerous world of the prison. When the benefits of participation in research are perceived as the only means of avoiding assault, rape, or financial destitution, inmates may not consider the potential risks involved in such research. Mounting concern over this covert coercion and the threat of lawsuits have resulted in a sharp reduction in this kind of research.

The problem of voluntary consent may be somewhat more subtle among other recipients of human services. Though refusal to participate may not be linked to termination of benefits, clients may not be sure of this and may be disinclined to take the risk of finding out. For example, the reading level of AFDC clients is often less than that of the eighth grade, yet the reading level necessary to comprehend many welfare documents is above 13 years of education. Thus, it is not unreasonable to suspect that clients who are accustomed to being confused by welfare requirements might not aggressively seek to determine their rights to refuse participation in a research project presented by official-looking people with official-looking forms. We are not suggesting that research never be conducted on prisoners or public welfare recipients. Rather, clinician-researchers need to exercise additional caution—and, in some cases, possibly forgo valuable research projects—in the interests of ensuring truly voluntary informed consent.

Withholding Treatment for Research Purposes

An issue of particular concern to human service providers involves the research practice of withholding treatment from some group, called a control group, in order to assess whether a given treatment is effective (see Chapter 10). The control group serves as a comparison group. If a group receiving the treatment shows more improvement than does the control group over a certain span of time, then we can feel justified in claiming that the treatment brought about the improvement. Presumably, we are studying the

treatment because we believe that it will be effective. And herein lies the ethical dilemma for some service providers who feel that it is unethical to withhold a treatment that might help people. They believe that it deprives people in the control group of the possibility of improvement. This is a serious problem that is not easy to resolve, but there are a number of issues to consider. First of all, we might ask whether it is ethical to proffer treatments that are untested. We pointed out in Chapter 1 that many contemporary approaches to human service professions explicitly caution against the use of treatments whose effectiveness has not been evaluated. Providing services is expensive and time-consuming, and it also raises clients' expectations for improvement. Is it ethical to do this when there is no evidence to document that it will be beneficial? We would not think of marketing drugs without a thorough test of their effects, both positive and negative. We should expect no less from the human services that we offer people.

There may be, in some cases, alternatives to withholding treatment. For example, we might offer the control group a treatment that is known to be effective and then see whether the new treatment provides more or less improvement. In this way, all clients are receiving a treatment that is either known to be, or suspected of being, effective. Another alternative would be to delay giving the treatment to the control group for a period of time and make the comparisons between those receiving treatment and the control group over this time period. A similar approach was used in a study of two different approaches to controlling people's smoking behavior (Coelho, 1983). All participants in the study were told that if they were randomly placed in the group that would not receive treatment they would receive treatment when the study was over and would receive the treatment the study showed to be most effective. This resolves the ethical problem by ensuring that all participants will receive treatment *at some point.* In fact, clients often confront a delay in receiving services when the resources of an agency are taxed.

In cases where such alternatives do not exist, however, clinician-researchers must use the risk-benefit approach: Does the benefit to be gained from the research outweigh the risks of withholding treatment from the people in the control group? If we were studying people at high risk of suicide, we would probably be cautious about withholding treatment. In the treatment of nonassertiveness, on the other hand, we might decide that a delay of a few weeks in treatment would not be terribly detrimental, and whatever damage occurred could be undone once treatment was initiated. As with so many other ethical issues, this is ultimately a judgmental one over which clinician-researchers will continue to agonize.

The ethical issues involved in withholding treatment can also arise in a more subtle fashion, namely, the extent to which research activities might interfere with the delivery of services to clients. Research activities might include, for example, administering questionnaires, making observations in clients' homes, or gathering data from agency records. If these activities take much of a client's time, the client may be reluctant to ask for services or cooperate with treatment. Likewise, the time necessary to interview a client for purposes of data collection might reduce the amount of time available to provide treatment. Given that a major concern of practitioners is to provide services, they would have to weigh the costs of any interference with service delivery against the benefits of conducting research. And they would also need to consider the costs of *not* carrying out the research in their assessment of whether the interference is unethically impairing service delivery.

Codes of Ethics

A point that has been emphasized in this chapter is that ethical judgments are difficult and often controversial because they involve interpretation and assessment. Most professional organizations establish written codes of ethics to serve as guides for their members to follow. Though these codes by no means settle all debate, they do stand as a foundation from which professionals can begin to formulate ethical decisions. In Appendix C we have presented those parts of the codes of ethics of the National Association of Social Workers and the American Sociological Association that relate to the conduct of research. The codes of ethics of other human service professions would be similar to these.

||||||||||||||||||||||||||||||||||||||||||||||||||||||||||||||||||||||||||||||||||||||||

≡ Main Points

• What is ethical in research practice is based on human values and varies as those values change.

• The mistreatment of minority peoples in research has been a major impetus to the development of ethical standards for research in the United States and abroad.

- Social research is typically evaluated in terms of risk versus benefits, with "questionable practices" being allowed if the research promises sufficient benefits.

- Informed consent refers to telling potential research participants about all aspects of the pending research before they agree to participate.

- Rigid adherence to the doctrine of informed consent can limit social research by eliminating some useful research methods and forcing the study of only those persons who volunteer.

- Confidentiality means that the researcher will not publicly identify individual participants and their responses or actions.

- Intrusion by third parties, such as courts of law, can occasionally be a threat to the guarantee of confidentiality.

- Privacy refers to the ability to control when and under what conditions others will have access to your beliefs, values, or behavior.

- Exposing subjects to physical or mental distress should be kept to a minimum and should never be done without fully informed consent. Subjects should be thoroughly debriefed at the conclusion of the research.

- When conducting research for a sponsor, many ethical difficulties can be avoided by a detailed research agreement that covers such things as the purpose and nature of the research, rights of publication, and revealing to participants the sponsor of the research.

- Researchers have an obligation to report their results fully and honestly.

- Replication is a major tool of science for correcting research errors and fraudulent reports.

- It is the researcher's own decision regarding the degree to which he or she will become an advocate; however, caution is required so that objectivity is not undermined.

- Because of their disadvantaged status, human service clients are often vulnerable to coercion to participate in research projects and, therefore, require special protection.

- Withholding treatment from control groups raises an ethical dilemma, but it is often justified when testing unproved approaches.

- Most professional organizations have established codes of ethics that provide useful guidelines for making ethical decisions.

≡ Important Terms for Review

anonymity
confidentiality
ethics
informed consent
privacy

≡ For Further Reading

Beauchamp, Tom L., et al., eds. *Ethical Issues in Social Science Research.* Baltimore: The Johns Hopkins University Press, 1982.
A volume of readings that covers the range of ethical issues one is likely to face in human service research.
Bermant, Gordon, Herbert C. Kelman, and Donald P. Warwick. *The Ethics of Social Intervention.* New York: Wiley, 1978.
A readable overview of ethical issues involved in social intervention involving research.
Blumer, Martin, ed. *Social Research Ethics,* London: Macmillan, 1982.
An anthology of essays dealing with virtually all of the major issues in research eth-

ics. Classic studies are used as the focal point of discussions of disguised observation, invasion of privacy, deception, and many others.

Broad, William, and Nicholas Wade. *Betrayers of the Truth: Fraud and Deceit in the Halls of Science.* New York: Simon & Schuster, 1983.

An enlightening book by two journalists about the many frauds perpetrated by scientists. In fact, they argue, in a thought-provoking way, that fraud is endemic in science.

Hearnshaw, L. S. *Cyril Burt, Psychologist.* Ithaca, N.Y.: Cornell University Press, 1979.

An intriguing book about the now infamous case of a psychologist who conducted identical twin studies, claiming to show that heredity was more important than environment in promoting intelligence. The studies have since been proved to be fraudulent, but they served as a foundation for much social and educational policy.

Kimmel, Allan J. *Ethics and Values in Applied Social Research.* Beverly Hills, Calif.: Sage, 1988.

An excellent overview of the ethical dilemmas that confront applied researchers.

Milgram, Stanley. *Obedience to Authority: An Experimental View.* New York: Harper & Row, 1973.

A summary of a controversial series of experiments on the conditions under which people will obey authority. The core ethical issues involved are the psychological harm to people and the "cost-benefit" of harm against scientific worth.

Miller, Arthur G. *The Obedience Experiments: A Case Study of Controversy in Social Science.* New York: Praeger, 1986.

An exhaustive discussion of the famous Milgram experiments into obedience to authority and their ethical implications. Other experiments involving deception and stressful conditions are also presented.

Tripodi, Tony. *Uses and Abuses of Social Research in Social Work.* New York: Columbia University Press, 1974.

Though mostly about how to put human service research to work effectively, this volume also sensitizes the reader to the many ways such knowledge can be abused.

Wilson, Suanna J. *Confidentiality in Social Work: Issues and Principles.* New York: The Free Press, 1978.

A detailed analysis of the issue of confidentiality as it relates to human service practice. Given the linkage between research and practice, however, the analysis is also relevant to the needs of clinician-researchers in the human services.

☰ Exercises for Class Discussion

3.1 A student majoring in criminal justice needs to do a research project as a course requirement. He is working part-time as an undercover store detective in a large discount department store. His idea is to do observational research on the shoplifting behavior that he encounters as a part of his job. In addition, he has access to store records on suspects apprehended for shoplifting in the past. He also plans to interview a sample of shoppers about shoplifting without disclosing that he is also a store detective.

Discuss how the issues of informed consent, confidentiality, and disclosure of results apply to this case.

3.2 What recommendations could you make to this student to safeguard the ethical standards for research in this case? Consider each of the ethical issues discussed in this chapter. Do you think the study could be done ethically at all? Support your conclusion.

3.3 Suppose that you are working in an alcoholism treatment unit, and a proposal is made to initiate a new treatment program that looks promising but is largely untested. Under what conditions do you think it would be acceptable to utilize a control group as a comparison group that does not receive any treatment? Under what conditions would it be ethically unacceptable? How might you avoid some of the ethical dilemmas that come from withholding treatment but still have some form of control group to use for comparison purposes?

3.4 Consider the Codes of Ethics presented in Appendix C. What changes in the codes would you recommend making in order to improve them? Why do you think these would be improvements?

4

Issues in Problem Formulation

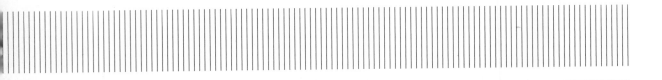

Suppose that you were required, as many students in courses on social research are, to design and conduct a research project. Our experience teaching research courses in the social sciences and human services is that some students respond to this assignment by drawing a total blank. Other students grasp eagerly onto a topic, such as "the cause of drug addiction," and rush off with total confidence that they are about to solve this enduring problem. In each case, the student is having difficulty adequately formulating a research problem. In the first case, the difficulty is in locating a problem to investigate, whereas in the second, it is in formulating a problem sufficiently specific that it is amenable to scientific research. We assure you that this problem is not unique to students. Every researcher must grapple with the issue of problem formulation. Because it is the initial step and provides the basis for the complete research project, problem formulation is of crucial importance. Many potentially serious difficulties can be avoided—or at least minimized—by careful problem formulation. In this chapter, we will present the major issues to be considered in problem formulation, beginning with how to select a problem on which to conduct research. Then we will analyze how to refine the research question so that it can be answered through research. Finally, factors relat-

ing to the feasibility of research will be discussed.

Selecting a Research Problem

The first hurdle confronting a researcher is to select a topic that is appropriate for scientific investigation. Actually, this is not as difficult as it may first appear because the social world around us is literally teeming with unanswered questions. Selecting a problem calls for some creativity and imagination, but there are also a number of places to which you can turn for inspiration. We will discuss the more common sources of research problems.

Personal Interest

Research topics are often selected because a researcher has an interest in some aspect of human behavior, possibly owing to some personal experience. One social scientist, for example, conducted research on battered women and women's shelters in part because of her own earlier experience of being abused by her husband; another researcher, who had grown up in the only black family in a small rural town, later did research on prejudice, discrimination, and the experience of minorities (Higgins and Johnson, 1988). Research frequently focuses on behavior that is unique or bizarre and thus compelling to some. Examples of such research abound, including studies of people's behavior in bars (Cavan, 1966) and nudist colonies (Weinberg, 1968), pool hustlers (Polsky, 1967), juvenile gangs (Horowitz, 1987), and striptease dancers (Dressel and Peterson, 1982).

Researchers who select topics out of personal interest must be careful to demonstrate the scientific worth of their projects. Recall from Chapter 1 that the goals of scientific research are to describe, explain, predict, and evaluate. The purpose of research is to advance our knowledge, not just satisfy personal curiosity. In his study of strippers, for example, sociologist James Skipper (1979) was interested in learning about how people adapt to a job that many people consider deviant. Such a focus placed his research firmly in an established area of study and amplified its scientific contribution. A researcher who chooses a topic based on personal interest—especially if it deals with some unusual or bizarre aspect of human behavior—should be prepared for the possibility that others will fail to see the worth of that research. Even though Skipper, as noted, established a scientific rationale for his study of strippers, he and his associates were subjected to much abuse by those who failed to appreciate its scientific value.

Social Problems

In selecting a topic for research, you often need look no further than the daily newspaper, where you can read about the many social problems that our society faces. Problems such as crime, delinquency, poverty, pollution, overpopulation, drug abuse, alcoholism, mental illness, sexual deviance, discrimination, and political oppression have all been popular sources of topics for social research. The Society for the Study of Social Problems—a professional organization to which many social scientists and human service providers belong—publishes a journal titled *Social Problems*, whose sole purpose is to communicate the results of scientific investigations into current social problems.

Within each of these general categories of social problems, there is a range of issues that can be studied. Many studies, for example, focus on the sources of a problem. Others are concerned with the consequences these problems have for individuals or for society. Still others deal with the outcomes of social programs and other intervention efforts intended to ameliorate these problems. People in the human services, who are routinely involved with many of these problems, can find opportunities for research that are directly related to their professional activities.

Testing Theory

Some research problems are selected on the basis of their relevance in testing the implications of a particular theory. We noted in Chapter 2 that theoretical concerns should be at issue to some degree in all research. At a minimum, nearly all research has some implications for existing theory. Certain research topics, however, are selected specifically for the purpose of testing some aspect of a given theory. Many theories relevant to the human services have not been thoroughly tested. In some cases, this means we do not know how valid the theories are, whereas in other cases it means that we do not know how wide the range of human behavior is to which the theory can be applied.

Evaluation Research

Evaluation research focuses on assessing the effectiveness or efficiency of some program or practice. As noted in Chapter 1, evaluation, in the form of program evaluation and practice effectiveness evaluation, has become an increasingly important activity of human service professionals. Agencies or organizations that fund the human services today typically demand that evaluation research be conducted if funding is to be granted or continued. Beyond any requirements, however, opportunities abound for evaluation studies to be conducted at the initiative of individual practitioners. Personal experience in practice settings can lead to questions that might be answered through research. A human service worker, for example, might feel that some of the services performed for clients seem more beneficial than others. He or she can then set up an experiment to evaluate which of the procedures was most effective and which the least effective. On the basis of the results, modifications in practice might be made that improve services to clients. Human service workers with a research orientation will be especially attuned to research opportunities that arise in practice settings.

Prior Research

One of the most fruitful sources of research problems is prior research because the findings of all research projects have limitations. Though some questions are answered, others always remain. In addition, new questions may be raised by the findings. It is, in fact, common for investigators to conclude research reports with a discussion of the weaknesses and limitations of the research, including suggestions for future research that follow from the findings that have been presented. Focusing on these unanswered questions or expanding on previous research is a good way to find research problems.

Prior research can also lead to new research problems if we have reason to question the findings of the original research. As we emphasized in Chapter 2, it is imperative that we not complacently accept research findings, especially when conclusions are based on a single study, because there are numerous opportunities for error or biases to influence results. If we have reason to suspect research findings, we have a ready-made problem on which to conduct research ourselves. One of our students, in fact, found his problem in just this way when faced with the course assignment of conducting a research project. The student had read a research article suggesting a number of differences between the social settings in which marijuana is used in contrast to those in which alcohol is used. The student disagreed, partly because of his own experiences, believing that the social environments in which the two substances were used were quite similar. He designed a study that allowed him to determine whether his hypotheses—or those presumably verified by the previous investigation—would better predict what he would observe. As it turned out, many of his hypotheses were supported by his findings.

Human Service Practice

The ongoing practice of human service professionals is probably one of the more important sources of research topics for clinician-researchers. Such research, developed for practical reasons, can take many forms. A social agency, for example, may require some needs assessment research to gather information about its clients if it is to efficiently deliver services to them. Or a practitioner may need to know which intervention strategy—group work, psychotherapy, behavior therapy, or some other—will be most effective with a particular problem. Prison officials need to know which criminal offenders are the riskiest to parole. Home health-care workers need information about how to ensure that people will take medications as prescribed. In all these cases, the practical information required by an agency or practitioner determines the focus of the research effort.

Research begun out of a need for this very practical information is often conducted in such a way that the results are less useful than they might be. The information needed is gathered, to be sure, but opportunities to gather data that would make the research useful to a broader audience are often missed because the researchers fail to link their practical research concerns with some broader theoretical issues. Recall the functions of theories, as discussed in Chapter 2. By designing research—even applied research—with theoretical issues in mind, it is possible to accumulate results that are applicable to a wide range of settings. This can often be done without adding substantially to the time or cost of conducting the study. Because research is expensive and time-consuming, it is important to maximize the utility of any research opportunity. This also illustrates a point stressed in Chapter 1 about the role of research in the human services. Although practitioners and agencies may be interested in learning something specific and practical through research, they should also view research as an opportunity to add to our growing knowledge base. In other words, efforts should be made to combine both pure and applied research.

The ability to find research problems in practice settings is limited only by the creativity and imagination of the practitioner. This was delightfully brought home to us by two of our students in a social research course. They were doing a field placement in a community mental health clinic while taking the research course, so they decided to search for some problem at the clinic to serve as the focus of their research paper. They noticed that one problem the clinic faced was the failure of clients to show up for appointments that had been previously scheduled. In addition to creating difficulties in achieving effective intervention, this also resulted in an inefficient use of staff resources because counselors were left idle by missed appointments. The students designed a very simple investigation in which some clients were given a "reminder" phone call a day or so before their appointment whereas other clients, as had been previous practice, were not contacted. The researchers' concern was to establish whether the "reminder" phone call increased the rate at which people showed up for their appointments. After implementing this procedure for a while, the students concluded that the phone call did help and would be a useful and efficient addition to the functioning of the agency.

Minorities in Research: The Political Context of Problem Selection

From the preceding discussion on how to select a research problem, one could get the impression that the problem selection process is largely a matter of personal preference. Guided by personal interest or experience, the prospective researcher identifies a worthy problem and sallies forth in the pursuit of knowledge. But problem selection, like most other types of human activity, cannot be explained solely in such individual terms. In fact, if you were to ask students in research courses why they chose the term paper topics they did, you might find that, in addition to personal interest, theoretical orientation, or practice interest, their choices were governed by such factors as these: "My instructor had a data set available on this problem." Or "I got financial aid to work as a research assistant." Or "I knew my prof was interested in this topic, so I hoped studying it might help me get a better grade." In other words, issues of political efficacy can influence problem selection.

In the world of professional research, the situation is not unlike that of the student. However, the stakes are much higher, and the consequences are much greater. Although the number of problems to be studied may be infinite, the resources society can allocate to research them are not. Research is a major societal enterprise in which universities, governmental organizations, private research corporations, and independent researchers compete with each other for limited resources. At the same time, there are forces working in society to make sure that the concerns of vested interest groups receive attention from the research community. Thus, problem selection is very much a political issue, and the problems that affect minorities and other groups with little clout may not receive the research attention they deserve.

Consider the example of spouse abuse. Men have been assaulting their wives since long before there was social research. Prior to the 1970s, however, one would have been hard pressed to find much research on the topic. Today the social science and human service literature

is replete with studies on the topic. What explains the change? Certainly, there is no single answer, but a major factor has been the women's movement. Before the 1960s, women as a group had considerably less political power than they do today, and the special problems of this minority often received little research attention. Spouse abuse is now a hot issue to the women's movement, and this politically powerful group has been able to translate their concerns into public policy. The government has allocated money specifically for domestic violence research. Human service and social science journals responded to the growing societal concern by selecting for publication studies on this topic over studies on other topics. Researchers seeking problems to study were attracted to the area by the availability of funds, the potential for publication, and the desire to contribute knowledge to an area of public concern.

So one major factor influencing the research funding allocation process is the existence of a powerful, articulate, and effective interest group that can push for research on a particular problem (Strickland, 1972; Lally, 1977). Other factors include the following:

- support for research by influentials at the national policy-making levels
- definition of a condition as a social problem by national influentials
- public awareness of and concern about the condition
- the severity, extent, and economic costs of the condition
- the amount of publicity about the condition
- the amount of support for research on the condition in the major funding agencies.

On this last point, it is important to recognize that major agencies of the government, such as the Department of Health and Human Services and the National Science Foundation dispense millions of dollars for research each year. Support of congressional leaders and key personnel in these major departments is essential for problem areas to be deemed worthy of financial backing for research. Typically, funding sources publish "Requests for Proposals" (RFPs), which outline the organization's funding priorities and requirements. Researchers are invited to submit proposals for competitive consideration with other researchers. Proposals may be for millions of research dollars, and the competition for funding is as intense and high-pressure as any big business deal.

Given that the political process plays a major role in determining which problems are sufficiently important to warrant research attention, it is not surprising that those people who lack access to social power in our society are also those whose interests are least likely to be served by the research conducted. Children, for example, are among the least powerful groups in our society, and where their interests conflict with those of adults, the children are typically the losers. Child abuse has been around for centuries, but it was not until recently that the research and practice communities began to pay attention to the needs of abused children (Radbill, 1980; Gelles, 1987). As another example, problem pregnancies have traditionally been viewed as a "female" problem despite the fact that it doesn't take a researcher to surmise that a male was involved somewhere. Only recently, possibly because more women are now conducting research, have researchers begun to use the couple as the unit of analysis rather than the teenage mother when studying problem pregnancies (Brown, 1983).

John Lally (1977) developed an imaginative research project to address the wide disparity in funding before 1972 for research on cancer in comparison to crib death, or sudden infant death syndrome (SIDS) as it is formally known. SIDS is suspected of being the leading killer of children between the ages of 28 days and one year. Upwards of 10,000 infants may die annually from the syndrome. Although the number of deaths from cancer was estimated to be 33 times greater than the SIDS death toll, the 1971 federal support for direct cancer research was more than 2,000 times greater than direct SIDS funding.

The differences between cancer and SIDS funding seemed to be especially affected by a number of factors. For example, SIDS was not as well perceived as a social problem as was cancer. Although there was a strong, active lobby for cancer research, there were only two small and recently formed organizations concerned with SIDS. Furthermore, SIDS has characteristics that made it less appealing than cancer as a research topic. For example, it was a frustrating and unexplainable condition to the medical establishment. It was also not covered in standard medical education, with the consequence that, when a physician did encounter a case, it was often incorrectly diagnosed and reported. The victims of SIDS are more likely to be poor and members of minority groups. However, unlike sickle-cell anemia, the disease is not so concentrated among blacks that it became a factor in the efforts of blacks to achieve equitable treatment in the allocation of research dollars. Given this set of circumstances, a serious killer of the newborn was allowed to prey on the children of America with relatively scant attention whereas another disease received far more resources devoted to its eradication than could be predicted by death toll alone.

One recent and particularly disturbing case where minority status influenced the funding of research was with Acquired Immune Deficiency Syndrome, or AIDS. In the United States, 90 percent of the AIDS cases occur among homosexual or bisexual men and intravenous drug users (Shilts, 1987; Boffey, 1988). Both groups are seen as marginal and highly stigmatized by many Americans, especially those in positions of power. In fact, AIDS was widely defined as a "gay disease" and, thus, something that most Americans need not worry about. The attitude of many could be summed up by the comment of a person who was later to be a staff member at the White House: "Those poor homosexuals. They have declared war on nature, and nature is exacting an awful retribution." As long as AIDS was defined as a disease of "those deviants," funds for research on the cause and prevention of AIDS was slow in coming. It wasn't until AIDS began to threaten the blood available for blood transfusions and the fear arose that AIDS was entering the heterosexual population that considerable research support was forthcoming. Even though gays have become a fairly powerful minority group in some cities—they are well educated and affluent—they do not have clout in the domains where decisions are made about the funding of research.

So, the selection of research problems is a highly political process. While powerful interest groups will always play a role in this process, researchers need to avoid the perceptual blinders that often hinder the ability of the powerful to see which problems are sufficiently important or serious to warrant attention. Human service professionals can play an

important role in the political issues surrounding problem selection whether they actually conduct research or not. In the course of practice, human service providers deal directly with the poor, those labeled as deviant, minorities, and the powerless. This puts them in a position to serve as advocates for the inclusion on the societal research agenda of problems relevant to their clientele.

We have discussed numerous sources of research topics for clinician-researchers. Although we have discussed them separately, they are often used in combination as an inspiration for finding researchable issues. A person might be compelled, for example, by personal, theoretical, and practical concerns toward a particular topic. Finding a research topic, however, is only the first step in problem formulation. The next step is to shape it into a problem that can be solved through empirical research.

Shaping and Refining the Problem

As we mentioned, one frustrating trap in which novice researchers often become ensnarled is choosing a topic that is so broad and encompassing that, by itself, it offers little guidance in terms of how to proceed. Finding the "causes of juvenile delinquency" or the "weaknesses of the modern family" sounds intriguing, but these topics provide little direction concerning specifically *where* to begin to look. The next step in the research process, then, is to begin translating a general topical interest into a precise, researchable problem. The scope of the problem needs to be narrowed to manageable proportions. One investigation is unlikely to uncover "the causes of juvenile delinquency," but it might provide some insight regarding the influence of particular variables on the emergence of particular delinquencies. Refining, narrowing, and focusing a research problem do not occur at once but rather form a continuous process involving a number of procedures. We will discuss some of the major influences on this shaping process.

Conceptual Development

In Chapter 2, we discussed the role of theories and hypotheses in the research process, pointing out that concepts are one of the central components of theories. In the refining of a research problem, one of the key steps is *conceptual development:* identifying and properly defining the concepts that will be the focus of the study. In exploratory studies, of course, we are entering areas where there is little conceptual development, and a major purpose of the research itself may be to identify and define concepts. In cases where there is existing theory and research to rely on, however, some conceptual development occurs as a part of formulating a research problem. One part of this process, already discussed in Chapter 2, is to clearly define the meaning of a concept. Another part of the process is to narrow the focus of the concept so that it encompasses something that is feasible to research in a single study. Practitioners in a youth home, for example, with an interest in juvenile delinquency might ask themselves: Are we interested in all forms of delinquent behavior or only in some types? In reality, the concept of delinquency is an extremely broad one that includes all actions by juveniles that violate criminal or juvenile codes. There is no reason to assume that *all* types of de-

linquency can be explained on the basis of a *single cause.* The concept of delinquency, therefore, might be narrowed so that it includes only certain behaviors, such as violence or truancy. The goal of this specification process, then, is to make clear *exactly* what the focus of the research effort is to be.

Once key concepts have been clearly defined, the next consideration is their measurability. Only concepts that are in some way measurable can be used in the research process. Eventually, of course, concepts will have to be operationalized, as is pointed out in Chapter 2, so any that are not readily measurable will have to be dropped. Measuring concepts can sometimes be difficult, as we will note in more detail in Chapter 5. In fact, theories at times include concepts that are extremely difficult to operationalize. Theorists are sometimes criticized for this practice although the criticism is misdirected. Theorists, of necessity, must be free to create and utilize whatever concepts are deemed necessary without regard to their immediate measurability. To do otherwise would limit theoretical development to those concepts that we currently have the skill to measure (Shearing, 1973; Denzin, 1978). Theorists' use of concepts that are not immediately measurable allows for theoretical advances, but it also confronts researchers with the task of creating ways to measure the concepts. However, if concepts in a proposed study cannot be measured, then some modification in the project—and possibly in the theory—will be necessary. This process of refining and developing concepts as a part of the research process illustrates a point made in Chapter 2 regarding the interplay between theory and research: Theories provide concepts and hypotheses for research while research modifies theories through conceptual development.

Review of the Literature

With concepts clarified and deemed measurable, we are ready to conduct a review of previous research that relates to our research problem. This "review of the literature" is a necessary and important part of the research process. We do it in order to familiarize ourselves with the current state of knowledge regarding our research problem and to learn how others have delineated similar problems. Unless we are planning a replication, it is unlikely that we will formulate our problem precisely like any one of these previous studies. Rather, we are likely to pick up ideas from several that can be integrated to improve our own. Through reviewing the relevant literature, we can further narrow the focus of the research project and ensure that we do not unnecessarily duplicate what others have already done. A thorough literature review calls for familiarity with basic library utilization skills, including how to locate books, professional journals, and public documents. To help with this important aspect of doing research, we have included Appendix A in this book on the use of the library. Even those students who have had some experience using the library will find some helpful new information in this appendix.

What one finds during the literature review can be just about anything. We may find that our selected topic has hardly been touched by previous research or that it has been quite thoroughly investigated. If there has been little previous research, we are relatively free to formulate our problem in any way we like. Given the paucity of research, however, the literature review will be less helpful

in refining our problem, and we will have to make more decisions ourselves. If we find that our topic has been lightly researched, we might consider a loosely structured exploratory study. If our review finds that we have selected a popular topic that has been heavily researched, we will find concepts, variables, and hypotheses well developed, and existing research will direct us to fairly specific questions for further research.

Most likely, the literature review will reveal that the volume of prior research falls somewhere between total neglect of the problem and complete knowledge about it. There will be some research, but all questions will not have been covered. If this is the case, researchers will undoubtedly find that pitfalls can be avoided by learning from others' experiences. It may be, for example, that one or more specific approaches to a topic have proved unproductive. That is, several studies have failed to find significant results or strong relationships. Unless there is good reason to believe that there were methodological weaknesses in these earlier studies, using the same approach is likely to lead once again to failure. Research is likely to be more productive if it focuses on studies that have achieved some positive results. There is simply little point in following the lead of those who have encountered failure.

During the literature review, a major focus should be on the methodology employed in previous research. Knowledge of others' methodological successes and failures can be of great value. As we have noted, successful operationalization of concepts is often difficult. Previous work in this area is invaluable in finding workable measures for concepts. Measures used in the past may require modification to meet current needs, of course, but making these modifications is likely to be easier than concocting a completely new measure because developing measures is a difficult and time-consuming process.

Previous research will also be useful in selecting the most appropriate data-gathering technique for a problem. Successful approaches by others should be noted, and unsuccessful ones should be avoided. It is of the utmost importance that the problem determine the data-gathering technique used, and not the other way around. All too often, beginning researchers decide to do a survey, an experiment, or some other type of study and then try to make the problem fit the method. This is the wrong approach. A variety of data-gathering techniques exists because no one method is always best. As will be noted in subsequent chapters, each technique has its strengths and weaknesses, and each is suitable for answering some questions but not others.

Previous research can also be useful in determining the sampling strategy that will be used and in avoiding sampling problems encountered by others. Suppose, for example, that the study we propose to do calls for the use of mailed questionnaires. An ever-present problem with mailed questionnaires is making sure that a sufficient number of people complete and return them. It would be useful for us to know what the experience of other investigators has been with people like those we plan to survey. Not all groups respond to mailed questionnaires with the same degree of enthusiasm. If the group we are proposing to sample has exhibited notoriously low return rates in the previous studies, we have to plan accordingly. We would likely increase the number of questionnaires mailed and would certainly use all available means of obtaining the highest response rate pos-

sible. Or, if very low return rates are anticipated, we may want to search for another group to study or even consider whether this particular project is feasible given the anticipated low return rate.

The literature review can also serve the very practical function of showing how other researchers have stated their research problems. The narrowing and focusing process can benefit from exposure to good examples. We have noted the importance of the problem's being clearly stated. Most research articles begin with an abstract, which is a brief paragraph describing in summary form the research that is more fully described in the body of the article. Contained in this abstract will be a concise statement of the research problem, such as the following:

> In this paper I consider family day care as a site in which to explore the personal and social consequences of home-based work. The data are from a questionnaire sent to all registered day care providers in Vermont ($N = 225$) and from interviews with 28 registered and 34 unregistered family day care providers. I describe the motivation for offering family day care. I discuss how the autonomy of family day care providers is constrained. Finally, I look at some additional economic, personal and political consequences of home-based work. Although, from one perspective, family day care might be considered a booming success, I argue that this success rests on the secondary status of women in the labor force and on the unpaid labor of women at home (Nelson, 1988).

> The clinical assessment or "clinical judgment" of clients has historically served as a guide for the interventions of social work practitioners. Yet, despite the critical importance of such judgments, very little is known about how certain variables influence the clinical judgment

process. This study explored the nature of the interaction between practitioner variables associated with differential judgments and the client variables of class and race. The paper describes specific strategies likely to increase practitioners' effectiveness with working-class and black clients, and the implications of these findings for future research endeavors (Franklin, 1985).

Notice that in each example the problem addressed in the study is clearly and directly stated. Notice also that the statements contain information about the data that are utilized in the studies. Before moving beyond the planning stages of a project, we will want to be able to state the problem in similar fashion.

Units of Analysis

An important element in the process of shaping and refining a research problem is the decision regarding the unit of analysis to be investigated. **Units of analysis** are the specific objects or elements whose characteristics we wish to describe or explain and about which data will be collected. Although there are many units of analysis, five that are commonly used in human service research are individuals, groups, organizations, programs, and social artifacts (see Table 4.1). (There are different units of analysis used in studying documents, and these will be discussed in Chapter 8.)

Much social research focuses on the *individual* as the unit of analysis. The typical survey, for example, obtains information from individuals about their attitudes or behavior. Anytime we define our population of inquiry with reference to some personal status, we are operating at the individual level of analysis. For example, unwed mothers, welfare recipients, mental patients, retarded children, and similar categories all identify individuals with reference to a status they occupy.

If we identify our unit of analysis as individuals, it is important to recognize that the entire analysis will remain at

TABLE 4.1   Possible Units of Analysis in Research on Juvenile Delinquency

Unit of Analysis	Example	Appropriate Variables	Research Problem
Individual	Adolescents arrested for larceny	Age, sex, prior arrests	Do males receive different penalties from females for similar offenses?
Groups	Delinquent gangs	Size, norms on drug usage	Are gangs involved in drug trafficking more violent than other gangs?
Organizations	Adolescent treatment agencies	Size, auspices, funding level	Do private agencies serve fewer minority and lower-class delinquents than public agencies?
Programs	Delinquency prevention programs	Theoretical model, type of host setting	What services are most frequently included in prevention programs?
Social artifacts	Transcripts of adjudication hearings	Number of references to victim injury	To what extent does the level of violence in the offense affect the kind of penalty imposed?

that level. For the sake of describing large numbers of individuals, it is necessary to utilize summarizing statistics such as averages. We might, for example, as a part of a study of unwed mothers, note that their average age at parturition (childbirth) was 16.8 years. Aggregating data in this fashion in no way changes the unit of analysis. Our data are still being collected from individuals.

Social scientists sometimes focus on social *groups* as their unit of analysis and collect data on some group characteristic or behavior. Many of these groups involve collections of individuals who share some social relationship with the other group members. In such groups as families, peer groups, occupational groups, or juvenile gangs, the members have some sense of membership or belonging to the group. If we study families in terms of whether they are intact or not, we are investigating the characteristics of a group—the family—not of individuals. Other groups of interest to social scientists are merely aggregates of individuals with no necessary sense of membership, such as census tracts, cities, states, or members of a particular social class. For example, we might study the relationship between poverty and delinquency by comparing rates of delinquency in census tracts with low income and those with high income. In this case, we have collected data regarding the characteristics of census tracts rather than individuals.

Social scientists also deal with *organizations* as the unit of analysis. Formal organizations are deliberately constructed groups organized for the achievement of some specific goals. Examples of formal organizations include corporations, schools, prisons, unions, government bureaus, and human service agencies. For example, our experience may lead us to suspect that organizations

providing substance abuse services can more effectively serve their clients if they have a more open and democratic communication structure in contrast to a closed and rigidly stratified one. If we compared the success rates of organizations with different communication structures, our study would be utilizing organizations, not individuals or groups, as the unit of analysis. Although individuals may experience *success* at overcoming substance abuse, only organizations can have a *success rate*.

Research in the human services can also focus on *programs* as the basic unit of analysis. The program may provide services for individuals, and it may exist as part of an organization, but it is still a separate unit of analysis about which data can be collected. Like organizations, programs can have success rates or be assessed in terms of overall costs. For example, one research project investigated 456 delinquency prevention programs across the nation, looking for whether there were different types of human services delivered to minorities as opposed to whites (Hawkins and Salisbury, 1983). Among other things, they found that whites were more likely to receive such services as family training and training in affective skills whereas blacks received remedial services and employment services. Programs might cut across a number of different organizations, such as social service agencies, in which case the unit being observed is the effectiveness of the combination of services provided by these organizations.

Finally, in fairly rare instances, the unit of analysis may be *social artifacts*, which are simply any material products produced by people. Examples are virtually endless: newspapers, buildings, movies, books, magazines, automobiles, songs, graffiti, and so on. Of all the units of analysis, social artifacts are the least frequent focus of human service research, but as reflections of people and the society that produces them, analysis of social artifacts can be useful. Books and magazines, for example, can be used as artifacts in the assessment of sex-role stereotyping. Children's books have been attacked for allegedly reinforcing traditional sex roles through their presentations of men and women (Weitzman et al., 1972; Kirk and Karbon, 1986; Dougherty and Engel, 1987). Any kind of legal or administrative statute can also be an artifact worthy of study. One effort, for instance, used the juvenile codes in states as the independent variable in a study of whether legal statutes made a difference in how the courts handled the cases of juveniles (Grichting, 1979).

Clearly specifying the unit of analysis in research is very important in order to avoid a serious problem: an illegitimate shift in the analysis from one unit to another. Careless jumping from one level to another can result in drawing erroneous conclusions. An example of this type of error is called the **ecological fallacy:** inferring something about individuals based on data collected about groups (Robinson, 1950). Suppose, for example, a study found that census tracts with high rates of teenage drug abuse also had a large percentage of single-parent families. We might be tempted to conclude that single-parent families are a factor promoting teenage drug abuse. Such a conclusion, however, represents an illegitimate shift in the unit of analysis. The data have been collected about census tracts which are at the group level. The conclusion drawn, however, is at the individual level, namely, that teenage drug abusers live in single-parent families. The data do *not* show this. They only show the association of two rates—substance abuse and single parenthood—in census tracts. It is, of course, possible that relationships found at the group level will hold at the individual level, but they may not. It is always an empirical question whether relationships found at one level of analysis will hold up at other levels. In our hypothetical study, it may be that some other characteristic of census tracts leads to both high rates of drug abuse *and* single-parent families. The error comes in the automatic assumption that correlations at the group level necessarily reflect relationships at the individual level. A clear awareness of the unit of analysis with which we are dealing can help ensure that we do not make such illegitimate shifts.

A final point needs to be made about the unit of analysis in contrast to the source of data. The unit of analysis refers to the element *about which* data are collected and inferences made, but it is not necessarily the source *from which* data are collected. A common example is the U.S. Census, which reports data on *households.* We speak of household size and income, but households don't fill out questionnaires; people do. In this case, individuals, such as the heads of households, are the *source* of the data, but the household is the unit of analysis *about which* data are collected. When the unit of analysis is something other than the individual, attention must be paid to the source of the data because this might introduce bias into the data analysis. For example, when the household is the unit of analysis, data are often collected from one member of the household. In single-parent families, which are headed primarily by women, we would be gathering data mostly from women. In two-parent families we would be obtaining data from both men and women since either could be the head of the household, and in some cases men might be the majority of those from whom data are collected. If men tend to give answers to some questions that are different from those women give, there could be a sex bias in the results even though our unit of analysis was not linked to sex. A difference that we attribute to single-parent as compared with two-parent families may be due to the fact that the former involves mostly women answering questions whereas the latter involves more men.

Reactivity

Another consideration in refining a research problem is the issue of "reactivity." The term **reactivity** refers to the fact that people can react to being studied and may behave differently from when they don't think they are being studied. In other words, the data collected from people who know they are the object of study might be different from that collected from the same people if they did not know. So, a reactive research technique changes the very thing that is being studied. Suppose, for example, that you are a parent and a researcher enters your home and sets up videotaping equipment to observe your interactions with your children. Would you behave in the same way that you would if the observer were not present? You might, but most people would feel strong pressures to be "on their toes" and present themselves as "good" parents. You might be more forgiving of your child, for instance, or give fewer negative sanctions.

Reactivity in research can take many forms, and it is a problem for virtually all sciences. However, it is especially acute in social research because human beings are so self-conscious and aware of what is happening to them. Refining a research problem and choosing a research design

are done with an eye toward reducing as much as possible the extensiveness of reactivity. We will consider this in assessing the various research strategies in later chapters.

Cross-Sectional Versus Longitudinal Research

In addition to deciding on the unit of analysis to be investigated, refining a research problem also requires a decision about the time dimension. The basic issue involved is whether you want a single "snapshot" in time of some phenomenon or an ongoing series of photographs over time. The former is called **cross-sectional research,** and it focuses on a cross-section of a population at one point in time. Many surveys, for example, are cross-sectional in nature.

Although all the data in cross-sectional research are collected at one time, such studies can nonetheless be used to investigate the development of some phenomenon over time. For example, to study the developmental problems of children of alcoholic parents, one could select groups of children of varying ages, say, one group at age 5, another at 10, and a third group at age 15. By observing differences in developmental problems among these groups, we may infer that a single youngster would experience changes as he or she grew up similar to the differences observed among these three groups. Yet one of the major weaknesses of such cross-sectional studies is that we have not actually observed the changes an individual goes through; rather, we have observed three different groups of individuals at one point in time. Differences among these groups may reflect something other than the developmental changes that individuals experience. Because of this disadvantage researchers sometimes resort to the other way of handling the time issue: longitudinal studies.

Longitudinal research involves gathering data over an extended period, which might span months, years, or, in a few cases, decades. To study the developmental changes mentioned in the preceding paragraph, the preferred longitudinal approach would be a **panel study,** in which the same people are studied at different points in time. This allows us to observe the specific changes that individuals go through over time. Another longitudinal approach is the **trend study,** in which different people are observed at different points in time. Public opinion polling and research on political attitudes are often trend studies.

The decision whether to use a longitudinal or cross-sectional approach is typically determined both by the nature of the research problem and by practical considerations. Longitudinal studies, especially panel studies, have the advantage of providing the most accurate information regarding changes over time. A research question regarding such changes, then, would probably benefit from this approach. A disadvantage of panel studies is that they can be reactive: People's responses or behavior at one time may be influenced by the fact that they have been observed earlier. For example, a person who stated opposition to abortion in one survey may be inclined to respond the same way six months later so as not to appear inconsistent or vacillating even though those attitudes had softened considerably. Another disadvantage is that people who participated early in a panel study may not want to, or be unable to, participate later. People die, move away, become uninterested, and in other ways become unavailable as panel studies progress. This loss of participants can adversely affect the validity of the re-

search findings. The disadvantages of all longitudinal studies are that they can be difficult and expensive to conduct, especially if they span a long period of time.

Cross-sectional research is cheaper and faster to conduct, and one need not worry about the loss of participants. However, cross-sectional research may not provide the most useful data for some research questions. Thus, the decision on the issue of time dimension should be based on considerations of both the nature of the research problem and practical issues. There are times, of course, when practical feasibility plays a large part in the decision. We will end this chapter with a discussion of factors related to the feasibility of research.

Research in Practice 4.1 discusses some other subtle, but important factors that can influence the development of a research problem.

Feasibility of a Research Project

By the time researchers have selected, shaped, and refined a research problem, the problem should be sufficiently clear that a consideration of practical issues involving the feasibility of the project is in order. Practical considerations of what can reasonably be accomplished given the time and resources available can force researchers, sometimes painfully, to reduce the scale of a project. A careful and honest appraisal of the time and money required to accomplish a project will be useful in determining the feasibility of the project as envisioned and reveal if a change in goals is called for. In making a feasibility assessment, one should keep in mind a couple of old axioms that apply to research projects: "Anything that can go wrong will" and "Everything will take longer than possibly imagined."

The practical aspects of a project's

RESEARCH IN PRACTICE 4.1
Behavior and Social Environments: Do Males and Females Have Different "Voices"?

We have analyzed some of the explicit elements that feed into the shaping and refining of research problems, such as conceptual development and the avoidance of reactivity. However, there may be much more subtle and unnoticed influences on problem development. Feminists have brought attention to one such area that has generated considerable controversy today in the human services, both in research and in practice: Are males and females socialized to perceive the world and acquire knowledge in fundamentally different ways? There is great debate over this issue, with strong advocates supporting each side. At the heart of the debate are fundamentally different ways of knowing the world, and these differences could translate into quite different approaches to problem formulation in research (Nielson, 1989).

In Chapter 2, we discussed the characteristics of science and emphasized the importance of objectivity. However, there are critics who claim that our knowledge of the world is always subjective and relative because knowledge is interpreted through a filter of human perceptions and meanings (Heineman, 1981). Nothing has meaning for human beings until we attach some social importance to it, and this makes all knowledge subjective. Because of our biology, socialization, and experiences, people attach a variety of meanings to knowledge and

events, and we are often unaware of these influences. One important influence, it is argued, is our socialization as males and females and possibly even biological differences (Davis, 1986; Ivanoff, Robinson, and Blythe, 1987).

The basic argument is that, because of differences between the sexes, there is a male model of knowledge development and a female one, and that the two are, to an extent, alien to one another. In developing some of these ideas, Carol Gilligan (1982) used the term "voice" to mean modes of thinking about the world and tried to describe the differences between male and female "voices." Women emphasize the importance of relationships and the danger of being separated from others. Women see connectedness between people and feel obliged to protect and nurture those to whom they feel connected. This leads to a concern about the needs of others, but the needs of self and others exist primarily in the context of their relationships with other people. So, women's voices focus on the individual embedded in a social network. This emphasis on connectedness and relationships means that problems and people are inextricably intertwined. Neither problems nor the people they affect can be fully understood if they are separated from one another.

By contrast, men's voices speak of separation and autonomy. They emphasize independence and to an extent

(Continued on next page)

alienation in the sense that people can be abstracted from their relationships, from their context, and even from their own uniqueness. For men, the separate individual has some meaning and importance, and possibly even more value than a person encumbered by relationships and connections. In this view, these abstracted individuals can all be treated the same, ignoring the unique needs or contexts of each person. To this extent, men's voices are abstract and formal. People and their problems can be separated.

A concrete example of this difference is supplied by Gilligan from her work on moral development. A boy and a girl, both age 11, were asked to evaluate a dilemma faced by "Heinz," who is confronted with choosing between stealing a drug that he cannot afford in order to keep his wife alive or obeying the law and letting her die without the drug. According to Gilligan, the boy's conclusion is that Heinz should steal the drug because a life is more valuable than property. For him, it's fundamentally a math problem: weigh the alternatives and take the highest value. In contrast, the girl sees a more complex problem. She responds, "I think there might be other ways besides stealing it, like if he could borrow the money or make a loan or something. . . . If he stole the drug, he might save his wife then, but if he did, he might have to go to jail, and then his wife might get sicker again, and he couldn't get more of the drug" (Gilligan, 1982, p. 28). In contrast to the boy's math problem perspective, the girl sees the moral problem in the context of "a narrative of relationships that extend over time" (Gilligan, 1982, p. 28).

Proponents of the male–female distinction argue that these male and female voices are fundamentally contrasting ways of perceiving and developing knowledge about the world. As for shaping research problems, the male voice will tend toward a research problem where separation predominates: The researcher extracts data from the "subject" or "respondent" and any personal relationship (or connectedness) between them is avoided in the interests of objectivity. All contact except that necessary to collect data is avoided. Standardized measuring instruments and procedures are used on the assumption that all people can be treated alike and this will produce the most valid and objective data. A number of procedures commonly used in research can be seen as efforts to strip away the context from the individual: placing them in laboratory settings, using random assignment to conditions, using aggregate responses from large-scale surveys, and isolating variables for study. All of these procedures assume that the context in which a person lives is merely interfering "noise" and that more meaningful information can be gotten without it. Through quantification, the male voice minimizes the uniqueness and subjectivity of experiences by providing summary responses of the aggregate; so the fact that Jane Doe got pregnant at age 13 under a certain set of unique and meaningful circumstances gets lost when we conclude that the average teen pregnancy in a high school occurs at age 14.7 years.

The key in the development of a research problem for the female voice is connectedness: Researcher and respondent are tied together in a relationship that influences the data that are produced. "Objectivity," in the traditional sense, is impossible because the meaning and importance of data relate to specific individuals and their relationships with one another. The researcher and subject are seen as partners in the relationship of producing research. Subjects are seen more as collaborators. "Female"-oriented researchers also disdain the notion of the objective, impartial researcher in favor of involvement with the topics of their research. "Thus, the researcher and subject can work in different ways to explore a 'truth' that they mutually create and define" (Davis, 1986, p. 38). Research questions will be developed in the direction of emphasizing connectedness: keeping people in their social contexts and studying the complexity of the whole. People can be studied in their homes or where they work and play. Some research methods, such as participant observation, as discussed in Chapter 9, are better suited to emphasizing this connectedness. Female perspective research also emphasizes a qualitative approach, such as in-depth interviews, where people have an opportunity to express the fullness and complexity of their lives in their own words.

Obviously, it is possible for men to speak with a female voice and women with a male voice. The point is that people's experiences can lead to fundamentally different ways of perceiving the world. In fact, some critics would argue that researchers, whether male or female, in the social sciences and human services tend to be trained in graduate school with a male voice because that is what has dominated over the years among graduate faculty. Yet, neither voice is inherently superior. Each is a valid way of gaining knowledge about the world. However, researchers need to be clear, as they shape a research problem and choose a research methodology, about which voice would best serve the research goals. In some cases, the most solid foundation of knowledge would be to use both voices. No single research method is complete or totally objective. They all involve a perspective that has some limitations. It is especially dangerous to assume that a single research method can provide all answers about a problem.

---

feasibility center primarily on time and money (Kelly and McGrath, 1988). For clarity, we will treat these two concerns separately, although they are related.

Time Constraints

In developing a research project, one of the major considerations is whether there will be sufficient time to complete adequately what you hope to do. In later chapters, as we consider specific research techniques, we will see how different techniques vary in terms of how much time they take. Here, we want to mention some of the major factors related to time considerations. One factor concerns the population that is the focus of the research. If the focus is a population with characteristics that are fairly widespread, then a sufficient number of people will be readily available from which to collect data. If we were studying the differing attitudes of men and women toward work-release programs for prison inmates, we could select a sample of men and women from whatever city or state we happened to be in. If, however, our study focuses on people with special characteristics that are somewhat rare, problems may arise. In general, the smaller the number of people who have the characteristics needed for inclusion in a study, the more difficult and time-consuming it will be to contact a sufficiently large number necessary to make scientifically valid conclusions. For example, a study of incestuous fathers, even in a large city, may encounter problems obtaining enough cases because relatively few such people will be openly known.

A second problem relating to time constraints involves the proper development of measuring devices. All techniques used for gathering data should be tested before the actual study is conducted, and this can be very time-consuming. A pretest, as we saw in Chapter 1, refers to the preliminary application of the data-gathering techniques for purposes of assessing their adequacy. A pilot study is a small-scale "trial run" of all the procedures planned for use in the main study. In some studies, several pretests may need to be conducted as data collection devices are modified based on the results of previous pretests. All in all, a lot of time can be consumed in such refining of data-gathering procedures.

A third major factor related to time considerations is the amount of time required for actual data collection, which can range from a few hours for a questionnaire administered to a group of "captive" students to the months characteristic of some observational research to the years that are necessary in many longitudinal studies. Because the amount of time required for data collection is so variable, it should be given close scrutiny when addressing the question of the feasibility of a particular research design.

A fourth consideration related to the time issue is the amount of time necessary to complete the analysis of the data. In general, the less structured the data, the more time will be required for analysis. The field notes that serve as the data for some observational studies, for example, can be very time-consuming to analyze (see Chapter 9). Likewise, the videotapes collected during an experiment or during single-subject research may take many viewings before they are adequately understood (see Chapters 10 and 11). However, highly structured data in quantified form can also be time-consuming, as we will see in Chapter 14. Although computers can manipulate the data rapidly, it takes considerable time to prepare the data for entry into the computer, and the amount of time needed increases as the number of cases increases. So, as with the time required for data collection, the time needed for analysis should be carefully considered owing to wide variation in the amount that may be necessary.

The fifth area in which time becomes a factor is writing the report itself. The amount of time this consumes depends on the length and complexity of the report and the skills of the investigator. Each researcher is in the best position, based on past writing experiences, to assess the amount of time he or she will require. As a final reminder, it will likely take longer than you expect.

Financial Considerations

A second consideration surrounding a project's feasibility is money. Just as the amount of time required for research varies widely, so does the amount of money. Many very valuable studies have cost little, whereas the price tag for large-scale projects can easily be hundreds of thousands of dollars. A consideration of the following factors will help in developing a cost estimate for the planned project.

One cost consideration is any payment that may be necessary to ensure the cooperation of people in your study. In an experiment, for example, because of the amount of time and cooperation required from participants, a fee of a few dollars will likely be needed to interest people in participating. Although the amount paid each person will likely be fairly nominal, the total cost can mount rapidly. For example, a study of 50 four-person groups, with each person paid five dollars to participate, adds up to $1,000 in subject fees. Studies using nonexperimental techniques usually require less cooperation from subjects, so payments in observational research and surveys (with the exception of panel designs) are rarely involved.

A second major cost consideration is expenditures for office supplies and equipment. Under this item are such things as paper, envelopes, stamps, recorders, tapes, printing, and the like. Paper products may seem inexpensive, but given the large samples characteristic of some surveys, their cost can become substantial. Postage for mailed questionnaires is also a large cost factor as each questionnaire will cost a minimum of 50 cents (postage to send the questionnaire and the prepaid envelope for its return, at today's postage rates). Additional postage will be required for large questionnaires or follow-up letters sent to those who fail to respond to the initial mailing. Researchers may also face several high-cost equipment items such as video cameras, recorders, and videotape. Unless these are already available, substantial outlays will be needed.

The third and potentially largest cost item is the salaries of those who conduct the study. Studies using interviewers have the highest costs in this area. Not only must the interviewers' wages be paid, but transportation costs, which can be sizable, must also be covered. Other types of studies may also require paid assistance. To get the work done in a reasonable amount of time and to help ensure reliability, investigators may have to hire people to organize the data into a form in which it can be analyzed. For any type of study using the computer for data analysis, there will be the added cost of having the data keypunched and made ready for the computer.

A fourth cost factor is computer time for the data analysis itself. Sometimes computer time can be obtained free or at reduced rates if a university computer is available. If no special arrangements can be made, computer time can become an item of high cost despite the marked decreases in unit computation costs that have occurred in recent years. If the researcher must pay full price for computer time, this item should be carefully estimated.

Anticipating and Avoiding Problems

Problems related to time and financial considerations arise during virtually all research projects, but their impact on the outcome of the research can be minimized if they can be anticipated as much as possible, especially during the planning stage when the details of the project are easier to change. There are a number of things that can be done to anticipate problems. First of all, learn as much as possible from the experiences of others. One way to do this is through the studies consulted during the review of the literature. We mentioned earlier that noting problems these other researchers encountered is one focus of this review. Personal advice from experienced researchers who might be available for consultation can also be solicited. A knowledgeable researcher may be able to identify potential trouble spots in your plans and suggest modifications to avoid them.

Second, obtain whatever permissions or consents may be needed early in the planning stages of the project. Depending on the people you wish to study, it may be necessary to obtain permission from them officially to collect data. For example, some studies are aimed at school-age children and seek to gather data while the children are in school. School administrators, to protect students from undue harassment and themselves from parental complaints, are frequently cool to allowing researchers into their schools. It may take considerable time to persuade whatever authorities are involved to grant the permissions you need—if they are granted at all. It is certainly wise to obtain any needed permissions before expending effort on other phases of the project, which might be wasted if permissions cannot be obtained.

The final—and perhaps most important—suggestion for avoiding problems is to conduct a pilot study. As we noted, a pilot study is a preliminary run-through on a small scale of all the procedures planned for the main study. For surveys, a small part of the sample, say 20 people, should be contacted and interviewed. The data should be analyzed as they will be in the complete project. In experiments, the researcher should run a few groups through all procedures, looking for any

unexpected reactions from participants. Observational researchers should visit the observation sites and make observations as planned for the larger study. The focus is again on problems that might force modifications in research plans. Any problems that surface during the pilot study can then be dealt with before the main project is launched.

Given all of the pitfalls that a project might encounter, it is quite possible that at some point one may conclude that the project is not feasible as planned. Before throwing up one's hands and calling it quits, however, one should give careful consideration to possible modifications in the project that would enhance its feasibility. If inadequate time or money is the problem, perhaps the project can be scaled down. It might be possible to reduce the sample size or reduce the number of hypotheses tested to make the project manageable. If interviewing were originally planned, consider a mailed questionnaire or even a telephone survey as cost- and time-reducing measures. If the problem is with procedures, such as may occur in an experiment, consider how they might be changed so that the project can proceed. For example, in an experiment conducted by one of the authors and two associates, a problem surfaced concerning a negative reaction to one of our experimental procedures (Norland et al., 1976). The reaction was so severe among some participants that for a while it appeared we would have to give up the project on ethical grounds. After considerable thought and some trial and error, however, it was found that the negative reactions could be eliminated by more thorough debriefing of the subjects after they had participated in the experiment. The point is that a project should not be abandoned until all efforts to make it feasible have been investigated.

||||||||||||||||||||||||||||||||||||||||||||||||||||||||||||||||||||||||||||||||||||||||||||||||||||||||||||||

☰ Main Points

• Suitable topics for research may be obtained from a variety of sources, including personal interest, social problems, theory testing, evaluation research, prior research, and human service practice.

• Problem selection is also influenced by political factors, which means that powerful interest groups encourage the expenditure of research resources on issues that are of interest to them and that may not serve the interests of less advantaged and minority groups.

• After a general topic for research is selected, it must be narrowed and focused into a precise, researchable problem.

• An important part of refining a research problem is conceptual development: identifying and defining the concepts that will be the focus of the study.

• Reviewing previous research related to the selected topic is a crucial step in problem development and preparing to conduct a research project.

• The nature of the research problem should dictate the choice of the specific research technique employed rather than attempt to make the problem fit a particular method of data gathering.

• The units of analysis must be clearly specified and may be either individuals, groups, organizations, programs, or social artifacts.

• Continual awareness of the operative unit of analysis is necessary to avoid errors such as the ecological fallacy: inferring something about individuals from data collected about groups.

• Reactivity refers to the fact that people may behave differently when being observed from when not, and the effects of reactivity must be considered when shaping a research problem.

• Cross-sectional research is based on data collected at one point in time, making accurate conclusions about trends or behavioral changes difficult.

• Longitudinal studies are based on data collected over a period of time and are particularly useful for studying trends or behavioral changes.

• Once a proposed research problem is fully refined, the practical feasibility of the project should be realistically assessed.

• Data analysis, including how to prepare a data set for computer analysis, must be considered when shaping a research problem in order to ensure that appropriate data are available to answer all research questions.

☰ Important Terms for Review

cross-sectional research
ecological fallacy
longitudinal research
panel study
reactivity
trend study
units of analysis

☰ For Further Reading

Bransford, John D., and Barry S. Stein. *The Ideal Problem Solver: A Guide for Improving Thinking, Learning, and Creativity.* New York: Freeman, 1984.
Sound thinking combined with creativity are clearly important to formulating re-

search problems. This guide assists you in improving thought processes, drawing logical deductions, enhancing creativity, and even improving your communications skills.

Golden, M. Patricia, ed. *The Research Experience*. Itasca, Ill.: F. E. Peacock, 1976.

A book of readings meant for introductory social research classes. The uniqueness of this book is that each contribution includes a personal "note" about how the investigator's research ideas emerged and evolved.

Gross, Ronald, *The Independent Scholar's Handbook*. Reading, Mass.: Addison-Wesley, 1982.

Contains many examples of how successful scholars developed personal hunches and notions into serious research inquiries. It is also filled with practical advice about such things as obtaining resources and communicating with other researchers who share similar research interests.

Journals in the Human Services.

An excellent source for research ideas and for well-formulated research problems is the many journals that publish research relevant to the human services. There are numerous journals listed in Appendix A. A good place to start would be the following: *Annual Proceedings of the National Conference on Social Welfare, Community Mental Health Journal, Educational Research Quarterly, Journal of Studies on Alcohol, Journal of Criminal Justice, Journal of Health and Social Behavior, Nursing Research, Social Problems, Social Work Research and Abstracts.*

≡ Exercises for Class Discussion

In working through the exercises in this chapter, we suggest that you review Appendix A, which covers the basic issues involved in conducting research in the library. We have also found it helpful for students in our research classes to schedule a one- or two-hour workshop with the

reference personnel in the library. This helps familiarize students with the materials available in their library, especially human service resource material.

4.1 There follow several broad topic areas that are relevant to the human services. Select one that has the greatest personal appeal to you. Identify the reasons why this topic interests you. How do your selection and the reasons for it compare with those of other students?
  a. child abuse
  b. nursing home care of the elderly
  c. emotionally disturbed children
  d. victims of crime
  e. violence in the family
  f. alcoholism
  g. discrimination against minorities
  h. adaptation to stress
  i. community living for the developmentally disabled
  j. effects of unemployment

4.2 Use your library resources to locate at least five research studies published in the professional literature on the topic you selected. Your search efforts should include, but need not be limited to, the following: *Social Science Index, Social Work Research and Abstracts, Monthly Catalog of Government Publications,* and the library public catalog. Be prepared to discuss with the class how you located your studies.

4.3 For each research study you locate, do the following:
  a. Indicate which factors seemed to influence the selection of topic in this study (that is, personal interest, social problems, theory testing, project evaluation, prior research, or practice experience).
  b. What was the unit of analysis for each study? Was it the same as,

or different from, the source of the data? If different, indicate the source. Can you think of any reasons for selecting a different unit of analysis?

c. What was the *specific* problem that the study addressed? From the presentation of the study, what factors influenced the final, actual problem formulation? In particular, were there issues of cost, time, or feasibility that necessitated a modification of the problem from what was initially proposed?

d. Chapter 3 presented a discussion of ethical issues in research. What ethical issues confronted the researchers in studying each problem? Did a concern for ethics impact on what specific research problem emerged from an interest in studying the general topic?

4.4 We have made the point that problem selection in research is a social process in which power, interest groups, and other factors play significant roles. One practice issue that has received considerable attention in recent years is the placement of minority children, especially Native American children, in white foster and adoptive homes.

a. Have one group of students imagine that they are members of an adoptive/foster parent association that has been asked to provide suggestions to the Department of Health and Human Services for research priorities. What research problems would this group want to have studied?

b. Have a second group of students imagine that they are tribal leaders representing Native American interests. What priorities would they have and what questions might this group suggest? Contrast the problems suggested by each group.

5

The Process of Measurement

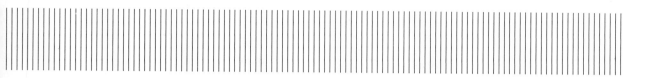

A crisis counselor working with a mental health agency receives a call from the county jail. The deputy there is concerned about an inmate whom he describes as severely depressed. The counselor responds by asking a number of questions such as the following: Has the inmate been eating his meals? Is he sleeping too much or too little? Is his affect flat when he responds to questions? Has he made any remarks about committing suicide? By asking these questions, the counselor is attempting to make an initial assessment of the severity of the inmate's depression. Later the counselor may interview the inmate directly, request psychological testing, or refer him to a psychiatrist for further evaluation. Assessments such as this are analogous to a process in research called *measurement*. Just as the clinician just mentioned used a variety of observations by the deputy as indicators of the inmate's condition, so researchers use various observations as indicators of the concepts of interest in a research project. **Measurement** refers to the process of describing abstract concepts in terms of specific indicators by the assignment of numbers or other symbols to these indicants in accordance with rules. At the very minimum, we must have some means of determining whether a variable is either present or absent, just as the counselor needs to know whether or not the inmate is eating. In many cases, however, measurement is more complex and involves assessing how much or to what degree a variable is present. This is illustrated by the counselor's asking how much the inmate is sleeping, "amount of sleep" being a variable that can take on many values.

Measurement is a part of the process of moving from the abstract or theoretical level to the concrete. Recall from Chapter 2 that scientific concepts have two types of definitions—nominal and operational. Before research can proceed, nominal definitions have to be translated into operational ones. The operational definitions indicate the exact procedures, or operations, that will be used to measure the concepts. Measurement is essentially the process of operationalizing concepts. Figure 5.1 illustrates the place of measurement in the research process. Measurement will be a topic of interest throughout this book.

In this chapter, we will discuss the general issues that relate to all measurement, beginning with some of the different ways in which measurements can be made. We will then analyze how measurements can be made at different levels, and their effects on the mathematical operations that can be performed on them. Finally, we will present ways of evaluating how good measures are and what the errors are that can occur in the measurement process.

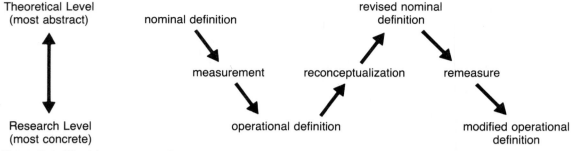

Figure 5.1 The Measurement Process

Ways of Measuring

The concepts and variables that are the focus of both research and practice cannot normally be directly observed. Such things as poverty, social class, mental retardation, and the like cannot be seen but only inferred from something else. Take something as seemingly obvious as child abuse. Can you directly observe child abuse? Not really. What you directly observe is a bruise on a child's back, an infant's broken leg, or a father slapping his daughter. Even the slap may not relate to child abuse because parents sometimes slap their children without its being a case of child abuse. However, all these things—the bruise, the broken leg, the slap—may be used as *indicators* of child abuse. In research and in practice, an **indicator** is an observation that is assumed to be evidence of the attributes or properties of some phenomenon. What we observe are the indicators of a variable, not the actual properties of the variable itself. Emergency room personnel may take a child's broken leg as an indicator of child abuse even though they have not observed the actual abuse.

Child abuse represents a good illustration of the difficulties of moving from nominal to operational definitions with variables involving social and psycholog-

ical events. At the nominal level, we might define child abuse as an occurrence in which a parent or caretaker injures a child, not by accident but in anger or with deliberate intent (Gelles, 1987; Korbin, 1987). But what indicators would we use to operationalize this definition? Some things would seem to indicate child abuse obviously, such as a cigarette burn on a child's buttock. What about a bruise on the arm? There are subcultures in our own society that view hitting children, even to the point of bruising, as an appropriate way to train or discipline a child. Furthermore, some people would argue that a serious psychological disorder suffered by a child is an indicator of child abuse because it shows the parents had not provided the proper love and affection for stable development. In short, one of the problems in operationalizing child abuse, as is true with many other variables in human service research, is that its definition is culture-bound and involves subjective judgments. This illustrates the importance of good conceptual development and precise nominal definitions for research. It also shows how the theoretical and research levels can mutually influence one another: As nominal definitions are shaped into operational ones, difficulties that arise often lead to a reconceptualization, or change in the nominal definition at the theoretical level (see Fig. 5.1). Research in Practice 5.1 describes a research project in the human services that involved some fairly complex measurement problems and shows how theoretical considerations can play a substantial role in operationalizing concepts.

The example of child abuse also makes another point, namely, that there can be more than one indicator of a variable. The term **item** is used to refer to a single indicator of a variable. Items can take numerous forms, such as an answer to a question or an observation of some behavior or characteristic. Asking a person her age or noting her sex, for example, would both produce "items" of measurement. In many cases, however, operationalizing variables involves combining a number of items into a composite score called an **index** or **scale.** (Although scales involve more rigor in their construction than do indexes, for our purposes we can use the terms interchangeably.) Attitude scales, for example, commonly involve asking a person a series of questions, or items, and then summarizing their responses into a single score that represents their attitude on an issue. A major reason for using scales or indexes rather than single items is that they enable us to measure variables in a more precise and usually more accurate fashion. In addition, they are more valid and reliable than single-item measures. To illustrate the value of scales over items, consider your grade in this course. In all likelihood, your final grade will be an index, or composite score, of your answers to many questions on many tests throughout the semester. Would you prefer that your final grade be determined by a one-item measure? Probably not, because it would not measure the full range of what you learned in the course. Fur-

thermore, an error on that question would indicate that you had not learned much in the course even if the error were due to ill health or personal problems on the day of the exam. For these reasons, then, multiple-item measures are usually preferred to single-item indicators. In this chapter, we will discuss general issues related to measurement, and then in Chapter 13 we will return to the issue of constructing indexes and scales.

We began this discussion by noting that variables are abstract and cannot normally be directly observed. Actually, variables differ in their degree of abstraction, and this affects the ease with which we can accomplish measurement. In general, the more abstract the variable, the more difficult it is to measure. For example, a study of child abuse might include the variable "number of children in family," on the theoretical presumption that large families create more stress for parents and are, therefore, more likely to precipitate abusive attacks on children. This is a rather easy variable to measure because the concepts "children" and "family" have readily identifiable empirical referents, and they are relatively easy and unambiguous to observe and count. Suppose, however, that the child abuse study also included as a dependent variable "positiveness of a child's self-concept." "Self-concept" is a difficult notion to measure because it can take many different forms, but we have narrowed it to the "positive–negative" dimension. It is still more difficult to measure than "number of children in family" because there is a whole variety of questions that could be asked to explore how positively people feel about themselves. Self-concept can also be measured by behaviors on the theoretical presumption that people who feel positively about themselves behave differently from those who do not.

RESEARCH IN PRACTICE 5.1
Behavior and Social Environment: Problems of Measurement in Spouse Abuse Research

A major problem today—and one that calls for the skilled intervention of human service professionals—is spouse abuse. And recent studies of spouse abuse illustrate some of the problems of measurement in social research. One study hypothesized that *status inconsistency* and *status incompatibility* might increase the risk of spouse abuse for a couple (Hornung, McCullough, and Sugimoto, 1981). Thus, the hypotheses to be tested in this research contained at least three highly abstract concepts: status inconsistency, status incompatibility, and spouse abuse. First of all, it was necessary to define the concept of "spouse" even though at first its definition would seem obvious. The data were collected in interviews with women, and women were considered eligible for the study if they were at least 18 years old and were married at the time of the interview or had lived with a male partner within the preceding 12 months. Thus, the concept of spouse abuse, as used in this study, was extended to cover abuse involving a cohabiting couple.

Next the investigators needed measures of their independent variables, status inconsistency and status incompatibility. Status inconsistency refers to possessing status characteristics that are not consistent with one another as when a highly educated person has a low-status occupation. To operationalize this concept, the investigators compared people in terms of

occupation and education. The U.S. Census Bureau makes available an occupational index that can be used to measure a person's occupational status. Educational status was measured by asking people how many years of school they had completed. However, what the researchers were really interested in was the *consistency* of these two statuses for each person in their study. When was a person's education "inconsistent" with his or her occupation? For guidance in measuring consistency, the researchers relied on a theoretical assumption, namely, that *most* people have levels of education that are consistent with the job they hold. People were divided into occupational groups of roughly equal status, using the Census Bureau's index. Within each occupational category, people were ranked according to their level of education. Then the middle 70 percent of the people in each occupational category were assumed to have educations consistent with their job. The 15 percent with the lowest levels of education in each occupational category were defined as status inconsistent-low in terms of education; and the 15 percent with the highest levels of education, as status inconsistent-high.

This operational definition of status inconsistency, only one of several used in this study, illustrates the complexity that can be involved in measuring social variables. It also illustrates how operational definitions are influenced by theoretical considerations, such as the assumption that most people will have consistent status characteristics. Status incompatibility was measured in much the same way although now it involved comparing the status characteristics of the husband with those of the wife. Again, the theoretical assumption that guided this measurement process was the assumption that *atypical* combinations of husband's and wife's status characteristics would be perceived and experienced as incompatible and thus stressful. Consistency in this regard does not mean that husband and wife have the same status, only that the status differences between them be typical and commonly found.

Next the researchers turned their attention to the problem of measuring spouse abuse, and they followed one of the principles we describe in this chapter: They borrowed and modified a measurement device that another researcher had used successfully and had already tested. Murray Straus (1974) had developed the Conflict Tactics (CT) scale. This instrument includes items that measure different types of abuse: psychological abuse (e.g., "Did or said something to spite the other person"); violent aggression (e.g., "Pushed, grabbed, or shoved the other one"); and severely violent aggression (e.g., "Beat up the other one"). With people's responses to these items, the researchers could compare levels of abuse among couples at varying levels of status inconsistency and status incompatibility. They found that both were associated with increased risk of spouse abuse, both psychological and physical. Some types of inconsistency had a greater impact. A couple with a

husband who was underachieving in terms of his occupation was, for example, at very high risk of abuse. An overachieving husband, on the other hand, seemed to buffer the couple against abuse.

While the CT scale was a valid way to measure spouse abuse for Hornung, et al., it has been criticized as misleading when used for some other types of research, especially comparisons of the levels of abuse perpetrated by women as opposed to men. A number of investigations using the CT scale have reported that women abuse men about as much as, and maybe more than, men abuse women (McNeely and Robinson-Simpson, 1987). The problem, however, is that the CT scale measures *actions*, such as hitting or shoving, but it ignores *motivations* and *effects* (Saunders, 1988). Women may hit men as much as men hit women, but the women's actions are more likely to be self-defensive rather than aggressive. They hit in order to ward off the assaults of men. In terms of effects, men's attacks are far more serious and injurious, largely due to their greater physical size and strength. Taking motivations and effects into account in measuring spouse abuse, one researcher and therapist concluded that "husband assault is not a major social problem because few males are injured by female violence. Wife assault, on the other hand, does produce serious injuries and physical risk" (Dutton, 1988, p. 20).

This illustrates some of the complex considerations that need to be taken into account in finding appropriate measures for social and psychological variables.

The point is that with highly abstract concepts there is usually no single empirical indicator that is clearly and obviously preferable to others as a measure of the concept.

We have emphasized the point that measurement involves the transition from the abstract conceptual level to the concrete and observable, and this is what most typically occurs in research. However, exploratory studies can involve measurement in the opposite direction: First, we observe empirical indicators and then formulate theoretical concepts that those indicators presumably represent. In Chapter 2, we called this "inductive reasoning." In a sense, you might think of Sigmund Freud or Jean Piaget as having done this when they developed their theories of personality and cognitive development, respectively. Piaget, for example, observed the behavior of children for many years as he gradually developed his theory of the stages of cognitive development, including concepts like egocentrism, object permanence, and reversibility (Phillips, 1969; Vander Zanden, 1985). Piaget recognized that what he observed could be understood only if placed in a more abstract theoretical context. In a sense, he had measured something before he knew what it was he had measured. Once his theories began to develop, he then tested them deductively by developing new concepts and hypotheses and formulating different measuring devices. The point is that whether one shifts from the abstract to the concrete, or vice versa, the logic is the same, involving the relationship between theoretical concepts and empirical indicators.

A major problem in most measurement has to do with which indicators are to be used in a particular research project. This depends in part, of course, on theoretical concerns, but there are other

matters to be considered. One such matter has to do with whether a particular measure permits one to perform mathematical operations on it, and we turn to this issue next.

Levels of Measurement

We have seen that there are numerous ways of measuring phenomena, such as by asking questions or noting observations. Measures also differ from one another in terms of what is called their **level of measurement,** or the rules that define permissible mathematical operations that can be performed on a set of numbers produced by a measure. There are four levels of measurement: nominal, ordinal, interval, and ratio. Before defining these, however, we need to distinguish discrete from continuous variables. If we keep in mind that variables are things that can take on different values, measurement basically involves assessing the value, or category into which a particular entity falls. Measuring age, for example, is the process of placing each person into a particular age category. **Discrete variables** are variables with a finite number of distinct and separate values. Religion is a discrete variable in that there are a finite number of religions that we might list and no person could be categorized as falling *in between* any of those religions (assuming that "no religion" is also a single, separate category). One either belongs to this religion, that religion, or no religion. **Continuous variables** are variables that, at least theoretically, can take on an infinite number of values. Age is a continuous variable in that people gradually move from one age to another as they grow older. Normally, we measure age in terms of years, but theoretically we could measure it in terms of months, weeks, days, minutes, seconds, or even nanoseconds! There is no theoretical limit to how precise the measurement of age might be. For most social science purposes, of course, the measurement of age in terms of years is quite satisfactory, but age is nonetheless a continuous variable.

It is important to recognize that a variable is continuous or discrete by its very nature, and the researcher cannot change that. It is possible to measure a continuous variable by specifying a number of discrete categories, as is typically done with age, but this does not change the nature of the variable itself. This characteristic of variables—whether they are continuous or discrete—has an impact on their level of measurement.

Nominal Measures

Nominal measures classify observations into mutually exclusive categories. They represent nominal variables at the theoretical level. Variables such as sex, ethnicity, religion, or political party preference are examples. Thus, we might classify people according to their religious affiliation by placing them into one of five categories: Protestant, Catholic, Jewish, other, or no religious affiliation. These are mutually exclusive categories because membership in one precludes membership in another. For purposes of data analysis, we might assign numbers to represent each of the categories. We could label Protestant as 1, Catholic as 2, Jewish as 3, other as 4, and none as 5. It is important to recognize, however, that the assignment of numbers is purely arbitrary; the numbers comprising a nominal measure have none of the properties, such as ranking, ordering, and magnitude, that we usually associate with numbers. None of the usual arithmetic opera-

tions such as adding, subtracting, multiplying, or dividing can legitimately be performed on numbers comprising a nominal scale. The reason for this is that the numbers in a nominal scale are merely symbols or labels used to identify a category of the nominal variable. Protestant could have been labeled as 2 as well as 1.

Ordinal Measures

When variables can be conceptualized as having an inherent order at the theoretical level, we have an ordinal variable and, when operationalized, an **ordinal measure.** Ordinal measures are considered of a higher level than nominal because, in addition to being mutually exclusive, the categories have a fixed order. Socioeconomic status, for example, constitutes an ordinal variable, and measures of socioeconomic status are ordinal scales. Table 5.1 illustrates how socioeconomic status might be divided into ordinal categories. With ordinal measurement, we can speak of a given category as ranking higher or lower than some other category; lower-upper class, for example, is higher than middle class but not as high as the upper-upper class. It is important to recognize that ordinal measurement does not assume that the categories are equally spaced. For example, the distance be-

TABLE 5.1 Ordinal Ranking of Socioeconomic Status

Category	Rank
Upper-upper	7
Lower-upper	6
Upper-middle	5
Middle	4
Lower-middle	3
Upper-lower	2
Lower-lower	1

tween lower-upper and upper-upper is not necessarily the same as between lower-middle and middle even though in both cases the classes are one rank apart. This lack of equal spacing means that the numbers assigned to ordinal categories do not have the numerical properties necessary for arithmetic operations. Like nominal scales, ordinal scales cannot be added, subtracted, multiplied, or divided. The only characteristic they have that nominal does not is the fixed order of the categories.

Interval Measures

The next highest level of measurement is called *interval*. **Interval measures** share the characteristics of ordinal scales—mutually exclusive categories and an inherent order—but also have equal spacing between the categories. Equal spacing comes about because some specific unit of measurement, such as the degrees of a temperature scale, is a part of the measure. Each of these units is considered to have a certain value, making for the equal spacing characteristic of an interval scale. We would have an interval scale if the difference between, say, scores of 30 and 40 was the same as the difference between scores of 70 and 80. A 10-point difference is a 10-point difference regardless of where on the scale it occurs.

The common temperature scales, Fahrenheit and Celsius, are true interval scales. Both of these temperature scales have, as units of measurement, degrees and the equal spacing characteristic of interval scales. A difference of ten degrees is always the same, no matter where it occurs on the scale. These temperature scales illustrate another characteristic of true interval scales. The point on the scale labeled zero is arbitrar-

ily selected. Neither 0°C nor 0°F is absolute zero, the complete absence of heat. Because the zero point is arbitrary in true interval scales, we cannot make statements concerning ratios. That is, we cannot say that a given score is twice or three times as high as some other score. For example, a temperature of 80°F is not twice as hot as a temperature of 40°F. Despite not having this ratio characteristic, interval scales have numbers with all the other arithmetic properties. If we have achieved interval level measurement, we can legitimately perform all the common arithmetic operations on the numbers.

Considerable controversy exists over which measures used in behavioral science research are true interval measures, with only a few measures clearly of interval level. One, for example, that is relevant to the human services is intelligence, as measured by IQ tests. With IQ tests, there are specific units of measurement—points on the IQ scale—and each point on the scale is mutually exclusive. Furthermore, the distance between IQs of 80 and 90 is equivalent to the distance between IQs of 110 and 120. However, there is no absolute zero point on an IQ scale, so we cannot say that a person with an IQ of 150 is twice as intelligent as a person with an IQ of 75. As with temperature scales, the IQ scale is in part an arbitrary construction that allows us to make some comparisons but not others. Beyond a few measures such as intelligence, however, the debate ensues. Some researchers would argue, for example, that attitude scales can be treated as interval scales. The questions that make up attitude scales commonly involve choosing one of five responses: strongly agree, agree, uncertain, disagree, or strongly disagree. The argument is that people see the difference between "strongly agree" and "agree" as roughly equivalent to the distance between "disagree" and "strongly disagree." This perceived equidistance, some argue, makes it possible to treat these scales as interval level. Other researchers would argue that there is no logical or empirical reason to assume that such perceived equidistance exists and, therefore, that attitude scales should always be considered ordinal measures rather than interval measures.

We will not presume to settle this debate here. Rather, we raise the issue because level of measurement influences which statistical procedures can be used at the data analysis stage of research. This matter will be discussed in Chapter 14. You should be sensitive to the issue of levels of measurement when utilizing research. The results of research in which an inappropriate level of measurement has been used should be viewed with caution (Miller, 1983; Kenny, 1986).

Ratio Measures

The highest level of measurement is *ratio*. **Ratio measures** have all the characteristics of interval measures, but the zero point is absolute rather than arbitrary. As the name implies, with ratio measures, we can make statements to the effect that some score is a given ratio of another score. For example, one ratio

variable with which human service workers are likely to deal is income. With income, we have the dollar as the unit of measurement. Also, as many are all too well aware, there is such a thing as no income at all, so the zero point is absolute. Because it is absolute, it is perfectly legitimate to make the kinds of statements about income that are commonly made: An income of $20,000 is twice as much as $10,000, but only one-third as much as $60,000. (Recognize, of course, that income is a ratio measure only as an indicator of the *amount* of money available to a person; if income is used as a measure of a person's *social status*, for example, then a difference between $110,000 and $120,000 does not necessarily represent a shift in status equivalent to that between $10,000 and $20,000.) Given that ratio scales have all the characteristics of interval scales, we can, of course, perform all arithmetic operations on them.

The characteristics of the four levels of measurement are summarized in Table 5.2. Keep in mind that, although researchers have no control over the nature of a variable (it is either continuous or discrete), they do have some control over how they will define variables, at both the nominal and operational levels, and this affects the level of measurement. Basi-

TABLE 5.2   The Characteristics of the Four Levels of Measurement

Level of Measurement	Mutually Exclusive	Possess a Fixed Order	Equal Spacing Between Ranks[a]	A True Zero Point[ab]
	Characteristics of Categories			
Nominal	y			
Ordinal	y	y		
Interval	y	y	y	
Ratio	y	y	y	y

y = possesses that characteristic

[a]Permits standard mathematical operations of addition, subtraction, multiplication, and division.

[b]Permits statements about proportions and ratios.

cally, continuous variables can be measured as if they were discrete, but not the reverse.

What determines the level of measurement that is achieved when measuring a given variable? In general, we should always strive for the highest level of measurement possible because higher levels of measurement generally enable us to measure variables more precisely. In addition, many of the most powerful statistical procedures, such as regression and analysis of variance, assume that the dependent, and sometimes the independent, variable is at the interval level of measurement (see Chapter 14). It is also desirable to measure at the highest possible level of measurement because it gives the researcher the most options: The level of measurement can be reduced during the data analysis, but it cannot be increased. Thus, choosing a level of measurement that is too low introduces a permanent limitation into the data analysis.

It is important to recognize, however, that the primary determinant of the level of measurement is the nature of the variable being measured. The major concern is to have an accurate measure of a variable (a topic discussed at length in the next section). Religious affiliation, for example, is a nominal variable because that is the nature of the theoretical concept "religious affiliation." There is no way to treat religious affiliation as anything other than merely nominal classification. It is sometimes possible, however, by changing the theoretical variable somewhat, to open up higher levels of measurement. If, instead of religious *affiliation*, we were to measure *religiosity*, or the strength of religious beliefs, we would have a variable that could be conceptualized and measured as ordinal and perhaps even interval. People could easily be ranked, on the basis of certain responses,

into ordered categories of greater or lesser religiosity. It should be clear from this example that the theoretical nature of the variable plays a large part in determining the level of measurement. This illustrates once again the constant interplay between theoretical and research levels (see Figure 5.1). The decision regarding level of measurement at the research level might affect the conceptualization of variables at the theoretical level.

It should be noted, finally, that there is nothing inherently undesirable about nominal variables. It would be quite wrong to get the impression that variables capable of being measured at higher levels are always better than nominal variables. The first consideration should be to select variables on theoretical grounds and not on the basis of their possible level of measurement. Thus, if a research study is really concerned with religious affiliation, the nominal variable is the correct one to use, and not the variable of religiosity which is ordinal or possibly interval. On the other hand, researchers do strive for more accurate and powerful measurement. Other things being equal, a researcher having two measures available, one ordinal and the other interval, would generally prefer the interval measure.

Evaluating Measures

We have seen that there are normally a number of indicators, sometimes a large number and at different levels of measurement, that can be used to measure a variable. How do we choose the best of these measures to use in a particular study? A number of factors come into play in making this decision, including matters of feasibility discussed in Chapter 4. Here we want to discuss two additional and very important considerations in this regard: the validity and reliability of measures.

Validity

Validity refers to the accuracy of a measure: Does it accurately measure the variable that it is intended to measure? If we were developing a measure of self-concept, a major concern would be whether our measuring device measures the concept as it is theoretically defined. There must be a fairly clear and logical relationship between the way a variable is nominally defined and the way it is operationalized. For example, if we propose to measure self-concept on the basis of how stylishly people dress, we would probably have an invalid measure. Many factors influence the way people may be dressed at any given time. The slight possibility that one of these factors might have something to do with self-concept would not be sufficient to make the suggested measure valid. The validity of measures is very difficult to demonstrate with any finality. However, several approaches to the question of validity exist, and they can offer evidence regarding the validity of a measure.

Content Validity. Content validity, also called **face validity,** involves assessing whether there is a logical relationship between the variable and the proposed measure. It essentially amounts to a rather commonsense comparison of what comprises the measure and the theoretical definition of the variable: Does it seem logical to use this measure to reflect that variable? We might measure child abuse in terms of the reports made by physicians or emergency room personnel of injuries suffered by children. Although this is not a perfect measure because health

personnel might be wrong, it does seem logical that an injury reported by such people might reflect actual abuse.

No matter how carefully done, content validity clearly is subjective in nature. All we have is logic and common sense as arguments for the validity of a measure. This serves to make content validity the weakest demonstration of validity, and it should usually be considered no more than a starting point. All measures must pass the test of content validity. If they do, we should attempt one of the more stringent methods of assessing validity.

One way to strengthen faith in content validity is to gather the opinions of other investigators, especially those knowledgeable about the variables involved, regarding whether particular operational definitions seem to be logical measures of the variables. This extension of content validity, sometimes referred to as *jury opinion,* is still subjective, of course. However, because there are more people to serve as a check on bias or misinterpretation, jury opinion is superior to using individual tests of content validity.

Criterion Validity. Criterion validity refers to establishing validity by showing a correlation between a measurement device and some other criterion or standard that we know or believe accurately measures the variable under consideration. Or we might correlate the results of the measuring device with some properties or characteristics of the variable the measuring device is intended to measure. For example, a scale intended to measure risk of suicide should correlate with the occurrence of self-destructive behavior if it is to be considered valid. The key to criterion validity is to find a criterion variable against which to compare the results of our measuring device.

Criterion validity moves away from the subjective assessments of face validity and provides more objective evidence of validity. One type of criterion validity is **concurrent validity,** in which the instrument being evaluated is compared to some already existing criterion, such as the results of another measuring device. (Presumably, any other measuring devices used in this assessment have already been tested for validity.) Lawrence Shulman (1978), for example, used a form of concurrent validity to test an instrument intended to measure the practice skills of human service practitioners. The instrument consisted of questions on a questionnaire, in which clients rated the skills of practitioners. Shulman reasoned that more skilled practitioners would be viewed as more helpful by clients and would have more satisfied clients. Thus, he looked for correlations between how positively clients rated a practitioner's skills and the perceived helpfulness of practitioners or satisfaction of clients. These correlations offered evidence for the validity of the measure of practitioner's skills.

There are numerous existing measures that can be used to establish the concurrent validity of a newly developed measure. One inventory, for example, found a total of 2080 such existing measures (Bonjean et al., 1967; Lake et al., 1973). Other compilations of existing measures can be found in Chun et al., 1975; Mitchell, 1985; Magura and Moses, 1986; and Corcoran and Fischer, 1987. (This also suggests, as pointed out in Chapter 4, that a thorough review of existing literature should be undertaken before going through all of the work of creating a new measure. An existing measure may be found that meets one's needs and that has already demonstrated adequate validity and reliability.) Should

a suitable measure for comparison be found, it is a matter of applying both measures to the same sample and comparing the results. If a substantial correlation is found between the measures, we have reason to believe that our measure has concurrent validity. As a matter of convention, a correlation of $r = .50$ is considered the minimum required for establishing concurrent validity.

The inherent weakness of concurrent validity is the validity of the existing measure that is used for comparison. All we can conclude is that our measure is about as valid as the other one. If the measure we select for comparison is not valid, the fact that ours correlates with it hardly makes our measure valid. For this reason, only those measures established by research to be valid should be used for comparison purposes in concurrent validity.

A second form of criterion validity is **predictive validity,** in which an instrument is used to predict some future state of affairs. In this case, the "criterion" used to assess the instrument is certain future events. The Scholastic Aptitude Test (SAT), for example, can be subjected to predictive validity by comparing performance on the test with how people perform in college. If people who score high on the SAT do better in college than do low-scorers, then the SAT is presumably a valid measure of "scholastic aptitude." Some measures are created for the specific purpose of predicting a given behavior, and these measures are obvious candidates for assessment by predictive validity. For example, attempts have been made to develop a measure that can predict which convicted criminals are likely to revert to high involvement with crime when released from prison (Chaiken and Chaiken, 1984). Predictions are based on information about the number and types of crimes people commit, the age at which they commit their first crime, and involvement with hard drugs. Ultimately, a measure such as this is validated by its ability to make accurate predictions about who experiences high crime involvement after release.

Because this may require numerous applications and many years, the scales can be initially assessed for validity on their ability to differentiate between high and low crime involvement among current criminals. It is expected that if a measure can make this differentiation, it can also predict future involvement in crime. This is called the *known groups* approach to validity. If it is known that certain groups are likely to differ substantially on a given variable, a measure's ability to discriminate between these groups can be used as an indicator of validity. Suppose, for example, we were working on a measure of prejudice. We might apply the measure to a group of ministers and to a group affiliated with the American Nazi Party. If these groups differed significantly in how they responded to the instrument, then we would have reason to believe that the measure is valid. If it failed to show a substantial difference, we would certainly have doubt about its validity.

Despite the apparent potential of the known groups approach, it does have its limitations. Frequently, there are no groups known to differ on the variable we are attempting to measure. In fact, the purpose of developing a measure is often to allow the identification of groups who do differ on some variable. The upshot of this is that the known groups technique cannot always be used. When it is used, it has a further limitation, namely, that it cannot tell us whether a measure can make finer distinctions between less extreme groups than those used in the val-

idation. It may be, for example, that the measure of prejudice just described shows the Nazis to be high in prejudice and the ministers low. With a broader sample, though, the measure may show that *only* the Nazis score high and *everyone else*, not just ministers, scores low. Thus, the measure can distinguish between groups only in a very crude fashion.

Construct Validity. Construct validity, the most complex of the three types of validity we have discussed, involves relating an instrument to an overall theoretical framework in order to determine whether the instrument is correlated with all the concepts and propositions that comprise the theory (Cronbach and Meehl, 1955). In this case, instruments are not assessed in terms of how they relate to one criterion but rather to the numerous criteria derivable from some theory. For example, if we develop a new measure of socioeconomic status (SES), we can assess construct validity by showing that the new measure predicts accurately the many hypotheses that can be derived from a theory of occupational attainment. In the theory, there would be numerous propositions relating occupational attainment and SES to a variety of other concepts. If some or all of the predicted relationships are not found, then we may question the validity of the new measuring instrument. (Of course, it may be that the theory itself is flawed, and this possibility must always be considered in assessing construct validity.)

There are some very complex forms of construct validity. One is called the **multitrait-multimethod approach** (Campbell and Fiske, 1959). This is based on two ideas. The first is that two instruments that are valid measures of the same concept should correlate rather highly with one another even though they are different instruments. Secondly, two instruments, although similar to one another, should not correlate highly if they measure different concepts. You can readily imagine that this approach to validity involves the simultaneous assessment of numerous instruments (multimethod) and numerous concepts (multitrait) through the computation of intercorrelations. This technique was used recently to assess the validity of children's self-reports about their negative emotions, such as aggressiveness and depression (Wolfe et al., 1987). The point is that assessing construct validity can become highly complex, but the complexity offers greater evidence of the validity of the measures.

The three types of validity we have discussed—content, criterion, and construct—involve a progression in which each builds on the previous one. Each requires more information than prior ones, but it also provides a better assessment of validity. Unfortunately, many studies limit their assessment to content validity, with its heavy reliance on the subjective judgments of individuals or juries. Although sometimes this is necessary, measures that have been subjected only to content validity should be used with caution.

Reliability

In addition to validity, measures are also evaluated in terms of their **reliability,** which refers to a measure's ability to yield consistent results each time it is applied. In other words, reliable measures do not fluctuate except because of variations in the variable being measured. An illustration of reliability can be found at most any carnival. At carnivals, there is usually a booth with a person guessing people's weight within a certain range of accuracy, say, plus or minus three pounds. The customer essentially bets that the carny's ability to guess weights is sufficiently unreliable, that his or her estimate will fall outside the prescribed range, and that the customer will win a prize. A weight scale, of course, is a reliable indicator of a person's weight because it will record roughly the same weight each time the same person stands on it, and a scale is provided by the carny to assess his or her guess of the customer's weight. Despite the fact that carnies who operate such booths become quite good at guessing weights, they do occasionally give the wrong weight. The unreliability of the guesses is mainly due to the carny's being influenced by aspects of the customer other than actual weight, such as loose clothing that obscures the customer's physique.

In general, a valid measure is a reliable one. So if we were certain of the validity of a measure, we would not need to concern ourselves with its reliability. We have seen, however, that evidence of validity is often lacking or weak, so we turn to other ways of evaluating measures, a major one being reliability. Fortunately, reliability can be demonstrated in a more straightforward manner than validity. There are many specific techniques for estimating the reliability of a measure, but they are all based on one of two principles: stability or equivalence. *Stability* is the idea that a reliable measure should not change from one application to the next, assuming the concept being measured has not changed. *Equivalence* is the idea that all items that make up a measuring instrument should be measuring the same thing and thus be consistent with each other. The first technique for estimating reliability, test–retest reliability, is based on the stability approach.

The others discussed use the equivalence principle.

Test–Retest   The first and most generally applicable assessment of reliability is called test–retest. As the name implies, this technique involves applying a measure to a sample of people and then, somewhat later, applying the same measure to the same people again. After the retest, we have two scores on the same measure for each person, as illustrated in Table 5.3. These two sets of scores are then correlated by using an appropriate statistical measure of association (see Chapter 14). Because the association in test–retest reliability involves scores obtained from two identical questionnaires, we fully expect a high degree of association. As a matter of convention, a correlation coefficient of .80 or better is normally necessary for a measure to be considered reliable. In Table 5.3, the *r* means that the particular statistic used was Pearson's correlation coefficient, and the value of .98 indicates that the measurement instrument is highly reliable according to the test–retest method.

Lawrence Shulman (1978), in addition to subjecting his measure of practice skills to the tests of validity mentioned earlier, also tested its reliability. He did so by sending versions of the questionnaire to a set of clients and then sending an identical questionnaire two weeks later to the same clients. This provided him with a test–retest assessment of reliability, and he obtained a correlation coefficient of .75. When a reliability coefficient is close to the conventional level, such as this is, the researcher must make a judgment about whether to assume the instrument is reliable (and the low coefficient due to factors other than the unreliability of the instrument) or to rework the instrument in order to obtain higher levels of association.

In actual practice, the test–retest method cannot be used quite as simply as just suggested because exposing people to the same measure twice creates a problem known as *multiple-testing effects* (Campbell and Stanley, 1963). Whenever a measure is applied to a group of people a second time, people may not react to it the same as they did the first. They may, for example, recall their previous answers, and this could influence their second response. People might respond as they recall doing the first time to maintain consistency or purposely change responses for the sake of variety. In either case, it can have a confounding effect on testing reliability. If people strive for consistency, their efforts can mask actual unreliability in the instrument. If they purposely change responses, they can make a reliable measure appear unreliable.

A solution to the dilemma posed by multiple-testing effects is to divide the test group randomly into two groups: an experimental group that is tested twice and a control group that is tested only once. Table 5.4 illustrates the design for such an experiment. Ideally, the measure will yield consistent results in all three testing sessions, and if it does, we have

TABLE 5.3   Hypothetical Test–Retest Data

Subjects	Initial Test	Retest
1	22	30
2	40	35
3	38	35
4	15	20
5	70	65
6	40	41
7	60	55
8	12	15
9	75	77
10	40	38

r = .98

TABLE 5.4   Design for Test–Retest

	Initial Test	Retest
Experimental group	Yes	Yes
Control group	No	Yes

solid reason to believe the measure is reliable. On the other hand, substantial differences among the groups may indicate unreliability. If, for example, the experimental group shows consistency in both responses to the measurement instrument, but the control group differs, the measure may be unreliable, and the consistency of the experimental group might result from the multiple-testing effects described earlier. On the other hand, if the experimental group yields inconsistent results, but the control group is similar to the results of the experimental group's initial test, this outcome could also be due to multiple-testing effects and result from the experimental group's purposely changing their answers during the retest. Despite the inconsistency in the experimental group, the measure still might be reliable if this outcome is observed. Finally, the results of all three testing sessions may be inconsistent. Such an outcome would suggest that the measure is not reliable. If either of the outcomes that leaves the reliability of the measure in doubt occurs, a second test–retest experiment should be conducted with the hope of obtaining clearer results.

The test–retest method of assessing reliability has both advantages and disadvantages. Its major advantage is that it can be used with many measures, which is not true of alternative tests of reliability. However, its disadvantage is that it is slow and cumbersome to use, with its required two testing sessions and the desirability of having a control group. In addi-

tion, as we have seen, the outcome may not be clear, leading to the necessity of repeating the whole procedure. Finally, the test–retest method cannot be used on measures of variables whose value might have changed in the interval between tests. For example, people's attitudes can change for reasons that have nothing to do with the testing, and a measure of attitudes might appear unreliable when it is not.

Multiple Forms   If our measuring device is a multiple-item scale, as is commonly the case, we can approach the question of reliability through the technique of *multiple forms.* When developing the scale, we create two separate but equivalent versions made up of different items, such as different questions. These two forms are administered successively to the same people at a single testing session. The results from each form are correlated with each other, as was done in test–retest, using an appropriate statistical measure of association, with the same convention of $r = .80$ required for establishing reliability. If the correlation between the two forms is sufficiently high, we can assume that each scale is reliable.

The advantage of multiple forms is that only one testing session is required and no control group is needed. This may be a significant advantage if either multiple-testing sessions or using a control group is impractical. In addition, one need not worry about changes in a variable over time because both forms are administered at the same time.

The multiple forms technique relies on the two forms' appearing to the respondents as though they were only one long measure so that the respondents will not realize that they are really taking the same test twice. This necessity of deluding people points to one of the disadvantages of multiple forms. To maintain the equivalence of the forms, the items in the two forms will likely be quite similar—so similar that people may see through the attempted deception and realize that they are responding to essentially the same items twice. If this occurs, it raises the specter of multiple-testing effects and casts doubt on the accuracy of the reliability test. Another disadvantage of multiple forms is the difficulty of developing two measures with different items that are really equivalent. If we obtain inconsistent results from the two forms, it may be due to differences in the *forms* rather than the unreliability of either one. In a way, it is questionable whether multiple forms really test reliability and not just our ability to create equivalent versions of the measure.

Split-Half Approach   In the *split-half approach* to reliability, the test group responds to the complete measuring instrument. The instrument is then divided into two halves by separating the odd-numbered items from the even-numbered ones. Each half is then treated as though it were a separate scale, and the two halves are correlated by using an appropriate measure of association. Once again, a coefficient of $r = .80$ is needed to demonstrate reliability. Shulman, in his study of practice skills mentioned earlier, utilized a split-half reliability test on his instrument in addition to the test–retest method. He divided each respondent's answers to his questions about practitioners' skills into two roughly equivalent sets, correlated the two sets of answers, and found a correlation (following a correction, to be mentioned shortly) of .79. This is an improvement over the reliabil-

ity he found by using the test–retest method, and it comes very close to the conventional level of .80.

One complication in using the split-half reliability test is that the correlation coefficient may understate the reliability of the measure. The reason for this is that, other things being equal, a longer measuring scale is more reliable than a shorter one. Because the split-half approach divides the scale in two, each half is shorter than the whole scale and will appear less reliable than the whole scale. To correct for this, the correlation coefficient is adjusted by applying the Spearman-Brown formula, which was the correction used by Shulman:

$$r = \frac{2r_i}{1 + r_i}$$

Where:

r_i = the uncorrected correlation coefficient

r = the corrected correlation coefficient (reliability coefficient)

To illustrate the effect of the Spearman-Brown formula, suppose we have a 20-item scale with a correlation between the two halves of $r_i = .70$. It will be noted that this value is smaller than the minimum needed to demonstrate reliability. Let us see if the Spearman-Brown formula will adjust this coefficient upward enough to reach the conventional minimum of $r = .80$:

$$r = \frac{(2)(.70)}{1 + .70}$$

$$r = \frac{1.40}{1.70} = .82$$

$$r = .82$$

It can be seen that the Spearman-Brown formula has a substantial effect, increasing the uncorrected coefficient from well below .80 to just over it. If we had obtained these results with an actual scale, we would conclude that its reliability was now adequate.

Using the split-half technique requires that two preconditions be met that can limit its applicability. First, all the items in the scale must be measuring the same variable. If the scale in question is a jumble of items measuring several different variables, it would be meaningless to divide it and compare the halves. Second, the scale must contain a sufficient number of items so that, when it is divided, the halves do not become too short to be considered scales in themselves. A suggested minimum is eight to ten items per half (Goode and Hatt, 1952, p. 236). As many measures are shorter than these minimums, it may not be possible to assess their reliability with the split-half technique.

You might have detected a certain indeterminacy with the split-half approach to reliability regarding exactly which items will make up each half. The convention, as we mentioned, is to divide them according to odd and even numbers. The point, however, is to ensure that items are assigned *randomly* to one half or the other, and this assignment can be accomplished in many ways. In fact, there are many different arrangements of items into two halves. For a 20-item scale, for example, there are 184,756 possible arrangements of the items into two halves. Thus, there are conceivably 184,756 different possible tests of reliability that could be made when using the split-half technique, and each would yield a slightly different correlation between the halves. Which should be used

to assess reliability? The most popular approach to this problem is to use *Cronbach's alpha*, which is the average of all possible split-half correlations. Essentially, you split the scale into all possible configurations of items in two halves, calculate a correlation for each possibility, and then compute the average of those correlations (Cronbach, 1951). Obviously, this calls for many statistical calculations, especially for a long scale. Fortunately, there are computer programs such as SPSS^X that can calculate Cronbach's alpha and other complex tests of reliability once individual responses to items have been fed into the computer.

The split-half reliability test has several advantages. It requires only one testing session, and no control group is required. It also gives the clearest indication of reliability. For these reasons, it is the preferred method of assessing reliability when it can be used. The only disadvantage, as we noted, is that it cannot always be used. A lesson should be learned, however, from Shulman's approach: It is preferable to use more than one test, if possible, in assessing both reliability and validity. The issues are of sufficient importance that the expenditure of time is justified.

Measurement of Minority Populations

The validity and reliability of measuring instruments is often first assessed by applying them to white, nonHispanic respondents since they are often the most accessible to researchers. However, it should almost never be assumed that such assessments can be generalized to minority populations (Becerra and Zambrana, 1985). The unique cultural characteristics and attitudes of minorities are, typically, not considered in the development of such instruments. For some minorities, such as Asians and Hispanics, language differences mean that an English-language interview would have some respondents answering in a second language. It cannot be assumed that such a respondent will understand words and phrases as well as, or in the same way as, a person for whom English is their first language. In addition, there may be concepts in English that do not have a precise equivalent in another language.

So, measuring instruments usually need to be refined if they are to be valid and reliable measures among minorities. A study of mental health among Native Americans, for example, had to drop the word "blue" as a descriptor of depression because that word had no meaning among the Native Americans (Manson, 1986). They also had to add a category of "traditional healer" to a list of professionals whom one might turn to for help. A study of Eskimos found that, because of the cultural context, the same question could be used but had to be interpreted differently. Since Eskimo culture emphasizes tolerance and endurance, they are less likely than white Americans to give in to pain by staying off work. So a positive response from an Eskimo to a question like "does sickness often keep you from doing your work" is considered a much more potent indicator of distress than the same answer by white Americans.

These illustrations should make clear that measurement in social research must be culture sensitive. When conducting research on a group with a culture different from that of the researchers, it is always desirable to get assistance from members of that culture on the development of measurement instruments. Furthermore, validity and reliability checks of instruments must be done on members of that culture.

Errors in Measurement

The range of precision in measurement is quite broad: from the cook who measures in terms of pinches, dashes, and smidgens to the physicist measuring in tiny angstrom units (0.003937 millionths of an inch)! No matter whether measurement is crude or precise, it is important to recognize that *all* measurement involves some component of error. There is no such thing as an exact measurement. In general, the kind of measurement devices used by social scientists are rather crude and contain substantial error components. The major reason for this is that most of our measures deal with abstract and shifting phenomena, such as attitudes, values, or opinions, which are difficult to measure with a high degree of precision. The large error component in many of our measurements means that researchers must be concerned with the different types and sources of error so they can be kept to a minimum.

Random Errors

In measurement, researchers confront two basic types of error, *random* and *systematic*. **Random errors** are those that are neither consistent nor patterned; the error is as likely to be in one direction as another. They are essentially chance errors, and tend to cancel themselves out. For example, a respondent may misread or mismark an item on a questionnaire; a counselor may misunderstand and thus record incorrectly something said during an interview; or a keypuncher may punch incorrect data into the computer. All these are random sources of error and can occur at virtually every point in a research project. Cognizant of the numerous sources of random error, researchers take steps to minimize them. Careful wording of questions, convenient response formats, and "cleaning" of keypunched data are some of the things that can be done to keep random error down. Despite all efforts, however, the final data will contain *some* component of random error. It simply cannot be completely avoided.

Researchers, however, are not overly concerned about random error. Because of their unpatterned nature, it is assumed that random errors tend to cancel each other out. For example, the careless keypuncher mentioned earlier would be just as likely to punch a score lower than the actual one as to punch a higher score. The net effect is that the random errors, at least in part, offset each other. Also, owing to its lack of pattern, random error is unlikely to cause us to come to false conclusions. The major problem with random error is that it weakens the precision with which a researcher can measure variables. The situation is analogous to clocking Olympic downhill skiers, whose times are so close that often only a few one-thousandths of a second separate the competitors. Attempting to determine the winner with a stopwatch, which only measures to tenths of a second, would result in some error in measurement. But the error is just as likely to affect the Russians as the Americans. The error does not single out any particular group, and over the long run of several heats, the best skier is most likely going to emerge the winner. The same cannot be said for a more serious enemy of measurement, systematic error.

Systematic Errors

Systematic error is error that is consistent and patterned. Unlike random errors, systematic errors may not cancel themselves out. If there is a consistent over- or under-statement of the value of a given variable, then the errors will accumulate. For example, it is well known that there is systematic error when measuring crime with official reports of crimes known to the police. The Uniform Crime Reports (UCR) of the Federal Bureau of Investigation counts only crimes that are reported to the police. The Department of Justice supplements these statistics with the National Crime Survey (NCS), which measures the number of people who claim to be the victims of crime. Comparisons of these two measures consistently reveal a substantial amount of "hidden" crime: crimes reported by victims but never brought to the attention of the police. For example, NCS data indicate a victimization rate for violent crimes nearly six times greater than that reported by the UCR (McCaghy and Cernkovich, 1987). So, there is a very large systematic error when measuring the amount of crime the way the UCR does because of the underreporting of most crimes.

Systematic errors are more troublesome to researchers than random errors because they are more likely to lead to false conclusions. For example, official juvenile delinquency statistics consistently show higher rates of delinquency among children of lower socioeconomic status families. Self-report studies of delinquency involvement suggest, however, that the official data systematically overstate the relationship between delinquency and socioeconomic status (Binder, Geis, and Bruce, 1988). It should be easy to see how the systematic error in delinquency data could lead to erroneous conclusions as to possible causes of delinquency as well as to inappropriate prevention or treatment strategies.

Researchers deal with error, both random and systematic, by eliminating as much of it as they can and accepting what remains as inevitable. Because systematic error is potentially the most damaging, reducing that type of error to the minimum is of greater concern. In the chapters that follow, where we present specific measurement techniques, procedures for reducing error will be a major focus.

In Research in Practice 5.2, we suggest ways in which concerns about measurement—problems of reliability, validity, and error—have direct parallels in practice intervention.

RESEARCH IN PRACTICE 5.2
Assessment of Client Functioning: Valid and Reliable Practice Measurement

At the beginning of this chapter, we emphasized the point that practitioners as well as researchers engage in a process of measurement, although for different purposes. We have discussed the evaluation of measurement primarily as it applies to research settings. Yet practitioners need to be equally concerned about such measurement issues to ensure that instruments used in practice are valid and reliable. This problem was brought to light dramatically by a now well-known study conducted by D. L. Rosenhan (1973).

Rosenhan was concerned with the ability of mental health practitioners to diagnose, or measure accurately, the presence of various mental disorders in people. To evaluate these abilities, he and a few other people attempted to gain admission to mental hospitals as patients. All these people, whom Rosenhan called "pseudopatients," had been given a variety of psychological tests and judged to have no serious mental disorders. Yet every pseudopatient gained entrance to the hospital he or she approached, and with suprising ease! All were diagnosed as schizophrenic based on their intake interview, in which they claimed they heard voices saying things like "thud" and "hollow." All were later released as "schizophrenia in remission."

It seems clear that the assessment tools used by these mental health practitioners were not completely valid measures of psychological disorder. (The diagnostic tool used here was the *Diagnostic and Statistical Manual*, or DSM, of the American Psychiatric Association.) It is possible, of course, that the psychological tests Rosenhan ad-

(Continued on next page)

ministered to the pseudopatients were invalid and the pseudopatients (including Rosenhan) were, in fact, schizophrenic! Yet we know from a host of research studies that the reliability of psychiatric diagnoses is highly variable (Kutchins and Kirk, 1986; Gallagher, 1987). In some cases, diagnoses vary little from one practitioner to another, whereas, in other settings, there is great variation. The reliability of psychiatric diagnoses is affected by the nature of the disorder, the skill of the practitioner, and the circumstances under which assessments are made as well as by the kinds of efforts that are made to reach agreement. This fluctuation in reliability certainly suggests that the assessments made by practitioners at the hospitals were unreliable and may very well have been invalid also.

The point, then, is that practitioners need to be concerned with measurement issues as much as do researchers. Problems of validity, reliability, and error can result in ineffective and possibly harmful practice intervention. By observing how researchers deal with such problems, practitioners can learn systematic ways of evaluating measurement instruments.

In addition, measures developed for practice are often used to measure the independent or dependent variable in research. Research on mental illness, for example, sometimes uses the DSM as a measurement tool for assessing the extent and type of mental illness. Corcoran and Fischer (1987) describe a host of practice measures that can be very useful in research. They also assess what reliability and validity information exists about each measure.

COMPUTERS IN RESEARCH
Transforming Data and Creating New Variables

In a simple model of the research process, measurement tools are designed, data are collected, and then analysis takes place. Measurement, however, need not be restricted to the data in the form that it is collected and entered into the computer. On the contrary, once the data are in computer format, the researcher can call on the computer's capabilities to create new variables, correct errors in data entry, and combine data from several variables into summary variables such as scale scores. Changing data and creating additional variables in a data set is known as *data transformation,* and this transformation capability is one of the features that makes computers so useful in the research process.

Statistical analysis software for mainframe computers are usually capable of doing complex and sophisticated data transformations. Microcomputer statistical packages also have transformation capabilities, but they vary substantially in the kinds of transformations they can do and the number of variables and transformations they can accommodate. The examples we will discuss are based on SPSS^x, which has features similar to those found in other large mainframe programs like SAS and BMDP. Other types of software may use different terms and symbols, but they all work with the same types of transformation procedures. Even if a transformation capability is lacking in a particular software, it may be possible to modify data by using a spreadsheet, data base, or other file management program to do the transformations and then import the revised data file into the statistical program for analysis.

We will discuss two basic kinds of transformations. The first is commonly referred to as a *recode,* in which a new value is substituted for an existing value.

Recoding is often done to reduce the number of categories into which a variable has been coded. For example, in studying education as an independent variable, we would normally be interested in the impact of certain educational accomplishments, such as completing high school or college, on people's lives. It is graduation from high school that has a big impact on job opportunities and income; on the other hand, a person who completed the eleventh grade would not have much additional opportunity compared with a person who had completed only ten years. In measuring education, however, people are typically asked to indicate the highest grade of schooling completed. So, we need to transform or recode our variable (called EDUCAT in SPSS^x language) as measured into a set of categories that has more meaning in terms of our theoretical understanding of the impact of education on people's lives. The following SPSS^x commands will do this:

```
RECODE EDUCAT (LO THRU
   7=1) (8=2) (9 THRU
   11=3) (12=4) (13 THRU
   15=5) (16 THRU HI=6)
```

From the first line, the command says: Recode the variable EDUCAT so that any respondents who said they had between one and seven years of education (LO THRU 7) are given a value of "1"; those who said they had completed 8 years are given a value of 2; those who said they had 9, 10, or 11 years (9 THRU 11) are given a value of 3; and so on. In this way, instead of 20 or more categories for the variable education, we now have only six. This kind of data reduction is very useful for grouping people who have made theoretically important transitions in education, such as graduating from college (value "6"), so that comparisons can be made with those who have not made the transition (those who have not graduated from college, or values "1" through "5"). With these few commands, then, an entire data set can be recoded almost instantly. It is important to note that the original values have not been modified or destroyed.

(Continued on next page)

By simply eliminating the recode command from the computer file, the original "years of education" values can be used for other analyses.

A second basic type of data transformation is the creation of new variables by combining or, in some fashion manipulating, the data that are already in a data set. In SPSS^x, this is sometimes done by means of the COMPUTE statement. COMPUTE statements create new variables by combining existing variables according to the specifications provided by the researcher. A typical illustration would be to develop a composite index score from several items that measure the same concept. For example, measuring loneliness is important in a mental health needs assessment. This could be done by having people respond to five items that tap how lonely they feel, such as "There are no people I can talk to," and "I feel left out." Response options are: 1 = Never, 2 = Rarely, 3 = Sometimes, and 4 = Often.

Although responses to the individual items may be of some interest, the person's responses to all five items is probably the best indicator of degree of loneliness. To obtain this measure, we could use the following COMPUTE statement, where the variable names L1 through L5 refer to each separate question on loneliness and the variable LTOTAL refers to the new variable, which is a summary measure of the five responses combined:

```
COMPUTE LTOTAL = (L1 +
   L2 + L3 + L4 + L5) - 5
```

This statement, first, causes the computer to create a new variable in your data set called LTOTAL and, second, gives each case in the data set a value for LTOTAL that is the sum of their responses to the five individual items minus 5. The result is a score that ranges from 0 for someone who answered "Never" to all five items, to 15 for someone who answered "Often" to all five. (Subtracting 5 in this computation simply adjusts the score to have a low value of 0. Incidentally, SPSS^x does the computations in parentheses before those outside parentheses.)

There are many other kinds of transformation available to the researcher who is able to exploit the file management capability of the computer. Exact program statements and symbols will vary from one software package to another, but the same general principles apply. In fact, one of the major criteria used in assessing statistical software is the complexity and sophistication of the data transformations that the software permits. (These transformations could be done by hand, of course, but it would be very time-consuming and expensive, and people would make far more errors than would the computer). Newly created variables have the same status as any other variable in the data set: They can be saved permanently in the data set, they can be subjected to statistical analysis, and they can be used in yet further data transformations. Any research project today is likely to involve some sort of data transformation (sometimes quite lengthy and involved) to develop a complete and accurate picture of a data set.

||||||||||||||||||||||||||||||||||||||||||||||||||||||||||||||||||||||||||||||||||||||||||||||||||

≡ Main Points

- Measurement is the process of describing abstract concepts in terms of specific indicators by assigning numbers or other symbols to them.
- An indicator is an observation that is assumed to be evidence of the attributes or properties of some phenomenon.
- Discrete variables have a limited number of distinct and separate values.
- Continuous variables theoretically have an infinite number of possible values.
- The four levels of measurement are nominal, ordinal, interval, and ratio.
- The level of measurement achieved with a given variable is determined by the nature of the variable itself and by the way it is measured.
- Validity refers to a measure's ability to measure accurately the variable it is intended to measure.
- Content validity, jury opinion, criterion validity, and construct validity are techniques of assessing the validity of measures.
- Reliability refers to a measure's ability to yield consistent results each time it is applied.
- Test–retest, multiple-forms, and split-half are techniques for assessing the reliability of measures.
- Measurement in social research must be culture sensitive, and it should never be assumed that a measurement instrument that is valid and reliable for majority group populations will be so for minorities.
- Random errors are those that are neither consistent nor patterned and are unlikely to lead to false conclusions.
- Systematic errors are consistent and patterned and, unless noted, can potentially lead to erroneous conclusions.
- A part of the measurement process is to use computer capabilities to create additional variables from the data as collected through a process known as data transformation.

≡ Important Terms for Review

concurrent validity
construct validity
content validity
continuous variables
criterion validity
discrete variables
face validity
index
indicator
interval measure
item
level of measurement
measurement
multitrait-multimethod validity
nominal measure
ordinal measure
predictive validity
random error
ratio measure
reliability
scale
systematic error
validity

≡ For Further Reading

Bracht, Neil F., ed. *Social Work in Health Care.* New York: Haworth, 1978.

This book contains measurement scales that assess the personal and social changes that accompany the onset of illness. These measurement instruments can be used in both research and practice.

Burgess, Robert G., ed. *Key Variables in Social Investigation.* London: Routledge & Kegan Paul, 1986.

This collection of essays is unusual in that it focuses on ten of the most commonly used social science variables analyzing their underlying concepts and how they have been operationalized.

Geismar, Ludwig L. *Family and Community Functioning: A Manual of Measurement for Social Work Practice and Policy.* 2d ed. Metuchen, N.J.: Scarecrow Press, 1980.

Another illustration of measuring devices that can be applied to both practice and research issues.

Hindelag, Michael J., Travis Hirschi, and Joseph G. Weis. *Measuring Delinquency.* Beverly Hills, Calif.: Sage Publications, 1980.

A good description of the development of a measuring device related to a human service issue. The volume covers all the issues related to problems of measurement.

Miller, Delbert C. *Handbook of Research Design and Social Measurement,* 4th ed. New York: Longman, 1983.

A good resource work for scales and indexes focusing on specific human service concerns.

Price, James L. *Handbook of Organizational Measurement.* Lexington, Mass.: Heath, 1972.

Using concepts that are a part of organizational theory, this book illustrates how to link concepts with indicators.

Social Work Research and Abstracts (special issue on assessment). 17:1 (Spring 1981).

This entire issue of the journal is devoted to assessment and measurement in the human services. It especially emphasizes the nontechnical issues such as the influence of the setting and practice-research differences.

≡ Exercises for Class Discussion

5.1 Here is an interesting way to illustrate measurement issues. Imagine that there is a new student at your college who is blind. He is trying to become independent of others and asks some students to help him measure the distance to such places as the nearest drinking fountain, the rest room, and the student lounge. To help this student out, select a destination that is at least 50 feet from the classroom and preferably around a corner or two. Have four or five students independently count the number of steps to the destination and write their count on the board. Compare the counts. How does this exercise illustrate the definition of measurement presented in this chapter? Given the responses of the volunteers, would the blind student be able to find the destination? Was this a valid and reliable measurement procedure?

5.2 Are there modifications that you could make in the "rules" of measurement presented in Exercise 5.1 that would improve the validity and reliability of the measure?

5.3 The following list contains variables that researchers and practitioners in the human services commonly encounter.

> race
> income
> health
> drug use
> school achievement
> number of arrests
> depression
> marital satisfaction
> employment status

assertiveness
parenting skill
client satisfaction

Which level of measurement is applicable to each of these variables? Which of these variables are discrete and which continuous? Which of these variables could be measured at more than one level of measurement? Which level would be best?

5.4 Working independently or in teams of two or three students, locate in your library some studies that have used one of the variables from the list in Exercise 5.3. Describe how the variable was operationalized in each study. Do you see any weaknesses in using this operational definition given the nominal definition of the variable? What problems might there be in obtaining valid and reliable measures of these variables based on the studies that you have reviewed?

6

Sampling

A number of correctional systems have established programs that use behavior modification techniques to shape inmate behavior, rewarding sought-after behavior and withholding privileges from inmates who are recalcitrant or hostile. Each inmate who is placed in such a program becomes, in a sense, a test of the hypotheses about behavior change derived from behavioral theory (see Chapter 11 on single-subject research designs). What can we conclude, however, if one inmate's behavior changes in a way that supports these hypotheses? Will the program work with other inmates? This is the issue at the core of this chapter: Can knowledge gained from one or a few cases be considered knowledge about a whole group of people? The answer to this question depends on whether the inmate is *representative* of some larger group, of which the inmate is a "sample." Does he or she represent all inmates? Only inmates in a particular prison? Just inmates who have committed certain offenses? Or is this inmate not representative of any larger group? These issues are at the center of the problem of *sampling*, or selecting a few cases out of some larger grouping for study. All of us have had experience with sampling. Cautiously tasting a spoonful of soup is a process of sampling to see how hot it is, and taking a bite of a new brand of pizza is sampling to see if we like it. All sampling involves attempting to make a judgment about a whole something—a bowl of soup, a brand of pizza, or an inmate population—based on an analysis of a part of the whole. Scientific sampling, however, is considerably more careful and systematic than casual, everyday sampling. In this chapter, we will discuss the fundamentals of sampling along with the benefits and disadvantages of various sampling techniques.

The Purpose of Sampling

When the subject of sampling is first encountered, a not uncommon question is, Why bother? Why not just study the whole group? A major reason for studying samples rather than the whole group is that the whole group is sometimes so large that it is not feasible to study it. For example, human service workers might be interested in learning about welfare recipients, the mentally ill, prison inmates, or some other rather large group of people. It would be difficult—and often impossible—to study all members of these groups. Sampling allows us to study a workable number of cases from the large group to derive findings that are relevant for all members of the group.

A second reason for sampling is that, as surprising as it may seem, information based on carefully drawn samples can be better than information from an entire group. This is especially true when the group being studied is extremely large. For example, a census of all residents of the United States is taken at the beginning of each decade. Despite the vast resources the federal government puts into the census, substantial undercounts and other errors occur. In fact, after the 1980 census numerous cities filed lawsuits complaining of alleged undercounts. Between the decennial censuses, the Census Bureau conducts *sample* surveys to update population statistics and collect data on other matters. The quality of the data gathered by these sample surveys is actually superior to that of the census itself. The reason for this is that, with only a few thousand people to contact, the task is more manageable: Better-trained interviewers can be used, greater control can be exercised over the interviewers, and fewer hard-to-find respondents are involved. In fact, the Bureau of the Census even conducts a sample survey after each census as a check on the accuracy of that census. Indeed, were it not a constitutional requirement, the complete census might well be dropped and replaced by sample surveys.

Much research, then, is based on samples of people. Samples make possible a glimpse at the behavior and attitudes of whole groups of people, and the validity and accuracy of research results depend heavily on how samples are drawn. An improperly drawn sample renders the data collected virtually useless. The overriding consideration is that the sample be *representative* of the population from which it is drawn. A **representative sample** is one that accurately reflects the distribution of relevent variables in the target population. In a sense, the sample should be considered a small reproduction of the population. Imagine, for example, that you were interested in the success of unmarried teenage moth-

ers in raising their children in order to improve the provision of services to these adolescents. Your sample should reflect the relevant characteristics of unmarried teenage mothers in your community. Such characteristics might include age, years of education, and socioeconomic status. To be representative, the sample would have to contain the same proportion of unmarried teenage mothers at each age level, education level, and socioeconomic status as exists in the community. In short, a sample should have all the same characteristics as the population. The representative character of samples allows the conclusions based on them to be legitimately generalized to the populations from which they are drawn. Before comparing the various techniques for drawing samples, we will define some of the major terms used in the field of sampling.

Sampling Terminology

Populations and Samples

A sample is drawn from a **population,** which refers to all possible cases of what we are interested in studying. In the human services, the target population is often people who have some particular characteristic in common, such as all Americans, all eligible voters, all school age children, and so on. A population need not, however, be composed of people. If our unit of analysis is something other than individuals, such as groups or programs, then the target population will be all possible cases of whatever our unit of analysis is. A **sample** consists of one or more elements selected from a population. The manner in which the elements are selected for the sample has enormous implications for the scientific utility of the research based on that sample. To select a good sample, you need to define clearly the population from which the sample is to be drawn. Failure to define the population clearly can make generalizing from the sample observations highly ambiguous and result in drawing inaccurate conclusions.

The definition of a population should specify four things: content, units, extent, and time (Kish, 1965, p. 7). We will illustrate these with the sample that was used by James Greenley and Richard Schoenherr (1981) to study the effects of agency characteristics on the delivery of social services. First of all, the *content* of the population refers to the particular characteristic that the members of the population have in common. For Greenley and Schoenherr, the characteristic held in common by the members of their population was that they were health or social service agencies. Secondly, the *unit* indicates the unit of analysis, which in our illustration is organizations rather than individuals or groups. Although Greenley and Schoenherr collected data from practitioners and clients in the organizations, their focus was on comparing the performance of agencies. Third, the *extent* of the population refers to its spacial or geographic coverage. For practical reasons, Greenley and Schoenherr limited the extent of their population to health and social agencies serving one county in Wisconsin. It would not have been financially feasible for them to define the extent of their population as all agencies in Wisconsin or the United States. Finally, the *time* factor refers to the temporal period during which a unit would have to possess the appropriate characteristic in order to qualify for the sample. Greenley and Schoenherr conducted a cross-sectional study, and only agencies that were in operation at the time they collected their data qualified. A longitudinal study might include agencies that came into existence during the course of the study.

So, with these four factors clearly defined, a population will normally be adequately delimited and what is called a sampling frame can be constructed.

Sampling Frames

A **sampling frame** is a listing of all the elements in a population. In many studies, the actual sample is drawn from this listing. The adequacy of the sampling frame is crucial in determining the quality of the sample drawn from it. Of major importance is the degree to which the sampling frame includes *all* members of the population. Although there is an endless number of possible sampling frames depending on the research problem, we will discuss a few illustrations to describe some of the intricacies of developing good sampling frames.

In human service research, some of the most adequate sampling frames consist of lists of members of organizations. If we wanted, for example, to expand the study of the impact of behavior modification on inmates mentioned at the beginning of this chapter, we could draw a larger sample of inmates in that prison. The sampling frame would be quite straightforward, consisting of all inmates currently listed as residents of that institution. Given the care with which correctional facilities maintain accurate records of inmates, the sampling frame would undoubtedly be complete and accurate. Other examples of sampling frames based on organizational affiliation would be the membership rosters of professional groups such as the National Association of Social Workers, the American Psychological Association, or the

American Society of Criminology. These lists would not be quite as accurate as the inmate roster because people who had very recently joined or resigned from the organization might not appear on the official list; also, clerical errors might lead to a few missing names. These few errors, however, would have little effect on the adequacy of the sampling frame.

When using organizational lists as a sampling frame, caution must be exercised regarding what is defined as the population and to whom generalizations are made. The population consists of the sampling frame, and legitimate generalizations can be made only to the sampling frame. There are many social workers, for example, who do not belong to the National Association of Social Workers. Thus, a sample taken from the NASW membership roster represents only NASW members and not all social workers. In the use of organizational lists as sampling frames, then, it is important to assess carefully whom the list includes and whom it excludes. Sometimes research focuses on a theoretical concept that is operationalized in terms of an organizational list that does not include all actual instances of what is intended by the concept. For example, a study of poverty could operationalize the concept "poor" as those receiving welfare payments. Yet many people with little or no income do not receive welfare. In this case, the sampling frame would not completely reflect the population intended by the theoretical concept.

Some research focuses on populations that are quite large, such as residents of a city or state. This is particularly true of needs assessment research and oftentimes of evaluation research. To develop sampling frames for these populations, three listings are commonly used: telephone numbers, utility subscribers,

or city directories (Lavrakas, 1987). A listing of telephone numbers in an area can be found in telephone books, but telephone books have a number of problems when used as sampling frames. Even today some people do not have telephone service, and others have unlisted numbers. The number of households that lack telephone service has diminished over the past few decades. As recently as 1960 13 percent of American households were without telephone service; today, probably no more than 2 percent lack such service (U.S. Bureau of the Census, 1987). Those without telephones, however, are concentrated among the poor, those living in rural areas, and transient groups such as the young. So for a research project in which these groups are important, sampling based on telephone books could be very unrepresentative. As for unlisted numbers, the extent varies from one locale to another, but it could be as much as 30 percent in some areas. Because of these problems with the listings in telephone books, they are typically not used, at least by themselves, for drawing samples. Instead, there are other techniques, such as *random digit dialing* (or RDD) that can assure that every household with telephone service has an equal chance of appearing in the sample. With RDD, telephone numbers are selected for the sample by using a table of random numbers or having a computer generate random telephone numbers (see Appendix B). (If the researcher knows the telephone prefix of the areas to be sampled, then only the last four numbers need be randomly chosen.) Because the phone numbers are randomly determined, RDD gives all telephone numbers an equal chance of being selected regardless of whether they are listed in the directory. It, therefore, removes the noncoverage due to unlisted numbers. Random digit dialing, of course, does nothing about the noncoverage due to the lack of telephone service in some households.

Another population listing that can be used for sampling is a list of customers from the local electric utility. Though some households do not have telephone service, relatively few lack electricity, and the problem of noncoverage is, therefore, less significant. Utility listings do, however, have their own problems that must be handled in order to draw a satisfactory sample. The major problem comes from multiple-family dwellings, which often have utilities listed only in the name of the owner rather than all the individual residents. Multiple-family dwellings are more likely to be inhabited by the young, the old, and the unmarried. Unless the utility listings are supplemented, samples will systematically under-represent people in these groups. This problem can be overcome by visiting the dwellings and adding the residents to the list of utility subscribers, but this is a very time-consuming task. Beyond the problem of multiple dwellings, the old, the poor, and those living in rural areas are more likely to be without utilities and thus not appear in the sampling frame.

As a source of population listings, city directories are quite useful. City directories can be found in most libraries, and they are generally divided into four sections. The first is a listing of commerical firms and is analogous to the yellow pages of the telephone book. The second section is an alphabetical listing of residents together with their addresses, phone numbers, and the head of household's occupation. This section of the directory is useful if the research problem calls for a sample of people or households with particular occupational characteristics. Next comes an alphabetical listing of streets and addresses with residents' names. For

sampling purposes, this is often the most useful section of the directory. The other sections become outdated rapidly whereas the address listing will exclude only new construction. The last section is a listing of telephone numbers in numerical order together with the name of the person to whom the number is assigned. The accuracy of city directories is quite high, certainly as good a sampling frame as a researcher could compile starting from scratch (Sudman, 1976). In addition, city directories are the least likely to exclude people with low incomes.

A Classic Sampling Disaster

There have been some disastrous mistakes in sampling in past investigations, often because of inadequate sampling frames. These mistakes result in special chagrin when the investigator makes some precise—and easily refutable—predictions based on the sample. A classic example of this was the attempt by the *Literary Digest* magazine to predict the outcome of the 1936 presidential race between Alfred Landon and Franklin Roosevelt. In election predicting, the target population is all eligible voters. The *Literary Digest,* however, did not utilize a sampling frame that listed all eligible voters. Rather, they drew their sample from lists of automobile owners and from telephone directories. On the basis of their sample results, Landon was predicted to win by a substantial margin. But, of course, Roosevelt won the election easily. Why the error in prediction? In 1936 the Great Depression was at its peak, and a substantial proportion of eligible voters, especially the poorer ones, did not own cars or have telephones. In short, the sample was drawn from an inadequate sampling frame and did not represent the target population. Because the poor are more likely to vote Democratic, most of the eligible voters excluded from the sampling frame—and thus having no chance to be in the sample—voted for the Democratic candidate—Roosevelt—resulting in his victory and the *Literary Digest's* embarrassingly inaccurate prediction. Although the *Literary Digest* was a popular and respected magazine before the election, it never recovered from its prediction and went out of business a short time later.

From this illustration, it should be clear that utilizing a sampling frame that adequately covers the target population is essential if the sample is to reflect that population accurately. In general, the larger the target population, the more difficult it is to obtain an adequate listing. Indeed, with very large populations, obtaining a sampling frame of individual elements may become impossible, and some form of sampling that does not require a list must be utilized. For many human service projects focusing on smaller populations, usable listings (such as those already mentioned) are available or can readily be created. Still, caution in using such things must be exercised because they may inadvertently exclude some people. In fact, human service research may be especially vulnerable to this because we study populations that are often difficult to enumerate. For example, undocumented aliens are by definition not listed anywhere. We know they comprise a large segment of the population in such urban centers as Los Angeles, but a study of the poor in these areas that relied on a city directory would obviously miss large numbers of such people. Studies of homosexuals have also fallen prey to this problem (Hooker, 1957; Bell and Weinberg, 1978). In some of these studies, the sampling frame was homosexuals who were listed as patients by

therapists who were participating in the research. The studies concluded that homosexuality was associated with personality disturbance. Yet it does not take great insight to recognize that many gays—those feeling no need to see a therapist—are not listed in the sampling frame, and the sample is thus strongly biased toward finding personality disorders among gays.

So sampling frames need to be assessed carefully to ensure that they include all elements of the population. The remainder of this chapter is a discussion of the different ways in which samples can be selected. First, we will discuss probability samples, for which we are most likely to have a sampling frame from which to draw the sample. Probability samples are often used in such human service research as needs assessment and evaluation research. Then we will discuss nonprobability samples, which are often used in such research as assessing client functioning and evaluating the effectiveness of intervention strategies.

Probability Samples

By chance, almost any sampling procedure could produce a representative sample. But that is little comfort to a researcher who wants to be as certain as possible that his or her sample is representative. Techniques that make use of probability theory can both greatly reduce the chances of getting a nonrepresentative sample and, what is more important, permit the researcher to estimate precisely the likelihood that a sample differs from the true population by a given amount. In these samples, known as **probability samples,** each element in the population has some chance of being included in the sample, and the investigator can determine the chances or probability of each element's being included (Scheaffer, Mendenhall, and Ott, 1986). In their simpler versions, probability sampling techniques ensure that each element has an *equal* chance of being included. In more elaborate versions, the researcher takes advantage of knowledge about the population to select elements with differing probabilities. The key point is that, whether the probabilities are equal or different, each element's probability of being included in a probability sample is nonzero and known. Furthermore, probability sampling enables us to calculate **sampling error,** which is essentially the extent to which the values of the sample differ from those of the population from which it was drawn. We will discuss the major types of probability samples, followed by an analysis of how to estimate the sample size needed to produce a given amount of sampling error.

Simple Random Sampling

The simplest technique for drawing probability samples is **simple random sampling** (SRS), in which each element in the population has an equal probability of being chosen for the sample. Simple random sampling treats the target population as a unitary whole. One begins with a sampling frame containing a list of the entire population or as complete a list as can be obtained. The elements in the sampling frame are then numbered sequentially, and elements are selected from the list by using a procedure known to be random. If the sampling frame is computerized, random selection can be accomplished by merely programming the computer to select randomly a sample of whatever size is desired.

If one is drawing the sample by hand,

the most common method of ensuring random selection is to use a table of random numbers, which consists of digits from zero to nine that are equally represented and have no pattern or order to them. Appendix B contains an illustration of a table of random numbers, and using one to draw a simple random sample from a sampling frame is a straightforward procedure. First, we note the size of the population. This will determine how many of the random digits we need when selecting each element. For example, if the population did not exceed 9999 elements, we would use four columns of random digits for each of the selections from the sampling frame. If the population exceeded 9999 elements, but not 99,999, we would take random digits five columns at a time.

The second step is to select a starting point in the table of random numbers. It is important that one not always start from the same place in the table, such as the upper left corner. If that were done, every sample, assuming the same number of digits were used, would select the same elements from the population. That would, of course, violate the randomness we seek to achieve. This problem can be easily avoided by merely starting in the table at some point that is itself randomly determined (close your eyes and point).

Assuming a population smaller than 9999, we would proceed through the table from the randomly selected starting point taking each set of four digits that is a part of the sampling frame until we had reached the desired sample size. (If the sampling frame contains 2000 elements, we just ignore any number between 2001 and 9999 that appears on the random number list.) This list of random numbers is then used to identify the elements to be included in the sample. If one of the random numbers is 426, for example, then the 426th element in the sampling frame would be a part of the sample.

Although simple random samples have the desirable feature of giving each element in the sampling frame an equal chance of appearing in the sample, they are often impractical. A major reason for this is the cost. Imagine doing a research project that calls for a national sample of 2000 households. Even if one could obtain such a sample using SRS, which is unlikely, it would be prohibitively expensive to send interviewers all over the country to obtain the data. Furthermore, alternatives to SRS may be more efficient in terms of providing a high degree of representativeness with a smaller sample. Simple random sampling is normally limited to fairly small-scale projects dealing with populations of modest size for which adequate sampling frames can be obtained. The importance of simple random sampling lies not in its wide application. Rather, simple random sampling is the basic sampling procedure on which statistical theory is based, and it is the standard against which other sampling procedures are measured.

Systematic Sampling

A variation on simple random sampling is called *systematic sampling*. **Systematic sampling** involves taking every *k*th element listed in a sampling frame. Systematic sampling uses the table of random numbers to determine a random starting point in the sampling frame. From that random start, we select every *k*th element into the sample. The value of *k* is called the *sampling interval*, and it is determined by dividing the population size by the desired sample size. For example, if we wanted a sample of 100 from a population of 1000, the sampling interval would be 10. From the random starting point, we would select every tenth element from the sampling frame for the sample. (Consider the sampling frame to be a circle: If the starting point is in the middle of the list, we proceed to the end, jump to the beginning, and end up at the middle again.)

In actual practice, dividing the population by the sample size will usually not produce a whole number. The decimal should be rounded upward to the next largest whole number. This will provide a sampling interval that will take us completely through the sampling frame. If we rounded downward, the sampling interval would be slightly too narrow, and we would reach the desired sample size before we had exhausted the sampling frame. This would mean that those elements farthest from the starting point would have no chance of being selected.

Systematic sampling is commonly used when samples are drawn by hand rather than by computer. The only advantage of systematic sampling over SRS is in clerical efficiency. In SRS, the random numbers will select elements that are scattered throughout the sampling frame. It is time-consuming to search all over the sampling frame to identify the elements that correspond with the random numbers. In systematic sampling, we proceed in an orderly fashion through the sampling frame from the random starting point.

Systematic sampling can sometimes yield strange and biased samples. The difficulty occurs when the sampling frame consists of a population list that has a cyclical or recurring pattern, called *periodicity*. If the sampling interval happens to be the same as that of the cycle in the list, it is possible to draw a totally worthless sample. For example, Earl Babbie (1986) reports the strange outcome of a systematic sample of soldiers. The sample was drawn from unit rosters with the members of each squad grouped and arranged in descending order of rank, that is, sergeants first, then corporals, with privates last. Unfortunately for the researchers, the size of each squad—ten—was the same as the sampling interval they were using. The result was a sample containing all sergeants! Had the starting point been different, they could have obtained samples of all corporals or all privates because of the arrangement of the sampling frame. Given this potential problem with systematic sampling, the sampling frame should be inspected carefully for any cyclical pattern that might confound the sample, and the list should be rearranged to eliminate the pattern. Alternatively, SRS could be used instead of systematic sampling.

Although systematic sampling can yield strange results, this outcome is not common. Sudman (1976, p. 56) reports that, in over 20 years of sampling experience, he encountered only one case where systematic sampling produced an unusable sample. In a practical sense, then, systematic sampling can be relied on to produce adequate samples.

Stratified Sampling

With simple random and systematic sampling methods, the target population is treated as a unitary whole when sampling from it. **Stratified sampling** changes this by dividing the population into smaller subgroups, called *strata,* prior to drawing the sample, and then separate random samples are drawn from each of the strata. Research in Practice 6.1 provides an illustration of a stratified random sample used in human service research.

Reduction in Sampling Error   One of the major reasons for using a stratified sample is that stratifying has the effect of reducing sampling error for a given sample size to a level lower than that of an SRS of the same size. This is so because of a very simple principle: the more homogeneous a population on the variables being studied, the smaller the sample size needed to represent it accurately. Stratifying makes each subsample more homogeneous by eliminating the variation on the variable that is used for stratifying. Perhaps a gastronomic example will help illustrate this point. Imagine two large commercial-size cans of nuts, one labeled peanuts and the other labeled mixed nuts. Because the can of peanuts is highly homogeneous, only a small handful from it would give a fairly accurate indication of the remainder of its contents. The can of mixed nuts, however, is quite heterogeneous, containing several kinds of nuts in different proportions. A small handful of nuts from the top of the can could not be relied on to represent the contents of the entire can. If, however, the mixed nuts were stratified by type of nut into homogeneous piles, a few nuts from each pile could constitute a representative sample of the entire can.

Although stratifying does reduce sampling error, it is important to recognize that the effects are modest. One should expect approximately 10 percent or less reduction in comparison to an SRS of equal size (Sudman, 1976). Essentially the decision to stratify depends on two issues: the difficulty of stratifying and the cost of each additional element in the sample. If the cost of each case is high, as in an interview survey, stratifying to minimize sample size is probably warranted. If each case is inexpensive, however, stratifying to reduce cost may not be worth the effort unless it can be easily accomplished.

Proportionate Sampling   When stratification is used for reducing sampling error, *proportionate* stratified sampling is normally used, in which the size of the sample taken from each stratum is proportionate to the stratum's presence in the population. Consider a sample of the undergraduate population at your college or university. Although students differ on many characteristics, an obvious one is their class standing in school. Any representative sample of the student body should reflect the relative proportions of the various classes as they exist in the college as a whole. If we drew an SRS, the sample size would have to be quite large in order for the sample to reflect accurately the distribution of class levels. Small samples would have a greater likelihood of being disproportionate. If we stratify on class level, however, the sample can easily be made to match the actual class distribution regardless of sample size. Table 6.1 contains the hypothetical class distribution of a university student body, based on university records. If one wished a sample of 200 students with these proportions of students accurately represented, stratifying could easily accomplish it. One would begin by developing a sampling frame with the students grouped according to class level. Separate SRSs are then drawn from each of the four class strata in numbers proportionate to their presence in the population: 70 freshmen, 50 sophomores, 40 juniors, and 40 seniors.

In actual practice, it is normal to stratify on more than one variable. In the case of a student population, one might wish to stratify on sex as well as class level. That would double the number of separate subsamples from four to eight: senior men, senior women, junior men, and so on. Even though stratifying on appropriate variables always improves a sample, it should be used judiciously. Stratifying on a few variables provides nearly as much benefit as stratifying on many. Because the number of subsamples increases geometrically as the number of stratified variables and their number of categories increases, attempting to stratify on too many variables can excessively complicate sampling without offering substantially increased benefits in terms of reduction in sampling error.

Disproportionate Sampling In addition to reducing error, stratified samples are used to enable one to make comparisons among various subgroups in the population when one or more of the subgroups are relatively uncommon. For example, suppose we were interested in comparing "two-parent" families receiving AFDC with other AFDC families. If "two-parent" families comprise only about 2 percent of families on the AFDC rolls, a large SRS of 500 AFDC families would be expected to contain only 10 such families. This number would be far too small to make meaningful statistical comparisons. Stratifying in this case would allow us to draw a larger sample of "two-parent" families to provide enough cases for reliable comparisons to be made. This is called *disproportionate* stratified sampling because the strata are not sampled proportionately to their presence in the population. This type of sample is different from most probability samples where representativeness is achieved by giving every element in the

TABLE 6.1 Hypothetical Proportionate Stratified Sample of University Students

Proportion in University		Stratified Sample of 200	
Seniors	20%	Seniors	40
Juniors	20%	Juniors	40
Sophomores	25%	Sophomores	50
Freshmen	35%	Freshman	70
	100%		200

population an equal chance of appearing in the sample. With a disproportionate stratified sample, each element of a *stratum* has an equal chance of appearing in the sample of that stratum, but the elements in some strata have a better chance of appearing in the overall sample than do the elements of other strata.

So far, we have said nothing about the selection of variables on which to stratify. If disproportionate stratifying is planned, the stratification variables will be dictated by our hypotheses, as in our example of comparing two-parent with one-parent AFDC families. If proportionate stratifying is planned to reduce sampling error, the stratification variables will be less clear, and the researcher will have some options. Stratifying has its greatest effect in reducing sampling error

when the stratification variables are related to the variables under study. We should, therefore, select stratification variables from those known or suspected of being related to the major variables in our study. For example, a study of delinquency might stratify on socioeconomic status because this variable has been shown to be related to delinquency involvement. Stratifying on a frivolous variable, such as eye color, would probably gain nothing, for it is unlikely to be related to delinquency involvement. It is worth noting, however, that stratifying never hurts a sample. The worst that can happen is that the stratified sample will have about the same sampling error as an equivalent-size SRS, and our stratifying efforts will have gone for naught. Research in Practice 6.1 illustrates a fairly complex use of a stratified sample.

||||||||||||||||||||||||||||||||||||||||||||||||||||||||||||||||||||||||||||||||||||||||||||||||||||||||||||||||||||||||||||||||

RESEARCH IN PRACTICE 6.1
Program Evaluation: Sampling for Direct Observation of Seat Belt Use

During the 1960s seat belts were mandated as standard equipment in all passenger cars. Millions of drivers, however, remained unimpressed by the belts and merely sat on them. There was talk of passive restraints and other mechanisms to ensure that people used their seat belts. Eventually a compromise emerged between the automakers and the federal regulators in the form of an agreement that if a majority of the states passed mandatory seat belt use laws and if the compliance rate was high enough, then there would be no passive restraints

required in new cars. This created the impetus for states to pass legislation requiring the use of seat belts by drivers and passengers. Do the laws work? Do people wear their seat belts in states that require them? To answer this question through observation has required the development of some creative sampling procedures.

One approach might be to take a random sample of drivers license holders and conduct a survey of seat belt use. Unfortunately, this is precisely the type of question that is likely to evoke a socially desirable response

(Continued on next page)

rather than the truth. Everyone knows they should wear their seat belts, so a survey is likely to produce results indicating substantially higher levels of belt use than is actually the case. Faced with the undesirability of a survey, researchers at the University of Michigan Transportation Research Institute turned to direct observation of drivers and passengers to accurately determine levels of seat belt use (Wagenaar and Wiviott, 1986). But direct observation had its own problems. Early on it was determined that to reliably code the desired information about each vehicle enough time was required that the vehicle had to be stopped, at least briefly. This requirement greatly affected both the sampling and observational procedures.

Because the major purpose of the study was to estimate seat belt use rates for the state of Michigan, a representative sample was crucial. Given the requirements for observation, the researchers needed a representative sample of places where vehicles would be temporarily stopped. They solved their unique sampling problem by selecting a sample of intersections controlled by automatic traffic signals. The signals held the traffic long enough for accurate observations to be made and were located in places with sufficient traffic to keep the observers efficiently busy. Specifically, 240 intersections were selected using a multistaged stratified probability sampling procedure. First, the researchers identified all counties in Michigan that had at least three intersections controlled by electronic signals. They discovered that 20 of Michigan's 83 counties did not meet this criterion, so those were

grouped with adjacent counties to form 63 counties or county groups.

The 63 areas were then grouped into seven regions which became strata for a stratified sample, with a separate sample drawn from each region. Given the great differences in population density, from high in the southeastern part of the state to very low in the north and northwest, a disproportionate sample was drawn to ensure some inclusion of the low population density areas. This was important as one might hypothesize that population density could be related to seat belt use rates. The counties and county groups in the seven regions constituted the primary sampling units (PSU). Sixty PSUs were selected, resulting in 32 of the county and county groups being included in the sample.

For the next stage, a complete list of all intersections equipped with electronic signals in the selected counties and county groups was constructed to serve as a sampling frame. From this sampling frame, the final sample of intersections was randomly selected for a total of 240 observation sites.

Sampling considerations did not end with the final sample of intersections. Because the goal was to estimate seat belt use at *all times* on Michigan roads, time sampling (discussed in more detail in Chapter 9) became important. Unfortunately, the researchers could not meet this ambitious goal because accurate observations could not be made during the night. Therefore, observations and conclusions were restricted to daylight hours. During the daytime, however, observations were distributed throughout the daylight hours and across all days of the week. The resulting observations of the sample of intersections, days of the week, and times of day could be expected to reasonably approximate the seat belt use rates for the population of Michigan motorists.

Care to know what the researchers found out? Well, actually three observational studies were conducted, one prior to passage of a mandatory seat belt use law, one shortly after such a law was passed, and a third approximately two years after the law went into effect. (This is called a time series design and is discussed in more detail in Chapter 10). Results of the first survey revealed a relatively low level of seat belt use, 19.8%. By the time the law went into effect, use had risen to 58.4%, clearly indicating that mandatory seat belt laws are effective in encouraging belt use. The last survey showed that the effectiveness of belt laws does wear off to some extent after the publicity dies down and some people revert back to their old habits. Two years after the law was passed, the seat belt use rate was down to 46.6%, still more than double the rate prior to the legal mandate. So, can motorists be coerced into doing what is good for them against their will? Apparently, over the long run, about half can be. The other half, rebels to the end, will be saved only by passive restraints or their own dumb luck.

Area Sampling

Area sampling (also called **cluster** or **multistage sampling**) is a procedure in which the final units to be included in the sample are obtained by first sampling among larger units, called *clusters*, in which the smaller sampling units are contained. A series of sampling stages are involved, working down from larger clusters to smaller ones. Imagine, for example, that we wanted to conduct a needs assessment survey to determine the extent and distribution of preschool children with educational deficiencies in a large urban area. Simple random and systematic samples would be out of the question because there would likely be no sampling frame that would list all such children. We could turn to area sampling which is a technique that enables us to draw a probability sample without having a complete list of all elements in the population. The ultimate unit of analysis in this needs assessment would be households. We get there in the following way (see Figure 6.1). First of all, we would take a simple random sample from among all census tracts in the urban area. The census bureau divides urban areas into a number of census tracts, which are areas of approximately 4000 people. At the second stage, we would list all the city blocks in each census tract in our sample and then select a simple random sample from among those city blocks. In the final stage, we would list the households on each city block in our sample and select a simple random sample of households on that list. With this procedure, we have what is called an *area probability sample* of households in that urban area. (Public opinion polling agencies, such as Roper, typically use area sampling, or a variant of it.) Each household in the sample is interviewed regarding educational deficiencies among children in the household. If we were sampling an entire state

Step 1:
Take a random sample of census tracts in an
urban area (the shaded tracts are those sampled).

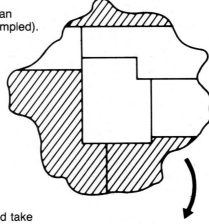

Step 2:
Identify city blocks in each census tract, and take
a random sample from a list of those city blocks
(the shaded blocks are those sampled).

Step 3:
Using a table of random numbers, select a
sample of five households from each city block
sampled in each census tract sampled (addresses
with an asterisk are those sampled).

1. 100 2nd St.*
2. 110 2nd St.
3. 120 2nd St.
4. 130 2nd St.*
5. 140 2nd St.*
6. 401 Ave. D
7. 415 Ave. D
8. 425 Ave. D
9. 435 Ave. D*
10. 201 3rd St.
11. 205 3rd St.
12. 209 3rd St.
13. 213 3rd St.*
14. 217 3rd St.
15. 400 Ave. C
16. 410 Ave. C
17. 420 Ave. C
18. 430 Ave. C

Figure 6.1 Drawing an Area Probability Sample

or the whole country, there would be even more stages of sampling, starting with even larger areas, but eventually working down to the household or individual level, whichever is our unit of analysis.

In practice there are a number of complicating factors in area sampling that our brief description ignores. For example, selected blocks often contain vastly different numbers of people—from high-density, inner-city areas to the low-density suburbs. The number of blocks and the number of households per block selected into the sample must be adjusted to take into account the differing population densities. Another complication involves the estimation of sampling error. With the simpler sampling techniques, there are fairly straightforward formulas for estimating sampling error. With area sampling, however, the many stages of sampling involved make error estimation exceedingly complex. It can be done, however, and those interested in the procedures are advised to see Kish (1965) or Scheaffer, Mendenhall, and Ott (1986).

Error estimation is quite important for area samples because they are subject to greater error than other probability samples. The reason is that some error is introduced at each stage of sampling. The more stages involved, the more the sampling error accumulates. Other factors affecting sampling error are the size of the areas initially selected and their degree of homogeneity. The larger the initial areas and the greater their homogeneity, the greater the sampling error. This may seem odd because, with stratified sampling, greater homogeneity leads to less error. Remember, however, that with stratified sampling, we select a sample from *each stratum*. With area sampling, we draw samples only from *a few areas*. If the few areas in a sample are very ho-

mogeneous in comparison to the others, they will be unrepresentative. Small and more numerous, heterogeneous clusters lead to more representative area samples. Despite the complexity, area sampling allows highly accurate probability samples to be drawn from populations that, because of their size or geographical spread, could not otherwise be sampled.

Estimating Sample Size

People new to the field of social research are often confused when confronted with the issue of how large a sample should be. This is so because they don't know what criteria should be used in assessing sample size. As we have seen, a key issue in selecting a sample is that it *represent* the population from which it was drawn. People sometimes assume that a larger sample is more representative than a smaller one, and thus one should go for the largest sample possible. Actually, deciding on an appropriate sample size is far more complicated than this. Five factors influence the sample size that a researcher will choose: the research hypotheses, level of precision, the homogeneity of the population, the sampling fraction, and the sampling technique used.

Research Hypotheses   One concern in establishing desired sample size is that we have a sufficient number of cases to examine our research hypotheses. Consider a hypothetical study in which we have three variables containing three values each. For an adequate test of the hypotheses, we need a cross tabulation of these three variables, and this would require a 3 × 3 × 3 table or 27 cells. If our sample were small, many cells would have few or no cases in them, and we could not test the hypotheses. Johann Galtung (1967, p. 60) has suggested that there should be from 10 to 20 cases in each cell in order to provide an adequate test of hypotheses. Disproportionate stratified sampling could be used here to ensure an adequate number of cases in each cell. When that is not possible, Galtung suggests the following formula to determine sample size:

$$r^n \times 20 = \text{sample size}$$

where r refers to the number of values on each variable, and n refers to the number of variables. Thus, for our hypothetical study:

$$r^n \times 20 = 3^3 \times 20 = 540$$

So we would need a sample of 540 in order to feel reasonably assured of having a sufficient number of cases in each cell. The formula works only if, as in our example, all variables have the same number of values. Furthermore, this technique does not guarantee an adequate number of cases in each cell. If some combination of variables is very rare in the population, then we may still find few cases in our sample.

Statistical procedures are often used in testing hypotheses, and most such procedures require some minimum number of cases in order to give accurate results. What is the smallest legitimate sample size? This depends, of course, on the number of variables and the values they can take, but generally 30 cases is considered the bare minimum, and some conservatively set 100 as the smallest legitimate sample size (Champion, 1981; Bailey, 1987). Anything smaller begins to raise questions about whether statistical procedures can be properly applied.

Precision Another factor influencing sample size is the level of precision, or the amount of sampling error, a researcher is willing to accept. Recall that sampling error refers to the difference between a sample value of some variable and the population value of the same variable. Suppose the average age of all teenagers in a city is 15.4 years. If we draw a sample of 200 teenagers and calculate an average age of 15.1 years, then our sample statistic is close to the population statistic, but there is an error of 0.3 years. Recall, however, that the ultimate reason for collecting data from samples is to draw conclusions regarding the population from which those samples were drawn. We have data from a sample, such as the average age of a group of teenagers, but *we do not have those same data for the population as a whole*. If we did, there would be no need to study the sample because we already would know what we want to know about the population. If we do not know what the population value is, how can we assess the difference between our sample value and the population value? We do it in terms of the likelihood or probability that our sample value differs by a certain amount from the population value. (Probability theory is discussed in more detail in Chapter 14.) This is done by establishing a confidence interval, or a range in which we are fairly certain that the population value lies. We can illustrate this without showing the actual computations. If we draw a sample with a mean age of 15.1 years and establish a confidence interval of $\pm$ 1.2 years, we are fairly certain that the mean years in the population is between 13.9 and 16.3 years of age. Probability theory also enables us to be precise about how certain we are. For example, we might be 95 percent certain, which is called the confidence level. (The computation of confidence levels is beyond the intent of this book.) Technically, what this means is that, if we draw a large number of random samples from our population and compute a mean age for each of those samples, approximately 95 percent of those means would have confidence intervals that include the population mean and 5 percent would not. What is the actual population mean? We don't know because we have not collected data from the whole population. We have data from only one sample, but we can conclude that we are 95 percent sure that the population mean lies within the confidence interval of that sample.

Precision is directly related to sample size: Larger samples are more precise than smaller ones. Thus, probability theory enables us to calculate the sample size that would be required to achieve a given level of precision. Table 6.2 does this for simple random samples taken from a very large population (over a million elements). Thus, with a sample of 9604 people, there is a 95 percent chance that the sampling error is 1 percent or less. Or in other words, there is a 95-percent chance that the sample value is within 1 percent of (above or below) the population value. Again, to be technical, it means that if we draw many random samples and determine a confidence in-

terval of 1 percent for each, 95 percent of those confidence intervals will include the population value. In actuality, of course, only one sample would be drawn; probability theory tells us the chance we run of a single sample's having a given level of error. There is a chance—5 times out of 100—that the sample will have an error level greater than 1 percent. In fact, there is a chance, albeit a very minuscule one, that the sample will have a very large error level. This is a part of the nature of sampling: Because we are selecting a segment of a population, there is always a chance that the sample will be very unrepresentative of the population. The goal of good sampling techniques is to reduce the likelihood of that error. (Furthermore, one goal of replication in science, as discussed in Chapter 2, is to protect against the possibility that the findings of a single study are based on a sample that unknowingly contains a large error.)

If the 95-percent confidence limits are not satisfactory for your purposes, you can raise the odds to the 99-percent level by increasing the sample size to 16,587. In this case, only 1 out of 100 samples is likely to have an error level greater than 1 percent. However, a sample size this large would be very expensive and time-consuming to gather data from. For this reason, professional pollsters are normally satisfied with a sample size that will enable them to achieve an error level in the 2 to 4 percent range. Likewise, most scientific researchers are forced to accept higher levels of error—often as much as 5 to 6 percent with 95 percent confidence limits. At the other end of the spectrum, exploratory studies can provide useful data even though they incorporate considerably more imprecision and sampling error. So the issue of sample size and error is influenced in

TABLE 6.2 Simple Random Sample Size for Several Degrees of Precision

Tolerated Error (Confidence Interval)	Confidence Level	
	95 Samples in 100	99 Samples in 100
1%	9,604	16,587
2%	2,401	4,147
3%	1,067	1,843
4%	600	1,037
5%	384	663
6%	267	461
7%	196	339

Source Reprinted with permission of Macmillan Publishing Company from *Survey Research*, 2nd ed., by C. H. Backstrom and G. D. Hursh. Copyright © 1981 by Macmillan Publishing Company. Table 2.2, p. 75.

part by the goals of the research project.

With smaller populations, the sample size needed to achieve a given level of precision declines below that in Table 6.2. Figure 6.2 shows the sample size needed for populations between 1000 and 500,000 with 95 percent confidence limits and 3 percent tolerated error. If your college enrolls 10,000 students, for example, and you wanted to conduct a crime victimization survey among the students, you would need a simple random sample of about 550 students in order to achieve the indicated precision.

A larger sample would increase the precision, and a smaller one would reduce it. The sample size you selected, then, would depend on how precise you wanted to be.

Population Homogeneity The third factor impacting on sample size is the variability of the population to be sampled. As we have noted, a large sample is more essential for a heterogeneous population than for a homogeneous one. Unfortunately, researchers may know little about the homogeneity of their target population. Accurate estimates of population variability can often be made only

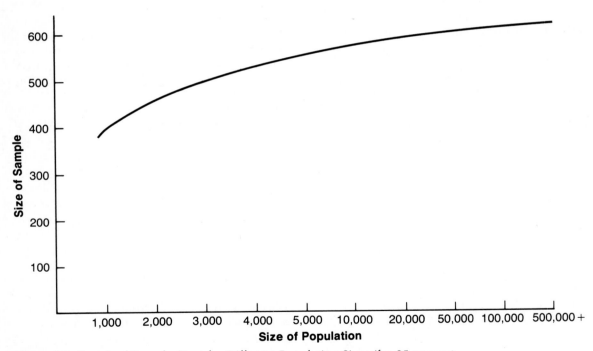

Figure 6.2 Required Sample Sizes for Different Population Sizes (for 95 percent confidence level and ±3 percent confidence interval and with the assumption of 50–50 percent split of the percentages for the characteristic in the population)

Source: Nan Lin, *Foundations of Social Research* (New York: McGraw-Hill, 1976); Figure 9.1, p. 160. Reprinted with permission of the author.

after the sample is drawn and data are collected and at least partially analyzed. On the surface, this would appear to preclude estimating sample size in advance. In fact, however, probability theory still allows sample size to be estimated by simply assuming maximum variability in the population. The estimates of sample size made in the preceding section were based on this assumption. (In Figure 6.2, the assumption of "50–50 percent split of the percentages" means that maximum variability is assumed.) Such estimates are, of course, conservative. This means that the sample size estimates will be larger than needed for a given level of precision if the actual variability in the population is less than assumed.

Sampling Fraction A fourth factor influencing sample size is the *sampling fraction,* or the number of elements in the sample relative to the number of elements in the population (or n/N, where n = estimated sample size ignoring sampling fraction and N = population size). With large populations, the sampling fraction can be ignored because the sample will constitute only a tiny fraction of the population. In Figure 6.2, for example, a population of 20,000 calls for a sample size of only 570, which is less than 3 percent of the population. For such samples, the research hypotheses, sampling error, and population homogeneity would be sufficient to determine sample size. With smaller populations, however, a sample that meets these criteria may constitute a relatively large fraction of the whole population and, in fact, may be larger than it needs to be (Moser and Kalton, 1972). This is so because a sample that constitutes a large fraction of the population would be likely to contain less sampling error than if the sample were a small fraction. In such cases, the sample size can be adjusted by the following formula:

$$n' = n/[1 + (n/N)]$$

Where:

n' = the adjusted sample size
n = estimated sample size ignoring the sampling fraction
N = population size

As a rule of thumb, this correction formula should be used if the sampling fraction is more than 5 percent. For example, suppose that a community action agency is conducting a needs assessment survey for an Indian tribal organization with 3000 tribal members. On the basis of the research hypothesis, sampling error, and population variance on key variables, it is estimated that a sample of 600 is needed. The sampling fraction, then, is n/N = 600/3000 = 0.2, or 20%. As this is well over 5 percent, we apply the correction.

$$n' = 600/[1 + (600/3000)]$$
$$n' = 600/1.20$$
$$n' = 500$$

Thus, instead of a sample of 600, only 500 are needed to achieve the same level of precision. At costs that often exceed $50 per interview, the savings of this adjustment could be significant.

Sampling Technique The final factor influencing sample size is the sampling technique employed. The estimates discussed thus far are for simple random samples. More complex sampling procedures change the estimates of sample size. Area sampling, for example, tends to increase sampling error in comparison with SRS. A rough estimate of sample sizes for area samples can be obtained by simply increasing the suggested sizes in

Table 6.1 by one-half (Backstrom and Hursh, 1981). That estimate will be crude and probably conservative, but it is simple to obtain. Stratified sampling, on the other hand, tends to reduce sampling error and decrease required sample size. Estimating sample sizes for stratified samples is relatively complex because the effect of stratifying on sampling error varies from one sample to another depending on such things as the number of stratification variables, homogeneity of strata, and the like. Accurate estimates of sample sizes for area and stratified samples can be calculated, but they involve fairly complex computations that are beyond the scope of this book. Readers interested in this are advised to consult Kish (1965) *or* Scheaffer, Mendenhall, and Ott (1986).

In an assessment of the implications of scientific work for clinical application, the issue of precision in sampling comes to the fore. Practitioners need to exercise judgment regarding how sound scientifically the research is and whether it is sufficiently valid to be introduced into practice. As we have emphasized, single studies should be viewed with caution, irrespective of how low the sampling error is. As numerous studies begin to accumulate, it is necessary to assess them in terms of how much error can be expected, given the sample size and the sampling technique. If the sampling errors appear to be quite low, then a few replications might confirm that the findings from these samples reflect the state of the actual population. With large sampling errors, however, the probability that the samples do not represent the population is increased. In such cases, confidence in the outcomes would be established only if a *number* of studies arrive at the same conclusions. More studies mean that more samples were drawn, which in turn reduces the likelihood that *all* the samples contain large sampling errors.

Nonprobability Samples

Probability samples are not required or even appropriate for all studies. Some research situations call for **nonprobability samples,** samples in which the investigator does not know the probability of each population element being included in the sample. Although nonprobability samples can be very useful, they do have some important limitations. First, without the use of probability in the selection of elements for the sample, no real claim of representativeness can be made. There is simply no way of knowing precisely what population, if any, a nonprobability sample represents. This question of representativeness greatly limits the ability to generalize findings beyond the level of the sample cases.

A second limitation is that the degree of sampling error remains unknown and unknowable. With no clear population being represented by the sample, there is nothing with which to compare it. The lack of probability in the selection of cases means that the techniques employed for estimating sampling error with probability samples are not appropriate. This also means that the techniques for estimating sample size are also not applicable to nonprobability samples. The only factor impacting on sample size for nonprobability samples is that sufficient cases be selected to allow the types of data analysis that are planned.

A final limitation of nonprobability samples involves statistical tests of significance. These commonly used statistics, to be discussed in Chapter 14, indicate to the researcher whether relationships found in sample data are sufficiently strong to be generalizable to the whole population. All these statistical tests, however, are based on various laws of probability and assume that a random process is utilized in selecting sample elements. Because nonprobability samples violate the basic assumption of these tests, they should not be used on data derived from such samples.

Availability Sampling

Availability sampling (also called **convenience** or **accidental sampling**) involves taking whichever elements are readily available to the researcher. These samples are especially popular and appropriate for research in which it is very difficult or impossible to develop a complete sampling frame. Sometimes it is too costly to do so, whereas in other cases it is impossible to identify all the elements of a population. Helen Mendes (1976), for example, used an availability sample in her study of single fathers. Because it would be practically impossible to develop a sampling frame of all single fathers, she turned to teachers, physicians, social workers, and self-help groups for assistance. She asked these people to refer single fathers to her. The limitation on generalizability, however, seriously reduces the utility of findings based on availability samples. It would be impossible for Mendes to argue, for example, that the single fathers she studied were representative of all single fathers. It may well be that only fathers with certain characteristics were likely to become a part of her sample.

Availability samples are often used in experimental or quasi-experimental research. This is because it is virtually impossible to get a representative sample of people to participate in an experiment—especially one that is lengthy and time-consuming. For example, Ronald Feldman and Timothy Caplinger (1977) were interested in factors that bring about behavior change in young boys who had exhibited highly visible antisocial behavior. Their research design was a field experiment calling for the youngsters participating in the study to meet periodically in groups over an 8-month period. Groups met an average of 22.2 times for 2 to 3 hours each. Most youngsters could be expected to refuse such a commitment of time and energy. Had the investigators attempted to draw a probability sample from the community, they probably would have had such a high refusal rate that the representativeness of their sample would have been questionable. They would have expended considerable resources and still had, in effect, a nonprobability sample. So they resorted to an availability sample. For the boys who had exhibited antisocial behavior, they sought referrals from numerous sources: mental health centers, juvenile courts, and the like. In order to have a comparison group of boys who had not been identified as antisocial, they sought volunteers from a large community center association. Given the purpose of experimentation, representative samples are less important. Experiments serve to determine *if* cause-and-effect relationships can be found. The issue of how generalizable those relationships are becomes important only after the relationships have been established.

Availability sampling is probably one of the more common forms of sampling used in human service research, both because it is less expensive than many other methods and because it is often impossible to develop an exhaustive sampling frame. For example, in all issues of the *Journal of Social Service Research* from 1980 through 1984, at least 52 of the 76 research articles could be classified as reporting some form of availability sample. The student can readily grasp the problems of trying to develop a sampling frame in the following studies:

- The evaluation of interviewer competence: Graduate students in an advanced social work methods course constituted the sample.
- The effect of using videotapes in training: The sample consisted of 55 non-MSW social workers in a public welfare agency.
- Techniques of assertion training: The sample contained people who responded to posters or advertisements in the local media.
- The assessment of sexual dysfunction: The sample was 190 couples who applied for treatment at a sex therapy clinic during a two-year period.
- The patterns of utilization of a prenatal clinic: The sample was 185 women who sought prenatal services at a clinic.

An exhaustive sampling frame that would make possible the selection of a probability sample in each of these studies might be, respectively, as follows:

- all interviewers
- all non-MSW social workers in public welfare agencies
- all people
- all couples with some sexual dysfunction
- all pregnant women

Clearly, such probability sampling is beyond the realm of most investigators. Availability samples, though less desirable, make it possible for scientific investigation to move forward in those cases where probability sampling is impossible or prohibitively costly.

Snowball Sampling

When a snowball is rolled along in wet, sticky snow, it picks up more snow, becoming larger and larger. This is analogous to what happens with **snowball sampling:** We start with a few cases of the type we wish to study and have them lead us to more cases, who, in turn, are expected to lead us to still more cases, and so on. Like the rolling snowball, the snowball sample builds up as we continue adding cases. Because snowball sampling depends on the sampled cases' being knowledgeable of other relevant cases, the technique is especially useful for sampling subcultures where the members routinely interact with one another. Snowball sampling can also be useful in the investigation of sensitive topics, such as child abuse or drug use, where the perpetrators or the victims might be hesitant to identify themselves if approached by a stranger, such as a researcher, but might be open to an approach by someone who they know shares their experience or deviant status (Gelles, 1978).

Snowball sampling allows the researcher to accomplish what Norman Denzin (1970, p. 87) calls *interactive* sampling—that is, the sampling of persons who interact with one another. Probability samples are all noninteractive because knowing someone who has been selected for the sample does not change the probability of being selected. Interactive sampling is often theoretically relevant because many social science theories stress the impact of one's associates on one's behavior. In order to study these associational influences, researchers often combine snowball sampling with a probability sample. For example, Albert Reiss and Lewis Rhodes (1967), in a study of associational influences on delinquency, drew a probability sample of 378 boys between the ages of 12 and 16. They then had the members of this sample indicate their two best friends. By correlating various characteristics of the juveniles and their friends, the researchers were able to study how friendship patterns affect delinquency.

This interactive element, however, also points to one of the drawbacks of snowball sampling: Though it taps people who are involved in social networks, it misses people who may be isolated from such networks. Thus, a snowball sample of drug users would be limited to those users who are a part of some social network, but would ignore those who use drugs in an individual and isolated fashion. It may well be that drug users involved in a social network differ from isolated users in significant ways. Care must be taken in making generalizations from snowball samples to ensure that we generalize only to those people who are like those in our sample.

Quota Sampling

Quota sampling involves dividing a population into various categories and setting quotas on the number of elements to be selected from each category. Once the quota is reached, no more elements from that category are put in the sample. Quota sampling is like stratified sampling in that both divide a population into categories, and then samples are taken from the categories, but quota sampling is a nonprobability technique, often depending on availability to determine precisely which elements will be in the sample. Quota sampling was at one time the method of choice among many professional pollsters. Problems deriving from efforts to predict the very close 1948 presidential election caused pollsters to

turn away from quota sampling and embrace the newly developed probability sampling techniques. With its fall from grace among pollsters, quota sampling also declined in popularity among researchers. Presently, use of quota sampling is best restricted to those situations in which its advantages clearly outweigh its considerable disadvantages. For example, quota sampling might be used to study crowd behavior, where it is not possible to establish a sampling frame given the unstable nature of the phenomenon. Quota sampling might be justified for a researcher who is studying reaction to disasters such as a flood or tornado, where the need for immediate reaction is critical and takes precedence over sample representativeness.

Quotas are normally established for several variables. Typically included among these variables are common demographic characteristics such as age, sex, race, socioeconomic status, and education. In addition, it is common to include one or more quotas directly related to the research topic. For example, a study of political behavior would likely include a quota on political party affiliation to ensure that the sample mirrored the population on the central variable in the study.

In quota sampling, interviewers do the actual selection of respondents. Armed with the preestablished quotas, interviewers begin interviewing people until they have their quotas on each variable filled. The fact that quota sampling utilizes interviewers to do the actual selection of cases is one of its major shortcomings. Despite the quotas, much bias can enter quota sampling owing to interviewer behavior. Some people simply look more approachable than others, and interviewers naturally gravitate toward the former. Interviewers are also not stupid.

They realize that certain areas of major cities are less than safe places to go around asking questions of strangers. Protecting their personal safety by avoiding these areas can introduce obvious bias into the resulting sample. Imagine yourself in the following situation described by Robert Rygor of the Census Bureau speaking of the 1980 census: "Any outlandish person was theoretically supposed to be approached. But imagine a person lying on the ground with wine all over and urine and a fly on his nose and asking if he had been counted" (Magnet, 1981). Would you interview him?

Because of the potential for large biases to enter quota samples, the technique is considered unreliable. Its major positive attributes, however, are that it is cheaper and faster than probability sampling. At times, these advantages can be sufficient to make quota sampling the logical choice. For example, if we wanted a rapid assessment of people's reactions to some event that had just occurred, quota sampling would probably be the best approach.

Purposive Sampling

In the sampling procedures discussed thus far, one major concern has been to select a sample that is representative of, and will enable generalizations to, a larger population. However, generalizability is only one goal, albeit an important one, of scientific research. In some studies, the issue of *control* may take on considerable importance and dictate a slightly different sampling procedure. In some investigations, control takes the form of choosing a sample that specifically *excludes* certain types of people because their presence might confuse the research findings. For example, if one were conducting an exploratory study of a psychotherapeutic model of treatment,

it might be desirable to choose people for the sample from among those who would be "ideal" candidates for psychotherapy. Because psychotherapy is based on talking about yourself and insight into feelings, "ideal" candidates for psychotherapy are people with good verbal skills and the ability to explore and express inner feelings. Because well-educated, middle-class people are more likely to have these characteristics, they might be chosen for the sample.

This is called **purposive** or **judgmental sampling:** The investigators use their judgment and prior knowledge to choose people for the sample who would best serve the purposes of the study (Bailey, 1987). Lest you think this is "stacking the deck" in your favor, consider the illustration given earlier. The basic research question is whether this type of psychotherapy can work at all. If we selected a random sample, we would have variation based on age, sex, education, socioeconomic status, and a host of other variables that are not of direct interest in this study but that might influence receptiveness to psychotherapy. Certainly, in a truly random sample, the effects of this variation would be washed out. The sample, however, would have to be so large that it would not be feasible to do psychotherapy on that many people. So rather than use some other sampling technique, we choose a group that is homogeneous in terms of the factors that are likely to influence receptiveness to psychotherapy. This enables us to see whether psychotherapy works better than some other form of therapy. If it does not work with this "ideal" group, then we can probably forget the idea. If it does work, then we can generalize only to *this group*. Further research would be required among other groups to see how extensively the results could be generalized.

In a study of social supports among elderly women, Gertrude Goldberg and her colleagues (1986) used a purposive sample. Their basic interest was to investigate the sources of support among women who face old age with neither a spouse nor a child to provide them with support. For this exploratory study, they selected a sample of women who were single or widowed, childless, and not working full time. Since the sources of support for women who are married or have children have been studied extensively, there was no need to repeat this. This enabled them to look directly at such questions as whether kin and friends provide different kinds of support for these childless, spouseless women and whether widowed or divorced women have social supports that are different from those of women who never married.

Dimensional Sampling

It is often expeditious, if not essential, that small samples be used. Small samples can be very useful, but considerable care must be exercised in drawing the sample. (The smallest sample size, of course, is the single case, which will be discussed in Chapter 11.) **Dimensional sampling** is a sampling technique for selecting small samples in a way that enhances their representativeness (Arnold, 1970). There are basically two steps to dimensional sampling: First, specify all the dimensions or variables that are important, and second, choose a sample that

includes at least one case representing each possible combination of dimensions. We can illustrate this with a study of the effectiveness of various institutional approaches to the control of juvenile delinquency (Street et al., 1966). The population consisted of all institutions for delinquents. To draw a random sample of all those institutions, however, would have called for a sample size that would tax the resources of most investigators. As an alternative, the researchers used a dimensional sample. The first step was to spell out the conceptual dimensions that were important. In terms of juvenile institutions, this investigation considered three dimensions, each containing two values as illustrated in Table 6.3: organizational goals (custodial or rehabilitative), organizational control (public or private), and organizational size (large or small). The second step was to select at least one case to represent each of the eight possibilities that resulted.

Dimensional sampling has a number of advantages that can make it an attractive alternative in some situations. First, it is faster and less expensive than studying large samples. Second, it is valuable in exploratory studies where there is little theoretical development to support a large-scale study. Third, dimensional sampling provides more detailed knowledge of each case than is likely to be gained from a large sample. With a large sample, data collection will necessarily be more cursory and focused (which is

TABLE 6.3   An Illustration of Institutional Dimensions for a Dimensional Sample

	Custodial Goals		Rehabilitative Goals	
	Public	*Private*	*Public*	*Private*
Large Size				
Small Size				

justified if previous research has nar-rowed the focus of what variables are important).

Despite their limitations, nonproba-bility samples can be valuable tools in the conduct of human service research. How-ever, two points need to be reiterated. First, some research uses both probabil-ity and nonprobability samples in a single research project, and we have given some illustrations of this. The point is that the two types of samples should not be con-sidered competitors for our attention. Second, findings based on nonprobability samples should be viewed as suggestive rather than conclusive, and opportunities to retest hypotheses using probability samples should be sought.

Research in Practice 6.2 illustrates how a complex research problem might call for the use of several sampling tech-

niques as discussed in this chapter for a single research study.

Sampling With Minority Populations

The key to selecting scientifically valid samples is to ensure their representative-ness so that valid generalizations can be made. Accomplishing this can be an es-pecially difficult challenge when research is conducted on racial or ethnic minori-ties. One problem is that some minorities have "rare event" status. That is, they constitute a relatively small percentage of our populace. Blacks, for example, con-stitute approximately 12 percent, His-panics around 7 percent (slightly higher if those in the country illegally are counted), Native Americans maybe 3 percent (U.S.

|||||||||||||||||||||||||||||||||||||||||||||||||||||||||||||||||||||||||||||||||||||||||||||||||||||||||||||||||||

RESEARCH IN PRACTICE 6.2
Needs Assessment: Mental Health Among the Homeless

With the implementation of the mental health policy known as "deinstitution-alization" over the past three decades, many people with mental disorders are outside of mental institutions rather than in them. Linked with this devel-opment has been a growth in concern over the number of homeless people in the United States. In fact, the rise in homelessness has been tied to mental health policies through the belief that many of the homeless are those with moderate-to-severe emotional disor-ders who in the past would have been institutionalized. Instead, many pre-

sume, these people have been released from the mental health system (or never placed there in the first place) even though they lack the financial or personal resources to maintain a home to live in. Needs assessment research has produced varying estimates of the percent of mentally ill among the homeless, from a low of 25 percent in a New York study to a high of 90 per-cent in a Boston investigation (New York Office of Mental Health, 1982; Bassuk, 1984). From the perspective of mental health planners and policy-makers, such widely varying estimates offer little assistance in assessing how adequately the system meets the needs of the homeless and mentally ill or what policies could overcome the shortcomings in service delivery.

For many obvious and some not so obvious reasons, homelessness is an extremely difficult phenomenon to study. A major problem in studying it is sampling, and this accounts in part for the widely varying conclusions that different studies have come to (Burnam and Koegel, 1988). Clearly, conventional probability samples are out of the question since it would be impossible to develop a complete sampling frame of all homeless people in a community. Most studies of the homeless have been limited to collecting data at one type of location, such as at shelters for the homeless, in one city. Mental health researchers in Ohio (Roth et al., 1985) developed a creative sampling procedure to try to overcome these problems. First of all, they found that the concept of "homelessness" was too simple to reflect the complexities of life for people without permanent residences. They developed an operational definition that classified people into four types or levels of homelessness:

1. Those with no shelter at all to spend the night in;
2. People living in public or private shelters or missions;
3. People living in cheap hotels or motels for 45 days or less;
4. Other unique situations, such as living with friends, in a tent city, or in jail.

Persons were classified into these categories based on where they had slept the night before the interview. (If the person became homeless on the day of the interview, then placement was based on where they intended to sleep during the coming night.) This illustrates once again the importance of conceptual development and the reconceptualization that often occurs in the process of operationalizing concepts (see Figure 5.1).

The goal of the sampling technique used in the Ohio study was to establish the highest probability that the sample was representative of the homeless in Ohio, including both urban and nonurban homeless. To achieve this they used a combination of stratified, purposive, and random sampling techniques. The state was stratified into five geographic regions, and four counties were selected from each region, one being the major urban center in the region. In addition, two rural counties and one mixed type were selected from each region through a random process. Through this method, the researchers increased the likelihood that their sample would be representative of the homeless in Ohio.

To further ensure that sufficient data were collected from the different types of homeless people, the sample in each county was stratified according to type of homelessness as spelled out in the operational definitions. Then, equal numbers of each type of homeless persons were interviewed in each county. Because of the small number of homeless in rural and mixed counties, all homeless persons identified in these counties were interviewed to ensure that there was a sufficient number of cases for data analysis in each

(Continued on next page)

county. In urban counties, purposive processes were used to develop sampling frames that listed sites at which homeless people of each type could be found, and sites were randomly selected for interviewing from these lists. At the sites themselves, the interviewers were trained to use random techniques, when possible, to select specific individuals to interview. For example, at shelters they interviewed the person at every tenth sleeping location. Had the interviewers selected who they wished to interview at these sites, they might be inclined to interview people who looked least dangerous, most approachable, or most articulate, and this would have biased the sample.

A research team in Chicago used an additional sampling technique to reduce bias in the sampling of homeless people (Rossi et al., 1987). They began with a list of census blocks in the city and asked police and others in a position to know which blocks would have many homeless and which only a few. They then stratified blocks by the number of homeless, choosing a larger random sample among blocks believed to contain many homeless. Then the interviewers, accompanied by off-duty police officers, looked for homeless people to interview in all of the non-dwelling places on the sampled blocks to which they could gain access between midnight and 6 A.M., including hallways, roofs, abandoned buildings, and parked cars. This strategy is obviously far more likely to produce a sample that is representative of all homeless people than are the many studies that limit their sampling to people in shelters.

To assess the mental status of the homeless, the Ohio researchers used an existing scale known as the Psychiatric Status Schedule, or PSS (Spitzer, Endicott, and Cohen, 1970). This enabled them to detect the presence of psychiatric symptoms that are commonly associated with psychiatric disorders warranting intervention. After analyzing the data, the researchers concluded that ". . . about 31 percent of the respondent group presented problems or symptoms that possibly required a mental health service" (Bean, Stefl, and Howe, 1987, p. 414). Since some people having symptoms detected by the PSS do not require treatment, the actual number of homeless needing mental health intervention in Ohio is probably somewhat less. This figure of 31 percent is at considerable variance with assessments of the problem in the popular literature, which typically reports much higher levels. These studies, of course, are not free of sampling problems. For example, the use of a police escort in the Chicago study may have caused many homeless people, understandably suspicious of someone seeking them out and possibly waking them up in the night, to flee, and this could have introduced a bias into the sample (Burnam and Koegel, 1988). Yet, the sampling procedures used in these needs assessments give us much more confidence that the results are accurate than does the more limited sampling typically done.

So, large-scale research on such difficult-to-find groups as the homeless is possible if care is taken in operationalizing concepts and if time and resources are used in developing representative sampling techniques.

Bureau of the Census, 1987). This means that a representative sample of 1500 Americans would, if it included the proper proportions of minorities, contain 180 blacks, 105 Hispanics, and 45 Native Americans. Unfortunately, the numbers of minorities in the sample are too small for most data analysis purposes. The Native Americans, especially, are so few in number that any analysis that breaks the sample down into subgroups would result in meaninglessly small numbers in each subgroup. Furthermore, these small numbers mean that the error rate will be much higher for the minorities than for nonminority groups since small samples are less reliable and have more error (Smith, 1987). These small sample sizes make it difficult to assess differences of opinion or behavior within a minority group, and thus, it is easy to falsely conclude that the group is homogeneous. As a consequence, we know little about sex, social class, regional, or religious differences among members of particular minorities. The outcome, according to one researcher, is "little more than a form of stereotyping, an *underestimation* of the variability of opinions among blacks. This leads to an *overestimation* of the contribution of race, per se, to black–white differences" in attitude and behavior (Smith, 1987, p. 445). The Committee on the Status of Women in Sociology (1986) makes the same recommendations regarding sex: "Research should include sufficiently large subsamples of male and female subjects to allow meaningful analysis of subgroups."

Some minorities have "rare event" status in another way that can cause problems in sampling. Because of substantial residential segregation of minorities in the United States, minorities who live in largely white areas are relatively small in number and can be easily missed by chance even in a well-chosen, representative sample. The result is a sample of minorities that is biased: It includes minorities living in largely minority communities but not minorities living elsewhere. Since minorities living in different communities probably vary in terms of attitudes and behavior, such a biased sample would give a deceptively homogeneous picture of the minority.

So efforts must be made in sampling to ensure that those "rare events" have a chance to be selected for the sample. In some cases this can be done with disproportionate sampling, in which some individuals or households have a greater probability of appearing in the sample than do other individuals or households. Another way to avoid some of these problems is to use both probability and nonprobability sampling techniques when studying minorities. One researcher suggests that purposive, dimensional, and snowball sampling can be effectively combined with some type of probability sample to ensure effective coverage of a minority population (Becerra and Zambrana, 1985). A dimensional sample of Hispanics, for example, might specify a series of dimensions that would all have to be covered by the sample. Thus, you might specify that certain age cohorts of Hispanic women (20–30 years of age, 31–40, and 41 and older) would have to be included in the sample, or a minimum number of single-parent and two-parent Hispanic families would have to be included. This would ensure that there were sufficient people with certain characteristics in the sample for valid data analysis. Another study of mental health among Asian immigrants used the snowball technique to ensure a complete sampling frame (Kuo and Tsai, 1986). Part of the sampling frame was developed by using local telephone directories and gathering names from ethnic and community organizations. However, given the dispersion of Asian Americans in the Seattle area where this study was done, they also used the snowball technique.

A Note on Sampling in Practice

Human service practitioners do not routinely engage in sampling procedures like those used for research purposes. Yet there are parallels between what occurs in practice and in research along these lines, and some of the principles of sampling discussed in this chapter can be applied to providing client services. The assessments and actions of practitioners are typically guided by the needs and characteristics of a particular client. However, to what extent are judgments about one client based on experiences with other clients? The issue being raised here, of course, is that of *generalizability*. As human beings, we constantly dip into our own fund of experience to help us cope with situations that we confront. Practitioners use their past experience with clients—sometimes very effectively—to grapple with problems of other clients. The critical judgment that needs to be made in this regard is whether it is legitimate to generalize those past outcomes to current situations.

In practice settings, you will not likely be dealing with probability samples. Irrespective of whether one's clients are welfare recipients, elderly people receiving nursing-home care, child abusers, or problem pregnancies, you have no way of knowing whether *all* people with such characteristics had a chance to be in your "sample" (that is, be one of your clients) or how great that chance was. For all practical purposes, then, you will be dealing with nonprobability samples, with all

the limitations that they entail. In most cases, you will have an availability sample—those people who happened to come to your attention because they are your clients. This means that you need to show caution in making generalizations from your observations. This is, however, no reason for despair. Remember that many scientific investigations are based on availability samples. One simply needs to recognize their limitations and use care in generalizing.

If your main concern is to generalize to other clients with similar problems, then a reasonable assumption is that the clients you see are representative of others with similar problems who seek the aid of a practitioner. Whatever propels people to see a practitioner is likely to be operative on many, if not all, of your clients. However, if your research interest concerns all people experiencing a certain type of problem, then agency clients would not be an appropriate sample. Agencies intentionally and unintentionally screen their prospective clients; thus, many people who could use services are not included in a sample of agency clients. The well-known study by Robert Scott (1975) on agencies serving the blind is a classic example. Scott found that these agencies concentrated their effects on young, trainable clientele even though most blind people are elderly or have multiple handicaps. If workers in such an agency assumed that the agency clientele represented all blind people, they would have a distorted perspective on the actual blind population.

There are, of course, ways of checking on such distortions. For example, you can compare notes with other practitioners. Do they find the same kinds of things among their clients? If so, that is support for your assumption that your clients are representative of all people with similar problems. You might also consider utilizing, at least in an informal fashion, other sampling techniques. For example, you could adopt a snowball technique by asking your clients to recommend someone they know who has a similar problem but is not receiving any services. Especially with people whose problems may be of a "sensitive" nature, this snowball approach is a mode of entry with a considerable likelihood of success. Another sampling technique that might be utilized effectively in practice is purposive sampling. For example, in dealing with unplanned pregnancies among teenagers, suppose that all your clients are members of ethnic minorities. It might occur to you that your clients' behavior, such as hostility toward practitioners, could either be due to the crisis of the pregnancy or to the animosity of a minority member toward the welfare bureaucracy. Your problem is that you have a sample that is homogeneous with respect to two variables that may be important: They all have problem pregnancies and they are all members of an ethnic minority. To get around this problem, you might begin to choose a purposive sample in which the problem pregnancies occur among nonminority teenagers. In this way, you would be in a better position to determine the source of the hostility.

In some ways, dimensional sampling might be the most feasible one for prac-titioners. In our previous illustration, for example, there are two variables—race and pregnancy—with two values each—white versus nonwhite and pregnant versus not pregnant. Thus, there are four possible cells in the analysis. If for some reason, such as past experience, you believe that these two variables interrelate in important ways in determining such factors as clients' hostility or adjustment, you could make sure that you had at least one client in each of those four cells. In this way, you would be able to make some preliminary judgments regarding the importance of these two factors.

In summary, every client you encounter is part of a sample and they are all a part of the larger population of clients that are of interest to you as a practitioner. In Chapter 11, we will discuss single-subject designs and the ways in which considerable scientific knowledge can be gained from studying changes in behavior of a single person. For now, however, it is important to have an awareness of how scientific sampling procedures can aid in assessing the validity of what is learned from a client. Once again, we can see that the gap between scientific research and human service practice is not nearly as large as is often assumed. They are both linked in a common endeavor—to gain useful knowledge of human behavior.

|||||||||||||||||||||||||||||||||||||||||||||||||||||||||||||||||||||||||||||||||||||||||||||||||||||||

COMPUTERS IN RESEARCH
Software for Sampling

One question that haunts any researcher embarking on a research project is, How big a sample do I need? Unfortunately, the only concise answer to this question is the frustrating reply: It depends. It depends on many things, as

(Continued on next page)

is evident from the five key factors detailed in this chapter. Although understanding these factors conceptually helps one understand what influences sample size, the researcher needs a number, not a general explanation. Because an appropriately sized sample is so important to research and because the problem of selecting a sample is one that readily lends itself to computerization, there are several software options available to assist the researcher with sampling decisions.

One such software program is Design Power, available from Scientific Software. This program helps researchers estimate several related factors in research planning. One is the design power or ability to detect an effect of an independent variable. Essentially, the program can tell the researcher how big a difference must occur between experimental and control conditions in order to conclude that a statistically significant difference exists. For example, imagine that an experimental treatment actually raises the reading scores of a group by 10 points on average. With a weak design, statistical results might lead the researcher to conclude that the difference is simply a chance variation and not a real difference. The researcher enters information about the study such as the proposed sample size and the desired level of statistical significance, and the program reports how big an effect must occur to reject the hypothesis that the change occurred by chance. Conversely, when the researcher specifies the power of the test, the program can specify how big a sample is necessary for an effect of a given size to be statistically significant.

The program operates through a series of menus that guide the user through making choices in the program. The researcher need only select the menu option for sample size and complete a limited number of information entries requested by the program, and the program will designate the sample size needed without requiring the user to provide complex formulas or large amounts of data.

Another sampling aid is the program Ex-Sample. This program also helps determine sample size by using information supplied by the researcher such as anticipated data analysis procedures, time, money, projected response rate, and so on. Besides generating a recommended sample size, this program leads the researcher through a structured decision-making system that reduces the possibility that some important consideration will be left out of the sampling decision.

In addition to sample size estimation, computers are also used to select the sample. One of the best applications is in random digit dialing for survey research. The convenience of random digit dialing is not limited to large-scale survey organizations with mainframe computers. One option has been for agencies to purchase telephone samples from outside organizations. Software is now available, however, for agencies to do the job themselves on microcomputers. One such program is THE SURVEY SAMPLER from Creative Research Systems. To use the system, the researcher must specify the area codes and three-digit prefixes to be included, and the percentages that these prefixes should represent in the sample. It is also possible to specify blocks of numbers that you do not want included. Telephone companies may be able to identify unassigned numbers to avoid a high frequency of nonworking numbers. The program will also eliminate numbers ending in a specified number of zeros, because these are often non-residential numbers.

Computer software will do more than merely generate the list of random numbers. In the next chapter we describe programs for conducting interviews with computer assistance. Some of these programs will keep track of the phone numbers that have been generated, record if and when calls are completed, and in cases where call-backs are needed, remind the interviewer when to place the call. Such features help assure that the sample actually obtained by the researcher will be faithful to the sample generated in the initial sample selection.

☰ Main Points

- A population consists of all possible cases of whatever one is interested in studying.

- A sample is composed of one or more elements selected from a population.

- A sampling frame is a list of the population elements used to draw some types of probability samples.

- The representativeness of a sample is its most important characteristic, referring to the degree to which the sample reflects the population from which it was drawn.

- Sampling error is the difference between sample values and true population values.

- Probability sampling techniques are the best for obtaining representative samples.

- The key characteristic of probability sampling is that every element in the population has a known chance of being selected into the sample.

- Simple random, systematic, stratified, and area samples are all types of probability samples.

- Nonprobability samples do not assure each population element a known chance of being selected into the sample and, therefore, lack the degree of representativenses of probability samples.

- Availability, snowball, quota, purposive, and dimensional samples are all types of nonprobability samples.

- Data based on properly drawn probability samples are reliable and generalizable within known limits of error to the sampled populations.

- In studies of racial and other minorities, care must be taken to ensure that sampling procedures do not result in unrepresentative samples, especially given the "rare event" status of many minorities.

- There is computer software available to assist in such sampling tasks as selecting a sample size and selecting the sample itself through random digit dialing.

☰ Important Terms for Review

area (cluster or multistage) sampling
availability (convenience or accidental) sampling
dimensional sampling
nonprobability samples
population
probability samples
purposive (judgmental) sampling
quota sampling
representative samples
sample
sampling error
sampling frame
simple random sampling
snowball sampling
stratified sampling
systematic sampling

☰ For Further Reading

Epstein, Irwin, and Tony Tripodi. *Research Techniques for Program Planning, Monitoring, and Evaluation.* New York: Columbia University Press, 1977.
  This book contains a chapter on sampling considerations when assessing the performance of agency workers, along with some other brief discussions of sampling.
Hess, Irene. *Sampling for Social Research Surveys, 1947–1980.* Ann Arbor: University of Michigan Institute for Social Research, 1985.
  Sometimes a good example can enhance the understanding of complex subjects and that is what Hess provides in her historical review of survey sampling. In addition, further discussion of many sampling issues is provided.
Jaeger, Richard. *Sampling in Education and the Social Sciences.* New York: Longman, 1984.
  A good introduction to sampling issues applied to the kinds of problems that human service professionals confront in research.

It includes information on computer programs for sampling.
Kish, Leslie. *Survey Sampling.* New York: Wiley, 1965.
  Considered the mainstay regarding sampling issues in social research, this book assumes that the reader has an elementary understanding of statistics.
Scheaffer, Richard L., William Mendenhall, and Lyman Ott. *Elementary Survey Sampling.* Boston: Duxbury Press, 1986.
  As the name implies, this book is meant as an introductory text on the design and analysis of sample surveys. Limited to coverage of probability sampling techniques, it provides the information necessary to successfully complete a sample survey.
Sudman, Seymour. *Applied Sampling.* New York: Academic Press, 1976.
  This book, along with the Kish work, will tell you almost all you need to know about sampling.

☰ Exercises for Class Discussion

A student is doing an internship with the Metropolis Senior Citizens Service Center (MSCSC), where she has been asked to help do a needs assessment. MSCSC is a publicly funded agency that is supposed to serve all residents of Metroplolis who are 60 years of age or older. Spouses of such individuals are also eligible to receive services if they are at least 50 years old. As a part of the internship, the director wants the student to conduct interviews with all senior citizens in this city of 25,000 inhabitants. The student, having taken a research methods course, knows that this would be time-consuming and inefficient as well as unnecessary. She suggests that selecting a probability sample and conducting careful interviews with those people selected will yield better information with less interviewing time. The director tells her to develop a plan to convince the agency board how this might be done.

6.1 What is the population for this project? Try to define the population as specifically as possible.

6.2 Three sampling frames that might be used are (a) the city directory, (b) the local telephone book, or (c) a Social Security Administration listing of recipients of benefits for the county. What might be the advantages and disadvantages of each? Can you think of any other sampling frames that might be useful for this project?

6.3 Could you use a random digit dialing method to sample this population? Indicate reasons for and against using such a technique.

6.4 A staff member at the agency suggests dispensing with the sampling and just running a series of public service announcements on the local radio station and in the newspaper in which senior citizens are urged to call the agency to express their concerns. Those people who call in

could be interviewed, and these interviews would constitute the "needs assessment." What kind of sampling process is being suggested? What are its advantages and disadvantages?

6.5 The elderly who reside in nursing homes make up a group of special interest to the center although they represent only 1.5 percent of the eligible residents. Describe how sampling procedures could address the problem of including a representative group of nursing-home elderly in the sample.

6.6 Use your local city directory to compile a simple random sample of 25 households, using the street address portion of the directory.

6.7 In the previous exercises, options included random digit dialing, the city directory, the telephone book, Social Security recipients, and respondents to radio announcements. Evaluate each of these options in terms of potential for under-representing minorities in the sample. Which method would be best?

7

Survey Research

A survey is a data collection technique in which information is gathered from individuals, called *respondents*, by having them respond to questions. It is probably the most widely used research method in social science research. One analysis of sociology journals, for example, found that approximately 90 percent of the articles involved survey research (Brown and Gilmartin, 1969). One of the earliest large-scale surveys in the human service field was a needs assessment survey in Pittsburgh in 1907 that focused on the extent of problems accompanying industrialization, like poor living conditions and industrial accidents. In the 1986 volume of *Social Service Review*, 17 of the 34 articles, or 50 percent, relied on survey research as a method of data collection. Likewise, in the 1987 volume of the *Journal of Health and Social Behavior*, 83 percent of the articles were based, at least in part, on survey data. In the human services, surveys have been used to investigate the functioning of clients, the effectiveness of practitioners, and the operation of human service agencies. In fact, surveys have been used to study all five of the human service focal areas discussed in Chapter 1. This illustrates a major attraction of survey research—its flexibility. Surveys can be used for all types of studies—exploratory, descriptive, explanatory, and evaluative.

There are a number of different techniques for conducting surveys. All, however, have certain characteristics in common. First, surveys typically involve collecting data from large samples of people, which means that they are ideal for obtaining data representative of populations too large to be dealt with by other methods. Indeed, the generalizability of survey findings is another major attraction of the method. Second, all surveys involve presenting respondents with a series of questions to be answered. These questions may tap matters of fact, attitudes and opinions, or future expectations. The questions may be simple single-item measures or complex multiple-item scales. In whatever form, however, survey data are basically what people say to the investigator in response to a question.

There are basically two ways in which data can be collected in survey research: with *questionnaires* or with *interviews*. A **questionnaire** contains written questions that people respond to directly on the questionnaire form itself, without the aid of an interviewer. A questionnaire can be handed directly to a respondent, or it can be mailed to the members of a sample, who then fill it out on their own and mail it back to the researcher. An **interview** involves an interviewer reading questions to respondents and recording their answers. Interviews can be conducted either in person or over the telephone. Some survey research uses both questionnaire and interview techniques, with respondents filling in some answers themselves and being asked other questions by interviewers. Because both questionnaires and interviews involve asking people to respond to questions, a problem central to both is what type of question is to be asked. We will discuss this issue first before analyzing the elements of questionnaires and interviews separately.

Designing Questions

Closed-ended Versus Open-ended Questions

There are basically two types of questions that can be used in questionnaires and interviews: closed-ended or open-ended. **Closed-ended questions** are those that provide respondents with a fixed set of alternatives from which they are to choose. The response formats of multiple-item scales, for example, are all closed-ended, as are multiple-choice examination questions, with which you are undoubtedly familiar. **Open-ended questions** are questions to which the respondents write their own responses, much as you do for an essay-type examination question.

The proper use of open-ended and closed-ended questions is important for the quality of data generated as well as for the ease of handling the data. Theoretical considerations play an important part in the decision about which type of question to use. In general, closed-ended questions should be used when all the possible, theoretically relevant responses to a question can be determined in advance and the number of possible responses is limited. For example, a question relating to marital status would

almost certainly be treated as a closed-ended question. There are a known and limited number of possible answers: married, single, divorced, separated, or widowed. In research today people are commonly offered another alternative in answering this question, namely, "living together" or cohabitation. Although cohabitation is not legally a "marital" status, it helps to reflect more accurately the living arrangements available to people today. Another obvious closed-ended question is about sexual status. To leave such questions open-ended runs the risk that some respondent will either purposefully or inadvertently answer in a way that provides meaningless data. Putting "sex" with a blank after it, for example, is an open invitation for some character with an overinflated sense of his comedic skills to write in "yes" rather than the information wanted.

Open-ended questions, on the other hand, would be appropriate in an exploratory study in which the lack of theoretical development suggests that we should place few restrictions on people's answers. In addition, when researchers cannot predict all the possible answers to a question in advance or when there are too many possible answers to list them all practically, then closed-ended questions are not appropriate. Suppose we wanted to know the reasons why people moved to their current residence. There are so many possible reasons for doing so that such a question would have to be treated as open-ended. If we were interested in the county and state in which our respondents resided, we could generate a complete list of all the possibilities and thus create a closed-ended question. But the list would consume so much space on the questionnaire that it would be excessively cumbersome, especially considering that respondents should be able to answer this question correctly in its open-ended form.

Some questions lend themselves to a combination of both formats. Religious affiliation is a question usually handled in this way. Although there are a great many religions, there are some to which only a few respondents will belong. Thus, religions with large memberships can be listed in closed-ended fashion with a category "other" where a person can write the name of a religion not found on the list (see Question 4, Table 7.1). Any question with a similar pattern of responses—numerous possibilities, but a few popular ones—can be efficiently handled in this way. The combined format maintains the convenience of closed-ended questions for most of the respondents, but also allows those with less common responses to express them.

When the option of "other" is used on a closed-ended question, it is a good idea to request respondents to write in their response by indicating "please specify." These answers can then be coded into whatever response categories seem appropriate for data analysis. However, the opportunity to specify an alternative should be offered even if, for purposes of data analysis, the written responses will not be used. The reason for this is that respondents who hold uncommon views or memberships may be proud of them and desirous of expressing them on the questionnaire. In addition, well-educated, professionals tend to react against completely closed-ended questions as too simple, especially when the questions deal with complicated professional matters (Sudman, 1985). The opportunity to provide a written response to a question will be more satisfying to such respondents and they will be more likely to complete the questionnaire.

Another factor in choosing between open- and closed-ended questions is the ease with which each can be handled at the data analysis stage. Open-ended questions can sometimes be quite difficult to work with. One difficulty is that poor handwriting or the failure of respondents to be clear in their answers can result in data that cannot be analyzed. It is not uncommon to find responses to open-ended questions that just do not make sense, so they end up being dropped from analysis. In addition, open-ended questions are more complicated to analyze by computer since a respondent's answers must first be coded into a limited set of categories and this coding is time consuming and can introduce error (see Chapter 14).

Another related difficulty with open-ended questions is that some respondents are likely to give more than one answer to a question. For example, in a study of substance abuse, people might be asked why they use or do not use alcoholic beverages. As a response to this question, a researcher might receive the following: "I quit drinking because booze was too expensive and my wife was getting angry at me for getting drunk." How should this response be categorized? Should the person be counted as quitting because of the expense or because of marital problems created by drinking? It may be, of course, that both factors were important in the decision to quit. Data analysis problems such as this are usually handled in one of two ways. First, all of the individual's responses can be accepted as data. This, however, creates difficulties in data analysis, for some people may give more reasons than others because they are talkative people rather than because there are actually more reasons for their behavior. A second way of handling multiple responses is to assume that each respondent's *first* answer is the most important one and consider it to be the only response. This assumption, of course, may not always be valid, but it does solve the dilemma in a systematic fashion.

The decision about whether to use open- or closed-ended questions is a complex one that often requires considerable experience with survey methods to assess. It is an important issue because it can have substantial effects on the type and quality of the data that are collected, as was illustrated in a survey of attitudes about social problems confronting the United States. The Institute for Social Research at the University of Michigan asked a sample of people open-ended and closed-ended versions of essentially the same questions (Schuman and Presser, 1979). The two versions elicited quite different responses. For example, with the closed-ended version, 35 percent of the respondents thought crime and violence were important social problems compared with only 15.7 percent in the open-ended version. With a number of other issues, people responding to the closed-ended questions were more likely to indicate that particular issues were problems. One reason that the type of question has such an effect on the data is that the list of alternatives in the closed-ended questions tends to serve as a "reminder" to the respondent of issues that might be problems. Without the stimulus of the list, some respondents would not even think of some of those issues. A second reason is that people tend to choose from the list provided in closed-ended questions rather than writing in their own answers even when provided with an "other" category.

It is possible, in some cases, to gain the benefits of both open- and closed-ended questions by using an open-ended format in a pretest or pilot study and then, based on the results, designing closed-ended questions for the actual survey. See Sudman and Bradburn (1982) for further discussion of open- versus closed-ended questions in surveys.

Wording of Questions

Because the questions that make up a survey are the basic data-gathering devices, they need to be worded with great care. Especially with questionnaires, where there may be no opportunity to clarify questions for the respondent, ambiguity in the design of questions can be a source of substantial trouble. We will review some of the major issues in developing good survey questions (Sudman and Bradburn, 1982). (In Chapter 13, we discuss some problems of question construction having to do specifically with questions that are part of multiple-item scales.)

The wording of questions should, whenever possible, be subject to empirical assessment to determine whether particular wording might be leading to unnoticed bias. Words, after all, have connotative meanings (that is, emotional or evaluative associations) that the researcher may not be aware of but that may influence respondents' answers to questions, as found in a survey of attitudes about public welfare policy (Smith, 1987). In surveying people's attitudes about spending public money for welfare, the question was asked in three different ways: Some people were asked whether we should spend more money on "welfare" while others were asked if we should spend more on "assistance for the poor" or "care for the poor." The question with the word "welfare" in it produced considerably more negative responses and less willingness to support the poor. While the different wordings of the question would seem to ask the same thing, the word "welfare" probably has some connotative meanings for many people of bureaucracy, waste, and possibly, fraud. On the other hand, "assist the poor" has positive connotations of charitableness, giving, and beneficence. These connotations lead to very different responses to the questions. In many cases, the only way to assess such differences is to compare people's responses with different versions of the same question during a pretest.

In general, questions should be stated in the present tense. An exception would be specialized questions that focus on past experiences or future expectations. In these situations, the appropriate tense would be used. Of major importance is that statements are not carelessly mixed with regard to tense. Failure to maintain consistent tense of questions can lead to an understandable confusion on the part of respondents and, therefore, more measurement error.

Questions should be simple, direct, and express only one idea. Complex statements expressing more than one idea should be avoided. For example, a statement that reads, "The city needs more housing for the elderly and property taxes should be raised to finance it" is poor because it is possible that some respondents might agree with the first part but disagree with the second. Statements such as this should be broken up into two separate statements, each expressing a single idea.

Statements that seem crystal clear to a researcher may very well prove unclear to many respondents. One common error is to overestimate the reading ability of the average respondent. H. L. Mencken is credited with this observation: "No one ever went broke underestimating the intelligence of the American public." Though this comment is perhaps overstated and slightly cynical, it is wise for researchers to keep it in mind when writing questions. This is especially true in the human services, where respondents of interest may have poor reading and writing skills. Accordingly, avoid the use of technical terms. For example, if would not be advisable to include a statement that read, "The current stratification system in the United States is too rigid." "Stratification" is a technical term in the social sciences that many people outside the field may not understand in the same way that social scientists do.

Another practice to avoid is reference to things that are not clearly definable or that depend on the respondent's interpretation. For example, "Children who get into trouble typically have had a bad home life" would be a poor statement because there are two sources of vagueness. The word "trouble" is unclear. What kind of trouble? Is it trouble with the law, trouble at school, trouble with parents, or what? The other problem is "bad home life." What constitutes a "bad home life" will again depend on the respondent's interpretation.

Finally, for the majority of questions designed for the general public, slang terminology should be avoided completely. The major reason for this is that slang usage tends to arise in the context of particular groups and subcultures. It may have a precise meaning within those groups, but people outside those groups are likely to be confused by it. Occasionally, however, the target population for a survey will be more specialized than the general population, and the use of their "in-group" jargon may be appropriate. It would demonstrate to the respondents that the researcher cared enough to "learn their language" and could increase rapport resulting in better responses. If the researcher decides to use slang, however, the burden is on him or her to be certain the slang is used correctly.

Once a survey instrument is developed, it must be pretested to see if questions are clearly and properly understood and are unbiased. Pretesting can be done by having people respond to the questionnaire or interview and then reviewing it with them to see if there are problems. The way in which a group responds to the questions themselves can also point to trouble. For example, if many respondents leave a particular answer blank, then there may be a problem with the question. Once the instrument is pretested, modifications should be made where called for, and it should be pretested again. Any time changes are made in the questionnaire, it should be pretested. Once it is pretested with no changes called for, it is ready to be used in research.

One of the key decisions to be made in survey research—and it is a complex decision—is whether to collect data through questionnaires or interviews. We will discuss both types of surveys with an eye on the criteria to be used in assessing which is more appropriate for a particular research project.

Questionnaires

Questionnaires are designed so that they can be answered without assistance. Of course, if a researcher hands a questionnaire to the respondent, as is sometimes done, the respondent then has the opportunity to ask the researcher to clarify anything that is ambiguous. The value of a good questionnaire, however, is that such assistance should not be necessary. In fact, questionnaires are often mailed to respondents, who, therefore, have no opportunity to ask questions. In other cases, questionnaires are administered to a large number of people at once in a classroom, auditorium, or agency setting. Such modes of administration make questionnaires quicker and less expensive than most interviews. But it also places a burden on researchers to design questionnaires so that they can be properly completed without assistance.

Structure and Design

Directions One of the simplest, but also most important, parts of questionnaire construction is the inclusion of precise directions for respondents. Good directions can go a long way toward improving the quality of data generated by questionnaires. If you want respondents to put an X in a box corresponding to their answer, tell them precisely that. Questionnaires often contain questions requiring different ways of answering. At each place in the questionnaire where the format changes, additional directions should be included.

Order of Questions An element of questionnaire construction that takes careful consideration is the proper ordering of questions. Careless ordering can lead to undesirable consequences such as a reduced response rate or biased responses to questions. Generally, questions asked early in the questionnaire should not bias answers to those questions that come later. For example, if we asked several factual questions regarding poverty and the conditions of the poor and later asked a question concerning what people consider to be serious social problems, more will likely include poverty than would otherwise have done so. These potentially biasing effects can sometimes be avoided by placing opinion questions first when a questionnaire contains both factual and opinion questions.

Ordering of questions can also increase a respondent's interest in answering a questionnaire—this is especially helpful for boosting response rates on mailed questionnaires. Questions dealing with particularly intriguing issues should be asked first. The idea is to interest the recipients enough to get them to start answering. Once they have started, they are more likely to complete the entire questionnaire. If the questionnaire does not deal with any topics that are obviously more interesting than others, then opinion questions should be placed first. People like to express their opinions and, for the reasons mentioned earlier, opinion questions should be first anyway. A pitfall definitely to be avoided is beginning a questionnaire with the standard demographic questions of age, sex, income, and the like. People are so accustomed to those questions that they may be disinclined to answer them again and may promptly file the questionnaire in the nearest wastebasket.

Question Formats All of our efforts at careful wording and ordering of the questions will be for naught unless the questions are presented in a manner that facilitates responding to them. The goal is to make responding to the questions as straightforward and convenient as possible and to reduce the amount of data lost because of uninterpretable responses.

When presenting response alternatives for closed-ended questions, best results are obtained by having respondents indicate their selection by placing an X in a box corresponding to that alternative, as illustrated in Question 1 of Table 7.1. This format is preferable to open blanks and check marks (✓) because it is too easy for respondents to get sloppy and place check marks *between* alternatives, leaving their response unclear and thus useless as data. Boxes force respondents to give unambiguous responses. Though this may seem a minor point, we can attest from our own experience in administering questionnaires that it makes an important difference.

Some questions on a questionnaire may apply to only some respondents and not others. These questions are normally handled by what are called *contingency questions:* Depending on the response to one question, the next question may or may not be relevant to that respondent. The question format must clearly guide respondents to the next relevant question for them. A good way to accomplish this is to set off the contingency questions from the main questions as illustrated in Question 2 of Table 7.1. This reduces the likelihood that questions will be missed by respondents. A different contingency situation requiring a different solution arises where whole sections of a questionnaire may not apply to some respondents. You need to provide instructions to skip to the next relevant question, as illustrated in Question 3 of Table 7.1. By sectioning the questionnaire on the basis of contingency questions such as this, the respondent can be guided through even the most complex questionnaire.

Response Rate

A major problem in many research endeavors is to gain people's cooperation so that they will provide whatever data are needed. In surveys, this cooperation is measured by the **response rate,** or the

TABLE 7.1 Formatting Questions for a Questionnaire

Please indicate your response to the following questions by placing an X in the appropriate box.

1. Which of the following best describes where you live?
   - ☐ In a large city (100,000 population or more)
   - ☐ In a suburb near a large city
   - ☐ In a middle-sized city or small town (under 100,000 population) but not a suburb of a large city
   - ☐ Open country (but not on a farm)
   - ☐ On a farm
2. Have you ever shoplifted an item with a value of $10 or more?
   - ☐ Yes
   - ☐ No

   > *If yes:* how many times have you taken such items?
   > - ☐ once
   > - ☐ 2 to 5 times
   > - ☐ 6 to 10 times
   > - ☐ more than 10 times

3. Have you purchased a *new* automobile between 1987 and the present?
   - ☐ Yes
   - ☐ No (If No, please skip to Section C, Question 1.)
4. Please indicate the religion to which you belong:
   - ☐ Protestant
   - ☐ Catholic
   - ☐ Jewish
   - ☐ Other. Please specify._____

proportion of a sample that completes and returns a questionnaire or agrees to be interviewed. With interviews, response rates are often very high—in the area of 90 percent—largely because people are reluctant to refuse a face-to-face request for cooperation. In fact, with interviews, the largest nonresponse factor is the inability of the interviewers to locate respondents. With mailed questionnaires, however, this personal pressure is absent, and people feel freer to refuse (Bridge, 1974). This can result in many *nonreturns,* or people who refuse to complete and return a questionnaire. Response rates with questionnaires, especially mailed ones, vary considerably, from an unacceptably low 20 percent to levels that rival those of interviews.

Why is a low response rate of such concern? This goes back to the issue of the representativeness of a sample discussed in Chapter 6. If we selected a representative sample and obtained a perfect 100-percent response, we would have confidence in the representativeness of the sample data. However, as the response rate drops below 100 percent, the sample may become less and less representative. Those who refuse to cooperate may differ from those who return the questionnaire in some systematic ways that affect the results of the research. In other words, any response rate less than 100 percent may result in a biased sample. Of course, a perfect response rate is rarely achieved, but the closer the response rate is to that level, the more likely it is that the data obtained are representative. A number of things can be done to improve response rates. Most of these apply only to questionnaires, but a few can also be used to increase response rates in interviews.

The Cover Letter A properly constructed cover letter can help increase the response rate. A **cover letter** is a letter that accompanies a questionnaire and serves to introduce and explain it to the recipient. Because, with mailed questionnaires, the cover letter is the researcher's only medium for communicating with the recipient, it must be carefully drafted to include information recipients will want to know and to encourage them to complete the questionnaire (see Table 7.2).

Prominent in the cover letter should be the sponsor of the research project. Recipients are understandably interested in who is seeking the information they are asked to provide, and research clearly indicates that the sponsoring organization influences the response rate (Scott, 1961; Heberlein and Baumgartner, 1978; Goyder, 1985). The highest response rates are for questionnaires sponsored by government agencies. University-sponsored research generates somewhat lower response rates, and commercially sponsored research produces the lowest of all. It would appear that, if the research is at all associated with a government agency, stressing that in the cover letter may have a beneficial effect on the response rate. The response rates of particular groups can be increased if the research is sponsored or endorsed by an organization that people in the group feel has legitimacy. For example, response rates of professionals can be increased if the research is linked to relevant professional organizations, such as the National Association of Social Workers, the American Nurses Association, or the National Education Association (Sudman, 1985).

The address and telephone number of the researcher should appear somewhere on the cover letter. In fact, it is a good idea to use letterhead stationery for the cover letter. Especially if the sponsor of the re-

TABLE 7.2 Items to Be Included in the Cover Letter of a Questionnaire or the Introduction to an Interview

Item	Cover Letter	Interview Introduction
1. Sponsor of the research	yes	yes
2. Address/phone number of the researcher	yes	if requested
3. How the respondent was selected	yes	yes
4. Who else was selected	yes	yes
5. The purpose of the research	yes	yes
6. Who will utilize or benefit from the research	yes	yes
7. An appeal for the person's cooperation	yes	yes
8. How long it will take the respondent to complete the survey	yes	yes
9. Payment	if given	if given
10. Anonymity/confidentiality	if given	if given
11. Deadline for return	yes	not applicable

search is not well known, some recipients may desire further information before they decide to participate. Although relatively few respondents will ask for more information, including the address and telephone number gives the cover letter a completely open and aboveboard appearance that may further the general cooperation of recipients.

The cover letter should also inform the respondent regarding how people were selected to receive the questionnaire. It is not necessary to go into great detail on this matter, but people receiving an unanticipated questionnaire are quite naturally curious about how they were chosen to be a part of a study. A brief statement that they were randomly selected or selected by computer (if this is the case) should suffice.

Recipients will also want to know the purpose of the research. Again, without going into great detail, the cover letter should inform them concerning such things as why the research is being conducted, why and by whom it is considered important, and the potential benefits anticipated from the study. Investigations have clearly shown that the response rate can be significantly increased if the importance of the research, as perceived by the respondent, is emphasized. This part of the cover letter must be worded very carefully, however, so that it does not sensitize respondents in such a way that their answers to questions are affected. Sensitizing effects can be minimized by keeping the description of the purpose very general and certainly not suggesting what any of the research hypotheses might be. Regarding the importance of the data and anticipated benefits, the researcher should resist the temptation of hyperbole and instead make honest, straightforward statements. Exaggerated claims about "solving a significant social

problem" or "alleviating the problems of the poor" are likely to be seen as precisely what they are.

The above information provides a foundation for the single most important component of the cover letter, a direct appeal for the recipient's cooperation. General statements about the importance of the research are no substitute for a more personal appeal to the recipient as to why he or she should take the time to complete the questionnaire. The respondent must believe that their individual response is very important to the outcome (as, in reality, it is). A statement to the effect that "your views are important to us" is a good approach. It emphasizes the importance of each individual respondent and emphasizes that the questionnaire will allow the expression of opinions, which people like.

The cover letter should indicate that the respondent will remain anonymous or that the data will be treated as confidential, whichever will be the case. "Anonymous" means that *no one*, including the researcher, can link a particular respondent's name to his or her questionnaire. "Confidentiality" means that, even though the researcher can match respondents to their questionnaires, the information will be treated collectively, and no individuals will be publicly linked to their responses.

With mailed questionnaires, there are two ways to assure anonymity (Sudman, 1985). The best way is to keep the questionnaire itself completely anonymous, with no identifying numbers or symbols, and provide the respondent with a separate postcard, including the respondent's name, to be mailed at the same time the completed questionnaire is mailed. In this way, the researcher knows who has responded and need not be sent reminders to respond; and no one can link a respondent's name with a particular question-naire. A second way to ensure anonymity is to attach to the questionnaire a cover sheet with an identifying number and assure the respondents that the cover sheet will be removed and destroyed once the receipt of the questionnaire has been recorded. This second procedure provides less assurance to the respondent since a highly unethical researcher might retain a link between questionnaires and their identification numbers. The first procedure, however, is more expensive because of the additional postcard mailing, so the second procedure may be preferred in questionnaires that do not deal with highly sensitive issues that would make respondents very concerned about anonymity. If the material is not very sensitive, assurances of confidentiality can be adequate to ensure a good return rate. There is no evidence that assuring anonymity rather than confidentiality will increase the response rate in nonsensitive surveys (Moser and Kalton, 1972).

Finally, the cover letter should include a deadline for returning the questionnaire, calculated to take into account mailing time and a few days to complete the questionnaire. The rationale for a fairly tight deadline is that it will encourage the recipient to complete the questionnaire soon after it is received and not set it aside where it can be forgotten or misplaced.

Payment   In addition to the cover letter, response rates can also be increased by offering a small payment as a part of the appeal for cooperation. Research indicates that, like most things, a recipient's cooperation can be bought—and not at a high price. One study reported that each increment of 25 cents up to one dollar added 6 percent to the response rate (Heberlein and Baumgartner, 1978). By of-fering recipients one dollar, the researcher with a bountiful treasury could increase the response rate approximately 24 percent over what it would be with no payment. For the payments to have their greatest effect, they should be included with the initial mailing and not promised on return of the questionnaire. One study found that including the payment with the questionnaire boosted the return rate by 12 percent over promising payment on return of the questionnaire (Berry and Kanouse, 1987). However, such payments are not always feasible because even small payments can add substantially to the cost of a survey with a large sample.

Response rate is also affected by the mailing procedures used. It almost goes without saying that a stamped, self-addressed envelope should be supplied for returning the questionnaire, making things as convenient as possible for the respondent. The type of postage utilized also affects the response rate, with stamps bringing about 4 percent higher return than bulk-printed postage (Scott, 1961). Presumably, the stamp makes the questionnaire appear more personal and less like unimportant junk mail. A regular stamped envelope also substantially increases the response rate in comparison with a business reply envelope (Armstrong and Luck, 1987).

Follow-ups   The most important procedural matter affecting response rates is the use of follow-up letters. A substantial percentage of nonrespondents to the initial mailing will respond to follow-up letters. With two follow-ups, 15 to 20 percent increases over the initial return can be achieved (Scott, 1961; Heberlein and Baumgartner, 1978). Such follow-ups are clearly essential, and they can be done by telephone, if budget permits and speed is important. With aggressive follow-ups, the difference in response rates between mailed questionnaires and interviews declines substantially (Goyder, 1985). (Obviously, follow-ups are impossible if the decision is made to keep the responses completely anonymous.)

In general, two follow-ups should be used. When response to the initial mailing drops off, follow-up letters should be sent to the nonrespondents encouraging them to return the questionnaire. The follow-up letter should include a restatement of the points in the original cover letter with an additional appeal for their cooperation. When response to the first follow-up declines, a second follow-up is then sent to the remaining nonrespondents, including another copy of the questionnaire because people may have misplaced the original. After two follow-ups, the remaining nonrespondents are a pretty intransigent lot, and additional follow-ups will generate relatively few further responses.

Length and Appearance Two other factors that affect the rate of response to a mailed questionnaire are the length of the questionnaire and its appearance (Miller, 1977). As length increases, the response rate declines. There is, however, no hard-and-fast rule regarding the length of mailed questionnaires. Much depends on the intelligence and literacy of the respondents, the degree of interest in the topic of the questionnaire, and other such matters. However, it is probably a good idea to keep the questionnaire less than five pages long. It should also take no more than 30 minutes to fill out. This means that great care must be taken to remove any extraneous questions or any questions that are not essential to the hypotheses under investigation (Epstein and Tripodi, 1977). Although keeping the

questionnaire under five pages is a general guide, this should not be achieved by cramming so much material onto each page that the respondent has difficulty using the instrument because the appearance of the questionnaire can also be important in generating a high response rate. As discussed earlier, the use of boxed response choices and smooth transitions through contingency questions help make completing the questionnaire easier and more enjoyable for the respondent, which in turn increases the probability that it will be returned.

Other Influences on Response Rate A number of other factors can work to lower response rates. In telephone surveys, for example, the voice and manner of the interviewer can have an important effect (Oksenberg, Coleman, and Cannell, 1986). Interviewers with higher pitched and louder voices and clear and distinct pronunciation have lower refusal rates. The same is true for interviewers who sound more competent and positive toward the respondent. Reminders of confidentiality can also affect the response rate (Frey, 1986). People who are reminded of the confidentiality of the information part way through the interview are more likely to refuse to respond to some of the remaining questions than are people who do not receive such a reminder. It may be that the reminder works to undo whatever rapport the interviewer has already built up with the respondent.

A survey following all the suggested procedures should yield an acceptably high response rate. Specialized populations may, of course, produce either higher or lower rates. Because there are so many variables involved, only rough guidelines can be offered for evaluating response rates with mailed questionnaires. Babbie (1989) suggests that a 50 percent rate is adequate for analysis. Rates in the 60 percent range are considered good, and anything over 70 percent is very good. A properly conducted general population survey should have little trouble surpassing the minimum needed for analysis and would be expected to do even better.

The response rate, as we have said, is an indicator that respondents have cooperated in the survey. However, cooperation involves more than merely a high response rate. It also has to do with how carefully and thoughtfully people respond to a questionnaire. Research in Practice 7.1 suggests a creative way in which this sort of cooperation can be enhanced.

RESEARCH IN PRACTICE 7.1
Behavior and Social Environment: Enhancing Respondent Cooperation Through Commitment

We have pointed out many parallels between research and practice, suggesting that practice efforts could be improved by incorporating some techniques commonly used in the research process. Now we find ourselves in the situation of recognizing that the research process might be improved by incorporating some practice techniques. A problem common to both research and practice is to encourage cooperation on the part of respondents and clients. One tool that practitioners sometimes use to enhance cooperation is a contract with a client that specifies the goals, obligations, and expectations of the intervention effort (Croxton, 1974; Connaway and Gentry, 1988). It may be possible to use a similar procedure in survey research to encourage commitment and full cooperation on the part of respondents. The basic idea here is that the contract generates a commitment on the part of a person to achieve a goal and increases the likelihood that the goal will be achieved.

Does it work? An experiment conducted by one team of researchers suggests that such contracts can make people into better survey respondents (Oksenberg, Vinokur, and Cannell, 1979). The basic question of this research was to assess the effectiveness of using commitment in the interviewing process in order to increase the effort respondents devote to completing the interview. "Effort" was operationalized as the following:

1. Provide more information.
2. Respond with greater exactness or precision.
3. Be more likely to perform overt actions that promote accuracy.
4. Give responses that reflect less positively on themselves.
5. Be more likely to complete and return a mailed questionnaire.

The method used to study this re-

(Continued on next page)

search question was an experiment within a survey project. An experimental group of 192 women were interviewed in a survey that began with an introduction stressing the importance of working hard to produce information and explaining that after a few questions the respondent would be asked to decide if she were willing to put in the thought and effort needed for the interview. After the first 8 questions, she was presented with an agreement, on university letterhead, which included the statement:

> I understand that the information for this interview must be very accurate in order to be useful. This means that I must do my best to give accurate and complete answers. I agree to do this.

The document included a place for the respondent to sign her name and explained that the agreement was hers to keep. If she signed, the interviewer also signed following a statement promising confidentiality. Thus, the respondent was given a clear understanding of what she was expected to do and also what the interviewer would do with the information provided. A control group

of 170 respondents received exactly the same survey questionnaire but without the contractual agreement. Assignment to groups was random, and the sample was selected from a relatively homogeneous population to ensure equivalency between groups. The survey procedure was highly controlled to ensure still further equivalence between groups.

Results were compared in terms of amount of information, precision of reported dates, overt activities to increase accuracy (such as respondents checking outside sources of information), response to embarrassing or threatening questions, return of a sendback questionnaire, and reaction to the interview. In general, the researchers concluded that the commitment procedure was a workable interviewing technique. Though many differences were not statistically significant, "contracted" respondents performed better than controls on nearly every measure used. The researchers were especially encouraged by the overall pattern of better performance.

Checking for Bias Due to Nonresponse

Even if a relatively high rate of response is obtained, possible bias due to nonresponse should be investigated by determining the extent to which respondents differ from nonrespondents (Wallace, 1954; Miller, 1977). One common way of doing this is to compare the characteristics of the respondents with the characteristics of the population from which

they were selected. If there is an already existing data base on the population, then this job can be simplified. For example, if you are studying a representative sample of welfare recipients in a community, the Department of Social Services is likely to have data on age, sex, marital status, level of education, and other characteristics for all the welfare recipients in the community. You can compare your respondents with this data base on the characteristics for which there is information. A second approach to assessing bias resulting from nonresponse is to locate a subsample of nonrespondents and interview them. In this way, the responses to the questionnaire by a representative sample of nonrespondents can be compared with those of the respondents. This is the preferred method because the direction and the extent of bias that are due to nonresponse can be directly measured. It is, however, the most costly and time-consuming approach.

Any check for bias due to nonresponse, of course, informs us only about those characteristics on which we make comparisions. It does not prove that the respondents are representative of the whole sample on any other variables—including those that might be of considerable importance to the study. In short, though we can gather some information regarding such bias, in most cases it is not possible to *prove* that bias due to nonresponse does not exist.

An Assessment of Questionnaires

Advantages As a technique of survey research, questionnaires have a number of desirable features. First, they can be used to gather data far more inexpensively and quickly than interviews. Only a month to six weeks is needed for mailed questionnaires, whereas obtaining the same data by personal interviews would likely take several months at a minimum. Mailed questionnaires also save the expense of interviewers, interviewer travel, and other such costs.

Second, mailed questionnaires enable one to collect data from a sample that is geographically dispersed. It costs no more to mail a questionnaire across the country than across a city. Costs of interviewer travel rise enormously as distance increases, making interviewing over wide geographic areas prohibitively expensive.

Third, with questions of a personal or sensitive nature, mailed questionnaires may provide more accurate answers than interviews. People may be more likely to respond honestly to such questions when they are not face-to-face with a person they perceive as possibly making judgments about them. There is evidence, for example, that questions about premarital sex are answered more honestly in a questionnaire than an interview (Knudsen, Pope, and Irish, 1967). However, this does not appear to be true for all topics, so the choice of questionnaire versus interview on these grounds would depend on the subject of the research (Moser and Kalton, 1972).

Finally, mailed questionnaires eliminate the problem of interviewer bias. Interviewer bias occurs when an interviewer influences a person's response to a question through what the interviewer says, his or her tone of voice or demeanor. Because there is no interviewer present when the person fills out the questionnaire, it is not possible for an interviewer to bias the respondent's answers in a particular direction (Cannell and Kahn, 1968).

Disadvantages Despite their many advantages, mailed questionnaires have important limitations that may make them less desirable for some research efforts (Moser and Kalton, 1972).

First, mailed questionnaires require a minimal degree of literacy and facility in English that some people do not possess. Substantial nonresponse is, of course, likely with such people. With most general population surveys, the nonresponse due to illiteracy will not seriously bias the results. Self-administered questionnaires are more successful among people who are better educated, motivated to respond, and involved in issues and organizations. However, some groups of interest to human service practitioners often do not possess these characteristics. If the survey is aimed at a special population where less than average literacy is suspected, personal interviews would be a better choice.

Second, the questions must all be sufficiently simple to be comprehended on the basis of printed instructions. Third, there is no opportunity to probe for more information or evaluate the nonverbal behavior of the respondent. The answers they mark on the questionnaire form are final. Fourth, there is no assurance that the person who should answer the questionnaire is the one who actually does so. Fifth, responses cannot be considered independent, for the respondent can read through the entire questionnaire before completing it. Finally, all mailed questionnaires face the problem of nonresponse bias.

Interviews

In an interview, the investigator or an assistant reads the questions directly to the respondents and records their answers. Interviews offer the investigator a degree of flexibility that is not available with questionnaires. One area of increased flexibility relates to the degree of structure built into an interview.

The Structure of Interviews

The element of structure in interviews refers to the degree of freedom the interviewer has in conducting the interview and respondents have in answering questions. Interviews are usually classified in terms of three levels of structure: (1) the *unstandardized*, (2) the *nonschedule-standardized*, and (3) the *schedule-standardized*.

The *unstandardized interview* has the least structure. All the interviewer typically will have for guidance is a general topic area, as illustrated in Figure 7.1. By developing his or her own questions and probes as the interview progresses, the interviewer explores the topic with the respondent. The approach is called "unstandardized" because different questions will be asked by each interviewer and different information obtained from each respondent. There is a heavy reliance on the skills of the interviewer to ask good questions and to keep the interview going, and this can only be done if experienced interviewers are available. This unstructured approach makes unstandardized interviewing especially appropriate for exploratory research. In Figure 7.1, for example, the interviewer is guided only by the general topic of parent–child conflicts. The example also illustrates the suitability of this style of interviewing for exploratory research as the interviewer is directed to search for as many areas of conflict as can be found.

Nonschedule-standardized interviews add more structure, with the topic narrower and specific questions asked of all respondents. However, the interview remains fairly conversational, and the interviewer is free to probe, rephrase questions, or take the questions in whatever order best fits that particular interview. Note in Figure 7.1 that specific questions are of the open-ended type, allowing the respondent full freedom of expression. As in the case of the unstandardized form, success with this type of interview requires an experienced interviewer.

The *schedule-standardized interview* is the most structured type. An **interview schedule** is used, which contains specific instructions for the interviewer, specific questions in a fixed order, and transition phrases for the interviewer to use. Sometimes the schedule also contains acceptable rephrasings for questions and a selection of stock probes. Schedule-standardized interviews are fairly rigid, with neither interviewer nor respondent allowed to depart from the structure of the schedule. Although some questions may be open-ended, most will likely be closed-ended. In fact, some schedule-standardized interviews are very similar to a questionnaire except that the interviewer asks the questions rather than having the respondent read them. Note, in Figure 7.1, the use of cards with response alternatives that are handed to the respondent. This is a pop-

---

The Unstandardized Interview

Instructions to the interviewer: Discover the kinds of conflicts that the child has had with the parents. Conflicts should include disagreements, tensions due to past, present, or potential disagreements, outright arguments and physical conflicts. Be alert for as many categories and examples of conflicts and tensions as possible.

The Nonschedule-Standardized Interview

Instructions to the interviewer: Your task is to discover as many specific kinds of conflicts and tensions between child and parent as possible. The more *concrete* and detailed the account of each type of conflict the better. Although there are 12 areas of possible conflict which we want to explore (listed in question 3 below), you should not mention any area until after you have asked the first two questions in the order indicated. The first question takes an indirect approach, giving you time to build up rapport with the respondent and to demonstrate a nonjudgmental attitude toward teenagers who have conflicts with their parents.

1. What sorts of problems do teenagers you know have in getting along with their parents?
   (Possible probes: Do they always agree with their parents? Do any of your friends have "problem parents"? What other kinds of disagreements do they have?)
2. What sorts of disagreements do you have with your parents?
   (Possible probes: Do they cause you any problems? In what ways do they try to restrict you? Do you always agree with them on everything? Do they like the same things you do? Do they try to get you to do some things you don't like? Do they ever bore you? Make you mad? Do they understand you? etc.)
3. Have you ever had any disagreements with either of your parents over:
   a. Using the family car
   b. Friends of the same sex
   c. Dating
   d. School (homework, grades, activities)
   e. Religion (church, beliefs, etc.)
   f. Political views
   g. Working for pay outside the home
   h. Allowances
   i. Smoking
   j. Drinking
   k. Eating habits
   l. Household chores

Figure 7.1 Examples of Various Interview Structures

(Continued on next page)

Source: Interviewing Strategy, Techniques, and Tactics, 4/E, by Raymond L. Gorden. Copyright © 1987 by the Dorsey Press. Reprinted by permission of Wadsworth, Inc.

The Schedule-Standardized Interview

Interviewer's explanation to the teenage respondent: We are interested in the kinds of problems teenagers have with their parents. We need to know how many teenagers have which kinds of conflicts with their parents and whether they are just mild disagreements or serious fights. We have a checklist here of some of the kinds of things that happen. Would you think about your own situation and put a check to show which conflicts you, personally, have had and about how often they have happened. Be sure to put a check in every row. If you have never had such a conflict then put the check in the first column where it says "never."

(*Hand him the first card dealing with conflicts over the use of the automobile, saying,* "If you don't understand any of those things listed or have some other things you would like to mention about how you disagree with your parents over the automobile let me know and we'll talk about it.") (*When the respondent finishes checking all rows, hand him card number 2, saying,* "Here is a list of types of conflicts teenagers have with their parents over their friends of the same sex. Do the same with this as you did with the last list.")

Automobile	Never	Only Once	More than Once	Many Times
1. Wanting to learn to drive				
2. Getting a driver's license				
3. Wanting to use the family car				
4. What you use the car for				
5. The way you drive it				
6. Using it too much				
7. Keeping the car clean				
8. Putting gas or oil in the car				
9. Repairing the car				
10. Driving someone else's car				
11. Wanting to own a car				
12. The way you drive your own car				
13. What you use your car for				
14. Other				

Figure 7.1 (continued)

ular way of supplying respondents with a complex set of closed-ended alternatives. Note also the precise directions for the interviewer as well as verbatim phrases to be read to the respondent. Schedule-standardized interviews can be conducted by relatively untrained, part-time interviewers because nearly everything they need to say is contained in the schedule. This makes schedule-standardized interviews the preferred choice for studies with large sample sizes requiring many interview-ers. The structure of these interviews also ensures that all respondents are presented with the same questions in the same order. This heightens reliability and makes schedule-standardized interviews popular for rigorous hypothesis testing.

Contacting Respondents

As with mailed questionnaires, interviewers face the problem of contacting respondents and eliciting their cooperation. Many interviews are conducted in the homes of the respondents, and locating and traveling to their homes are two of the more troublesome and costly aspects of interviewing. It is estimated that as much as 40 percent of a typical interviewer's time is spent traveling (Sudman, 1965). Because so much time and cost are involved and because high response rates are desirable, substantial efforts are directed at minimizing the rate of refusal. The way prospective respondents are first contacted has substantial impact on the refusal rate.

Two approaches to contacting respondents that might appear logical to the neophyte researcher, in fact, have an effect opposite of that desired. It might seem that *telephoning* to set up an appointment for the interview would be a good idea. In reality, it greatly increases the rate of refusal. In one experiment, for example, the part of the sample that was telephoned had nearly *triple* the rate of refusal of those contacted in person (Brunner and Carroll, 1967). Apparently it is much easier to refuse over the relatively impersonal medium of the telephone than in a face-to-face encounter with an interviewer. *Sending people a letter* asking them to participate in an interview has much the same effect (Cartwright and Tucker, 1967). The letter seems to give people sufficient time before the interviewer arrives to develop reasons why they do not want to cooperate. Those first contacted in person, on the other hand, have only those excuses they can muster on the spur of the moment. Clearly, then, the lowest refusal rates are obtained by contacting interviewees in person.

There are additional factors that can affect the refusal rate (Gorden, 1987). For example, information regarding the research project should blanket the total survey population through the news media. The purpose of this is to demonstrate general community acceptance of the project that it is hoped will increase cooperation among people chosen for the sample. The information provided should be essentially the same as that of a cover letter for a mailed questionnaire, with a few differences (see Table 7.2). Pictures of the interviewers and mention of any props they will be carrying such as clipboards or zipper cases should be included. This information assists people in identifying interviewers and reducing possible confusion with salespeople or bill collectors. In fact, it is a good idea to equip the interviewers with identification badges or something else that is easily recognizable so that interviewers are not mistaken for others who go door-to-door. When the interviewers go into the field, they should take along copies of the news coverage. If they encounter an interviewee who has not seen the media coverage, it can be shown to him or her during the initial contact.

The timing of the initial contact also affects the refusal rate. It is preferable to contact interviewees at a time convenient for them to complete the interview without the need for a second call. Depending on the nature of the sample, predicting availability may be fairly easy or virtually impossible. For example, if the information required can be obtained from any household member, almost any reasonable time of day will do. On the other hand, if specific individuals must be contacted, timing becomes more difficult. If the breadwinner in a household must be interviewed, for example, then contacts should probably be made at night or on weekends unless knowledge of the person's occupation suggests a different time of greater availability. Whatever time the interviewer makes the initial contact, it still may not be convenient for the respondent, especially if the interview is lengthy. If the respondent is pressed for time, it is better to use the initial contact to establish rapport and set another time for the interview, even though call-backs are costly. This is certainly preferable to the rushed interview that results in inferior data.

When the interviewer and potential respondent first meet, there are certain points of information the interviewer should include in the introduction. One suggestion is the following (Smith, 1981):

> Good day. I am from the Public Opinion Survey Unit of the University of Missouri (shows official identification). We are doing a survey at this time on how people feel about police-community relationships. This study is being done throughout the state, and the results will be used by local and state governments. The addresses at which we interview are chosen entirely by chance, and the interview only takes 45 minutes. All information is entirely confidential, of course.

Respondents will be looking for much the same basic information as with mailed questionnaires. As the preceding example illustrates, respondents should also be informed of the approximate length of the interview. After giving the introduction, the interviewer should be prepared to elaborate on any points the interviewee questions. Care must be exercised, however, when discussing the purpose of the survey to avoid biasing responses.

Conducting an Interview

A large-scale survey with an adequate budget will often turn to private research agencies to train interviewers and conduct interviews. Smaller research projects, however, may not be able to afford

this and will have to train and coordinate their own team of interviewers, possibly with the researchers themselves doing some of the interviewing. It is important, therefore, to know how to conduct an interview properly.

The Interview as a Social Relationship
The interview is a social relationship designed to exchange information between respondent and interviewer. The quantity and quality of information exchanged depend on how astute and creative the interviewer is at understanding and managing that relationship (Bradburn and Sudman, 1979). Human service workers are generally knowledgeable regarding the properties and processes of social interaction, and in fact much human service practice is founded on the establishment of social relationships with clients. There are, however, a few elements of the research interview that are worth emphasizing because they have direct implications for conducting the interview.

The research interview is a secondary relationship in which the interviewer has a practical, utilitarian goal. It is easy, especially for an inexperienced interviewer, to be drawn into a more casual or personal interchange with the respondent. Especially with a friendly, outgoing respondent, the conversation could drift off to sports, politics, or children. That, however, is not the purpose of the interview. The goal is not to make friends or give the respondent a sympathetic ear but rather to collect complete and unbiased data following the interview schedule.

We all recognize the powerful impact that first impressions can have on our perceptions of other people. This is especially true in interview situations, where the interviewer and respondent are likely to be total strangers. The first thing that impacts on a respondent is the physical and social characteristics of the interviewer. Thus, considerable care needs to be taken to ensure that the first contact enhances the likelihood of cooperation by the respondent (Warwick and Lininger, 1975). Most research suggests that interviewers are more successful if they have social characteristics similar to those of their respondents. Thus, characteristics such as socioeconomic status, age, sex, race, and ethnicity might influence the success of the interview—especially if the subject matter of the interview relates to one of these topics. In addition, the personal demeanor of the interviewer plays an important role, and interviewers should be neat, clean, and businesslike, but friendly.

After initial pleasantries have been exchanged, the interviewer should begin the interview. The interviewee may be a bit apprehensive during the initial stages of an interview. In recognition of this, the interview should begin with fairly simple, nonthreatening questions. If a schedule is used, it should be designed to begin with these kinds of questions. The demographic questions that are reserved until the later stages of a mailed questionnaire are good to begin an interview. Respondents' familiarity with these questions makes them nonthreatening and a good means of reducing tension in the respondent.

Probes   If an interview schedule is used, the interview will progress in accordance with the schedule. As needed, the interviewer will use **probes,** or follow-up questions, that are intended to elicit clearer and more complete responses. In some cases, suggestions for probes will be contained in the interview schedule. In less structured interviews, however, interviewers must be prepared to develop and use their own probes. Probes can take the

form of a pause in conversation that encourages the respondent to elaborate. Or a probe could be an explicit request to clarify or elaborate on something. A major concern with any probe is that it not bias the respondent's answer by suggesting how he or she should answer.

Recording Responses   A central task of interviewers, of course, is to record the responses of respondents. There are four common ways of accomplishing this: classifying responses into predetermined categories, summarizing the "high points" of what is said, taking verbatim notes, or recording the interview with a tape recorder or videotape machine.

Recording responses is generally easiest when an interview schedule is used. Since the closed-ended questions are typical of such schedules, responses can simply be classified into the predetermined alternatives. This simplicity of recording is another factor making schedule-standardized interviews suitable for use with relatively untrained interviewers as no special recording skills are required.

With nonschedule interviewing, the questions are likely to be open-ended and the responses, longer. Often all that need be recorded are the key points that the respondent makes. The interviewer condenses and summarizes what the respondent says. This requires an experienced interviewer familiar with the research questions who can accurately identify what should be recorded and do so without injecting his or her own interpretation, thus biasing the summary.

Sometimes it may be desirable that everything the respondent says be recorded verbatim in order to avoid the possible biasing effect of summarizing responses. If the anticipated responses are reasonably short, competent interviewers can take verbatim notes. Special skills such as shorthand, however, may be necessary. If the responses are lengthy, verbatim note-taking can cause difficulties such as leading the interviewer to fail to monitor the respondent or to be unprepared to probe when necessary. It can also damage rapport by making it appear that the interviewer is ignoring the respondent. Problems such as this can be eliminated by recording the interviews. This, however, increases the costs substantially. Though individual cassettes and recorders are not very expensive, the number needed for a large-scale survey would certainly drive costs up considerably. The really big cost comes, however, when transcribing the tapes into a written transcript. Vast amounts of secretarial time are required for this (Gorden, 1987).

The fear of some researchers that tape recorders will increase the refusal rate appears unwarranted (Gorden, 1987). If the use of the recorder is explained as a routine procedure that aids in recording complete and accurate responses, few respondents object to it. You should avoid asking the respondents if they mind if you record the interview. The interrogative almost invites the respondent to object and implies that there may be legitimate reasons for objecting. The interviewer should assume that the tape recorder will be accepted unless the respondent raises the issue.

Controlling Interviewers Once interviewers go into the field, the quality of the resulting data is heavily dependent on them. It is a naive researcher indeed who assumes that, without supervision, they will all do their job properly, especially when part-time interviewers who have little commitment to the research project are used. Proper supervision begins during interviewer training. The importance of contacting the right people and meticulously following established procedures should be stressed. Interviewers should be informed that their work will be carefully checked, and failure to follow procedures will not be tolerated.

One particularly serious problem with hiring people to conduct interviews is a practice variously known as "curbing," "curbstoning," or "shade-treeing." These terms refer to interviewers' filling in the responses themselves without contacting respondents. In large-scale surveys, this can be a real problem. For example, a New York City reporter serving as a census enumerator for the 1980 census observed for eight days in a row as a carload of census takers "parked . . . turned the radio on, and boogied—just had a good time—talked—took drugs—ate—slept—and basically just loafed" while falsely filling in census forms (Magnet, 1981). Fortunately, with projects of a smaller scale than the census, curbing can be controlled with adequate supervision. Completed interviews should be scrutinized for any evidence of falsification. Spot-checks can be made to see if interviewers are where they are supposed to be at any given time, and respondents can be telephoned to see if they have, in fact, been interviewed.

Minorities and the Interview Relationship

The typical interviewer in survey research is probably a white, middle-class woman with a white-collar occupation. Certainly many respondents in surveys, probably most, have different characteristics than these. Does it make a difference in terms of the quantity or quality of data collected in surveys? It appears to. In survey research, three elements interact to affect the quality of the data collected: the minority status of the interviewer, the minority status of the respondent, and the minority content of the survey instrument. The interrelationships among these elements need to be considered carefully to ensure that the least amount of bias enters the data-collection process.

As we have emphasized, an interview is a social relationship in which interviewer and respondent have cultural and subcultural expectations for appropriate behavior. One set of expectations that comes especially into play in this regard is the social desirability of respondents' answers to questions. Substantial research documents that there is some tendency for people to choose more desirable or socially acceptable answers to questions in surveys (DeMaio, 1984). This stems in part from the desire to appear sensible, reasonable, and pleasant to the interviewer. In all of our contacts with people, including an interview relationship, we typically prefer to please someone rather than offend or alienate. In cases where interviewer and respondent are from different racial, ethnic, or sexual groups, respondents tend to give answers they perceive to be more desirable, or at least less offensive, to the interviewer; and this is especially true when the content of the questions is related to racial, ethnic, or sexual issues. A second factor that comes into play is the social distance between interviewer and respondent, or how much they differ from one another on important social dimensions such as age or minority status. Generally, the less social distance there is between people, the more freely, openly, and honestly they will talk. Racial, sexual, and ethnic differences often indicate a degree of social distance.

The impact of cross-race interviewing has been studied extensively with black and white respondents (Hyman, 1954; Bradburn and Sudman, 1979; Schaeffer, 1980; Cotter, Cohen, and Coulter, 1982; Bachman and O'Malley, 1984). Black respondents, for example, are less likely to express dissatisfaction or resentment over discrimination or inequities against blacks to white interviewers. White respondents tend to express more "pro-black" attitudes when interviewed by a black than a white. This race-of-interviewer effect can be quite large and occurs fairly consistently, but it seems to play a part mostly when questions involve some racial content. Nonracial items seem not to be affected.

The impact of ethnicity on interviews has been studied much less, probably because the ethnicity of both interviewer and respondent is not as readily apparent in most cases as is race, which is very visibly signified by skin color. One study used both Jewish and non-Jewish interviewers asking questions about the extent of Jewish influence in the United States (Hyman, 1954). Respondents were much more willing to say that Jews had too much influence when they were being interviewed by a non-Jew.

So, the cross-race interview effect results in respondents giving more socially desirable answers to interviewers on questions relating to racial topics. Some researchers recommend routinely matching interviewer and respondent for race for both blacks and whites in interviews on racial topics, and this is generally sound advice. Sometimes, however, a little more thought is called for. The problem is that we are not always sure in which direction the bias is occurring. If white respondents give different answers to white as opposed to black interviewers, which of their answers most accurately reflects their attitudes? For the most part, we aren't sure. It is generally assumed that the same-race interviewer will gather more accurate data. A more conservative assumption is that the truth falls somewhere between the data that the two interviewers collect.

When minorities speak a language different from that of the dominant group, the quality of data collected can be affected if the interview is conducted in the dominant group's language. For example, a study of Native American children in Canada found that these children expressed a strong white bias in racial preferences when the study was conducted in English; the bias declined significantly when the children's native Ojibwa language was used (Annis and Corenblum, 1986). This impact of language should not be surprising, considering that language is not solely a mechanism for communication; it also reflects cultural values, norms, and a way of life. So when interviewing groups where a language other than English is widely used, it would be appropriate to consider conducting interviews in that other language.

An Assessment of Interviews

Advantages   First, interviews can help to *motivate* respondents to give more accurate and complete information. There is little motivation for respondents to be especially accurate or complete when responding to a mailed questionnaire. They can hurry through it if they want to. The control afforded by an interviewer encourages better responses. This becomes especially important as the information sought becomes more complex.

Second, interviewing affords an opportunity to *explain* questions that respondents may not otherwise understand. Again, if the information sought is complex, this can be of great importance,

and the literacy problem that was a limitation of mailed questionnaires is virtually eliminated. Even lack of facility in English can be handled by using multilingual interviewers. (When we conducted a needs assessment survey in some rural parts of Upper Michigan a few years ago, we employed one interviewer who was fluent in Finnish because there were a number of people in the area who spoke Finnish but little or no English).

Third, the presence of an interviewer allows *control* over factors uncontrollable with mailed questionnaires. For example, the interviewer can ensure that the proper person responds to the questions and that questions are responded to in sequence. Furthermore, the interviewer can arrange for the interview to be conducted such that the respondent does not consult with, or is not influenced by, other people before responding.

Fourth, interviewing is a more *flexible* form of data collection than questionnaires. The style of interviewing can be tailored to the needs of the study. A free, conversational style, with much probing, can be adopted in an exploratory study. In a more developed study, a highly structured approach can be utilized. This flexibility makes interviewing suitable for a far broader range of research situations than are mailed questionnaires.

Finally, the interviewer can add *observational information* to the responses of the respondent. What was the respondent's attitude toward the interview? Was it essentially cooperative, indifferent or hostile? Did the respondent appear to be fabricating answers? Did he or she react emotionally to some questions? This additional information helps to evaluate better the responses given, especially when the subject matter is highly personal or controversial (Gorden, 1987).

Disadvantages   There are some disadvantages associated with personal interviews that may lead one to choose another data collection technique.

The first disadvantage is *cost*. Interviewers must be hired, trained, and equipped; and their travel must be paid for. All of these together can be very expensive.

The second limitation is *time*. Traveling to respondents' homes requires much time and limits each interviewer to only a few interviews each day. If particular individuals must be contacted, several time-consuming callbacks may be needed to complete many of the interviews. Considerable time is also required for start-up operations such as developing questions, designing schedules, and training interviewers.

A third limitation of interviews is the problem of interviewer bias. Especially with unstructured interviews, there is the possibility that interviewers will misinterpret or misrecord something because of their own personal feelings about the topic. Furthermore, just as the respondent is affected by the interviewer's characteristics, so the interviewer is similarly affected by the characteristics of the respondent. Sex, age, race, social class, and a host of other factors may subtly shape the way in which the interviewer asks questions and interprets the words of respondents.

A fourth limitation of interviews, especially with less structured interviews, is that there may be significant but unnoticed variation in wording from one interview to the next or among interview-

---

RESEARCH IN PRACTICE 7.2
Needs Assessment: Response Bias in Mental Health Surveys

An important element of both scientific research and human service practice is the assessment of the traits and states of people, and this is often accomplished with questionnaire or interview surveys. When making such assessments, we must keep in mind that survey data are merely what people say about something: their feelings, their intentions, or their beliefs. One glaring and unsettling limitation with survey data is that people's responses to survey questions may not be thoroughly "honest." Now "honesty" is a notoriously difficult concept to delineate. One person's truth is often another's falsehood. Our concern here is not with intentional, conscious efforts by respondents to deceive interviewers. Such deceit happens, but it is relatively rare and can be detected in a number of ways.

Instead, our focus is on the much more subtle ways in which responses to questions may be influenced by factors other than the person's true feelings, intentions, and beliefs. When this occurs in surveys, it is called **response bias**, and it can lead to erroneous conclusions about the relationship between independent variables and dependent variables. For example, in

(Continued on next page)

studies of mental health, it has been commonly found that women report more psychiatric symptoms than do men (Gallagher, 1987). From this, it might be concluded that women are less mentally healthy than men and, at a more general level, that one's gender has an impact on one's mental health. However, critics of these studies have suggested that women report more psychiatric symptoms in survey interviews because it is more socially acceptable for women in our society to "complain," show weakness, and the like. In other words, the actual rates of mental health and illness might be the same for both sexes, but women report more symptoms than do men. The relationship between an independent variable (gender) and a dependent variable (mental health status) may be an artifact due to response bias: People are answering questions in terms of the social acceptability of their responses rather than in terms of their actual feelings.

The sociologists Walter Gove and Michael Geerken (1977) tackled this issue with regard to three potential sources of response bias in the study of mental health: (1) the tendency for people to answer questions in either a positive or negative way irrespective of the content of the question (a form of "response set"), (2) the tendency to choose the socially desirable response to questions, and (3) the degree of a person's need for approval from others.

Gove and Geerken did find some intriguing relationships. For example, younger respondents tended to choose negative answers more than older respondents, and they showed less need for approval. In terms of gender, there were no differences between men and women on these two factors. However, the critical focus was on whether these response bias factors changed the relationship between independent variables (demographic factors) and dependent variables (psychiatric symptoms). Gove and Geerken's findings in this realm were thoroughly negative. They could find no instances in which response bias significantly changed the relationship between any demographic variable and reports of psychiatric symptoms. This gives us some confidence that findings in this area of study reflect true relationships rather than being artifacts of response bias.

However clear these findings are, they do not permit us to dismiss the issue of response bias altogther. We must keep in mind that this is only one study. It needs to be replicated in order to increase confidence in the findings. In addition, this investigation deals with only three sources of response bias. There are many other possible elements that might contribute to response bias in this and other realms of study. Finally, and especially important for practitioners, this study deals with aggregates, not individuals. Although there may be no relationships at the aggregate level, we still may find response bias important when screening and assessing individuals. Thus, when we assess the mental health status of individuals in clinical settings, it is important to know the extent to which their responses to items that comprise the assessment tools are due to factors such as the need for approval or social desirability rather than to their true mental health status.

ers. We know that variations in wording can produce variations in response, and the more freedom interviewers have in this regard, the more of a problem it is. Wording variation can affect both reliability and validity (see Chapter 5).

Telephone Surveys

The rapidly rising costs of conducting personal interviews has prompted researchers to consider telephone surveys as a cost-cutting alternative (Lavrakas, 1987). Travel time and costs for interviewers are totally eliminated, which enables each interviewer to conduct more interviews (see Table 7.3). Fewer interviewers are needed, therefore, and the cost of supervisory personnel and training is reduced. This cost advantage essentially means that research that otherwise would be prohibitively expensive may be affordable if the telephone is used.

The speed with which a telephone survey can be completed also makes it preferable at times. If we wanted people's reactions to some event, for example, or repeated measures of public opinion, which can change rapidly, the speed of telephone surveys makes them preferable in these circumstances.

Certain areas of the country and many major cities contain substantial numbers of non-English-speaking people. These people are difficult to accommodate with mailed questionnaires and personal interviews unless we know ahead of time what language a respondent speaks. Non-English-speaking people can be handled fairly easily with telephone surveys, however. All that is needed are a few multilingual interviewers. (Spanish-speakers account for the vast majority of non-English-speaking persons.) If an interviewer contacts a non-English-speaking respondent, that respondent can be conveniently transferred to an interviewer conversant in the respondent's language. Though multilingual interviewers can be and are used in personal interviews, this is far less efficient, probably involving at least one callback so that an interviewer with the needed language facility can be sent out.

TABLE 7.3 Cost Comparison for Telephone and Personal Interview Surveys

Item	Telephone		Personal	
	Cost	%	Cost	%
Sampling	$ 955	2.5%	$ 8,547	10.1%
Pretest	723	1.9	1,113	1.3
Training and prestudy	2,066	5.4	9,524	11.2
Materials	1,375	3.6	3,660	4.3
Field office	1,395	3.7	4,160	4.9
Field salaries	12,545	33.1	32,278	38.0
Field travel	0	0	16,815	19.8
Communication	15,794	41.6	5,980	7.0
Other	3,087	8.1	2,787	3.3
Total	$37,940		$84,864	
Cost per I'W	23.45		54.82	

Source Adapted from Robert M. Groves and Robert L. Kahn, *Surveys by Telephone* (New York: Academic Press, 1979), pp. 189–193. Used with permission of authors and publisher.

A final advantage of telephone interviews is that supervision of the interviewers is far easier. The problem of curbing is eliminated because supervisors can monitor the interviews any time they wish. This makes it easy to ensure that specified procedures are followed and that any problems that might arise are quickly discovered and corrected.

Despite these considerable advantages, telephone surveys have several limitations that may make the method unsuitable for many research purposes. First, they must be quite short in duration. Normally, the maximum length is about 20 minutes, with most of them being even shorter. This is in sharp contrast to personal interviews, which can extend to an hour or more. The time limitation obviously restricts the volume of information that can be obtained and the depth to which issues can be explored. Telephone surveys work best when the information desired is fairly simple and the questions are uncomplicated.

A second limitation stems from telephone communication's being only voice-to-voice. Lack of visual contact eliminates several desirable features characteristic of personal interviews. The interviewer is unable to supplement responses with observational information, and it is harder to probe effectively without seeing the respondent. Furthermore, the use of cards with response alternatives or other visual stimuli is precluded. The inability to present complex sets of response alternatives in this format can make it difficult to ask some questions that are important.

Finally, as we noted in Chapter 6, surveys based on samples drawn from telephone directories may have considerable noncoverage because some people are without telephones and others have unlisted numbers. Although modern telephone sampling techniques, such as

random digit dialing, eliminate the problem of unlisted numbers, the approximately 2 percent of households without telephones remain unreachable, and they are concentrated among the poor and transient segments of the population. So some sampling bias remains even if random digit dialing is used. Because some human service clients are heavily concentrated in the population groups with lower rates of telephone service, special caution should be exercised before deciding on a telephone survey.

Practice and Research Interviews Compared

The interview is undoubtably the most commonly employed technique in human service practice. Thus, it is natural for students in the human services to question how research interviewing compares with practice interviewing. The fundamental difference is in the *purpose* of the interview. Practice interviews are conducted for the purpose of helping a client, while research interviews are done for the purpose of gaining knowledge about a problem or population under study. Whereas the practitioner seeks to understand the client as an individual and often uses the interview as a means of effecting change, the researcher uses the data collected on individuals to describe the characteristics of, and variations in, a population. To the practitioner, the individual client system is central. To the researcher, the respondent is merely the unit of analysis; the characteristics and variability of the population are of primary concern.

The difference in purpose is the basis for differences between practice and research interviewing. Whereas *respondents* are selected to represent a population, *clients* are accepted because they have individual needs that the agency is designed to serve. Research interviews are typically brief, often single encounters, whereas practice relationships may be intensive, long-term relationships. Clients (or the client's needs) often determine the topic and focus of a practice interview, whereas the content of the research interview is predetermined by the nature of the research project. The ideal research interview presents each respondent with exactly the same stimulus in order to obtain comparable responses. The ideal practice interview provides the client with a unique situation that maximizes the potential to help that individual.

An emphasis on differences between the two forms of interviewing, however, should not obscure many of the similarities. Both require that the interviewer make clear what the general purpose of the interview is. Both require keen observational skills and disciplined use of self according to the purpose of the interview. This last point is the key to answering another question about interviewing: Do practitioners make good research interviewers? The answer to this depends on the nature of the particular interview task and the capacity of the interviewer

to perform that particular task. Some situations may best be served by interviewers who display warmth, patience, compassion, tolerance, and sincerity, whereas other situations would require interviewers who are reserved and controlled and who bring an atmosphere of objective, detached sensitivity to the interview (Kadushin, 1972). Some researchers found that using verbal reinforcement—both positive comments to complete responses and negative feedback to inadequate responses—resulted in obtaining more complete information from respondents (Vinokur, Oksenberg, and Cannell, 1979). Although successful in terms of amount of information gained, such techniques might be foreign to the style of interviewing that a practitioner uses. Thus, for the structured, highly controlled interview, the practitioner who is used to improvising questions and demonstrating willingness to help may be a poor choice of interviewer. In other situations, where in-depth, unstructured exploratory interviews are needed, the practitioner's skills might be ideal. Again, it is the purpose of the interview and the nature of the task that determine the compatibility of human service skills with the research interview.

COMPUTERS IN RESEARCH
Survey Design and Data Collection

A popular truism about the computer is, "Garbage in; garbage out." For the researcher, it is a fact that the quality of the research produced can be no better than the quality of the data used to do the analysis; and in survey re-

search, the computer is rapidly becoming an essential tool in the effort to elicit valid and reliable data from respondents and to accurately record these data for analysis.

Probably the most intensive appli-

(Continued on next page)

cation of computer technology to survey research is Computer Assisted Telephone Interviewing, or CATI (Groves et al., 1988). With CATI, the interview is conducted over the telephone as the interviewer reads questions from a computer monitor instead of a clipboard and records responses directly into the computer via the keyboard instead of using a paper form. On the surface, CATI replaces the paper and pencil format of interviewing with a monitor and keyboard arrangement, but the differences are much more significant than this. Some of the special techniques that are possible with CATI include personalizing the wording of questions based on answers to previous questions and automatic branching for contingency questions. For example, in a study on sibling relations, if a respondent reported that she has a son named David who is 14 and another named Peter who is 11, the computer can automatically insert the name "David" into questions to refer to the older child. If there is one subset of questions for the same-sex siblings, and a different set for boy–girl relations, the computer will automatically select the former subset and skip the latter. These features speed up the interview and improve accuracy because the interviewer can concentrate fully on the questions at hand instead of searching through pages of items that do not apply. The CATI program may also include enforced probing when respondents give incomplete answers, editing of responses, and automatic call scheduling.

In computer terminology, such programs are "interactive," that is, the interview schedule changes and presents customized instructions for the interviewer depending on the responses that are recorded. While these CATI features are common for large-scale survey organizations with custom software such as the U.S. Bureau of the Census, a variety of microcomputer software now makes the technology feasible for smaller organizations that need to do frequent surveys.

Computer-assisted interviewing really involves two steps. The first is to design a computer program application that contains the interview schedule. To accomplish this task, the researcher can turn to specialized software for designing data collection programs such as the Viking Forms Manager program, which is available for a variety of mini- and microcomputers and is designed to permit nonprogrammers to develop the interactive screen formats that make CATI effective.

The second step is actually to conduct the interviews. To do this, the interactive forms are used by means of a companion software program, the Viking Data Entry System, to actually collect and enter the data from respondents into a data file for analysis.

Besides customizing questions and utilizing branching routines, the program helps prevent errors from entering the data during the collection phase. For example, with a question that requires numeric data such as, "How old are you?" the program can require that only numeric characters be entered. If the interviewer accidentally hits an alphanumeric character, the program responds with an error message and requires the interviewer to reenter the response. Range checks can also be used to catch errors. Assuming one is interviewing adults, the age range might be set to 18–99. Any response outside that range would result in an error message or a request to recheck the entry.

Data entry can be simplified by prerecording responses where most people will give the same answer. For example, when asking about health status, very few respondents may have had heart attacks. A "no" response can be prerecorded for this item so that data need be changed only for those few individuals who respond *yes.*

The interview schedule can be further refined to warn of logical inconsistencies. If a respondent lists three family members as being employed during the year, an error message would result if the interviewer attempts to enter zero annual income for one of those persons at a later point in the survey. The program will also catch errors such as a February 29 birthday in a non-leap year.

In some situations, the order in which questions are asked can affect the responses in a survey. Because of this, it is common to administer scale items in a random order in a questionnaire. Some software now includes a special feature to take the principle of randomized question ordering a step farther. In administering a scale, it will randomly order the items separately for each respondent to eliminate possible bias due to question order.

A special problem in survey research is coping with open-ended or narrative responses. Even here, computer software is available to aid in survey research. The Survey System is a microcomputer application designed with the survey researcher in mind. In addition to many of the features already described, it has available a special component known as the Verbatim Module. It will search for key words in the narrative responses and even accept approximate spelling of names or key words. The program will then generate reports that display narrative responses.

Although telephone interviewing is undoubtedly the most intensive application of computerized interviewing, it is not the only application. Respondent-completed questionnaires can also be computerized in some situations. Hudson (1988) describes the use of his Clinical Assessment System by clients in social work settings. When clients come to the agency for their appointments, they can use a computer to complete various assessment instruments. Personal interviews can also be adapted to computerized interviewing. With the advent of truly portable personal computers with high memory capacity, questionnaires developed with the help of programs like the Viking Form Manager can be taken into the field. Probably the ultimate application of this concept is the survey research package, INTERV, which uses a design called "tele-interviewing," for panel studies. With tele-interviewing, inexpensive microcomputers are placed in the sampled homes. Respondents get to keep them if they stay in the panel for the duration of the study. Games and other software are provided to the respondents in each panel period as an additional incentive to stay with the

(Continued on next page)

study. A central computer polls the panel respondents who record data on the computers in their homes (News and Notes, 1987).

Of course, any organization contemplating the expense of computerized interviewing has to ask the question: Is it worth it? Two recent reports on an evaluation of CATI suggest that it clearly has some advantages over traditional methods but is not without its problems (Catlin and Ingram, 1988; Weeks, 1988). Statistics Canada, in cooperation with the U.S. Bureau of the Census, conducted a controlled experiment in which over 10,000 household interviews were conducted with approximately equal numbers receiving either CATI treatment or traditional paper and pencil interview schedules.

The costs of the two approaches proved to be about equal. However, CATI had a lower overall response rate. This was due mainly to the fact that CATI interviews took longer, especially when conducted by interviewers who were unfamiliar with the procedure. However, as the interviewers gained practice, interview time was cut dramatically. Another problem was computer down time. Monday through Wednesday were the most productive interviewing days. If the computer system happened to be inoperable during that time, there was no way to make up the difference later in the week. Where CATI had its greatest benefit was in reducing the error rate. It was 50% less overall with CATI, and 60% less in the portion of the questionnaire that required complex branching. The researchers concluded that studies that require complex branching would benefit the most from CATI. With the rapid development of microcomputer capacity and the development of more sophisticated software, it is expected that the computer will play an expanded role in the conduct of survey research.

☰ Main Points

• Surveys are of two general types: (1) questionnaires completed directly by respondents and (2) interviews with the questions read and responses recorded by an interviewer.

• Closed-ended questions provide a fixed set of response alternatives from which respondents choose.

• Open-ended questions provide no response alternatives, leaving respondents complete freedom of expression.

• Clear directions must be provided on questionnaires to indicate what respondents are to do and to guide them through the questionnaire.

• Questions should be ordered so that early questions maximize the response rate, but do not affect the responses to later questions.

• Obtaining a high response rate, the percentage of surveys actually completed, is very important for representativeness in survey research.

• Central to efforts to maximize the response rate with the mailed questionnaire is the cover letter, the use of payments and follow-up letters, and the length and appearance of the questionnaire.

- Interviews are classified by their degree of structure as unstandardized, nonschedule-standardized, or schedule-standardized.

- Probes are used to elicit clearer and more complete responses during interviews.

- Telephone surveys offer significant time and cost savings compared with interviews or mailed questionnaires and are a suitable alternative in many cases.

- Computer software now enables telephone surveyors to input responses directly to a computer file, and it can check for errors or inconsistencies in the data.

≡ Important Terms for Review

closed-ended questions
cover letter
interview
interview schedule
open-ended questions
probes
questionnaire
response bias
response rate
survey

≡ For Further Reading

Converse, J. M., and H. Schuman. *Conversations at Random: Survey Research as Interviewers See It.* New York: Wiley, 1974. A sensitive portrayal of survey research through the eyes of the interviewer. A delightful and insightful look at this most crucial link in the survey research chain.

Cormier, William H., and L. Sherilyn Cormier. *Interviewing Strategies for Helpers,* 2d ed. Monterey, Calif.: Brooks/Cole, 1985. The four major stages of the helping process, relationship assessment, goal-setting, strategy selection and implementation, and evaluation-termination are presented with an eye toward tactics for improving each stage through improved interviewing skills. Not just for social workers, this book is a "must read" for anyone in the helping professions, including counseling.

De Vaus, D. A. *Surveys in Social Research.* Boston: Allen & Unwin, 1986. A very useful book that gets to the heart of designing survey instruments. It includes numerous design recommendations and more practical hints for developing questionnaires that work.

Gorden, Raymond L. *Interviewing Strategy: Techniques, and Tactics,* 4th ed. Chicago: Dorsey, 1987. One of the most comprehensive books on interviewing available. A particularly useful feature is the presentation of different specific interview settings ranging from the research interview to police interrogation. With the information contained in this book, one can learn to tailor the interviewing approach to best fit the setting.

Klein, Philip, et al. *A Social Study of Pittsburgh: Community and Social Services of Allegheny County.* New York: Columbia University Press, 1938. The "second" Pittsburgh survey. This book details the social and economic life of the community, along with the social and health services available. It is a classic illustration of a needs assessment survey.

Lansing, J. B., and J. N. Morgan, *Economic Survey Methods.* Ann Arbor, Mich.: Survey Research Center, Institute for Social Research, 1980. Detailed coverage of survey research issues including design, sampling, methods of data collection, how to prepare data for analysis, and some very practical information on organizing and estimating costs of surveys. Applicable to many types of surveys, not just the economic type.

Lockhart, D. C., ed. *Making Effective Use of*

Mailed Questionnaires. San Francisco: Jossey-Bass, 1984.

An excellent text on the design and administration of mailed questionnaires published by the Evaluation Research Society.

Rosenberg, M. The *Logic of Survey Analysis*. New York: Basic Books, 1968.

A presentation of the logic of surveys, understanding relationships between variables, and analyzing the findings of surveys that requires very little statistical background to comprehend.

Rossi, Peter, James Wright, and Andy Anderson, eds. *Handbook of Survey Research*, New York: Academic, 1983.

A collection of articles from experts on their various areas of specialization in survey research. A useful research work that should be a part of any researcher's library.

Turner, Charles F., and Elizabeth Martin, eds. *Surveying Subjective Phenomena*. New York: Russell Sage, 1986.

This two volume set pursues numerous issues that plague survey research such as the complexity of measuring attitudes, socially desirable responses, how wording can affect responses, the impact of interviewer-respondent relations, and many more. A very thought-provoking book for anyone who deals with surveys or survey data.

≡ Exercises for Class Discussion

The state Health and Human Services Department has recently released a controversial study that concludes that the state is able to provide better quality foster care for less cost than private agencies can provide under a ''purchase of services'' contract. The private agencies are outraged and point out some serious flaws in the study. For example, the state study was done by people who might lose their jobs if the state contracts out for services. Furthermore, the study compared a state program in an urban area with a rural private agency program. To resolve these concerns, the independent research firm by which you are employed has been asked to conduct a survey that will generate results that are respresentative of the entire state.

The following exercises explore some of the tasks and decisions you would face in undertaking such a survey.

7.1 Would you use mailed questionnaires, telephone surveys, or personal interviews with: (a) foster parents, (b) adolescents in care, (c) line workers? Defend your choices. What additional information would help you make this decision?

7.2 If your organization decides to send a mailed questionnaire to foster parents, what things could you suggest to improve the response rate?

7.3 One of the topics to cover with foster parents would be their satisfaction with the services provided by the foster care worker. Write a closed-ended question and an open-ended question to deal with this topic. Which type of question would, in your opinion, be best?

7.4 For interviewing the foster children, would you think a nonstandardized, a nonschedule-standardized, or a schedule-standardized format would be best? Why?

7.5 In what ways would interviewing the adolescents in foster care be different for a researcher or a line worker for the agency? How would the interviewing be similar?

7.6 You are given the task of selecting the interviewers to conduct face-to-face interviews with the adolescents. You are given the following options: Department of Health and Human Services workers, interviewers from a political polling organization who are mostly middle-aged women, or teenagers between 16 and 19 who are eligible for a state-sponsored summer jobs program. Which group would you pick and why? What would be the advantages and disadvantages associated with each of these groups as interviewers?

7.7 Approximately 30% of the young people in foster care are known to be black-Americans and another 15% are Hispanic. What differences does the racial composition of the population make in terms of the way you would suggest doing the study?

7.8 In Chapter 6, we described a study in which a sample of homeless people were interviewed. In some cases, the homeless people were found as they slept in doorways or abandoned buildings during the night. Is it ethical for an interviewer to intrude on the homeless in this fashion? We would not intrude on the sleep of more respectable people by phoning them in the middle of the night. The homeless, of course, are in public areas. Nonetheless, discuss the extent to which this is an unacceptable invasion of their privacy.

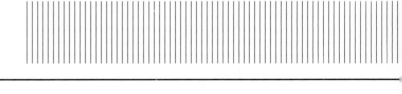

8

Analysis of Available Data

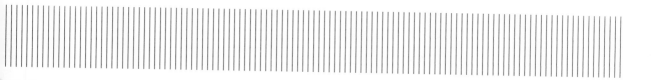

Normally, researchers prefer to organize and direct the collection of the data themselves. This enables them to tailor the nature and form of the data collected to the research hypotheses and the state of knowledge in the field (see Chapter 4). In some cases, however, it may be far too costly and time-consuming for researchers to collect their own data. In other cases, it may simply be impractical or unnecessary to do so. Consider, for example, a study by Deborah Wingard (1987) of the characteristics of adopted children and their parents in California. Wingard could have gotten a list of the children and their parents from agencies and then conducted mailed questionnaires or interviews. As we saw in Chapter 7, however, the former suffer from nonresponse problems, and the latter are expensive. Furthermore, as a routine part of service delivery, adoption agencies gather information about the characteristics of children and both their birth and adoptive parents. So, in this case, data collection by Wingard was unnecessary because the data to test the hypotheses already existed in an agency computerized information file.

Data of this type are referred to as **available data**: observations collected by someone other than the investigator for purposes that differ from the investigator's, but that nonetheless are available to be analyzed. A vast array of this type of data is available for scientific analysis.

In some cases, it takes the form of *statistical data*, or quantified observations of some element of human behavior. Large amounts of statistical data, for example, are collected by the various branches of government and provide quantified information about crime, health, birth rates, death rates, and the like. *Documents* are another form of available data and refer, in their broadest sense, to any form of communication that is nonquantitative in format. They include such things as books, magazines, letters, memoranda, diaries, and other media of communication such as radio, television, movies, and plays. Documents can also make up a part of records maintained by various institutions, such as military records, police records, court records, social work case records, and agency records. Some such records, of course, include statistical data as well as information in nonstatistical form.

Available data are a rich source of data for human service research, and they are sometimes used in conjunction with data collected from other sources, such as surveys. Furthermore, available data can often be treated as if they were data the researchers had collected themselves. Wingard, for example, could work with the agency data much as if they were survey data that she had collected. However, there are some situations in which available data present researchers with some new problems, and these problems are the topic of this chapter. We will first review sources of available statistical data and problems associated with their use. Then we will discuss content analysis, a mechanism for analyzing the nonstatistical data in documents. Finally, we will weigh the advantages and disadvantages of using available data.

Statistical Data

Human service professionals often complain about the mountains of paperwork associated with the procedures of trying to help people. But the facts and figures generated by these procedures can be a rich source of data for research. Unfortunately, the statistical data available to human service agencies is often either overlooked, or it is found to be deficient in some critical respects. An important contribution that the research-knowledgeable human service professional can make to both practice and research is to help develop data collection procedures that generate useful statistical data. This was a major theme of Research in Practice 1.2, where the social agency was described as a "research machine." To make such a contribution, human service professionals must have an understanding of how available statistical data are used in research and what qualities enhance the usefulness of available data for research.

Sources of Statistical Data

Statistical data are collected for a number of reasons, and much of these data are available to human service researchers. First of all, some statistical data are collected as part of many research projects. Many research organizations, such as the Institute for Social Research at the Uni-

versity of Michigan or the Institute for Research on Poverty at the University of Wisconsin, collect large amounts of very useful data that may be reanalyzed by others with different research questions in mind. In this way, data collected for one project may be reanalyzed by a number of different people in the years that follow. This reanalysis of data collected for some other research project is called **secondary analysis.** In fact, some universities have organized a national system of **data archives,** which are essentially libraries that lend or sell sets of data much as other libraries lend books. Two of the better-known data archives are the Roper Center at Williams College and the Inter-University Consortium for Political Research at the University of Michigan. Three useful guides to publicly available data sets are Hakim (1982), Taeuber and Rockwell (1982), and Kiecolt and Nathan (1985). One of the most up-to-date lists of such data sets can be found in *American Demographics,* which includes in each February issue a section called "Directory of Commercial Data Suppliers." Data collected for research purposes and made available for secondary analysis tend to be of fairly high quality because they were collected by professional researchers. Nonetheless, such data still suffer from some of the problems to be discussed shortly.

A second source of statistical data is the federal, state, and local human service agencies that collect data for either administrative purposes or for purposes of client service. Community mental health centers, head start programs, departments of social services, and health and educational institutions are repositories of vast amounts of available data. Figure 8.1, for example, illustrates some of the data regarding clients that are routinely collected by human service agen-

2–7　Client No.: _____

13–40　Name: _____　97–102　Date: _____
　　　　　　　　　　　　　　　　　　　　　　　　　　　　　　　　　　　Mo.　　　Day　　　Yr.

41–68　Address: _____　103–112　Telephone: _____ / _____

69–91　City, State: _____ Zip _____　113–121　S.S.N.: _____
　　　　　　　　　　　　　　　　　　　92–96

Who can we contact if we need to get in touch with you in a hurry?

13–37　Name: _____　38–47　Telephone: _____ / _____

Background

48　Sex (circle one):　male$_1$　female$_2$

49　Race:　White$_1$　Black$_2$　Indian$_3$

Spanish surname$_4$　Other$_5$

50–55　Date of Birth: _____ Age: ____
　　　　　　　　　　Mo.　Day　Yr.

Circle your highest level of education:

56–57　Grades　3　4　5　6　7　8　9　10　11

12　GED$_{13}$

58　College?　　1　2　3　4

Grad. Schl.　5　6　7　8

Have you had Voc. Tech. training?

59　yes$_1$　no$_2$　If yes—

Where? _____

_____

In what? _____

_____

Last school attended? _____

_____

Degree? _____

60　Are you a veteran?　yes$_1$　no$_2$

Type of discharge: _____

Family

Marital status (circle one):

61　married$_1$　　unmarried$_2$

Maiden or former name: _____

62–63　Number of dependents: _____

64–65　Number of people in your current household:

_____

(If married)

Spouse's name: _____
Spouse's employment (if employed):

Occupation: _____

_____

Employed by: _____

_____

66–69　Spouse's earnings per month: $ _____

_____

70–71　Number of dependent children in family: ____

How many are ages　0– 5? _____

ages　6–12? _____

ages 13–16? _____

over age 16? _____

Figure 8.1　A Confidential Client Information Survey　　　(Continued on next page)

Source: James B. Taylor, *Using Microcomputers in Social Agencies*, pp. 20–21. Copyright © 1981 by Sage Publications, Inc. Reprinted by permission of Sage Publications, Inc.

Referral	10) Cystic Fibrosis
	11) Muscular Dystrophy
72–73 Referral Source (circle one):	12) Multiple Sclerosis
	13) Diabetes

Referral

72–73 Referral Source (circle one):

1) VR	9) Priv Phys.
2) CETA	10) CMHC
3) SR	11) KC
4) Job Serv. Ctr.	12) Break Thro.
5) TS	13) Family
6) TM	14) Self
7) VA	15) Friend
8) GM&C Hosp.	16) Other

Specific Source: _____

_____

74 VR certified? yes_1 no_2

VR counselor: _____

75 Referred to VR from PWI? yes_1 no_2

Medical

76–77 Type of disability (circle one): if more than
one, circle the primary disability.

1) Visual
2) Hearing
3) Amputation or limb absence
4) Psychiatric
5) Alcohol/Drugs
6) MR
7) Paraplegia
8) Hemiplegia
9) Quadriplegia

10) Cystic Fibrosis
11) Muscular Dystrophy
12) Multiple Sclerosis
13) Diabetes
14) Blood disorder
15) Cancer
16) Renal failure
17) Spinal cord injury
18) Back injury
19) Colostomy
20) Speech impediment
21) Cerebral Palsy
22) Learning disability
23) Epilepsy
24) Stroke
25) Other circulatory or cardiac impairments
26) Respiratory
27) Digestive (Ulcer)
28) Muscular degeneration
29) Arthritis
30) Brain damage
31) Other (specify)

_____

_____

78 Is client severely disabled? yes_1 no_2

Primary Physician: _____

Address: _____

Figure 8.1 (continued)

cies. Many of these data are in a quantified form, such as the number of grades of school completed or the number of dependent children, and they are amenable to statistical manipulation. These data are stored in data banks and may be available to investigators. Some states, for example, routinely store information regarding the client loads of caseworkers, the size of agencies, and the errors made in providing assistance to clients (Baker and Vosburgh, 1977). Such data can be used to test hypotheses regarding the effect of agency characteristics, such as the size of an agency or the caseload, on caseworker errors. Unfortunately, data from human service agencies are often not efficiently catalogued and indexed so that they may be difficult for investigators to locate and use. Such data have, nonetheless, grown to voluminous proportions in the past two decades. This has occurred because human service agencies have increasingly been required to engage in needs assessment, planning, accountability, and evaluation. In addition, the strides made in computer technology, along with the widespread use of management information systems in social agencies, have contributed to the growth and increased availability of data produced by social agencies (Hoshino and Lynch, 1981).

A third source of statistical data is the organizations and government agencies that collect data as a public service or to serve as a basis for social policy decisions. Such agencies as the Federal Bureau of Investigation and the National Center for Health Statistics, for example, collect vast amounts of data, as do state and local governments. The U.S. Bureau of the Census also collects enormous amounts of data to be used for establishing and changing the boundaries of political districts and allocating government funds that are based on population size. Often data from this source can be used in conjunction with other types of data— from questionnaires, for example, or from agency records—to test hypotheses. In one study of caseworker accuracy, it was hypothesized that caseworker errors might be influenced by the political and economic characteristics of the local community (Piliavin, Masters, and Corbett, 1977). Data were based on interviews, questionnaires, and other sources. In addition, the political and economic characteristics of each community were measured with data from the Bureau of the Census regarding the percentage of poor people in the county, how the county voted in the most recent gubernatorial election, and the percentage of poor families that were headed by women. In this way, data from multiple sources can be combined to measure variables and test hypotheses in a single study.

Data collected by private organizations are distributed less widely than government statistics and for that reason may be more difficult to locate. Professional associations, such as the American Medical Association, the American Bar Association, and the National Association of Social Workers, produce statistics relating to their membership and issues of concern to their members. Additionally, statistical data are produced by research institutes and commercial polling firms. Research in Practice 8.1 illustrates one way in which available data of a statistical type can be used in human service research.

Using Statistical Data

When using available statistical data, you should remember that most such data were not collected for research purposes or at least not for the specific research questions for which you now intend to use them. They were collected to meet the needs of whatever agency, organization, or researcher originally collected them, and you are limited by whatever form in which the data were collected. This leads to some special problems that call for caution.

Missing Data   For a variety of reasons, a data set may not include complete data for every person studied or may fail to collect data from the entire population or sample of interest. For example, a person may refuse to answer certain questions, which results in a gap in his or her data set. Or data may not be collected in a particular neighborhood because it is considered too dangerous for interviewers to enter. Such gaps in a data set are referred to as **missing data** and are found to some degree in practically all studies. The

RESEARCH IN PRACTICE 8.1
Program Evaluation: Do More Serious Offenses Result in More Serious Punishments?

One of the major attractions of available data to researchers is that it is available for less work and less cost than is the case with data collected from scratch. In fact, its convenience alone may make it attractive to researchers. Also, as noted in the chapter, there is a vast amount of such data generated, covering a variety of social issues. With all of these data so readily available, a substantial amount of research is conducted using them. As good as all of this sounds, researchers contemplating using available data should approach them with caution and should look for anything in the production of the data that could affect its validity for the purpose of answering particular research questions. Some of the pitfalls of available data are well illustrated in research on how effectively the criminal justice system disposes of the cases of juvenile delinquents. After a two-year period of observing a large city's probation office, Carolyn Needleman (1981) suggests that several researchers in the area of delinquency may have fallen victim to some traps found in juvenile court data.

Juvenile court records have been a popular source of data for research into the disposition of delinquency cases (see Terry, 1967; Meade, 1974; Cohen, 1975; Thomas and Sieverdes, 1975). One main issue addressed by these studies has been the influence of various factors on a probation officer's decision whether to refer an offender to the courts or to handle the case informally. Among the variables considered have been the nature of the offense, the delinquent's prior record, the delinquent's demeanor during an interview with the probation officer (PO), and the delinquent's family situation. Let us take just one of these: the seriousness of the offense. It seems logical to assume that the more serious the offense, the more severe the disposition of the case would be. That is, after all, a fundamental principle of our whole criminal justice system: that the punishment should fit the crime. As an indicator of severity of disposition, it is common to assume that being sent to court constitutes a more severe sanction than having the case handled informally by the PO at the intake unit.

Surprisingly, researchers over the years have found either no relationship or a very small one between offense and disposition, pointing to a possible flaw in the criminal justice system. Actually, the researchers had stumbled onto one of the many traps in using juvenile court data: The people producing the court data, particularly the POs, had a different definition of what was a more "severe" punishment than did the researchers, and only through observation of the POs at work could this be detected by Needleman. Typically, the POs view the juvenile court with a degree of contempt. They express a low opinion of Family Court and the judges who preside over it, and they see it as likely to be *more lenient* and *less effective* than diversion from the court. Because of this, they try to divert from Family Court as many cases as they can, with little concern for the severity of the offense. In addition, with the waiting period for a court date approaching six months, the POs feel that many serious cases need intervention immediately; so they divert them from court for this reason also. The result is that juveniles who have committed more serious offenses are no more likely, and may even be less likely in some jurisdictions, to go to court than are juveniles who have committed less serious offenses.

We can see, then, that the anomolous finding of little or no relationship between severity of offense and severity of disposition resulted from a lack of understanding concerning the social context in which juvenile court data are generated. So, it is crucial to investigate factors affecting the production of the data that might in any way adversely affect its use for research purposes. In our example, the PO's opinions about the lack of effectiveness of the courts led them to make organizational decisions which resulted in data that seemed to violate the idea that the punishment should fit the crime. The true import of the court data could be understood only when researchers understood the meaning that various decisions and actions have for the people involved, and those meanings may not be contained in such available data as court records. This does not mean that available data should be avoided; rather, one needs clearly to recognize that organizational or agency records are *social products,* which means that they are influenced by the motives and meanings of the people who create them. Researchers must be careful about assessing how those motives and meanings could influence research results.

problem when using available data files is that you have no control over this failure to collect a complete set of data. Missing data result in incomplete coverage, which, if extensive, can throw into question the representativeness of the data. Furthermore, because statistical procedures are based on the assumption of complete data, missing data can result in misleading statistical conclusions. As we dig back into data from the past, it is not uncommon to find data for whole periods of time missing. This can occur for many reasons such as data destroyed by fires, lost data, changes in policy, and the like. Finding data that cover only a portion of one's target population is also quite common. For example, the researchers in a study of marriage rates among older Americans in the United States were forced to do without data from three states—Arizona, New Mexico, and Oklahoma—because those states did not maintain central marriage files (Treas and VanHilst, 1976). Given the high concentration of retirees in Arizona, however, it is possible that the exclusion of data from that state might have affected their results. When working with data that suffer from noncoverage, one should assess the implications that noncoverage has for the results of the research.

Inductive Versus Deductive Analysis

In research investigations in which data are collected firsthand, a deductive approach is commonly used. That is, hypotheses are deduced from a theory, variables in the hypotheses are operationally defined, and data are collected based on these operational definitions. In short, research moves from the abstract to the concrete: The kind of data collected is determined by the theory and hypotheses being tested (see Chapter 2). In the analysis of available data, however, such a deductive approach is often impossible because the data necessary to measure the variables derived from a theory may not have been included when the original data were collected. For example, a theory regarding caseworker effectiveness with clients might include the variable of the intensity of the casework relationship. Although intensity of relationship is a crucial concept in interpersonal helping, it is unfortunately not the type of variable that is included in routine agency data collection procedures. In circumstances such as this, it is not possible to operationalize the variable in the way most appropriate to the theory. If this dif-

ficulty is encountered, a compromise is often made. In Chapter 5, we saw that the measurement process often calls for modifying nominal and operational definitions (see Figure 5.1). Here operational definitions and, in some cases, hypotheses are revised so that they can be tested with the data available (see Figure 8.2). In the previous example, we might measure intensity of relationship by looking at the amount of time a worker spends with a given client over the course of treatment, the frequency of contacts, or the duration of contacts. Although none of these variables may be the best measure of "intensity of relationship," each is readily derived from the worker time sheets that are mandatory in many agencies. Total contact time, frequency of contact, duration of contact, or some combination of these may be used even though they are not thoroughly accurate measures of the variable of interest.

In other words, we have modified our research to fit the data. When this occurs, research takes on a somewhat inductive character. In inductive research, we move from the concrete to the abstract: Starting with data collected for some reason, we develop hypotheses and theories to explain what we find in the data. The situation we have described is actually somewhere in limbo between induction and deduction. We have begun with the-

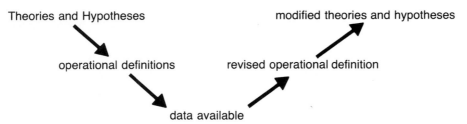

Figure 8.2 The Measurement Process with Available Statistical Data

ories and hypotheses, but we have also been forced to let the available data influence how we test the hypotheses. This is a frequent problem in the analysis of available statistical data and has led some to argue that available data are most appropriately used in purely inductive research that has an exploratory purpose (Hoshino and Lynch, 1981). Although this caution is well taken, there are many areas in which available data can be used in deductive research, provided that care is exercised in how extensively hypotheses and operational definitions are changed to fit the data. The major danger when extensive changes are made is one that has been discussed in relation to other data collection techniques: validity.

Validity Validity refers to whether a measurement instrument actually measures what it is intended to measure (see Chapter 5). Many data in existing statistical files can be considered valid indicators of certain things that they directly describe. The age, sex, and racial profiles of clients along with the amounts of different kinds of services provided would be examples of these. There are three areas, however, in which validity problems frequently arise.

First, there are many elements of agency operation—such as achievement of goals, success of programs, or satisfaction of clients—that may not be measured directly by any data normally collected by an agency. To study these, one would have to search for indirect measures among the agency data that might enable one to infer such things as goals, success, or satisfaction. These situations create the same kinds of validity problems that confront researchers using other methods except that, when avail-

able data are used, validity problems cannot be considered and resolved *before* the data are collected. Because the data have already been collected, the problems are entrenched.

A second area where validity problems frequently arise is where data analysis becomes inductive, as we have just discussed—that is, when operational definitions are changed so that variables can be measured with the data available. The more the definitions are changed, the more the validity of the measures is called into question. The operational definitions may be changed so drastically that they no longer measure the theoretical concepts they were first intended to measure.

Finally, validity questions arise when procedures used in gathering data by an agency or organization have changed over the years. Changing modes of collecting data, such as dropping some questions or developing new definitions of something, are quite common in any agency or organization. These procedural changes can, however, affect the comparability of data collected at various times and the validity of using the same operational definitions. An example of this is found in crime statistics for New York City (Crime Records, 1952). Prior to 1951, crime reporting was the responsibility of each precinct in the city. In 1951 a centralized system was established on a city-wide basis. In the month after the system was in operation, the volume of many reported crimes increased 200 to 300 percent. The apparent reason for this was that individual precincts had in the past been endeavoring to make themselves look good by keeping the appearance of crime in their districts low by underreporting. The centralized system clearly produced more accurate and complete data, but the later data are not comparable with the earlier data. Researchers using existing data must be careful not to fall prey to similar traps, with the result that research findings are an artifact of changes in record keeping.

The amount of available statistical data from various sources is likely to grow astronomically in the future. In addition, the increasing availability and sophistication of computer technology, along with the growing expertise of human service workers in using computers, are likely to make these data more readily available for research (Taylor, 1981; Parker et al., 1987). Such data represent vast, but currently much underutilized, sources for research. When contemplating a research project, you would be wise to consider whether there is some source of available data that might serve as a legitimate source of data.

Content Analysis

Whenever activity is recorded in some document—whether it be a book, diary, case record, film, or tape recording—it is amenable to scientific analysis. Although the data discussed in the previous section were already quantified when made available for research, the documents now being considered have basically *qualitative* data that must be quantified. **Content analysis** refers to a method of transforming the symbolic content of a document, such as words or other images, from a qualitative, unsystematic form into a quantitative, systematic form (Holsti, 1969; Krippendorff, 1980; Weber, 1985). Audrey Smith (1982) and Paula Allen-Meares (1984) discuss some of the many uses of content analysis in human service research and practice. Content analysis is a form of coding, a practice we discuss as a way of transforming data

used in some surveys and observational research in Chapters 7 and 9. **Coding** refers to categorizing behaviors or elements into a limited number of categories. In surveys and observational research, coding is performed on data that are collected firsthand by the investigator for particular research purposes. In content analysis, coding is performed on documents that are produced for purposes other than research and then made available for research purposes. In both survey data coding and content analysis, categories and coding schemes are developed in order to quantify verbal or symbolic content.

Coding Schemes

A major step in content analysis is to develop a coding scheme that can be used in analyzing the documents at hand. Coding schemes in content analysis, like those in coding observed behavior, can be quite variable, and their exact form depends on the documents being studied and the hypotheses being tested in the research project.

Existing Coding Schemes In some cases, it is possible to find existing coding schemes that can be used for content analysis. For example, the coding categories developed by Bales (1950) for the analysis of interaction in small groups can be applied to documents if they suit the purpose of the study (see Chapter 9). Another example of a general scheme is one commonly used for categorizing themes in fiction and drama. The basic themes are these: (1) love, (2) morality, (3) idealism, (4) power, (5) outcast, (6) career, and (7) no agreement (McGranahan and Wayne, 1948). There are also categories for classifying endings, temporal settings, spacial settings, and patterns of love in the love theme. In the human services, coding schemes have been developed to analyze the content of a clinician's responses to patients in interviews. In a study of the impact of a clinician's responses on whether clients continued with treatment, described in more detail in Research in Practice 8.2, a coding system utilizing three categories was developed:

1. Substantive congruent responses: clinician responses that referred to the client's immediately preceding response or contained some elements of that response;
2. Nonsubstantive congruent responses: clinician responses, such as "I see" or "Yes," that indicate that the clinician is aware of and paying attention to the client's verbalizations;
3. Incongruent responses: clinician responses that appear unrelated to what the client has said.

Others interested in similar aspects of the practitioner–client interview might be able to utilize the same coding scheme.

In conducting content analysis, then, one will find it beneficial to search for an existing coding scheme that might be applicable to the research problem at hand. Not only does the use of an existing coding scheme result in considerable savings for the researcher in terms of time, energy, and money, but it also serves to make the research project comparable with other studies that have also used the same coding system.

Coding schemes can be found in the many journals that report research relevant to the human services or in books, such as Holsti's (1969) or Krippendorff's (1980), that are devoted to the study of content analysis. Whether one is using an existing coding scheme or developing a new one, these schemes should possess certain characteristics.

Characteristics Like categories in any measurement process, those used in content analysis should be exhaustive and mutually exclusive. Categories are *exhaustive* when there is a category available for every relevant element in the documents. Meeting this guideline may be easy or quite impossible depending on what we are trying to measure. If there are only a few possibilities and they can be clearly defined, an exhaustive set of categories will not be difficult to develop. If what we are trying to measure is rather open-ended with many possibilities, however, developing an exhaustive set of categories may well be difficult. For example, presidential speeches have been analyzed in terms of the values expressed. Obviously, there are so many values that an exhaustive list is unlikely to be developed. One such list contained 14 value categories, which undoubtedly cover the most important or commonly mentioned values (Prothro, 1956). It is doubtful if even that many categories are really exhaustive, however. If it is impossible to be exhaustive, then the most common or most important categories should be used, and a residual category should be made available for those items that do not fit any of the other categories.

Coding categories should also be *mutually exclusive*, which means that each coded item can fall into one—and only one—category. This requirement forces one to have precise definitions for each category so that there is no ambiguity concerning which items it includes and which it does not. Failure to meet this requirement can totally befuddle the measurement process because items will be placed every which way by coders confused with overlapping categories. Lack

RESEARCH IN PRACTICE 8.2
Practice Effectiveness: Communication Between Practitioner and Client

A nagging problem confronting human service workers is a client's abandonment of treatment before treatment goals have been achieved. It has been variously estimated that between 28 and 80 percent of clients leave treatment prematurely. Such abandonment means that the treatment process has failed and leads to wasted resources and reduced staff morale. However, one study showed how data that are readily available in practice settings can be useful for research on how to solve this problem in the delivery of services. Wayne Duehn and Enola Proctor (1977) decided to use data that were available from other sources rather than collect data themselves. In an agency to which they had access, the initial interviews with clients were routinely tape recorded. They selected a random sample of these recordings to serve as their data base.

Assuming that communication patterns between practitioner and client might play a role in the problem, they hypothesized that two independent variables—the *congruence* between what is said by the practitioner and by the client and the *relevance* of the practitioner's comments—would affect the rate of premature defection.

"Response congruence" is the extent to which the response of the practitioner to a statement by the client indicates that the client's message was received by the practitioner. For example, if the client asked, "How long will treatment take?" and the practitio-

ner responded, "It is too early to tell at this point," the response would be considered congruent because it answered the client's question. If, however, the practitioner responded, "Tell me what your problem is," that would be an incongruent response. A congruent exchange provides positive feedback to the client, whereas an incongruent exchange does not. "Response relevance" is the extent to which the responses of the practitioner are perceived by the client as being relevant to his or her treatment needs. A reasonable hypothesis is that congruent and relevant responses by practitioners in initial interviews produce greater satisfaction in the client and thus a willingness to maintain the relationship.

Response congruence was operationally defined as a practitioner's response that acknowledges the content of a client's statement. Practitioner responses were coded into three categories: (1) substantive congruent, (2) nonsubstantive congruent (simple responses such as "mm-humm" or "I see," which convey no information, but indicate acknowledgment of the client's statement), and (3) incongruent responses.

Response relevance was operationalized by having the clients indicate on a questionnaire, completed prior to the interview with the practitioner, which of 24 subject areas they believed would be relevant to their treatment. The practitioner's responses were then coded into one of three categories: (1)

relevant content—responses fell into one of the subject areas selected by the client, (2) nonsubstantive responses, and (3) irrelevant content—responses that did not fall into one of the subject areas selected by the clients.

Thirty-two interviews with clients who prematurely defected were randomly selected from a total of 109 cases. Another 32 interviews of clients who continued treatment were randomly selected from a total of 139 cases. Coders, who were unaware of whether the client defected or continued, applied the coding categories to the practitioner's responses. Coder reliability was high, averaging 0.88.

The results of the content analysis indicated that practitioner behavior during the initial interview was significantly related to whether clients prematurely defected or continued treatment. The mean number of incongruent responses from the practitioners was 14.3 with defectors, and only 6.9 with those who continued treatment. The relevancy of responses revealed a similar pattern. Practitioners averaged 21.7 irrelevant responses with defectors, but only 12.1 with continuers. Duehn and Proctor suggest that these results indicate that practitioners may be able to reduce the number of clients who prematurely cease treatment by modifying their own behavior during initial interviews. Of course, further research needs to be done to show that there is a causal relationship between relevance or congruence and defection. It may be, for example, that counselors tend to behave in a nonrelevant or incongruent fashion with clients who, for other reasons, are poor risks to continue therapy.

of mutual exclusiveness will likely show up in low levels of reliability as the coders disagree on the placement of items into categories.

Units of Analysis

With the categories established, the next research decision concerns precisely what aspects of the documents will be recorded. Generally, there are four units of analysis: a word, a theme, a major character, or a sentence or paragraph. (The units of analysis commonly found in research other than content analysis are discussed in Chapter 4.) An often convenient unit of analysis is a *single word*. Coding the presence of certain words in documents can be accomplished easily and with a high degree of reliability. If a single word qualifies as a valid indicator of what you wish to measure, it is a good choice for the unit of analysis. For example, as a part of their study of colonial families, Herman Lantz and his colleagues (1968) counted the frequency with which the word "power" was associated with men or women in colonial magazines. In this context, the single word was used as a measure of the perceived distribution of power between men and women during colonial times. When using single words as the unit of analysis, it is often helpful to make use of a context unit, which is the context in which a single word is found. The words surrounding the word used as the unit of analysis modify it and further explain its meaning. This contextual information is taken into account when coding the unit of analysis. For example, in the study just mentioned, the investigators needed to know whether the word "power" referred to men or to women. The context surrounding the word supplied this crucial information. The amount of context needed to explain the use of a given word adequately is, of course, variable.

The *theme* as a unit of analysis refers to the major subject matter of a document or part of a document. An entire document can be characterized as having a primary theme. Novels, for example, can be described as mysteries, science fiction, historical, and so on. In a study of the images of women during World War II and their treatment by government propaganda agencies, one researcher analyzed themes relating to the role of women in the work force found in fiction pieces in two magazines that were popular during the war, *Saturday Evening Post* and *True Story* (Honey, 1984). Themes can, however, be difficult to delineate. The overall theme may or may not be clear, or there may be multiple themes. Coder reliability is likely to be lower than when easily identifiable words are the unit of analysis.

A third unit of analysis in documents is the *main character*. The use of this unit of analysis is, of course, limited to documents that have a cast of characters, such as plays, novels, movies, or television programs. A study of children's television programs, for example, used the major dramatic character as the unit of analysis. The study, funded by the Ford and Carnegie foundations, found that only 16 percent of the major characters were women and "females were por-

trayed as married, less active, and with lower self-esteem" (Corry, 1982).

The fourth unit of analysis is a *sentence* or *paragraph*. The study described earlier regarding congruency in clinician–client interaction used a similar unit of analysis: Each clinician response, preceded and followed by a client comment, was considered the unit to be coded as congruent or incongruent. A paragraph or even a single sentence, however, often contains more than one idea, and this may make these larger units more difficult to classify while maintaining mutually exclusive categories and intercoder reliability. Indeed, reliability may well be lower than with the word or main character units. Yet the larger units are often more theoretically relevant in the human services. In clinician–client interaction, for example, it would make little conceptual sense to characterize an interchange as congruent on the basis of one word. Meaning in social interaction normally arises from a whole block of words or sentences. So, as we emphasized when discussing units of analysis in Chapter 4, the primary consideration in selecting a unit of analysis is theoretical: which unit seems to be preferable given theoretical and conceptual considerations.

Issues in Content Analysis

When developing coding categories for content analysis, researchers confront several issues. It is important to remember that content analysis is a form of measurement—measurement of aspects of a document's contents. As such, we encounter the familiar concerns regarding validity and reliability, along with problems of choosing a level of measurement and a sample (see Chapters 5 and 6).

Validity

In content analysis, validity refers to whether the categories we develop and the aspects of the content coded are meaningful indicators of what we intend to measure. Developing coding schemes that are valid indicators can be a challenging task. Anne Fortune (1979), for example, reported on an effort to study communication patterns between social workers and their clients in which recordings of interviews were content analyzed. The goal of the research was to discover which interview techniques used by practitioners would bring about cognitive and affective change in clients. Fortune was concerned, in particular, with how techniques varied when clients were adults rather than children. First, a typology of communication techniques was developed based on William Reid's work on task-centered casework. As there are many ways to execute a particular verbal technique in a therapeutic setting, it was impossible to base the content analysis on a single word or phrase. Instead, coders were provided with a description of each technique and examples of the verbal forms that each technique might take. For example, the communication technique of "exploration" was described as "communication intended to elicit information, including questions and restatements or 'echoes' of client's communications." Examples of this technique provided to the coders were such phrases as "What class was that?" and "You said your son misbehaved. . . ." The communication technique of "direction" was exemplified by "I think the first step would be to talk this over with your

daughter" (Fortune, 1979, p. 391). By a provision of specific examples of how to code comments, it was hoped that the resulting coding would have greater validity than if coders were left on their own.

Depending on the nature of the research and the documents to be analyzed, any of the methods of assessing validity may be applicable (see Chapter 5). The logical approaches of content validity and jury opinion are the most generally used assessments of validity in content analysis although criterion validity is sometimes used. For example, in a content analysis of suicide notes, an attempt was made to identify aspects of the content of real suicide notes that would differentiate them from simulated ones written by people who had not attempted suicide (Ogilvie, Stone, and Shneidman, 1966). The researchers compared half of the genuine notes with half of the simulated ones and found that genuine notes made more references to concrete things and greater use of the word "love." The simulated notes, on the other hand, contained more references to the thought processes that went into the decision to kill oneself. Using these observations to predict which of the remaining notes were genuine, the researchers were able to do so at a 94-percent level of accuracy. The ability to predict at such a level suggests that the content aspects of the notes they discovered were valid indicators of genuine suicide notes.

Researchers must be able to argue convincingly that indicators are valid if scientific outcomes are to be accepted. Though most content analyses do not go beyond content validity or jury opinion, it is important to remember that these are the weakest demonstrations of validity. Whenever possible, more rigorous tests should be attempted.

Reliability

Reliability refers to the ability of a measure to yield consistent results each time it is used. In content analysis, reliability relates to the ability of coders to apply consistently the coding scheme that has been developed. That is, can several coders code the documents according to the coding scheme and obtain consistent results? Reliability in content analysis depends on many factors, including the skill of the coders, the nature of the categories, the rules guiding the use of the categories, and the degree of clarity or ambiguity in the documents (Holsti, 1969; Weber, 1985). The clarity of the documents in any given study is largely fixed, so our discussion of control over reliability is limited to the coders and the categories utilized.

First, reliability can be enhanced by a thorough training of the coders and by practice in applying the coding scheme. Coders who continually deviate from the others in their coding during this practice period should not be relied on as coders. One must be cautious, however, about eliminating coders without assessing whether their deviation indicates poor performance or an ambiguous coding scheme.

Second, the nature of the categories to be applied to the document is also important for reliability. The simpler and more objective the categories, the higher the reliability will be. Vaguely defined categories or those requiring substantial interpretation will decrease reliability because they create greater opportunity for disagreement among the coders.

Measuring reliability in content analysis is much the same as measuring reliability when coding observed behavior (see Chapter 9). One simple way to do this is to calculate the percent of judgments on which coders agree out of the total number of judgments that they must make:

$$\text{percent of agreement} = \frac{2 \times \text{no. of agreements}}{\text{total no. of observations recorded by both observers}}$$

This measure of intercoder reliability, however, does not take into account the extent to which intercoder agreement can occur by chance. Paula Allen-Meares (1984) presents other ways of measuring intercoder reliability. Accepted levels of reliability are 75-percent agreement between coders or better. Well-trained coders using well-constructed coding schemes should achieve better than an 85-percent agreement.

There is a certain tension between validity and reliability in content analysis. The simplest coding schemes—such as those employing word frequency counts—produce the highest reliability because they are very easy to apply in a consistent manner. As we have noted, however, word frequency counts may not validly measure what we want to measure. It may be necessary to sacrifice some degree of reliability for the sake of validity. Researchers often end up performing a balancing act between the dual requirements of validity and reliability.

Level of Measurement

Like other methods of collecting data, content analysis involves a decision about the level of measurement to be used (see Chapter 5). The level of measurement achieved depends on the variable being measured and on the process used to measure it. The variable being measured puts an upper limit on the level of measurement that can be reached. For example, if we rate main characters in a book according to marital status, the highest level of measurement would be nominal because marital status is a nominal variable. No amount of measurement finesse can change this once the key variables have been selected. There is, however, some control over the level of measurement depending on the process used to measure the variables. The key factor is how the unit of analysis is quantified in the coding process. Coding systems in content analysis generally fall into one of four categories: (1) presence or absence of an element, (2) frequency of occurrence of an element, (3) amount of space devoted to an element, and (4) intensity of expression.

The simplest rating system is to indicate merely *the presence or absence of an element* in a document. For example, we might rate interviews as to whether the clinician mentions certain subjects, such as sexual behavior or parent–child relationships. This simple system would yield nominal data and convey a minimum of information about content. Several important questions would remain unanswered. We would not know whether the subject was addressed in a positive or negative light nor how the client reacted. Also unknown would be how much time was devoted to that subject or how frequently it was repeated. Consideration of these factors would make the study more informative.

Frequency counts are very common methods of rating. We simply count up how often an element appears. For example, Jack Levin and James Spates (1970) sought to compare the dominant values expressed in middle-class publications with those in the so-called underground press. The investigators rated the frequency with which statements of various values appeared in the two types of publications. On the basis of the frequency counts, the study concluded that the underground press emphasized values related to self-expression, whereas the middle-class publications stressed values related to various types of personal achievement. Frequency counts reveal more information about the document than does the simple present-or-absent approach. They also open the way for more sophisticated statistical analysis because they can, with the appropriate theoretical concepts, achieve an interval level of measurement.

Coding systems based on *amount of space devoted to an element* have proved useful for analyzing the mass media. In the case of newspapers or magazines, the normal approach is to measure column inches. The equivalent for films or television would be time. For example, for a study of the contribution of social work writers to the development of professional knowledge, Merlin Taber and Iris Shapiro (1965) counted the number of column inches in selected social work journals that were devoted to a discussion of different types of knowledge, such as theoretical versus empirical knowledge. We could measure the amount of space devoted to a topic, such as family violence or the problems of lesbian mothers, over the years in order to assess the impact of popular trends or political events on professional concern about various issues. The major attraction of space/time measures is the ease of their use. The amount of space devoted to a given topic can be measured far more rapidly than word frequency counts or even whether key words are present or absent. As each document takes only a short time to analyze, space/time measures allow a larger sample size, possibly leading to greater representativeness. Space/time measures also can yield interval level measurement with theoretical concepts that are amenable to such a level of measurement.

Unfortunately, space/time measures are still somewhat crude. Other than the volume of space devoted to the particular topic in question, they reveal nothing further about the content. For example, time measures applied to the network news could tell us which types of news are allotted the most coverage, but nothing about more subtle issues such as whether the news coverage was biased or not. As Ole Holsti (1969, p. 121) notes, "a one-to-one relationship between the amount of space devoted to a subject and the manner in which it is treated cannot be assumed."

The most complex rating systems involve a *measure of intensity*—the forcefulness of expression in the documents. However, developing intensity measures is difficult. Intensity of expression can be quite subtle and dependent on many aspects of word usage. This makes it extremely difficult to clearly specify the conditions for coding content elements. The coders will have to make many judgments before deciding how to categorize the content, and this leads to disagreements and low reliability.

Developing intensity measures that will produce reliable results is quite similar to constructing measurement scales. We could, for example, have coders rate documents along a scale (as in the semantic differential or the Likert scales discussed in detail in Chapter 13). Newspaper editorials dealing with public assistance programs might be rated as (1) very unfavorable, (2) unfavorable, (3) neutral, (4) favorable, or (5) very favorable. The options for intensity scales are nearly endless given the vast variety of intensity questions that can arise concerning the contents of documents. Despite their complexity, intensity measures are the most revealing concerning a document's contents and represent the highest measurement level of content analysis.

Sampling

In document analysis, the number of documents is often too vast for all to be analyzed, and it is then necessary to take a sample from a whole group of documents. For example, we might wish to study the extent to which concern for family violence has changed among human service providers between the 1950s and the 1980s. We could do this by studying the extent of coverage of the topic in human service journals over the years. Considering the number of journals and thousands of pages involved, sampling would clearly be necessary to make such a project feasible. As with other types of sampling, a key issue is representativeness. In order to generalize the findings of our document analysis, the sample must be representative, which is often difficult to achieve with documents. One problem is that the elements of the population of documents may not be equal. In the case of family violence, some journals would be more likely to publish articles on this topic than would others. Such journals as *Child Welfare* or *Family and Child Mental Health Journal*, for example, would be more likely to receive and publish an article on child or spouse abuse. A more general journal, like *Social Service Review*, would include a much smaller proportion of articles dealing with family violence. Likewise a journal specializing in a different area, such as the *Journal of Gerontology*, would probably publish few if any articles on family violence. A random sample of all human service journals, then, might include only a few of the ones most likely to publish articles on this topic. Thus, the sample would be dominated by journals having a small likelihood of publishing family violence articles, making it more difficult to measure changes in practitioner concern for family violence. This problem could be solved by choosing our sample from among those journals specializing in areas related to family violence. Or we could stratify the journals by type and then select a stratified random sample, taking disproportionately more journals that are likely to publish articles on family violence (see Chapter 6).

A second issue in sampling documents is the difficulty in defining the population of documents. For example, for a study of the changing image of the social work profession, James Billups and Maria Julia (1987) conducted a content analysis of advertisements for job vacancies in social work positions. Since such ads are published in many different places—in local, state, and national publications—it would have been difficult to define what that whole population of documents is. To get around this problem, they limited themselves to advertisements in national publications on the grounds that they would be most likely to reflect national trends in the changing image of social work. At a national level, most ads were placed in *Social Casework* in 1960 and 1970 and in the *NASW News* in 1980. In order to assess trends over time, it was not necessary to sample documents from every year. Instead, they took a random sample of 10 percent of the ads appearing in these journals in 1960, 1970, and 1980, which covered the period in which they were interested. The changing trends in practice that Billups and Julia found in their content analysis research reflected what had been discovered in other research: The distinction between casework and group practice

has become less important over time, and social workers, especially those with graduate degrees, are more likely to find themselves in supervisory or administrative positions.

Assuming that the population to be sampled can be adequately defined, the normal procedures of sampling discussed in Chapter 6 can be applied to documents. Of those, simple random sampling is probably most common and most generally applicable (Holsti, 1969). As we have seen, however, stratified sampling may be required to avoid bias when sampling from a population of unequal elements. Systematic sampling should be approached cautiously as it is easy to be trapped by *periodicity* in documents. Periodicity is the problem in which elements with certain characteristics occur at patterned intervals throughout the sampling frame. For example, the size and content of newspapers varies substantially with the days of the week. If the sampling interval were seven or a multiple of seven, a systematic sample would include only papers published on the same day of the week and could be very biased depending on what aspects of content we were studying.

Sampling documents often involves multistage sampling. As in all multistage sampling, we start with large units and work down through a series of sampling stages to smaller and smaller units. Levin and Spates's (1970) sample of the underground press illustrates multistage sampling. The first stage was selecting a sample of publications from the membership of the Underground Press Syndicate. This was done by choosing the top five in terms of circulation. The second stage involved randomly selecting a single issue of each publication for every other month from September 1967 through August 1968. This produced 6 sample issues of each of the 5 publications for a total of 30 issues. The final stage was to select every other nonfiction article appearing in the sample issues for analysis. The resulting sample contained 316 articles to represent the underground press.

Assessment of Available Data Analysis

Like other research techniques, the use of available data has both advantages and disadvantages. A consideration of these will assist in determining when such analysis is the most appropriate choice, as well as in pointing out some potential problems associated with its use.

Advantages

Lower Costs Document analysis can be one of the least costly forms of research, and using available statistical data can help hold down the costs of a research project. The major expense of data gathering is borne by the producers of the documents and statistics rather than by the researcher. The sheer volume of data collected by the U.S. Bureau of the Census, the National Association of Social Workers, or the many local and state social agencies is so massive that only the best-endowed research projects could possibly duplicate their data collection efforts. In the study of caseworker accuracy that used the political and economic characteristics of the community as one of its independent variables, for example, the costs of the investigation would have escalated tremendously if the researchers had had to collect these data themselves (Piliavin, Masters, and Corbett, 1977). Fortunately, they were able to use Census Bureau data, which is virtually cost-free.

Document analysis can become expensive if the documents of interest are widely scattered and difficult to obtain or if very large samples are employed. Also, the more complex the coding process, the more expensive the study will become. Overall, however, available data offer an opportunity to conduct valuable research at reasonable cost.

Nonreactivity Like simple observation and unobtrusive measures, available data are nonreactive (see Chapter 9). Unlike the case of surveys or experiments where the participants are aware that they are being studied, producers of documents do not normally anticipate a researcher's coming along at some later date to analyze those documents. The contents of the documents are, therefore, unaffected by the researcher's activities. This does not mean, of course, that those producing the documents are not reacting to some elements that might result in biased documents. For example, police officers might be more likely to record an instance of physical or verbal assault in an arrest report when the suspect is nonwhite than when the suspect is white, thus generating data that make nonwhites appear more abusive and introducing bias into arrest records. In addition, people who compile documents may be reacting to how people other than researchers, such as a supervisor or politician, may respond to their document. Likewise the preparation of a document might be shaped by the preparer's hope for a "place in history." Despite all of this, researchers are not a source of reactivity with available data.

Inaccessible Subjects Properly cared for, documents can survive far longer than the people who produce them. Document analysis allows us to study the ways of society long ago and the behavior of people who are long dead. Several of the examples cited in this chapter illustrate the use of document analysis for this purpose. The Lantz et al. (1968) study of the colonial family and the study of suicide notes by Ogilvie, Stone, and Shneidman (1966) dealt with the behavior of persons quite inaccessible by research techniques other than document analysis.

Longitudinal Analysis Many statistical data are collected routinely over a period of years—even centuries. This contrasts sharply with the typical "one-shot," cross-sectional survey data. With such longitudinal data, trend analysis—looking for changing patterns over time—can be accomplished. For example, a longitudinal analysis of available data was used in an evaluation of the progress of blacks in the United States since the 1950s by Reynolds Farley (1984). Using census data from the 1950s, 1960s, and 1970s, Farley compared the position of blacks relative to whites over three decades. He found mixed results. The census data revealed that blacks as a whole had made substantial gains in the quality of employment, family earnings, and educational attainment. Other indicators were less encouraging, however, showing little or no improvement. In the areas of residential integration, unemployment rate, and school integration, blacks' position relative to whites had not improved over 30 years. In general, Farley's analysis reveals that although blacks have experienced significant gains in some areas, substantial gaps remain and appear quite persistent. This type of research is obviously valuable in putting today's conditions into a historical perspective, and just as obviously this type of longitudinal

analysis of *past* trends can be done only through the analysis of available data. Existing statistical data often lend themselves to the kind of time series analysis described in Chapter 10. In fact, the illustration of the multiple time series analysis by Campbell and Ross (1968) in that chapter utilized existing data on traffic fatalities in Connecticut and its surrounding states.

Sample Size Many types of documents are highly abundant. As we commented when discussing sampling, a researcher is likely to confront far more documents than can be analyzed rather than too few. This means that large samples can be employed to increase one's confidence in the results. The low cost associated with document analysis also contributes to the researcher's ability to use substantial sample sizes without encountering prohibitive costs.

Disadvantages

Variable Quality Because documents are produced for purposes other than research, their quality for research purposes is quite variable. Unless the limitations of the documents are known, as with crime statistics, researchers may have little idea of the conditions under which the data were collected or the amount of attention to quality that went into them. Researchers should, of course, investigate the issue of quality where possible so that any deficiencies in the data are discovered. When this cannot be done, we simply have to draw conclusions cautiously.

Incompleteness Documents, especially those of a historical nature, are frequently incomplete. Gaps of weeks, months, or even years are not uncommon. In addition, there can be missing data in available statistical data. What effect these gaps have on a study is often impossible to know except that confidence in the findings is reduced somewhat. Incompleteness is simply a common characteristic plaguing available data that researchers have to work around if they can.

Lack of Comparability over Time
Even though documents are commonly used in longitudinal analysis, this can be problematic. Things can change over time that create statistical artifacts in the data and render comparisons useless. We illustrated this with the New York City crime rates, which increased several fold in one month due to a change in recording procedures. Researchers need to be careful of similar kinds of changes in other data.

Bias   Because documents are produced for purposes other than research, there is no assurance that they are objective. Data from private sources, for example, may be intentionally slanted to present a particular viewpoint. A researcher blindly accepting these data could be walking into a trap. Nonstatistical documents may suffer from biased presentation as well. A good example is the corporate annual reports to stockholders, which are filled with glowing praise for management, impressive color photographs, and bright prospects for the future, with anything negative presented in the most favorable light or camouflaged in legalese.

Sampling Bias   Bias may creep into otherwise objective data during the sampling process. As we noted, sampling documents is often difficult owing to unequal population elements and hard-to-define

populations. We also commented that document sampling is frequently complex, requiring several stages. If errors or bad decisions are made in the sampling process, it is quite possible to end up with a highly biased sample that will produce misleading results.

Using Available Data in Research on Minorities

When studying emotionally charged topics such as racism or sexism, reactivity can be a very serious problem since people may be inclined to disguise their true feelings or motives if these might result in disapproval. People may deny feelings of prejudice toward minorities or women, when asked by a survey researcher about such feelings, even though they may feel some prejudice and it influences their behavior. However, one of the major benefits of available data is that it is often less reactive than other ways of studying behavior. For this reason, it may be the preferred research method, or a valued adjunct to other research methods, when studying such emotion-laden topics. We will illustrate some of the uses to which available data have been put in the study of racism and sexism.

The records of agencies and organizations often contain evidence of sexism even when those who run the organizations vehemently deny its existence. For example, David Fanshel (1976) studied sex differences in salaries and in representation in leadership positions in social work by using a membership survey conducted by the National Association of Social Workers (NASW) and data routinely collected with the application for membership to the NASW. He found that the status of women in social work is quite different from that of men. First, men were more heavily concentrated in administrative positions whereas women were more common in casework positions. Second, men earned substantially higher salaries than did women, even among those who entered the profession at the same time. Third, single women and previously married women without children were most likely to be in administrative positions, while married women with children were least likely to be administrators.

So there may be some lingering elements of sexism in the human services, and it probably would have been more difficult to detect if agency directors had been asked directly about their promotion or salary policies. It is often less reactive and more valid to measure the consequences of organizational decisions. Another way to detect the persistence of prejudices and stereotypes is to study the portrayal of people in various cultural productions such as books, magazines, or movies. During the 1970s, a study by the Michigan Women's Commission revealed that boys far outnumber girls in school books and adult males outnumber adult females (Michigan Women's Commission, 1974). In addition, many elementary school books portray men as capable of performing many more jobs than women: Men appeared in 213 different occupations, while women were pictured in only 39. The women were typically portrayed in stereotypically female occupations such as nurse or secretary, and they were frequently portrayed as working only if they were unmarried (Fisher, 1974). Even television programs reflect these attitudes: 75 percent of the male roles in prime time reflect the images of unmarried men who are "tough" and "cool." A survey of the Screen Actors Guild found that 72 percent of all roles portrayed in prime time television were played by men (Richmond-Abbott, 1983). There have been improvements in all of

this, of course, especially when efforts are made to produce materials that are clearly nonsexist in their presentation (Davis, 1984; Sullivan and O'Conner, 1988). Yet, stereotyped differences in the portrayal of men and women in books, magazines, and movies can still be found, and they offer a valuable unobtrusive measure for the detection of persistent sexism in society. (Many issues of the journal *Sex Roles* contain articles about research that used available data, typically content analysis, to explore issues of sex roles and sexism.)

Some differences in the portrayal of men and women in cultural products can be very subtle. In a creative series of studies involving an intriguing application of available data, Dane Archer and colleagues (1983) measured the amount of space in photographs devoted to people's faces. They divided the distance from the top of the head to the bottom of the chin by the distance from the top of the head to the lowest point of the body visible in the depiction. The result is a proportion with an upper limit of 1.00 (face fills entire picture) that indicates the degree to which the face is prominent in the picture. The first application of this measure was on 1750 photographs drawn from the magazines *Time, Newsweek,* and *Ms.,* and the newspapers *The San Francisco Chronicle* and *The Santa Cruz Sentinel.* Before even measuring the photos, they discovered an interesting finding: Over 60 percent of the photos were of men! When they applied their facial prominence indicator, they found another difference between the sexes: The average "face-ism" value for men was .67 and only .45 for women, indicating that the pictures of males tended to feature the face more prominently, whereas pictures of women featured more of the body; and more recent studies show that this tendency has persisted in the 1980s (Nigro et al., 1988). A subsequent study by Archer and colleagues found that this pattern held across pictures in publications from 11 other countries. Applying the indicator to paintings going back as far as 600 years showed that the pattern they had found had a long history and the difference seemed to be increasing. Just how deeply ingrained this tendency is was illustrated in another part of the study where subjects were instructed to draw a picture of a man or a woman. Consistently, and regardless of the sex of the subject, the subjects drew men with faces more prominent than for women.

What is the significance of this face-ism? It may represent another mechanism for perpetuating stereotypes about the sexes. The researchers followed up their available data study of the existence of face-ism by collecting data regarding its consequences. They printed up two sets of pictures of the same individuals, varying only in facial prominence. Sub-jects then rated the people in the pictures on a variety of characteristics. Sure enough, those depicted with more prominent faces were rated more intelligent, more ambitious, and as having a better physical appearance. In other words, the faces of men are more prominently displayed in the pictures we are surrounded with every day, and a more prominent facial display leads people unwittingly to the perception of the person as more intelligent and ambitious. The authors conclude that this face-ism could contribute to unconscious stereotyping of women as less intelligent and capable and contribute to discrimination against women. They suggest that face-ism may contribute to another stereotype: "that essential aspects of personal identity are thought to be centered in different anatomic locations in men and women. Men are represented by their heads and faces; women are represented using more of their bodies" (Archer et al., 1983, p. 733).

COMPUTERS IN RESEARCH
Computer-Assisted Content Analysis

Of all research strategies, content analysis would seem to be an unlikely candidate for computer application. The task of objectively coding communication messages to obtain data for testing hypotheses about the content of documents does not appear readily to lend itself to computerization, which is typically characterized by an emphasis on numerical codes, not words, phrases, themes, or meanings. Although the computer is not suited to all content analysis tasks, recent advances in computer technology are expanding the contribution of computer-aided content analysis to human service research activities. For example, it can be applied to analyze and monitor clinical social worker performance (Tripodi and Epstein, 1980). Other potential applications in human service settings include log entries in such settings as spouse abuse shelters and other residential facilities, self-report client logs, disciplinary proceedings in correctional institutions, as well as more traditional applications such as evaluating the content of professional journals. Computer application to such tasks has been made feasible through the development of relatively low cost microcomputers and, more importantly, the development of devices for making printed texts machine readable.

Weber (1984) describes early experiences with the problem of text encoding, that is, transforming written documents into a format that the computer can read. One project took about nine person-months to prepare a half million words and punctuation for computer analysis by using punch cards. Such an experience is hardly motivation for a human service organization to embrace content analysis! This problem of encoding is being eliminated through the development of optical scanner technology. Optical scanners can now be used to read almost any typed or printed page and transfer the text to an electronic storage medium such as tape or disk. In contrast to the labor-intensive punch card process, a sophisticated scanner such as the Kurzweil Data Entry Machine is very fast and accurate. These machines can easily cost $30,000 or more, so this is not the kind of equipment that human service organizations are going to purchase themselves. However, the Kurzweil Company in Cambridge, Massachusetts, can provide a listing of over 20 KDEM service bureaus around the country. These firms will provide scanning service for a typical price of $1 or $2 per 1000

characters. Scanners vary in their capacity to handle different kinds of type. There are modestly priced, hand-held models available for as low as $500, but these machines are not nearly as flexible or accurate as the expensive models. Because there is great interest in many fields to have technology that enables computers to read printed material, we will no doubt see advances in technology and a lowering of costs in the future.

Getting documents into the computer is only the beginning. The computer can also aid with a variety of useful analysis tasks. A basic procedure is to produce word frequency lists. The computer can rapidly produce a listing of specified words and the frequency with which they appear in the documents. It can also supply a printout of key words in their context. For example, a portion of one analysis compared 1980 Republican and Democratic Party platforms by focusing on the word "rights." The computer supplied a listing of every occurrence of the key word, including the preceding and following phrase. Researchers could then analyze these data to determine if one party used the term more than the other and if there was a difference in the kind of rights each emphasized.

A clear advantage of computerization is the ability to search through text and retrieve portions that meet specified criteria. For example, a content analysis program can readily provide all paragraphs that contain the words "poverty" and "cause" or "causes". Computer programs are now being refined to apply various category systems for classifying content of documents

(Continued on next page)

by computer. This has been a very challenging process because it is one thing to have a computer search for occurrences of single words, and quite another to devise a program that can distinguish between "mine," meaning a hole in the ground, and "mine" used as a personal pronoun. Such distinctions as these require the ability to apply meaning to words according to their context. The ability of machines to make such distinctions is known as *artificial intelligence*, or AI. It is expected that more complex content analysis will be done by computer as AI becomes more available.

Although exotic computer technology may be the answer to advanced content analysis problems, it is also possible to do some content analysis using standard data-base programs on microcomputers. Certain kinds of documents such as case records readily lend themselves to storage in data-base programs for agency administrative purposes. Because record sorting is a basic function of data-base programs, such procedures as identifying key words and sorting records based on them for content analysis purposes is a logical extension of the record management function for which the programs were designed.

≡ Main Points

• Available data include both statistical data collected by others and documents, which include any form of communication.

• Content analysis quantifies and organizes the qualitative and unsystematic information contained in documents.

• Content analysis is essentially a form of measurement making the issues of validity and reliability paramount.

• Document analysis will normally include some form of sampling procedure, which must be performed carefully for the sake of representativeness.

• Document analysis offers the advantages of low cost, nonreactivity, ability to study otherwise inaccessible subjects, easy longitudinal analysis, and often large samples.

• Problems in using available data include the variable quality of the data, incomplete data, changes in data over time, possible bias in data, and possible sampling bias.

• The analysis of available data is often less reactive than other research methods, and this can make it very useful in the study of emotionally charged topics such as racism and sexism where people may be inclined to hide their true feelings and emotions.

≡ Important Terms for Review

available data
coding
content analysis
data archives
missing data
secondary analysis

For Further Reading

Fanshel, D. *On the Road to Permanency: An Expanded Data Base for Service to Children in Foster Care.* New York: Child Welfare League of America, 1982.
This book is an illustration of the type of human service research project that can be carried out by using a well-constructed agency information system data base.

Jacob, H. *Using Published Data: Errors and Remedies.* Beverly Hills, Calif.: Sage, 1984.
An excellent guide to the problems and pitfalls of using existing data sets. The book focuses primarily on issues of validity and reliability.

Price, J. *Handbook of Organizational Measurement.* Lexington, Mass.: Heath, 1972.
This volume describes a diversity of ways of measuring organizational variables, many of which are based on available data.

Rutman, L., ed. *Evaluation Research Methods*, 2d ed. Beverly Hills, Calif.: Sage, 1984.
Although devoted to evaluation in general, it also contains an excellent discussion of how to make agency information systems of maximum utility for research purposes.

Webb, J., D. Campbell, R. Schwartz, L. Sechrest, and J. Grove. *Nonreactive Measures in Social Research*, 2d ed. Chicago: Rand McNally, 1981.
A discussion of the advantages and problems in the use of nonreactive measures, with two chapters devoted to archival records.

Exercises for Class Discussion

8.1   A valuable source of available data is agency records. If you are in a field placement, an internship, or doing volunteer work in a human service agency, ask the agency to provide sample copies of required and routine data collected on clients. Of course, you should be certain to obtain the forms and reports in a way that will not infringe on client or service-user confidentiality.

a.   Compare the types of information gathered in the agency with which you are affiliated to that gathered by other students in other agencies. Can you think of some specific research questions you could explore with these data? Can you suggest some changes in agency data-gathering procedures that might produce more data for research at little additional effort?

b.   What steps are required in order to obtain existing data on clients so as to meet ethical safeguards for confidentiality?

8.2   A researcher is interested in studying the impact of changing economic conditions on the retention of minority students in college. The researcher's hypothesis is that an economic recession will have a greater negative effect on the retention and graduation of minorities than on nonminority students.

Using your own institution as the site for the project, what sources of data, already available in some data bank in your institution, might be used in such a study? What problems do you envision with these data in terms of sampling, unit of analysis, and levels of measurement?

8.3   A concern of human service professionals is the negative portrayal of public welfare service users in the media. Is the image of welfare recipients really negative? Has there been a trend toward improvement? Does the image portrayed improve or deteriorate in conjunction with changes in the national economy?

These are questions that might be approached through a content analysis of the news media. Develop a research project that could be conducted in your community that would utilize content analysis to answer these questions.

a. Suggest what elements you think the population being studied contains.

b. Identify some sampling issues the researcher would confront.

c. What different problems are involved in answering the second and third questions posed in the above paragraph in contrast to the first question about negative image?

d. Assume the research is confined to daily newspapers. Suggest some possibilities for the unit of analysis.

e. How could operational definitions of "negative image" and "welfare recipient" be developed?

9

Observational Techniques

All methods of data collection involve some form of observation, but the term *observational technique* is used in this chapter to delineate a special type of data collection. **Observational techniques** refer to the collection of data through direct visual or auditory experience of behavior. With observational techniques, which include video or audio recordings of behavior, the researcher actually sees or hears the behavior or words that are the data for the research. Surveys, in contrast, involve people's *reports* to the researcher about what they said, did, or felt. With surveys and available data, the researcher does not directly observe what will be the focus of the research.

People often believe that direct observation provides us with a more accurate or honest picture of reality because we "see it ourselves" without anything to interfere with our perceptions. This belief, however, can be highly misleading, as Alice's experiences before her journey through Wonderland illustrate. Alice introduced her black kitten to a place seen through the mirror above her fireplace, a place Alice called the "Looking-glass House":

> Now if you'll only attend, Kitty, and not talk so much, I'll tell you all my ideas about Looking-glass House. First, there's the room you can see through the glass—that's just the same as our

drawing-room, only the things go the other way. I can see all of it when I get upon a chair—all but the bit just behind the fireplace. Oh! I do so wish I could see *that* bit! I want so much to know whether they've a fire in the winter: you never *can* tell, you know, unless our fire smokes, and then smoke comes up in that room too—but that may be only pretence, just to make it look as if they had a fire. Well then, the books are something like our books, only the words go the wrong way: I know *that*, because I've held up one of our books to the glass, and then they hold up one in the other room (Carroll, 1946, pp. 8–10).

In her quest to know the Looking-glass House, Alice is inextricably trapped and limited by her perspective. She has tantalizing glimpses of that other world, but she can't see all of it no matter how hard she struggles. Distressingly, the clues she does observe—such as smoke seeming to come from a fire—are difficult to interpret. Do they mean what she thinks (or wants) them to mean? The Looking-glass House is forever partially shrouded in mystery and dissimulation.

Scientific research and practice in the human services also involve peering through a looking glass—making observations of a world with our own, admittedly frail, perceptual apparatus. What is outside ourselves is as alien to us as the Looking-glass House is to Alice. We, too, are trapped by our perspective. We, too, cannot see all that we are convinced is "out there." Observation is difficult, it is tricky, and it can be faulty—but it is at the core of both scientific investigation and human service practice. Because of this, we need to take a lesson from Alice and approach observation in a careful and systematic fashion. Alice seems serenely unaware that it is *her perspective* that shapes the world she observes through the mirror. We need to recognize the force of our own perspectives and adopt observational techniques that minimize their distorting effect. This chapter will discuss observational techniques in scientific research, beginning with the different types of observations that can be made. Next a discussion will follow of some important issues related to observation, such as how to record observations and the validity and reliability of observations. The advantages and disadvantages of observational techniques will also be assessed. Finally, we will suggest some lessons that scientific observation can provide for those making observations in practice settings.

Designs for Observation

Observational methods vary in terms of the extent to which the investigator *participates* in the activities of the people being observed. There are two general possibilities: that of participant observer and that of nonparticipant observer. Each technique has its unique difficulties, advantages, and disadvantages.

Participant Observation

Participant observation is a method in which the researcher is a part of, and participates in, the activities of the people, group, or situation that is being stud-

ied (Burgess, 1984; Lofland and Lofland, 1984). In some cases, the investigator may have belonged to the group prior to the start of the research and can use this position as a group member to collect data. For example, a social worker might be interested in staff adaptation to antidiscrimination legislation in hiring. If this person is on the agency personnel committee, such a position might serve as the context for participant observation. As new staff are hired, the social worker could observe the reactions of the other staff in dealing with the new regulations. In other cases, a researcher must first gain access to a group in order to be a participant observer. This was done by the anthropologist Sue Estroff in an effort to learn more about the daily lives and problems of ex-mental patients. She joined for two years in the lives of a group of deinstitutionalized mental patients, experiencing the drudgery and degradation of their daily routine (Estroff, 1978). She worked at low-paying jobs (such as slipping rings onto drapery rods) that were the lot of these ex-patients. She took the powerful antipsychotic drugs that were routinely administered to them and that had distinctive side effects such as hand tremors and jiggling legs. And she experienced the extreme depression and despair that result when one suddenly stops taking these potent drugs. From her position as participant in the subculture of these mental patients, she could observe the con games that characterized the relationships between patients and mental health professionals.

Through this type of participant observation, practitioners have access to a view of client groups that cannot be gained in an interview or therapy session. It is a unique view because it is seen from the perspective of the client, a perspective that is especially valuable to anyone who works with groups that are stigmatized or commonly misunderstood by both practitioners and laypeople. Like Alice, who could not clearly see the whole room in the Looking-glass House, human service workers can by no means clearly see the lives of their clients from their position as practitioners. In a sense, Estroff climbed *through* the "mirror" in much the same way little Alice did. Though many practitioners may not have the opportunity to engage in such observations personally, there are many such research efforts by behavioral scientists that can be utilized to develop a better understanding of client groups with whom the practitioner will be working. And human service professionals should seek out opportunities to conduct this kind of research themselves in order to understand particular groups or subcultures. In fact, practitioners might consider periodically engaging in participant observation of their clients, if it is possible, in order to detect ways in which the practitioner perspective may limit understanding of client groups.

Verstehen versus Positivism   Proponents of participant observation argue that it is the only approach that offers the investigator access to a particular type of data: the subjective experiences of those under study. This reflects a controversy in social research concerning the proper orientation toward human behavior. In a simplified form, this controversy pits the *verstehen* approach against the *positivist* approach.

The sociologist Max Weber posited that the subjective meanings that people attach to what they do are an important part of human social behavior (Weber, 1957). In order to understand human behavior, he argued, we must study not only what people do, but also how they think,

feel, and subjectively experience what happens to them. Weber proposed the method of *verstehen* to accomplish this goal. **Verstehen** refers to subjective understanding, or the observer's effort to view and understand a situation from the perspective of the people themselves. Given their culture, values, and past experiences, how do they feel about what is happening to them? Weber argued that we cannot really understand social behavior until we achieve such subjective understanding.

The opposite orientation toward human social behavior is **positivism:** the position that human behavior should be studied only in terms of behavior that can be observed and recorded by means of some objective technique. Positivists do not necessarily deny the existence or importance of subjective experiences, but they do question whether the subjective interpretations of the verstehen method have any scientific validity. By limiting study to observable behaviors and using objective techniques, positivists hope to ensure that research methods are systematic, repeatable, and open to refutation by other scientists.

Proponents of participant observation argue that it is the only method that enables the researcher to approximate verstehen, an understanding of the subjective experiences of people. Of course, actual access to such experience is impossible; thoughts and feelings, by their very nature, are private. Even when someone *tells* you how he or she feels, this person has objectified that subjective experience into *words* and thus changed it. Participant observers, however, can gain some insight into those subjective experiences by immersing themselves in the lives and daily experiences of the people they study. By experiencing the same culture, the same values, the same hopes and fears, researchers are in a better position to take on the point of view of these people. However, despite its focus on subjective experiences, participant observation is still empirical in the sense that it is grounded in observation, and those who use this method are also concerned about issues of reliability and validity. Those who use participant observation consider it no less systematic or scientific than the more positivistic research techniques.

Consider an example. An investigator interested in the causes of poverty and unemployment might gain great insight into this problem by using participant observation to study such conditions. Anthropologist Elliot Liebow (1967) did precisely this. After spending considerable time with a group of black men who hung around a street corner in Washington, D.C., Liebow wrote an account of their lives that is filled with compassion and understanding. He gained considerable comprehension of how the social conditions these men faced generated intense feelings of hopelessness that permeated all parts of their lives. He learned why these men worked little, if at all. The only jobs open to them were either physically demanding or very menial and low-paying. He also came to understand how their past history of failure had left them lacking in the self-confidence necessary to address new challenges. Their conception of themselves as failures was reinforced daily by their inability to support a family or keep a good job. Through using the participant observer technique, Liebow was better able to discover why, from their own perspective, these men found it difficult to change their lot in life. Proponents of participant observation argue that other, more "objective" methods, such as interviews or available statistical data on unemployment, would not have

been able to uncover this depth of feelings.

So once again, we see that the research question—in this case, the need for subjective understanding to explain something—influences the selection of a participant observation research design over other types of observation or over nonobservational techniques. Had the research question called for data of a more positivist nature, then a different design might have been called for. We will see later in this chapter that some observational techniques do lend themselves to the positivist approach.

There is another way in which the research question influences the choice of participant observation. This observational technique is often selected when the research question is exploratory in nature and theoretical development does not enable researchers to spell out relevant concepts or develop precise hypotheses. Participant observation permits the researcher to view human behavior as it occurs in the natural environment without the restrictions of preconceived notions or explanations. Through observation, the researcher can begin to formulate concepts, variables, and hypotheses that seem relevant to the topic and grounded in the actual behavior of people.

Observer Roles In many types of research, the relationship between the researcher and those participating in the research is fairly clear-cut. In surveys, for example, participants know who the researchers are and that they as respondents are providing data to the researchers. In observational research—and especially with participant observation—the researcher–participant relationship becomes more problematic in that it can take a number of different forms. There are two critical issues here: the extent to which the observer will change the setting that is being observed and the extent to which people should be informed that they are being used for research purposes. The way in which a researcher resolves these issues determines the nature of the observer–participant relationship for a given research project.

A participant observer is a part of the activities being studied and so is in a position to influence the direction of those activities. For example, the anthropologist Sue Estroff might have been inclined to organize the deinstitutionalized mental patients she studied into a lobbying group demanding better living conditions and improved treatment from mental health professionals. Yet had she done this early in her participant observation, would it have interfered with her research goals? Would she have learned all the sources of despair and degradation that these people experienced? Would she have learned how such groups, without benefit of an intervening anthropologist, adapt to their plight? The resolution of this issue of the extent of intervention, of course, rests partly on the research question. If Estroff were interested in how such groups adapt without outside aid, then she should limit her influence on the group, even though humanitarian values might push her toward involvement. On the other hand, if she wanted to assess effective strategies for improving the lot of such groups, then intervention on her part would be called for by the research question. Human service providers, in particular, need to be sensitive to this issue because an important part of their role is intervention. Providers need to recognize that intervention may at times be counterproductive to research goals.

This problem of the degree of intervention is often referred to as a question of whether the researcher is, first and foremost a *participant*, or an *observer* (Gold, 1958). Which of these two aspects of the role should one emphasize? Let us look at each side of the issue. Those who would emphasize the importance of the *participation* of the observer argue that the investigator plays two roles—that of scientist *and* that of group member. In order to comprehend fully the activities of the group and the dynamics of the situation, the researcher must become fully involved in the group. Otherwise, group members may not confide in the researcher, or he or she may not become aware of the meanings that various actions and objects have for the group. In order to become fully involved, the researcher must act like any other group member—and this means intervening in those situations in which other group members might do so.

On the other side of the issue, those who emphasize *observation* over participation would argue that the more fully one becomes a group member, the less objective one becomes. The real danger is that researchers will become so immersed in the group that they take on completely the perspective of the group and can no longer view the situation from a scientific perspective (Shupe and Bromley, 1980). This is always a danger in participant observation. In fact, some researchers caution against the use of participant observation for this very reason. For example, one criminology professor joined a local police force in order to learn more about the police work that he talked about in his lectures. Over a period of time, he became so caught up in the world of the police that he could no longer view them objectively and critically, and any semblance of scientific investigation was lost. He identified with the police and viewed the world as a police officer rather than as a researcher (see Kirkham, 1976, and Manning, 1978, for a discussion of this case). Similarly, human service practitioners must guard against becoming so identified with their clients that they lose objectivity in evaluating situations. Imagine a counselor in a rape crisis center who sees many women who have experienced the terror and humiliation of sexual assault only to be further humiliated by a clumsy or insensitive police staff. Improving the capacity of the criminal justice system to respond with sensitivity to victims would be an appropriate goal. However, the counselor's empathy with victims could so arouse her hostility that the worker might become incapable of working with police on a professional basis. Most participant observers attempt to strike a balance between total immersion and loss of objectivity on the one hand and total separation with its consequent loss of information on the other.

The second critical issue in the researcher–participant relationship is both practical and ethical: To what extent should the people being studied be informed of the investigator's research purposes? (Punch, 1986.) This is an especially troubling problem in participant observation because in some cases fully informing people would undermine the researcher's ability to gather accurate data. For example, a study of staff treatment of patients in a mental hospital was conducted by having researchers admitted to the hospital as patients without informing the staff of their research purposes (Rosenhan, 1973). There seems little doubt in this case that the hospital staff would have behaved quite differently had they known they were under surveillance. Thus, some researchers take the position that concealment is sometimes necessary in order to conduct scientific work and that researchers must

judge whether the scientific gain justifies the deception of human beings and any potential injury—social or psychological—they might suffer. Others, however, hold adamantly to the position that any research on human beings must include "informed consent": The people involved should be fully informed concerning the purposes of the research, any possible dangers or consequences, and the credentials of the researcher. Anything less, they argue, would be unethical and immoral because it tricks people into cooperation and may lead to undesirable consequences of which they are not aware. This ethical dilemma is a complex one and is dealt with at greater length in Chapter 3.

In a classic piece on observational research, Raymond Gold (1958) has identified three distinct observer roles that can emerge depending on how the issues of observer influence and informed consent are resolved: complete participant, participant-as-observer, and observer-as-participant. The major distinguishing feature of the *complete participant role* is that the observer's status as observer is not revealed to those who are being studied. The observer enters a group under the guise of being just another member and essentially plays that role while conducting the study. The researcher must be able to sustain this pretense for long periods because studies using the complete participant role are usually characterized by lengthy involvement with the group studied. The complete participant role has proved itself valuable in studying groups that otherwise might be closed to research if the observer's true identity were known. Drug users (Becker, 1953), homosexuals (Humphreys, 1970), drug dealers (Adler, 1985) and members of the Satanic Church (Moody, 1976) are among such groups that have been studied by using the complete participant role.

The *participant-as-observer* differs from the complete participant role in that the researcher's status as observer is revealed to those who are being studied. In this role, the observer enters a group and participates in their routines but is known to be doing so for research purposes. As in the case of the complete participant role, the participant-as-observer will spend a considerable amount of time observing in the group being studied. The participant-as-observer role has found its major use in community research. This is probably due to the large size of the groups involved and the need for direct access to information that the complete participant might find difficult or too time-consuming to obtain while maintaining a disguise. Whyte's (1955) classic study *Street Corner Society* is a fine example of the use of the participant-as-observer role. Research in Practice 9.1 illustrates the use of the participant-as-observer role in a human service context.

RESEARCH IN PRACTICE 9.1
Program Evaluation: Participant Observation of a Token Economy Program Among Schizophrenics

> Remember, these are locked wards. These are the worst patients. We chose the worst so we could prove our program works.
> —organizer of a token economy program

> I think this system stinks. They can go shove the whole thing as far as I'm concerned.
> —patient in a token economy program (Biklen, 1976, pp. 53, 59)

These starkly contrasting views of a token economy program illustrate one dimension of the controversy that has swirled around such change efforts. Token economy is a form of behavior modification that has been trumpeted by some as a corrective for many social and personal ills and denounced by others as an instrument of coercion and repression. Token economy programs have been used as therapeutic efforts with many types of people, such as the developmentally disabled, the mentally ill, and criminal offenders.

There are a number of questions that could be asked about these programs. Do they work? Is it ethical to use such admittedly manipulative therapies with involuntary clients? While these issues are being debated in the professional literature, there is another dimension of the problem that often receives little attention: What do the recipients of behavior modification programs think of them? Do they share the optimistic views of the program organizers that token economies will usher in positive changes in behavior? Or do the patients echo, each in their own distinctive style, that they should "shove the whole thing"?

This concern for the client's view of behavior modification was the catalyst for a research project designed and carried out by Douglas Biklen (1976). To gain this important, but too often neglected, client view, Biklen developed a research strategy based on unstructured participant observation. He spent five months observing a token economy program among schizophrenic women in a locked ward of a state mental hospital. Biklen adopted an observer role that fell somewhere between that of participant-as-observer and that of complete observer. He explained his presence to the patients by saying that he was there "to study mental hospital life and change in an institution" (Biklen, 1976, p. 54). However, he did not participate in the token economy program. He observed staff–patient interchanges that were a part of the program, and patients knew they were being observed. With such a stance, he hoped to avoid being identified with any one faction, such as the patients, the attendants, or the supervisory staff. This would place him in the most advantageous position to collect data regarding how both staff and patients perceived the program.

Participant observation was appropriate for Biklen's research because his study was exploratory in nature and specific hypotheses had not yet been developed. Biklen observed patient–staff encounters in three-hour shifts, taking detailed field notes of his observations immediately after each session. He analyzed the field notes himself but guarded against unreasonable bias by subjecting his analysis and interpretation to the critical scrutiny of his colleagues—social scientists, educators, and psychologists. From this, he was able to develop hypotheses grounded in his data.

From his position as an outsider, Biklen observed elements of the token economy program that those organiz-

ing the program failed to perceive. For example, staff and client perceptions of the program were quite different from one another. The staff placed great emphasis on what they called "activation" of patients, and helping became operationalized as "activating" the patient—getting them to move, talk, play checkers, or do anything else. In many cases, Biklen found, the patients didn't want to be "activated" and didn't perceive it as "helping" them. Their response to this program—which they perceived as being thrust unwanted into their lives—was one of anger, ironic humor, or withdrawal. In addition, the patients viewed the rewards offered by the staff—cigarettes and canteen privileges—as dehumanizing.

From his observations, Biklen raises a vexing issue: Do token economy programs—with their complex system of rewards, privileges, and denials meted out by the staff based on their judgment of the patient's conformity to certain standards—help the patient? Or do they merely intensify institutional control over patient behavior under the guise of "scientific" behavior change? Biklen's participant observation research makes us acutely aware that clients—all clients—have a legitimate perspective that needs to be considered:

> I sought to treat the patients not as "psychotics" but as people who, like other participants in the setting, had perspectives that were relevant for themselves [Biklen, 1976, p. 54].

Participant observation research is one very valuable scientific tool for learning about that perspective.

The *observer-as-participant role* is similar to the participant-as-observer role in that the observer's true status is known to those being studied but differs with regard to the length of time the observer spends with the group. As noted, the participant-as-observer role assumes a lengthy period of observation. The observer-as-participant role involves brief contact with the group being studied, possibly for as short as one day. This brief contact tends to preclude the deep, insightful results that characterize studies utilizing the two previous roles. The observer-as-participant role is likely to generate more shallow, superficial results. In fact, the brief contact that characterizes this role may lead the observer to misunderstand aspects of the group being studied. Because of these problems, the observer-as-participant role has been less popular for conducting serious social research.

Steps in Participant Observation Research Any participant observation research will encounter certain common problems. These problems are dealt with by organizing the investigation into a series of steps (Bailey, 1987). The first step, of course, is to establish the specific goals of the research and to decide that participant observation is the most appropriate research strategy to use. If you are trying to gain a comprehensive understanding of the values, perceptions, and other subjective elements of a particular group or subculture, then participant observation may well be the most appropriate mode of attack.

The second step is to decide which specific group to study. If you are interested in ex-mental patients living in residential care centers, with which groups of people will you be involved? One way this issue is commonly decided is simply by the accessibility of the group, but representativeness may also be considered.

The third step is the very challenging one of gaining entry into the group to be studied. In the complete participant role, this step may be less of a problem because the people do not know they are being studied. However, you must be sufficiently like those studied to gain access. In the other participant roles, however, you must find some way to convince the people to agree to accept your involvement as a researcher. There are a number of ways in which the likelihood that people will cooperate can be increased (Dean, Eichhorn, and Dean, 1969; Johnson, 1975). One way is to gain the cooperation of those with more status and power in the group and use your relationship with them to gain access to others. It would be best, for example, to approach the directors of a mental health center and enlist their aid before contacting caseworkers and ward staff. Another way to increase cooperation is to present your reasons for conducting the research to people in a way that seems plausible to them and makes sense in their frame of reference. Esoteric or abstract scientific goals are unlikely to be very appealing to an agency director or to a single parent struggling on welfare. You should emphasize that your major concern is understanding their thoughts and behaviors as legitimate, acceptable, and appropriate. Nothing will close doors faster than the hint that you intend to *evaluate* the group. The door of a welfare recipient may be opened if you tell him or her you are studying the difficulties confronting parents on welfare; it will surely be slammed if you say you want to separate the "good" welfare recipients from the "bad."

Cooperation is also enhanced if you have some means of legitimizing yourself as a researcher. This might be done through an affiliation with a university that supports the study or an agency that has an interest in the research. In a study of a venereal disease clinic, for example, Joseph Sheley (1976) gained entrance because he was involved with a larger community study of venereal disease. Such legitimation can backfire, of course, if the group you hope to study is suspicious of, or hostile toward, the organization with which you are affiliated. (Sheley, for example, although allowed into the clinic, found himself having a degree of "outsider" status because of his association with the communtity VD study.) Finally, it may be necessary to use informants to gain entry into some groups. An informant is an insider who can introduce you to others in the group, ease your acceptance into the group, and help you interpret how the group views the world. Especially with informal subcultures, the informant technique can be a valuable approach.

The fourth step in participant observation is to develop rapport and trust with the people being studied so that they will serve as useful and accurate sources of information. This can be time-consuming, trying, and traumatic. It is a problem with which the human service professional can readily identify. The community organizer attempting to gain the trust of migrant workers, the substance abuse worker dealing with a narcotics addict, and the child welfare worker running a group home for girls can all attest to the importance of establishing rapport. Although in many cases the human service worker can express a sincere desire to help as a means of establishing rapport, the researcher cannot always employ this approach because the research goals may not include the provision of such help. In the initial stages of the re-

search, people are likely to be distant if not outright distrustful. You are likely to make errors and social gaffes that offend the people you have joined. More than one participant observation effort has had to be curtailed because the investigator inadvertently alienated the people being studied.

There are a number of elements involved in developing rapport or trust among one's informants (Wax, 1952; Dean, 1954; and Johnson, 1975). Rapport can emerge if the informants and group members view the investigator as a basically nice person who will do them no harm. It matters little if the informants know of or agree with the research goals—only that they develop a positive attitude toward the investigator. Trust and rapport can also emerge if the investigator shows through behavior that he or she agrees with, or at least has some sympathy for, the perspective of the people being studied. If you join your field contacts in some of their routine activities, such as drinking beer or playing cards, they are likely to view you as one who accepts them and can be trusted. Here, of course, the researcher must balance the need for acceptance against personal and professional standards of behavior. Finally, rapport can be enhanced if the relationship between investigator and group members is reciprocal; that is, both the observer and the group members have something that the other needs and wants. You might, for example, gain scientific data from your informants while they, in turn, hope to gain some publicity and attendant public concern from the publication of your results.

The fifth step in participant observation is to observe and record. This can only truly begin once you have established sufficient rapport to ensure that you are gathering useful data. We will discuss recording observations later in this chapter, but first we need to look at nonparticipant forms of observation.

Unobtrusive Observation

Some research questions call for or require the investigator to refrain from participation in the group being investigated. There may be concern, for example, that the intrusive impact of an outsider might change the behavior of group members in ways detrimental to the research question. In such cases, the relationship adopted by the investigator would be what Gold labels the *complete observer* role—the observer has no direct contact with those being observed. One way of doing such nonparticipant observation is to use an observational technique that has been called **unobtrusive** or **nonreactive observation:** Those under study are not aware that they are being studied, and the investigator does not change their behavior by his or her presence (Webb et al., 1981; Sechrest and Belew, 1983). Unobtrusive observation can take a number of forms: hidden observation, disguised observation, and physical traces.

Hidden Observation In some research projects, it is possible to observe behavior from a vantage point that is obscured from the view of those under observation. This might be done by observing people through a one-way mirror or by filming them with a hidden camera. For example, one could study the interaction between a client and a practitioner by recording interactions without their knowledge. However, there are problems with this type of observation. First, it is not *truly* unobtrusive if the counselor (who is presumably a part of, or at least willing to cooperate with, the research project) is aware of the

observation. All people, including trained counselors, have a tendency to react differently when they are being observed—they try to put their best foot forward or to behave in a fashion that will be acceptable to the observer. So, in the ideal hidden observation, all subjects should be unaware that they are being watched. One way that this can be achieved is to inform the counselor that he or she will be observed at some point during a given time period, say, one month. In this way, the counselor is unsure at any particular time whether observation is in progress. Furthermore, if a sufficiently long time period is specified, it becomes more difficult for people to behave "unnaturally" throughout the study.

A second problem with hidden observation is with one-way mirrors: People have become more sophisticated about such devices. Through watching police interrogations on television or being a subject in some experiment, many people have come to realize that mirrors can be used in this fashion and immediately become suspicious when in the presence of a mirror in a setting in which someone might be interested in studying them. When weighing the use of such a device, investigators should consider whether people are likely to see through the guise. If they do, the unobtrusive nature of the observation has been compromised.

Disguised Observation With some types of behavior, it is possible to observe people in a natural setting, but without participating and without revealing that one is observing them. Any setting in which one can be present and not participate without calling attention to himself or herself is a potential scene for disguised observation. One setting, for example, that might lend itself to such disguised observation is a drop-in center

(Westhues, 1972). Because the atmosphere of such centers is usually casual with people constantly coming and going or sitting and waiting, it is possible for an investigator to be present and observe without raising much suspicion. There are many data that can be collected in such settings simply through observation: sex and age of clients, frequency of visits to the center, and the like. Such data might be part of an exploratory study, or they might be part of an hypothesis-testing effort.

One intriguing type of disguised observation was done by a group of investigators interested in alcohol-related aggressive behavior (Graham et al., 1980). They decided that information could best be gathered through an unobtrusive observation of the behavior of people as they consumed alcohol in various bars in Vancouver, British Columbia. Teams of observers spent from 40 to 56 hours per week making observations in drinking establishments. Each team consisted of a male–female pair. They would enter an establishment, locate a table with a good view of the saloon, and order a drink. They made every effort not to influence the people in the bar in any way. We would consider such research nonparticipant, rather than participant, because the investigators made efforts to have no contact with, or influence on, the behavior of the patrons. At times, this would be impossible—a patron would wander over to their table and engage them in a conversation. In those cases, they quickly terminated the observations and left the bar. In some other ways, one might question the unobtrusive character of their observation: The female observer was often the only white female in the bar (the others being Native Americans), the observers were sometimes a small island of sobriety in a sea of drunkenness, and

there were often social class differences in the dress and behavior of the observers. Nonetheless, their impact on the behavior of the clientele was probably minimal, so we can consider this disguised, nonparticipant observation.

Physical Traces.   Physical traces refer to the physical objects or evidence that result from people's activities that can be used as data to test hypotheses. This is commonly done in police investigations in which fingerprints, tire tracks, dirt stains, and the like are investigated. (It is in this realm that a scientific investigator is most likely to feel like a fledgling Sherlock Holmes.) Although such methods are less common in social research, an investigator with ingenuity and an unrestrained imagination can devise ways to utilize such observation. There are two types of physical traces. *Erosion measures* involve the degree to which some materials are worn, eroded, or used up. For example, nurses making home visits commonly observe the level of medicine in medicine bottles as an unobtrusive indicator of whether the patient is taking the prescribed amount.

Accretion measures are those involving materials that are deposited or accumulated because of human activity. For example, the archaeologist William Rathje (Rathje and McCarthy, 1977) directed a project devoted to the study of modern household refuse as an accretion measure. Sometimes called "garbology," this research had as its purpose learning more about contemporary civilization by studying the things that we throw out in our garbage. Rathje provided his assistants with lab coats, surgical masks, gloves, and appropriate immunizations before sending them out to inspect people's garbage. The items in the refuse were sorted along a number of dimensions: whether an object was food, drugs, or something else; how much it weighed; cost; brand name; and the like. Such a study can serve a number of purposes. First, it can serve as a check on what a respondent tells an interviewer. If a person claims to consume a few cans of beer a day, inspection of refuse can validate or refute that claim. Second, it can measure people's responses to various social and economic changes. As food prices rise, one can measure the changing patterns of food consumption by people of various social classes. Kinsey used accretion studies in the form of graffiti in public toilets as part of his classic study of human sexuality (Kinsey et al., 1953). From such graffiti one can learn much about a populace, such as prejudice and animosity toward certain groups. There is a tendency to ignore things such as garbage as unimportant by-products of human activities and to disparage accretions such as graffiti as simply the pornographic meanderings of a demented mind. Yet we should constantly remind ourselves that these things—no matter how odd or repugnant they may be to some—are the traces of human social activity, and in that context they have meaning. Human service workers should be sensitive to the meaning and importance of all human behavior. Many of these products can be the focus of unobtrusive research.

Physical traces are not commonly used by themselves. However, in conjunction with other data collection efforts, they can add a valuable dimension to one's knowledge of certain social phenomena. Through such nonreactive techniques, it is possible to discover some aspects of a problem that one is unlikely to find through more reactive measures.

Nonparticipant observation can be a valuable observational technique because it provides the investigator with access to behavior in social settings that has not been disturbed or changed as a result of scientific scrutiny. However, nonparticipant observation is highly behavioristic in that it is largely limited to the observation of visible behaviors. As such, it is not conducive to linking behavior with subjective or symbolic meanings important to people. Thus, nonparticipant observation is often used as an adjunct to research methods more capable of discovering these meanings.

Other Types of Observation

There are many forms of observation other than participant and unobtrusive. In fact, any time researchers look, listen, and record what they observe, they are engaging in observational research. For example, observation can be the primary mode of data collection in experimental settings where we would record the changes in behavior that result from our manipulation of an independent variable. (Experiments will be discussed in detail in Chapter 10.) Observation also plays an important part in the activities of practitioners who are seeking some behavior change in clients. This can often take the form of single-subject designs, which will be presented in Chapter 11.

One way in which observational settings differ from one another is in terms of the degree of structure imposed by the researcher on people's activities in the setting. In participant and unobtrusive observation, people are usually left to behave as they wish, with little guidance from the researcher. Experimental observation, on the other hand, is a more systematic observation in which researchers assign people very precise tasks to accomplish. Normally, the degree of structure imposed is greater in hypothesis-testing research and less in exploratory research. Whatever their specific form, all observational techniques raise certain issues that must be addressed by the researchers. It is to these issues that we now turn our attention.

Issues in Observation

Because human perceptions are limited and frail—recall Alice's view of the Looking-glass House—observational research needs to be conducted in a way that reduces misperception and increases the accuracy of the data. We will discuss problems of accuracy in terms of four issues: recording observations, sampling, the validity and reliability of observations, and the problem of reactivity.

Recording Observations

Modes of recording observations vary in terms of how structured they are. In their more systematic form, they involve coding sheets whereas field notes are the less structured variety.

Coding Sheets Observational research normally involves a process of **coding,** or categorizing behaviors into a limited number of categories. To do this, it is desirable to specify as clearly as possible the behaviors to be observed or counted during data collection. When this can be done, the use of coding sheets is desirable. A *coding sheet* is simply a form designed to facilitate categorizing and counting of behaviors. For example, a typical coding sheet would have a listing of various behaviors with blanks following them in which the behaviors could be checked as they occur. If duration of a behavior is also important, additional blanks would be provided to record the timing of the behaviors.

The code sheet for a particular research project is likely to be a unique and highly specific document that reflects the special concerns of that project. Nevertheless, there are a number of coding schemes that have sufficient generality that they can be useful in a number of different settings. For example, one coding scheme that has been applied to a diversity of research projects was developed by the sociologist Robert F. Bales (1952) to study the elements of social interaction in small, face-to-face groups. As can be seen in Figure 9.1, Bales's categories are very specific and behavioral: They refer to behaviors that the coder is to look for, such as jokes, laughs, concurs, withholds help, and the like. Bales's coding categories emerged from his operationalization of social processes and interactional strategies common to all groups. Bales argues that all behavior in groups can be classified as relating to either task issues (instrumental or goal-oriented behavior) or social–emotional issues (behavior relating to the expression of feelings or the integration of motivations). Furthermore, all groups must contend with six separate problem areas in accomplishing these task and social–emotional goals (listed at the bottom of Fig. 9.1). With this coding scheme, a profile of any group can be developed in relation to these issues and processes.

Table 9.1 presents a coding scheme, with similarities to that of Bales, that was used in a study of group work among institutionalized elderly. The goal of the research was to devise and evaluate intervention strategies that would increase people's participation in group activity. At each group meeting, two observers sat

Problem Areas:

Observation Categories:

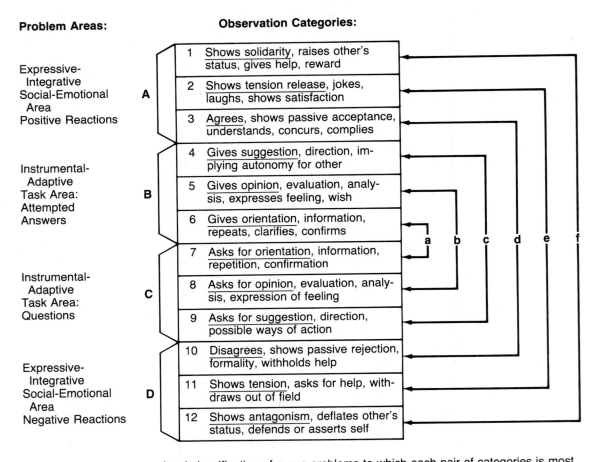

Expressive-
Integrative
Social-Emotional
Area
Positive Reactions

A

1 Shows solidarity, raises other's status, gives help, reward

2 Shows tension release, jokes, laughs, shows satisfaction

3 Agrees, shows passive acceptance, understands, concurs, complies

Instrumental-
Adaptive
Task Area:
Attempted
Answers

B

4 Gives suggestion, direction, implying autonomy for other

5 Gives opinion, evaluation, analysis, expresses feeling, wish

6 Gives orientation, information, repeats, clarifies, confirms

Instrumental-
Adaptive
Task Area:
Questions

C

7 Asks for orientation, information, repetition, confirmation

8 Asks for opinion, evaluation, analysis, expression of feeling

9 Asks for suggestion, direction, possible ways of action

Expressive-
Integrative
Social-Emotional
Area
Negative Reactions

D

10 Disagrees, shows passive rejection, formality, withholds help

11 Shows tension, asks for help, withdraws out of field

12 Shows antagonism, deflates other's status, defends or asserts self

A subclassification of group problems to which each pair of categories is most relevant:

a Problems of orientation   d Problems of decision
b Problems of evaluation   e Problems of tension-management
c Problems of control   f Problems of integration

Figure 9.1 Categories for the Observation of Social Interaction

adjacent to the group where they could observe interaction without interfering with the group (a modified form of non-participant observation). Each observer had a stopwatch and a coding sheet (see Fig. 9.2). Behaviors were recorded on the coding sheet at one-minute intervals for the group members and at one-half minute intervals for the group worker who led each group. In this fashion, the researchers developed a running account of the verbal and nonverbal interaction between group members and group workers. The effect of various strategies by the group worker, such as directing questions at individuals or using tangible rewards for specific behaviors, could then be measured in terms of changes in interaction patterns. The parallels between Bales's and Linsk's categories should be clear: Linsk's categories of "questions," "statements," "positive comments," and "negative comments" are virtually identical with Bales's categories of "asks for orientation," "gives orientation," "shows solidarity," and "shows antagonism" respectively. This illustrates the utility of examining existing, general coding schemes to determine the extent to which they can be used directly or modified to serve one's purposes.

The development of an efficacious coding scheme requires considerable care. The coding categories should derive from the hypotheses being tested in the research. In the Linsk study, the researchers' concern was with the nature and quality of verbal and nonverbal interaction in a group, and the categories chosen reflect that focus. In addition, coding categories should be highly specific and behavioral. The degree to which this can be achieved is obviously limited because overspecificity would become cumbersome and meaningless. For example, in Linsk's study, a category of "speaks" would be too general because it does not inform us of the type of verbal contribution the person makes. At the other extreme, a category such as "raises eyebrows" is so specific that we cannot determine the meaning of the behavior. It is essential to walk a fine line between being too specific and too general—providing a coding scheme that enables us to answer our research questions. It is important to recognize that, although coding behavior with such schemes may appear quantifiable and objective, there is still a considerable degree of subjective interpretation involved. The coder must decide, for example, whether a given response is positive or negative and shows solidarity or antagonism, and these judgments are necessarily subjective.

The use of coding schemes is not limited to situations in which a group is small, well organized, or engaging in highly structured behavior. If it is possible to specify concepts and hypotheses very precisely—in other words, if the research is clearly hypothesis testing rather than exploratory—then it may be possible to develop a precise coding scheme for data collection. In their disguised observation study of alcohol-related aggression, Kathryn Graham and colleagues (1980) were able to do this. Their basic hypothesis was that aggressive behavior among men when they drink is due to situational factors as much as to psychological predispositions toward violence. They hypothesized that aversive stimuli in bars (their independent variable) serve as cues that allow or encourage aggressive behavior (the dependent variable). The dependent variable was coded by using a dichotomous coding scheme: nonphysical aggression (swearing or other forms of abusive language) and physical aggression. Within the physical category, behavior was

TABLE 9.1 Behavioral Definitions and Symbols Used to Record Data

Behavior	Recording Symbols*	Definition
		—*Social Group Workers Behaviors*—
Questions	G, I	Verbal behavior that demands or suggests a response from one or more group members, indicated by words that suggest a question (i.e., why, how) or a direct request or demand for a response
Statements	G, I	Verbal behavior that gives information and does not call for a response from group members and is not a direct consequence of a previous behavior of individual or group of residents. Includes reading to residents.
Positive Comments	G, I	Verbal behavior that followed the behavior of one or more group members and relates to this behavior to encourage similar responses. Suggests recognition, approval, or praise.
Negative Comments	G, I	Verbal behavior that followed the behavior of one or more group members and relates to this behavior to discourage similar responses. Suggests disapproval or displeasure.
Listening	✓	Silence on the part of the worker either while a group member verbalizes or while waiting for resident response in the absence of other worker behavior.
Demonstration/ Participation	✓ (with slash)	Demonstrating equipment or activity or participating in activity.
Attending to External Events	✓ (with slash)	Watching, listening to, or talking to a stimulus outside of the activity.
		—*Group Member Behaviors*—
Appropriate Verbal	○	Verbal behavior related to current group task (subject under discussion, activity, or relating to activity stimuli, e.g., phonograph recording).
Verbal Behavior Related to Environment	○	Verbal behavior related to another person present at activity or related to the room or other aspects of the environment, but not related to the current group task.
Inappropriate Verbal Behavior	⊘	Verbal behavior that does not relate to group task or other residents or staff present or the environment. Verbalizations not audible to the entire group or observers.
Appropriate Attention	△	Visual or apparent listening attention, indicated by head orientation or other observable response, that is directed toward social worker, a resident who is making or has just made an appropriate verbal response, or activity stimulus.
Appropriate Activity	□	Manipulating equipment related to activity as worker has demonstrated or similar appropriate use, helping another resident to do so, nodding or head-shaking appropriately, raising hand for recognition.
Inappropriate Activity	╱	Repetitive actions, aggressive actions, manipulating materials not related to group task or activity stimuli, leaving activity, sleeping, talking to oneself, any attention directed away from worker, group task, activity stimuli, or a resident making a verbal response.

*Questions, statements, and comments were judged as to whether directed to an individual (I) or to the group (G).

Source N. Linsk, M. W. Howe, and E. M. Pinkston, "Behavioral Group Work in a Home for the Aged." Copyright © 1975, National Association of Social Workers, Inc. Reprinted with permission from *Social Work*, Vol. 20, No. 6 (November 1975), p. 456, Fig. 1; p. 457, Fig. 2.

Group Activity Study—Observation Form—Observer I   Date _____ Page _____

Observer _____

Leader Behavior:

	1		2		3		4		5	
Questions	*G*									
Statement		*G*		*G*		*G*				
Comment +			*I*							
Comment −										
Listening					✓					
Demo/Part										
Att/Ext										

Residents Present:

1. _____   6. _____
2. _____   7. _____
3. _____   8. _____
4. _____   9. _____
5. _____   10. _____

Resident Behavior:

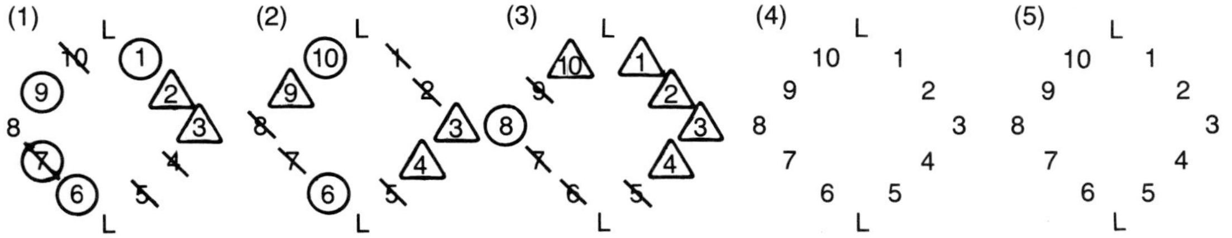

Figure 9.2 Sample Observation Form (Used to Record Data During 3-Minute Observation Periods at Group Meetings)

Source: N. Linsk, M. W. Howe, and E. M. Pinkston, "Behavioral Group Work in a Home for the Aged." Copyright © 1975 by National Association of Social Workers, Inc. Reprinted with permission from *Social Work,* Vol. 20, No. 6 (November 1975), Fig. 1, p. 456; Fig. 2, p. 457.

coded as physical threats or challenges to fight but no actual contact, aggressive but noninjurious physical contact (for example, grabbing and pushing), and actual physical violence (punching and kicking).

The independent variable—situational factors eliciting aggression—was, needless to say, more complex to code. First, they spent some weeks in the field observing and developing precise definitions and coding schemes for the situational variables. Here are a few of the coding categories they developed:

location: 1 = downtown bar
          2 = suburban bar

time of day: 1 = 9 A.M. to noon
             2 = noon to 3 P.M.
             3 = 3 P.M. to 6 P.M.
                 and so on

noise level: 1 = very quiet
             2 = medium quiet
             3 = medium loud
             4 = loud

sexual bodily
    contact: 1 = none, very casual
             2 = discreet necking
             3 = heavy necking, touching
             4 = flagrant fondling

friendliness
    to strangers: 1 = open, lots of conversation with strangers
                  2 = closed, people talk only to members of their own group

Each two-person observation team would spend from two to two and a half hours in an establishment. Most recording of observations was done after leaving the establishment so that note-taking would not attract attention.

This unobtrusive observation illustrates the manner in which a precise, quantifiable coding scheme can be used in field observation if the hypotheses to be tested are sufficiently developed. The investigators found, however, that while they were in the field, more variables of importance began to emerge, and these were added to the coding scheme. The investigators also decided that coding, although the major form of data collection, was not sufficient by itself. They found it useful to record descriptive accounts of aggressive incidents in order to ensure a complete record.

Coding schemes can become highly complex, involving many categories of behavior, timing of the behaviors, measures of intensity, and the like. However, more complex coding schemes can be used only in situations where it is possible to record accurately all that is necessary. Linsk's study of a single, small, task-oriented group enabled the use of a complicated coding scheme. In Graham's study, this would have been considerably more difficult, for the group (the clientele of a bar) was large and shifting in composition, much was going on, and actual recording had to be reserved until after the observation was concluded. This research setting necessitated a simpler coding scheme. Furthermore, investigations using complex coding schemes that require intense concentration on the part of the observer often require a number of observers, each of whom records for a short period and then is relieved by another observer. This reduces error due to observer fatigue or fluctuations in concentration. In some investigations, group behavior is recorded on videotape in order to reduce error and to allow researchers to view the group as often as needed to code behavior properly. In developing a coding scheme, in short, one must make sure that it does not become more complex than is usable given the resources at hand. Research in Practice 9.2 presents an observational study that effectively used a relatively simple coding scheme.

Coding schemes are not appropriate forms of recording observations in all observational research. In some cases, as with exploratory research, hypotheses cannot be developed with sufficient precision to make possible the operationalizing of concepts. The research is intended to explore and discover rather than explain and predict. In other cases, the hypotheses involve variables and relationships that require considerable interpretive effort on the part of the observer in the field and cannot easily be condensed to a few coding categories. In still other cases, the complexity and lack of structure in the group being observed render coding schemes useless. When these considerations lead to the conclusion that coding schemes are not appropriate, the investigator is likely to turn to field notes as a means of recording observations.

Field Notes. **Field notes** are detailed, descriptive accounts of the observations made during a given period. Whereas the precise nature of field notes will vary greatly from one study to another, John Lofland (1971) suggests five elements that all field notes should include: (1) a running description, (2) previously forgotten happenings that may be recalled while still in the field, (3) analytical ideas and inferences, (4) personal impressions and feelings, and (5) notes for further information.

1. A *running description* will make up the bulk of the field notes and is pretty much self-explanatory. It is simply the record of the day's observations. The primary concern of the running description

is to record accurately the concrete events that are observed. The observer should avoid *analyzing* persons or events while in the field because there is not the time, and it will interfere with observation of the ongoing scene. Instead, one should concentrate on faithfully recording what occurs.

2. Field notes also include *accounts of previous episodes that were forgotten or went unnoticed* but were remembered while the investigator was still in the field. When the field notes from any observation session are being prepared, it is likely that certain events may be forgotten and left out. During subsequent observations, events may transpire that bring the forgotten episodes back to mind. These events should be recorded when remembered, with the proper notation concerning when they originally occurred.

3. *Analytical ideas and inferences* refer to spur-of-the-moment ideas concerning such things as data analysis, important variables, speculation regarding causal sequences, and the like. "Flashes of insight" regarding any aspect of the study should be recorded when they occur. Reviewing these ideas after the completion of observations can be of great benefit to the final data analysis and writing of the report. Although most data analysis will be reserved until after the observation period is over, you would not want to forget whatever analytical ideas occurred to you while in the field.

4. *Personal impressions and feelings* should be noted, for the possibility for bias to color one's observations is always present. Recording personal impressions and feelings helps to minimize this bias by giving a sense of the perspective from which the observer is viewing various persons, places, or events. Does the observer just plain dislike a certain

RESEARCH IN PRACTICE 9.2
Assessment of Client Functioning: A Systematic Observational Study of Child Abuse

In the past decade, there has been an outpouring of research focused on uncovering the conditions under which child abuse and neglect are likely to occur. Much of this research has utilized indirect measures of behavior such as clinical assessments, rating scales, and questionnaires. Although such approaches can be valuable sources of data, Robert Burgess and Rand Conger (1978) reasoned that we might benefit more from direct observation of behavior than depending solely on what people say about their behavior. So, they focused their research on the everyday family interaction patterns that might contribute to, or serve as indicators of, abuse and neglect. Calling their approach a social–psychological model, they argue that studies should examine the patterned forms of interaction within the entire family: between parents, between parents and children, and between siblings. To this end, Burgess and Conger proposed to examine whether there are significant behavioral differences among abusive families (those in which there has been an authenticated incident of child abuse), neglectful families (those in which child neglect was sufficiently severe to reach the attention of authorities), and normal families (those with no record of abuse or neglect).

They developed a systematic observational research design in which a sample of 17 abusive, 17 neglectful, and 19 normal families was studied. Each family was observed by a team of two observers for a total of six hours over a one-week period. The observations occurred in the homes of the families. In order to introduce some consistency and control into the observations, Burgess and Conger provided each family with a set of specified tasks to accomplish while being observed: construct something using a set of building blocks, play games requiring skills such as ringtoss, and discuss some issue such as what to do on a family vacation. Burgess and Conger were interested in the kinds of interaction patterns that emerged as family members related to one another while carrying out these tasks. (The student might recognize that similar exercises are often used by practitioners in family therapy. Burgess and Conger's goal, however, was not to provide therapy for the families in their sample but rather to gain knowledge regarding the sources of child abuse and neglect.)

Data collection was based on a coding scheme developed by the researchers. During each two-minute interval of family interaction, the following information was coded for a particular family member.

1. Type of interaction:

    1 = gives verbal response
    2 = receives verbal response

3 = gives physical contact
4 = receives physical contact

2. Emotional affect of interaction:

   1 = neutral
   2 = positive
   3 = negative

3. The identity of a person interacting with the particular family member

4. Occurrence of a command:

   1 = gives prescriptive command
   2 = gives proscriptive command
   3 = complies with command
   4 = refuses command
   5 = neither

Using a stopwatch, a ten-digit keyboard, and a modified tape recorder, observers recorded their observations for each two-minute period as electrical impulses on a magnetic tape, enabling the investigators to code data for each time interval rapidly. This tape could then be deciphered by a special computer program.

Burgess and Conger recognized that observers might be influenced in their coding if they were aware of whether the family under observation was abusive, neglectful, or normal. To reduce observer bias from this source, they kept the status of the families secret from the observers. After observation, each observer was asked to guess the status of the family he or she had just watched, which they were unable to do with any accuracy. As a safeguard of reliability and validity of observations, the composition of observer pairs was changed frequently to pre-

vent the development of unique definitions of the behavior codes by observer teams. Also, comparisons between observer codings of the same behavior served to estimate inter-observer reliability.

As Burgess and Conger had hypothesized, there were distinctive interaction patterns in the three types of families. Mothers in abusive families were most different behaviorally from mothers in normal families. The former were less verbal and had less positive contact with their children. In general, both abusive and neglectful families showed more negative interaction and less positive interaction than did normal families. Furthermore, the researchers found little evidence that the children in abusive families behaved markedly differently from children in normal families. Finally, the neglectful mothers were the most negative in general and the least positive in their relationships with other family members.

The authors of this research are quick to caution against overgeneralizing their findings. The sample of families was small, and the researchers did not consider the problem of reactivity. A further problem is that of determining causality. Were the interaction patterns the causes of abuse, or were they produced by the abuse? Despite these problems, their study illustrates the potential for highly structured observations to yield insights into problems of central concern to human service practitioners.

person in the setting who is being observed? If so, the observer should honestly record such a feeling when it first occurs. This can prove beneficial when reviewing accounts relating to this person to see if one's personal feelings may have influenced the description.

5. *Notes for further information* are notes observers write to and for themselves: plans for future observations, specific things or persons to look for, and the like. It is risky to rely on memory for anything important relating to the study.

Recording field notes is particularly problematic for participant observers whose status as observer is disguised. Because such observers must constantly guard against having their true identity revealed, note-taking must be accomplished surreptitiously. In some settings, a bit of ingenuity on the part of the researcher can handle the problem quite nicely. For example, in her study of people's behavior in bars, Sheri Cavan (1966) solved the note-taking problem by making frequent trips to the rest room and recording her observations there. Given the well-recognized effect of alcoholic beverages on the human body, her trips probably raised little suspicion among the other bar patrons. The study mentioned earlier conducted by researchers who were admitted as patients to mental hospitals found another wrinkle on note-taking in participant observation: They could take notes openly because the staff defined note-taking as the meaningless activities of people who were "crazy"! (Rosenhan, 1973).

In many participant observation settings, no amount of innovation will allow the researcher to record observations on the scene. In these situations, there is no alternative but to wait and record observations after one has left the observational setting. Relying on memory in this fashion is less than desirable because memory is quite fallible. The observer should record observations as soon as possible to minimize the likelihood of forgetting important episodes. Persons interested in a more detailed discussion of the problems of taking field notes in participant observation are advised to see Lofland and Lofland (1984) and Bogdan and Taylor (1975).

What to Record   For someone who has never conducted participant observation research, collecting data through field notes can be a particularly frustrating and confusing affair. What to watch for? What to include in the field notes? These can be very difficult questions even for veteran observers. In addition, because participant observation research may be exploratory, one is often only partially aware of what might be relevant. It is possible, nevertheless, to organize one's thoughts around some general categories of things to be observed and recorded (Sellitz et al., 1976; Runcie, 1980):

1. *The setting:* Field notes should contain some description of the general physical and social setting being observed. Is it a bar, restaurant, or ward of a mental institution? Are there any physical objects or barriers that might play a role in the social interaction in the setting? Bogdan and Taylor (1975) suggest beginning each day's field notes with a drawing of the physical layout being observed. Such things as time of day, weather, or the presence of others who are not the focus of your observations might be useful information in some field research. In short, the field notes should serve to remind you—when you review them weeks, months, or years later—of the characteristics of the setting in which you observed behavior.

2. *The people:* Field notes should include a physical and social description of the main characters who are the focus of your observations. How many people? How are they dressed? What are their ages, genders, and socioeconomic characteristics (as well as you can observe from physical appearance)? Again, field notes should tell you, for each separate day of observation, who was present, who entered and left the setting during observation, and how the cast changed from one day to the next.

3. *Individual behavior:* The central observations in most studies are the behaviors of the people in the settings. How do people relate to one another? Who talks to whom, and in what fashion? What sequences of behavior occur? In addition, you may want to record the duration and the frequency of interaction among people. Are there repetitive cycles of behavior that occur? Is there a particular sequencing of behavior?

4. *Group behavior:* In some cases, the behavior of groups may be an important bit of information. How long does a group of people remain on the scene? How does one group relate to another? It might, for example, be useful to know what cliques have formed in a setting.

It should be clear that there is an enormous amount of information that might be gathered in any setting. In addition, the more exploratory the research, the more information must be recorded because it is more difficult to be sure what is relevant. With experience in the field and the development of more narrowly focused hypotheses, it is often possible to reduce the amount of information collected.

Time Sampling

Many observational strategies involve the continual recording of observations throughout the length of the study. Participant observers record things as they happen, and more systematic observers mark coding schemes for as long as an interchange or social setting persists. There are situations, however, where such continuous data collection is costly and unnecessary. In addition, as we discussed with other forms of sampling in Chapter 6, it is often not necessary to collect data from *all* elements of a population. In studies of child development, for example, it may not be necessary to record all that occurs during an hour, a day, or a week. Instead, we can gather valid data through **time sampling,** or making observations only during certain selected time periods (Irwin and Bushnell, 1980). In a study of the extent of disturbed behavior in mental hospitals, for example, Murray Melbin (1969) divided the waking hours of the day into 2-hour units and then selected from those time periods randomly to make observations. This provided sufficient time for observation as well as a representative sampling of periods to reduce the bias that could occur because of the time of day during which observations were made.

When conducting time sampling, there are some guidelines to keep in mind (Suen and Ary, 1986). The length of each time-sampling interval and the distance between intervals depend on the nature of the behaviors being observed: They should occur with sufficient frequency that they are likely to be seen during the sampled time periods. Very infrequent behaviors might call for continual observations. The more frequently a behavior occurs, the smaller the number of intervals that will need to be sampled. Furthermore, the time interval should be long enough for the behavior to occur and for the observer to make whatever recordings are called for.

Many of the considerations in time sampling are like the issues in sampling subjects or respondents as discussed in Chapter 6. If the primary concern of the researcher is to be assured of observing *some* occurrences of the behavior under study, it is advisable to use the equivalent of a purposive sample. For example, in studying domestic violence, a researcher would want to observe instances of family quarreling. Doing observations at mealtime would be one way to increase the probability of witnessing the desired events. On the other hand, if the researcher is concerned with accurately estimating the frequency of occurrence of a particular event or with studying the pattern of responses over a time period, it would be necessary to use the equivalent of a probability sample. For example, in observing nursing home residents for frequency of contacts with nonresidents, the week could be divided into hourly segments, and a random selection of hours could then be used as the basis for doing the observations.

Particularly when the observation process is highly complex and difficult to sustain for long periods of time, some form of time sampling can be a considerable help in improving the quality of data collected.

Validity and Reliability

Observational techniques, like other forms of data collection, need to be assessed in terms of how valid and reliable they are (Kirk and Miller, 1986). Observation rests on human sense organs and human perceptions—both of which are notoriously fallible. Just as Alice had difficulty perceiving the Looking-glass House, we have profound problems in perceiving the world around us. This is an especially difficult and insidious problem because we are so often totally unaware of the ways in which our senses and our perspective can lead us to misperceive situations. Especially with observational methods, people are inclined to resolutely say, "I was there. I saw it. I comprehend what was going on." Yet, as any trial lawyer will readily attest, eyewitnesses are often very unreliable spectators to events, and there is considerable experimental evidence that firsthand accounts of events are often partially inaccurate (Buckhout, 1974). Given these problems, we need to consider the validity and reliability of observations carefully.

There seems little question that observational techniques have greater face validity as measures of behavior and events than do many techniques that rely on second-hand accounts. Surveys or questionnaires depend on someone else's perception and recollection, which can be shaped and clouded by many factors beyond the control of the researcher. Observational techniques, on the other hand, provide first-hand accounts of occurrences under conditions that are partially controlled by the investigator. Misperception may still occur, of course, but the researcher is in a position to recognize its impact and possibly control its magnitude. For these reasons, observation is considered to have greater face validity than many other data collection techniques.

We saw in Chapter 5 that it is sometimes possible to measure the validity of an instrument through such means as correlating the results of the instrument with the results achieved by some other instrument known to measure the variable validly. When such direct measures of validity are not possible in observational research, it is helpful to evaluate the observational efforts in terms of factors that exist that might work to *reduce* validity:

1. If the people being observed do not have *anonymity,* their behavior may not be a true reflection of how they behave normally. Especially when controversial, sensitive, or potentially embarrassing issues are investigated, validity will decline substantially if anonymity has not been ensured. For this reason, hidden or disguised observation and observation in which the researcher takes the complete participant role are more valid than other types of observation.

2. Our perceptions are drastically shaped by our *expectations or lack of them.* If we expect something to occur, we are much more likely to observe it—whether it actually occurs or not. If we expect welfare recipients to be lazy, then we will be acutely aware of all those behaviors among welfare recipients that seem to indicate laziness. Thus, validity of observations will be reduced to the extent that our expectations—whether recognized or not—mold our perceptions. On the other side of the coin, a lack of expectations may lead us to miss something of importance in a setting. This is especially a problem in participant observation research that is characterized by a lack of structure and organization.

3. Validity of observations is also influenced by *the condition of the observer.* Hunger, fatigue, stress, or personal problems can lead to very distorted perceptions and interpretations. Likewise, physical characteristics, such as the lighting in an establishment, may lead to invalid observations. (This is another good reason for keeping complete field notes—field conditions affecting validity can be assessed at a later point.) If a number of these conditions exist, it may be judicious to terminate observation and resume when conditions are more favorable.

Although many of the conditions influencing validity may be beyond the control of the investigator, it is important to assess their impact on the research honestly so that accurate appraisal of the results can be made.

There are, of course, a number of guides that one can use to determine how confident we are of the validity of our results. First, some of the ways of assessing validity discussed in Chapter 5 can be adapted for use with observational techniques. For example, criterion validity might be assessed by comparing the results we achieve through observation with the results gained with other methods, such as surveys or experiments. If the various methodologies yield the same conclusions, then we have greater confidence that our observations have validity.

Second, the behavior of the people being observed may offer some hint as to how valid the observations are. If they engage in actions that are illegal or deviant or that might result in sanctions if publicly known, then you can assume that their behavior is an honest reflection of how they would act were you not present. In a study of police officers in a juvenile division, for example, Irving Piliavin and Scott Briar (1964, p. 207) made this argument:

> While these data do not lend themselves to quantitative assessments of reliability and validity, the candor shown by the officers in their interviews with the investigators and their use of officially

frowned upon practices while under observation provide some assurance that their behavior accurately reflects the typical operations and attitudes of the law-enforcement personnel studied.

Likewise, in his study of a venereal disease clinic, Joseph Sheley (1976, p. 116) argued that the validity of his data was quite strong because "staff members dropped their professional masks and displayed quite unprofessional behavior and ideas in the company of the researcher." Under such conditions, you can assume that people are reacting to environmental stimuli that normally guide their behavior rather than shaping a performance for the benefit of the investigator.

Assessing the reliability of observational research may be quite easy and straightforward or impossible, depending on the type of observation employed. In the case of an individual researcher who is studying a single group or setting through participant observation, there is no practical way to assess reliability (Kirk and Miller, 1986). When observations are more structured, as when using a coding scheme, reliability can be readily assessed through tests of *intercoder reliability,* or the ability of observers to code behaviors consistently into the same categories of the coding scheme. Two or more observers code the same behavior and the resulting codes are correlated to determine the degree of agreement between them. For example, in their study of barroom aggression, Graham and her colleagues (1980) did this by correlating the coding results from the two observers who visited each bar. They achieved reliabilities ranging from $r = .57$ to $r = .99$. Many experts suggest that structured observation should achieve an intercoder reliability of $r = .75$ or better (Bailey, 1987).

Reactivity

A major concern in any research is **reactivity,** or the degree to which the presence of the researcher influences what is being observed (Webb et al., 1981). To take an extreme example, suppose a researcher enters a group for the purpose of studying it through participant observation. Suppose, in addition, that the researcher takes a very active role in the group's proceedings by talking a great deal, offering suggestions, and the like. It should be clear that an observer behaving in this fashion will exert considerable influence on what occurs in the group, making the observer's presence highly reactive. This affects the validity of the observations because you do not know whether you have measured the group's *natural* activities or their *reactions* to the observer. One is never sure if events very different from those observed may have taken place had the observation been conducted in a less reactive manner. Reactivity also relates to the generalizability of findings. If the observer's presence is reactive, it is difficult to generalize findings to similar groups which have not had an observer in attendance.

It is generally agreed that participant observation generates the best results when reactivity is kept to a minimum. This is a major argument in favor of the complete participant role where the observer's true status is concealed (Johnson and Bolstad, 1973). It is logical to assume that a group will be less affected by observation if they are unaware of the observer's role-as-observer than if they are aware. Using the complete participant role will not, however, guarantee a lack of reactivity. The role must be played properly. The complete participant should play as passive a role in the group as possible without raising suspicion. Even when the beginning of an observational study is accomplished without undue re-activity, the researcher must be careful that reactivity does not increase during the course of the project. Such a situation occurred in a study of a group that had predicted the end of the world (Festinger, Riecken, and Schachter, 1956). On numerous occasions situations arose that forced the observers to become active participants to the point where subsequent group activity was influenced by their actions.

Human service workers should be aware that reactivity is a problem that is confronted more frequently than just when they are conducting formalized observational research. Practitioners are routinely called on to make intervention decisions based on observational data. For example, a home visit may be called for in a case of suspected child neglect. The worker's presence during the home visit will undoubtedly cause a change in the interactional patterns of the family. The realization that their child-rearing practices are under scrutiny will likely place all family members on their best behavior during the visit. An appreciation for the reactivity of such a visit might help the practitioner avoid making an erroneous decision.

Observational Research on Minority Populations

In the last chapter, we noted that the use of available data was good for studying sensitive topics because it minimized the problem of reactivity. The same can be said for the use of some observational techniques, especially unobtrusive observation. Studies of the extent of racism in the United States, for example, have often relied on survey research, and the findings have shown a considerable decline in racism over the years, particularly in the late 1960s and 1970s (Crosby,

Bromley, and Saxe, 1980). However, these surveys have been criticized on the grounds that they reflect not an actual decline in racist attitudes but rather a change in the social atmosphere so that it is frowned on to *express* prejudice or racism overtly. To get around this problem of reactivity, some researchers have used unobtrusive observations to measure racism.

The most common approach has been to present people with the opportunity to assist someone who is obviously in need of help and then measure how much or what kind of help is preferred. These studies are often conducted in field settings with the subjects unaware that they are part of a research project. The help needed might be to pick up some groceries that have been dropped, to give spare change to a panhandler, or to contribute money to a charity. The race of the person needing help is varied in order to see whether blacks receive less or more assistance than do whites (virtually all of these studies are of racism directed toward either blacks or whites). Then, the extent and type of help offered is noted by the researcher unbeknownst to the subject. These studies suggest strongly that prejudicial attitudes are more common among Americans than the surveys would indicate and that Americans express those prejudices when there are few negative consequences to doing so.

Other unobtrusive studies of racism have used willingness to exhibit aggression as a measure of prejudice and discrimination. Most often, subjects are asked to give a person a series of electrical shocks as a part of an alleged experiment on learning. While no one actually receives any shocks, the subject is convinced that they will. The intensity of the shock given is used as a measure of direct aggression while the duration of the shock is a measure of indirect aggression.

Then, comparisons can be made of whether more intense or longer shocks are given to blacks than whites. These studies again find antiblack hostility to be pervasive but subtle. For example, they find that the race of the subject was more likely to influence levels of indirect aggression but not direct aggression.

An overall assessment concluded that "discriminatory behavior (among Americans) is more prevalent in the body of unobtrusive studies than we might expect on the basis of survey data" (Crosby, Bromley, and Saxe, 1980, p. 557). Americans today are more likely to say that they are not prejudiced but then behave in a discriminatory fashion. So, it is only by combining survey and observational investigations that we can see this complexity.

While observational studies improve our understanding in this area, they also need to be conducted with care. Especially when dealing with social characteristics like race or sex that are value-laden in themselves, it is easy for bias to enter. Observations need to rest as much as possible on objective, quantifiable indicators. In the studies using aggression as a dependent variable, for example, subjects sit at a shock machine and turn a lever to give the bogus shocks. There is no judgment needed to assess whether the lever was turned or how much: It is recorded by the machine. Aggression is operationally defined as providing more electrical shocks. At the other extreme, if people are given no guidelines or training for judging whether actions are aggressive, bias is likely to intrude. In one study, people were presented with drawings showing a number of children playing (Lyons and Serbin, 1986). With no training, they were asked to say which children were behaving aggressively. The people, particularly males, were more

likely to rate the behavior of male children as more aggressive than the behavior of female children, even though the drawings differed only in the gender of the children depicted. So, observations related to minority status can often be biased in the direction of cultural or subcultural stereotypes if the observations are not carefully and systematically conducted.

Assessment of Observational Techniques

As much as one might desire simplicity and clarity, it should be understood that the choice of research methodology is precisely that—a *choice* among competing alternatives. Often this choice is a difficult one to make as there is no "perfect" or even "best" research technique. Here we will review the advantages and disadvantages of observational research.

Advantages

1. The advantage most often claimed for observational research is that it provides deeper and more insightful data than those generated by most other methods. Especially with participant observation, researchers immerse themselves in the daily activities of those studied to a greater degree than with other techniques. This places them in a position to gain information that would likely be missed with techniques such as a questionnaire or a survey. This is especially so for the complete participant who, as an accepted member of the group, sees people behaving freely and naturally, unaware that they are being studied. The interviewer may generate socially acceptable responses and a carefully orchestrated presentation of self. The participant observer, however, is better able to go beyond these public fronts and penetrate the nether regions of human behavior.

2. Observational research is capable of studying groups and behavior that would be closed to other forms of research. Many studies cited in this chapter involve groups that, for various reasons, would not be open to research by other methods. They may have something to hide, or they may view intrusion by a stranger as threatening to their cohesion and values. The ability of the complete participant to conceal his or her identity and conduct research where it could otherwise not be conducted is a major advantage of this observational technique.

3. Unlike surveys, which are limited to dealing with verbal statements, observational research can focus on both verbal and nonverbal behavior. This is an advantage because *actual* behavior is being studied in addition to people's *statements* about how they behave. By dealing with behavior, observational research avoids a potential source of error: the gap between what people say they do and what they actually do. The ability of observational techniques to consider both verbal and nonverbal behavior puts the researcher in a better position to link the verbal statements with behavior.

4. A frequently overlooked, but nevertheless significant, advantage of observational research is that the most qualified person is often directly involved in the collection of data because the senior researcher is often one of the observers (Denzin, 1978, p. 212). This is very different from surveys, for example, in which the project director may rarely conduct interviews, leaving this to part-time interviewers hired for the job. This places the most knowledgeable person the furthest from the data collection effort.

5. Much observational research is longitudinal in nature and thus enables researchers to make statements concerning changes that occur over the time of the research. In addition, by following activities over time, observers will have less trouble establishing the correct causal sequence than would be the case with surveys. As we noted in Chapter 2, establishing the causal order with survey data can at times be difficult.

Disadvantages

Most of the disadvantages of observational research relate to the more unstructured types. With less structure, the quality of the results of an observational study depends heavily on the individual skills of the researcher, and this leads to several criticisms.

1. A nagging concern with participant observation research has always been the possible effect of observer bias on the results. Such research does not have the structured tools of other methods that help ensure objectivity. If researchers are not careful, personal attitudes and values can distort research findings, rendering them virtually useless for scientific purposes.

2. Closely related to the issue of observer bias is the problem of the observer over-identifying with those who are studied (Shupe and Bromley, 1980). As the observer frequently becomes a part of a group for a substantial period of time, this possibility is quite real. Overidentification with subjects was first noted in anthropology, which contains much observational research, and was given the label "going native." Going native and allowing the research to deteriorate into a propaganda piece for the group studied can surely have as disastrous results for the utility of a study as would observer bias.

3. The lack of structure also makes exact replication—an important part of scientific research—virtually impossible. Observational studies are often such individualized projects that the possibility for exact replication is slight. Any observer in a natural setting will be forced to record what occurs selectively owing to sheer volume. There is little chance that a replication attempt would select precisely the same aspects of a given setting on which to focus.

4. The nature of the data gathered in some observational research makes it very difficult to quantify. We noted that some participant observers generate field notes that are basically rambling descriptions. Data in this form are quite difficult to code or categorize in summary form. This makes traditional hypothesis testing exceedingly problematic. As a result, many observational studies fail to get beyond a description of the setting observed.

5. Although unrelated to its lack of structure, the ethics of participant observation have been called into question by some critics, with the complete participant role generating the most controversy. Some social scientists see it as unethical to conceal one's identity for the purpose of conducting research. The strongest statement against concealed observation is that of Erikson (1967), who completely rejects all field studies that do not inform those being studied in advance. Whether or not disguised observation is ethical is still an open controversy in the social sciences. As we noted in Chapter 3, disguised observation is considered a "questionable practice" that requires approval by an institutional re-

view board. So long as the research is not trivial and the identities of participants are not revealed, disguised observation would likely be allowed.

6. As has been mentioned earlier, participant observation affords the researcher little control over the variables in the setting. There may be a great deal occurring, and the researcher will not be in a position to control or moderate these influences. This often leads to situations where the researcher is at a loss to select the important causal factors in a situation.

7. Because of the physical limitations on the observing capabilities of human beings, a participant observation study will almost certainly study a limited sample of people. Although one could, with a sufficient number of observers, study a large sample, this is rarely done. Observation is more commonly limited to a small group (such as a family or gang) or one setting (such as a bar or restaurant). The explanatory power that comes from a large sample size is, therefore, not available.

Observation in Human Service Practice

Observation is at the foundation of human service practice, and our analysis of scientific observation in this chapter has some important implications for observation in practice settings. Even though the goals of practice and research are somewhat different, some of the observational techniques developed by researchers can be carried over into practice. We will illustrate a few of the lessons to be learned.

1. It is critical for practitioners to realize that the type of observation engaged in affects the kind of information one can gather. Structured observation in a therapeutic setting offers practitioners considerable control over what occurs and comparability of information from one setting to the next. Yet it is a somewhat artificial setting (from the client's perspective) and may not capture the dynamics of real-life situations as experienced by the client. For this, participant observation would be more valuable.

2. Reactivity is a serious concern in any observation—whether done by a researcher or a practitioner. Human service workers must be sensitive to the extent to which their presence affects, possibly profoundly, the behavior of others. Clients may put their best foot (or their worst foot!) forward when a caseworker is present. The effect may be subtle, and even the client may not be aware of the change. A concern about reactivity may dictate the use of observational techniques that reduce the extent of the problem. One may choose unobtrusive observation or the disguised observer role as a means of reducing the extent of reactivity.

3. Good observational techniques rest on sound methods of recording information. This means that the practitioner should spell out as clearly as possible beforehand the kinds of behaviors that will be observed. The more specificity, the better: "Aggression" is too general; one should plan to look for "hitting, kicking,

or verbal insults." Thus, a precise and specific coding scheme is an important tool in both research and practice observation. This leaves fewer decisions to be made during observation when one is likely to be rushed and concerned about other matters.

4. Observation in research and practice have different purposes: The former focuses on hypothesis testing and knowledge accumulation while the latter is intended primarily as a tool for change or amelioration of undesirable conditions. However, as we stressed in Chapter 1, practice observations, if done properly, can add to our body of scientific knowledge.

5. Both research and practice observations should be done systematically, which means that certain explicit and publicly agreed upon rules are followed so that others know precisely how the observations were made and could repeat them if desired. At times, departure from a previously established, systematic plan of observation may be called for in practice. As a practitioner–client relationship develops or circumstances change, the intuition of the practitioner may call for such departures in order to maintain progress toward the goals of practice. However, such departures are rarely justified in research and are practically always detrimental to the research process because observations made using different procedures are not comparable.

||||||||||||||||||||||||||||||||||||||||||||||||||||||||||||||||||||||||||||||||||||||||

≡ Main Points

• Observational techniques involve the collection of data through direct visual or auditory experience of behavior.

• Verstehen refers to observers' efforts to view and understand a situation from the perspective of the people involved.

• Positivism holds that human behavior should be studied only by objective means.

• A major decision for the participant observer is whether his or her status as observer will be revealed to those studied (participant-as-observer) or will be concealed (complete participant).

• A problem faced by observational researchers is reactivity: the extent to which the observer's presence influences what is observed.

• Unobtrusive measures, including hidden observation, disguised observation, and the analysis of physical traces are designed to minimize reactivity.

• Coding schemes identify which behaviors are relevant to a study and how they will be recorded.

• Coding sheets contain the categories of the coding scheme and are designed to facilitate the recording process.

• Some participant observers record data as field notes, which are detailed, descriptive accounts of the observations made during a given period.

• Time sampling is often used in observational research to reduce the volume of observations that have to be made.

• Validity in observational research means that the observations correctly and accurately reflect reality.

• Some observational techniques, especially unobtrusive observation, minimize reactivity and are thus good for studying sensitive topics such as racism and sexism.

• Observational techniques are relevant to both research and practice settings.

≡ Important Terms for Review

coding
field notes

observational techniques
participant observation
physical traces
positivism
reactivity
time sampling
unobtrusive (or nonreactive) observation
verstehen

≡ For Further Reading

Bogdan, R., and S. Taylor. *Introduction to Qualitative Research Methods.* New York: Wiley, 1975.
A text on participant observation studies, including several illustrative cases that present an interesting account of how to do all aspects of observational research.

Emerson, Robert M., ed. *Contemporary Field Research.* Boston: Little, Brown, 1983.
A collection of articles that focus on a range of issues confronted in field research. Experts discuss such things as the role of theory in field research, ethical considerations, and political issues.

Goffman, Erving. *Asylums.* Garden City, N.Y.: Anchor Books, 1961.
A classic participant observation study of a human service delivery system—in this case, a mental hospital. There is little doubt that other research designs could not have achieved the rich insight available in this work.

Irwin, D. M., and M. M. Bushnell. *Observational Strategies for Child Study.* New York: Holt, Rinehart and Winston, 1980.
An excellent coverage of all types of observational studies of children with valuable exercises to give direct experience in doing observation. It includes structured observation, rating scales, and sampling procedures.

Johnson, J. M. *Doing Field Research.* New York: Free Press, 1976.
A thorough coverage of the full process of doing observational research in field settings.

Wilson, S. J. *Recording: Guidelines for Social Workers.* New York: Free Press. 1976.

Though not a research text, this book contains many useful insights with regard to recording observations made during clinical sessions with clients. As such, it is useful for improving one's technique of collecting observational data.

Whyte, William Foote. *Learning From the Field: A Guide From Experience.* Beverly Hills, Calif.: Sage, 1984.

A delightful book by one of the premier field researchers in the social sciences. Whyte has used his 50 years of experience in the field to produce a practical and accessible volume on the gamut of issues related to field research.

≡ Exercises for Class Discussion

9.1 A school counselor is asked by a teacher to assist her in controlling the behavior of four boys in her fifth grade class. The teacher complains that the boys "horse around" a great deal. They don't work on their assignments, throw paper wads, disrupt other children, get out of their seats, and make "smart remarks" instead of answering questions. The counselor suggests setting up a behavioral intervention but first wants to observe the class.

a. What problems will the counselor face in doing an observation?

b. One idea is to observe at random intervals throughout the week. Another is to observe for one full morning. What do you think would be the advantages and disadvantages of each approach? Can you think of a better method of time sampling for this situation?

c. Develop a coding sheet that the counselor could use to record the frequency of the problems mentioned by the teacher.

d. Besides the occurrence of these specific behaviors, what other things should the counselor attempt to observe?

e. What ethical issues would need to be addressed in conducting and reporting on this type of observation? For example, would it be necessary to have the student's permission? What about parents? What steps should be taken to assure confidentiality of the data that are collected as a result of the observation?

9.2 Select one of the following locations for an observational study, and spend approximately one hour there in actual observation: a veterinarian's waiting room, a beauty shop, a shoeshine stand, an adult bookstore, a fast-food restaurant, a bus stop, a hospital emergency room, or a garage sale.

Answer each of the following questions:

a. For the location selected, what general categories of data will you look for?

b. How will you gain entry to the setting? Whose permission will you need, and how will you obtain it?

c. Are there any particular time periods that would be preferable for making observations at the setting you have selected?

d. Which observational approach will you use—nonparticipant or one of the participant forms?

e. Conduct the observations, and report your experiences to the class.

f. For the observational setting you have selected, would it be more appropriate to collect data in the form of field notes or to develop a coding scheme? Why?

9.3 For the observational settings discussed in Exercise 9.2, consider the issue of when a participant observer should intervene and bring about some changes in the setting. What kinds of things would have to occur to warrant such intervention even though intervening would be detrimental to research goals? Given the examples that you and others in the class have developed, can you deduce any principles that might help others make the decision about when intervention is justified?

10

Experimental Research

When people think of "science" and "research," experiments are often the first things that come to mind. The terms conjure up images of laboratories and white coats and electronic gear that are often associated with experiments. Yet this points to a considerable misunderstanding of the nature of experimentation. In fact, we all engage in casual experimenting in the course of our everyday lives. For example, when a mechanical device malfunctions, we probe and test its various components in an effort to discover the elements responsible for the malfunction. In essence, we are experimenting to find the component (or variable) that *caused* the device to malfunction. Human service practitioners also often engage in casual experimentation. For example, in working with clients with particular problems, human service workers often try new intervention strategies to see if they will prove beneficial to the client. If behavior modification or role rehearsal do not bring about the desired effect, then a cognitive learning strategy might be tried. While these illustrations are of casual rather than systematic experiments, they do point to the essence of **experimentation:** It is a controlled method of observation in which the value of one or more independent variables is changed in order to assess its causal effect on one or more dependent variables.

The term "experimentation" as used in research, then, refers to a logic of analysis rather than to a particular location, such as a laboratory, in which observations are made. In fact, experiments can be conducted in many settings. **Laboratory experiments** are conducted in artificial settings constructed in such a way that selected elements of the natural environment are simulated and features of the investigation controlled. **Field experiments,** on the other hand, are conducted in naturally occurring settings as people go about their everyday affairs (Nachmias and Nachmias, 1987).

The logic of scientific experiments can be illustrated by taking a more careful look at two elements of the impromptu or casual experimenting that may occur in everyday human service practice. First, many casual experiments fail. That is, manipulating the variables involved does not produce the desired result. No matter which approach to a client is used, for example, improvement in functioning is not forthcoming. In part, failures in casual experiments stem from the fact that they are *casual* and thus not carefully planned. For example, the wrong variables may have been selected for manipulation such that no matter how they were changed, the desired result could not be obtained. In scientific experimentation, criteria exist to increase the likelihood of success by ensuring that the experiment is soundly planned and that crucial procedures are carried out. Not that following the formalized procedures will guarantee success—it will not. Failure—in the sense of not achieving desired results—is an unpleasant, but fully expected, outcome of experimenting. Actually, it may be best not to conceive of failure to achieve predicted results as "failure." Rather, not achieving predicted results serves to rule out one possible explanation, assuming the results are not due to poor research techniques.

The second feature of casual experimenting is a tendency to jump to conclusions that later prove incorrect. An effort to improve the performance of a client, for example, may have produced temporary changes, but later the improvement disappeared. What went wrong? It may be that the practitioner's change in intervention strategy was not the real source of the change in the client's behavior. Rather, it may have been something else that actually caused the temporary changes. For example, the client may have found a job or his or her mother-in-law recovered from surgery, and these could have led to temporary improvements in performance. Or, it may be that *any change* from one intervention strategy to another will result in short-term improvements that quickly dissipate. The point is that there are many things that influence people's behavior, and casual experimentation is not organized to sort out these influences. Scientific experimentation is designed to do this and thus reduce the likelihood of reaching false conclusions.

The focus of this chapter is experimental research, but it should be clear that the techniques learned here can be carried over into practice settings. Although the impromptu experimenting attributed to human service practice certainly has its place, a thorough grasp of the principles of experimentation can enhance the practitioner's knowledge-building and decision-making efforts. In this chapter, we will first discuss the underlying logic of experimentation, including a presentation of the major terms associated with experimental research. Then we will present the major factors that can lead to incorrect inferences in experiments and discuss how these problems can be avoided by properly designing the experiment. Finally, we will analyze the problem of generalizing experimental findings to other settings and review the advantages and disadvantages of experiments.

The Logic of Experimentation

Causation and Control

The strength of experiments as a research technique is that they are designed to enable us to make inferences about causality. The element that makes this possible is *control*: In experiments, the investigator has considerable control over determining who participates in a study, what happens to them, and under what conditions it happens. In order to appreciate the importance of this, let us look at some of the key terms in experimental research (Kirk, 1982).

At the core of experimental research is the fact that the investigator exposes the people in an experiment, commonly referred to as *experimental subjects*, to some condition or variable, called the *experimental stimulus*. The **experimental stimulus,** or experimental treatment, is an independent variable that is directly manipulated by the experimenter in order to assess its effect on behavior. Recall from Chapter 2 that independent variables are those variables included in a study that are hypothesized to produce change in another variable. The variable affected by the independent variable is the dependent variable—so called because its value is dependent on the value of the independent variable. An **experimental group** is a group of subjects who are exposed to the experimental stimulus. **Experimental condition** is the term used to describe the group of people who receive the experimental stimulus.

We can illustrate the logic underlying experimentation by means of a series of symbols. The following symbols are commonly used to describe experimental designs:

O = an observation or measurement of the dependent variable

X = exposure of people to the experimental stimulus or independent variable

R = random assignment to conditions

In addition, the symbols constituting a particular experimental design are presented in time sequence, with those to the left occurring earlier in the sequence than those further to the right. With this in mind, we can describe a very elementary experiment in the following way:

$$O \quad X \quad O$$

In this very elementary experiment, the researcher measures the dependent variable (this is called a pretest), exposes the subjects to the independent variable, and then remeasures the dependent variable (the posttest) to see if there has been a change. So, one major yardstick for assessing whether the independent variable in an experiment has had an effect is a comparison of the pretest scores or measures with the posttest. (Note that this is a slightly different use of the term

"pretest" from its use in Chapters 1 and 7. In those contexts, the purpose of the pretest was to assess the adequacy of a data collection instrument before actual data collection ensued. In this context, the pretest involves actual data collection, but before the introduction of the experimental stimulus.)

Suppose, for example, that we were interested in the ability of developmentally disabled children to remain attentive and perform well in classroom settings (Frankel and Graham, 1976). We might hypothesize that behavior modification techniques, in the form of reinforcement with praise, would improve the children's performance. To test this hypothesis, we would first measure the children's performance so as to have a baseline against which to assess change. Then we would expose the children to rewards for performance, the independent variable. For a specified period, children would be given praise each time they showed certain specified improvements in performance. Finally, we would again measure their performance—the dependent variable—to see if it had changed since the first measurement.

This illustration shows one of the major ways that experiments offer researchers control over what happens: The researcher manipulates the experimental stimulus. In this illustration, the researcher is using praise as the reinforcer. The experimenter specifies how and under what conditions the reinforcement is delivered, including how much reinforcement is delivered for a given response. The researcher might use one standard level of reinforcement or use multiple levels of reinforcement to assess the impact of such variation. The key point here is that the "when" and "how much" of the experimental stimulus are *controlled* by the researcher.

The purpose of an experiment, as we

have said, is to determine what effects independent variables produce on dependent variables. Variation in the dependent variable produced by the independent variable is known as **experimental variability,** and this is what is of interest in experiments. However, variation in the dependent variable can occur for many reasons other than the impact of the independent variable. For example, measurement error may affect the dependent variable (see Chapter 5). Or the people in the experiment may have some peculiar characteristics that influence the dependent variable separately from any effect of the experimental stimulus. It is also possible that chance factors can affect the dependent variable. Variation in the dependent variable from any source other than the experimental stimulus is known as **extraneous variability,** and it makes inferences about change in the dependent variable difficult to make. Every experiment contains some extraneous variability since there will always be things other than the experimental stimulus that influence the dependent variable. Researchers need some way of discovering how much variation is experimental and how much extraneous, and experiments can be designed to provide this information through the use of *control variables* and *control groups*. **Control variables** are variables whose value is held constant in all conditions of the experiment. By not allowing these variables to change from one condition to another, any effects they may produce in the dependent variable should be eliminated. In the study of developmentally disabled children, for example, we might have some reason to believe that the environment in which learning occurs—such as the lighting and heating—could affect how well the children perform in addition to the presumed impact of the experimental stimulus. To control for

this, we would conduct all the observations in the same setting with no changes in lighting or heating. With such controls, we have greater confidence that changes in the dependent variable are caused by changes in the independent variable and not by the variables that are controlled.

A **control group** refers to a group of research subjects who are provided precisely the same experiences as those in the experimental condition with the single exception that the control group receives no exposure to the experimental stimulus. **Control condition** refers to the state of being in a group that receives no experimental stimuli. When we include the control group in the elementary experimental design just described, we end up with a common experimental design:

Experimental group: *O X O*
Control group: *O*   *O*

The control group is very important in experiments because it provides the baseline from which the effects of the independent variable are measured. For example, in the study of developmentally disabled children, the experimental condition involves receiving reinforcement in terms of praise. However, it might be possible that the children's performance would increase even in the absence of praise, possibly because of the attention received by being a part of an experiment. To test for this it would be desirable to have a control group that receives the same attention as the children in the experimental group but is not rewarded with praise. Because both experimental and control groups experience the same conditions with the exception of the independent variable, it can be more safely concluded that any differences in the posttest value of the dependent variable between the experimental and control groups is due to the effect of the independent variable. So a second yardstick, in addition to the pretest–posttest comparison, for assessing whether an independent variable has an effect is the posttest–posttest comparison between experimental and control groups.

It is important that the ideas of a control variable and a control group be kept distinct because they serve quite different functions. The use of a control variable is an attempt to minimize the impact of a single, known source of extraneous variability on the dependent variable. The use of a control group, on the other hand, is an effort to assess the impact of extraneous variability from any source—including variables that are not known to the researcher—on the dependent variable.

Matching and Randomization

When comparisons are made between the experimental and control groups to determine the effect of the independent variable, it is of crucial importance that the two groups be composed of people who are as much alike as possible. If they are not, any comparison could be meaningless as far as the effects of the independent variable are concerned. For example, imagine that a teacher decides to experiment with a new teaching technique. As luck would have it, she has two classes on the same subject, one meeting in the morning and the other in the afternoon. She uses the new teaching technique in the afternoon—the experimental group—and her conventional teaching methods in the morning section—the control group. At the end of the term, she notes that the afternoon class did substantially better on tests than the morning class. Can she conclude that the new technique is more effective than her old methods? The answer is this: not with any great certainty. The students in the

two classes may have differed from one another in some systematic ways, and it may have been these differences between students, rather than variation in teaching technique, that caused differences in performance. It may be, for example, that students involved in extracurricular activities take morning classes so that their afternoons are free for those activities. Furthermore, students active in extracurricular affairs may have less time to study or be less academically inclined. Thus, given the kind of students who tend to take morning classes, we would expect the afternoon class to perform better even if there had been no variation in teaching technique.

There are two methods used to avoid the problem encountered by the teacher and ensure that the experimental and control groups are equivalent: matching and random assignment. The first has a certain intuitive appeal, but on closer inspection, it proves to be the less desirable of the two. As the name implies, **matching** involves matching individuals in the experimental group with similar subjects for a control group. People are matched on the basis of variables that we presume might have an effect on the dependent variable separate from the effect of the independent variable. By matching, we make the experimental and control groups equivalent on these variables so that these variables could not account for any differences between the two groups on the dependent variable. For example, the teacher described earlier might use an IQ test as a matching tool. A high IQ student in the morning class would be matched with a high IQ student in the afternoon class. Any students without equivalent matches on IQ in the other class would simply not be used in the data analysis. But there are other variables in addition to IQ that could affect the outcome. Race, sex, socioeconomic status, study habits, reading ability, math proficiency—the list goes on and on. Though matching on IQ would not be too big a problem, the difficulty of matching would increase geometrically with the addition of more variables. For example, the teacher might need to find a match for a black female of middle-class background with good study habits and a ninth-grade reading ability who is also in the ninety-fifth percentile in math proficiency.

This illustration points to one of the problems with matching: There are so many variables that might be used in matching that it is usually impractical to consider more than a few at a time. A second problem with matching is that the researcher needs to know in advance which factors might have an effect on the dependent variable so that these can be included in the matching process, but often such prior knowledge is not available. On the positive side, matching is better than no attempt to control at all and may be the only type of control available. In our illustration, the teacher may very well have no control over which students get assigned to which class. Consequently, the best she could do is to select subgroup members in one class who have counterparts in the other class on a few key variables.

The second approach to assuring equivalent groups is random assignment. As the name implies, **random assignment** uses chance to reduce the variation between experimental and control groups. This can be done in a number of ways. For example, each person in the experiment can be given a random number, then the numbers are arranged in order and every other person on the list is placed in the experimental condition. Or the names of all the people in the experiment can be listed alphabetically and given a number, then a computer can

randomly assign each number to either the experimental or the control group. (See Chapter 6 and Appendix B on the use of random numbers tables.) The point is to make sure that each person has an equal chance of being placed into either the experimental group or the control group. In the long run, this technique offers the greatest probability that experimental and control groups will have no systematic differences between them so that differences on the outcome measures can be confidently attributed to the effect of the independent variable. Chance rather than a priori knowledge of other variables is the foundation of random assignment.

The problem with relying on chance is that, even though in the long run and over many applications randomization generates equivalent groups, this approach can still yield nonequivalent groups on occasion. This is especially so when the study sample is very small. Table 10.1 illustrates the extreme difference between groups that is possible by chance using randomization. In this hypothetical data, there are eight subjects who have been identified by sex and height. The subjects are ranked according to their true position on the dependent variable prior to the experiment with scores ranging from 2 to 18. The mean score for the entire group is 10. Thus, when divided into an experimental and a control group, the ideal situation would be for each group to have the same mean score of 10, or at least very close to it, on the dependent variable. While probability theory tells us that, with random assignment, it is most likely that experimental and control group means will be close to the overall mean, it is possible to obtain groups with very different means since, by chance, any combination of subjects in the two groups is possible. Table 10.1 shows how one could obtain one group

TABLE 10.1   Randomization and Blocking Illustration

Subject	Sex	Height	True Dependent Variable Score
A	Male	Short	2
B	Male	Tall	4
C	Male	Tall	6
D	Male	Short	8
E	Female	Tall	12
F	Female	Short	14
G	Female	Short	16
H	Female	Tall	18
Total $N = 8$			Mean = 10

	Possible Groupings			
	Group 1	*Group 1 mean*	*Group 2*	*Group 2 mean*
Ideal groups	B C F G	10	A D E H	10
Worst random	A B C D	5	E F G H	15
Worst block on sex	A B E F	8	C D G H	12
Worst block on height	A B C D	5	E F G H	15

with a mean score of 5 and the other with a mean score of 15 (labeled "Worst random").

To reduce the likelihood of such occurrences, researchers often use a combination of matching and randomization known as **blocking.** In blocking, the subjects are first matched on one or more key variables in order to form blocks. Members of each block are then randomly assigned to the experimental and control conditions. Blocking works by reducing the extreme range of groups that are possible. For blocking to be effective, it is necessary that the variable on which cases are blocked be associated with the dependent variable. Notice in Table 10.1 that males have low scores and females have high scores; so, the variable, sex, and the dependent variable are clearly associated. There is no such association between height and the dependent variable. When blocking is done on the basis of sex, two males are randomly assigned to each group and two females are randomly assigned to each group. The most

extreme difference between groups that is possible in our hypothetical illustration with sex as the blocking variable are group means of 8 and 12 (labeled "Worst block on sex"). This is a considerable improvement over the extremes of 5 and 15 that are possible with randomization alone. Notice, however, that when the groups are blocked on the basis of height, there is no improvement; the worst possible group difference is still 5 and 15, as it was under randomization (labeled "Worst block on height"). This demonstrates that blocking on an appropriate variable can help reduce differences between groups. Choosing a variable for blocking that is unrelated to the dependent variable won't make matters any worse than random assignment, but it also won't improve the chances of achieving equivalent groups. Whether or not it is worth it to use blocking basically comes down to the anticipated improvement in group equivalency versus the cost and complexity of carrying out the blocking procedure.

Internal Validity

The central issue in experimentation is its utility in enabling us to make statements about causal relationships between phenomena. This is the reason for such things as control variables, control groups, randomization, and matching. In what has come to be considered the definitive work on experiments and experimental designs, Donald Campbell and Julian Stanley (1963) discuss the importance of *internal validity* in experiments (*see also* Cook and Campbell, 1979). Recall from Chapter 5 that the "validity" of a measure refers to whether it accurately measures what it is intended to measure. Likewise, **internal validity** in experiments refers to whether the independent variable actually produces the effect it appears to have had on the dependent variable; it is concerned with ruling out extraneous sources of variability to the point where we have confidence that changes in the dependent variable were caused by the independent variable. In the preceding discussion, we presented the basic logic involved in designing experiments that have internal validity. However, the problem is much more complex than we have so far stated because internal validity can be threatened in many ways. We now turn to the seven most serious threats to internal validity, as identified by Campbell and Stanley.

History The threat of history concerns events that occur during the course of an experiment, other than the experimental stimulus, that could affect the dependent variable. History is more of a problem for field experiments than for those conducted in the confines of a laboratory because field experiments typically last longer, allowing more time for events to occur that could affect the outcome. Fur-

thermore, the subjects in field experiments are roaming about free to experience and be affected by whatever events happen. For example, many commentators have made the observation that the reduction in the nation's highway speed limit in the early 1970s to 55 miles per hour appeared to have produced a reduction in deaths in traffic accidents. This conclusion may not be warranted, however, for contemporaneous with the reduction of the speed limit there occurred rapidly rising fuel prices and a reduced fuel supply. These two events produced a sharp cutback in the number of miles people drove. It should be evident that the effects of these historical events make it very difficult to ascertain what effect the reduction of the speed limit actually had on accident rates.

Maturation Maturation refers to changes occurring within experimental subjects that are due to the passage of time. Such things as growing older, hungrier, wiser, more experienced, or more tired are examples of maturation changes. If any of these changes are related to the dependent variable, their effects could confuse the effect of the independent variable. For example, many believe that people pass through a natural series of stages when grieving over the loss of a loved one: First, there is shock, then intense grief and sense of loss, followed by recovery (Kamerman, 1988). In other words, time brings its own change, or maturation, to the grieving individual. If we wanted to assess the effectiveness of some therapeutic intervention in helping people cope with the death of a loved one, any improvements people show over time might be due to maturation, or the natural progression of the grief process, rather than to the therapeutic intervention.

3. **Testing** The threat of testing may occur at any time subjects are exposed to a measurement device more than once. Because many experiments use paper-and-pencil measures and "before" and "after" measurements, testing effects are often of concern. For example, people taking achievement or intelligence tests for a second time tend to score better than they did the first time. This improvement occurs even when alternative forms of the test are used. Similar changes occur on personality tests. It should be quite clear that these built-in shifts in paper-and-pencil measures could lead to changes in the dependent variable that are due to testing rather than to the impact of the independent variable.

4. **Instrumentation** The threat of instrumentation refers to the fact that the way in which variables are measured may change in systematic ways during the course of an experiment, resulting in the measurement of observations being done differently at the end from the way they were in the beginning. In observing and recording verbal behavior, for example, observers may become more adept at recording and do so more quickly. This means that they could record *more* behaviors at the end of an experiment than at the beginning. If the observers do learn and become more skillful, then changes in the dependent variable may be due to instrumentation effects rather than to the impact of the independent variable.

5. **Statistical Regression** The threat of statistical regression can arise any time subjects are placed in experimental or control groups on the basis of extremely high or low scores on a measure in comparison to the average score for the whole group. When remeasured, those extreme groups will tend, on the whole, to score less extremely. In other words, they will *regress toward the overall group average.* For example, suppose the bottom 10 percent of scorers on a standard achievement test are singled out to participate in a special remedial course. On completing the course, they are measured with the achievement test again and show improvement. Could we conclude that the remedial course was responsible for the higher scores? You would certainly be hesitant to make this inference because of the effects of testing and maturation that we have already discussed. But, in addition, there would also be a regression effect. Some of those people scoring in the bottom 10 percent undoubtedly did so for reasons other than their actual level of ability—because they didn't get enough sleep the night before, were ill, or were upset over a quarrel. (How many times have you scored lower on an exam than you normally do because of factors like these?) If these people take the exam a second time, the conditions mentioned will have changed, and they will likely perform better—even without the special remedial course. Recognize that many, possibly most, people at the lowest 10 percent *are* performing at their normal level. However, in any such group based on a single test administration, a certain number of people can be expected to be scoring lower than their normal level. If the whole group repeats the exam—even without any intervening experimental manipulation—they can be expected to perform better and thus the average score of the group will improve.

Statistical regression can be an especially serious concern in studies done in practice settings. Clients are likely to seek help when their problems are particularly serious and troubling, as when they are severely depressed. If some intervention is followed by improvement in the client's situation, the improvement might have been due to the intervention, or it might have been due to the fact that severe depression could be expected to ease somewhat even without intervention.

(6) **Selection** Selection is a threat to internal validity when the kinds of people selected for one experimental condition differ from the people selected for other conditions. The threat of selection derives from experimental and control groups being improperly constituted. Recall the importance of random assignment or matching to equalize these groups. As previously noted, improper composition of these groups can make findings based on comparisons between them meaningless.

(7) **Experimental Attrition** The attrition threat occurs when there is a differential dropout of subjects from the experimental and control groups. Especially in experiments that extend over long time periods, some people will fail to complete the experiment. People will die, move away, become incapacitated, or simply quit. If there is a notable difference in attrition rates between the comparison groups, the groups may not be equivalent at the end of the experiment although they were at the beginning. An example of the attrition threat can be found in a study of the effects of sex composition on the patterns of interaction in consciousness-raising counseling groups (Carlock and Martin, 1977). One group was all women while the other was composed of both men and women. The women were randomly assigned to one or the other of the groups. Originally the all-female group contained 9 members, and the male–female group had 16 members. Before the experiment was completed, however, two female

members of the male–female group dropped out. When the interactional patterns in the groups were compared, substantial differences were found. The authors conclude that these differences were due to the differing sex composition of the groups, but, as they note, their findings are weakened because of the dropouts from the female–male group. With such small groups to begin with, the loss of two members from one group could have substantially affected the results.

With this lengthy list of threats to the internal validity of experiments, can one ever have confidence that changes in the dependent variable are due to the impact of the independent variable and not to some extraneous variability? In fact, such confidence can be established—and threats to internal validity controlled—through the use of a good experimental design, and it is to this topic that we now direct our attention.

Experimental Designs

There are three categories of experimental designs. **Preexperimental designs** lack the random assignment to conditions and the control groups that are such a central part of good experimental designs. While they are still sometimes useful, they illustrate some inherent weaknesses in terms of establishing internal validity. The better designs are called *true experimental* designs and *quasi-experimental* designs. **True experimental designs** are more complex ones that use randomization and other techniques to control the threats to internal validity. **Quasi-experimental designs** are special designs for use in the approximation of experimental control in nonexperimental settings.

Preexperimental Designs

On the surface, the design on page 270 might appear to be an adequate design. The subjects are pretested, exposed to the experimental condition, and then post-tested. It would seem that any differences between the pretest measures and post-test measures would be due to the experimental stimulus.

P.1 The One-Group Pretest–Posttest Design

Experimental Group: $O \: X \: O$

However, there are serious weaknesses in this design as it stands. With the exceptions of selection and attrition, which are irrelevant owing to the lack of a control group, Design P.1 is subject to the other five threats to internal validity. If a historical event related to the dependent variable intervenes between the pretest and the posttest, its effects could be confused with those of the independent variable. Maturation changes in the subjects could also produce differences between pretest and posttest scores. If paper-and-pencil measures are used, a shift of scores from pretest to posttest could occur owing to testing effects. Regardless of the measurement process utilized, instrumentation changes could produce variation in the pretest and posttest scores. Finally, if the subjects were selected because they possessed some extreme characteristic, differences between pretest and posttest scores could be due to regression toward the mean. In all of these cases, variation on the dependent variable produced by one or more of the validity threats could easily be mistaken for variation due to the independent variable.

The other preexperimental design—the Static Group Comparison—involves comparing one group that experiences the experimental stimulus with another group that does not.

P.2 The Static Group Comparison

Experimental group: $\underline{X} \: \underline{} \: \underline{O}$
Control group: $ \underline{O}$

In considering this design, it is important to recognize that the comparison group that appears to be a control group is not, in the true sense, a control group. The major validity threat to this design is selection. Note that no random assignment is indicated that would make the comparison groups comparable. In Design P.2, the group compared with the experimental group is normally an intact group picked up only for the purpose of comparison. There is no assurance of comparability between it and the experimental group. For example, we might wish to test the impact of a local assistance program by comparing a city in which the program exists with one that does not have the program. Any conclusions we might reach about the effects of the program might be inaccurate because of other differences between the two cities.

Despite their weaknesses, preexperimental designs are used when resources do not permit the development of true experimental designs. Human service practitioners especially are likely to be faced with this dilemma. It should be evident, however, that conclusions based on such designs are to be regarded with the utmost caution and the results viewed as suggestive at best. We would also want to be sure to avoid these designs if at all possible. When they are used, efforts should be made to test the validity of those findings further by using one of the true experimental designs.

True Experimental Designs

Probably the most common true experimental design is the Pretest–Posttest Control Group Design with random assignment, which is identical to the design on page 271 but with randomization. This design is used so often that it is frequently referred to by its popular name: the "classic" experimental design. In all of the true experimental designs, the proper test of hypotheses is the comparison of posttests between experimental and control groups.

T.1 The Pretest–Posttest Control Group Design with Randomization—the "classic" experimental design

Experimental group: R O X O
Control group: R O O

This design utilizes a true control group, including random assignment to equalize the comparison groups, which eliminates all the threats to internal validity except certain patterns of attrition. Because of this, we can have considerable confidence that any differences between experimental and control groups on the dependent variable are due to the effect of the independent variable. Let us take a closer look at how the classic design avoids the various threats. History is removed as a rival explanation of differences between the groups on the posttest because both groups would experience the same events with the one exception being the experimental stimulus. Because the same amount of time passes for both groups, maturation effects can be assumed to be equal and, therefore, do not account for posttest differences. Similarly, as both groups are pretested, any testing influences on the posttest should be the same for the two groups. Instru-

mentation effects are also readily controlled with this design because any unreliability in the measurement process that could cause a shift in scores from pretest to posttest should be the same for both comparison groups.

In situations where regression could occur, the classic experimental design can control it through random assignment of subjects with extreme characteristics. This ensures that whatever regression does take place can be assumed to be the same for both groups. Regression toward the mean should not, therefore, account for any differences between the groups on the posttest. Randomization also controls the validity threat of selection by making sure that the comparison groups are equivalent. Furthermore, the pretest results can be used as a check on precisely how similar the two groups actually are. Because the two groups are very similar, attrition rates would be expected to be about the same for each group. In a lengthy experiment with a large sample, we would fully expect about the same number of subjects in each group to move away, die, or become incapacitated during the experiment. These can be assumed to be, more or less, random events. Attrition due to these reasons, therefore, is unlikely to create a validity problem. Attrition due to voluntary quitting is another matter. It is quite possible that the experimental stimulus may affect the rate of attrition. That is, subjects might find something about the experimental condition either more or less likable than the subjects find the control condition, so the dropout rate could differ. If this occurs, it raises the possibility that the groups are no longer equivalent at the time of the posttest. Unfortunately, there is no really effective way of dealing with this problem. About all one can do is to watch for its occurrence and interpret the results cautiously if attrition bias appears to be a problem.

A second true experimental design—the Solomon Four-Group Design—is more sophisticated than Design T.1 in that four different comparison groups are used.

T.2 The Solomon Four-Group Design

Experimental group 1:	R	O X	O
Control group 1:	R	O	O
Experimental group 2:	R	X	O
Control group 2:	R		O

As should be evident, the first two groups of the Solomon design constitute Design T.1, indicating that it is capable of controlling the same threats to internal validity as did that design. The major advantage of the Solomon design is that it can tell us whether changes in the dependent variable are due to some *interaction effect* between the pretest and the exposure to the experimental stimulus. Experimental group 2 is exposed to the experimental stimulus but without being pretested. If the posttest of experimental group 1 differs from the posttest of experimental group 2, it may be due to an interaction effect of receiving both the pretest and experimental stimulus—something we would not find out with the classic design. Suppose, for example, that we wanted to assess the effect on prejudice toward racial minorities (the dependent variable) of receiving positive information about a racial group (the independent variable). So we pretest groups by asking them questions regarding their prejudice toward particular groups. Then we expose them to the experimental stimulus: newspaper articles reporting on civic deeds and rescue efforts of members of those racial groups. If we find lower levels of prejudice in ex-

perimental group 1 than in control group 1, it might be due to the independent variable. But it could also be that filling out a pretest questionnaire on prejudice sensitized people in the first group to these issues and they reacted *more strongly* to the experimental stimulus than they would have without such pretesting. If this is so, then experimental group 2 should show less change than experimental group 1. If the independent variable has an effect separate from its interaction with the treatment, then experimental group 2 should show more change than control group 1. If control group 1 and experimental group 2 show no change but experimental group 1 does show a change, then change is produced only by the interaction of pretesting and treatment.

It should be apparent that the Solomon design enables us to make a more complex assessment of the causes of changes in the dependent variable. In addition, the combined effects of maturation and history cannot only be controlled (as with Design T.1) but also measured. By comparing the posttest of control group 2 with the pretests of experimental group 1 and control group 1, these effects can be assessed. However, our concern with history and maturation effects is usually only in terms of *controlling* their effects, not *measuring* them.

Despite the superiority of the Solomon design, it is often bypassed for Design T.1 because the Solomon design requires twice as many groups. This effectively doubles the time and cost of conducting the experiment. Not surprisingly, many researchers decide that the advantages are not worth the added cost and complexity. If a researcher desires the strongest design, however, Design T.2 is the one to choose.

There are times when pretesting is either impractical or undesirable. For example, pretesting might sensitize subjects to the independent variable. In these cases, it is still possible to use a true experimental design, the Posttest-Only Control Group Design.

T.3 The Posttest-Only Control Group Design

Experimental group:	R X	O
Control group:	R	O

Despite the absence of pretests, Design T.3 is an adequate true experimental design that controls validity threats as well as do the designs with pretests. It uses random assignment to conditions, which distinguishes it from the preexperimental Design P.2. The only potential validity question raised in conjunction with this design is selection. The absence of pretests means that random assignment is the only assurance that the comparison groups are equivalent. Campbell and Stanley (1963), however, argue convincingly that pretests are not essential and that randomization reliably produces equivalent groups. Furthermore, they argue that the lack of popularity of Design T.3 stems more from the tradition of pretesting in experimentation than from any major contribution to validity produced by its use.

The preceding experimental designs are adequate for testing hypotheses when the independent variable is either present (experimental group) or absent (control group). Yet many hypotheses involve independent variables that vary in terms of *degree* or *amount* of something that is present. For example, *how much* treatment of a client (intensity level) is needed to produce some desired behavioral change? In a study of abusive parents, for example, the independent variable was

exposure to positive parenting sessions (Burch and Mohr, 1980). Rather than just assess the effect of the presence or absence of such sessions, the researchers exposed some groups to *more* sessions than others. In cases such as this, an extension of Design T.1 with multiple experimental groups and one control group is used.

T.4 The Multiple Experimental Group with One Control Group Design

Experimental group 1:	R O	X_1	O
Experimental group 2:	R O	X_2	O
Experimental group 3:	R O	X_3	O
Control group:	R O		O

The symbols X_1, X_2, and X_3 refer to differing amounts or intensities of a single independent variable or treatment. Comparing the posttests of the experimental groups enables us to determine the impact of the differing amounts of the independent variable.

The experimental designs considered thus far can assess the impact of only a single independent variable at a time on the dependent variable. We know, however, that variables can *interact* with one another, and the combined effects of two or more variables may be quite different from the effects of each variable operating separately. For example, one experimental study investigated the impact of both social class and race on people's stereotypes of women (Landrine, 1985). People in the study were asked to describe society's stereotype of four different women: a middle-class black, a middle-class white, a lower-class black, and a lower-class white. They found that social class and sex did affect stereotyping: Lower-class people received more negative stereotyping than did middle-class people, and blacks were viewed less favorably than whites. They did not find an interaction effect, however. In other words, various class/race combinations did not produce more changes in stereotyping than the effects of class and race separately. To assess the effect of such interactions, experimenters have to expose the subjects to more than one independent variable. A convenient experimental design for accomplishing this is what is called the Factorial Design. Design T.5 illustrates the simplest factorial design in which two independent variables (X_1 and X_2) are involved, each with only two values (present or absent.)

T.5 The Factorial Design

Experimental group 1:	R	X_1 X_2	O
Experimental group 2:	R	X_1	O
Experimental group 3:	R	X_2	O
Control group:	R		O

Factorial designs involve enough groups so that all possible combinations of the independent variables can be investigated. Assessment of interaction is accomplished by the comparison of experimental group 1, which is exposed to both independent variables, with experimental groups 2 and 3. We can see whether the combined effects of the independent variables differ from their separate effects.

Factorial designs can be expanded beyond the simple example used here. More than two variables can be investigated, and each variable can have more than two values. However, as the complexity of factorial designs increases, the number of groups required rapidly increases and can become unmanageable. For example, with three independent variables, each with three values, we would need a $3 \times 3 \times 3$ factorial design or 27 different groups in the experiment. However, field experiments designed to assess the impact of social programs sometimes involve such complex designs.

We have covered the major types of true experimental designs in this section. However, circumstances often require researchers to use a variant of one of these designs. Research in Practice 10.1 illustrates such a variation that, nonetheless, retains randomization. The designs presented here also form the basis for many other more complex designs capable of handling such problems in experimenting as multiple independent variables and order effects. Those interested in further elaboration of these and other complex designs are advised to consult the excellent treatment given them by Roger Kirk (1982).

Quasi-Experimental Designs

There are many times when it is impossible, for practical or other reasons, to meet the conditions necessary for the development of true experimental designs. The most common problems in this regard are an inability to assign people randomly to conditions or the difficulty of creating a true control group with which to compare the experimental groups. Although this can be a problem in experiments in any context, it is especially acute in field experiments and in practice settings. Rather than rule out experimentation in such settings, however, one may be able to use a *quasi-experimental design*. These designs allow the researcher to approach the level of control of true experimental designs in situations where the requirements of the latter cannot be met. Quasi-experimental designs afford considerable control, but they fall short of the true experimental designs and should, therefore, be used only when conditions do not allow the use of a true ex-

||||||||||||||||||||||||||||||||||||||||||||||||||||||||||||||||||||||||||||||||||||||||||||||||||||||||||||||

RESEARCH IN PRACTICE 10.1
Program Evaluation: A Field Experiment on Police Handling of Domestic Violence Cases

Experiments, if done properly, have the benefit of enabling us to make statements about causal relationships between phenomena with some confidence. The reason for this is the control that researchers have over the variables—independent, dependent, and extraneous—in experimental research. Yet it is this very element of control—or lack of it—that seems to rule out experimental designs as unworkable in many field settings. Experiments may be dismissed too quickly, however, before all the possibilities have been considered. Sometimes it is a lack of creativity rather than the absence of opportunities that leads researchers to ignore experimental designs in such settings. Consider, for example, whether it would be possible to evaluate experimentally the response of police officers to domestic violence calls. Should the officers arrest an alleged spouse abuser? Or would a brief period of separation for the couple be sufficient to ward off future episodes of abuse? Such decisions are usually left to the discretion of officers responding to a domestic violence call, but would it be possible to assess the various options available to police officers with some degree of experimental control?

Criminologist Lawrence Sherman and sociologist Richard Berk (1984) designed a randomized field experiment in Minneapolis that they hoped would accomplish this goal. The independent variable was the mode of police intervention, which could take on one of three values: arrest of the alleged perpetrator, separation of the couple by ordering the abuser out of the premises, or offering advice and mediation but no arrest. The dependent variable was whether or not the perpetrator was involved in another domestic violence incident in the six months following the police intervention. The really difficult problem in this field experiment was how to achieve random assignment to experimental conditions. First of all, for ethical and practical reasons, Sherman and Berk limited their study to cases of simple, or misdemeanor, domestic assault where there was no severe injury or life-threatening situation. Then, they achieved randomization in the following way. Each police officer carried a pad of report forms, color-coded for the three different experimental treatments: arrest, separation, and mediation. The researchers randomly ordered the forms in the pad, and then the officers took whatever action was called for by the form on the top of the pad when they were called out on a disturbance that fitted the experiment's criteria.

One of the major problems the researchers faced, as you can well imagine, was how to ensure that the officers followed the randomization process by

(Continued on next page)

using the intervention indicated by the forms for a given domestic violence call. The researchers tried riding patrol with the officers on a sample of days to make sure they didn't tamper with the order of the forms. This proved impractical, however, because long periods of time would sometimes go by before a domestic assault call would occur. Another approach they used was to have officers fill out a brief form after each call telling what had occurred. Because the researchers knew which intervention should have been used on that call, they could assess whether the proper sequence was being followed. Although there were some violations of the randomization process, most cases were done properly, and the data analysis was performed on those cases.

Another problem the researchers faced was that some officers turned in more cases for the experiment than did others. This was so partly because some officers patrolled more violent beats. But it also occurred because some were more committed to the experiment. Some of the less committed officers, for example, would leave their report pads at the police station when they went on patrol, and cases were, therefore, lost to the experiment. The differential rates of reporting do not raise issues of internal validity because treatments are still randomized by officers, but they do raise the issue of validity discussed in Chapter 5. Recall that validity refers to how accurately a measurement tool measures some theoretical concept. In this study, the critical question is how well the independent variables of arrest, separation, and mediation are measured. The treatments were measured basically by

assuming that all the officers properly applied a given treatment when they said they did. The question can be raised, however, of whether one officer's exercise of mediation, for example, is the same as another's. Mediation, in particular, is difficult to operationalize because police officers may differ in how effectively they mediate. It may have been that those officers who turned in much data for the experiment were particularly capable at making an arrest effective and less capable in effectively using separation or mediation. The other officers, who did not provide many cases, may have been more effective separators or mediators. If this were the case, then the study was really measuring variations in the skills of police officers rather than variations in the effectiveness of different treatments. And because the poor mediators were turning in most of the data, the results would be skewed toward finding mediation less effective and arrest more effective. The differential reporting rates of officers leave this question unresolved.

Despite the problems in this experimental field study, it represents a creative way to use experimentation in a setting that would at first not seem amenable to such research. What did Sherman and Berk discover? Basically, they found that arrest was a more effective mode of intervention than either separation or mediation. People who were arrested were significantly less likely to perpetrate a repeat episode of domestic violence in the following six months, and this was true despite the fact that those arrested were released very soon and thus were as free to commit abuse as were those who were not arrested. The impact of the other two interventions depended on how the dependent variable was measured. When a repeat offense was measured by the appearance of the person in a police record, then mediation was somewhat more effective than separation. When the dependent variable was measured by a victim's self-report of future episodes, then separation was somewhat more effective. As a result of this experiment, the Minneapolis police were ordered in 1984 "to aggressively utilize arrest powers" in dealing with domestic assault cases, which resulted in a threefold increase in such arrests ("Arrests of Wife-Beaters . . ." 1984). Other urban police departments—including New York,

Houston, and Dallas—have followed suit (Barth, 1984); and a number of other field experiments are currently being conducted on this problem in cities across the country (Barth, 1984; Garner and Visher, 1988).

This field experiment illustrates the importance of assessing internal and external validity in experiments. It also reinforces a point we have made repeatedly, namely, that the results from a single study should be viewed with caution—in this case, because of the potential problems with validity. This experiment also suggests that multiple measures are important to use, a point to which we will return in Chapter 11.

perimental design (Achen, 1986). As we will see in Chapter 11, quasi-experimental designs also form the basis of single-subject designs used in clinical practice.

One of the simplest and most useful of the quasi-experimental designs is the Time Series Design. This design involves a series of repeated measures, introduction of the experimental condition, and then another series of measures.

Q.1 The Time Series Design

Experimental group:
$$O_1\ O_2\ O_3\ O_4\ X\ O_5\ O_6\ O_7\ O_8$$

The number of pretest and posttest measurements can vary, but it would be unwise to use fewer than three of each. Time series designs can be analyzed by graphing the repeated measures and inspecting the pattern produced. We can conclude whether the independent vari-

able produced an effect by observing when, over the whole series of observations, changes in the dependent variable occur. Figure 10.1 illustrates some possible outcomes of a time series experiment. Of major interest is what occurs between O_4 and O_5, as these are the measures that immediately precede and follow the experimental stimulus. The other measures are important, however, as they provide a basis for assessing the change that occurs between O_4 and O_5. As Figure 10.1 illustrates, some outcomes suggest that the stimulus has had an effect whereas others do not. In cases A, B, and C, stimulus X appears to produce an effect. In each case the differences between measures O_4 and O_5 are greater than the differences between any other adjacent measures. Cases E and F illustrate outcomes where we can infer that changes result from something other than the stimulus because the differ-

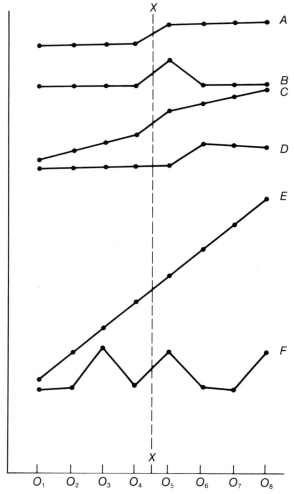

Figure 10.1 Hypothetical Examples of Time Series Data

Source: Adapted from Donald T. Campbell and Julian C. Stanley, *Experimental and Quasi-Experimental Designs for Research* Copyright © 1963 Houghton Mifflin Company. Used with permission.

The sharp change between measures O_5 and O_6 could be a delayed effect of X, or it could be due to something else. More careful analysis would be required to come to a firm conclusion in that case.

In field studies involving a time-series analysis, the experimental stimulus is often not something that the researcher manipulates, rather it is something that occurs independently of the research. So, any natural event that is presumed to cause changes in people's behavior could serve as an experimental stimulus. In a study of the mass media and violence, for example, the experimental stimulus was the heavyweight championship prize fights that occurred between 1973 and 1978 (Phillips, 1983). The dependent variable was the daily counts of all homicides in the United States provided by the National Center for Health Statistics, so an assessment could be made of the daily homicide rates after championship prize fights. They found a sharp increase in homicides after such fights, peaking on the third day after each fight. Apparently, in some Americans viewing heavyweight prize fights stimulates aggressive behavior that turns fatal in a few cases.

The time series design fares quite well when evaluated on its ability to control threats to internal validity. With the exception of history, the other threats are controlled by the presence of the series of premeasures. Maturation, testing, instrumentation, regression, and attrition produce gradual changes that would be operating between all measures. As such, they could not account for any sharp change occurring between O_4 and O_5. Because this design does not use a control group, the issue of selection is not a factor. Thus, history is the only potential threat to internal validity. It is always possible that some extraneous event

ences between measures O_4 and O_5 are not substantially different from those between some other adjacent measures. The results of a time series design are not always clear-cut, as illustrated by case D.

could intervene between measures O_4 and O_5 and produce a change that could be confused with an effect of X. In many cases, there may not be an event that plausibly could produce the noted effect, and we could be quite sure it was due to X. Nevertheless, the inability of the time series design to control the threat of history is considered a weakness.

The time series design requires that we be able to measure the same group repeatedly over an extended period of time. As this requires considerable cooperation from the subjects, there may be times when the time series design cannot be used. A design that avoids this problem and yet maintains the other characteristics of the time series is the Different Group Time Series Design. Rather than make repeated measures on one group, this design substitutes several randomly selected groups, each of which is measured only once but at different times.

Q.2 The Different Group Time Series Design

$$R \; O_1$$
$$R \qquad O_2$$
$$R \qquad\quad O_3$$
$$R \qquad\qquad O_4$$
$$X$$
$$R \qquad\qquad\qquad O_5$$
$$R \qquad\qquad\qquad\quad O_6$$
$$R \qquad\qquad\qquad\qquad O_7$$
$$R \qquad\qquad\qquad\qquad\quad O_8$$

Design Q.2 produces the same type of data as the regular time series and can be analyzed using the same graphing procedure. In terms of internal validity, Design Q.2 controls the same threats as the time series. Random sampling is relied on to equate the several comparison groups. Design Q.2 also has the same weakness as the time series design. Historical

events can intervene between O_4 and O_5, possibly confusing the results.

Because of the many random samples required by this design, it is limited to situations where the cost of those samples is inexpensive. For example, if it is possible to draw the samples and collect data by telephone, this design is ideal. This is essentially the approach used by commercial pollsters as they repeatedly measure public opinion by conducting monthly telephone surveys of different random samples. Although the pollsters do not conduct experiments, their repeated measures allow the assessment of the impact of events on public opinion. The event in question becomes the X in the design, and levels of opinion are compared before and after it occurred. For example, after President Reagan was shot by a would-be assassin in the spring of 1981, his popularity increased dramatically. Because of the series of before-and-after measures, there was little doubt that it was the assassination attempt that heightened his popularity.

As we have noted, both of the preceding designs suffer from the validity threat of history. By the addition of a control group to that time series design, this last remaining threat is controlled. Design Q.3 illustrates this and is known as the Multiple Time Series Design.

Q.3 The Multiple Time Series Design

Experimental
group: $O_1 \, O_2 \, O_3 \, O_4 \, X \, O_5 \, O_6 \, O_7 \, O_8$

Control
group: $O_1 \, O_2 \, O_3 \, O_4 \quad\; O_5 \, O_6 \, O_7 \, O_8$

Design Q.3 controls all of the threats to internal validity, including history. Events other than X should affect both groups equally, so history is not a rival explanation for differences between the groups after the experimental group has been exposed to *X*. A design that uses a control group without random assignment might be thought suspect on the threat of selection. This is less of a problem than with preexperimental designs, however, as the series of before measures affords ample opportunity to see how similar the comparison groups are.

Data from Design Q.3 are plotted and analyzed in the same way as with the two preceding designs. This time, however, there are two lines on the graph, one for the experimental group and one for the control group. The patterns of the two groups are compared to see what effect *X* produced. As a demonstration of the utility of quasi-experimental designs, Donald Campbell and H. Laurence Ross (1968) studied the impact of a crackdown on speeding on the highway fatality rate in Connecticut. After a particularly bloody year of traffic accidents in 1955, Connecticut instituted a crackdown on speeders in 1956. As Figure 10.2 illustrates, the fatality rate fell in the years following the crackdown. But was the decrease due to the crackdown or something else? By pooling fatality data from contiguous states where there was no similar crackdown on speeders, Campbell and Ross were able to produce a control group for comparison. Because no similar decline in fatality rates was evident in the surrounding states, it became safer to conclude that the crackdown on speeders was what produced the reduction in Connecticut. However, given the fluctuation in fatality rates in Connecticut in previous years, which is not evident in the control states, the conclusion is still not certain.

Quasi-experimental designs have considerable potential for human service research, much of which involves re-

peated contact with the same clients. Records of clients' situations and progress are routinely kept, which means that the repeated measures required by the time series designs might not be difficult to obtain. Various treatments or programs used with the clients would constitute the experimental condition. Plotting the data as suggested for time series analysis would reveal whatever impact those procedures produced. Some of these topics and the intricacies of such designs will be discussed in more detail in Chapter 11.

External Validity

In experiments, researchers make something happen that would not have occurred naturally. In laboratory experiments, for example, they construct a social setting that, they believe, simulates what occurs in the everyday world. In addition to being artificial, this setting is typically more simple than what occurs naturally because researchers try to limit the number of social or psychological forces operating in order to observe more clearly the influence of the independent variables on the dependent variable. Even field experiments, which are considerably more natural than those in the laboratory, involve a manipulation of an independent variable by the researcher—a change in the scene that would not have occurred without the researcher's intervention.

This "unnaturalness" raises a validity problem different from internal validity discussed earlier in the chapter. **External validity** concerns the extent to which causal inferences made in an experiment can be generalized to other times, settings, or groups of people (Cook and Campbell, 1979). The basic issue is

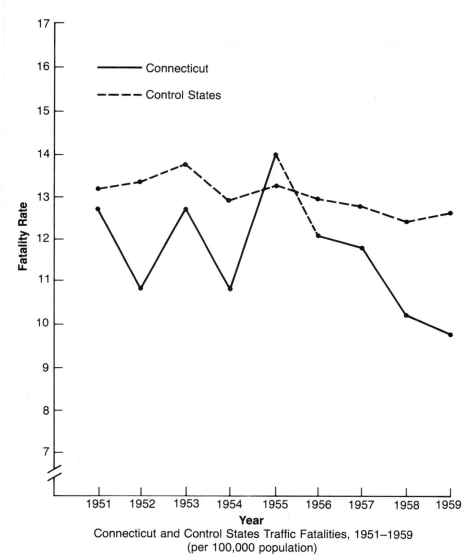

Connecticut and Control States Traffic Fatalities, 1951–1959
(per 100,000 population)

Figure 10.2 Example of Multiple Time Series Data: Connecticut and Control States Traffic Fatalities, 1951–1959 (per 100,000 population)

Source: Donald T. Campbell and H. Laurence Ross, ''The Connecticut Crackdown on Speeding: Time Series Data in Quasi-Experimental Analysis,'' *Law and Society Review*, 3:1 (1968). Copyright © 1968 by the Law and Society Association. Used with permission.

whether an experiment is so simple, contrived, or in some other way different from the everyday world that what we learn from the experiment does not apply to the natural world. This problem is a part of the problem of generalizing findings from samples to populations discussed in Chapter 6. With experiments, however, some special problems arise that are not found with sampling in other types of research methods. Indeed, resolving the problem of external validity can be difficult and is less straightforward than is the case with internal validity. As Campbell and Stanley (1963, p. 17) succinctly state the problem:

> Whereas the problems of internal validity are solvable within the limits of the logic of probability statistics, the problems of external validity are not logically solvable in any neat, conclusive way. Generalization always turns out to involve extrapolation into a realm not represented in one's sample.

We will review four major threats to external validity and ways in which these threats can be reduced.

Reactive Effects of Testing

In any design using pretesting, the possibility exists that experiencing the pretest can alter subjects' reactions to the independent variable. For example, items on a paper-and-pencil pretest measure might make subjects more or less responsive to the independent variable than they would have been without exposure to those items. The problem this raises for generalizability should not be difficult to understand. The populations to which we wish to generalize findings are composed of people who have not been pretested. Therefore, if the subjects are af-

fected by the pretest, findings may not accurately generalize to the unpretested population.

Whether reactive effects of testing are a threat to generalizability depends on the variables involved in the experiment and the nature of the measurement process used. Paper-and-pencil measures may be quite reactive whereas unobtrusive observation is likely not to be reactive. When one is planning an experiment, therefore, it is important to consider whether reactive effects of testing are likely to be a problem. If they are, then it would be desirable to choose a research design that does not call for pretesting, such as Design T.3, or one that includes groups that are not pretested, such as the Solomon design. With the latter design, it is possible to measure the extent of any pretesting effects.

Unrepresentative Samples

As we emphasized in Chapter 6, the representativeness of the people studied in any form of research is crucial to the issue of generalizability. Unfortunately, it is often difficult to experiment on truly representative samples of any known population. Often experimental subjects are volunteers, people who are enticed in some way to participate, or people who happen to be available to the researcher. The implications of this for generalizing experimental findings are quite serious. For example, one review of a large number of studies concluded that people who volunteer for experiments differ systematically from the general population in the following ways: The volunteers are better educated, come from a higher social class, have higher intelligence, have a greater need for social approval, and are more sociable (Rosenthal and Rosnow,

1975). Clearly, these differences could be related to any number of the variables likely to be used in human service research. Generalizing findings from such volunteer subjects could be quite hazardous.

Although the use of coerced subjects may reduce the differences between experimental subjects and the general population from which they are drawn, it has problems of its own as far as generalization is concerned. Coerced subjects are likely to have little interest in the experiment and may be resentful about the coercion used (Cox and Sipprelle, 1971). This effect has been found even where the nature of the coercion was quite mild, such as gaining extra credit in a college class for agreeing to participate in an experiment. It is reasonable to assume that these effects would be amplified where the level of coercion was greater, such as court-ordered participation in a treatment program under threat of incarceration. In fact, a study of a drug treatment program involving court-ordered clients found this anticipated pattern (Peyrot, 1985). The coerced clients were resentful, uncooperative, and unwilling to commit to the therapeutic objectives of the program.

The threat to external validity created by unrepresentative samples is of great importance to human service workers because most efforts to evaluate the effectiveness of treatment approaches are conducted on volunteers or coerced subjects. Volunteers may make programs look good because they are interested in the treatment and motivated to change in the direction promoted by the treatment. It should come as no surprise that apparently effective treatment approaches on volunteers often fail when applied to non-volunteer groups. Alternatively, because of their lack of interest and resentment, coerced subjects tend to make treatments appear ineffective when they might be effective on persons who are not coerced.

Reactive Settings

In addition to the reactivity produced by testing, the experimental setting itself may be reactive, leading people to behave in ways that are different from their behavior in the everyday world. One reason for this is that experimental settings contain *demand characteristics:* subtle, unprogrammed cues that communicate to subjects something about how they should behave. For example, people in experiments tend to be highly cooperative and responsive to the experimenter. In fact, the psychologist Martin Orne (1962) deliberately tried to create boring and repetitive tasks for subjects so that they would rebel and refuse to do them. One task was to perform a series of additions of random numbers. Each page required 200 additions, and each person was given 2000 pages. After giving instructions, the experimenter told them to continue working until he returned. Five and one-half hours later the subjects were still working, and it was Orne who gave up and ended the experiment! On the basis of this and other research, it has become evident that experimental settings exercise a powerful influence on subjects that can damage the generalizability of experimental findings. This has been labeled as the problem of the ''good subject''—that is, the subject who will do whatever the investigator asks, even to the point of confirming the experimenter's hypotheses if they are communicated to the subject (Wuebben, Straits, and Schulman, 1974).

Subjects' reactions are not the only

way in which experimental settings can be reactive. Experimenters themselves can introduce distortion into the results that can reduce generalizability. Experimenters, of course, usually have expectations concerning the results of the experiment, wanting it to come out one way or another. These *experimenter's expectations* can be communicated to subjects in such a subtle fashion that neither experimenter nor subjects are aware that the communication has taken place (Rosenthal, 1967). A classic illustration of how subtle this can be is recounted by Graham (1977) and involves a horse, not humans. The horse was called Clever Hans because of his seeming ability to solve fairly complex arithmetic problems. Hans and his trainer toured Europe in the early 1900s, amazing audiences and becoming quite famous. Hans would stand on stage pounding out the answers to problems with his hoofs. Amazingly, Hans was hardly ever wrong. Hans would perform his feats as well even when his trainer was not present. Could Hans really do arithmetic? After very careful observation it was discovered that Hans was picking up the subtle cues given off by those who asked him questions. As Hans approached the correct number of hoofbeats, questioners would move or shift just enough to cue the horse that it was time to stop.

The same phenomenon has been thoroughly investigated in the physician–patient relationship (Kline, 1988). When giving a patient a treatment known to be effective, a physician exudes confidence, and the patient picks up on this and expects to get better. The patient's hopeful mood then increases the likelihood that the patient will actually improve. However, when a physician is giving a patient a placebo—an inert substance the physician doesn't expect to work—his or her

manner communicates doubt, and the patient helps that expectation become a reality. So the patient senses, without being aware of it, what the physician's expectations are and then helps create that reality. People in experiments do the same thing. They react to cues unconsciously given off by an experimenter. What happens is that experimenters give off subtle cues to subjects that tell subjects how to behave in a way that researchers would like them to.

Reactive experimental settings can threaten external validity because changes in the dependent variable might be due to demand characteristics or experimenter expectancies rather than to the independent variable. One procedure for reducing the problem of reactivity in experimental settings is to conduct the experiment in such a way that subjects are "blind"—that is, unaware of the experimental hypotheses—so that this knowledge will not influence their behavior. In fact, subjects are commonly given a false rationale for what they are to do in order to reduce the reactions of subjects that might interfere with the generalizability of the findings. As an ethical matter, subjects should be informed of the experiment's true purpose during the postexperimental debriefing session.

The surest way of controlling reactivity due to the experimenter is to run what is called a *double-blind* experiment. In a **double-blind experiment,** neither the subjects nor the experimenter know which people are in the experimental and which are in the control condition. This makes it impossible for the experimenter to communicate to subjects how they ought to behave because, for any given subject, the experimenter would not know which responses would confirm the experimental hypotheses. Though it is simple in theory, maintaining a double-blind procedure in practice can be difficult. Another layer of personnel must be added to accomplish the assignment of subjects, issue sealed instructions to the experimenter, and keep track of the results. Furthermore, all information relating to these activities must be kept from those actually running the experimental groups. It is easy for this structure to break down so that the double-blind feature is lost. However, for true protection against such reactivity, double-blind experiments need to be used. Unfortunately, there are times when the nature of the treatment interferes with the use of the double-blind approach. Because of the different activities involved, it may be obvious which condition is experimental and which is control. Clearly, this would prevent the use of a double-blind experiment.

Multiple-Treatment Interference

In an experiment in which there is more than one independent variable, it may be the particular combination and ordering of experimental treatments that produce change in the dependent variable. If this same combination and this same ordering do not occur outside the experimental setting, the findings from the experiment cannot be generalized. Suppose, for example, that an experiment calls for subjects to experience four independent variables in succession. Furthermore, suppose that the last variable in the series appears to produce an interesting effect. Could the effect of that fourth variable be safely generalized on the basis of the experimental findings? The answer would be no. The subjects in the experiment would have experienced three other independent variables first. Experiencing those other variables first might have affected the way they reacted to the last

one. If people outside of the experimental setting do not experience all the variables in sequence, generalization concerning the fourth variable is risky. The problem of multiple-treatment interference is similar to reactive effects of testing in that the subjects in the experiment experience something that the people in the population at large do not.

The threat of multiple-treatment interference can be effectively eliminated through the use of complex designs in which the independent variables are experienced by the different experimental groups in every possible sequence. If a given variable produces a consistent effect regardless of the ordering of the variables, then multiple-treatment interference is not a threat to the generalizability of the findings. An alternative is to isolate the variable of interest in a multiple-treatment experiment and conduct a follow-up experiment with that variable as the only treatment. If it produces an effect similar to that found when it was a part of a series of treatments, multiple-treatment interference can be ruled out.

In designing experiments, especially those to be conducted in laboratory settings, problems of external validity need to be considered. Properly designed experiments can offer researchers substantial confidence in generalizing from an experimental sample to other settings or groups. However, efforts to enhance external validity may impact on our ability to achieve internal validity, which brings us to the importance of replication for external validity.

The Importance of Replication

Although both internal and external validity are important to experimental research, there is a tension between the two. On the one hand, internal validity is enhanced through greater control. Consequently, the researcher seeking internal validity is attracted to the laboratory experiment and to precise testing. Yet we have just seen that the reactive effect of testing is a threat to external validity. Seeking control, the researcher may use a homogeneous sample to avoid the confounding effects of other variables. In the effort to achieve internal validity, one might, for example, use a sample of white, male 18-year-olds. Although the effects of race, sex, and age are now controlled, the external validity threat of unrepresentative samples is increased. We have suggested the use of complex designs to reduce the threat to external validity of multiple-treatment interference. However, complex designs are more difficult to implement in a way that retains the integrity of the research design. Thus, there appears to be a dilemma between seeking internal validity on the one hand and external validity on the other.

The basic solution to this problem is not to seek a solution to both internal validity and external validity in one single study. As Thomas Cook and Donald Campbell (1979, p. 78) put it with regard to experiments: "In the last analysis, external validity . . . is a matter of replication." Confidence in generalizing from experimental findings increases as the same hypotheses are tested and supported in a variety of settings with a variety of designs. Often this takes the form of initial testing in the laboratory under ideal conditions to see if the hypothesis is supported at all. Then the same hypothesis can be tested under the less-than-ideal conditions of the field. Through replication, the dual objectives of internal and external validity can be achieved.

Lack of Minority Participation and Analysis

Depending on the setting in which an experiment is conducted, women and minorities may well find themselves underrepresented in laboratory or field experiments. This is a problem that can affect external validity as well as internal validity. Researchers often choose as subjects for experiments college students who are easily accessible to them. Further, it is often students in introductory psychology or sociology classes who are selected. The sex ratio of college students is fairly even: 47 percent male and 53 percent female. However, nonwhites constitute only 15 percent of all college students while they are 25 percent or more of our total population (U.S. Bureau of the Census, 1987). This means that experiments using a representative sample of college students will tend to underrepresent blacks, Hispanics, and some other minorities. And this underrepresentation is more severe at some colleges than at others: Some major research universities even today have only 1- or 2-percent black enrollment. So, whenever experimental subjects are selected from a setting, care must be taken to ensure representation of minorities in a sample if the minorities are to be included in the generalizations made from the data. Otherwise, mention should be made that no special procedures were used in the sampling to enhance minority involvement.

A related problem is what one sociologist calls "gender insensitivity": "ignoring gender as an important social variable" (Eichler, 1988, p. 66). In experiments, this can happen when no mention is made about the sex ratio of the subjects in the experiment or data are not analyzed separately for each sex. Eichler reports one issue of a psychology journal in which the only article to mention the sex of the subjects was one that used rhesus monkeys; none of those using human subjects did so. This was true despite the fact that practically all of those articles focused on variables (such as perception, verbal ability, and learning) on which people's gender might well have an influence.

A final problem relating to minority participation in experiments is the failure to consider the gender or minority status of all participants in the experiment. In addition to the researcher and the subject, this might include interviewers, confederates of the experimenter, and any others who interact with the subject during data collection. We know, for example, that people of the same gender interact differently from people of the opposite gender. So, a male interviewer will respond differently when asking questions of a female subject from when interviewing a male subject. In the former case, he might be more friendly, attentive, or engaging without even realizing it, and this could influence the subject's response to questions.

These threats to external validity can be reduced by reporting the sex or minority status of the various people involved in experiments and analyzing the data with sex or minority status as an experimental or control variable. There are, of course, reasons to have a homogeneous sample in an experiment: It can reduce extraneous variation when trying to establish a causal relationship between independent and dependent variables. However, if the results are to be generalized to all racial and ethnic groups and both sexes, then experiments need to be replicated using subjects from these groups. For example, Research in Prac-

tice 10.2 describes a program of experimental evaluation of social work intervention in which replication was done to improve external validity.

Assessment of Experiments

By now you should more fully appreciate the extent to which experimentation can be used in human service research. In addition, you should recognize how the logic of experimentation can be translated into valuable guidelines that can enhance human service intervention. We will close the chapter with a brief summary of the advantages and disadvantages of experiments.

Advantages

Inference of Causality The major advantage of experimental research is that it places us in the most advantageous position from which to infer causal relationships between variables. Recall from Chapter 2 that causality can never be directly observed. Rather we infer that one thing caused another by observing changes in the two things under the appropriate conditions. A well-designed and controlled experiment puts us in the strongest position to make that causal inference because it enables us to control the effect of other variables, which raises our confidence that it is the independent variable that is bringing about changes in the dependent variable. Experiments also permit us to establish the time sequence necessary for inferring causality. We can measure the dependent variable to see if it has changed *since* the experimental manipulation. With other research methods, such as the survey, it is often not possible to determine whether the

RESEARCH IN PRACTICE 10.2
Practice Effectiveness: A Program of Knowledge Building Through Experimental Design

For reasons presented in this chapter, the experimental design is clearly the best approach social scientists have devised for demonstrating causality, and it is therefore a preferred choice for researchers seeking to test practice theory. However, barriers such as difficulty in applying randomization, restricted sampling opportunities, and issues of external validity present significant obstacles to implementing experiments in the quest for practice knowledge. Even when experiments are undertaken, the knowledge derived can easily be fragmented because of the limited findings produced by any one experiment alone. Unless there is some way of coordinating experiments into a unified program of research, much of the potential for this design can go unrealized.

An excellent example of both overcoming the obstacles to using experimental design and organizing studies into a unified program of knowledge building comes from the field of social group work in which a program of doctoral study has made significant advances in the application of the experimental model to practice issues. Over an 11-year period, Sheldon Rose (1988) supervised 18 doctoral dissertations through a process described as "thematic research" as a part of the Interpersonal Skill Training and Research Project of the School of Social Work of the University of Wisconsin–Madison.

Rose uses the term "thematic research" to describe an approach to knowledge building in which a series of projects are generated around a practice approach or theme as a way of investigating an area more fully than could be accomplished with a single study. The 18 projects represent three such thematic efforts. One series of experiments was designed to test the effectiveness of assertiveness training in groups; a second investigated social skills and problem-solving training with school children; and five new studies have been created that build on the assertiveness studies and evaluate a multimethod group approach to managing stress, anger, and pain. All the studies used treatment and control conditions. In some cases randomization was used; in other studies matching was relied on to establish comparisons. Several studies employed waiting lists to achieve a no-treatment comparison group, while comparison with an existing treatment was used in others.

In the course of achieving precision and control by such techniques as using homogeneous samples, the researcher often sacrifices the ability to generalize findings. The eight studies on assertiveness illustrate this point. Treatment and control groups were typically small (under 40) and homogeneous in nature, so generalization on the effectiveness of a method based on any one study would be especially ill-advised. To address this disadvantage, very different samples were used in the various studies. Target populations included the general population, women, elderly, couples, families with adolescents, parents, and parents of handicapped children. In the case of the series of studies on social skills and problem-solving training, one study (Hepler, 1986) used a sample comprised of white sixth graders. A later study (Hayden, 1988) replicated the study with mixed racial and socioeconomic groups. Thus, the issue of external validity of findings was addressed through replication with quite different groups.

Another limitation of a single study is that the necessity of specifying a precise independent variable restricts the degree to which a given intervention can be evaluated. Even a fairly explicit intervention such as assertiveness training has many subcomponents, so several studies may be required to fully evaluate the method. This aspect of knowledge building is exemplified by the more recent studies on multiple component treatments. Earlier projects focused on assertiveness training only (Schinke, 1976), while later works involved a multimethod package of interventions designed from the earlier experience with assertiveness training (Hall, 1981). Working in the area of managing stress, anger, and pain, a study by Tallant (1986) was used to assess whether social support contributed to the effectiveness of a multimethod approach investigated by Tolman (1985) that included relaxation training, assertion training, group methods, operant techniques, and cognitive restructuring. Again, the more complex interventions were built on the successful experiences with the earlier efforts.

Rose points out that thorough preparation and extensive background work form the foundation of a well-done practice evaluation experiment. The doctoral researchers follow these steps in completing an experimental design for their dissertations:

1. Carefully describe the attributes of the clinical population who will be served through the project.
2. Articulate an intervention and explicate how it derives from an intervention theory.
3. By building on experiences from prior projects, prepare assessment and intervention protocols, obtain approval for human subject research, and develop client–subject recruitment plans.
4. Undertake a pilot study to check the recruitment, assessment, intervention, and generalization strategies before the actual experiment is put into operation.
5. Design a control group or matched group experiment with a follow-up period of at least three months.
6. Conduct the experiment while monitoring the group process through post-session questionnaires, observation of interactions, rates of assignment completion, attendance, and promptness.

A major advantage of the thematic approach is that it avoids "reinventing the wheel" with each study. For example, techniques that worked in one study for recruiting subjects can be applied to the next. A relationship cultivated with human service agencies to

(Continued on next page)

provide referrals or therapists can be further relied on for future studies. Students who will eventually head research projects of their own work as assistants on studies that are in progress by advanced students. Conducting true experiments is a complex, time-consuming, and expensive undertaking; and the experience base of earlier studies does much to make the experimental research process more feasible.

Although undertaking a program of experimental research for practice development purposes is extremely challenging, Rose identifies some significant achievements. He reports that the three series of studies undertaken in this project represent the only extended evaluation of interventions in social work. In general, they provide support for the effectiveness of the approaches that were evaluated. Beyond the results of the studies themselves, the research process has also generated useful products for practice. In-

tervention manuals that detail the treatment techniques used in the experiments have been adopted by the therapeutic community. Not only can practitioners make use of the findings of the studies, but they can use many of the tools for measurement and assessment in their own practice as well. For example, one article based on the research experience details group monitoring techniques that practitioners can use (Rose, 1984) and another provides explicit directions for evaluating client outcomes in groups (Rose and Tolman, 1985).

So, there are real benefits for the advancement of practice to be derived from a sustained program of experimentation. In a time when the human services are being confronted with the demand to be accountable, there is more need than ever for well-designed studies that assess the effectiveness of our interventions.

changes in one variable preceded or followed changes in another variable.

Control   Experimenters are not limited by the variables and events that happen to be naturally occurring in a particular situation. Rather, they can decide what variables will be studied, what values those variables will take, and what combination of variables will be included. In other words, they can create precisely what their hypotheses suggest are important. This is in sharp contrast to other research methods, such as the use of available data (see Chapter 8) or some observational techniques (see Chapter 9), in which hypotheses need to be reshaped to fit the existing data or observations.

The Study of Change   Many experimental designs are longitudinal, which means that they are conducted over a period of time, and measurements are taken at more than one time. This makes it possible to study changes over time. Many other research methods, such as surveys, tend to be cross-sectional—they are like "snapshots" taken at a given point in time. In cross-sectional studies, we can *ask* people how things have changed over time, but we cannot *directly observe* that change.

Costs   In some cases, experiments—especially those conducted in laboratory settings—can be considerably cheaper than other research methods. Because of the element of control, the sample size can be smaller and this saves money. The costly travel expenses and interviewer salaries found in some surveys are eliminated. Some field experiments, however, can be expensive because they may require interviewing—possibly more than once—to assess changes in dependent variables.

Disadvantages

Artificiality The laboratory setting in which many experiments are conducted is an artificial environment created by the investigator, and it raises questions of external validity. We often do not know what the relationship is between this artificial setting and the real world in which people live out their daily lives. We cannot be sure that people would behave in the same fashion on the street or in the classroom as they do in the laboratory. (Field experiments, of course, do not suffer from this problem.) The laboratory setting, in addition to being artificial, is also a much simpler environment in terms of the range and interaction of social and psychological forces playing on a person at any given time. In the real world, such simplicity rarely exists. The problem is that the interaction of a number of factors may significantly change the way in which the variables of interest to us would operate.

Sampling Problems Because many experiments, especially those in the laboratory, can normally be conducted with only a few subjects at any given time, the time and cost considerations rise considerably as sample size increases. Thus, experiments are normally limited to fairly small samples—a few hundred at best and often much smaller. These small samples increase the problems of measurement error and make generalization of the findings more difficult. In addition, experiments very commonly have unrepresentative samples because they use availability samples. It is often assumed that representative sampling is not as essential in experiments as in other types of research because of the randomization and control available to experimenters. Although these help, one still must be cautious regarding the population to which one makes generalizations.

Experimenter Effects We have just pointed out the artificiality of experimental settings in comparison to the real world. Yet there is another side to this coin: The experimental setting itself is a real world—a social occasion in which social norms, roles, and values exist and shape people's behavior (Wuebben, Straits, and Schulman, 1974). Social processes that arise within the experimental setting—and that are not a part of the experimental variables—may shape the research outcome. Thus, changes in the dependent variable may be due to the demand characteristics of experiments or to the impact of experimenter expectations—factors, obviously, that do not influence people in the everyday world.

||||||||||||||||||||||||||||||||||||||||||||||||||||||||||||||||||||||||||||||||||||||||||||||||||||||||

☰ Main Points

• Experiments are a controlled method of observation in which the value of one or more independent variables is changed in order to assess the causal effect on one or more dependent variables.

• Owing to the great control afforded

by experiments, they are the surest method of discovering causal relationships among variables.

• Major elements of control in experiments include control variables, control groups, matching, and randomization.

• Internal validity refers to whether the independent variable does in fact produce the effect it appears to produce on the dependent variable.

• Numerous conditions may threaten the internal validity of experiments, but all of them can be controlled by using true experimental designs.

• Quasi-experimental designs are useful for bringing much of the control of an experiment to nonexperimental situations.

• External validity concerns the degree to which experimental results can be generalized beyond the experimental setting.

• Threats to external validity are generally not controllable through design, being more difficult and less straightforward to control.

• Double-blind experiments, in which neither the subjects nor the experimenters know which groups are in the experimental or control condition, are used to control both experimental demand characteristics and experimenter bias.

• To avoid race, ethnicity, or gender "insensitivity," the minority composition of experimental groups should be reported, consideration should be given to analyzing the data by controlling for minority impact, and the minority status of all experimental participants should be considered.

• An understanding of experimental procedures can contribute to practice effectiveness as well as research endeavors.

☰ Important Terms for Review

blocking
control condition
control group
control variables
double-blind experiment
experimental condition
experimental group
experimental stimulus
experimental variability
experimentation
external validity
extraneous variability
field experiments
internal validity
laboratory experiments
matching
preexperimental design
quasi-experimental design
random assignment
true experimental design

☰ For Further Reading

Adair, J. *The Human Subject: The Social Psychology of the Psychological Experiment.* Boston: Little, Brown, 1973.
A good analysis of the many kinds of reactivity and experimenter expectancies that can be found in experimental settings.

Fairweather, George W., and William S. Davidson. *An Introduction to Community Experimentation: Theory, Methods, and Practice.* New York: McGraw-Hill, 1986.
An interesting book ideally suited to those involved in community action programs. It outlines the reasons for experimentation and supplies the designs to evaluate the effectiveness of various intervention programs.

Gamson, William A., Bruce Fireman, and Steven Rytina. *Encounters with Unjust Authority.* Homewood, Ill.: Dorsey Press, 1982.
An experimental design to study how people respond to requests to assist an otherwise respectable organization to do some-

thing reprehensible or unethical. It suggests a creative way to study the relationships between human service organizations and their members and clients.

Gottman, John M. *Time-Series Analysis: A Comprehensive Introduction for Social Scientists.* New York: Cambridge, 1981.

Comprehensive is certainly the operative word in describing this book as it details the mathematical analysis of time-series designs. The author also argues persuasively against the common "eyeballing" approach to time-series analysis.

Pechman, Joseph, and P. Michael Timpane, eds. *Work Incentives and Income Guarantees: The New Jersey Income Tax Experiment.* Washington, D.C.: The Brookings Institution, 1975.

An excellent discussion of methodological and political problems in conducting an applied experiment in a controversial field setting.

Schwartz, Edward E., and William C. Sample. *The Midway Office: An Experiment in the Organization of Work Groups.* New York: National Association of Social Workers, 1972.

A field experiment intended to assess the most effective use of caseworkers in human service organizations.

☰ Exercises for Class Discussion

A senior citizens service organization is concerned about the large number of purse snatchings and other attacks on elderly people in the community and decides to apply for a Department of Justice grant intended to assist local communities in fighting crime. A requirement for receiving such a grant is that an evaluation be done to assess the effectiveness of any program established.

The idea of the staff of the center is, first, to hire local teenagers to work out of the center as escorts to those people who request the service. Second, they plan to use the teenagers as a crime watch in those areas where attacks have been fairly frequent. Initially, the center will not be able to serve everyone, and the crime watch staff will only be able to cover some of the neighborhoods.

The senior center staff believes that this program will serve two objectives. First, it will reduce the threat of crime to the elderly. Second, if young people are put into positions where they can work with and help the elderly, it will increase feelings of understanding between the generations.

You have been asked to help the center develop a research design whose purpose is to assess how well the program attains its objectives.

10.1 What would be the independent and dependent variables for such a project? Give some examples of possible indicators for these variables. Given the various types of experimental designs available—preexperimental, quasi-experimental, and true experimental—which two would be the most appropriate to the research question and the most feasible?

10.2 One decision that needs to be made is whether to use the presence or absence of the program as the independent variable or to test different combinations of the independent variables. List some possible combinations of intervention efforts that could be used in a factorial design.

10.3 A major issue in experimental research is how to assign participants to experimental and control conditions.

   a. Consider just the escort service. How could participants be assigned to treatment and control conditions? Would random assignment be ethical? Indicate why or why not.

b. Now consider the crime watch component, which serves anyone who happens to be in the patrolled area. Assume the center serves about a 50-block area of the city. Suggest some ways of developing experimental and control conditions.

c. Are there any control variables that might be usefully considered in this study? How would these control variables assist you in making causal inferences?

10.4 How would you collect data to evaluate the effectiveness of the program in meeting its goals of reducing crime and increasing intergenerational understanding? Consider the alternatives of personal interviews, mailed questionnaries, observations, and existing data.

Now there's trouble in River City. It seems a local, very influential politician has gotten wind of the project. His mother lives in the impact area, and under no circumstances will he support an evaluation where his mother may wind up as a control subject who will not be provided services. Without his support, there will be no grant.

10.5 How could you design a quasi-experimental study that would not involve designating certain people or areas as experimental and control? What deficiencies would this design have in comparison to a true experiment?

10.6 What are the major threats to internal and external validity in this research project? How have the designs considered in the preceding exercises helped to reduce these threats?

11

Single-Subject Designs

Much human service work occurs in clinical settings in which practitioners attempt to improve the functioning of individual clients. This one-to-one relationship may at first appear far removed from research settings involving the experimental groups, independent variables, and matching described in the preceding chapter. Although research findings are clearly useful in such practice settings, can the practitioner–client encounter itself be considered a part of that research process? Increasingly, the practitioner–client relationship is becoming an arena for social research. Not only is this individual client interaction being recognized as able to serve the purposes of scientific research and knowledge accumulation, but practitioners are also calling on research practices to help enhance their intervention efforts (Fischer, 1981).

We saw in Chapter 1 that there is a growing tendency for human service professionals to view their role as that of clinician-researchers. The purpose of this chapter is to present a fundamental tool of this role and a central mechanism through which valid research can be conducted in clinical settings: the *single-subject design*. **Single-subject designs** are quasi-experimental research designs that involve assessing change in a dependent variable on a single research subject. The dependent variable is measured during a baseline phase and during one or more intervention phases when the independent variable is manipulated. Experimental effects are inferred by comparisons of the subject's responses across baseline and intervention phases. We will begin by discussing how and why a "clinical-research model" has emerged in the human services. Then, we will analyze the clinical-research process, showing how research can be merged with clinical practice. Building on the discussion of experimental designs in Chapter 10, we will then present the various kinds of single-subject designs that are available to clinician-researchers. Finally, we will analyze the advantages and disadvantages of single-subject designs.

The Clinical-Research Model

As with advances in many other areas, interest in single-subject designs grew out of dissatisfaction with existing sources of knowledge (Barlow and Hersen, 1984; Levy and Olson, 1979; Jayaratne and Levy, 1979). Prior to single-subject designs, one major source of new knowledge for many practitioners was group experiments. Group experiments, however, are often inappropriate or impossible to conduct in clinical settings. It is often too time-consuming and costly to assemble clients with similar problems and randomly assign some to treatment and others to control groups. A second problem with group experiments in terms of practice implications is that the results are often an average of the whole group's response, obscuring individual reactions. It is, of course, precisely the effects on individuals that are of most interest to clinicians. For example, knowing that a given treatment was effective on 70 percent of an experimental group may be interesting, but it helps relatively little in predicting the reaction of a particular client seated in a practitioner's office.

Another problem in some traditional group experimentation is the failure of the research design to capture the process by which change was induced. Thus, traditional research has sometimes been referred to as "black box" research because subjects receive some treatment and are then compared with other subjects who did not receive the treatment. With only a pretest and posttest measure, experimenters may not have information on the process of how change occurred but only on whether or not it occurred. It is as if the subjects passed through a mysterious black box and came out either improved or not improved. A fourth complaint about traditional group experiments has been that the complicated nature of the statistical analysis associated with data interpretation necessitate that quantitative methodologists, not regular practitioners, carry out the research. This reliance on direction from outside of practice may have contributed to studies' being viewed as not relevant to practice. Finally, the use of control groups, from whom treatment is withheld, has been a source of ethical concern to human service professionals. Thus, although group experiments are appropriate for some purposes, the deficiencies inherent in the method have led both practitioners and researchers to seek an alternative approach for evaluating individual change and refining intervention techniques. Single-subject designs, as we shall see, effectively avoid the unattractive features of group experiments.

A second source of clinical knowledge prior to single-subject designs was case histories. A case history, of course, is a report from a clinician about a client who has undergone treatment. Whereas many of these reports are intriguing, they often do not provide a sound basis for the accumulation of knowledge. First of all, they exhibit to only a limited degree the characteristics that distinguish science from other sources of knowledge (see Chapter 2). For example, vague treatments are often reported to have produced vague improvements. Because of this, other practitioners would have grave difficulty replicating the procedures if they wished. And the ability to replicate is, of course, a fundamental characteristic of the scientific method, especially when one is working with a single case at a time. In addition, case histories are often prepared only on successes, so information about failures, which may be of equal importance, is not communicated to other practitioners. Another problem with case histories is a failure to report valid and reliable data to support conclusions. In the absence of hard data, exaggerated claims of success become commonplace (Barlow and Hersen 1984). Finally, these studies, with no controls, fail to consider the possible impact of extraneous variables on the client.

So it was against this backdrop of unsatisfactory research techniques for clinical settings that the clinical-research model emerged. The **clinical-research model** became an effort to merge research and practice, and it includes much more than single-subject designs. It involves a stance toward practice that includes the following basic points (Bloom and Fischer, 1982):

1. The human service professional views service delivery as a problem-solving experiment in which a major responsibility of the practitioner is to hypothesize and test relationships between client problems and intervention effects.
2. The professional incorporates single-subject designs as a routine strategy in the monitoring and evaluation of all clients.
3. In the selection of practice strategies, the clinician-researcher gives preference to knowedge that has been substantiated by empirical testing in contrast with knowledge that is primarily of a traditional, intuitive, or experiential nature.
4. The practitioner places a high value on the professional responsibility to continue learning and evaluating practice techniques in order to improve intervention.

The systematic evaluation of practice through the use of single-subject designs is a core component of this model of practice. It is through the mechanism of single-subject designs that research and practice merge into one enterprise. (The parallels between the clinical-research model and our discussion of "clinical scientists" in Research in Practice 1.1 should make this point clear.) It should be noted, however, that this approach does not reject traditional large-group research. Such research is necessary for testing total programs and for confirming the generalizability of intervention effectiveness. With this note of clarification, we now turn to examining the stages in the clinical-research process and how

single-subject designs are incorporated into practice.

The Clinical-Research Process

At the outset, we wish to make it clear that the clinical-research model is not a radically new approach to intervention. In fact, there are many parallels between this model and traditional practice. Much of what the model calls for many practitioners are likely to do anyway. The model does, however, inject greater specificity, objectivity, and empiricism into the clinical process. By following the model, clinician-researchers are in a position to know precisely what treatment was applied and how much effect was produced and to have supporting data for proof. The model links research and practice by putting the practitioner in the enviable position of not only bringing about change but also having valid evidence as to why the change occurred. What follows in this section is an outline of the clinical-research process divided into five stages, which are summarized in Figure 11.1.

Establish Problems and Goals

As in all practice approaches, the clinical-research model begins with an assessment of the client's problem. Typically, the problem will involve some aspect of the client's functioning: behaviors, perceptions, attitudes, or feelings. During the initial stage, the practitioner strives to obtain as clear and specific an understanding of the problem as possible, using assessment strategies, such as interviewing or paper-and-pencil assessment tools, commonly used by practitioners.

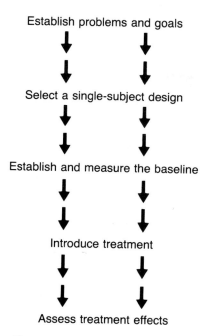

Establish problems and goals

Select a single-subject design

Establish and measure the baseline

Introduce treatment

Assess treatment effects

Figure 11.1 Steps in the Clinical Research Process

After the problem is identified, the next step is to determine what goals are to be achieved through treatment. At this point, the first real difference between the clinical-research model and traditional practice is encountered. The model requires, first, that goals be more specific and precisely defined than is often done in conventional practice, and second, that they be measurable in some way (Kazdin, 1985). Although these requirements of specificity and measurability are more rigorous under the clinical-research model than in traditional practice, they are best seen as an extension of normal practice procedures rather than as something strangely different. As to the requirement for measurability of outcomes, some practitioners would argue that some beneficial outcomes of intervention are so subtle that they are un-

measurable. Countering this attitude in the field of social work, two researchers contend: "When the outcome is not measurable, social workers are probably engaging in self-delusion" (Newman and Turem, 1974, p. 16). The self-delusion is believing that a real but unmeasurable change has occurred when actually it has not. Rather than try to settle this debate, we make the important point that the clinical-research model places strong emphasis on measurable outcomes.

One common problem encountered in establishing goals is that they are often long-term, making it impractical for the clinician-researcher to monitor progress all the way to achievement of the final goal. In these cases, it may be necessary to identify proximate, intermediate goals whose achievement is evidence of progress toward the final goal. For example, the final goal for an underachiever might be improved academic performance—a long-term goal. Proximate goals that would evidence progress might include improved note-taking, longer study hours, and more regular class attendance. Achievement of these proximate goals would be expected to be related to achievement of the final goal. Which measurable, intermediate goals can serve as valid indicators of long-term goals depends, of course, on a theoretical understanding of the long-term changes sought through intervention.

Select a Single-Subject Design

Once a problem and a corresponding goal for intervention have been identified, the next phase of the clinical-research process is to select an appropriate single-subject design. Whereas the general principle of single-subject research consists of comparing a series of preintervention measurements with a series of postintervention measurements, there are many variations on this basic scheme. Later in the chapter we will present several common designs and discuss their strengths and limitations. At this point, however, we simply want to alert you to the fact that there are many design options from which to choose and also to point out that, early in the process, the practitioner should be thinking about the design choices that will best suit the goals and constraints of a particular clinical case. For example, if the practitioner's primary objective is to provide treatment and simply monitor the client's progess, then a simple design will be adequate. In other cases, there may be a general behavior deficit where the proposed intervention involves working on increasing the desired behavior in different realms of the client's life such as at home, in school, and in visiting with friends. There are designs that take advantage of such an intervention strategy both to monitor client behavior and maximize validity for research goals.

The point is that single-subject designs are very flexible and adaptive to many practice situations. To take advantage of this flexibility requires that the practitioner have a clear notion of the problem to be addressed, an understanding of how the proposed intervention is supposed to effect changes, and an awareness of single-subject design strengths and limitations. Once a particular design has been chosen, the practitioner can address the next step in the clinical-research process, establishing and measuring a baseline.

Establish and Measure the Baseline

Single-subject designs are based on the quasi-experimental time-series designs discussed in Chapter 10, although modified to make them more appropriate for use with a single subject. As such, single-subject designs call for repeated measures of the client's condition so that trends and changes can be noted. Typically, what is measured is the frequency, intensity, or duration of some behavior of the client, such as how many cigarettes are smoked, the severity of pain, or how long a depression lasts. Thus, the third step in the clinical-research process is to establish a **baseline,** or a series of measurements of the client's condition prior to treatment; the baseline is used as a basis from which to compare the client's condition after treatment is implemented. By comparing measurements after treatment with those of the baseline period, the clinician can trace the effect the treatment is having. Typically, three measurements are needed, as an absolute minimum, to establish a baseline (Barlow and Hersen, 1973). More measurements are better, especially if the client's condition is unstable, It is important to note that all single-subject designs rule out the simple procedure of using only two measurements—one pretest and one posttest—because this results in a preexperimental design that is extremely weak on internal validity.

Figure 11.2 illustrates how baseline measurement can serve as a basis for assessing treatment effects. The hypothetical data show a high level of undesirable client behavior prior to treatment. After treatment is instigated, this drops sharply. Results are not always as dramatic as these, so making interpretations can be more difficult. We will deal with the issue of assessing treatment effects in more detail later.

Two major issues to be settled in establishing the baseline are what to measure and how to measure it. Typically, the

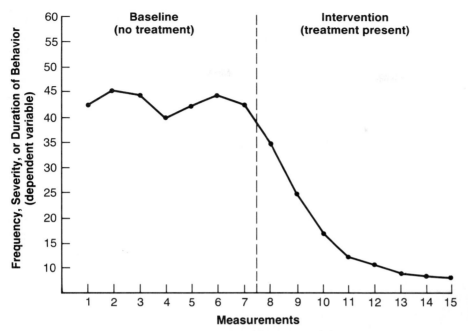

Figure 11.2 Hypothetical Baseline Followed by Successful Treatment

clinical problem itself will suggest the appropriate trait to measure. In general, what we seek to change through treatment is what needs to be measured. For example, a child whose problem is disruptive behavior in school could be monitored as to the frequency of disruptions he or she causes each day. On the other hand, treatment philosophy might suggest monitoring frequency of *appropriate* behavior as a means of not only measuring behavior but also setting the stage for change. As we emphasized in Chapter 5, measurement and operational definitions should be deduced from theoretical concepts, whether those concepts emerge from research or practice theories.

Client problems that do not have specific behavioral outcomes or manifestations are more difficult to measure. Depression, for example, can be displayed in many different behavioral forms, and in such cases it is preferable to use several measures (Jayaratne and Levy, 1979). Also, where there is such an indirect link between a concept and behavioral manifestations, the use of multiple indicators helps to reduce the effects of error in those measures. In the case of depression, we might establish a separate baseline for a behavioral indicator (say, percent of day spent alone), a paper-and-pencil measure of depression, and a self-report from the client about his or her subjective assessment. If the treatment produced positive gains on all measures, we would have greater evidence of the treatment's effectiveness than if we relied on only one indicator.

Having decided on what aspects of the client's condition to measure, we confront the question of *how* to measure them. Basically, the clinician-researcher has four choices: observation, existing records, paper-and-pencil measures, and client self-reports. Of these, observation is of most general utility and is the most valid and reliable (Jayaratne and Levy, 1979; Weiss and Frohman, 1985). Unfortunately, as we noted earlier, many client problems are not directly observable, so there is a limit to the applicability of observation. When it is used, however, there are three important considerations. (These issues regarding observation are discussed in greater detail in Chapter 9.) First, the observations should be unobtrusive. If they are not, the client may behave differently owing to the presence of the observers. This could result in faulty baseline data, which could obscure treatment effects. Second, multiple observers should be used where possible in order to assess the extent of observer reliability. In some cases, videotapes might be substituted for multiple observers, but in natural settings their use is likely to be difficult. Third, if possible, observers should not be aware of when treatment is begun. If they are, their expectations for improvement might affect the objectivity of their observations. For example, borderline behaviors that were counted as disruptive during the baseline phase might be ignored during the treatment phase. This shift would tend to overstate the apparent effectiveness of the treatment to reduce disruptive behavior.

A second measurement approach is existing records. Some client problems relate to matters on which data are routinely gathered by people other than the clinician or client. For example, existing records, such as grades and school attendance, are often used in assessing a child's school performance. Where existing records are appropriate, they are often a good choice. They are unobtrusive

because they are collected whether the client is under treatment or not. Furthermore, because they are collected by persons other than the clinician-researcher, time and cost factors are likely to be favorable. There are several problems associated with using existing records for research purposes, however, that can be reviewed in Chapter 8.

A third common measurement approach is paper-and-pencil measures, which are often used when the client's problem does not lend itself to direct observation. If the decision is made to use a paper-and-pencil measure, it is advisable to use an existing one, if available, rather than devise a new one. In addition to the practical benefits of avoiding the time and trouble of developing a new measure, existing measures usually have established levels of validity and reliability. Furthermore, their use contributes to the accumulation of knowledge because the standardized measuring devices make for greater comparability across studies. Fortunately, there are a large number of measures available, covering a wide array of client problems. For example, *Measures of Social Psychological Attitudes* (Robinson and Shaver, 1973), *Measuring Human Behavior* (Lake et al., 1973), *Measures for Psychological Assessment* (Chun et al., 1975), *Outcome Measures for Child Welfare Services* (Magura and Moses, 1986), and *Measures for Clinical Practice* (Corcoran and Fischer, 1987), to name just a few, present many paper-and-pencil measures. Research in Practice 11.1 discusses such measures in detail.

Paper-and-pencil measures have some characteristics that make them less than ideal for use in single-subject designs, however. First, they are obtrusive, because clients obviously know they are

RESEARCH IN PRACTICE 11.1
Assessment of Client Functioning: Rapid Assessment Instruments

This chapter describes the exciting use of single-subject research designs in practice settings. While the design holds much promise for improving the precision with which practitioners evaluate the outcomes of intervention with individual clients, a stumbling block to reliable and valid applications from the time this design was first advocated has been the lack of sound measurement tools. While a practitioner could rely on direct observation or available records, many existing standardized measures were not suitable for the repeated measurements required by the single-subject design. This situation is no longer the case, thanks to the development of a variety of measurement tools known collectively as *rapid assessment instruments*, or RAIs.

RAIs are distinguished from other measures by several main features. They are short, easy to administer, and easy to complete. RAIs are written in clear, easy-to-understand language with uncomplicated directions so that disruption of the intervention process is kept to a minimum. Scoring can normally be done in a few minutes without the need for special equipment. They have been applied in family service agencies (Toseland and Reid, 1985) and in agencies serving children and youth (Edlesen, 1985). Levitt and Reid (1981) identify sources for RAIs covering anxiety, depression, assertiveness, social interaction, and marital problems. Probably the best current reference for the practitioner seeking measurement instruments to aid in single-subject evaluation in practice is the book *Measures for Clinical Practice: A Sourcebook*, compiled by Corcoran and Fischer.

One can gain an appreciation for the effort and creativity required to develop sound measurement tools for single-subject designs from the ongoing work of Walter Hudson and colleagues, who set out to design a measurement package that would be appropriate for single-subject work, easy to administer and score, and relevant to the clinical problems likely to be encountered in practice (Hudson, 1982). In the early 1970s, they began work on this project, culminating in the *Clinical Measurement Package* (CMP). This manual includes nine 25-item paper-and-pencil scales for the assessment of (1) depression, (2) self-esteem, (3) marital discord, (4) sexual discord, (5) parent–child relationships as seen by the parent, (6) mother–child relationships as seen by the child, (7) father–child relationships as seen by the child, (8) intrafamilial stress, and (9) peer relationships.

With regard to research, the CMP illustrates several key points. First, good data collection techniques are essential for both research and practice. Recall from Chapter 2 that theory pro-

(Continued on next page)

vides hypotheses for research and interventions for practice and that the outcomes of research and interventions contribute to theory development (see Figure 2.1). Without good data-collection strategies and sound measurement procedures, utilization of single-subject designs is doomed to failure. Efforts to overcome these problems culminated in the development of this scale package, and creation of the scales involved repeated application of the scales in various research projects to determine reliability and validity. Second, the package illustrates the kind of achievements that are necessary to link practice and research more closely in the human services. The scales are relevant to the clinical problems practitioners face, they are easy to administer, they are relatively innocuous in work with clients, and they yield reasonably clear interpretations. Third, the manual illustrates some of the differences in applying such scales for practice as compared with research. For example, one difference, Hudson argues, is in the type of design chosen. For practice purposes, a simple design with a single baseline and a single treatment can be extremely powerful for documenting client improvement and for making clinical decisions. As we point out in this chapter, however, such a simple design is weak for research purposes. Another difference between practice and research, Hudson argues, is in reliability: Practitioners require higher reliability in a measurement tool than do researchers. The reason for this is that researchers, even in single-subject work, may be able to combine cases and use statisti-

cal analysis to determine significance of effect, thus easing the distortions of a somewhat unreliable measure. The clinician, on the other hand, is concerned with helping one client, not in simply knowing what in the long run would be the probability of a certain effect on a group of people. According to Hudson, the estimates for reliability of the CMP scales are all over .90, suggesting that they should be well suited to the needs of both practice and research.

The CMP manual illustrates another issue in research, namely, that the construction of good instruments is a painstaking, time-consuming process that goes far beyond simply making up a list of questions (*see* Chapters 5 and 13). We mention in this chapter problems with data based on self-reports. The CMP manual overcomes many of these problems through careful tests for reliability and validity. Because of this, the package of nine instruments illustrates that careful assessment of client functioning and single-subject design are well within the reach of human service providers in a wide variety of practice settings. Since the publication of the Clinical Measurement Package, Hudson has continued his work to provide the practice community with tools for single-subject data collection. He has developed the Clinical Assessment System (CAS), which is a computer software package for maintaining client records and evaluating client progress. In addition to the scales described in the CMP, the CAS contains many new scales, some of which are still being evaluated for reliability and validity.

Some of the new scales measure (1) personal stress, (2) anxiety, (3) alcohol abuse, (4) sexual attitude, (5) homophobia, (6) partner abuse: nonphysical, (7) partner abuse: physical, and (8) peer relations. Information on the scales and their administration by computer using the CAS is available in *Computer-Assisted Practice: Theory, Methods, and Software* (Hudson and Nurius, in press).

being measured, and this can create many problems. For example, completing a questionnaire concerning family relationships might sensitize parents that they have been paying less attention to their children than they should, and they could change their behavior because of this awareness. Recall from Chapter 10 that this is the "testing" threat to internal validity in experiments. (Although such change may be desirable, the problem from a research standpoint is that it is not possible to determine if the treatment or the measurement process caused the change.) The second problem with paper-and-pencil measures is that of "demand characteristics," also discussed in Chapter 10. Clients may deliberately change responses in the direction indicating improvement. This effect can occur out of a desire to fulfill the expectations that the clinician has for improvement in the client. Furthermore, because of frequent exposure to the measure, the client will become familiar with it, raising the specter of multiple-testing effects also discussed in Chapter 10. Finally, some paper-and-pencil measures are projective tests, such as the Rorschach Inkblot Test, the Thematic Apperception Test, sentence completion tests, and figure drawings. These tests all rely heavily on the examiner's interpretation of client responses. After reviewing the evidence, Barlow and Hersen (1984) strongly advise against the use of these types of measures because they do not have sufficient validity and reliability to provide a sound basis for single-subject experiments.

The last measurement alternative is to use self-reports of clients who monitor their own behavior or feelings. Although client's perceptions of their condition are important, there are many problems associated with overreliance on self-reports.

First, there is evidence that self-reports do not correlate well with objective indicators. For example, studies of assertiveness among female college students have made use of people's own reports of how assertive they are and of trained observers' assessments of how assertively these people actually behave. Generally, they find that the self-reports do not correlate with the observers' assessments (Frisch and Higgins, 1986).

Second, self-monitoring is reactive because it sensitizes the client to some aspect of his or her behavior (Barlow et al., 1984). Research has indicated that the mere process of monitoring can change one's behavior. In one study, for example, objective baselines were gathered on how many cigarettes were consumed by a group of smokers (McFall, 1970). Half the subjects were then asked to monitor and record the extent of their smoking. The other half were to keep track of the times when they didn't smoke. Both groups showed a change from their baseline levels but in the opposite direction. Those monitoring instances of smoking smoked *more* whereas those monitoring instances of nonsmoking smoked *less!* Similar self-monitoring effects have been noted concerning study habits among college students (Johnson and White, 1971). This phenomenon has been put to use in a variety of treatment programs, which include self-monitoring as the intervention that brings about behavior change. This effect, however, is hardly desirable when the goal is to assess the effects of treatments other than self-monitoring. Because of the multitude of problems associated with self-report data, they should be used with caution, preferably as an adjunct to other measures that are less subject to false reports.

From our discussion of measurement options available to clinician-researchers, it is evident that some are better than others. The most objective, valid, and reliable measure available in a given research context should be selected. As we noted, direct observation is usually best if the client's problem lends itself to such observation. Otherwise, a more indirect measure will be necessary, but these have the limitations we have outlined. However, by using multiple measures, the weaknesses of the indirect measures can be reduced and the quality of the single-subject experiment improved (Gottman, 1985).

Introduce Treatment

Once the baseline is established, the next stage in the clinical-research process is to begin treatment. When the treatment is applied, it is important that only a *single, coherent* treatment be applied during any treatment phase (Barlow and Hersen,

1984). The reason for this derives from the fact that each application of the clinical-research model is essentially an experiment, with the treatment being the independent variable in that experiment. If more than one treatment is used and the client exhibits behavior change in comparison to the baseline, we would not know *which* treatment produced the change and would have learned nothing that might be valuable with similar clients in the future. In order to assess the effects of the independent variable, we must be able to specify precisely what the treatment consisted of and also be consistent in its application during the treatment phase.

The demand for a single, specific treatment is one aspect of the clinical-research model that has led to a cold reception in some human service circles, particularly among nonbehaviorists (Nelsen, 1981). Nonbehavioral treatments often lack the specificity that allows practitioners to trace a particular treatment over the period of the treatment phase. In addition, nonbehavioral treatments can be very complex and may even mix a number of treatment modes together, making it difficult to identify the precise factors that presumably resulted in change. However, this is less a criticism of the clinical-research model than a challenge to those using nonbehavioral treatments: "[nonbehaviorists] must work hard at choosing interventions that may be effective and at defining their interventions precisely, preferably by addressing both what they do and how they do it" (Nelsen, 1981, p. 35).

Resistance to the discipline imposed by the clinical-research model appears to be greatest among those who are least familiar with it. After some initial frustration with the specificity and single treatment required by the model, practitioners learning to apply the model come to accept it (Johnson, 1981). They come to appreciate that the model increases rationality in the selection of treatments, forces an explicit consideration of the assumptions on which treatment is based, and requires the use of specific practice skills rather than a reliance solely on their own intuition or ingenuity. Greatest satisfaction, however, comes from the fact that the model provides solid evidence regarding whether the client benefited from treatment. Whereas it is rewarding to feel that one has been of assistance, it is even more rewarding to have some objective evidence to support those feelings.

During the treatment phase, the measurement of the client's condition, started during the baseline phase, is continued. This, of course, is done to track what changes (if any) the treatment is producing in the client's condition. It is crucial that the conditions under which measurements are made during the treatment phase remain consistent with those under which the baseline measurements were obtained (Jayaratne and Levy, 1979). Any change in such things as observers, settings, examiners, or instructions could confound apparent treatment effects. Remember that a single-subject design is an experiment, and only one variable—the treatment—should be allowed to change from one phase to another.

Assess Treatment Effects

When is a treatment judged effective? This seemingly simple question, which is addressed in the last stage of the clinical research process, has a surprisingly complex answer. Assessing effectiveness depends, first of all, on the pattern produced during the baseline measure-

ments: The ease and clarity with which baseline measures can be compared with treatment measures depends in part on the *stability* of the baseline measures. Figure 11.3 illustrates four possible baseline patterns: (1) a stable baseline, (2) a rising trend (client worsening), (3) a descending trend (client improving), and (4) an unstable baseline. (In this discussion of baseline stability, we will assume that lower measurement scores represent improvement, as in the case of reducing the incidence of some problem behavior. If the goal of treatment is to increase some aspect of client functioning, as it often

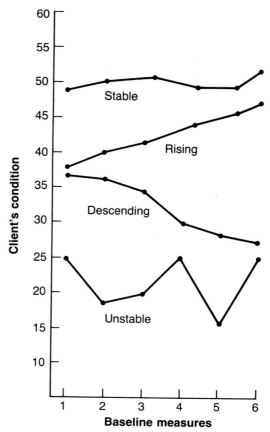

Figure 11.3 Types of Baseline Patterns

is, improvement would be indicated by higher measurement scores.) A stable baseline is the ideal since posttreatment comparisons will then readily reveal treatment effects. If the treatment is helpful, there should be a pronounced downward move in measurement levels. A treatment producing negative effects would yield an upward move in measurement levels. Ineffective treatment would be revealed by little change from the baseline levels. The value of a stable baseline is that it allows all three possible treatment outcomes to be readily noted.

Unfortunately, client conditions are often not stable. Their condition may worsen, improve, or be highly variable. Assessing treatment effects with baselines of these types is more difficult and often puts limits on what can be inferred. A baseline with a rising trend (client worsening) is not too problematic because an effective treatment will produce a reversal of the baseline trend. Such a change provides strong evidence that the treatment was effective. With ineffective or harmful treatments, however, it is difficult to tell if this is just a continuation of the baseline trend (ineffective treatment) or if the continued deterioration is due to some harmful treatment. A baseline with a decreasing trend, showing client improvement, has the opposite effect. If the treatment proves harmful, the trend will reverse, and the negative effect will be readily apparent. But if the client continues to improve during treatment, it is unclear whether the treatment produced that improvement (effective treatment) or whether it was just a continuation of the baseline trend (ineffective treatment).

The most troublesome baseline is one that is unstable. With the client's condition changing from one measurement to another, it becomes very difficult to iden-tify changes due to treatment. There are, however, a couple of strategies for dealing with an unstable baseline (Barlow and Hersen, 1984). One is to extend the period of baseline measurements with the hope that a stable pattern wll emerge. There is no guarantee, of course, that it will. In addition, there may be practical as well as ethical constraints on how long treatment can be postponed while awaiting baseline stability. A second strategy is the application of statistical techniques that can reveal trends and differences between pre- and posttreatment that are too subtle to be noted by visual inspection (Gottman, 1981; Achen, 1986). These statistics are of limited effectiveness, however, if the pattern is very unstable.

The use of statistics in assessing treatment effects also raises a problem beyond that of baseline stability, namely, how much change is necessary before one can say that a treatment is effective? From a research perspective, any change from pretest measures to posttest measures is evidence that the treatment was effective in the sense of bringing about change in the dependent variable. However, in clinical settings, *change* can take the form of improvement *or* deterioration in a client's status. Practitioners are seeking improvement, of course, so treatment effectiveness in single-subject designs is normally defined as an improvement in performance after treatment. Yet assessing whether improvement has occurred can be complex because it can be based on three different criteria: therapeutic, experimental, or statistical.

A treatment is *therapeutically effective* when it leads clients to achieve fully the goals set for them to accomplish. The disruptive student is no longer disruptive, the underachiever is now achieving, or the teenage mother can care for her infant independently. When treatment produces these kinds of improvements in a client's condition, its effectiveness is obvious. Visual inspection of the measurements taken during the treatment phase will clearly reveal the improvement wrought when compared with the baseline measurements.

A treatment is *experimentally effective* when it produces a pronounced improvement in the client's condition although ultimate goals have not been reached. For example, a claustrophobic may have come to the point where he or she can use an elevator alone but remains unable to use a crowded one. As with therapeutic effectiveness, the change in the client's condition from baseline to treatment phase is sufficiently dramatic that visual inspection is normally adequate to reveal it. One criterion for establishing experimental effectiveness through visual inspection is nonoverlapping data (Kazdin, 1982). All the measurements taken during the treatment phase are higher or lower (whichever direction represents improvement) than those taken during the baseline phase. Stated another way, performance during treatment does not overlap with that of the baseline period. This is a fairly severe guideline and one that, if met, is a strong demonstration of experimental effectiveness. A second criterion is somewhat less rigorous: All the measurements taken during the treatment phase are higher or lower than the *average* level of the baseline. This guideline would be preferred over the first if the baseline were not especially stable. It is important to emphasize that these are only guidelines, not rigid rules. It is quite possible that a given single-subject experiment could evidence clear experimental effectiveness and achieve neither of these guidelines. Following them, however, does make visual inspection more systematic and less

a matter of judgment on the part of the clinician-researcher.

Statistical effectiveness is achieved when the treatment produces statistically significant improvement in the client's condition. In other words, the difference between baseline and treatment levels is too great to be due to chance variation. (The concept of statistical significance is discussed in detail in Chapter 14.) Because statistics are sufficiently sensitive to detect smaller changes than can visual inspection, statistical effectiveness sometimes requires the least improvement in the client. This raises the issue of the difference between statistical significance and therapeutic or experimental significance. A treatment judged effective because it produced a statistically significant improvement in the client might be judged a near failure according to the other criteria. For example, reducing an alcoholic's consumption from 20 ounces of whiskey a day to 15 might be a statistically significant reduction, but we would hardly call the treatment a rousing success. Because statistical significance may be only remotely related to treatment success, statistical analysis is usually limited to cases with an unstable baseline, which makes visual analysis difficult. When statistical analysis is used, single-subject data require the use of special statistical techniques. The reason for this is that many commonly used statistics assume that each measurement is independent of the others. Because all the measurements in a single-subject experiment are from the same person, statistical tests based on the assumption of independence would be inappropriate. Fortunately, statistics specifically designed for analyzing single-subject data are available (*see* Barlow and Hersen, 1984; Jayaratne and Levy, 1979; Kazdin, 1982; Marascuilo and Busk, 1988; Gottman, 1981; Achen, 1986). Furthermore, several of these techniques are fairly easy to apply without the need of a computer or other equipment to do the analysis.

So we see that the question of treatment effectiveness depends in part on the particular criterion of effectiveness applied. With the varying criteria, it is important to be aware of the differences and to be precise when discussing what is meant by effectiveness. Furthermore, it is important to recognize that there are both short-term effectiveness and long-term effectiveness. In other words, the effect of a treatment may be relatively permanent, or the effect may decrease after treatment is withdrawn. To test for this, the posttreatment measurements become, in effect, a new baseline. Deviation from this baseline as time passes suggests that there is a limit to how long the treatment is effective.

Types of Single-Subject Designs

Although there are numerous types of single-subject designs, all involve repeated measurements during baseline and treatment phases and a comparison across phases as evidence of treatment effects. The designs differ in the number of phases involved, the number of treatments applied, and the number of baselines employed. Perhaps the most important differences are in the internal validity of the designs. Some are more capable of providing evidence for the effect of a treatment when such an effect actually exists. Ideally, of course, clinician-researchers should select the most valid design that fits their particular case (see the discussions of validity in Chapters 5 and 10).

Single-Treatment Designs

The Basic AB Design   It has become customary to present single-subject designs by using the first letters of the alphabet to symbolize various phases of the design. The letter *A* signifies a phase in which the client is not receiving treatment. This would be the baseline period in all designs, but it could also refer to a period when treatment is withdrawn in some of the more complex designs. The letter *B* indicates a treatment phase during which some specific intervention is in progress. Subsequent letters of the alphabet, *C*, *D*, and so on, are used as needed to symbolize the application of treatments different from *B*.

With this notation in mind, the *AB* design is the simplest of the single-subject designs and forms the basis for the others. The *AB design* consists of one baseline phase followed by one treatment phase. Treatment effectiveness is determined by comparing the client's condition during treatment with that of the baseline. The basic *AB* design is less than ideal because its validity is threatened by *history:* Events other than the intervention could be responsible for the change in the client. Despite the limitations of the *AB* design, it provides better evidence of treatment effects than nonexperimental case histories. It also has the advantage of being applicable to most clinical situations, especially in cases where more rigorous designs might be precluded.

Reversal Designs   The *AB* design can be strengthened substantially by moving to a *reversal design*, so called because, after one treatment phase, the treatment is withdrawn for a period of time. There are basically two versions of the reversal design; *ABA* and *ABAB*. The two versions differ only in that the *ABA* design ends in a no treatment phase whereas, in the *ABAB* design, the treatment is reintroduced a second time (see Figure 11.4).

The value of the reversal designs stems from their ability to demonstrate more conclusively that it is the treatment and not some extraneous factor that is producing change in the client's condition. If the client's condition deteriorates when the treatment is withdrawn, we

THE ABA DESIGN

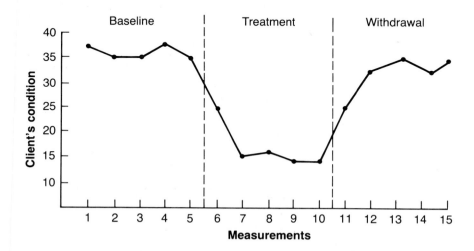

THE ABAB DESIGN

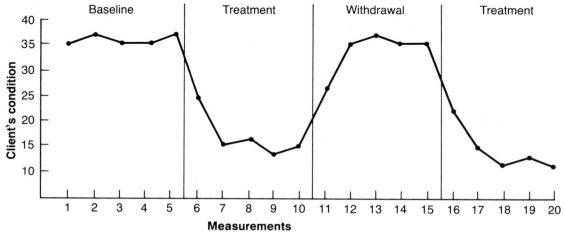

Figure 11.4 Hypothetical Examples of Reversal Designs

have evidence that the treatment is the controlling factor. Even more evidence is provided with the *ABAB* design if the reintroduction of the treatment coincides with renewed improvement of the client. Although it is possible for a set of extraneous factors to produce the first client improvement, it is less likely that the same set of factors would recur at precisely the right time to produce improvement on reintroduction of the treatment. As Figure 11.4 illustrates, especially with the *ABAB* design, we would have great confidence in the efficacy of a treatment that produced similar real-life results.

Despite their strengths on internal validity, there are often practical considerations that restrict the use of reversal designs. First, treatments that produce permanent changes in clients—which is often the goal of intervention—are not reversible. For example, if the treatment involves clients' learning something, it is obvious that they cannot "unlearn" it at the command of the clinician-researcher. In such cases, reversal designs are simply not applicable. Second, it might be unwise or unethical to attempt returning clients to their pretreatment state. An obvious example would be a case where the suicidal tendencies of a client were alleviated. It is up to the clinician-researcher to decide on a case-by-case basis whether a reversal design can be ethically justified.

Multiple-Baseline Designs The multiple-baseline design involves establishing baselines for more than one aspect of the client's condition. Multiple baselines can be established for different behaviors, for one behavior in multiple settings, or for different clients who suffer from a similar problem. For example, a practitioner working with several alcoholics could establish separate baselines for each, thus applying the multiple-baseline design across individuals. Although it is recommended that a minimum of three baselines be utilized, clinician-researchers should not be deterred from using only two if conditions do not permit more. The more baselines that are used, however, the stronger in terms of internal validity the design becomes (Barlow and Hersen, 1984; Jayaratne and Levy, 1979).

The multiple-baseline design is essentially a stacked set of *AB* designs, with the same treatment being introduced sequentially into each of the baseline conditions:

First client: A_1B
Second client: A_1A_2B
Third client: $A_1A_2A_3B$

In the illustration, the initial baseline measurement (A_1) is made on each client, and then the treatment is introduced to the first client only. A second baseline measurement is taken from the remaining two clients, and then treatment is introduced to the second client. A third baseline measurement is taken from the third client who then receives treatment. Figure 11.5 illustrates the multiple-baseline design with a successful outcome. In each of the three conditions, the introduction of the treatment is followed by improvement. The multiple-baseline design is fairly strong on internal validity. The efficacy of the treatment is assessed across three or more behaviors, settings, or individuals. Furthermore, the sequential introduction of treatments makes it highly unlikely that extraneous factors can account for apparent treatment effects across the several baseline conditions. So, the multiple-baseline design is generally superior to the *AB* design, but the *AB* design with replication also overcomes some of the threats to internal validity, such as history (Harris and Jenson,

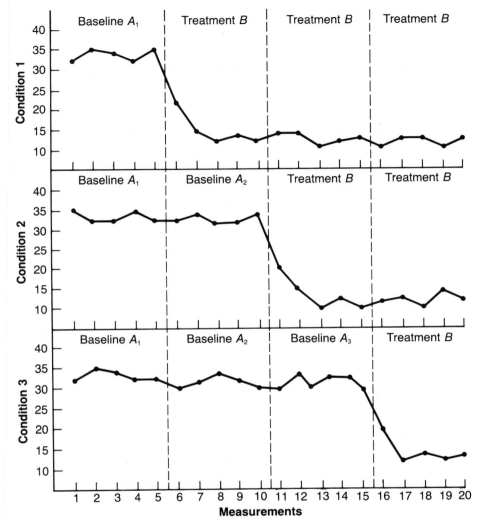

Figure 11.5 Hypothetical Example of Multiple-Baseline Design

1985). However, the multiple-baseline design is not as strong on internal validity as are the reversal designs; but where reversal designs are inappropriate, the multiple-baseline design is a good alternative.

The application of the multiple-baseline design is sufficiently complex to warrant a detailed example, illustrating the design as applied across settings (Allen,

1973). The client was an eight-year-old boy with a bizarre fascination with penguins. He would fantasize about them for up to eight hours a day and had an imaginary menagerie populated with the creatures, each with its own name. The child talked about his imaginary pets with great frequency. Quite naturally, his bizarre verbalizations made him an object of scorn and ridicule among other children and interfered with his interpersonal relations with adults. The experiment was conducted while the boy was attending summer camp. For the first six days, camp counselors made baseline observations of the frequency of penguin statements in four settings around the camp: evening-activity, dining-hall, cabin, and education settings. On the seventh day, treatment—consisting of ignoring the penguin statements and showing attention when he interacted more appropriately—was instituted during evening-activity. At successive intervals, the treatment was extended to cover another setting until it was operative in all four (see Figure 11.6).

Every time treatment was introduced in a setting, there was a decline in bizarre responses in that setting, some quite dramatic. Only in the education setting was the effect modest. This setting, however, had the lowest baseline rate to begin with, and it is probable that treatment effects from the other settings carried over to education where treatment was introduced last. Overall, the pattern across baselines provides very strong evidence that it was the treatment that brought about behavior change.

Multiple-baseline designs can provide strong evidence for the validity of single-subject outcomes, and they can be used in conjunction with group experiments, as Research in Practice 11.2 illustrates, to further our knowledge of phenomena. They do have weaknesses, however. The seepage of treatment effects from one setting to another, as in the "penguin" case, illustrates a major limitation of the multiple-baseline design. The behaviors, settings, or individuals traced by the several baselines must be relatively independent, or the treatment effects in one condition can produce changes in other, as yet untreated, conditions. For example, it would be unwise to attempt a multiple-baseline design with members of the same family. Because of their routine interaction, treatment applied to one family member could affect the others. If the baseline conditions are highly interrelated, the treatment will show effects after the initial introduction not only in the condition where it is applied, but in one or more of the other conditions as well. If interrelatedness is sufficiently severe, the power of the multiple-baseline design can be destroyed, rendering it little more than an *AB* design with multiple indicators.

One final note concerning the multiple-baseline design is its ability to reveal *contravariation:* positive changes in one area, but negative changes in another (Jayaratne and Levy, 1979). For example, a multiple-drug abuser might respond to treatment by reducing intake of one substance but increasing intake of another. If we traced only one drug, perhaps the most dangerous, the contravariation would remain undetected. A multiple-baseline design covering all the abuser's drugs would readily reveal such an occurrence.

Specialized Designs

The designs just discussed comprise the simplest and most generally useful single-subject designs and have in common the use of only a single treatment (although applied more than once in the *ABAB* design). There are, however, situations that call for variations of these simpler designs to handle special problems. There are so many complex and specialized designs that we can touch on only a few.

Multiple-Treatment Designs In some settings it may be necessary to apply sev-

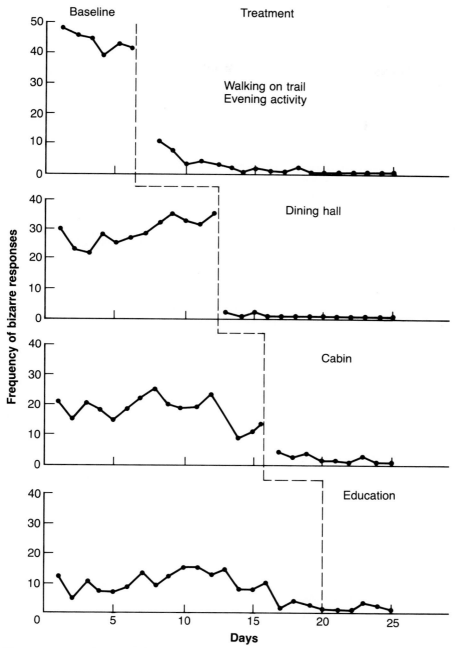

Figure 11.6 Reduction of Bizarre Verbalizations Through a Multiple-Baseline Experiment

Source: Adapted from Srinika Jayaratne and Rona J. Levy, *Empirical Clinical Practice* (New York: Columbia University Press). Copyright © 1979 by Columbia University Press. Used with permission.

RESEARCH IN PRACTICE 11.2
Practice Effectiveness: Studying Marital Problems with a Single-Subject Design

We have presented the single-subject design approach largely as an alternative research strategy to traditional group experimental designs. However, single-subject designs can also be used in combination with group experiments. This point is creatively illustrated in a study on the use of problem solving and contingency contracting in the treatment of marital problems (Jacobson, 1977). Ten couples seeking help for marital difficulties were randomly assigned to a treatment condition or to a waiting list that served as a control group. Couples in the treatment condition received training in problem-solving skills and the use of contingency contracts—the independent variables. There were two measures of improvement. First, videotape recordings of couples interacting while attempting to solve problems were coded for improved problem-solving behavior by research assistants ignorant of the experimental conditions for both a pretest and a posttest. Second, the couples were compared on the basis of the Marital Adjustment Scale, an index of global marital satisfaction. These measures formed the basis of the between-group comparisons. Both revealed a significant difference between treatment and control groups, providing evidence of the efficacy of the treatment.

In addition to comparing the two groups, each couple in the treatment group was studied by means of a multiple-baseline, single-subject design.

Thus, coupled with securing the benefits of a true experimental design, the study also overcomes certain problems of the experimental approach through the single-subject component. First, the design allows the clinician-researcher to trace the progress of *each* couple, not just the group, offering practitioners an assessment of clinical effectiveness. Second, marital discord is an exceedingly complex phenomenon, and the single-subject approach permits definition of the problem in terms of behaviors specific to each couple.

For the single-subject component of the study, spouses collected data on their mates at home. For example, improved marital satisfaction in one case was operationalized as an increase in the amount of time a husband engaged his wife in conversation and a decrease in the number of demanding statements he made. This is a multiple-baseline design in that it involves measurements across individuals and across different behaviors that could operationalize marital satisfaction. The figure in this section shows the outcome of one single-subject experiment with a couple in which the husband talked rarely with his wife and, when he did talk, made demanding statements. After a 14-day baseline period, the husband agreed to a contract that awarded him one hour of watching sports on television for every two hours that he spent talking with his wife. As can be seen, this intervention increased conversation but had little effect on demanding statements. A week later, the husband agreed to another contract that allowed him to host a card game in the couple's home if he made no more than one demanding statement a week. Again, the intervention had the intended effect on demanding statements but little impact on the amount of talking beyond the effect of the first intervention.

This study presents an imaginative approach to research in which the potentially competing goals of individualizing treatment to meet the needs of the client and operationalizing a research problem to cover a study population were achieved simultaneously. The single-subject design component allowed marital problems to be defined in terms of the needs of each couple. At the same time, the researcher was able to combine cases to do experimental and control group comparisons.

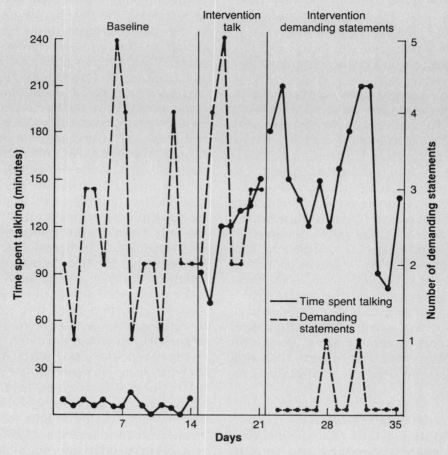

Source: Neil S. Jacobson, "Problem Solving and Contingency Contracting in the Treatment of Marital Discord," *Journal of Consulting and Clinical Psychology*, 45:1 (1977), p. 97. Copyright © 1977 by the American Psychological Association. Reprinted by permission of the author.

eral treatments before an effective one is found. By an extension of the reversal designs, *multiple treatments* can be accommodated. A fairly simple extension is the *ABACA* design. It should be apparent that the *ABA* segment comprises a basic reversal design. To that is added a second treatment phase and another return-to-baseline phase. This design can be extended to include as many treatments as a given case requires. One important limitation of this design is that it is not possible to determine which is most effective if both treatments show some effect (Barlow and Hersen, 1984). The culprit is history, as extraneous variables occurring during the *B* phase cannot be assumed to be the same as those occurring during the *C* phase.

Special designs can also be used when treatments are not applied individually, but in combination. In these cases, it is desirable to assess the relative effects of the components of the treatment package. The *A-B-A-B-BC-B-BC* design, a complex extention of the reversal designs, allows this to be accomplished. The first half, *ABAB*, is one of the basic reversal designs. This part provides a strong demonstration of component *B*'s effects. The *BC-B-BC* segment indicates the effects of *C* beyond those of *B* alone. This design can, of course, be extended further to indicate additional treatments. Because both of these design extensions are based on reversal designs, they cannot be used with treatments that are irreversible or that are unethical to reverse.

Changing-Criterion Designs Another specialized design that has considerable utility is called the *changing-criterion design* (Hall, 1971). With this design, the goal or criterion of success changes over time as the client is led to attainment of the final treatment goal in stages by achieving a series of subgoals. For example, a smoker could be brought to the final goal of abstinence through phased withdrawal. Figure 11.7 illustrates what a successful application of treatment with a changing-criterion design might look like with such a case. Following the baseline measurement of cigarettes smoked per day, treatment is instituted. For example, let us assume the treatment consists of reinforcement. During the first treatment phase, the client is reinforced for achieving the first subgoal, say, a reduction of eight cigarettes a day. In the second treatment phase, reinforcement is received for achieving a reduction of an additional eight cigarettes—the second subgoal. The third treatment phase would require another reduction to receive the reinforcement. The process is continued until the client has progressed through the subgoals and achieved the final goal of no longer smoking.

The changing-criterion design is related to the multiple-baseline design. In the multiple-baseline design, intervention was independently implemented in relatively distinct areas of the subject's environment. In the changing-criterion design, each time a subgoal is achieved and a new, more stringent subgoal is established, the preceding level essentially becomes a new baseline from which further improvement is measured. Like the multiple-baseline design, the changing-criterion design provides greater evidence of treatment effectiveness than the simple *AB* design. Each time the treatment leads to the achievement of another subgoal, further evidence of its effectiveness is obtained. The only major limitation associated with the changing criterion design is that it cannot be applied to

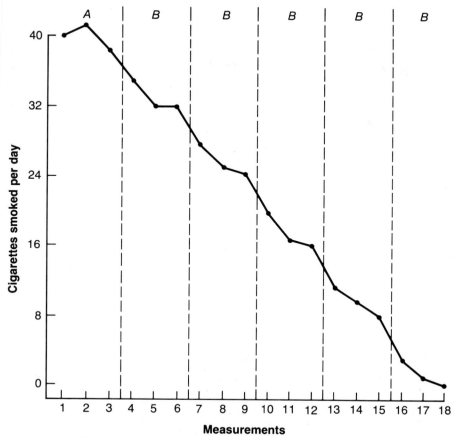

Figure 11.7 Hypothetical Example of the Changing-Criterion Design Applied to Phased Withdrawal of Smoking

all client problems. Unless the problem can be meaningfully broken up into subgoals, the changing-criterion design is not applicable.

Generalizability of Single-Subject Designs

In order to build a knowledge base for clinical practice, researchers must have research findings that are generalizable to a wide variety of situations and cases.

It should come as little surprise that *one* successful single-subject experiment has very little generalizability beyond that particular case. Despite success and hard evidence to prove that the treatment produced it, there is no assurance that the same treatment would be effective on other clients, in different settings, or when used by another practitioner. This lack of generalizability, however, does not detract from the value of single-subject experiments because generalizability can be achieved through replication. It requires many replications before a knowledge base is developed concerning which clients can be helped by a given treatment, which settings it will work in, and what the clinician must do to apply it successfully. As you may gather, this is a process of slow accretion. Each replication provides a little more knowledge concerning the extent of generalizability of treatment effectiveness.

It is valuable in this context to make a distinction between *direct* and *systematic* replication (Sidman, 1960). **Direct replication** involves the repeated application of the same treatment by the same clinician to clients suffering from the same basic problem. In direct replication, only the individual clients vary, with all other conditions remaining constant. Direct replication serves two important functions (Barlow and Herson, 1984). First, it increases confidence in the reliability of findings. For example, a clinician with a series of successes in treating claustrophobics would have far greater confidence in the effectiveness of the treatment than was present after success with the first case. Second, direct replication builds generalizability across clients. We discover that the initial success was not a fluke, as the treatment repeatedly proves effective with additional clients. Direct replication is the beginning of establishing the generalizability of a treatment. It cannot, however, answer questions concerning generalizability across settings, practitioners, or other client problems.

Systematic replication is an attempt to extend the treatment to different settings, practitioners, or client disorders by varying one of these conditions or any combination of them. It is normally conducted after there is evidence from direct replication that the treatment may work.

For example, the clinician mentioned earlier with the successful history of intervention with claustrophobics might begin systematic replication by applying the treatment to agoraphobics. If this is successful, it would indicate that the treatment was generalizable to a different client disorder from that with which success was originally obtained. Additional replications that vary settings and clinicians would, of course, be required to establish generalizability across these conditions.

An example of a successful systematic replication where all three conditions—change agent, setting, and client disorder—were varied is provided by the earlier example of the eight-year-old boy with the penguin fixation (Allen, 1973). Recall that treatment consisted of having counselors ignore the penguin remarks and show attention when the boy interacted more normally. Prior to this case, James Gardner (1967) reported success with the same treatment applied to a client suffering from a different disorder, in a different setting, and using different change agents. The client was a ten-year-old girl suffering from seizures. When examinations failed to locate a physical cause, the interaction patterns within the girl's family were observed. It was discovered that she and her sister were fiercely competitive for attention from their parents. Furthermore, it was observed that the seizures never failed to attract attention. Treatment consisted of the same type of reinforcement later used with the eight-year-old boy—ignoring the seizures and showing attention during normal behavior. Following intervention, the rate of seizures markedly decreased. Further proof of treatment effectiveness was obtained by applying an *ABAB* reversal design. The parents returned to paying attention to the seizures, and the rate increased. When treatment was reinstated, the girl's seizure rate dropped to zero. Permanent cessation of seizures was apparently achieved as a follow-up a year later revealed that no additional seizures had occurred.

When, as in this case, the same treatment evidences effectiveness in a replication with so many differences from a previous situation, it suggests that the treatment may have broad generalizability. Many more successful replications, of course, would be needed before the parameters of effectiveness for this or any other treatment would be firmly established.

When single-subject experiments and their replication are conducted, two practices are crucial. First, substantial information about client characteristics and backgrounds should be collected. This information can serve as *control variables* in assessing the complex effects that treatment can have on dependent variables. The necessity for this arises from the fact that replications often show that treatment is not consistently effective or ineffective. The background information may be useful in sorting out the reasons for these mixed results. A simple example would be a treatment that was effective with men but either ineffective or less effective with women. A second practice that is essential is that treatments be kept uniform from case to case so that the results of replications are truly comparable. In addition, reports must be clear and include all information relevant for future replication efforts. At the outset we noted that one source of dissatisfaction with traditional case histories is the tendency of reports to be too vague to allow for replication. The full potential of single-subject experiments will not be re-

alized if reports include inadequate information for sound replication.

Assessment of the Clinical-Research Model

Advantages

Promotes Better Service for Clients
The requisites of the clinical-research model—careful assessment of treatment goals, use of specific treatments, and continuous monitoring of client progress—tend to promote more effective treatment for clients and encourage the use of scientifically tested intervention strategies (Nelsen, 1981; Johnson, 1981). The model encourages the use of specific practice skills applied in a systematic and rational fashion rather than a reliance on personal idiosyncrasy, intuition, or vague and shifting treatment efforts. Furthermore, the model promotes a consideration of the assumptions underlying various treatment approaches, such as why a given treatment should produce positive results with a particular case. The net result is an increased likelihood that a successful intervention will be selected and that the client will be helped.

Promotes Research Activity   The merger of practice and research in the clinical-research model allows practitioners, who might otherwise not conduct research, to do so. For quite obvious and practical reasons, the opportunities for most human service practitioners to be involved in traditional group research are limited. The clinical-research model makes each client a possible subject for a single-subject experiment. In addition, single-subject research is more practical for the typical clinician because it is research on a small scale, involving minimal cost and avoiding the complexities of group research. Furthermore, involvement in single-subject research can enhance the status of the practitioner since publication of results is often possible. On a broader scale, increased research activity can promote the image of the human services as scientifically based professions.

Results Are of Both Immediate and Future Value Following the clinical-research model provides hard evidence of a client's progress, which is of immediate value to the practitioner. The tracking of progress aids in the selection and application of treatments that prove effective. After successful treatment, the data provide a clear demonstration that the client has been helped. In an age of increasing accountability, vague feelings of having helped clients or even client testimonials are no longer adequate. The value of casework, after all, has been questioned (Segal, 1972; Fischer, 1973; Reid and Hanrahan, 1982). In order to prove that intervention does work, critics will increasingly demand scientifically based evidence, and single-subject experiments hold the promise of providing that evidence.

Disadvantages

Impracticality Under current practice conditions, the application of the clinical-research model may often be impractical (Barth, 1981). Some of the most rigorous of the single-subject designs, such as the reversal designs, are especially difficult to apply because irreversible treatments and ethical considerations may preclude their use. Furthermore, some designs contain many phase segments that may require too much time to complete. Beyond these problems is the fact that some client disorders are of a crisis nature and call for immediate attention, precluding baseline measurements so crucial to single-subject designs.

Limited Generalizability of Results As we noted, results from one single-subject experiment have virtually no generalizability beyond that particular case, and they provide less powerful tests of therapeutic effects than do traditional group experiments (Barlow and Hersen 1984; Jayaratne, 1977), Generalizability is obtained only through successful replication across clients, settings, disorders, and practitioners. This is a slow process, meaning that the potential of single-subject research to increase the knowledge base of the profession will not be realized quickly.

|||||||||||||||||||||||||||||||||||||||||||||||||||||||||||||||||||||||||||||||||||||||||||||||||||||||||||

Computers in Research
Computer-Aided Single-Subject Data Analysis

In the discussion of analyzing the data on single-subject designs, the point was made that visual analysis is often preferred for single-subject data but that statistical analysis can be used. Whichever one chooses, the computer can be a big help in the analysis. One can simply adapt existing software, tailor it to the demands of single-subject design analysis, or select special packages designed specifically for evaluating clinical data.

While visual analysis may be simple and straightforward, it is still a labor intensive undertaking if data must be plotted by hand on graph paper. There are many software packages available for personal computers that will quickly provide line graphs, histograms, pie charts, and other visual displays for data. One of the most popular is the spreadsheet. With it the researcher can graph data and do statistical calculations. The spreadsheet derives its name from the common accounting system of organizing financial data on special grids of columns and rows known as spreadsheets. In the computerized version, the display format of the screen is organized into columns and rows of cells, with letters designating the horizontal axis and numbers the vertical axis, looking somewhat like this:

	A	B	C	D
1	NAME	AGE	TEST 1	TEST 2
2	John	19	97	86
3	Mary	26	82	88
4	Tina	18	75	84
5	Bret	20	92	81
6				
7		sum(b2..b5)/4		

Thus, the first row consists of cells A1, B1, C1, etc., and the first column consists of cells A1, A2, A3, etc. Users can enter words into cells, referred to as "labels," such as NAME and AGE on the first row; they can enter numer-

ical data, designated as "values," such as the people's ages in cells B2 through B5; or they can enter "formulas" that perform computations using values in other cells. Cell B7 contains a formula that says to sum up the ages in cells B2 through B5 and divide by 4 to obtain the mean age of these persons. Building on these basic features, a spreadsheet can be customized to do whatever calculations are required for a particular situation.

Although accounting applications were the impetus for spreadsheets, many other uses have been discovered for this ubiquitous program, including social science research. Here, we describe a spreadsheet application to single-subject research.

While anyone familiar with spreadsheets might set up a program for his or her own needs, it is also possible to rely on applications that have been developed and tested by others. Computer Assisted Practice Evaluation, or CAPE, developed by Denise Bronson at the School of Social Work, State University of New York at Buffalo, is a good example (Bronson and Blythe, 1987). CAPE is based on the Lotus 1–2–3 program, currently one of the most popular spreadsheets available. To use it, one needs only a rudimentary knowledge of spreadsheet design because all the complicated steps have been built into the program.

As a source for statistical procedures, Bronson relied on procedures reported in *Social Work Research and Abstracts* (Jayaratne, 1978). The specific techniques for statistical analysis of single-subject data are rather specialized, and consequently, many of

(Continued on next page)

these techniques are not yet available in standard statistical packages. However, by using the data manipulation and calculation capabilities of a spreadsheet, these statistics can be readily obtained. The heart of Bronson's program is what is referred to as a "template," which is a spreadsheet containing all the necessary formulas and explanatory labels but no data. Once the template is designed, one simply needs to input the data from a given single-subject experiment, and the program will plot the data on a graph and do the statistical tests that the user specifies from a menu of options.

Because of the ease of using such a program, the practitioner need not wait until treatment is completed before making use of the program. Baseline data can be input as it is received, a printed graph can be produced from the computer, and that visual data can be used in planning the intervention. As intervention proceeds, the intervention data can be included and either interpreted visually or, if appropriate, via statistics.

Another computer option for the practitioner wanting to incorporate single-subject designs into practice is the Clinical Assessment System (CAS) from Walter Hudson, the scales of which were described in Research in Practice 11.1. This system is much more than a collection of scales; it is a software package that incorporates the capacity to do single-subject analysis with the scales provided or any others that the user may wish to include with the package. CAS will provide graphs for visual analysis. The system is designed in such a way that clients can complete the computerized scales on a regular basis and see a printout of their progress. Because many clients can complete the scales on their own, interruptions and interference with treatment is kept to a minimum while still providing good data for monitoring client progress.

As more human service settings install personal computers and as software such as CAPE and CAS becomes available, the incorporation of single-subject design as a routine part of practice becomes increasingly feasible. Many agencies already have programs such as Lotus 1–2–3, so there is almost no cost involved in adding CAPE, which is available from the designer. The specialized CAS program not only permits single-subject evaluation but opens the door to using the computer as an integral part of human service delivery and evaluation.

☰ Main Points

• Single-subject designs are quasi-experimental designs used to trace changes induced by treatments to individual clients in a clinical setting.

• Interest in single-subject designs developed out of dissatisfaction with group experiments and case histories as sources of knowledge useful in clinical settings.

• The clinical-research model utilizing single-subject designs is not a radical departure from traditional clinical practice, but rather an effort to increase the specificity and objectivity of practice and to enhance opportunities for replication and knowledge accumulation.

• Although there are many specific single-subject designs from which to choose, all involve a series of pretreatment measures (the baseline) and a series of posttreatment measures that are then compared with the baseline.

• Measurements typically consist of observations, available records, paper-and-pencil measures, or self-reports, with observations usually being the most desirable and self-reports the least desirable.

• Effectiveness may be judged against three different standards—therapeutic, experimental, or statistical—with therapeutic effectiveness demanding the greatest client improvement and statistical effectiveness the least.

• The simple *AB* design is highly flexible, but is not strong on internal validity.

• Reversal designs, such as *ABA* or *ABAB*, are strong on internal validity, but are often impractical to apply.

• Multiple-baseline designs are quite strong on internal validity and are reasonably flexible, making them a good choice when a reversal design cannot be used.

• In addition to these basic designs, there are many specialized designs that can accommodate such things as changing treatments, combined treatments, or phased achievement of the treatment goal.

• Positive results from one single-subject experiment are not generalizable, but generalizability can be built up over time through replication.

• Computer software is available that can simplify and speed up both the visual analysis and the statistical analysis of data from single-subject research.

≡ Important Terms for Review

baseline
clinical-research model
direct replication
single-subject design
systematic replication

≡ For Further Reading

Bloom, M., and J. Fischer. *Evaluating Practice: Guidelines for the Accountable Professional.* Englewood Cliffs, N.J.: Prentice-Hall, 1982.
A textbook devoted entirely to single-subject applications in social work.

Fischer, J. *Effective Casework Practice: An Eclectic Approach.* New York: McGraw-Hill, 1978
A social work practice text that is highly compatible with practice assessment via single-subject designs.

Haynes, S. N., *Principles of Behavioral Assessment.* New York: Gardner, 1978.
A thorough coverage of a variety of issues important to single-subject designs, including the design of measurement instruments.

Journal of Social Service Research, 3:1 (Fall 1979).
This entire issue is devoted to assessment of practice with single-subject designs.

Kazdin, A. E. *Single-Case Research Designs.* New York: Oxford University Press, 1982.
A concise overview of single-subject research with illustrative applications in several areas of human service practice.

Tawney, J. W., and D. L. Gast. *Single Subject Research in Special Education.* Columbus, Ohio: Charles C. Merrill, 1984.
This book covers the applications of single-subject designs in educational settings.

This is a readable book, although it is intended for graduate students.

≡ Exercises for Class Discussion

11.1 A foster parent complains to the foster care worker that the 14-year-old child placed in her home chronically oversleeps in the morning and is late for school. She calls him every morning about 7 A.M., and he has two hours to get ready for school and be there on time.

   a. Establish the problems that the foster care worker might tackle with this youngster and the goals to be accomplished. As you do this, keep in mind the importance of specificity and measurability.

   b. Identify some alternative ways of measuring a baseline for assessing change in this case.

   c. What would be the advantages and disadvantages of having the foster parent versus the foster son do the data collecting? Can you identify any outside sources of data?

11.2 Select a behavior from one of the following, devise a means of measuring it, and collect baseline data for a week, using yourself or someone else as the client. Report your results to the class.

   a. Cigarette smoking
   b. Speeding while driving
   c. Snacking
   d. Feeling depressed
   e. Praising your child
   f. Completing homework

11.3 A counselor in a Spouse Abuse Shelter has been working with women in the shelter on assertiveness in dealing with men. She would like to do a single-subject design with a woman client to evaluate the effectiveness of the assertiveness training. She intends to have the staff collect data on the client's level of assertiveness in a variety of situations, using a coded observation form.

   What would be the advantages and disadvantages of the following designs for this research?
   a. *AB*
   b. *ABA*
   c. *ABAB*

   What steps would need to be taken to conduct this study in an ethical manner? Are there any special problems that are unique to each design type (*AB*, *ABA*, or *ABAB*)? Are there more complex designs that you might want to use in this situation?

11.4 An intensive foster care worker is responsible for six adolescent clients in separate foster homes. She has been receiving complaints from most of the foster parents that the kids do not pick up their clothes or do other chores around the house such as washing dishes, mowing lawns, or cleaning walks. She decides to implement a reinforcement program by enabling the foster children to earn points toward special activities such as a trip to a large amusement park. One such activity would be scheduled each week.

   a. Describe how this worker might design a multiple-baseline study across clients.

   b. Describe how the worker might design a multiple-baseline study across behaviors.

   c. How might she devise a changing-criterion design?

12

Evaluation Research

A major theme of this book is the benefits accorded to the human service field by linking human service practice with scientific research to form a single endeavor seeking common goals. In various places, we have labeled this "scientific practice" (see Chapter 1) or the "clinical-research model" (see Chapter 11). In this chapter we encounter a new element of this linkage in the form of *evaluation research,* which really points to a reason for conducting research rather than a new research methodology. **Evaluation research** refers to the use of scientific research methods to plan intervention programs, to monitor the implementation of new programs and the operation of existing ones, and to determine how effectively programs or clinical practices achieve their goals. Although evaluation research has been around for many years, it has risen to considerable prominence over the past two decades as the amount of public and private funds channeled into social programs has grown. As funding has increased, those providing the funds have sought valid and reliable evidence regarding whether programs achieve their goals, how efficiently they do so, and whether they produce any unintended consequences. Evaluation research is a mechanism for gathering evidence regarding these issues, and it has become an integral part of most social programs today.

In this chapter, we will provide an overview of the field of evaluation research. First, we will discuss in more detail what evaluation research is, distinguishing it from basic research. Then we will discuss the two major forms of evaluation research, formative and summative. This will be followed by a review of how evaluation research is conducted, including an assessment of the various research designs commonly used. We will conclude with a discussion of the problems that often arise when it comes time to utilize the outcomes of evaluation research.

What Is Evaluation Research?

Evaluation research is a means of supplying valid and reliable evidence regarding the operation of social programs or clinical practices—how they are planned, how well they operate, and how effectively they achieve their goals. For example, a medical care facility may need to know if there is a community need for a day-care program for the elderly. Corrections officials may wish to know the size at which a probation officer's caseload becomes too large to provide effective services to those on probation. Or hospital administrators may need to assess the impact on patient care of a 15-percent reduction in the nursing staff. In these situations and others like them, evaluation research utilizes many of the research techniques discussed in other chapters in this book to provide evidence regarding the workings of programs and practices in the human services. A typical evaluation effort might involve some combination of interviews, questionnaires, observation, available data, and an experimental design. In fact, we have already discussed evaluation research in many places in this book without calling it by name. In Chapter 11, for example, many of the single-subject design studies described can be considered evaluation research of the effectiveness of clinical interventions.

Why Evaluate?

Evaluation research is conducted for three major reasons (Rossi and Freeman, 1985). First, it can be conducted for *administrative purposes*, such as to fulfill an evaluation requirement demanded by a funding source, to improve service to clients, or to increase efficiency of program delivery. Evaluations done for administrative reasons tend to focus on assessing the daily operations of a program rather than its overall impact, and the goal is typically to find the most efficient means of running a program or agency. A second reason for conducting evaluation research is *impact assessment:* A program is assessed to see what effects, if any, it is producing. Typically, the goals of the program are identified, and the program is measured in terms of how well it achieves those goals. The results of the impact assessment are then used to make policy decisions regarding whether to expand, change, or curtail a program. Third, evaluation research may be conducted to *test hypotheses* or *evaluate practice approaches.* These are, in reality, often one and the same thing because practice strategies are typically based on

hypotheses derived from social and psychological theories. Such evaluation not only provides information about a particular practice intervention but also adds to the fund of social scientific knowledge, which may be useful in the design of new intervention strategies.

Evaluation Research and Basic Research

Evaluation research is a form of applied research discussed in Chapter 1, and as such it involves a special application of the general research techniques used in basic research. Because of this, there are similarities between the two, but there are also some important differences (Weiss, 1972). First of all, the results of evaluation research have immediate practical use in assessing operating programs. Basic research, on the other hand, is oriented toward more general information gathering and hypothesis testing.

Second, the basic researcher has more control over which issues are to be investigated in contrast to evaluation research, where the needs of the decision makers sponsoring the study are paramount in shaping the form and content of the research. In most evaluations, there is latitude for the evaluator to expand beyond the issues of direct interest to the decision makers, but control over the content of the research is shared with them. This is an area that may become a source of conflict between researchers and sponsors of the evaluation.

A third difference is that evaluation, by its very nature, has a judgmental quality about it that is often not a part of basic research. The evaluation may judge a program as a "success" or "failure" on the basis of how well it achieved its purposes, and this judgmental quality can be a source of tension between an evaluator and the sponsors of the evaluation. Understandably, the sponsors are concerned that a negative evaluation could have dire consequences for the existence of the program and for their own livelihoods and careers.

The fourth difference between basic and evaluation research relates to the issues given priority in the research process. In basic research, quite naturally, the requisites for producing a scientifically sound study are given strong weight. Evaluation research, on the other hand, takes place in a context in which an ongoing program is in operation, and the demands of the program may conflict with the demands for sound scientific practices. When this happens, the program administrators may give higher priority to the program than to the evaluation. The scientific demands of an evaluation, for example, might call for the random assignment of nurses from a home health care agency to each new client of the agency. The agency administrator, on the other hand, may prefer to assign nurses on the basis of his or her assessment of their competencies and "fit" with the client, and the agency head will likely be able to override the requests of the evaluators, forcing the latter to modify their scientific procedures. These conflicts can be aggravated by differences in approach sometimes found between practitioners and researchers (Blenkner, 1950; Weiss, 1972). Practitioners tend to emphasize the importance of providing services to people and the role of empathy and concern in the intervention process. Researchers, on the other hand, may give more weight to the understanding provided by rigorous scientific analysis and objectivity. Although these differences should not be overdrawn—for researchers do have empathy and practitioners do recognize the value of scientific analysis—there is a difference in emphasis between practitioners and researchers, and it can be a source of tension. In fact, one of the beneficial outcomes of developing linkages between practice and research is that it encourages people to develop ways of combining the two approaches so that advantages accrue to both.

A final difference between basic and evaluation research relates to making the results of the research public. One of the canons of science is that research results be made public for others to see and criticize in order to reduce the likelihood that errors or personal bias might find their way into scientific research (see Chapter 2). In the past, wide dissemination of evaluation results was uncommon. A review of the journals *Social Work* and *Social Casework* between 1958 and 1972 found not one article describing a carefully conducted evaluation. The few references to evaluation were more in the nature of "afterthoughts" (Segal, 1972). It was not until 1976 that a journal specifically devoted to evaluation reports, *Evaluation Quarterly,* came into existence. Today there are a number of journals devoted to this topic and a number of professional organizations that serve as outlets for the dissemination of the results of evaluation research. However, what still occurs all too frequently is that sponsors of an evaluation are supplied with a few copies of the report, which are promptly filed away where they gather dust on shelves and clutter already overcrowded offices. This has the effect of thwarting the accumulation of information so necessary for progress. Even if evaluation results show no effect, those findings are valuable in preventing ineffective programs from proliferating.

Despite the differences between evaluation research and basic research, there are important similarities. First, both may choose from the entire array of data-gathering techniques those that best fit their needs. In fact, as we have noted, evaluation projects often involve a synthesis of data gathered in a variety of ways. Second, both forms of research can focus on determining cause-and-effect relationships. In basic research, researchers seek cause-and-effect relationships between variables of their own choosing whereas in evaluation research the invesigation is focused on variables that are a part of the program being assessed.

In a review of these similarities and differences, it should be apparent that the differences are of a practical nature, deriving mainly from the context in which evaluation research is conducted. Although these differences are important—and the potential conflicts alluded to are quite real—the actual process of inquiry is very much the same in both types of research. In fact, evaluation research illustrates the dynamic and flexible quality of basic social research methods in that the core methods and techniques can be stretched and changed to confront new problems and issues. Evaluation research is a novel and challenging application of methods that have been used in many other contexts. As such, the distinction between basic and evaluation research is really one of degree rather of kind.

Types of Evaluation Research

The term "evaluation research" is somewhat misleading in that there is not a separate set of research techniques that are distinctly applied for a single purpose.

Rather, the term applies to a diverse collection of strategies that can be used for a broad range of evaluative purposes. One way in which evaluation research methods may be classified is in terms of the unit of analysis. For example, the single-subject designs covered in Chapter 11 may be considered evaluation methods where the unit of analysis is a single individual. Because of the unique features involved in doing such individual studies, we have chosen to devote a separate chapter to them and consider in this chapter those evaluations that focus on programs or organizations as the unit of analysis.

Another useful way of conceptualizing the diversity of evaluation research is in terms of the goals of the study. There are two basic goals that evaluation research can achieve. **Formative evaluation research** focuses on providing information to guide the planning, development, and implementation of a specific program. It is primarily concerned with ensuring a smooth-running, well-integrated program rather than with the ultimate worth or impact of the program. **Summative evaluation research** is concerned with the program's effects. Here the purpose centers on assessing the effectiveness and efficiency of programs and the extent to which the outcomes of the project are generalizable to other settings and populations. Formative evaluation research has traditionally received less attention in the evaluation literature than has summative. However, the two forms are closely linked and may be likened to a foundation and a building. The formative component of evaluation may not be especially glamorous or attract much attention, but, unless it is carefully prepared and well done, it will be very difficult to carry out the summative type of study and obtain high quality results. We will discuss each type of evaluation research separately.

Formative Evaluation Research

Formative research involves applying research to the types of questions that arise in the planning, implementation, and operation of programs. For initiating a program, certain basic information is essential. First, it is necessary to gather data on the target population and their characteristics. The nature of the problems they have, the number of potential program users, their location in the community, and other demographic information would also be essential to planning a good program. Second, it is important to be aware of existing services that the program under development might duplicate or on which it may rely for referrals or auxiliary services. Third, the program planners need to be knowledgeable about the specific intervention strategies that might be applied to the problems. Fourth, the program operators must be able to specify the skills that staff must have to deliver the program. Fifth, it must be determined if it is feasible to offer and monitor the program as it has been conceptualized.

To provide answers to these problems, formative research may rely on a diversity of research techniques. To answer the first question, for example, researchers commonly utilize a sampling strategy and then survey members of the target population. Thus, survey research methods form the backbone of such needs assessments. However, one could also rely on direct observation or utilize existing data to gain a profile of the population and identify needs. Essentially,

any techniques used for descriptive research may be used for answering this question. Knowledge of existing and related services might be gained through interviewing potential clients and representatives of existing agencies. Knowledge of possible intervention strategies and program components often comes from conducting a thorough literature search, which is a fundamental step in any research project. Appendix A in this book, on the use of the library, is directly applicable to such a task. Feasibility determination may essentially involve pretesting of program components and conducting a pilot study.

An example of a formative evaluation research project can be found in a program to provide financial aid to newly released offenders (Rossi, Berk, and Lenihan, 1980). They began with a very modest project involving six released inmates who received six weekly payments of $60 and 20 controls who received no payment. In addition to relying on a review of the literature and existing statistics on the problems of released offenders, this modest project helped prepare for a large-scale program in several ways. It helped determine that it was logistically possible to make the payments and to interview and keep track of ex-inmates in the community. Had this pilot project shown that these operational elements could not be accomplished effectively, then it would have been foolish to continue with a larger project even though one might be convinced of the overall effectiveness of the program.

Because the questions addressed in formative research are often modest in scope, the research is frequently conducted by the staff of the agency administering the program. However, such research may also be done on a national scale in conjunction with large programs. Programs such as AFDC, food stamps, and vocational rehabilitation involve large sums of money, and initiation of such programs involves estimating the number of potential recipients, which can vary considerably depending on what definition of poverty is applied. Before initiating such programs, formative research based on needs assessment is essential. There are many examples of programs that failed because there really were no potential users of the program or the design of the program precluded clients from using it. A fascinating account of one such program is in the book *Implementation: Or How Great Expectations in Washington Are Dashed in Oakland* (Pressman and Wildavsky, 1973). The authors describe the pitfalls encountered in an effort to develop a major antipoverty job creation program. After initial fanfare and allocation of several million dollars, only a few jobs had been created. Although formative evaluation cannot ensure success, it can help reduce instances of unnecessary intervention and increase the potential for success among those programs that are initiated.

Besides serving as a tool for the planning of an intervention program, formative research may also be used to monitor the implementation of new programs and the ongoing operation of existing ones. Experience with evaluations for program effectiveness has shown that a major factor in program failure is often the fact that the program as planned was never really implemented (Berman and Pauly, 1975). There are several basic issues in program monitoring that are the counterparts to program planning. First, it is necessary to determine if the target population is, in fact, being served. Second, are the services that are supposed to be delivered actually being delivered? Third, is the quality of the service adequate? As a means of supplying answers to the first problem, it is common to use a census of program users and compare their characteristics with the characteristics of the population for whom services were intended. Any discrepancy suggests that some members of the target population are not receiving services intended for them. Service delivery may be assessed in a variety of ways, including questionnaires and direct observation. Just as in single-subject designs, time samples may be used to determine if behaviors associated with service delivery are occurring as planned. Quality control techniques not unlike those used in industry are used to monitor the delivery of services in many settings. Major financial assistance services such as AFDC are routinely monitored by state departments of social services. Typically, this process involves selecting a random sample of recipients and examining the most recent action on their files to determine if the action resulted in a correct payment, an overpayment, or an underpayment. States are expected to keep their error rate within certain specified limits. Other settings may use follow-up questionnaires to service users to determine if expected services were delivered.

Finally, agencies commonly use a time-reporting system to make sure that staff are spending the expected amount of time on specified aspects of the program. Figure 12.1 illustrates one type of time-reporting system. Such studies do not address the question of whether or not the program is actually doing any good. Rather, they address the narrower issue of the extent to which the services actually being delivered are true to the intended plan.

Case Name _____
Case No. _____
Worker _____   Page _____

Date	Type	Time	

Code: Time Interval—
   1—Telephone Contact   8—Foster Parent Training   1–15 Min.
   2—In-office Visit   9—Court Visit
   3—School Visit   10—Visit to Family of Origin
   4—Foster Home Visit   11—Case Staffing & Supervision
   5—Referring Worker Visit 12—Other Collateral
   6—Paperwork   13—Client
   7—Driving Time

Figure 12.1 Example of a Time-Reporting Form

Summative Evaluation Research

Summative evaluation research involves assessing the impact of a program although good summative evaluations usually investigate other matters concerning the program's operation. The results of summative evaluations are intended to be used for policymaking decisions, such as whether to continue, expand, or cancel a program, and furthermore whether to generalize the findings of this project to other settings and populations. Summative evaluations are typically large-scale projects involving considerable time, personnel, and resources. For this reason, as well as to avoid the biasing effect of personal interest, summative evaluations are often conducted by outside consultants rather than by agency staff.

Although the steps in the research process are much the same for all types of research, including evaluation research, there is some special planning called for to take into consideration the unique problems of evaluation research.

Evaluability Assessment

During the planning of evaluation research, an **evaluability assessment** is often conducted to enable investigators to decide whether a program has the necessary preconditions to be evaluated. An evaluability assessment involves four steps (Rutman, 1984). First, the purpose of the evaluation—from the standpoint of the eventual users of the results—is determined. This identifies which aspects of the program are to be assessed for impact. To be evaluated, a program needs clearly specified goals. Having clear goals is necessary because they are the major criteria of a program's success. Goals are the dependent variables that the input variables are supposed to affect. Unfortunately, the goals of many programs are either vague or so global (improving family functioning, for example) that they are unusable for evaluation purposes. As we will see, it may be necessary for an evaluator to become actively involved, together with the staff, in developing a set of clear goals before a program is evaluable.

Second, an evaluator studies and gathers information about the program. What are the inputs, the expected results or goals, and the linkage between the two? This linkage is essentially the theory on which the program is based. It involves answering the question, Why, given these program inputs, should certain outcomes be expected? This theoretical linkage may be explicitly recognized as the basis of the program, or it might be implicit but derivable from the program's operation. The purpose of identifying this rationale is that it is important in understanding the success or failure of the program. For example, some programs may identify certain outcomes as goals but not direct any effort toward realizing them. (Quite obviously, if evaluated against these goals, the program would likely turn out to be a failure.) If we do not specify the linkage, the reason for failure may be unclear, and, in the case of a success, we would be at a loss to explain why. Knowledge of the linkage would reveal the source of the problem as the failure to direct input resources toward those particular goals. During this step, it is important to monitor the program *as implemented*, as gaps sometimes develop between the stated program and the program as operated.

Third, information gathered during the second stage is used to develop a flow-model of the program. This model traces program inputs, clients, and the interventions as they affect the expected results, specifying any assumed causal linkages along the way. Modeling of programs is extremely useful in evaluation research because it provides a clear picture of the structure and operation of the program. It can also help explain a program's successes or failures. For example, as a part of an evaluation of a group counseling program in a correctional system, a careful model of the program was developed (Kassebaum et al., 1971). When the results of the evaluation showed that inmates in the counseling program did not have lower recidivism rates than other inmates, the evaluators were hardly surprised. Their model revealed that counselors were poorly trained and unmotivated, counseling sessions tended to be unfocused "bull" sessions, inmate participation was motivated largely by a desire to impress the parole board, and the inmates did not view the sessions as likely to be helpful to them. Against this backdrop, the failure of counseling to reduce recidivism is understandable. The flow-model of the program helped identify these elements.

The final stage of the evaluability assessment is to review the program model to identify those aspects of the program that are sufficiently unambiguous in terms of inputs, goals, and linkages that evaluation of them appears feasible. The end result of the assessment may be that the whole program can be evaluated, none of the program can be evaluated, or, most commonly, only certain parts of the program are amenable to evaluation.

Specification of Variables

As in any research, an important part of evaluation research is the specification of variables and how they will be measured. In some evaluations, the variables of interest take the form of independent and dependent variables. The inputs to a social program, for example, might constitute the independent variables. In some cases, the independent variable takes the form of a dichotomous variable: participation or nonparticipation in a program. In other cases, the independent variable might be the degree or duration of participation in a program, such as the frequency of contact with a counselor, the level of financial aid received, or the length of time a service is provided. Commonly, the dependent variables in evaluation research are the goals of a program: precisely what it is supposed to accomplish. Some evaluation research, of course, especially the formative type,

would not involve independent and dependent variables. Whatever form the variables take, a central issue in evaluation research is that the variables be clearly and properly specified, and numerous problems can arise along these lines. This is especially true when measuring the goals of a program, and we will illustrate some of the measurement problems in evaluation research in this realm.

An often-encountered problem is that the goals, as articulated by program administrators, do not easily lend themselves to evaluation. They may be vague, overly broad, or so long-term that evaluation is not feasible. For example, a goal of Head Start preschool education is to develop capable and functioning adults who can rise out of poverty. Although the success of Head Start in achieving this goal may be its ultimate test, it would be necessary to wait 20 to 30 years before evaluating the program. Although this may be a laudable and essential part of the program, funding agencies are understandably reluctant to expend funds for that length of time with no evaluation. Thus, such programs normally include what are called *proximate* goals, or goals that can be realized in the short run and that are related to the achievement of the long-term goals (Weiss, 1972). In the case of Head Start, academic achievement would be a reasonable proximate goal because performance in school is associated with social and occupational success in adulthood.

There are programs, of course, in which it is possible and desirable to assess the long-term impact. For example, there was a 30-year follow-up of the Cambridge-Sommerville Youth Study, a 5-year experiment in delinquency prevention begun in Boston in 1939 (McCord, 1978). This field experiment focused on 506 young boys, half receiving counseling and other assistance while the other half served as a control group. The experimental condition consisted of counseling sessions every two weeks, tutoring, medical and psychiatric assistance, summer camps, and organized youth activities. Thirty years later, 95 percent of the participants in the experiment were located. Many of the comparisons showed no differences between the two groups. But what differences were found suggested that the experimental variables had the *opposite* effect from what was expected! The experimental group committed more crimes as adults, had higher rates of alcoholism, poorer mental and physical health, and less occupational success. The only positive result for the program appeared to be the participants' own subjective evaluations. Two-thirds of the experimental group indicated that they thought the program had been helpful to them even though their objective situation was worse than that of people in the control group. The reason the program produced harmful effects may have been that it raised participants' expectations to an unrealistically high level. When those expectations were not realized, they suffered frustration and added stress, which resulted in a greater tendency toward criminality and alcoholism as well as the deleterious effects on their mental and physical health (McCord, 1978). Despite the need for early program evaluations, long-term evaluation, accomplished so well in this study, is still essential in assessing many programs.

When goals are vague or overly broad, it is necessary that they be clarified or reduced in scope so that they are amenable to evaluation. In this regard, it is helpful if program administrators consult with evaluators in developing the goals for a program. During discussions with program administrators, it is important that evaluators not simply accept as all-inclu-

sive the goals articulated by the administrators. In fact, one of the major reasons for finding that a program does not have the intended result is that program goals are too limited (Chen and Rossi, 1980). Too often, administrators state program goals from the standpoint of what they desire, resulting in goals that are unattainable given program inputs. When evaluated against these goals, the program naturally appears to be a failure. Evaluators should "cast a wide net" in seeking program effects, including not only those suggested by administrators but also others logically expected given the nature of the program. The model developed during the evaluability assessment and the theoretical basis of the program are productive places to look for possible program effects to be included in the evaluation. This "multigoal, theory-driven" approach promises to provide a better chance of finding nonzero program effects and supplying information on what the program does as well as what it does not do.

Measuring Variables

Once the goals have been specified and agreed on, the evaluator must set about developing outcome measures for the program's effects. Some goals can be readily measured because they have clearly quantifiable outcomes. For example, the academic effects of compensatory education programs can be readily measured by standard achievement tests. Such effects of Head Start as improved self-esteem, better adjustment to the classroom environment, or enhanced parent–child relationships will likely require more inventiveness on the part of the evaluator to measure.

When measures for program effects are being considered, there may be alternative indicators of the same program effect. For example, in measuring the effects of a family planning program, we might use as a measure: (1) the proportion of participants adopting contraceptive practices, (2) average desired number of children, (3) average number of children actually born, or (4) attitudes toward large families (Rossi and Freeman, 1985). All these indicators are logically related to the effects of a family planning program. If the budget allows, multiple indicators are more useful than relying on a single one. Multiple indicators are more sensitive and, therefore, more likely to show an effect if the program produced one (Weiss, 1972, p. 36). If multiple indicators are impractical, a decision must be made as to which of the alternatives is best. In the case of the four alternatives for the family planning program, the clearest indicator of program success would be a low birth rate among participants. This indicator, however, might be impractical for some purposes because we would have to wait many years before the evaluation could be completed. The two indicators dealing with attitudes would not be the best choices because attitudes can change, and there is sometimes only a weak relationship between attitudes and behavior. Indeed, attitudinal measures should be avoided whenever a behavioral alternative is available. Of the four possible measures, then, the proportion of participants who adopt contraception is probably the best single indicator of the effectiveness of the family planning program. It would not be perfect, however, as contraceptives must be used conscientiously for them to be effective, but for a short-run measure it would be adequate.

As we have recommended on a number of occasions (for example, in Chapter 11), it is preferable to use existing measures where possible. This avoids the work involved in creating new measures, pretesting them, and establishing their validity and reliability. Furthermore, existing measures contribute to the accumulation of knowledge because they make evaluations of different programs more comparable. The preference for existing measures extends only to the point where good existing measures for the variables of interest can be found. If existing measures are only tangentially related to what one seeks to measure, then it is far better to develop new measures. Good measurement is so crucial to meaningful evaluation that shortcuts that compromise quality should not be tolerated.

Assuming that some new measures must be created, it is important to keep in mind the dual criteria for assessing them: validity and reliability. Measures used in evaluation research must meet the same standards of validity and reliability as those used in basic research, and the methods for assessing those characteristics that we considered in Chapter 5 apply here.

The Evaluation of Minorities in Evaluation Research

One area in which evaluation research has played an important role is in assessing the operation and impact of policies and programs that affect minorities. When the women's movement hit full stride in the 1970s, women began rapidly to enter what had long been considered exclusively male occupations. Before long, studies were being done assessing the relative performances of men and women working the same jobs. As more and more of this research was amassed, serious questions began to be raised concerning the quality and fairness of these evaluations, particularly toward the women in the traditionally male occupations.

Take the case of evaluating male and

female police officers. Merry Morash and Jack Greene (1986) reviewed the nine major evaluations of women police officers that had been conducted up to that time. Not surprisingly, given the varying methodologies of the several studies, results were inconsistent. With one exception, however, the studies concluded that female police officers were neither better nor worse than their male counterparts, but they were different. That is, women were better than the male officers at some policing activities, but they were not as good as the male officers at others. If these differences are real, such information could be quite valuable in allocating police personnel to maximize the strengths and minimize the weaknesses of the male and female officers. But what if the differences are merely artifacts of faulty study design? Because assignments in police departments have implications for career advancement, we had better be sure that the findings of such evaluations are indeed valid before we proceed to use them as a basis for allocating personnel, or for any other reason for that matter.

Morash and Green's review of the nine studies is not encouraging on the validity issue, but it does point out issues that future researchers should address. Among the problems they found were a tendency to emphasize conformity to male stereotypes (such as marksmanship or the frequency of arrests), a failure to evaluate performance on a representative sample of police tasks, an overemphasis on the violent and dangerous aspects of police work, a failure to consider the differences between men's and women's experiences in the workplace (there is greater camaraderie among male officers, for example), a failure to evaluate variations in performance among male officers as well as variation between sexes, and unclear or unspecified definitions of what

constituted good police work. Quite a litany of criticisms!

The authors also found that performance evaluations may be subject to deliberate political manipulation. A study conducted in Philadelphia concluded that women performed at least as well as did the men. In a second study certain behaviors that had been positively evaluated in the first study were now negatively evaluated. This time the results came out against the female officers.

Morash and Green's analysis clearly indicates that conducting performance evaluations of men and women in job settings can be very difficult and fraught with possibilities for invalid conclusions. The fact that such evaluations will continue to be done and their results acted upon means that those who conduct evaluations must be cognizant of the potential pitfalls that await and be ready to guard against biased results through the use of sound study designs and a firm resistance to any efforts at political manipulation.

Designs for Evaluation Research

Summative evaluation research is often concerned with cause-and-effect relationships. For example, the program being evaluated is presumed to bring about some changes in such factors as client behavior. A research design developed for such an evaluation needs to be based on an awareness of this cause-and-effect dimension. In Chapter 10, we noted that true experimental designs involving randomization are the best approach for establishing cause-and-effect relationships because they best control the validity threats that can lead to false causal inferences. The ideal approach to determining the effects of a program, therefore, is the randomized experiment (Saxe and Fine, 1981; Berk et al., 1985). Any of the true experimental designs discussed in Chapter 10 is appropriate for evaluation purposes.

Randomized Experimental Designs
As you recall, the requirements of a true experiment are two randomized equivalent groups, one that experiences the experimental condition and one that does not and serves as a control group. In summative evaluation research, the experimental condition is some level of participation in the program under consideration. The crucial feature of the true experiment is that members of the comparison groups are randomly assigned. This is the surest and most reliable way of producing equivalent groups.

Virtually all randomized experiments in evaluation are field experiments, taking place in the setting where the actual program is administered. Because of this, evaluators may encounter a number of impediments to conducting a randomized experiment. The first impediment centers around the control group and the randomization procedure used to obtain it. It is necessary, in order to have a control group, to deny some members of the target population access to the program under evaluation, and that denial must be on a random basis. Evaluators may encounter substantial resistance to such denials. For example, the enabling legislation of some programs requires that all persons who meet the eligibility requirements have a legal right to participate in the program. If such is the case, random denial of service is ruled out.

In other programs, resistance to random denial of services may spring from program administrators and staff. Practitioners are used to providing services on the basis of need and may be disinclined to use a table of random numbers instead. It seems cold, insensitive, even im-

moral to withhold available services from people who need them, especially if intuition leads us to believe that the provision of services would have beneficial effects. In advocating a randomized experiment, evaluators sometimes find themselves in a "no win" situation. If they discover that the program produces harmful effects, they are blamed for subjecting the experimental group to the harmful program. If the program produces positive results, they are blamed for withholding this valuable service from the control group. Imagine the ethical implications of a randomized experiment for evaluating something like a suicide prevention program where there are life-and-death issues at stake!

Along these lines, it is important to keep in mind that our intuition regarding the impact of programs is often faulty. In fact, the literature on evaluation research strongly suggests that practitioners' assumptions of positive program effects are often wrong. For example, casework practitioners commonly believe that casework is effective while the relevant research is much more equivocal about its impact. One review of numerous efforts to evaluate social casework concluded: "Not only has professional casework failed to demonstrate it is effective, but lack of effectiveness appears to be the rule rather than the exception across several categories of clients, problems, situations, and types of casework" (Fischer, 1973, p. 14). A broader review of attempts to evaluate group work, individual and group psychotherapy, behavior therapy, and multiple-impact therapy came to a similar conclusion, making a strong ethical case in favor of randomized experiments: "It is not unethical to deprive someone of treatment when that treatment is not an established or proven one in the agency. It is unethical to grant such treatment when no systematic assessment for possible negative effects has been carried out. . . . It might, in fact, be the most ethical step an agency can take since the literature now indicates that treatment can have negative effects'' (Segal, 1972, p. 10). When viewed from this stance, the arguments against withholding services in a randomized experimental design are severely weakened, and as we demonstrate in Research in Practice 10.2, studies involving true control groups are clearly feasible.

A second impediment to conducting randomized experiments in evaluation research is that they may be more time-consuming and expensive than other designs. Experimental evaluations of programs are typically longitudinal—sufficient time must pass for programs to have an effect. With many social programs, such as compensatory education or job training, the minimum length of the experiment might be at least a year. Furthermore, a listing of the target population, required for randomization, may be difficult or expensive to obtain. These practical considerations mean that randomized experiments are limited to those cases where the money and time are available for an elaborate, rigorous evaluation.

Despite these impediments, it is important to consider true experimental designs in evaluation research because these are the best designs from which to assess causality, and many statistical procedures are based on the assumption of equivalent experimental and control groups. Reports in journals such as *Evaluation Quarterly* document the widespread use of these designs today. With some inventiveness on the part of evaluators, much of the resistance to randomized experiments can be overcome. Indeed, there is a growing consensus about the desirability of randomized experiments and an expanding literature documenting their use. This should work to reduce the barriers to future randomized experiments in evaluation (Berk et al., 1985; Rossi and Freeman, 1985).

One common situation in particular contributes to the possibility of a randomized experiment. When the target population is larger than the program's capacity to serve it—in short, when demand for services exceeds supply—services must be denied to some people. Because many programs are initially instituted on a small scale, this excess demand often occurs. Because some members of the target population will not be served anyway, the determination of who will be served might as well be random unless there is some other clear-cut and defensible criterion that could be used, such as severity of need. In fact, a reasonable argument can be made that random allocation of services is the fairest method when resources are inadequate to serve all and no other criteria seem applicable.

If an evaluator is successful in getting a randomized experiment approved, it is important that the random assignment process be carefully monitored to ensure that it is properly implemented. Lack of such monitoring can destroy the experimental design. For example, an employment and training program, with which one of the authors once consulted, had agreed to a randomized study. However, when a large group of eager youths appeared at the agency on the first day, the staff was overwhelmed and simply threw the program open to all of them, thus totally destroying the randomization procedure. When such events go undiscovered, the comparison groups will not be equalized and the eventual results may be misleading. A two-step procedure is desirable in which client information is gathered by different personnel from those who do the random assignment. In this way, those doing the assignment would do so without knowledge of client identities or characteristics. Insulating the assignment process in this way reduces the opportunity for deviations from randomness to creep in and eases the monitoring task (Cook et al., 1977).

The Alternatives to Randomized Experiments The barriers to randomized experiments may be sufficiently formidable that an alternative design must be utilized. It is important to remember that anything other than a randomized experiment will produce results in which confidence is reduced because such alternative designs are weaker on internal validity (see Chapter 10). Properly conducted, however, these designs can allow evaluation with a reasonable degree of certitude (Achen, 1986).

One alternative to the randomized experiment is to use a quasi-experimental design. When a program is meant to affect behavior about which data are routinely collected, a time-series design may be appropriate. One research group, for example, used a time-series design to evaluate the impact of a Massachusetts gun control law that mandated a one-year minimum prison sentence for anyone convicted of carrying a firearm without a permit (Deutch and Alt, 1977). The law went into effect in April of 1975. The researchers, therefore, traced the monthly occurrences of homicide, assault with a gun, and armed robbery in Boston from 1966 to October 1975. This provided a baseline of gun-related offenses for about nine years prior to the introduction of the gun control law. Their analysis revealed that in the first seven months that the law was in effect, statistically significant

decreases in both armed robbery and assault with a gun occurred. No change was registered for homicide, however. Depite their frequent utility for evaluation, it is important to remember that the chief weakness of time-series designs is the validity threat of history. Unless it is possible to use a control group, as in the multiple time-series design, it is always possible that some extraneous variable can intervene and confound the results.

A second alternative to randomized experiments is matching. If randomization is not feasible, it may be possible to match persons in the experimental group with persons having similar characteristics in a control group. Recall, however, that matching can be unreliable because relatively few variables can be used for matching, which leaves uncontrolled variables that might confound the results.

An example of an evaluation in which a form of matching was used is a study of the effects of a housing allowance program implemented by the Department of Housing and Urban Development (HUD) in 1970 (Jackson and Mohr, 1986). Because of the nature of the program, people could not be assigned to experimental and control groups. Instead, for the experimental group, a random sample of clients enrolled in the program was used. For a control group, a sample was selected from the Annual Housing Survey administered by HUD. The HUD survey contained data similar to that collected from the experimental group. The matching involved selecting clients from the Annual Housing Survey who were eligible for, but not enrolled in, the housing allowance program. This provided a comparison group to assess the impact of enrollment in the housing allowance program on such things as changes in housing quality and the extent of the rent burden.

A third alternative to the randomized experiment, really another form of matching, is the use of cohort groups. Cohorts are groups of people who move through an organization or treatment program at about the same time. For example, the following are cohorts: students in the same grade in a school, people receiving public assistance at the same time from a particular agency, and people in a drug rehabilitation program at the same time. Cohorts are valuable alternatives to randomized experiments because we may be able to assume that each cohort in an organization or program is similar to the cohort preceding it in terms of the characteristics that might affect a treatment outcome. In other words, each group should be alike in age, sex, socioeconomic status, and other characteristics that may be important. However, there can also be very significant differences, and cohorts should always be assessed to detect any possible systematic variation between one cohort and another.

An elaborate cohort study evaluating curriculum revision and televised instruction was conducted in El Salvador from 1969 to 1973 (Mayo et al., 1976). Seventh grade classes in 1969, 1970, and 1971 made up three separate cohorts of students. Within the cohorts, some classes received a new curriculum, some received the new curriculum with televised instruction, and some received the old curriculum. The cohorts from 1969 and 1970 were followed for three years, and the one from 1971 was followed for two years. Comparisons among the groups produced mixed results. The new curriculum was consistently superior to the old one, and televised instruction was supe-

rior during the first year it was experienced. However, the superiority of televised instruction wore off as the students became accustomed to it.

The major weakness of cohorts is, again, the threat to validity from history. Because the measurements are taken at widely spaced times, extraneous variables may intercede and possibly affect the results. The El Salvador example is instructive on this point. It would be unlikely that a similar cohort study could have been reliably conducted ten years later as the country became unstable owing to guerrilla warfare. Comparing a cohort from a period of peace with one from a period of near civil war would have obvious problems.

A fourth alternative to the randomized experiment is called the regression discontinuity design: People are selected to receive a treatment based on their score on a test, their eligibility for a program, or some other criterion. The study of recidivism in California discussed in Research in Practice 12.1 was a regression discontinuity design in which prison inmates were eligible for the experimental group if they had worked sufficient hours in prison to be eligible for unemployment benefits when released. Inmates who had worked fewer hours were put in the control group. This design is often implemented for evaluation research field experiments, and it can be very useful. However, regression discontinuity designs suffer from some of the threats to internal validity, particularly selection and in some cases statistical regression. (Incidentally, the summative evaluation described in Research in Practice 12.1 was an outgrowth of the formative evaluation project, described earlier in this chapter, about the provision of financial aid to newly released prisoners.)

RESEARCH IN PRACTICE 12.1
Program Evaluation: The Effectiveness of Financial Assistance in Reducing Recidivism

Even the most reformed and well-intentioned former prisoner faces a host of obstacles in his or her efforts to begin a new life outside prison. Family members are often not supportive or too poor to help, or the ex-inmate has no relatives or friends outside prison on whom to rely. The newly released prisoner suddenly becomes responsible for innumerable decisions: where to live, buy clothes, obtain meals, find work, and how to make friends and keep out of trouble. These problems are frequently compounded by an uncertain financial status: no job prospects, a bus ticket to one's hometown, and $25 to $200 gate money.

Policymakers concerned about the welfare of former prisoners and hoping to reduce recidivism have considered programs that provide financial assistance to former prisoners to help them make the transition to civilian life. The thrust of such programs is typically to provide a payment, like unemployment insurance, to provide financial support while the ex-inmate gets settled and finds a job. Because many crimes are economically motivated, it seems reasonable to hypothesize that such financial assistance would reduce the likelihood that a newly released inmate would turn to such crimes.

To test this hypothesis, the Baltimore Living Insurance for Ex-prisoners (or Baltimore LIFE) Project was developed (Lenihan, 1977; Rossi, Berk, and Lenihan, 1980). This field experi-

ment was an intermediary stage between a small pilot project involving only six people and a much larger program involving several thousand inmates in Texas and Georgia. In the Baltimore LIFE project, high-risk inmates who were scheduled for release by the Maryland Department of Corrections were randomly divided into four groups, three experimental groups and one control group. One experimental group received financial assistance of $60 per week for 13 weeks after release and was offered job placement services. A second received the financial assistance but no job placement services. The third experimental group received only the job services whereas the control group received neither financial assistance nor job services. The intent of this phase of research was to determine if the two independent variables—financial assistance and job placement services—would have any positive effect on recidivism. For two years, the ex-prisoners were observed and their experience in employment and criminal activity was noted. When the analysis was done, a number of factors were considered such as race, age at first arrest, number of prior arrests, education, marital status, parole status, and work experience.

The Baltimore LIFE Project illustrates several key features of careful program evaluation. First, the project was preceded by a much smaller exploratory study that enabled the project staff to test and refine some of their procedures. Second, the evaluation utilized a variety of research techniques. In addition to the basic experimental design, the research relied on structured interviews and case studies of several participants to provide insight into the problems, reactions, and frustrations of these men as they attempted to cope with life in the community. Third, a cost–benefit analysis was conducted to ascertain if the program was worthwhile. Finally, great care was taken in selecting participants, in explaining the program to the participants, and in dispensing the financial aid and job counseling according to the design.

The results of the study indicated that the men who received financial aid had an 8-percent lower rate of arrest for charges of theft. Arrests for other types of crime were not significantly different. Also, those not receiving financial aid were arrested earlier, were more likely to be convicted, and were more likely to be returned to prison. Job placement services had no apparent impact on recidivism or occupational success.

Based on the modestly optimistic findings of this research, a much larger program, which involved dispensing financial aid through the existing Employment Security Offices in the states of Texas and Georgia, was implemented. In that project, the overall findings were not positive. The researchers concluded that one reason for the disappearance of positive outcomes may have been in the way the larger program was administered, thereby emphasizing the need for care-

ful program implementation as well as research. Thus, evaluation research focuses not only on the outcome of programs but also on how they can be best implemented.

The LIFE experiment also served as a model for a legislatively-mandated program in California (Berk and Rauma, 1983; Berk et al., 1985). It was designed much like the LIFE program except that the inmates actually applied for unemployment benefits once released from prison and were eligible if they had worked sufficient hours per week in prison. Because of this, however, the random assignment of inmates to experimental and control groups for evaluation purposes was not done, and thus, the best research design for assessing program impacts—the randomized experiment—was not used. Instead, they used a regression discontinuity design in which the experimental group consisted of those inmates who had worked enough to be eligible for unemployment benefits, and the control group contained those who had not. This did not affect the operation of the program, but it did make the evaluation of it more difficult and less certain. Nonetheless, a conservative evaluation of its effects concluded that it saved California $2000 for each inmate released into the program. In other words, the costs of the program were far outweighed by the money saved because some inmates in the program did not commit further crimes and the state saved the cost of incarcerating them. Despite this, the program was ended, partly because of ideological hostility to the idea of giving support to inmates and partly because California was facing a budget crisis.

The last major alternative to random-ized experiments is the use of statistical controls, which are procedures that allow the effects of one or more variables to be removed or held constant so that the effects of other variables can be observed. These procedures allow comparisons to be made between groups that differ from one another on some characteristics thought to be important. The effects of the variables on which the groups differ are removed through statistical manipu-lation so that they cannot obscure the re-sults. Statistical controls, however, even in their most elaborate application, can only approximate the level of control achievable in randomized experiments. Like matching, only variables known to the researcher to be potentially important can be statistically controlled, so there is always the possibility of important extra-neous variables left uncontrolled. Fur-thermore, statistical controls tend to un-deradjust for differences between groups because of the error component in the measurement of the control variables (Weiss, 1972). The error allows at least some of the effects of the control vari-ables to remain even after the statistical controls have been applied. Because of these limitations, statistical control alone may not be appropriate. However, it is well suited as an adjunct to the physical control obtained through design. For ex-ample, in a matched design we might find out after-the-fact that an important vari-able was left unmatched. Assuming the necessary data were collected, we could make up for this error by applying statis-tical control to that variable.

The use of both design control and statistical control is probably the best overall approach for evaluation, since statistical control can even be useful in randomized experiments (Rossi and Free-man, 1985).

Cost–Benefit Analysis

One particular type of evaluation re-search—one that has become the darling of some policymakers and the bane of others—is cost–benefit analysis. Be-cause it involves some unique issues and premises, it warrants special attention. In an era of increasing accountability for social programs, this controversial ap-proach to program evaluation is probably here to stay. If it is going to be used, it is important that it be used properly, with its limitations well understood.

On the surface, **cost–benefit analy-sis** appears seductively simple (Yates, 1985). All we need do is add up the costs of a program, subtract them from the dol-lar value of the benefits, and we have the result: either a net gain (benefits exceed costs) or a net loss (costs exceed benefits). Such an approach is very appealing to many policymakers because it seems to clarify complex issues and programs through quantification. They would logi-cally support and perhaps expand pro-grams showing a net gain and curtail those producing a net loss. If only it were that simple. As we shall see, quantifying benefits and costs can be extremely diffi-cult and often involves a number of un-proved assumptions and estimates.

Cost–benefit analysis can be applied to a program during its planning stages (called *ex ante* analysis) or after it has been in operation (*ex post* analysis) (Rossi and Freeman, 1985). The major dif-ference between the two is that an ex ante analysis requires the use of more es-timates and assumptions because there are no hard data on either costs or bene-fits. In an ex post study, there are records of actual cost outlays, and benefits can be empirically determined through normal evaluation research procedures. The use of estimates in ex ante analyses means that results are far more tentative. This also accounts for why ex ante analyses conducted by different parties sometimes come to widely divergent conclusions: They use different estimates and assumptions. Sorting out whose estimates are most valid has produced some lively debates among policymakers. Ex post analyses require fewer estimates and are, therefore, more reliable.

Estimating Costs The easiest part of cost–benefit analysis—although by no means simple—is determining the **direct costs** of a program. There is either a record of actual expenditures (in ex post analysis) or a proposed budget for the program (in ex ante analysis). A budget proposal, however, is based on certain assumptions that may not turn out to be accurate. For example, the budget for a supplemental unemployment compensation program must assume a certain unemployment rate. If the actual rate changes, the cost of the program could skyrocket or fall dramatically.

Considerably more difficult to estimate than the direct costs of programs are what economists call *opportunity costs*. **Opportunity costs** are the value of forgone opportunities. Suppose, for example, that you are fortunate enough to win a $1000 prize in a contest. You can invest the money and receive a monetary return or spend it on anything you like. Suppose you decide to spend it on a stereo. The direct cost of the stereo is the $1000 you spent on it, but there are opportunity costs. The opportunity costs are what you forgo by buying the stereo. You lose the return that you could have received by investing it or the value of other items you might have purchased, such as new clothes or the down payment on an automobile.

A similar situation applies to the funding of social programs. Agencies have limited resources. If they decide to fund a given program, the cost of the program includes the opportunity costs of not funding alternative programs. Normally, the estimated value of benefits of competing programs is used as the basis for computing the opportunity costs of the program being analyzed. It can be very complex computing the benefits that are lost by not initiating a program, which makes it difficult to calculate the opportunity costs of the funded program. It needs to be done, however, to provide an accurate picture of the total costs of a program.

Estimating and Monetizing Benefits The really difficult and often unreliable part of cost–benefit analysis comes in determining program benefits and monetizing, or attaching a dollar value to, them. This may be a fairly straightforward process or a mystical one, depending on the program. In general, if a program's benefits are related to some economic activity, they are easier to monetize. For example, the value of subsidized day care can be easily monetized. The market price of private day care plus the added income of the parent who otherwise could not work would constitute the major dollar benefits from the program. But what about program benefits less related to economic activity? How can a dollar value be placed on program benefits like improved mental health, improved self-esteem, reduced domestic violence, or other noneconomic outcomes? Cost–benefit analysis attempts, through complex procedures, to place a dollar value on practically anything. Doing so, however, requires many assumptions and value judgments that are likely to be controversial. Because of this, cost–benefit analysis is of the greatest utility when the relationship between program benefits and a certain dollar value is fairly clear.

Another complicating factor in cost–benefit analysis is that benefits and costs do not accrue at the same time. Costs are incurred immediately upon the program's implementation whereas benefits may accrue at some later date, possibly far in the future. In some programs, such as education or job training, at least part of the benefits may be very long-term indeed. This temporal gap is a problem because the value of both costs and benefits changes with time. We are well aware, for example, that a given number of dollars today does not have the same purchasing power that it did ten years ago. To make meaningful comparisons over time, we must adjust costs and benefits so that comparisons are made in constant dollars. This involves the calculation of what is called the *discount rate*. The discount rate is the amount that future costs and benefits are reduced to make them comparable to the current value of money. Actual determination of the discount rate involves some highly complex accounting procedures. There are also several competing approaches to its calculation (Rossi and Freeman, 1985). As many saddened investors will attest, predicting the future value of money is a risky business. Furthermore, the discount rate used has a marked effect on the outcome of the analysis. For all these reasons, it is common place to run several analyses with differing discount rates to see how the program fares under different sets of assumptions.

Whose Costs, Whose Benefits? An important consideration in cost–benefit analysis is that costs and benefits are calculated from particular perspectives. Three different perspectives may be used: program participants, the funding source, or society as a whole. A comprehensive cost–benefit analysis would include all three.

Let us take the example of subsidized day care and consider its costs and benefits from the three perspectives. For the parents who utilize the day-care service so that they can work at paying jobs, the costs are the loss of other public assistance they would receive if they stayed home or did not work. Their benefits would be the income received by working, together with less tangible benefits such as enhanced social status, job satisfaction, and freedom from child-care responsibilities. In general, from the standpoint of participants, benefits usually outweigh costs because program costs are paid by others. However, there may be many intangible costs for participants such as inconvenience, negative labeling, and concern over adequacy of care received by children. Consequently, participants may view the ''price'' as not worth it.

From the perspective of the funding source—in this case we will assume it is the federal government—the costs and benefits are quite different. The costs would be the direct costs of running the day-care service, together with the opportunity costs of not using the money for something else. The benefits would be the reduced costs of other public assistance programs and an increase in tax revenues on the incomes of working parents.

The societal perspective is the broadest and frequently the most difficult to calculate. (Furthermore, if the funding source is the government, we should not assume that the government's perspective coincides with the societal perspective. The government represents those groups that happen to control a particular government agency.) The costs to society of the day-care service would be the increased taxes or federal borrowing necessary to fund the program plus the opportunity costs involved. They would also include lost jobs to private child-care providers and lost income of workers displaced by the parents who now compete for their jobs. Benefits would be increased productivity of parents who are now freer to make economic, social, and cultural contributions to society (although we need to remember that performing as a parent or homemaker is also an essential contribution in our society). Other less direct benefits might accrue if working and the additional income it provides have positive effects on family relationships, the children's well-being, future aspirations, and the like. If day care happened to produce negative effects in these or other areas, they would be considered additional social costs.

An important contribution of the societal perspective is that it leads to a consideration of the distribution of costs and benefits across society. Most social programs involve some redistribution of wealth. In other words, program costs are typically not borne by the same segments of society that receive the benefits. Farm subsidy programs redistribute wealth from urban areas to rural areas, whereas Social Security transfers wealth from the young to the old, to cite only two of many possible examples. Whether these transfers are in the best interests of society is ultimately a political decision. A comprehensive cost–benefit analysis will make that a more informed decision. Some of the complexities and attributes of a cost–benefit analysis are illustrated in Research in Practice 12.2.

Cost-Effective Analysis

Because it is difficult to monetize benefits, interest has developed in an alternative approach that does not require that benefits be ascribed a dollar value. **Cost-effective analysis** compares program costs measured in dollars with program effects measured in whatever units are appropriate, such as achievement test scores, skill-performance level, coping abilities, or whatever effect the program is supposed to produce (Peterson, 1986). This is of greatest utility for choosing among competing programs rather than evaluating a single program. For example, a cost-effective appraisal of a compensatory education program might reveal that total per pupil costs of $300 raised reading performance by one point on a standard achievement test. This can then be compared with other programs in terms of the cost to raise reading performance a similar amount. A cost-effective comparison of remedial programs for disadvantaged children conducted by the General Accounting Office (GAO) found programs with wide-ranging cost-effectiveness (Socolar, 1981). The average per pupil cost of all such programs was $778. Interestingly, GAO found that six especially effective programs cost only $180 per student. Such cost-effective analyses of many competing programs make it possible to select the most efficient approach. Interpreting a single cost-effective analysis, however, is less clear-cut than a cost–benefit analysis because the costs and benefits are not expressed in the same units. For this reason, cost-effective analysis is not an interchangeable substitute for cost–benefit analysis. They answer very different questions.

Whereas cost–benefit analysis is a valuable tool in assessing programs, it is important that it not be oversimplified or overemphasized. Results must be carefully interpreted in light of the data used to produce them. The complex components that go into a cost–benefit analysis need to be considered when interpreting

RESEARCH IN PRACTICE 12.2
Program Evaluation: Cost–Benefit Analysis of a Personnel Program

A major goal of personnel programs is to improve the earning capacity of the people receiving training. One such program is the Supported Work Program (SWP), designed to provide work experience for several groups of people with long-standing employability problems (Kemper, Long, and Thornton, 1981). The target population included AFDC recipients, high-school dropouts, former drug users, and ex-inmates. The program provided temporary employment (up to 18 months) and utilized various approaches to improve functioning, such as peer support and graduated stress, in which job demands are increased gradually as the participant becomes more accustomed to the job. The SWP was a large-scale project involving sites at 15 locations across the country. Understandably, a question often asked of such programs is this: Are the expenditures for the program worth the results? To answer this question, a cost–benefit evaluation was conducted. A sample of eligible applicants was randomly assigned to either a treatment group receiving the supports just mentioned or a control group not receiving them. Both participants and controls were interviewed at 9-month intervals for a period of 36 months.

Whereas an employment program may seem more straightforward than other types of intervention in terms of computing costs and benefits in dollars, the table on page 359, which shows expected benefits and costs, clearly illustrates that it can be a challenging task. Benefits and costs are considered from three alternative perspectives: the participants, the funding source (taxpayers), and society as a whole. An important element of conducting cost–benefit analyses, as the table illustrates, is specifying the range of possible costs and benefits of a program and then clearly indicating which ones will be used in the assessment and how they will be estimated. Some benefits and costs can be readily translated into dollar values. It is relatively easy, for example, to monetize the earnings of program recipients who find employment and the taxes they would pay on their earnings. It is considerably more complex, however, to place a dollar amount on the reduced cost of operating the criminal justice system when program recipients avoid committing crimes or on the improved health status of people who are working and eating well. Finally, some benefits are probably impossible to monetize, such as the reduction in fear and psychological tension that results from a lower crime rate.

The results of the Supported Work Program were mixed. From the perspective of society as a whole, the long-term benefits exceeded costs by over $8000 per recipient. For former drug addicts, the net benefit was $4000 per participant. For high-school dropouts, the cost exceeded the benefits by about $1500 per participant. For ex-inmates, on the other hand, the researchers were unable to specify a clear net cost or benefit. In drawing their conclu-

Expected Effects of Benefits–Cost Analysis Components, by Accounting Perspective

	Accounting Perspective		
	Social	Participant	Funding Source (Nonparticipants)
Benefits and Costs			
I. Produced by Participants			
Value of in-program output	+	0	+
Increased postprogram output	+	+	0
Preference for work over welfare	+	+	+
II. Increased Tax Payments	0	−	+
III. Reduced Dependence on Transfer Programs			
Reduced transfer payments	0	−	+
Reduced administrative costs	+	0	+
IV. Reduced Criminal Activity			
Reduced property damage and personal injury	+	0	+
Reduced stolen property	+	−	+
Reduced justice system costs	+	0	+
Reduced psychological costs	+	+	+
V. Reduced Drug and Alcohol Use			
Reduced treatment costs	+	0	+
Psychological benefits	+	+	+
VI. Reduced Use of Alternative Education, Training, and Employment Services			
Reduced education and employment costs	+	0	+
Reduced training allowances	0	−	+
VII. Other Benefits			
Improved participant health status	+	+	+
Income redistribution	+	+	+
VIII. Program Operating Cost			
Overhead cost	−	0	−
Project cost	−	0	−
IX. Central Administrative Cost	−	0	−
X. Participant Labor Cost			
In-program earnings plus fringes	0	+	−
Foregone earnings plus fringes	−	−	0
Foregone nonmarket activities	−	−	0
XI. Increased Work-Related Cost			
Child care	−	−	−
Other	−	−	0

Note A plus (+) indicates an expected benefit from a given perspective whereas a minus (−) indicates a cost, with a zero (0) indicating neither a cost nor a benefit. **Source** Adapted from P. Kemper, D. Long, and C. Thornton, *The Supported Work Evaluation: Final Benefit-Cost Analysis* (Princeton: Mathematica Policy Research, Inc., 1981), p. 12. Used with permission.

sions, the researchers caution that the estimates are partially based on extrapolating future benefits, that some of the benefits in participant earnings may have been at the expense of other workers who were displaced, and that many benefits are not inherently evaluable in financial terms.

the results. Like all forms of analysis, cost–benefit is only as good as the data, the estimates, and the assumptions on which it is based. All these components should be explicitly discussed in the report, and the users should be encouraged to evaluate the soundness of them. The real risk associated with cost–benefit analysis comes when bottom-line results are accepted blindly and become the overriding factor in decision making. At its current level of development, cost–benefit analysis can be very useful, but it must be cautiously interpreted as only one of many factors in the decision-making process concerning social programs.

Barriers to the Use of Evaluation Research

At the beginning of this chapter, we described the purposes of evaluation research as improving service to clients, aiding in the policymaking process, and testing social science theories and practice approaches. In all these areas, the assumption is made that the research results will be used to produce some change in the status quo. In actuality, this is often not the case since there are many barriers to the use of the results of evaluation research (Siegel and Tuckel, 1985; Pollard, 1987).

One barrier is the fault of evaluators. Owing to poor design or execution, the evaluation may not produce clear-cut results. It is obviously difficult to overcome resistance to change unless the reasons for change are strong and the direction that change should take is clear. All too often, the basic conclusion of an evaluation is this: ''The program as currently operated is not achieving its intended goals.'' What is one to do with such a conclusion? There is no indication of why the

program is failing nor any suggestions for improving it. It is to avoid results such as this that we suggested that evaluation be broadly conceived so that findings indicate not only what the program does not do, but also what it does do and why. Such detailed findings are of far greater utility for pointing the way for the future and for producing positive program changes (Bedell et al., 1985).

A second barrier to the use of evaluation research results is poor communication on the part of evaluators (Miller, 1987). Researchers are used to communicating with other researchers who share a common technical language and background. When communicating with each other, researchers assume those commonalities and write their reports accordingly. If this is done in an evaluation report, the results may be quite unclear to practitioners, program administrators, and policymakers who are supposed to use those results. Rather than dump a technical report on a person's desk and bid farewell, evaluators should work through the report, explaining it thoroughly and answering all questions. Those sponsoring an evaluation or using the results should demand such accountability from evaluation researchers.

A third barrier to the use of evaluation research is the failure of evaluation researchers to press for the adoption of their research findings. Such an advocacy role is foreign to many researchers who feel that their job terminates once the data have been analyzed. However, implementation of modifications to a program is often complex, and program staff are faced with competing interests. Without active participation by the researcher, adoption of recommendations may very well not take place.

A fourth barrier is the resistance found in many quarters. People become accustomed to established procedures and may be disinclined toward change. There are vested interests that are difficult to overcome. One of the most arrogant rejections of research was President Richard Nixon's reaction to the findings of the President's Commission on Pornography. Nixon appointed the commission to study the societal impact of pornography, fully expecting negative effects to be found, thus justifying a crackdown. When the commission reported no negative effects of viewing pornography and possibly even some salutary ones, Nixon simply dismissed the report as wrong.

Such blatant dismissals are rare. More common is what happened to a study of group counseling in a correctional system (Kassebaum et al., 1971). This was a very well-conducted study that not only found few positive effects of counseling, but also provided many suggestions as to why these effects did not occur. The reaction to the report by the Department of Corrections was swift, but not what would be predicted given its contents. The counseling program was not dropped but was expanded to every prison in the system, and the expanded program was not modified to take into account suggestions in the report (Ward and Kassebaum, 1972). The evaluators speculated in a rather discouraged tone that the main effect of their report would be to limit future outside evaluations of prison programs.

One change suggested to improve research utilization is increased dissemination of results (Weiss, 1972). Earlier we expressed concern over the fact that evaluation reports are often not widely circulated. Broader dissemination may bring a report to the attention of someone willing to use the results. Another change that has been shown to increase the use of the results of evaluations is to involve the potential users in the evaluation research itself. Users can help design the research or serve as interviewers. When they do, there is better communication between evaluators and users, the users perceive the evaluation as more relevant and credible, and they are more committed to the evaluation (Dawson and D'Amico, 1985; Greene, 1988).

What is really needed to improve research utilization is for policymakers and program administrators to develop an increased willingness to put evaluation results to use. In fact, resistance to research utilization appears to be declining, and there may be a growing awareness that common sense and conventional wisdom are inadequate bases for designing and operating effective social programs (Rossi and Freeman, 1985). Years of experience with ineffective programs have made this conclusion quite evident. Such changing perspectives are encouraging for the future of evaluation research and its increased utilization.

☰ Main Points

• Evaluation research is the use of scientific research methods to plan intervention programs, to monitor the implementation of new programs and the operation of existing ones, and to determine how effectively programs or clinical practices achieve their goals.

• Formative evaluation focuses on the planning, development, and implementation of intervention programs.

• Summative evaluation assesses the effectiveness and efficiency of programs and the extent to which program effects may be generalized to other settings and populations.

• Prior to beginning evaluation, an evaluability assessment is conducted to gain knowledge about the program as operated and to identify those aspects of it that can be evaluated.

• Proximate goals are evaluable short-run goals that are logically related to the achievement of long-term goals that are impractical to evaluate.

• Despite frequent difficulties associated with their use, randomized experiments constitute the strongest, most desirable designs for assessing program impact.

• Cost–benefit analysis, through the use of complex assumptions and estimates, compares the costs of a program with the dollar value of its benefits.

• Cost–benefit analysis and cost-effective analysis are not interchangeable. Cost–benefit analysis is useful for evaluating a single program whereas cost-effective analysis is useful for choosing the most efficient program from among competing approaches.

• It is important that bottom-line results from either cost–benefit or cost-effective analyses not be accepted blindly, but that the data, estimates, and assumptions on which the results are based be carefully considered.

Important Terms for Review

cost–benefit analysis
cost-effective analysis
direct costs
evaluability assessment
evaluation research

formative evaluation research
opportunity costs
summative evaluation research

For Further Reading

Alkin, Marvin C. *A Guide for Evaluation Decision Makers.* Beverly Hills, Calif.: Sage, 1985.
This book is intended for administrators who commission evaluation research or who are responsible for seeing that evaluations are performed properly. It is a useful guide for developing meaningful and useful evaluations.

Bennett, Carl A., and Arthur A. Lumsdaine, eds. *Evaluation and Experiment.* New York: Academic Press, 1975.
This book of readings is a good resource for students interested in evaluation research. It covers a very wide range of problems and offers many illustrations.

Boruch, Robert F., and Werner Wothke, eds. *Randomization and Field Experimentation.* San Francisco: Jossey-Bass, 1985.
Numerous examples of evaluations of social programs in which randomized assignment was used are presented. The illustrations show that randomized experiments can be successfully carried out in a variety of field settings.

Carley, Michael. *Social Measurement and Social Indicators: Issues of Policy and Theory.* Boston: Allen & Unwin, 1983.
This book presents an in-depth look at various social indicators that may be monitored to assess aspects of social change. These indicators may be useful in measuring the impact of social programs for evaluation purposes.

Epstein, I., and T. Tripodi. *Research Techniques for Program Planning, Monitoring and Evaluation.* New York: Columbia University Press, 1977.
A nontechnical coverage of research applications to a wide range of evaluation issues, from formative program planning to effectiveness evaluation.

Glaser, Daniel. *Evaluation Research and Decision Guidance: Correctional, Addiction Treatment, Mental Health, Education, and Other People-Changing Agencies.* New Brunswick, N.J.: Transaction, 1987.
This is very much a "how to" book to guide those who need to evaluate the effectiveness of interventions.

House, E. R. *Evaluating with Validity.* Beverly Hills, Calif.: Sage, 1980.
This volume organizes a variety of evaluation techniques into a convenient taxonomy of models and presents a good coverage of fundamental issues such as standards for evaluation and the political context of evaluation.

Journal of Applied Behavioral Science
This journal, as the title implies, publishes applied social science research and is a good source for up-to-date reports on evaluation research projects.

Kershaw, David, and Jerilyn Fair. *The New Jersey Income Maintenance Experiment.* Vol. 1. New York: Academic Press, 1976.
An illustration of evaluation research focusing on the outcome of a large social program.

Rossi, P., and H. Freeman. *Evaluation: A Systematic Approach.* 3d ed. Beverly Hills, Calif.: Sage, 1985.
This book covers evaluation for planning programs, monitoring existing programs and assessing impact and also provides a discussion of design options.

Schneirer, M. A. *Program Implementation: The Organizational Context.* Beverly Hills, Calif.: Sage, 1981.
A discussion of evaluation program implementation with a specific case illustration of a token economy program in a mental health setting.

Stake, Robert E. *Quieting Reform: Social Science and Social Action in an Urban Youth Program.* Urbana, Ill.: University of Illinois Press, 1986.
This is an excellent case study of a program for disadvantaged youth; the evaluation of it and the politics that surrounds the whole process. It examines the many pressures on evaluation researchers, the many interests that get involved in such a process, and the varying definitions of what constitutes success.

Thompson, Mark S. *Benefit–Cost Analysis for Program Evaluation.* Beverly Hills, Calif.: Sage, 1980.
This book provides a thorough coverage in relatively nontechnical terms of the logic and techniques of benefit–cost analysis.

Tripodi, Tony. *Evaluation Research For Social Workers.* Englewood Cliffs, N.J.: Prentice-Hall, 1983.
This book makes the scientific method and applied research technology available to social work administrators and practitioners to help them make decisions about program evaluations.

≡ Exercises for Class Discussion

It is a commonly known fact that many elderly people have strong emotional attachments to their pets. However, the necessity of moving into a nursing home or medical care facility generally entails severing the relationship that the older person has developed with a dog or cat. Recently, experts in gerontology have been "discovering" the important role that animals can play in making residents feel at home in residential facilities. Consequently, some facilities have begun experimenting with pet therapy, a program in which volunteers bring pets to the nursing home on a regular basis so that interested residents may pet and play with the animals. The idea of having dogs and cats running around in a nursing home may seem contrary to the medical goals of a sterile, clean environment, but has proved to be quite popular with the patients.

Assume you are a human service worker with a nursing home, and you have been approached by some residents or staff about starting such a program.

You are aware that there may be some local foundation money available to support the project, and some local organizations such as the Humane Society, the area kennel club, and a cat fanciers group could probably be induced to provide both the animals and the volunteers to help with the project. You also know that to get the money for the program, you will have to convince the administration that the program is worth the trouble and also show the foundation that you have a well-designed program that is effective in meeting its goals.

12.1 In order to make a formal proposal for funding, you must first do some formative evaluation research to determine if the program is needed and, if so, feasible. What are some research questions you think would be important to ask in this regard?

12.2 What kinds of data would be necessary, and how might you collect them?

12.3 State some specific goals that such a program might be expected to achieve.

Assume you have done some formative evaluation work, and the facility administrator has given the go-ahead to apply for a grant for the project. However, the board was somewhat skeptical about the idea, so the compromise that resulted specifies that the program is to be tried for six months, at the end of which time a thorough evaluation must be done to determine the effects of the program and the relative costs and benefits.

12.4 What are some possible effects that the program might have? Remember to look for both positive and negative impacts. How would you suggest measuring these potential effects?

12.5 In terms of doing a cost–benefit analysis, make a list of both costs and benefits. For each list, do as follows: Make a column for three different accounting perspectives: society, the nursing home residents, and the funding source. For each cost and each benefit you identify, place a plus (+) sign in the column if that party stands to benefit, a zero (0) if the impact is neutral, or a minus (−) if that party stands to have a net cost. (See the table in Research in Practice 12.2 for an example.)

12.6 Given the kinds of benefits that might result from such a program, which ones lend themselves to cost accounting? Which ones are not readily translatable into dollars? All things considered, do you think a cost–benefit analysis is appropriate for this project?

12.7 The program as planned will be available to any resident in the facility who wants to participate. Thus, it will not be possible to assign residents randomly to receive or not receive the program. Given this condition, what are some alternate ways of providing experimental control for the project? What potential validity problems do your suggestions pose?

13

Scaling

The topic of measurement in research was discussed at some length in Chapter 5. In that context, we pointed out that some measurement is fairly straightforward and involves the use of only a single *item*, or indicator of a variable. We can, for example, measure a person's age with one question that asks how old the person is. Likewise, such variables as marital status or number of children in a family would normally be measured with a single item. These variables refer to phenomena in the world that are fairly unambiguous and for which a single indicator provides a valid and reliable measure. There are many other variables, however, that are much more difficult and complex to measure. In some cases, there may be more than one indicator of a variable. In other cases, the variable may involve a number of dimensions that call for multiple indicators. In still other cases, we may be concerned with the *degree* to which a variable is present. In these cases, a single-item measuring instrument would probably be inadequate, and we would use a **scale,** a number of items that are combined to form a composite score on a variable. To measure people's attitudes toward having children, for example, we could ask them how much they agree with a series of questions, which are the items that make up the scale. Their composite score on the scale would be their overall attitude toward having children.

The purpose of this chapter is to provide an introduction to how scales are constructed. We begin by discussing the benefits of scales as opposed to single-item measures, and then we present some basic considerations involved in selecting scale items. Following this, we assess the various scaling techniques and the reasons for choosing a particular format. Finally, we consider some of the special scaling needs likely to be confronted by human service practitioners.

Advantages of Scaling

Scales have four major advantages over single-item measures.

Improved Validity When measuring abstract or complex variables, a multiple-item measure is generally more valid than a single-item measure. Consider the variable "self-concept." The Twenty-Statements Test for measuring self-concept involves 20 statements (Kuhn and McPartland, 1954). It does so because no single question or statement could possibly measure something as complex, multifaceted, and constantly changing as a person's self-concept. What single question could we ask you that might encompass all the feelings that you have about yourself? Clearly, self-concept involves many aspects of a person's life situation—family, occupation, financial and social status, to name a few. Multiple-item scales provide us with more valid measures of such complex phenomena.

Improved Reliability In general, as we pointed out in Chapter 5, the more items contained in a measure, the more reliable it will be. This is so because the statements comprising a scale are actually just a sample of the entire universe of statements that could have been used. A single-item measure is a sample of one, and it is less likely to be *representative* of the universe of statements than more than one item would be. Multiple-item scales are larger samples from this universe and are, therefore, more likely to be representative. Being more representative, they are more reliable than single-item scales (Goode and Hatt, 1952).

Increased Level of Measurement Single-item measures are likely to produce data that are nominal, or, at the very best, partially ordered. The term "partially ordered data" refers to data with a few ordered categories but with many cases "tied" for each category. Although superior to nominal, these data are less desirable than fully ordered data in which every, or nearly every, case has its own rank (see Chapter 14). Multiple-item scales, on the other hand, are capable of producing fully ordered and possibly interval-level data. A higher level of measurement means better measurement in terms of precision and increased flexibility in data analysis.

Increased Efficiency in Data Handling Because the items in a scale are all related (in that they all measure the same variable), responses to these items can be summarized into a single number or score for each respondent. This achieves the quantification goal of measurement and means that all the separate responses to each of the items do not have to be analyzed individually. Each score summarizes a great deal of information about each respondent and facilitates analysis of the data.

So, when the concept to be measured is complex, multiple-item scales offer substantial advantages for the researcher—advantages that often outweigh the difficulty of their construction.

Developing Scales

Once it is decided to use scales as a measuring device, an appropriate scale needs to be found or developed. In most cases, scales consist of questions to which people respond or statements to which they indicate their level of agreement. In Chapter 7, we present guidelines for wording questions in questionnaires or interviews, and those same general rules apply to the development or selection of scale items. It would be beneficial for the reader to review those guidelines now, considering them in the context of scale construction. In many cases, it is possible to use a complete scale developed by someone else if it is a valid and reliable measure of the variables under investigation. Or a scale can be made up of statements or even of whole sections that are taken from previously developed scales. A major advantage of using existing items or scales is that their validity and reliability have usually already been established. A few of the many compilations of measurement scales are listed in the For Further Reading section of this chapter. In addition, scales are reported in the many research journals in the behavioral sciences.

If there is no existing scale that will do the job, then a new scale should be developed. There is a common logic to the development of scales, which generally involves the following steps:

1. Developing or locating many potential scale items, far more than will appear in the final scale.
2. Eliminating items that are redundant, ambiguous, or for some other reason inappropriate for the scale.
3. Pretesting the remaining items for validity, reliability, or other measurement checks to be described shortly.
4. Eliminating items that do not pass the tests of Step 3.
5. Repeating Steps 3 and 4 as often as necessary to reduce the scale to the number of items required.

Sources of Scale Items

One of the most accessible sources of scale items is a researcher's own imagination. Once a concept has been developed and refined, the researcher has a pretty good idea of what is to be measured. The researcher can then generate a range of statements that seem to satisfy the criteria to be discussed. At this early stage in scale construction, one need not be too concerned with honing and polishing the statements until they are perfect because there is much pretesting still to be done before any statement is ever seen by an actual respondent.

A second source of scale items is people, sometimes called "judges," who are considered to be especially knowledgeable in a particular area. If one is seeking out items for a delinquency scale, it would seem reasonable to discuss the issue with juvenile probation officers and others having daily contact with delinquents. Two social psychologists, for example, used a unique approach to finding items for a scale to measure people's tendency

to manipulate others for their own personal gain (Christie and Geis, 1970). They turned to the writings of Niccolò Machiavelli, a 16th-century adviser to the prince of Florence in Italy. In his classic book *The Prince*, Machiavelli propounded essentially a con artist's view of the world and politics: People, according to Machiavelli, are to be manipulated for one's own benefit, in a cool and unemotional fashion. Lying, cheating, and underhandedness are justified if they advance one's own personal position. In the writings of this Florentine of four centuries ago, these social psychologists found statements such as: "It is safer to be feared than to be loved" and "Humility not only is of no service but is actually harmful." They constructed a scale made up of Machiavelli's statements, somewhat revised, and asked people whether or not they agreed with each statement. The scale is now known as the Machiavellianism Scale and has been used widely in scientific research. One is tempted to wonder whether Signore Machiavelli, were he able to peer through the mists of time, would consider this scale a sufficiently cunning and beguiling use of his prose. In any event, this illustrates a particularly creative use of "judges" in the development of scales.

A third source of scale items is the people who are the focus of the research project. Coulton (1979), for example, was interested in person–environment fit among consumers of hospital social services. In developing her scale, she obtained a large number of verbatim statements from hospital patients and then began to form these into a scale. In like manner, if one were interested in attitudes among teenagers toward unwanted pregnancies, an excellent beginning would be to discuss the topic with teenagers and gather from them as many statements as possible regarding the issue. When items are garnered from people in this fashion, only rarely would statements be usable without editing. Many statements would ultimately be rejected, and most would have to be considerably rewritten. Such people, however, are likely to provide a range of statements that have meaning from the perspective of the group under investigation.

Characteristics of Scale Items

Once a large number of scale items have been found, the best ones have to be selected for the final scale. Good scale items have the following characteristics.

Validity A primary concern in item selection is the validity of the statements (see Chapter 5 on validity). Each statement considered for inclusion should be assessed for content validity. For example, if we were creating a self-report delinquency scale, each statement would be assessed as to how it related to measuring delinquent activity. Statements concerning a person's participation in various delinquent acts would be reasonable as valid measures of how delinquent that person is. On the other hand, an item relating to how well the respondent gets along with his or her siblings would probably not be a valid indicator of delinquency.

Range of Variation Variables that are measured with multiple-item scales are normally considered to consist of a number of possible values or positions that a person could take. If we wanted to measure people's attitudes toward growing old, for example, people's positions on that variable could be extremely positive, extremely negative, or anywhere in between. In selecting items for measure-

ment scales, we should ensure that the items cover the actual range of possible variation on the variable being measured. Failure to do so will result in a poor scale. When selecting items on the basis of variability, the researcher needs to exercise care to avoid defining the range either too narrowly or too broadly. Failure to include a sufficiently wide range of items will result in respondents' "piling up" at one or both ends of the scale's range. If many respondents tie with either the lowest or highest possible score, the range in the scale is inadequate. This "piling up" effect reduces the precision of the measurement because we are unable to differentiate among the respondents with tied scores.

Going to extremes with items to define the range is not desirable either. If we include items that are too extreme, they will apply to few, if any, respondents. In the case of a delinquency scale, for example, an item pertaining to engaging in cannibalism would be such an extreme item as to warrant exclusion. The act is so rare in our culture that it is unlikely that any juvenile has done it, and it thus contributes nothing of benefit to the scale. The goal is to select items with enough range of variation to cover the actual range of alternatives that people are likely to choose, without including items that are so extreme that they do not apply to anyone.

Unidimensionality In the construction of a multiple-item scale, the goal is to measure one specific variable, and we do not want the results confounded by items on the scale that actually measure a different, although possibly related, variable. A **unidimensional scale** is one whose items measure only one variable. If a scale actually measures more than one variable, then it is called multidimensional. In creating our delinquency scale, we might be tempted to include an item about school performance on the grounds that delinquents seem to perform poorly in school. Although there may be an empirical relationship between delinquency and school performance, they are separate variables and should be treated and measured as such.

In assessing the unidimensionality of scales, one must distinguish between *different variables* and *different aspects of the same variable*. A single variable may have more than one aspect, and we need to be careful to recognize these so that they can be measured appropriately. Delinquency, for example, contains at least two aspects: severity and frequency. In terms of severity, it seems reasonable to distinguish between an adolescent who committed petty theft and one who committed aggravated assault. In terms of frequency, an adolescent who regularly commits petty theft might be properly considered as delinquent, or even more delinquent, than one with a single case of assault.

The different aspects of a variable need to be distinguished and analyzed carefully because one may correlate with an independent or dependent variable whereas another does not. This again suggests the complexity of some variables. In a study of person–environment fit, for example, Claudia Coulton (1979) distinguished between the many aspects that might be parts of this variable. "Person–environment fit" refers to the extent to which an individual's needs can be satisfied and aspirations fulfilled in the context of the demands and opportunities available in a particular environment. Coulton distinguished between "fit" in relation to one's economic activities, "fit" in terms of the amount and relevance of information available to a person, "fit" in terms of one's family relations, and the

like. In this case, the "person–environment fit" scale is unidimensional in that it measures one underlying variable, but it also contains a number of distinct aspects that are a part of that variable.

To gain systematic evidence of the unidimensionality of a scale, the researcher can intercorrelate each item in the scale with every other scale item. This is often done during a pretest. If some items do not correlate with the others, it is possible that they do not measure the same variable or that they are separate aspects of the variable that vary independently of one another. If we suspect that these items measure a different variable, then they should be eliminated from the scale. If we find a few items that have nearly perfect correlations, we only need to use one of them in the scale. Two items to which people respond identically are simply redundant, and using both adds nothing to the measurement abilities of the scale. Occasionally, however, highly correlated items will be included to detect response inconsistency or random answering. That exception notwithstanding, the final scale will be composed of statements that correlate fairly highly, but not perfectly, with each other.

A knowledge of the characteristics and sources of scale items provides an important and necessary foundation for the development of scales. By themselves, however, these offer only a general guide to scale development. There are more complex intricacies to developing scales that can best be grasped by looking at specific types of scales and illustrations of how they have been developed. In addition, some types of scales have unique requirements that are not adequately covered by our previous discussion. We turn our attention, then, to a discussion of the most important types of scales used in human service research.

Scaling Formats

Scaling can utilize a number of formats, and each format calls for some unique elements in its design.

Likert Scales

One of the most popular approaches to scaling is that developed by Rensis Likert (1932). A **Likert scale** consists of a series of statements, each followed by five response alternatives. An illustration of a Likert scale is presented in Table 13.1. More or fewer than five alternatives can be used in a Likert scale, but five is the most common number because it offers respondents a sufficient range of choices without requiring unnecessarily minute distinctions in attitudes. Notice in Table 13.1 the small numbers ranging from 1 to 5 next to each of the response alterna-

tives. These numbers are included on the scale here for purposes of illustration only; they would not be printed on a scale for actual use because their presence might influence respondents' answers. The numbers are used when scoring the scale. The numbers associated with each response are totaled to provide the overall score for each respondent. In this case— a 6-item scale—individual scores can range from a low of 6 (if alternative "1" were chosen every time) to a high of 30 (if alternative "5" were chosen every time). (Note that, as we discussed in Chapter 5, each item in a Likert scale is an ordinal measure, ranging from a low of strongly disagree to a high of strongly agree. Because the total score of a Likert scale is the sum of individual, ordinal items, many researchers contend that a Likert scale is therefore ordinal in nature. Technically, one should refrain from using

---

TABLE 13.1   Selected Items from the *Reid–Gundlach Social Service Satisfaction Scale*

1. *The social worker took my problems very seriously.*

    Strongly agree[5] Agree[4] Undecided[3] Disagree[2] Strongly disagree[1]

2. *If I had been the social worker, I would have dealt with my problems in just the same way.*

    Strongly agree[5] Agree[4] Undecided[3] Disagree[2] Strongly disagree[1]

3. *The worker I had could never understand anyone like me.*

    Strongly agree[1] Agree[2] Undecided[3] Disagree[4] Strongly disagree[5]

4. *If a friend of mine had similar problems, I would tell them to go to the agency.*

    Strongly agree[5] Agree[4] Undecided[3] Disagree[2] Strongly disagree[1]

5. *The social worker asks a lot of embarrassing questions.*

    Strongly agree[1] Agree[2] Undecided[3] Disagree[4] Strongly disagree[5]

6. *I can always count on the worker to help if I'm in trouble.*

    Strongly agree[5] Agree[4] Undecided[3] Disagree[2] Strongly disagree[1]

Source Adapted from P. N. Reid and J. H. Gundlach. "A Scale for the Measurement of Consumer Satisfaction with Social Services," *Journal of Social Service Research*, Vol 7, pp. 37–54, 1983. Used with permission.

statistics such as the mean and standard deviation with ordinal level data. However, especially with well-established Likert scales, it is common to see published studies in which scores are treated as if they were interval level. Whether this application of interval procedures is appropriate is a debated topic among researchers and cannot be resolved here.)

The Likert scale is one example of scales known as **summated rating scales.** These are scales in which a person's score is determined by summing the number of questions answered in a particular way. We could, for example, ask respondents to agree or disagree with statements and then give them a "1" for each statement they agree with and a "0" for each disagreement. Their scale score is then the sum of their responses. Summated rating scales can take a number of different forms although the Likert format is the most common.

Constructing a Likert scale, as with all scales, requires considerable time and effort. One begins by developing a series of statements relating to the variable being measured. The general criteria for statements outlined previously should be carefully considered during this stage. No matter how diligent we are in following those guidelines, however, some of the statements will turn out to be inadequate for a variety of reasons. Because we anticipate having to drop some unacceptable items, substantially more statements than desired in the final scale should initially be written. A common rule of thumb is to start with three times the number of statements desired for the final scale.

Likert scale items are designed to avoid certain kinds of response patterns that affect the validity of the scale. You will notice in the items in Table 13.1 that choosing "strongly agree" on items 1, 2,

4, and 6 would be an expression of high satisfaction with social services; choosing "strongly agree" on items 3 and 5, on the other hand, would be an expression of low satisfaction. If "strongly agree" were an expression of high satisfaction for all items, some respondents would have to choose the same alternative on every item in order to express their opinion. This is not desirable because it can cause *response pattern anxiety:* Some people become anxious if they have to repeat the same response all the time and change their responses to avoid doing so. If this occurs, then their reactions to statements do not reflect their actual attitudes but rather their reaction to a certain response pattern, and the validity of the scale is reduced. As students, you have probably had this experience when taking a multiple-choice exam. If several consecutive questions all have the same answer, you become concerned and may doubt answers that you are fairly sure of just because the pattern of responses differs from the more random pattern you expect. If both positive and negative statements are provided in a scale, all respondents will find some statements with which they agree and others with which they disagree so that response pattern anxiety is avoided.

Having the same response alternative be an expression of the same opinion or feeling on all items can produce another problem with scales: *response set.* Some people tend to be either "yea-sayers" or "nay-sayers," tending either to agree or disagree with statements regardless of their content. If the satisfaction with social services scale were constructed so that "strongly agree" always indicated high satisfaction, then people who tend to agree with statements would score higher on satisfaction than they actually should because they tend to agree with statements irrespective of content. This again would throw into question the validity of the scale. Mixing the response pattern of items is taken into account in scoring Likert scales. The alternatives that indicate an expression of the same opinion or feeling are given the same numerical score. In our example, for instance, all high-satisfaction alternatives (whether they be "strongly agree" or "strongly disagree") are given a score of 5. Then each person's responses to all items can be summed for a total scale score.

In deciding which items will ultimately be used in a Likert scale, researchers use a final and very important criterion. This criterion is based on the fact that we want the scale items to *discriminate* among people. That is, we want people's responses to an item to range over the five alternatives rather than bunch up on one or two choices. Imagine a scale with an item that reads: "Persons convicted of shoplifting should have their hands amputated." If such an item were submitted to a group of college students, it is likely that most would respond with "strongly disagree" and maybe a few "disagrees." It is highly unlikely that any would agree. Of what use is this item to us? We cannot *compare* people—assess who is more likely to agree or disagree—because they all disagree. We cannot correlate responses to this item with the social or psychological characteristics of the students because there is little or no variation in responses to the item.

We want, then, to eliminate nondiscriminating items from consideration for our scale. *Nondiscriminating items* are those that are responded to in a similar fashion by both people who score high and people who score low on the overall scale. Nondiscriminating items in a scale can be detected on the basis of results

from a pretest in which people respond to all the preliminary items of the scale. One way of identifying nondiscriminating items is by computing a **discriminatory power score** (or DP score) for each item. The DP score essentially tells us the degree to which each item differentiates between respondents with high scores and respondents with low scores on the overall scale. Although this approach is now used less in actual practice because of the availability of other, more complex, procedures that depend on computer support, it is a straightforward technique that illustrates well the principles of item selection.

The first step in obtaining DP scores is to calculate the total scores of each respondent and rank the scores from highest to lowest. We then identify the upper and lower quartiles of the distribution of total scores. The *upper quartile* (Q_3) is the point in a distribution above which the highest 25 percent of the scores fall, and the *lower quartile* (Q_1) is the point below which the lowest 25 percent of the scores fall. With the quartiles based on *total* scores identified, we compare the pattern of responses to *each* scale item for respondents whose scores fall above the upper quartile with the pattern for respondents who fall below the lower quartile. Table 13.2 illustrates the computation of DP scores for one item in a scale to which 40 people responded. Ten respondents are above the upper quartile, and 10 are below the lower quartile. It can be seen that the high scorers tended to agree with this item because most had scores of 4 or 5. Low scorers tended to disagree because they are totally concentrated in the 1 and 2 score range. The next step is to compute a weighted total on this item for the two groups. This is done by multiplying each score by the number of respondents with that score. For example, for

TABLE 13.2 Calculation of Discriminatory Power Score for One Item in a Scale

Quartile	N	Response Value					Weighted Total	Weighted Mean	DP Score
		1	2	3	4	5			
Upper	10	0	1	2	4	3	39	3.90	
Lower	10	2	8	0	0	0	18	1.80	2.10
								2.10	

those above the upper quartile, the weighted total is: $(1 \times 0) + (2 \times 1) + (3 \times 2) + (4 \times 4) + (5 \times 3) = 2 + 6 + 16 + 15 = 39$. Next, the weighted mean (average) is computed by dividing the weighted total by the number of cases in the quartile. For the upper quartile we have $39 \div 10 = 3.9$. The DP score for this item is then obtained by subtracting the mean of those below the lower quartile from the mean of those above the upper quartile. In this example, we have $3.9 - 1.8 = 2.1$ DP. This process is repeated for every item in the preliminary scale so that each item has a DP score calculated for it. It should be clear that figuring DP scores for all preliminary items would be extremely tedious if done by hand. Fortunately, computers can be readily programmed to accomplish this task.

Once we have DP scores for all of the preliminary items, final selection can begin. The best items are those with the *highest* DP scores because this shows that people in the upper and lower quartiles responded to the items very differently. As a general rule of thumb, as many items as possible should have DP scores of 1.00 or greater, and few, if any, should drop below .50. Applying this rule to the item in Table 13.2, we would conclude that it is a very good item and would include it in the final scale.

Occasionally one will encounter DP scores with negative signs. Under no circumstances should an item with a nega-

tive DP score be included because this means that high scorers on the overall scale scored lower on this item than did the low scorers. If the size of the negative DP score is small, it is probably an ambiguous statement that is being variously interpreted by respondents. If the negative DP score is large, however, it is possible that the item was accidentally misscored; that is, a negative item was scored as if it were positive or vice versa.

Many computer software packages have procedures for item analysis that rely on other principles but accomplish largely the same task. For example, the popular package SPSS[X] includes the procedure RELIABILITY, which performs an item analysis on the components of additive scales by computing commonly used coefficients of reliability. The procedure computes a correlation matrix that shows how each item correlates with every other item. It also provides the reliability coefficient Alpha (see Chapter 5) for the proposed scale, with each item deleted. Using the output of this procedure, the researcher can exclude from the scale those items that detract from or contribute little to the overall reliability of the instrument.

The Likert scale is one of the most popular multiple-item scales because of the many advantages it possesses. First, it offers respondents a range of choices rather than the limited "yes–no" alternatives possible in some other scales.

This makes Likert scales valuable if our theoretical assessment of a variable is that it ranges along a continuum rather than being either present or absent. Second, data produced by Likert-type scales are considered to be ordinal level, which enables us to use more powerful statistical procedures than with nominal-level data. Third, Likert scales are fairly straightforward to construct.

Although its advantages make the Likert scale one of the most widely used attitude scales, it has the same disadvantages as many other scales. In particular, one must be careful in interpreting a single score based on a Likert scale because it is a summary of so much information (separate responses to a number of items). Whenever we summarize data we lose some information. (Your grade in this course is a summary measure of your performance, and in calculating it your instructor loses information regarding those high—or low—scores you received on individual exams.) The summary score might hide information about patterns of variation in responses or about possible multidimensionality of the scale.

Research in Practice 13.1 discusses the development of a Likert scale to be used for research in human service practice settings.

RESEARCH IN PRACTICE 13.1
Program Evaluation: Developing a Scale to Measure Client Satisfaction

In our efforts to evaluate the human services, one important group whose opinion is often neglected is that of the clients themselves, in spite of the fact that the jargon of the human services is filled with such phrases as "start where the client is" and "promote client self-determination" and labels such as "client-centered" therapy. This lack of a client focus in evaluation has been attributed in part to the fact that services are delivered through public settings where agencies are not dependent on the client for financial support. It has also been suggested that the user of social services is viewed as a patient in need of treatment rather than as a consumer who is making use of professional services in pursuit of his or her own personal goals (Rein, 1970). A consequence of this oversight has been a lack of measurement tools to assess what clients think of the services they receive.

Recognition that client evaluation of services should be an integral part of program evaluation efforts served as the challenge to a team of researchers who set out to develop a Likert scale that would serve as a valid and reliable indicator of client satisfaction (Reid and Gundlach, 1983). The process they followed in developing their scale illustrates many of the points made in our discussion of scale construction.

The first step in the process involved collecting possible scale items that would reflect social service consumer attitudes. The researchers relied on two main sources for scale items. First, one of the authors had extensive experience in practice and consulta-

(Continued on next page)

tion with service users, so this personal expertise served as a source of items. Second, the authors consulted the provocative book *The Client Speaks,* which was based on interviews with family service agency users in London (Timms and Mayer, 1971).

Items were developed to measure three attributes of a service:

1. Relevance—did a service correspond to the client's perception of his or her problem and needs?
2. Impact—did the service reduce the problem?
3. Gratification—did the service enhance self-esteem and contribute to a sense of power and integrity?

The items were included in a study of social service use involving 166 families in a mid-size Michigan community. The respondents were heads of households served by the Head Start program. The authors describe this sample as a high-service user group. During the three months prior to the study 78 percent had received AFDC, 75 percent had received Medicaid, and 56 percent had received food stamps. The sample had also used a variety of other public services.

To analyze the scale items, the authors turned to the SPSS^x statistical package and used its procedures for item analysis. They used Cronbach's alpha to determine which items to eliminate. A full explanation of the process is beyond the scope of this book. However, it basically involves comparing the reliability coefficient of the scale with an item included with the reliability coefficient obtained when an item is dropped from the scale. If the reliability is greater without a given item included, it is dropped from the scale. Items that contribute very little to the overall reliability may also be dropped to make the scale as concise and convenient to complete as possible.

On completion of the scale construction process, the authors reported that the total scale had a reliability of .955. Reliability for the Relevance subscale was .848; Impact was .821, and Gratification was .857.

Additional analysis was conducted to determine relationships between the subscales and background characteristics of the service users such as race, sex, and marital status. Comparisons were also made between respondents based on the particular service they viewed as most important. The authors concluded that a measurement tool for client satisfaction was feasible and recommended that the scale could be used by agencies seeking to assess the effect of differing services on client attitudes.

Thurstone Scales

Another approach to scaling was developed by L. L. Thurstone and E. J. Chave (1929). **Thurstone scales** are constructed so that they use *equal-appearing intervals*—that is, it is assumed that the distance between any two adjacent points on the scale is the same. This provides us with data of interval-level quality and enables us to use all the powerful statistical procedures that require interval-level data. (You may want to review levels of measurement in Chapter 5 to ensure that you understand the importance of this characteristic of Thurstone scales).

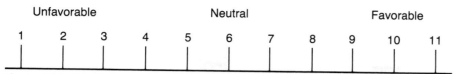

Figure 13.1 Equal-Appearing Intervals as Used in Thurstone Scale Construction

Construction of a Thurstone scale begins in much the same way as for Likert scales, with the selection of many statements that relate to the variable being measured. Once again, many of these preliminary statements will prove unsatisfactory and will be dropped. Starting with three times more items than will be used in the final scale, as was suggested for Likert scaling, should supply a sufficient number of usable items. Actually, beginning with more items than in Likert scaling is desirable because Thurstone scales, in their final form, tend to be longer. Once a sufficient number of statements is at hand, the next step is to provide a value between 1 and 11 for each statement. As illustrated in Figure 13.1, Thurstone scales utilize an 11-point scale ranging from 1, or the most unfavorable statement regarding an object, event, or issue, to 11, or the most favorable. Point 6 on the scale is called "neutral" and is used for statements that are neither favorable nor unfavorable. For example, the statement "teenage girls who get pregnant are immoral" would be considered very unfavorable toward teenage pregnancies.

The task of rating each statement as to how favorable or unfavorable it is with regard to the measured variable is assigned to a group of people known as "judges." With each of the preliminary statements printed on a separate card, the judges rate the items by placing them in piles corresponding to points on the 11-point scale. The judges place in each pile statements that they assess to be roughly equivalent in terms of their favorableness. The judgment as to whether a statement is favorable or unfavorable is made with regard to the judge's own personal opinion about the object of the statements. Irrespective of how one feels about teenage pregnancy, most people would agree that the previously mentioned statement is quite unfavorable.

Once the scale values are computed for all the preliminary items, the next step is to determine which items are the least ambiguous and, therefore, best for inclusion in the final scale. If the judges differed widely in their ratings on an item, it is likely that there is something unclear about the statement itself that leads to varying interpretations. Therefore, the degree of agreement among judges about the rating of an item is used as one indicator of ambiguity.

Scales should include the items with the most agreement among judges, and there should be a roughly equal number of items for each of the 11 scale values ranging from unfavorable to favorable, moving upward in half-point increments. This would mean that a minimum of 21 items is required although some argue that if reliability of .90 or better is desired, as many as 50 statements may be needed (Seiler and Hough, 1970). Regardless of the number actually used, the last step in Thurstone scale construction is to order the items randomly for presentation to respondents.

Table 13.3 presents the first 13 statements contained in the original 45-item Thurstone scale developed by Thurstone

TABLE 13.3   Attitude Toward Church Scale

Check (✓) every statement below that expresses your sentiment toward the church. Interpret the statements in accordance with your own experience with churches.

(8.3)*   1. I think the teaching of the church is altogether too superficial to have much social significance.

(1.7)   2. I feel the church services give me inspiration and help me to live up to my best during the following week.

(2.6)   3. I think the church keeps business and politics up to a higher standard than they would otherwise tend to maintain.

(2.3)   4. I find the services of the church both restful and inspiring.

(4.0)   5. When I go to church, I enjoy a fine ritual service with good music.

(4.5)   6. I believe in what the church teaches but with mental reservations.

(5.7)   7. I do not receive any benefit from attending church services, but I think it helps some people.

(5.4)   8. I believe in religion, but I seldom go to church.

(4.7)   9. I am careless about religion and church relationships, but I would not like to see my attitude become general.

(10.5) 10. I regard the church as a static, crystallized institution, and as such it is unwholesome and detrimental to society and the individual.

(1.5) 11. I believe church membership is almost essential to living life at its best.

(3.1) 12. I do not understand the dogmas or creeds of the church, but I find that the church helps me to be more honest and creditable.

(8.2) 13. The paternal and benevolent attitude of the church is quite distasteful to me.

*Scale value

Source   L. L. Thurstone and E. J. Chave, *The Measurement of Attitude* (Chicago: University of Chicago Press, 1929). Used with permission of the University of Chicago Press.

and Chave, with the scale value of each item indicated in parentheses. This particular scale is designed so that items with high scale values are "unfavorable" toward the church, and items with low scale values are "favorable." The scale values would not, of course, be included on a working version of the scale and are presented here for purposes of illustration. Note that all the respondents are required to do is to check the statements with which they agree, making the Thurstone format particularly easy for respondents.

Scoring a Thurstone scale is different from the simple summation procedure used with Likert scales. Because the respondents will agree to differing numbers of statements with different values, the simple sum of the item values is worthless. Rather, a respondent's score is either the mean or median of the scale values associated with the items that the person agrees with. For example, if a person agreed with Statements 2, 4, 8, and 12 in Table 13.3, that person's Thurstone scale score would be 3.13. Another person choosing 1, 7, 10, and 13 would have a score of 8.18. This scoring procedure distributes respondents along the original 11-point scale.

Thurstone and Likert scaling techniques are essentially interchangeble methods of measuring attitudes. A major advantage of the Thurstone technique is that it provides interval-level data. However, if the interval-data properties are not needed, the Likert technique is probably preferable owing to its higher reliability with fewer items and its reputed greater ease of construction. A second advantage of Thurstone scales is that people can respond to the items more quickly than with a Likert scale because they need only indicate whether they agree with an item and need not ponder how much they agree or disagree. However, because reliability calls for Thurstone scales to be longer, this advantage may be minimal. In fact, this can become a disadvantage if the longer scale leads people to be overly quick or careless in responding to statements. Another major disadvantage of Thurstone scales is that they are costly and difficult to construct. However, modern data-processing techniques have substantially reduced the construction time of Thurstone scales (Seiler and Hough, 1970).

Semantic Differential Scales

Another scaling format, which has proved quite popular, is the semantic differential (SD) developed by Osgood, Suci, and Tannenbaum (1957). The **semantic differential** format presents the respondent with a stimulus, such as a person or event, that is to be rated on a scale between a series of polar opposite adjectives. Normally, the scale has 7 points, but scales can have fewer or more points if theoretical or methodological considerations call for it. Table 13.4 illustrates an SD designed to measure people's attitudes toward the elderly. In this study, college students were shown pictures of people of varying ages and then asked to describe the characteristics of each person by placing an X on the line between each adjective pair that best represented their assessment of the person. So, on the first line, placing an X over the 6 means that you view the person as quite active, while placing an X over the 1 is an assessment of very passive. In this example, all of the "positive" adjectives are on the left and the "negative" adjectives are

TABLE 13.4 A Semantic Differential Scale Assessing Attitudes Toward the Elderly

				Scale				
	7	6	5	4	3	2	1	
Active	____	____	____	____	____	____	____	Passive
Competent	____	____	____	____	____	____	____	Incompetent
High IQ	____	____	____	____	____	____	____	Low IQ
Powerful	____	____	____	____	____	____	____	Weak
Healthy	____	____	____	____	____	____	____	Sickly
Secure	____	____	____	____	____	____	____	Insecure
Creative	____	____	____	____	____	____	____	Uncreative
Fast	____	____	____	____	____	____	____	Slow
Attractive	____	____	____	____	____	____	____	Ugly
Pleasant	____	____	____	____	____	____	____	Unpleasant
Reliable	____	____	____	____	____	____	____	Unreliable
Energetic	____	____	____	____	____	____	____	Lazy
Calm	____	____	____	____	____	____	____	Irritable
Flexible	____	____	____	____	____	____	____	Rigid
Educated	____	____	____	____	____	____	____	Uneducated
Generous	____	____	____	____	____	____	____	Selfish
Wealthy	____	____	____	____	____	____	____	Poor
Good memory	____	____	____	____	____	____	____	Poor memory
Involved	____	____	____	____	____	____	____	Socially isolated

Source. William C. Levin, "Age Stereotyping: College Student Evaluations," *Research on Aging,* 10 (March, 1988), pp. 134–148. Used with Permission.

on the right. Sometimes the positive responses to some adjectives are put on the right in order to discourage uninterested respondents from placing all their responses in the same column. If we found a respondent who had done so, we would probably discard that case because he or she obviously had not marked the scale seriously. (Incidentally, this study found considerable age stereotyping still persisting among college students: The elderly were consistently evaluated more negatively than younger people on most of these adjectives.)

Based on their research with the SD, Osgood and colleagues have suggested that, depending on the sets of adjectives used, three different dimensions of a concept are commonly measured. These dimensions are evaluation, potency, and activity. Semantic differentials can be designed to measure any one or all three of these dimensions. The measure illustrated in Table 13.4 contains adjectives relating to all of those dimensions.

One major problem in constructing an SD is the selection of relevant adjectives for rating a given concept. For example, the adjective pair "alive-dead" would not be very relevant for an SD rating self-concept. If one is unsure about the relevance of a set of adjectives, it is possible to supply the adjectives to a group of subjects and have them rank-order them according to their relevance to the concept to be rated. One would then use the pairs of adjectives ranked highest by the subjects (Mitsos, 1961).

A second problem with SDs is determining which of those three dimensions a given pair of adjectives is measuring. Generally, intuition is not reliable for making this determination (Heise, 1970). Accurate identification of the dimension measured by a given adjective pair can be accomplished through the use of a rather complex statistical procedure called factor analysis, which correlates each variable with every other variable. Its use in SD construction is to indicate which of the three dimensions a given set of adjectives correlates with most highly and hence which dimension is being tapped by those adjectives. Unfortunately, it is often impractical to do a factor analysis every time we wish to construct an SD because of the very large sample size needed for reliable results. A number of researchers, however, have factor-analyzed many adjectives and determined their SD dimension. When one is constructing an SD, it is wise to consult one or more of these sources: DiVista, 1966; Osgood, Suci, and Tannenbaum, 1957; Wright, 1958.

Many SDs are set up like the one in Table 13.4 with only the ends of the scale labeled with the adjectives. Some scales, however, employ adverbs such as "extremely," "quite," and "slightly" at appropriate points between the adjectives. One study found that the use of adverbs improved the quality of responses to SD scales (Wells and Smith, 1960). In light of these findings, it appears advisable to include adverbs when constructing SDs.

Scoring an SD can be done in a variety of ways depending on the researcher's needs. One way is to treat the response to each adjective pair separately. This procedure is not common, however, because usually we want a summary score for each respondent. For this to be accomplished, responses on the adjective pairs that constitute each dimension can be summed to provide an overall score on each of the dimensions measured—another variant of the summated ratings scale.

Semantic differentials have several advantages in comparison with both Likert and Thurstone formats. Unlike the other scaling techniques that require 20 or more items for adequate reliability, SDs require only 4 to 8 adjective pairs for each dimension to reach reliabilities of .80 or better. Approximately 10 adjective pairs are often used to ensure adequate validity. This brevity means that many concepts can be rated by respondents in a reasonable amount of time. In addition, because it is fairly easy to respond to, people can be expected to make from 100 to 400 judgments in one hour (Heise, 1970; Miller, 1977). Another advantage is that SDs are much easier and less time-consuming to construct than either Likert or Thurstone scales. Adjective pairs are easier to develop than are unambiguous and unbiased statements about an issue. In addition, adjective pairs from prior studies are more readily adaptable to other studies because of the general and nonspecific nature of the adjectives. This is particularly important if a measuring scale is needed quickly. If, for example, we wanted people's reactions to some unanticipated event, time would be of the essence. We would have to get their reactions while the event was still fresh in their minds. Only an SD-type scale could be readied in time.

About the only disadvantage of an SD is that, like Likert scales, SDs generate data considered to be ordinal. If interval data are desired, a Thurstone scale would be preferable.

Guttman Scales

A scaling technique considerably different from the preceding ones was developed by Louis Guttman (1944). At the outset of this chapter, we noted that efforts are made to create scales that are unidimensional—that is, they measure a single variable or a single aspect of a variable. With **Guttman scaling,** the pro-

cedures used in constructing the scale help ensure that the resulting scale will truly be unidimensional.

Researchers using Guttman scaling achieve unidimensionality by developing the items in such a way that, in a perfect Guttman scale, there is only one pattern of response that will yield any given score on the scale. For example, if an individual's score is 5, we would expect that he or she had agreed with the first five items on the scale. This can be contrasted with other scaling techniques where people can obtain the same score by agreeing or disagreeing with any number of items and having completely different response patterns. Guttman scaling is able to do this because the items in the scale have an inherently progressive order, usually relating to the intensity of the variable being measured. In the parlance of Guttman scaling, the least intense items are referred to as "easy" because more people are likely to agree with them and the most intense items are considered "hard" because fewer are expected to agree with them. If a person agrees with a certain item, we would expect him or her also to agree with all the less intense items; conversely, if a person disagrees with a particular item, we would also expect that person to disagree with all the more intense items.

Table 13.5 contains a Guttman scale designed to measure the degree of satisfaction foster mothers receive from caring for neglected children. The items are arranged with the "easiest" first and the "hardest" last. Note that only two response categories, either "agree" or "disagree," are provided. This or variations such as "yes" or "no" are the most common response formats. Some Guttman scales, however, make use of the Likert-type response categories. Because these categories are collapsed to a dichotomy at

TABLE 13.5   Benefactress of Children Scale

1. People who neglect or mistreat their children should be severely punished by society.
    Agree ＿＿＿＿＿＿＿   Disagree ＿＿＿＿＿＿＿

2. Being a foster parent requires a very strong love for children, which only a few people have.
    Agree ＿＿＿＿＿＿＿   Disagree ＿＿＿＿＿＿＿

3. The money foster parents receive is very inadequate considering the service they are asked to perform.
    Agree ＿＿＿＿＿＿＿   Disagree ＿＿＿＿＿＿＿

4. Adoptive parents do not appreciate the contributions of the foster parents to the child's welfare.
    Agree ＿＿＿＿＿＿＿   Disagree ＿＿＿＿＿＿＿

Source   Adapted from David Fanshel, *Foster Parenthood* (Minneapolis: University of Minnesota Press, 1966), pp. 61–62. Used with permission of the author and the publisher.

a later point in working with the scale, little is gained by their inclusion other than allowing the respondents greater freedom of expression.

The fact that the items in a Guttman scale are progressive and cumulative leads to the basic means of assessing whether a set of items constitutes a Guttman scale. This criterion is called *reproducibility*, or the ability of the total score of all respondents to reproduce the pattern of the responses to the scale items of each individual. For example, all persons with scores of 2 will have agreed with the two "easiest" items and disagreed with the rest, persons with scores of 3 will have agreed with the three "easiest" items and disgreed with the rest, and so

on. In a perfect Guttman scale, each respondent's score will reproduce one of these patterns, as is illustrated in Table 13.6. In actual practice, perfect Guttman scales are virtually nonexistent. There will usually be some respondents who deviate from the expected pattern. Nevertheless, Guttman scales with very high levels of reproducibility have been developed.

Constructing a Guttman scale is difficult and to an extent risky because we will not know whether the scale we have devised will have sufficient reproducibility to qualify as a Guttman scale until after we have applied it to a sample of respondents. As with the other scaling techniques, a basic first step is creating

TABLE 13.6   Example of Guttman Scale Response Pattern

1. Slapping a child's hand is an appropriate way to teach the meaning of "No!"
2. Spanking is sometimes necessary.
3. Sometimes discipline requires using a belt or paddle.
4. Some children need a good beating to keep them in line.

| | Guttman Scale Patterns | | | | |
	0	*1*	*2*	*3*	*4*
Slap hand (easier items)	no	yes	yes	yes	yes
Spank	no	no	yes	yes	yes
Belt or paddle	no	no	no	yes	yes
Beat (harder items)	no	no	no	no	yes

and selecting items for inclusion in the scale. In Guttman scaling, this task is further complicated by the need for the items eventually selected to have the characteristic of progression. The procedure for selecting items for a Guttman scale is very involved (Edwards and Kilpatrick, 1948). Known as the *scale discrimination technique*, it combines elements of both Likert and Thurstone scaling. As was done with both of those scaling techniques, we begin by writing a large number of statements relating to the variable to be measured. These statements are rated by a group of judges along the 11-point Thurstone equal-appearing interval scale. Scale values and interquartile ranges (upper quartile minus lower quartile, or $Q_3 - Q_1$) of the judges' ratings are obtained for each item. The half of the items with the lowest interquartile ranges are kept, with the remainder being discarded. The items on which judges were in the greatest agreement are given a Likert-type response format and presented to a pretest group. The pretest results are used to calculate discriminatory power (DP) scores as described under Likert scaling. Items for inclusion in the final Guttman scale are selected so that they cover the full Thurstone scale range and have the highest DP scores. Despite the effort involved in this approach, all it accomplishes is to increase the likelihood that the selected items will have sufficient reproducibility to constitute a Guttman scale; it does not guarantee reproducibility.

The only way to determine if we have succeeded in developing a true Guttman scale is to administer it to another pretest group and see if it has adequate reproducibility (Dotson and Summers, 1970). Guttman (1947) suggests that the pretest group contain a minimum of 100 persons. Table 13.7 illustrates the most common way of assessing reproducibility of items. For the sake of simplicity, the illustrated scale contains only 4 items and data from only 20 subjects. As can be seen from the table, subjects are arrayed according to their total score for the four statements, from highest (4) to lowest (0). Subjects' responses to each statement are indicated by an X under either 1 or 0 corresponding to an agree or disagree response, respectively. The statements are arranged from left to right from "hardest" (most disagreements) to "easiest" (most agreements). The lines drawn across each of the statement columns are called *cutting points* and indicate where the pattern of responses tends to shift from agree to disagree. The position of the cutting points must be carefully determined since they form the basis from which error responses are counted. Any "1" (agree) response below the cutting points and any "0" (disagree) response above the cutting points constitute error responses. Cutting points are drawn at positions that minimize the number of error responses. Inspection of the cutting points in Table 13.7 will reveal that locating them in any other position will not reduce the number of error responses.

With the cutting points established, tabulating error responses is a rather straightforard matter. In the example, under statement 1 there are three "1" responses below the cutting point with no "0" responses above it. Note that in the row marked "error," these responses are tabulated as 3 and 0, respectively. The same counting procedure was followed for the other statements. As Table 13.7 illustrates, the error responses for individual statements are summed to indicate the total number of error responses. It should be clear that tabulating error responses for a longer scale with the necessary 100 or more respondents by hand

TABLE 13.7 Example of Error Computation for a Guttman Scale

	Statements								
	1		*2*		*3*		*4*		
Subjects	*1*	*0*	*1*	*0*	*1*	*0*	*1*	*0*	**Scores**
1	x		x		x		x		4
2	x			x	x		x		3
3	x			x	x		x		3
4		x	x		x		x		3
5		x	x		x		x		3
6		x	x		x		x		3
7		x	x		x		x		3
8		x	x		x		x		3
9		x		x	x		x		2
10	x			x		x	x		2
11		x		x	x		x		2
12		x		x		x	x		2
13	x			x		x	x		2
14		x	x			x	x		2
15	x			x		x		x	1
16		x		x		x	x		1
17		x		x	x			x	1
18		x	x			x		x	1
19		x		x		x	x		1
20		x		x		x		x	0
Frequency	7	13	8	12	12	8	16	4	
Error	3	0	2	2	1	1	2	0	*e* = 11

would be exceedingly tedious. There is, however, computer software, such as the SAS package, that can assess the reproducibility of even a long scale quite rapidly (*SAS User's Guide*, 1979).

The total number of errors is used in the following simple formula to calculate the coefficient of reproducibility (R_c):

$$R_c = 1 - \frac{\text{Number of Errors}}{\text{No. of Items} \times \text{No. of Subjects}}$$

Inserting the values from Table 13.7 we have:

$$R_c = 1 - \frac{11}{(4)(20)} = 1 - .14 = .86$$

Guttman (1950) suggested that a coefficient of reproducibility of .90 is the min-

imum acceptable for a scale to qualify as a Guttman scale. According to this criterion, our example would not qualify. However, scales with reproducibility coefficients of somewhat less than .90 have given satisfactory results. In general, the more items in a Guttman scale, the more difficult it is to achieve a high level of reproducibility. For a very short scale, such as the Benefactress Scale in Table 13.5, .90 would certainly be the minimum acceptable, and its reported coefficient of reproducibility is .91. If the scale we are working with is somewhat longer, the minimum reproducibility level can be adjusted downward slightly.

Suppose that we developed a scale of 11 items, submitted it to a pretest group, determined the reproducibility coeffi-

TABLE 13.8 Misleading R_c Example

| | Statements | | | | | | | | |
| | 1 | | 2 | | 3 | | 4 | | |
Subjects	1	0	1	0	1	0	1	0	Scores
1	X		X		X		X		4
2		X	X		X		X		3
3		X	X		X		X		3
4		X	X		X		X		3
5		X	X		X		X		3
6		X	X		X		X		3
7		X	X		X		X		3
8		X	X		X		X		3
9		X		X	X		X		2
10		X		X		X	X		1
Frequency	1	9	8	2	9	1	10	0	

cient, and found it too low. The game is not over because of this initial failure. It is perfectly legitimate to rearrange the order of the items or drop items in an effort to achieve the necessary reproducibility. We might, for example, drop 3 or 4 of the items containing the most error responses, leaving us with a 7- or 8-item scale with adequate reproducibility to qualify as a Guttman scale.

One must be cautious about depending on the coefficient of reproducibility alone in assessing a Guttman scale. The reason is that when a high percent of responses to an item is in the modal category (the category with the most responses), the coefficient of reproducibility can be misleading. This problem is illustrated in Table 13.8. Notice that most of the responses are in the same category for a given item. There is only one "1" for the first item, and no "0" at all for the last item. When a very high percent of responses is in the modal category, there is very little room for possible error. Consequently, a high coefficient of reproducibility in this situation would not be a good indicator of the adequacy of our scale. Having selected items on the basis of discriminatory power scores is of some help

in avoiding this situation, but it is best to compute another statistic known as *minimal marginal reproducibility*, or *MMR* (Edwards, 1957). This statistic gives an indication of how low it is possible for the coefficient of reproducibility to go. A large difference between R_c and *MMR* indicates that R_c is not determined simply by high modal categories and is a good assessment of reproducibility.

To compute *MMR*, one first determines the proportion of responses in the modal category for each item. These proportions are used in the formula:

$$\text{MMR} = \frac{(p1 + p2 + \ldots + pn)}{N}$$

where N = the number of items in the scale, and

$p1$ = the proportion in the modal category for the first item

pn = the proportion of responses in the modal category for the nth item.

Computing MMR for the data in Table 13.7 yields the following results:

For the first item, 13 out of 20 responses are "0" while only 7 are "1." Therefore, the modal proportion is

13/20. Likewise, there are 12 "0"'s for item 2, so the proportion is 12/20. The remaining proportions are 12/20 and 16/20.
Entering these values in the formula, we obtain:

$$\text{MMR} = \frac{(13/20) + (12/20) + (12/20) + (16/20)}{4}$$

MMR = 2.65/4 = .66

Since our R_c = .86, it is considerably better than what can be expected based on modal frequencies alone; so we can be more confident about the adequacy of our scale.

It is important to note that a given Guttman scale may be group specific. This means that if we achieve adequate reproducibility with a given set of items with one sample of respondents, there is no guarantee that the same items will scale when applied to another sample. Only after-the-fact analysis of each sample will reveal if the Guttman scale properties hold for subsequent applications of a scale.

Regarding the data generated by Guttman scaling, it is of ordinal level. Given the relatively few items characteristic of these scales and the common "agree–disagree" format used, there are few possible scores for respondents to achieve. This means that large numbers of ties will be encountered. Guttman scales are unique, however, for the characteristics of unidimensionality and reproducibility. If these attributes are desired, they are apt to more than outweigh the presence of all the tied scores.

Given the extreme complexity of creating Guttman scales, it is unlikely that most human service workers will have occasion to develop one. There are, however, a substantial number of such scales in existence, making an understanding of their operating characteristics worthwhile. This is especially true because of the need to check the reproducibility level of a scale each time it is applied to a new sample.

Multidimensional Scales

As you may have noticed, all the scaling techniques presented so far were developed a number of years ago; even the more recent semantic differential scale is about 30 years old. More recent activity in scaling techniques has centered on what is called the **multidimensional scale,** which is a scale measuring variables that are composed of more than a single dimension. These scaling techniques are too complex for full presentation here, but we can discuss the basic logic that underlies them.

Recall that one purpose of the preceding scaling techniques is to locate people along some continuum. Accomplishing this, we are able to determine that various groups or people exhibit more or less of the variable measured. With these unidimensional techniques, the straight line of a single scale is sufficient to indicate the location of all people on a given variable. When we come to variables of more than one dimension, however, this single line is no longer adequate. We have to think of locating people somewhere in either two-, three-, or N-dimensional space. A common analogy is made between multidimensional scaling and cartography, or mapmaking. Just as the cartographer locates various places along the dimensions of a map, multidimensional scaling locates people along the various dimensions of a variable. For example, if we conceive of people's motivation as composed of the two dimensions of "discomfort" and "hope," then Figure 13.2 illustrates how multidimensional

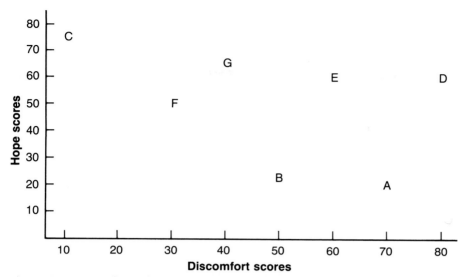

Figure 13.2 Hypothetical Two-Dimensional Space of Client Motivation

scaling might serve to locate these people with regard to these dimensions (Kogan, 1975). It might, for example, be possible to use multidimensional scaling of client motivation to predict chances of success with clients undergoing various forms of treatment.

Multidimensional scaling can, of course, deal with variables composed of many more than two dimensions. As more dimensions are added, however, presentation and interpretation become increasingly complex. Persons interested in a detailed presentation of multidimensional techniques are advised to consult Shepard et al., *Multidimensional Scaling* (1971). Be forewarned that multidimensional scaling utilizes some fairly sophisticated statistical techniques that you may need to review before you develop a thorough understanding of it.

Scales are most commonly used in research problems in which the unit of analysis is the individual (*see* Chapter 4), and this emphasis is reflected in the pre-

ceding discussion. However, it would be highly misleading to leave the impression that scales cannot be used with other units of analysis, such as the characteristics of organizations.

Scaling in the Human Services

In the past few decades, the use of scaling techniques has become quite widespread in the human services, both for clinical and for research purposes. In some cases, practitioners are called on actually to develop a scale themselves to measure a variable that is of interest for some clinical or research reason. More commonly, however, practitioners find it desirable to use a scale that has been developed by someone else. Many scales, for example, are useful tools in assessing the functioning of clients or organizations. Recall the Rapid Assessment Instruments and Walter Hudson's *Clinical Measurement Package* discussed in Research in Practice 11.1. In other cases, practitioners find themselves involved in survey or evaluation research where scales are used as data collection techniques. At the very least, human service providers utilize research related to intervention strategies that can be incorporated into practice, and increasingly this research involves the use of scales. For any of these uses, it is essential to know how to develop, evaluate, and use scales because their misuse can have devastating consequences.

The major danger in the uninformed use of scales is that a poorly constructed measuring device will provide false or inaccurate information about the world. And false data are in some ways worse than no data at all because people *believe* they have gained some understanding when, in fact, they have not. Social policy or practice techniques based on such erroneous data may actually exacerbate problems rather than alleviate them. For these reasons, one needs to be exceedingly cautious about using scales that have been developed without the extensive pretesting and analysis outlined in this chapter. Many people are under the very mistaken impression that one can gather usable data from statements that have been constructed with no pretesting or analysis. It is tempting to believe that a couple of intelligent people can sit down and write unbiased, valid, and reliable statements to measure variables. This is a dangerously erroneous belief. Great care is always called for in constructing scales. These concerns regarding scale construction illustrate the profound responsibility of social researchers to take all steps necessary to ensure that their findings are valid. Scientific results can have a powerful influence on the way we deal with other people, including clients, and such results

must therefore be approached cautiously and rigorously. Any investigator—including a human service practitioner—who casually develops scales without rigorous safeguards and distributes results based on those scales is, many would argue, engaging in unethical behavior.

This point is aptly illustrated by a study that reported on the validity of several measures of aggression in children (Seibert and Ramanaiah, 1978). The authors comment that there has been a proliferation of aggression measures involving self-report, teacher ratings, peer ratings, and projective techniques. However, there had been very little research to test the validity of these measures. Because lack of demonstrated validity both limits the usefulness of these scales and also makes it difficult to compare results from studies using different scales, the researchers set out to investigate the validity of three of the more commonly used aggression measures and three measures of impulsivity. For both impulsivity and aggression, teacher ratings, peer ratings, and self-report data constituted the three measures. The researchers found strong empirical support for the validity of peer ratings and teacher ratings, but only marginal support for self-report measures.

The researchers suggest that a strong tendency of children to respond in a socially desirable way may be the cause of the low validity of the self-report methods. In other words, children may respond to items not in terms of their true feelings, but rather in terms of what they believe the researchers or other adults would find socially acceptable. They also comment that the fact that the teacher and children had known each other for eight months contributed to the validity of the peer and teacher rating scales, presumably because experience enabled them to learn which behavioral manifestations represented aggression or impulsivity in particular individuals. This example illustrates not only the importance of testing the validity of a scale but also the importance of considering the characteristics of the subjects in the research. Suppose you were doing a research study on aggression in children and the research design included the use of one of the scales discussed here. According to this research, the best results would be achieved by using a peer or teacher rating scale near the end of the school year rather than at the beginning. Furthermore, you would probably be best off not using self-report measures.

In short, human service providers need to be in a position to assess whether research is methodologically sound. In the case of scale construction, this means considering how rigorous the investigator was in developing items, whether pretesting was conducted, and whether validity and reliability were tested. If you encounter a discriminatory power, or DP, score, you need to be able to evaluate it in deciding whether to accept the research results as scientifically sound. In some cases, after reviewing a piece of research, you may decide that, although the results are tantalizing, the study lacks the methodological rigor necessary to convince you to incorporate those results into your practice. Just as the U.S. Food and Drug Administration is very cautious about approving new drugs for medical use, you should also be prudent about adopting research results for practice purposes—especially results based on a single study or studies that do not meet strict scientific standards. Research in Practice 13.2 illustrates a case where issues of validity and reliability of scales, along with the time and cost necessary to administer them, were taken into account in deciding which scales to incorporate into practice.

RESEARCH IN PRACTICE 13.2
Client Functioning: Measurement for What? Benefits of Sequential Assessment

Although there is no one-to-one correlation, it is generally true that the most reliable and valid measurement procedures are also the most expensive to develop and use. Because of this, human service agencies sometimes find themselves confronting the question of whether the added cost of using a more valid and reliable scale is worth it.

One agency dealt with this issue in the assessment of alcohol-related problems of new clients in a treatment organization. There were three differ- ent levels of client problem screening in the organization: brief screening, basic assessment, and specialized assessment (Skinner, 1981).

The first consisted of a structured interview, conducted by a professional, for intake purposes. It included only a few questions about alcohol usage in addition to demographic items, work history, family background, legal status, and so on. The second level, basic assessment, consisted of a scale to measure involvement with alcohol

(Continued on next page)

called the Michigan Alcohol Screening Test (MAST). This scale contained 25 items on various problems associated with problem drinking, including the social, legal, medical, and interpersonal consequences of alcohol abuse for the individual. This scale has been tested for reliability and exceeds the conventional rule of .80. The third level of measurement, specialized assessment, consisted of the Alcohol Use Inventory (AUI). This is a multiscale inventory of 147 questions and is designed to measure styles of alcohol use, unfavorable consequences of use, and perceived benefits of drinking. Within the instrument are 22 separate scales. This instrument also has been found to meet acceptable levels of reliability and validity. The overall research question was whether the longer, more valid and reliable scale was worth the added cost of administering it.

The researcher administered the three forms of measurement to a sample of 327 individuals who had problems with alcohol in order to assess the relative benefits and liabilities of each approach. In addition, several other instruments were used to assess further the validity of the three procedures. These included the Lifetime Drinking History, which is a detailed, structured interview procedure that yields quantitative indexes of drinking patterns. Other measures included several scales to test for understanding of scale items and measures of the tendency to present oneself in a favorable light.

The study found that asking individuals a few simple questions during the intake process was effective in obtaining useful data about alcohol usage. However, although the intake interview permitted one to detect the existence of a potential problem, the MAST procedure produced reliable information on the severity and nature of the alcohol problem. More important, this additional information was gained at only a slight increase in time and money required for the assessment process. In contrast, the AUI procedure required considerably more time in order to complete the 147-item, multiscale instrument and also considerable time and skill to score and interpret the results. For the added cost, it provided detailed information about styles of use, patterns of symptoms, and perceived benefits of use.

The researcher concluded that human service professionals who are in a position to detect alcohol-related problems would definitely benefit from including a procedure such as MAST in their client screening routine. The added reliability and validity over and above what can be obtained in a brief screening are obtained for very little additional cost. On the other hand, the added precision and fine distinctions that are possible through use of the AUI cannot be justified for referring agencies. The AUI is better suited for specialized treatment facilities that can set up efficient procedures for scoring and analysis and that can make use of the added information in treatment planning for alcoholics. Thus, the selection of measurement tools and the decision to incorporate scales into practice should be based on the demonstrated capacity of the measurement tools weighed against the added costs in terms of time, money, and skill required for their use.

|||||||||||||||||||||||||||||||||||||||||||||||||||||||||||||||||||||||||||||||||||||||||||||||||||||||||||||||||||||

☰ Main Points

• Multiple-item scales are particularly valuable for measuring complex variables because they enhance validity and reliability, can increase the level of measurement, and improve the efficiency of data handling.

• The five basic steps common to most scaling techniques are these: develop many preliminary items, eliminate obviously bad items, pretest the remaining items, eliminate bad items on the basis of pretest results, and select items for the final scale.

• Likert scaling is a very popular scale format involving a series of statements to which respondents select from five alternatives ranging from strongly disagree to strongly agree.

• An important consideration in selecting items for inclusion in a Likert scale is their discriminatory power: the ability of each item to differentiate between high and low scorers on the overall measurement scale.

• Thurstone scaling uses judges to assign a scale value from 1 to 11 to each item in the scale, which results in a scale capable of producing interval-level data.

• Items for inclusion in a Thurstone scale have scale scores that cover the full 1 to 11 range and were most agreed on by the judges.

• The semantic differential scaling format presents respondents with a concept to be rated and a series of opposite adjective pairs separated by a 7-point scale that is used to evaluate the concept.

• Semantic differentials are a convenient scaling format as they are considerably easier to construct than the alternatives.

• Guttman scales have the unique characteristic of reproducibility, meaning that a given total score reflects one and only one pattern of responses to the items in the scale.

• Multidimensional scaling uses two or more dimensions or components of a complex variable to locate people with regard to the various components of the variable.

• The use of scales or the results of research based on measurement scales should be approached cautiously with careful consideration given to whether adequate development has gone into the scale, particularly in terms of assessing its validity and reliability.

☰ Important Terms for Review

discriminatory power (DP) score
Guttman scale
Likert scale
multidimensional scale
scale
semantic differential
summated rating scales
Thurstone scale
unidimensional scale

☰ For Further Reading

Corcoran, Kevin, and Joel Fischer. *Measures for Clinical Practice: A Sourcebook.* New York: The Free Press, 1987.
    Although this book is about practice scales, many of them were developed for research

purposes and are still quite useful for research.

Magura, Stephen, and Beth Silverman Moses. *Outcome Measures for Child Welfare Services: Theory and Applications.* Washington, D.C.: Child Welfare League of America, Inc., 1986.

Another compendium of scales that can be used in both research and practice.

Miller, Delbert C. *Handbook of Research Design and Social Measurement*, 4th ed. New York: Longman, 1983.

The latest edition of a classic in the field of measurement. Miller's book provides an overview of the various types of scale construction along with many examples of proven scales.

Mueller, Daniel J. *Measuring Social Attitudes: A Handbook for Researchers and Practitioners.* New York: Teachers College Press, 1986.

A step-by-step guide to developing any of the major scaling formats (Likert, Thurstone, Semantic Differential, etc.). It also contains many useful examples of existing scales.

Oppenheim, A. N. *Questionnaire Design and Attitude Measurement.* New York: Basic Books, 1966.

An excellent presentation of scale construction, particularly with regard to its use in questionnaires. In addition to detailed coverage of the scaling formats discussed in this chapter, it presents many less commonly used scaling techniques.

The following are some other useful compilations of scales that can be of utility in human service research:

Bonjean, C., R. Hill, and D. McLemore. *Sociological Measurement: An Inventory of Scales and Indices.* San Francisco: Chandler, 1967.

Lake, D. G., M. B. Miles, and R. B. Earle. *Measuring Human Behavior.* New York: Teachers College Press, 1973.

Robinson, J. P., and P. R. Shaver. *Measures of Social Psychological Attitudes.* Ann Arbor, Mich.: Institute for Social Research, 1973.

Straus, M. A. *Family Measurement Techniques.* Minneapolis: University of Minnesota Press, 1969.

≡ Exercises for Class Discussion

One point we have made in this chapter on scaling is that the human service professional may not have occasion to construct new scales. However, there are many situations in which you could use scales that have already been developed and that are reported in the literature.

13.1 For one of the following topics, find one or more scales that are included in the professional literature. We suggest using *Psychological Abstracts, Sociological Abstracts,* and *Social Work Research and Abstracts* as aids in your research. See also Appendix A (on the use of the library) in this volume.

Depression	Life satisfaction
Alcoholism	Stress
Child abuse	Marital satisfaction or adjustment

13.2 For each scale you locate, indicate what kind of scale it is, for example, Likert, Guttman, and the like. Is there reliability and validity information available on the scale? If you wanted to use a scale on this topic, what would be the problems with, and advantages of, using the one you found?

One source of scales for human service practice is the *Clinical Measurement Package* by Walter Hudson. As a class project, have members complete and score the Generalized Contentment Scale. (A trial set of the scales may be obtained from the Dorsey Press, 1820 Ridge Road, Homewood, Ill. 60430).

13.3 What value does such a scale have over and above data that might be gathered in interviews?

13.4 These scales are intended for repeated use with single-subject designs. How do you envision clients might respond to such a scale, especially with repeated applications?

14

Data Analysis and Statistics

All research involves some form of **data analysis,** which refers to deriving some meaning from the observations that have been made as a part of the research project. Data analysis can take many forms. In some cases, it is qualitative in nature, such as a summary description of an investigator's field notes from a participant observation study. Our focus in this chapter, however, is with quantitative data analysis, in which observations are put into numerical form and manipulated in some way based on their arithmetic properties. The analysis of quantitative data typically involves the use of **statistics,** which are procedures for assembling, classifying, tabulating, and summarizing numerical data so that some meaning or information is obtained.

This chapter is intended to familiarize readers with some common techniques of data analysis. It is primarily designed for those students who have not taken a course in statistics, but it may also be valuable for those who have taken such a course by serving as a refresher of things they may have forgotten. Actually to learn how to do statistical analysis would require at least a full course devoted solely to that topic. However, our goal is more basic: to acquaint you with the issues of selecting the most appropriate statistics to accomplish a particular task and interpreting statistical results. This will prepare you to understand various statistics when you run across them in research reports and to assess whether investigators have used the statistics

properly. We will begin by discussing how observations are put into a form that makes it possible to perform statistical procedures on them. Then we will present the major issues in deciding what statistics can be appropriately used in a given research project. The remainder of the chapter will be devoted to a discussion of various statistical procedures.

Before we proceed, an important point should be mentioned. In this chapter, we will assume that the data have already been collected and our task is now analysis. Recall from Chapter 1, however, that data analysis is a part of the overall research process and that many questions regarding data analysis should be resolved before any data are actually collected. Furthermore, we have emphasized, especially in Chapters 2, 4, and 5, that theoretical and conceptual considerations are very important in determining the nature of the data to be collected, and it is the nature of the data that determines the kinds of statistics that can be applied. In other words, whereas the actual data analysis may occur toward the end of a research project, most of the issues discussed in this chapter will have been settled *before* any data are actually collected.

Computers in Research: Data Preparation and Input

Imagine that you have completed a survey of sample size 400. The completed questionnaires are neatly stacked on your desk. Presumably, the questionnaires contain much information and contain the data for assessing the hypotheses you set out to test with the survey. But, as long as the data are on the questionnaires or in any other raw form for that matter, they are useless. In such a state, the data are in a highly inconvenient form from the standpoint of deriving some usable meaning from them. Indeed, even if we tediously read through the 400 questionnaires, we would have little idea of the overall contents when we were finished. The data were collected in an organized way that made sense in terms of the collection process, but this format is inconvenient for drawing conclusions. The collected data must be reorganized before we can go on and apply the necessary statistics for their analysis.

Coding Schemes

Today, virtually all quantitative data analysis is done with computers. This means that organizing the data for analysis requires getting it into a form that can be accessed by the computer. One element in this process is to code the data. We saw in Chapters 8 and 9 that coding refers to categorizing a variable into a limited number of categories. Sometimes this coding is built into the way a question is asked and answered (see Chapter 7). This is the case with the following question format:

Which of the following best describes where you live? (Circle the number of your choice.)

1. Large city.
2. Suburb of a large city.
3. City of 50,000 or less.
4. Rural but nonfarm.
5. Rural farm.

In this case, the number circled would be the code for how a particular respondent answered a question. This example also illustrates one reason why coding and data analysis issues need to be considered before data collection is initiated. The number of options in the question predetermines the maximum number of response categories that can be used later in looking at possible relationships between "residential area" and other variables. Because we did not provide an option for "City of 50,000 to 300,000," we could not use this as a category in our data analysis.

With some variables, the actual value of the response is a number and can be used to code the data. Family size, income, and number of arrests are variables where this is the case. However, when the data take the form of responses to open-ended survey questions, field notes, or other nonnumerical entities, the translation of data into numbers can be quite challenging. Nevertheless, this process is essential for most data analysis because the substitution of numbers for observations greatly reduces the volume of data that must be stored and facilitates its analysis, especially by computer. Many computer programs permit you to use words or letters to stand for categories, but these are generally more cumbersome and only infrequently used. (Recall from Chapter 5, however, that assigning a number to coding categories does not necessarily mean that we can perform the various mathematical functions, such as addition and subtraction, on them. Whether we can do this or not depends on the level of measurement.)

When coding categories are being established, two general rules should be followed. First, the coding categories should be *mutually exclusive;* that is, a given observation is coded into one and only one category for each variable. The universal practice of categorizing people by sex as either male or female exemplifies mutually exclusive categories. Second, the coding categories should be *exhaustive,* which means that there is a coding category for every possible observation that was made. For example, it might be tempting not to bother to code the "no opinion" response with Likert-type questions on the grounds that you will probably not include those responses in the data analysis. You might very well decide not to analyze those responses in the end, but the coding stage is not the time to make such decisions. If you fail to code a response and later decide to include it in the analysis, it would be necessary to develop a new coding scheme and reenter the data into the computer. A good rule of thumb when coding is to do it in such a way that *all* information is coded. Coding is usually a tedious, repetitive task that can cause the coder to become careless and fatigued. But even though it is not the most intellectually challenging part of research, it is critical that the job be done well. Searching out errors after the fact is often time-consuming and expensive. Unless caught and rectified, coding errors can ruin the most carefully collected data set by causing distortions in relationships and resulting in meaningless or misleading results.

Once a coding scheme is developed, it is normal to enter it into a *codebook,* which is a recording of how the various responses to a questionnaire were coded. This is done so that any researcher can determine what the numbers used as coding symbols mean. Normally, the next step is to enter the data into a computer file or data set. Today this is typically done with a computer keyboard and monitor (see Figure 14.1). Each case in the data set (for example, each person an-

swering a questionnaire) would be given one or more lines on the screen for their responses. Each line on the screen is divided into a certain number of columns, and the researcher specifies which columns contain data for which variables. So consider just three variables: respondent's identification number, respondent's gender, and respondent's age. We could specify in the computer program that, for all cases, columns 1–3 contain the respondents' identification numbers, column 4 contains the code for gender, and columns 5–6 contain data on their ages. So, in the first case in Figure 14.1, we can see that "304" was input as the identification number. A variable like gender would likely be coded "0" for male and "1" for female, so the respondent whose data are on line 1 is a female. If age is coded as the number of years since birth, then it would need two adjacent columns on the screen in order to contain all possible ages. (All respondents over 99 years of age could be coded as 99 with little effect on the outcome of the analysis since so few people are older than that.) The first respondent in Figure 14.1, then, is 27 years old. The inputting of data would continue like this until all the variables for all respondents had been entered. In a small research project, each respondent might have only one line of data; in a large-scale project, each might have 5, 10, or more adjacent lines of data. Once all the data have been input, they are saved on a disk or tape for easy access. While this line-by-line organization of the data is still used today, the actual entry of the data is often done slightly differently, using data-entry programs. These programs protect against errors because the range of values that each variable can take can be specified, and if any value outside this range is entered, it will not be accepted and the program will

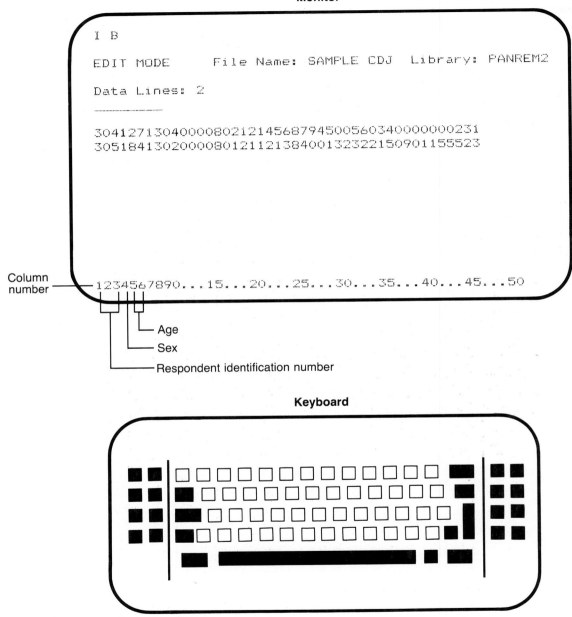

Figure 14.1 Illustration of CRT Data Input

TABLE 14.1   Sample Codebook

Item	Columns	Variable Name	Value Codes
Respondent identification number	1–3	IDENT	
What is R's gender	4	GENDER	0 = male 1 = female
What is R's age?	5–6	AGE	age in years

wait until an acceptable value is entered. These programs also ensure that a value is entered for every variable, and values cannot be entered into the wrong columns (an easy error with line-by-line entry). A similar form of data-entry program, computer-assisted interviewing, was described in the Computers in Research section of Chapter 7. With these programs, the interviewers actually sit at computer terminals, which display the questions to be asked; the interviewers then enter the data into the computer as the answers are given, making for a very efficient data collection and entry process.

The codebook can be further elaborated so that it contains information about how data are organized in the computer. The codebook in Table 14.1 shows what questions were asked in the survey as well as what columns the data are in for each person. It also shows the variable name by which the computer knows the variable, which is necessary in order to retrieve information about a variable from the computer. (Each software has different conventions for naming variables.) Finally, it shows the actual numbers that are entered into the computerized data set for each response to each variable. All of this information is essential in order to generate data analysis from the computer and understand what

it means. With the codebook, a researcher is guided in the access and manipulation of variables in a data set.

Cleaning the Data

If the data have been entered without using a data-entry program that has protections against errors, then the final task prior to statistical analysis involves checking the data for possible coding errors or other mistakes that could interfere with analysis.

One way of locating errors is to inspect the computer file visually. However, with large data files of several hundred or more respondents, it is very easy to miss coding errors with this procedure. Another common technique is to use a standard statistical analysis program such as SPSS[x] to generate a frequency distribution for all variables. To do this, the computer must read all entries, and letters that have been typed instead of numbers and other similar errors will thus be detected. An additional procedure uses the coding categories to detect errors. We know the expected range of values there will be for each variable, and any values outside that range must be errors. A conditional selection procedure in many statistical programs will print out the identification numbers of any cases where the value falls outside the defined range. For example, if the variable "sex" is coded as "0" for males and "1" for females, then the computer will scan the data and print out any cases where the value of sex is more than "1." Such a process does not catch all errors, but it can help eliminate some serious ones. It is important to note that though we are using statistical procedures here such as frequency distributions (discussed later), at this stage we are not actually analyzing the data, but only using the procedures to locate coding errors that might interfere with analysis.

Choosing Statistics

Once the data are coded and in a computer file, we are ready to begin analysis to unlock the information they contain. One of the major errors that occurs in data analysis is the selection of inappropriate statistics. This can be avoided by careful consideration of two factors. First, the level of measurement of the data plays a key role in determining the statistical techniques that are appropriate. In Chapter 5, we discussed four levels of measurement: nominal, ordinal, interval, and ratio. The numbers associated with some nominal data, for instance, have none of the usual arithmetic properties, so statistics that require the addition, subtraction, multiplication, or division of these numbers are not suitable for such data. Attempting to apply such statistics on nominal data will produce meaningless results.

The second consideration in assessing the appropriateness of statistics is to determine what the statistic is to accomplish. Each statistical technique performs a particular function, revealing certain information about the data. A clear conception of analytical goals is a prerequisite for selecting the best statistics for achieving those goals.

Statistical techniques have one of two goals: *description* and *inference*. **Descriptive statistics** are procedures that assist in organizing, summarizing, and interpreting the sample data we have at hand. **Inferential statistics** are procedures that allow us to make generalizations from sample data to the populations from which the samples were drawn.

Descriptive Statistics

One of the first steps usually taken with a data set is to look at the range of values for each variable. To accomplish this, a *frequency distribution* is constructed. In Table 14.2, the variable is the grade for a college class, with the traditional five categories. The frequency column shows the number of class members who received each grade. Of particular interest is the *shape* of a frequency distribution. A distribution's shape derives from the pattern the frequencies produce among the various categories of the variable. A number of labels are used to describe the shapes of distributions. First of all, distributions may be symmetrical or asymmetrical (see Fig. 14.2). *Symmetrical distributions* are balanced, with one half of the distribution being a mirror image of the other half. Quite naturally, most distributions only approach perfect symmetry. *Asymmetrical distributions* have

TABLE 14.2 Hypothetical Grade Distribution for a Social Science Research Class

Grade	Frequency
A	4
B	7
C	10
D	5
F	3
	N = 29

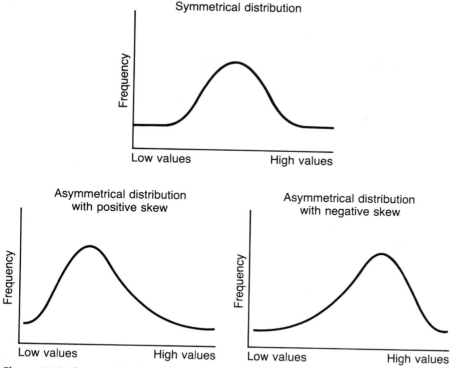

Figure 14.2 Symmetrical and Asymmetrical Distributions

cases bunched toward one end of the scale, with a long "tail" caused by a small number of extreme cases trailing off in the other direction. Asymmetrical distributions are said to be *skewed,* with positively skewed distributions having long tails extending in the direction of the higher values and negatively skewed distributions having tails going in the direction of lower values. (Note that the concepts of positive and negative skewness apply only to distributions of data of ordinal level or higher. Because the categories of nominal data have no inherent order, the shape of a distribution of nominal data is purely an arbitrary matter of how one chooses to arrange the categories.) Determining the amount of skewness is an important preliminary step for

later analysis. Certain inferential statistics, for example, are based on the assumption that the variables are normally distributed. One of the basic properties of a normal distribution is that of being symmetrical. Thus, our analysis at this stage may be critical for helping to decide later which inferential procedures are appropriate.

Measures of Central Tendency

Although valuable for revealing patterns within the data and the shape of the distribution, frequency distributions can be cumbersome. In fact, with variables that can take on many values such as age or income, a frequency distribution can become so massive that it is difficult to detect patterns in it. **Measures of central tendency,** more commonly known as *averages*, summarize distributions by identifying the "typical" or "average" value. They are one of the most commonly used statistics. The three most widely used measures of central tendency are the *mode, median,* and *mean,* each designed for use with a particular level of measurement and having unique qualities.

The mode is the category in a frequency distribution that contains the largest number of cases. The mode for the grade distribution in Table 14.2 is *C* because more people received that grade than any other. Although the mode can be determined for data of any level of measurement, such as the grade distribution, which is ordinal, it is usually used with data of the nominal level. There are two reasons for this. First, the mode is the least stable of the three measures, which means that its value can be changed substantially by rather minor additions, deletions, or changes in the values making up the distribution. With the other measures of central tendency, adding more cases produces less dramatic shifts in their values. Second, if two or more categories are tied with the largest number of cases, we could have two, three, or more modes, none of which would necessarily be very "typical" of the distribution. The presence of several modes also undermines its utility as a summary statistic to describe the average case.

With ordinal data, the median is the appropriate measure of central tendency. The median is the point in a distribution below which 50 percent of the observations fall. For example, a distribution of six scores—10, 14, 15, 17, 18, 25—would have a median of 16. Note that when the distribution contains an even number of values, an observed score may

not fall on the median. The median is then the value halfway between the two central scores. If we added another score greater than 16 to the preceding distribution so that it contained 7 cases, the median would be 17, an observed score. Because the median does not take into account the actual value of the scores, only the number of observations, it would make no difference if the score we added were 17, 100, or 1000—the median would still be 17. This makes the median very stable because the presence of extremely high or low scores in a distribution has little effect on the value of the median.

The mean, the measure of central tendency most people think of when they hear the word "average," is calculated by summing all of the scores in a distribution and dividing by the number of scores. The mean, however, is only suitable for interval-level data, where there is equal spacing along a scale and various mathematical functions can be performed (*see* Chapter 5). (There is one exception to this: dichotomous nominal or ordinal level variables that have only two values. Many interval-level statistics, such as the mean, can be meaningfully computed on such variables. This is called dummy variable analysis and is beyond what we wish to introduce in this chapter.) Because the mean takes into account the actual value of all scores in a distribution, it is less stable than the median. The presence of a few extreme scores will "pull" the mean in that direction. Because of this, the median is often the preferred average when summarizing skewed distributions, even with interval level data, as it more accurately reflects the central value. For example, although the mean could be used to summarize income data, the U.S. Bureau of the Census typically reports median income because the presence of the relatively few wealthy people tends to pull the mean to such a high level that it overstates the average family income. Because it is less affected by extreme scores, the median is also often preferred in clinical practice research, where treatment and control groups are usually small and violate conditions required for statistics based on the mean.

Selecting the most appropriate measure of central tendency for a given set of data is not difficult. Level of measurement and skewness are the primary considerations. With relatively symmetrical distributions, the only factor is level of measurement.

Measures of Dispersion

Like measures of central tendency, measures of dispersion are used to describe and summarize distributions. Whereas central tendency indicators describe the middle or average of the distribution, **measures of dispersion** indicate how dispersed or spread out the values are in a distribution. Measures of dispersion add valuable information about distributions. On the basis of central tendency measures alone, we might assume that two distributons with similar averages were basically alike. Such an assumption would be erroneous, however, if the spread of the distributions were different. As illustrated in Figure 14.3, distribution A is more dispersed, with values deviating widely from the central value. The values in distribution B are more tightly clustered near the average. For avoiding possible erroneous assumptions about the spread of distributions, it is desirable to report a measure of dispersion along with a measure of central tendency.

Three commonly used measures of dispersion are the *range, semi-inter-*

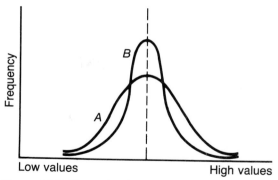

Figure 14.3 Two Distributions with the Same Average but Different Dispersions

quartile range, and the *standard deviation.* The *range* is the simplest of these, referring merely to the difference between the highest and lowest scores in the distribution. As such, the range indicates the total spread of a distribution. Knowing the end points of a distribution, however, tells us nothing about how the remainder of the values are dispersed within the distribution. In addition, because the range is based on only two values, it is unstable. Adding or deleting extreme scores causes the range to vary widely whereas the bulk of the distribution may change little. Furthermore, despite its simplicity, the range is suitable only for interval data. The operation of subtraction used to obtain the range assumes that the values of the scores in a distribution have meaning, and that is true only for interval- and ratio-level data. Because of these limitations, the range is usually used as an adjunct to other measures of dispersion and not reported alone.

The *semi-interquartile range* (sometimes called the quartile deviation) is conventionally symbolized by the letter Q. The semi-interquartile range is obtained by first dividing a frequency distribution into fourths, or *quartiles.* The first quartile is the score below which 25 percent of the scores fall, and the third quartile is the score below which 75 percent of the scores fall. Q is calculated by subtracting the first quartile from the third quartile and dividing by two. The semi-interquartile range is closely related to the median and is the measure of dispersion usually reported with it. In fact, the median is actually the second quartile, the point below which 50 percent of the scores fall. The semi-interquartile range shows the average spread of the distribution around the median. The larger the value of the semi-interquartile range, the more dispersed the scores are from the median.

The *standard deviation*, symbolized by the letter *s*, indicates the average (or mean) spread of the scores from the mean and is, therefore, the measure of dispersion usually reported along with the mean. The larger the value of the standard deviation, the more dispersed the scores are from the mean. Actual calculation of the standard deviation is relatively complex and beyond the scope of this chapter. In addition to its use as a descriptive statistic, the standard deviation has important applications in inferential statistics.

One final note on measures of dispersion. Although their overall purpose is to assist in the description of distributions, a single dispersion value from a single distribution is not particularly revealing. The major utility of dispersion indicators is in comparing several distributions because they enable us to tell at a glance which has more or less spread.

Bivariate Relationships

The statistics we have considered so far are used to describe the distribution of a single variable and are, therefore, called **univariate statistics.** Most data analysis in research, however, involves dealing with two or more variables simultaneously. Statistical procedures used to describe the relationship between two variables are called **bivariate statistics** whereas **multivariate statistics** deal with three or more variables. When two or more variables are analyzed with descriptive statistics, the major feature of interest is the relationship between the variables, especially the extent to which they covary, or vary together. If two variables are related, a change in one of the variables is associated with a change in the other.

Contingency and Percentage Tables

A convenient way of investigating bivariate relationships is to cross-tabulate the data in the form of a table. A *contingency table* contains raw frequencies, whereas in a *percentage table* the frequencies have been converted to percentages. Both types of tables are useful for studying relationships. We will discuss these tables for two variables. However, you should be aware that contingency table analysis can be applied to three or more variables.

Table 14.3 illustrates the general form of a contingency table. We will utilize two conventions to standardize the construction of contingency tables. First, when there is an independent variable and a dependent variable, the vertical *columns* are used to represent categories of the independent variable, with the horizontal *rows* representing categories of the dependent variable. Second, when ordinal-level or higher data are cross-tabulated, the categories should be ordered as illustrated in Table 14.3, with columns running from lowest on the left to highest on the right and rows from lowest at the

TABLE 14.3   Contingency Table

		Independent Variable			
		Low	Medium	High	Totals
Dependent Variable	High	21	47	12	80
	Medium	38	41	20	99
	Low	79	14	28	121
	Totals	138	102	60	$N = 300$

bottom to highest at the top. Be advised that these conventions are not universally applied, and you may encounter tables constructed differently. Following the conventions, however, contributes to consistency and ease of interpretation. Furthermore, the computational routines for some statistics assume that tables are constructed according to this convention and must be modified to produce correct results with tables structured differently.

Several labels are used to refer to the various parts of tables. The squares of the table are called *cells,* with the frequencies within the cells labeled *cell frequencies.* Values in the "totals" column or row are called *marginals.* Tables are often identified according to the number of rows and columns they contain. A table with two rows and two columns becomes a 2 × 2 (read "2 by 2") table. A

table such as Table 14.3 is a 3 × 3 table. In addition, because the number of rows is always designated first, a 2 × 3 table is *not* the same as a 3 × 2.

Contingency tables are generally used as a starting point for creating percentage tables or as the basis for applying many statistics. By themselves, contingency tables are difficult to interpret if there are varying numbers of cases in each column and row. Converting a contingency table to a percentage table makes interpretation far easier, and this can be done by dividing each cell frequency by the appropriate marginal total and multiplying the result by 100. The column margins would be used if we were interested in seeing how the dependent variable is distributed across categories of the independent variable. Table 14.4 illustrates Contingency Table 14.3 converted to a percentage

TABLE 14.4   Percentage Table

		Independent Variable		
		Low	Medium	High
Dependent Variable	High	15.2%	46.1%	20.0%
	Medium	27.5%	40.2%	33.3%
	Low	57.3%	13.7%	46.7%
	Totals	100%	100%	100%
		(138)	(102)	(60)

TABLE 14.5   Relative Effectiveness of Two Treatments for Depression

	Treatment A	Treatment B	
Improved	35.3%	42.1%	
No improvement	64.7%	57.9%	
	100%	100%	%d = 6.8%
	(34)	(38)	

table. Percentages in the first column were obtained by dividing the cell frequencies 21, 38, and 79 by the column marginal 138, with the result multiplied by 100. Below each column, the percentages are totaled and indicated as equaling 100 percent. This informs the reader that the column marginals were used to compute the percentages. The numbers in parentheses are the column marginals from the original contingency table. They supply valuable information regarding the number of cases on which the percentages are based and should always be presented with a percentage table.

Reading percentage tables is a straightforward process similar to constructing them. Whereas we computed the percentages down the columns, we read percentage tables by comparing percentages along the rows. Of particular interest is the *percentage difference* (% d) between any two categories within a given row. For example, Table 14.5 presents hypothetical data on the relative effectiveness of two different treatments for depression. The difference between the two cells in the top row is 6.8 percent, meaning that more of those receiving treatment B improved than those receiving treatment A. The % d suggests that treatment B was somewhat more effective on this sample of clients. Note that with a 2 × 2 table such as Table 14.5, the same % d will result by subtracting within the bottom row, so a single % d

summarizes the complete 2 × 2 table. As the number of rows and columns in a table increases, the number of % d's that can be calculated increases rapidly.

The magnitude of % d's is a crude indicator of the strength of relationships. It should not be surprising that small differences of 1 or 2 percent indicate very weak and possibly meaningless relationships. On the other hand, % d's of 15 percent or more usually indicate substantial relationships. Unfortunately, no hard and fast rules concerning evaluating the magnitude of % d's can be offered because of the complicating factor of sample size. For example, if we are dealing with employment data for the entire nation, a difference of 1 percent or less could represent a million more workers with or without a job. With very large samples, smaller % d's are more important. Alternatively, with small samples, % d's must be large before they indicate a substantial relationship.

Multivariate Analysis

As we noted in Chapter 2, analyzing an independent and a dependent variable and finding a bivariate relationship between them does not prove that the independent variable actually *causes* variation in the dependent variable. To infer causality, the possible effects of extraneous variables must be investigated. Although research projects may focus pri-

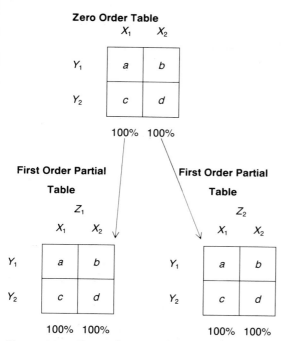

Zero Order Table

First Order Partial Table Z_1

First Order Partial Table Z_2

Figure 14.4 General Format for Partialing Tables. X = Categories of the independent variable; Y = categories of the dependent variable; Z = categories of the test variable.

for the sake of simplicity and space we will use dichotomous variables throughout this presentation.

The subtables Z_1 and Z_2 are referred to as *partial tables* and the relationships within them as *partial relationships*. So a partial relationship is the relationship between an independent and a dependent variable within one category of the test (or control) variable.

The original table that is divided into partials is called the *zero order table* and the relationship contained within it is known as a *zero order relationship*. The "zero" in these labels indicates that there are no test variables being controlled. As we introduce test variables, partial tables are referred to by the number of test variables being controlled at one time. If we are controlling one test variable in our partial tables, they would be referred to as *first order partials*, clearly indicating that the number of variables controlled is one. If more variables than one are simultaneously controlled, the tables would be called second order partials, third order partials, etc.. Although it is possible, it is rare to go beyond the first order with contingency control. One reason is that as we add more test variables, the number of partial tables that are generated increases rapidly and interpreting all of these tables may be extremely difficult. The other reason table elaboration is rarely taken beyond the first order is that the sample gets divided up quickly to the point that individual cell frequencies may become too small and reduce our confidence in the results. We literally run out of cases. This effect can be seen in Figure 14.4 where in the zero order case the sample is divided among the four cells of that table; but when we move to the partials, the same number of cases is spread among eight cells, thus reducing the magnitude of the cell frequencies. For

mary attention on two variables, they will typically consider others to assess the full complexity of social phenomena. A set of procedures for conducting this kind of multivariate analysis is called either *table elaboration* or *contingency control* (Rosenberg, 1968). Contingency control involves examining a relationship between an independent and a dependent variable while holding a third variable constant. Three variable tables are constructed such that the relationship between the independent and dependent variable can be examined within each category of that third variable. The general format of contingency control is illustrated in Figure 14.4. Although contingency control can be applied to variables with any number of categories,

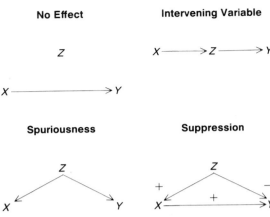

Figure 14.5 Diagrams of Four Possible Outcomes When Partialing

analyzing multivariate relationships beyond the first order, techniques other than table elaboration would normally be used.

When a test variable is introduced and partial tables created, the tables will reveal that one of four possible results has occurred. First, there may be *no effect*. This result is indicated when the relationship in the partial tables is approximately the same in terms of strength as it was in the zero order table. What has happened in this case is that we have tested a variable that is unrelated to either the independent or the dependent variable, thus it could not affect the relationship between those variables. In all cases, it is the direction and the strength of the relationships among the three variables that determines which result occurs when partialling. Figure 14.5 illustrates the no-effect condition by indicating no linkage between the test variable and either the independent or the dependent variable.

A second possibility when doing table elaboration is that the strength of the relationship found in the zero order table may be substantially reduced or even disappear entirely in the partials. This result may be difficult to interpret because there are two possibilities and we need more information (which may or may not be available) to choose between the two. One possibility is that in terms of temporal order, the test variable intervenes between the independent and the dependent variable (Figure 14.5). When such an intervening variable is controlled, the relationship between the independent variable and the dependent variable is effectively blocked, so the partial tables show little relationship.

The other possibility, is that the zero order relationship is either all or partly *spurious*. In this case, the test variable is temporally located before either the independent or dependent variable and is related directly to both (Figure 14.5). When the effects of the test variable are controlled, the apparent relationship between the independent variable and the dependent variable is reduced, because the operation of the test variable was to inflate the actual relationship between the other two variables in the zero order table. In a case of complete spuriousness the only reason the independent and dependent variables appear to be related in a zero order table is due to the influence of the test variable. With this influence blocked in the partials, the zero order relationship disappears. Be sure to note the importance of being able to establish the appropriate temporal location of the test variable relative to the other two variables. If that cannot be done, as might occur with survey data, we would not be sure whether the partials were indicating the presence of an intervening variable or that of a spurious relationship. As we noted in Chapter 2, determining temporal order is crucial in sorting out causal relationships among variables.

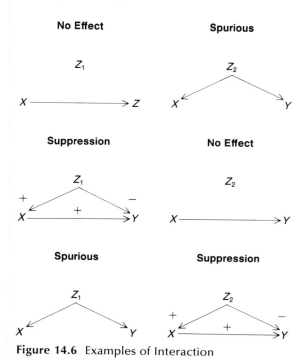

No Effect

Z_1

$X \longrightarrow Z$

Spurious

Z_2

$X \longleftarrow \quad \longrightarrow Y$

Suppression

Z_1

$+ \quad \swarrow \quad \overset{+}{\longrightarrow} \quad -$

$X \longrightarrow Y$

No Effect

Z_2

$X \longrightarrow Y$

Spurious

Z_1

$X \longleftarrow \quad \longrightarrow Y$

Suppression

Z_2

$+ \quad \swarrow \quad \overset{+}{\longrightarrow} \quad -$

$X \longrightarrow Y$

Figure 14.6 Examples of Interaction

Another possibility can occur when controlling on a third variable. The partial tables may show an even stronger relationship between the independent and dependent variables than was indicated by the zero order table. This outcome occurs because the action of the uncontrolled test variable in the zero order table is to suppress the relationship between the independent and the dependent variables. In fact, variables that produce this result are called *suppressor variables*, and the result itself is known as *suppression*. Figure 14.5 illustrates one way suppression can occur. Note that positive relationships are indicated between the independent and dependent variables and between the independent variable and the test variable. A negative relationship exists between the test variable and the dependent variable. It should be evident that the test variable and the inde-

pendent variable are exerting forces on the dependent variable that are, at least in part, offsetting. That is, as values of the independent variable increase, they influence the dependent variable to increase, but as the test variable increases, it is influencing the dependent variable to decrease, thus masking part of the relationship between the independent and the dependent variables. When the influence of the test variable is controlled, this masking effect is removed and the relationship between the independent variable and the dependent variable is now revealed to be stronger than in the zero order table.

The last, but often most intriguing of outcomes, is that of *interaction*. Interaction refers to a relationship between an independent and a dependent variable that is inconsistent. That is, the relationship between the variables differs depending on the condition of the test variable. For example, one partial table might show a no-effect result while another might show a "spurious" result. This result means that the relationships among the three variables are more complex than in the previous outcomes. When interaction is present, we can no longer speak of a simple, singular relationship between the independent variable and the dependent variable with the effects of the test variable controlled. Because the condition of the test variable affects the relationship, we must specify the condition of the test variable before discussing the independent–dependent relationship. In the above example, we would have to indicate that in condition 1 of the test variable the relationship found between the independent variable and the dependent variable at the zero order stayed roughly the same and controlling on the test variable had "no effect." In condition 2, however, controlling on the test variable caused the zero order relationship to disappear, indicating that it was "spurious" or possibly the test variable operates as an intervening variable. Be sure to note that this combination of "no effect" and "spurious" is only one possible combination of the various outcomes that may indicate interaction. Any combination that produces inconsistent results across the partial tables could be interaction. Figure 14.6 illustrates some of these combinations. Interaction results are not at all uncommon in social research. One common test variable—gender—routinely produces interaction effects because men and women react to numerous independent variables differently.

Measures of Association

Measures of association describe the nature of relationships between variables, particularly the *strength* of the relationship or how closely variables are related. The strongest relationship is a *perfect* one in which a given change in one variable is always associated with a given change in the other variable. Perfect relationships are only rarely found in human service research. A less than perfect relationship means that there is only a tendency for the variables to vary together. With ordinal or higher level data, relationships between variables can also be positive, negative, or curvilinear. Recall that a positive relationship is one in which the change in value of the variables is in the same direction; that is, both increase or both decrease. And recall that a negative relationship is one in which one variable increases while the other decreases. Finally, recall that a curvilinear relationship is one in which the drection of change in one variable is not

consistent with changes in the other. For example, in a U-shaped curvilinear relationship, both low and high values of the independent variable may be associated with high values of the dependent variable. In this case, there is a negative relationship between the two variables for low values on the independent variable and a positive relationship with high values on the independent variable. Most measures of association indicate a perfect positive relationship by 1.00 and a perfect negative one by −1.00. The closer the value of the measure is to −1.00 or 1.00, the stronger the relationship is. The closer the value is to zero, the weaker the relationship.

The overriding determinant in selecting a measure of association is the level of measurement of the data at hand, so we will consider measures of association according to the level of measurement for which each was designed.

Nominal Data   Some data are dichotomous in form. That is, the variables have only two values, such as yes or no, male or female. A useful measure of association for two dichotomous variables is the *phi* (pronounced *phee*) coefficient (ϕ). The data are cast into a 2×2 table as illustrated by Table 14.6. Phi indicates the strength of the relationship between variables by yielding a value between −1.00 and 1.00. Although phi may yield negative values, the negative sign is simply ignored because it has no meaning in the case of nominal data.

Phi is considered a good measure of association for three reasons. First, it is quite easy to compute. Second, it is mathematically related to measures of association suitable for other levels of measurement, which makes comparing the strength of different relationships possi-

TABLE 14.6   Nominal Data Suitable for Phi

		Independent Variable (X)	
		X_1	X_2
Dependent Variable (Y)	Y_1	15	35
	Y_2	40	18

ble. Measures of association that are not mathematically related have different operating characteristics and produce values that are not comparable, precluding meaningful comparisons. Third, phi is a member of a group of measures of association that can be given what is called a *proportional reduction in error* (PRE) interpretation. The PRE interpretation means that the measure shows how much the independent variable helps to reduce error in predicting values of the dependent variable. To interpret phi in this way, it is first necessary to square it (ϕ^2). For example, $\phi = .39$ is squared to become $\phi^2 = .15$. This latter value is treated as a percentage and is interpreted to mean that the independent variable reduced the error in predicting values of the dependent variable by 15 percent. All PRE statistics are interpreted in this way.

Since phi is suitable only for two dichotomous variables, a different measure of association must be used for nominal data with more categories. The most generally useful measure for data of this type is lambda (λ). As with phi, the data are cast into tabular form, as illustrated in Table 14.7.

Lambda is a bit different from most measures of association in that its value can range only from 0 to 1.00. Lambda is never negative, but this is not a disadvantage because the negative sign is meaningless with nominal data anyway. The reason lambda is always positive is that it is a direct reading PRE statistic. That is, lambda indicates the proportional reduction in error as calculated and need not be squared as phi was. This is an important point to remember as the values lambda produces usually look rather small. The reason is not that lambda understates relationships, but that the lambda values are "presquared," which makes them appear small.

Although phi and lambda are generally the most common nominal measures of association, there are several others available. For two dichotomous variables, an alternative to phi is Yules's Q. However, Q cannot be given the PRE interpretation and tends to make relationships appear stronger than they actually are. For nominal data with more categories, an alternative to lambda is the contingency coefficient (C). This measure cannot be recommended because it does not always vary from -1.00 to 1.00 and can-

TABLE 14.7   Nominal Data Suitable for Lambda

		Independent Variable (X)		
		X_1	X_2	X_3
Dependent Variable (Y)	Y_1	200	60	40
	Y_2	50	90	10
	Y_3	10	10	50

TABLE 14.8 Ordinal Data Suitable for Spearman's Rho

Independent Variable Ranks	Dependent Variable Ranks
10	9
8	10
1	1
3	5
2	2
9	6
4	7
6	3
5	4
7	8

not be given the PRE interpretation. These factors make values generated by the contingency coefficient rather difficult to interpret.

Ordinal Data   There are many commonly used measures of association for ordinal data. A major consideration in selecting one to use has to do with whether or not the data are *fully ordered*. In situations where every or nearly every case has its own unique rank and there are no or few ties, the data are said to be fully ordered. Table 14.8 illustrates fully ordered data. The most popular measure of association for fully ordered data is Spearman's rho (r_s). Rho, like phi, is

mathematically related to other measures and thus facilitates comparisons of relationships. It also has the desirable characteristic of varying between -1.00 and 1.00. Note that now, with ordinal data, the negative sign has meaning and indicates a negative relationship. Rho also may be squared (r_s^2) and given the PRE interpretation.

When there are only a few ordered categories and many cases to place into them, the data will contain many ties, far too many for Spearman's rho to be usable. Data of this type are called *partially ordered* and are handled in tabular form, as illustrated in Table 14.9. There are several alternative measures of association available for data of this type. Gamma (γ), Somer's *D*, and Kendall's tau (τ) are all suitable and vary between -1.00 and 1.00. There are, however, some subtle differences among them that make one or another most appropriate in a given situation.

Gamma is the easiest of the three to compute, but unfortunately it does not take into account any of the tied scores and tends to overstate the strength of the relationship. Indeed, on the basis of a positive gamma alone, we cannot safely assume that as *X* increases, *Y* also increases, which is a normal assumption of a positive relationship. Because of its failure to consider ties, all a positive gamma

TABLE 14.9 Ordinal Data Suitable for Gamma, Somer's *D*, or Kendall's Tau

		Independent Variable (X)		
		Low	*Medium*	*High*
Dependent	*High*	8	10	12
Variable	*Medium*	10	14	8
(Y)	*Low*	18	11	4

allows us to conclude is that as X increases, Y does not decrease, which, of course, is a much weaker conclusion.

Somer's D is used when we are only interested in our ability to predict Y from X (or less commonly X from Y). When predicting Y from X, Somer's D takes into account ties on the dependent (Y) variable. This has the effect of reducing the value of D in comparison with gamma when the two are computed on the same data. Somer's D, however, gives a more accurate indication of how much the independent variable reduces error in predicting the dependent variable.

Lastly, Kendall's tau takes into account all the tied scores. It indicates the degree to which the independent variable reduces error in predicting the dependent variable *and* how much the latter reduces error in predicting the former. Because it considers the relationship both ways, tau is particularly appropriate where we do not have a clearly identifiable independent and dependent variable and merely wish to determine if two variables are related. By including all of the ties, a positive tau allows us to conclude correctly that as X increases, Y also increases. As this is the type of statement we expect to make on the basis of a positive result, Kendall's tau is more generally useful than gamma.

Interval Data   The most used measure of association for interval data is the *correlation coefficient* or *Pearson's r*. The correlation coefficient is mathematically related to both phi and Spearman's rho, making comparisons among them possible. As with the other two, Pearson's r varies between -1.00 and 1.00 and may be squared (r^2) and given the PRE interpretation. When squared, this value is called the *coefficient of determination.*

The correlation coefficient has a unique characteristic that is important to remember when applying or interpreting it. Pearson's r indicates the degree to which the relationship between two interval level variables can be described by a straight line when plotted on a scattergram as in Figure 14.7. The formula for r mathematically determines the best fitting line and then considers the amount the scores deviate from perfect linearity. This feature of Pearson's r means that, if the relationship between the two variables is somewhat *curvilinear, r* will understate the actual strength of the relationship. Because of this, it is advisable to plot, or have the computer plot, a *scattergram*. A scattergram is a table with the scores of both variables plotted on it. The scattergram provides a visual indication of the relationship between the two variables and is useful for uncovering curvilinearity that might adversely affect the correlation coefficient. Figure 14.7 illustrates three typical scattergrams. In those instances where curvilinearity is discovered, a measure of association other than Pearson's r should be selected. Curvilinear measures of association do exist, but they are beyond the scope of our discussion. They may be found in more sophisticated textbooks about statistics.

Before we leave measures of association, one important matter requires emphasis. Association or correlation does not mean causality! Just because one variable is labeled independent and another dependent and a relationship is found between them does not prove that changes in one variable caused changes in the other. As we emphasized in Chapter 2, correlation is only one step toward inferring causality. In addition, it is necessary to affirm the appropriate temporal

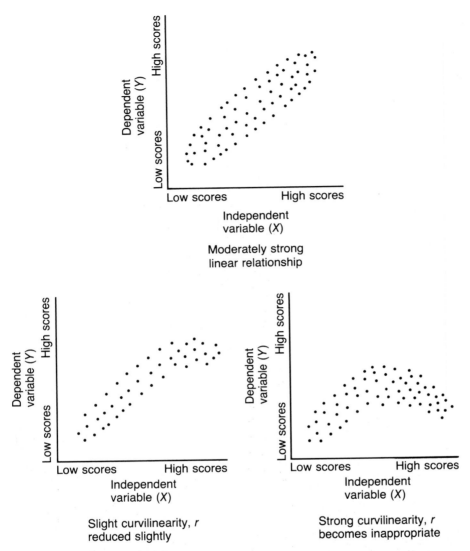

Figure 14.7 Three Typical Scattergrams

sequence and rule out rival causal variables.

Inferential Statistics

We noted in Chapter 6 that most social research is conducted on relatively small samples drawn from much larger populations, and all of the statistical procedures discussed so far are designed to assist in describing, summarizing, and interpreting data from samples. Findings from sample data, however, would be of little scientific value if they could not be generalized beyond the members of the sample to the larger population from which the samples were drawn. For example, it would do other practitioners little good to learn that a researcher had successfully raised the school performance of 50 underachievers unless they could reasonably expect the new approach to work on children who were not in the researcher's sample. In other words, for the new technique to be worthwhile, it must be generalizable to members of the population of underachievers.

Probability Theory

How do we know when research findings are generalizable? Generalization is always an uncertain business, but inferential statistics can reduce the uncertainty to the point where reasonably safe generalizations can be made and the probability of a given amount of error estimated. Inferential statistics are based on probability theory, the same probability theory that works to make probability samples representative. Because of this, inferential statistics can be meaningfully applied only to data based on probability samples or experiments where random assignment has been implemented.

Probability theory allows the mathematical calculation of the likelihood or probability that random events or outcomes will occur. For example, if 10,000 raffle tickets are issued and the winning ticket is chosen in such a way that each ticket has an equal chance of being selected, then each person who purchases one ticket has one-in-ten-thousand chances of winning. However, if you buy ten tickets, then you have ten-in-ten-thousand or one-in-a-thousand chances of winning. You have increased the probability of your winning even though the mechanism for selecting the winner is unchanged. This does not mean, of course, that you *will* win. Less likely events do occur, although with less frequency than more likely ones, and a person who purchased one ticket could certainly win the raffle. In other words, probability theory tells us the *likelihood* of something's occurring; it does not tell us what *will* occur. For this reason, inferential statistics can tell us whether the odds are on our side that a particular generalization is accurate, but they do not make it a sure bet.

As we noted in Chapter 6, probability samples are supposed to represent the populations from which they were drawn, but we expect differences between a sample and its population owing to chance alone. Because these differences are due to the random process used in the selection of samples, their probability can be readily calculated. For example, suppose a researcher draws a probability sample of 50 delinquent boys and applies a special intervention designed to reduce future delinquency involvement. At the end of one year the success rate of the sample is 75 percent whereas for the population of untreated delinquents, the rate is 60 percent. Can we conclude that the experimental intervention was a success? At the level of the sample alone, it is clear that the treated boys had a better rate, but the differences could be due, all or in part, to sampling error. Even with random sampling, the researcher could have obtained a sample of boys who were on average better risks than those in the general population of delinquent boys. The question that inferential statistics answers is whether the difference between the sample results and the population results is too great to be due to chance alone. In the example, running the appropriate inferential statistic would tell us what the chances are of obtaining, through random error, a 15-

percent difference between a population and a probability sample drawn from that population. If such a difference were highly probable, we would conclude that the seeming effect of the experimental treatment was due to chance differences between sample and population. On the other hand, if the result indicated that there was only a small likelihood that a 15-percent differential was due to chance, we would conclude that the treatment did produce a generalizable effect.

Statistical Hypothesis Testing

When utilizing inferential statistics, we are engaging in a special form of hypothesis testing in which two hypotheses that are precisely opposite of each other are developed. The outcome of a statistical test is then used to determine which hypothesis is most likely correct. One of the competing hypotheses, called the *null hypothesis*, states that there is no relationship between two variables in the population or that there is no difference between a sample statistic and a population statistic. "There is *no* relationship between variable X and variable Y in the population" or "There is *no* difference between the mean of the sample and the mean of the population" would be two examples of possible null hypotheses. Alternatives to null hypotheses are called *research hypotheses.* Suitable research hypotheses to go with the two preceding null hypotheses would be: "There *is* a difference between the sample mean and the population mean" and "There *is* a relationship between variable X and variable Y at the level of the population." In each application of a statistical test, we assess the research hypothesis by determining whether the opposite null hypothesis is probable or improbable.

It is not uncommon, upon first exposure to statistical hypothesis testing, to question the utility of null hypotheses. If we believe the research hypothesis is true, why not just test that hypothesis? The need for null hypotheses stems from the fact that it is not possible with inferential statistics to prove research hypotheses directly. However, by determining that it is very likely that the null hypotheses are false, we indirectly provide evidence that their opposite, the research hypotheses, are probably true. To illustrate this point, we will use an example where there is a clear criterion to use in testing a hypothesis. Imagine attempting to determine whether or not a die is unbiased. If the die is unbiased, each side should appear approximately an equal number of times—about one-sixth of the times the die is thrown. If the die is biased, one or more outcomes would occur a disproportionate number of times—one or more numbers occurring substantially more than one-sixth of the time. Suppose the die is tossed 12 times, with each outcome occurring twice or one-sixth of the time. Would this prove the die unbiased? The answer is no. The bias, if it exists, might be too slight to appear after only 12 trials. What if the die were tossed 144 times and still each outcome occurred one-sixth of the time? Such a result would still not make it certain that the die is unbiased, for a slight bias might be revealed by even more trials. Indeed, no number of trials would provide absolute assurance that the die is unbiased. However, a large number of trials with no evidence of bias would make the hypothesis of a biased die so unlikely that it would be rejected. By finding no evidence of support for one hypothesis, we indirectly obtain support for its alternative. In all applications of statistical hypothesis test-

TABLE 14.10   Illustration of Type I and Type II Errors

	Condition in Population	
Decision	Null Hypothesis Is True	Null Hypothesis Is False
Reject null hypothesis	Type I (alpha) error prob. = alpha	Correct decision (power of test) prob. = 1 − beta
Fail to reject null hypothesis	Correct decision prob. = 1 − alpha	Type II (beta) error prob. = beta

ing, if the evidence fails to support the null hypothesis, then the opposing research hypothesis is accepted as probably true.

Although their computational routines vary, all inferential statistical tests yield a result indicating the probability that the null hypohesis is true. In choosing between the competing hypotheses, we ask, How unlikely must it be for the null hypothesis to be true before we are willing to reject it as false and accept the research hypothesis? This is determined by the *alpha level,* or the probability at which the null hypothesis will be rejected (*see* Table 14.10). Researchers have some discretion in setting alpha levels but must guard against the two types of inferential errors that can be made. *Type I* or *alpha error* is the probability of rejecting a null hypothesis that is actually true. The alpha level selected determines the amount of alpha error we are willing to tolerate, so the researcher directly controls type I error by setting alpha. Alpha levels are usually written as "$p < .20$" and read as "a probability of less than 20 percent." Alpha levels can be understood in the following way. Suppose the null hypothesis is that "there is no relationship between variable X and variable Y in the population." We draw a sample from that population to test the hypothe-

sis and indeed find a relationship in the sample data. An alpha level of .20 means that we would find a relationship as large as we did in 20 percent of the samples we draw even though the null hypothesis is actually true and there is no relationship between the variables in the population. We are now faced with a difficult dilemma: Is the null hypothesis true and our sample an unusual one, or is the null hypothesis false? Inferential statistics can't answer that question for us. What it can tell us is that, in the long run and testing many hypotheses, we would be correct 80 percent of the time by rejecting null hypotheses in situations where differences of a given size have an alpha level of .20.

So setting an alpha level as low as .20 makes it easy to reject the null hypothesis, but we are also assured of rejecting true null hypotheses quite frequently. To avoid so much type I error, we might establish a very stringent alpha, such as .001, meaning that we would reject the null hypothesis only if its odds of being true were less than one in one thousand. If the null hypothesis can be rejected at such an alpha level, we would be quite confident that it was false and that we were not committing type I error.

But setting extremely rigorous alpha levels raises the probability of making the other possible inferential error. *Type II* or *beta error* is the probability of failing to reject null hypotheses that are actually false. Alpha levels such as .001 make it so difficult to reject null hypotheses that many false ones, which should be rejected, are not. Thus, in selecting suitable alpha levels, we face a dilemma. Guarding against one type of error increases the chances of making the other type. Fortunately, conventions regarding appropriate alpha levels have developed. In general, social researchers operate with alpha levels of .05, .01, or .001. Although these levels are the most common ones you will see in research reports, there is nothing sacred about them. The researcher must consider what the purpose of the research is and what the alternative risks are in selecting a given level. For example, medical research into the

safety and effectiveness of new drugs or treatments typically operates with very stringent alpha levels because there are matters of life and death at stake. If the null hypothesis in a research project is "Drug X is not safe," then we would want to reject it only if we were very sure that it is false. If it is wrongly rejected, people would be exposed to an unsafe product. On the other hand, a practitioner with a null hypothesis of "Reminder phone calls do not reduce the number of no-shows for clinic appointments" might select an alpha level as low as .10. If the procedure shows any chance of working, the clinic may want to try it. In this case, the consequences of rejecting a true null hypothesis would not be very severe. Some additional issues related to hypothesis testing and alpha and beta errors are discussed in Research in Practice 14.1.

RESEARCH IN PRACTICE 14.1
Program Evaluation: Designed for Failure: Statistical Power in Human Service Research

Although much attention is given to the issue of statistical significance or alpha levels in evaluation research, a related and equally important issue, statistical power, is often overlooked (Kraemer and Thiemann, 1987). *Statistical power* refers to the probability of *correctly* rejecting a null hypothesis in a research study (see Table 14.10). Another way of looking at statistical power is to conceptualize a study designed with low power as being a study with a high probability of failure because it cannot detect an intervention that works. For example, if family in-

tervention does actually reduce the extent of problems in families, does the statistical test we apply to a sample of families tell us this? This is a very real problem as evidenced by examinations of published human service research that indicate that almost half of the studies reviewed could not detect even a medium-sized effect (Orme and Combs-Orme, 1986). A consequence of this shortcoming is that policy decisions may be made to curtail or not implement potentially useful innovations. Another important consideration is that a research effort is wasted if it is unable to detect a program effect when it is present.

In the typical human service program evaluation, the investigator formulates a null hypothesis, such as "There is no difference between the treatment group and the control group," expecting to reject it at the specified level of statistical significance or alpha level. The sample data are analyzed and the null hypothesis is then rejected if the difference between the experimental group and the control group is sufficiently large to be considered an improbable event at the preselected alpha level such as .05, .01, or .001. An unfortunate error of interpretation is to assume that failure to reject the null hypothesis is equivalent to "proving" that the treatment had no effect. A more correct assessment is that the data generated from this study, *as designed,* failed to detect a difference between the treatment and the control conditions. Unless care is taken in the design of the study, it could well be that the study could not detect an effect, even if it were present.

One reason why inadequate attention has been paid to the issue of statistical power in the past has been that estimating statistical power was a difficult undertaking. Fortunately, this is no longer the case. One major advance was the publication of texts on the subject that included tables making determination of power relatively straightforward (Cohen, 1977). More recently, the task has been simplfed even further by the introduction of computer software such as Design Power, previously discussed in Chapter 6 in relation to sampling. Statistical power is determined quantitatively as:

$$1 - beta$$

or

$$1 - \text{(the probability of a Type II error)}.$$

The beta level is complex to calculate and beyond the scope of this book. For a particular research problem, beta can be looked up in a reference work such as Cohen (1977) or calculated by appropriate computer software. Once this is done, the adequacy of beta can be assessed by the following rule of thumb: The minimum acceptable ratio of type II errors to type I errors should be about four to one. Thus, if alpha is set at .05, beta should be $4 \times .05$ or .20. Because power equals $1 - $ beta, power equals $1 - .20$, or .80. (This means that there is an 80-percent chance that we will correctly reject the null hypothesis.) Similarly, if alpha is .01, power should be a minimum of .96, and if alpha is .001, power should be a minimum of .996. However, the four-to-one rule is only a general guideline. What power level is acceptable in a particular research project should be determined by the nature of the research project and its implications.

Reviews of published research studies in the human services and other fields have consistently reported that the actual power of a large proportion of studies is well below these standards of .80, .96, and .996 (Orme and Tolman, 1986). What can be done to improve the power of a research project? Although the concept of power is complex, it has three major determinants: sample size, alpha level, and effect size (ES). By manipulating them, one can improve statistical power.

The larger the sample, the greater the statistical power of a research pro-

(Continued on next page)

ject. Therefore, a simple solution to increasing power may be to increase the sample size. Another potential solution is to reduce the alpha level or probability of a type I error. Because type I and type II errors are related, it may be preferable to use a lower alpha level such as .1 instead of .05 as a way of increasing the power.

Although these two strategies may be an important part of a solution, the best approach may be to take steps to increase the effect size of the independent variable in the study sample. Other things being equal, the larger the effect of the independent variable relative to other factors, the more likely will the null hypothesis be rejected. One way to increase effect size is to select samples that minimize error and assure that a high proportion of the difference between treatment and control groups is due to the independent variable (see Chapters 6 and 10 on error). Another solution lies in taking steps to eliminate as much extraneous variation as possible. Thorough training of service providers, careful rehearsal of procedures, and attention to program detail can all serve to eliminate varia-

tion due to factors other than the program effect. We don't often think of social interventions in terms of "dosage," but the evaluation researcher should also make sure that the participants receive a sufficient dose of the independent variable to make a difference. If the program is financial aid, it might be better to give a small sample large amounts of aid instead of giving a little aid to many. If the program is counseling, the program should provide ample counseling experience. Using the most valid and reliable measurement tools can help detect a difference that exists between groups.

The issue of statistical power in research underscores the necessity of planning projects thoroughly from the initial stage of problem formulation. By the time data analysis is conducted, it is probably too late to take steps to achieve adequate power. The solutions lie in the design formulation, the sampling procedure, and the conduct of the study. Only by envisioning the data analysis requirements from the beginning of the project can studies achieve their goal of determining the effect of an intervention effort.

A common way of expressing that the null hypothesis was rejected is to indicate that a given result is "statistically significant" at some specified alpha level. Unfortunately, the use of the word "significance" can cause some confusion. In popular usage, "significant" means important or notable. Its meaning in statistics, however, does not have the same connotation. Whether a set of research findings is important or notable depends

far more on the topic, theory, sample, and quality of measurement than it does on statistically rejecting null hypotheses. Research on trivial matters or research that is procedurally flawed cannot produce important results no matter how many "statistically significant" findings it might contain. Be sure to remember that all significance means in statistics is that a null hypothesis has been successfully rejected.

Statistical Procedures

There are some basic considerations for selecting inferential statistical procedures much like those for descriptive statistics. One important consideration is the nature of the dependent variable. For nominal dependent variables, there are commonly used procedures such as chi-square, discussed later. There are many additional procedures such as log-linear analysis that go beyond the scope of this book, but that are rapidly gaining prominence in the research literature. With ordinal dependent variables, there are many procedures that, in addition to being applicable to ordered data, are compatible with small clinical samples. Many procedures that are technically appropriate for interval-level data are also used with ordinal variables because they are "robust," or not readily affected by violation of their theoretical assumptions. Finally, there are many procedures that have been developed to handle interval-level data such as Student's t, ANOVA (analysis of variance), and regression, which we discuss later.

Besides the level of measurement in the dependent variable, another consideration is the character of the independent variable. Some procedures are designed for single independent variables with only two levels. Other procedures handle two or more independent variables simultaneously as well as estimating combined effects.

Finally, another issue concerns how the data were generated. Some procedures such as ANOVA are intended for data generated by an experiment where you are comparing one or more control groups with one or more treatment groups. Other procedures, such as regression analysis, are well suited for analyzing large samples, such as surveys, in order to estimate effects. There are still other procedures, such as MANOVA (multivariate analysis of variance and covariance), that are suitable for both statistical control of nonexperimental variables and analysis of experiment-generated variables at the same time. Many of these procedures are highly complex and beyond the scope of this text. However, our point is that there are specific factors that favor the use of some statistical procedures over others. It is important to select the appropriate procedures. Through other courses, you may learn to utilize and select the procedures yourself, or, as a human service professional, you may rely on outside consultants to assist you with this aspect of your research.

In experimentation, one often makes comparisons between a control group and a treatment group. If these two groups are comparable in all respects except for the treatment received, a commonly used statistic is Student's t. This statistic compares the mean of one group against the mean of the other. From the chapter on sampling, it will be recalled that the groups may have different means by chance alone. Large differences, however, suggest that there is a treatment effect. But what is a large difference? The answer depends on the scale of the variable being measured and on the size of the samples. The t test results in a statistical value that is referred to a table for samples of different sizes. The table indicates the probability of obtaining a value that is as large or larger by chance. If the table value is less probable than the alpha level, one rejects the null hypothesis and concludes that the difference is significant. Tables indicating the value of t and of other inferential statistics necessary for rejecting null hypotheses at various alpha levels may be found in any introductory statistics textbook. If you are using a computer package such as SPSS^x, the significance value is provided for you.

In many experimental situations, the research involves more than just two groups. The researcher may also want to know how much difference there is between groups. For example, if four treatment groups each receive different amounts of tutorial help, we might be interested in what effect each level of help has on the number of problems the members of the different groups can solve. For this situation, involving an experimental design and an interval-level dependent variable (number of problems solved), a commonly applied statistical procedure is analysis of variance (ANOVA). ANOVA compares the variability in the scores of members within each group (within group variance) with variability between treatment groups. We would not expect all members of a treatment group to do equally well. In fact, even if one level of treatment works better than another, some members of a lower group might do better than some members receiving a better tutorial program. ANOVA permits the researcher to estimate how much of the variance in performance between groups is due to the treatment.

Another commonly used statistical procedure is multiple regression analysis. Multiple regression is used for a variety of purposes, but a typical application involves estimating the effect of multiple independent variables. For example, we might be interested in determining if a person's income is influenced by sex, race, and age and *how much* each of these variables affects income. As discussed earlier, correlation will indicate whether or not two variables are associated, but regression permits one to estimate how much change in the dependent variable is produced by a given change in an independent variable. Multiple regression is especially useful in that it can handle a large number of independent variables simultaneously, thus permitting researchers to estimate the effects of one variable while controlling for others. We know, for example, that income is correlated with race, education, age, and occupation, among many other variables. If we collect these data from a number of respondents, regression permits us to estimate the contribution of each independent variable to income. Multiple regression produces coefficients that indicate the direction and amount of change in the dependent variable to be expected from a unit change in the independent variables. Thus, if the dependent variable is dollars of income, a regression coefficient of $+580$ for the variable "years of education" indicates that one more year of education is "worth" an additional $580 in income, assuming the other independent variables are held constant. In our illustration, regression would produce an equation as follows:

$$Y' \text{ (income)} = a + b_1 \text{ (race)} + b_2 \text{ (education)} + b_3 \text{ (age)} + b_4 \text{ (sex)}$$

where a = value of Y before other factors' effects are considered, b_1 is an estimate of the effect of race on income, b_2 is the estimated effect of education, b_3 is the estimated effect of age, and b_4 is the estimated effect of sex.

A widely used inferential statistic suitable for nominal data is chi-square (χ^2), which is applied to data in tabular form. There are several versions of chi-square that allow its application to data of different types. All of these versions, however, operate by comparing the number of cases actually found in the cross classification of two or more variables

TABLE 14.11   Hypothetical Data Relating Race and Religion

Religion	Race			
	White	Black	Other	
Protestant	actual: 50 expected: 123	actual: 120 expected: 61.5	actual: 35 expected: 20.5	205
Catholic	actual: 150 expected: 108	actual: 20 expected: 54	actual: 10 expected: 18	180
Jewish	actual: 100 expected: 69	actual: 10 expected: 34.5	actual: 5 expected: 11.5	115
	300	150	50	N = 500

with what would be expected by chance. For example, Table 14.11 shows a sample of 500 community residents cross classified by religion and race. Chi-square compares the actual values in a table such as this with what would be expected if the variables were unrelated. Table 14.11 also contains these expected values, which can be determined from the marginals in the table. For example, because whites make up 60 percent of the whole sample, we would expect 60 percent of the Jews, or 69 out of 115, to be white if the variables of religion and race were unrelated. By chance, of course, one would expect that the actual values will not be exactly the same as the theoretically expected values even when there is no relationship. However, the more the actual cell frequencies in a sample diverge from the expected frequencies, the more likely it is that an association exists between the two variables at the level of the population.

Small values of chi-square indicate little or no association whereas large values indicate that an association is likely. With chi-square, the value of the statistic is influenced by sample size and by the number of categories on each variable. Computer data analysis packages automatically take this into account in reporting significance level; however, when doing hand calculations, one must refer the statistical value to a special table that states the probability of obtaining a χ^2 of that magnitude by chance, given the sample size and number of variable categories. Chi-square does not indicate how strong the association is but only whether or not one exists at the level of the population.

In this chapter, we have presented a basic introduction to the statistical analysis of data. For the consumer of research, this introduction provides some basic guidelines for interpreting statistical analyses that you will encounter in reading research. Those who will conduct research and engage in statistical analysis themselves will need to go beyond the materials presented in this chapter. For such people, we have suggested a few valuable books to consult in the For Further Reading section at the end of the chapter.

COMPUTERS IN RESEARCH
Evaluating Statistical Software

Although it is possible to compute statistics by hand or by pocket calculator, most data analysis today is done by computer. In the past, and sometimes even today, statistical analysis was done on mainframe computers. Four of the more popular statistical packages for mainframe computers are $SPSS^X$, SAS, BMDP, and MINITAB. With the advance in computer technology, however, microcomputers are slowly replacing mainframes for many of these tasks. This has placed computerized statistical capability at the disposal of virtually anyone who wishes to use it. At the same time, the bewildering array of software has made program selection a complicated choice.

Because researchers now use the computer for so many different tasks, one can no longer evaluate statistical software solely on the basis of the number of statistical procedures it can run but must also consider the other applications of the software. Fortunately, there are some excellent sources to which one can turn for assistance in selecting statistical software. Many popular periodicals about computers, such as *Byte* and *Infoworld*, publish articles evaluating software (see, for example, Carpenter, Deloria, and Morganstein, 1984; Fridlund, 1986; Lehman, 1987). These and other magazines are widely available in bookstores and at newsstands. In addition, many professional journals also contain articles on statistical software. One of the better ones for social research applications is *Social Science Computer Review*. Because of rapid innovation in software, it is best to consult current issues for up-to-date developments.

Because any attempt to list specific statistical software packages and their features in a text of this sort would be out of date by the time of publication and because the number of such programs available is simply too large, we will not do so here. Instead, it is more useful for beginning students to be aware of the features of statistical software for microcomputers that make them more or less useful to a data analyst. Clearly, there is no one program for everyone, and features that are very important to one user may be of low priority to another.

1. USER FRIENDLY Some statistical software is easier to use than other software. For example, some programs display a menu of command options. Such a program is an excellent choice for inexperienced operators or infrequent users because one need not memorize commands. For more experienced users, working through several menus in order to execute a simple command may negate the value of this feature.

2. PROGRAM COMPATIBILITY Some statistical software is more compatible with other software the researcher may be using. It is seldom that one program will do everything a researcher wants a computer to do.

3. DATA ENTRY/TRANSFER CAPACITY Some statistical software has more flexible and sophisticated data entry and transfer capabilities. The ability to rapidly and accurately enter data for statistical analysis becomes increasingly critical with larger data sets.

4. DATA AND DATA FILE RESTRUCTURING The capacity to transform data by combining and recoding variables or creating new variables is essential to most applied social research. For the researcher whose data may come from several different files, the capacity to merge data sets and to create new data sets may be essential.

5. QUALITY OF OUTPUT Software varies considerably in terms of quality of output. For the user who expects to prepare reports containing graphs, charts, and display data, the visual appearance of the output can be as important as the capacity to do the statistical procedures.

6. HELP CAPACITY AND TUTORIALS The availability of assistance in the form of a well-written and well-documented manual is very important, especially for those not thoroughly familiar with computer use. Much software also provides built-in, easy-to-use tutorials that help one learn to use the program. Some programs also have "help" screens which can be called up at any time and display the various program commands and what they do. When using a complex program with many procedures and a variety of features, even a seasoned user appreciates such help.

7. DATA AND VARIABLE CAPACITY Although mainframe programs typically can handle very large data sets with thousands of cases and hundreds of variables per case, microcomputers are often restricted in capacity. In selecting statistical software, you must make sure that it can handle the number of cases and variables in your project and that computer memory and storage is adequate for the job.

8. STATISTICAL PROCEDURES Programs vary both in terms of the number of statistical procedures they include and how these procedures are packaged. Some contain only a small number of the most common procedures while others include the equivalent of a large mainframe package.

9. TECHNICAL SUPPORT With some programs, you buy the software, read the manual, and you are on your own. A manufacturer may replace a damaged product but not be of much help with statistical questions or understanding problems that you run up against. Large programs often offer technical support so that the user can receive consultation when problems occur. There may be newsletters and users groups that not only cover such technical issues as how to install a program on a computer, but provide suggestions for conducting special kinds of data analysis. Some manufacturers provide toll-free numbers where assistance is available.

These, then, are the major considerations to be taken into account in choosing statistical software for microcomputers. (While the same issues would apply to choosing software for mainframe computers, these programs, such as SPSS^X or SAS, are so large and well developed that they are

(Continued on next page)

adequate to most tasks.) Evaluating these considerations in the light of the data analysis tasks that the researcher expects to encounter can help to simplify the software selection process. With the wide diversity of computer programs now available, the capacity for sophisticated statistical analysis is in the hands of most researchers and practitioners. The technological innovations in both computers and software are eliminating a serious constraint on the capacity to implement the concept of scientific practice.

≡ Main Points

• Data analysis refers to deriving some meaning from the observations that have been made as a part of a research project; quantitative data analysis involves putting observations into numerical form and manipulating them based on their arithmetical properties.

• Most data analysis is currently performed by computer, with data entered into a computer file from a CRT terminal.

• Data analysis begins by developing a coding scheme and a codebook, which is a set of mutually exclusive and exhaustive numerical codes into which the raw data are categorized.

• After the data have been entered into a computer file, they must be carefully checked for coding or input errors.

• Descriptive statistics are procedures that assist in organizing, summarizing, and interpreting sample data.

• Frequency distributions reveal the pattern the frequencies produce among the various categories of the variable and may be symmetrical or asymmetrical.

• Measures of central tendency, or averages, summarize distributions by locating the central value of frequency distributions.

• Measures of dispersion indicate how dispersed or spread out the values are in a distribution, with most indicators revealing the average spread of the scores around the central value.

• Contingency tables and percentage tables are particularly useful for analyzing bivariate and multivariate relationships with categorical or partially ordered data.

• Measures of association indicate the strength of relationships, and, with ordinal- or higher-level data, they also indicate the direction of relationships.

• Inferential statistics are procedures that allow generalizations to be made from sample data to the populations from which the samples were drawn.

• In inferential statistics a research hypothesis is paired with an opposite null hypothesis and the results of a statistical test are used to decide which is most likely correct.

• Although most data analysis is performed by computer, a knowledge of statistics is still essential for selecting appropriate statistics and properly interpreting the numerical results.

• Statistical software has become sufficiently sophisticated so that its utility cannot be evaluated solely on the basis of how many statistical procedures it can compute. There are many other features of software that must be considered.

≡ Important Terms for Review

bivariate statistics
data analysis
descriptive statistics
inferential statistics
measures of association
measures of central tendency
measures of dispersion
multivariate statistics
statistics
univariate statistics

≡ For Further Reading

Besag, Frank P., and Peter I. Besag. *Statistics for the Helping Professions.* Beverly Hills, Calif.: Sage, 1985.
This text focuses on the human service significance of concepts and procedures rather than on computational issues. It is useful for readers with a limited math background.

Blalock, H. M. *Social Statistics.* rev. 2d ed. New York: McGraw-Hill, 1979.
A straightforward presentation of basic statistics including computational routines as well as theoretical concepts. Includes coverage of everything from frequency distributions to log-linear analysis.

Computers in Human Services. New York: Haworth Press, Quarterly.
A new journal that began publication in 1984, focusing on the potential of computer technology to help us deal with mental health, developmental disabilities, and other human problems. It promises to be a timely contribution to this area.

Elifson, K., R. Runyon, and A. Haber. *Fundamentals of Social Statistics.* Reading, Mass.: Addison-Wesley, 1982.
One of many readily available, introductory-level statistics books that provides detailed coverage of the statistics discussed in this chapter.

Hanushek, E., and J. Jackson. *Statistical Methods for Social Scientists.* New York: Academic Press, 1977.
A more advanced textbook primarily devoted to a thorough discussion of regression and multiple-regression estimation.

Jendrek, Margaret Platt. *Through the Maze: Statistics with Computer Applications.* Belmont, Calif.: Wadsworth, 1985.
In addition to a general discussion of the nature and use of computers in the social sciences, this book provides an introduction to the popular SPSS^X statistical program that is far more comprehendible than that found in the company's manuals.

Kachigan, S. *Multivariate Statistical Analysis,* New York: Radius Press, 1982.
Another advanced textbook covering a variety of more sophisticated statistics, with primary emphasis on multivariate techniques.

Marascuilo, L., and M. McSweeney. *Nonparametric and Distribution-Free Methods for the Social Sciences.* Monterey, Calif.: Brooks/Cole, 1977.
A book devoted to a large number of statistical techniques especially suitable for the analysis of nominal- and ordinal-level data.

Schwartz, Marc D., ed. *Using Computers in Clinical Practice: Psychotherapy and Mental Health Applications.* New York: Haworth Press, 1983.
A good review of the clinical applications of computers in word processing, accounting, psychological testing, clinical assessment, and so on in a mental health context.

Schoech, Dick. *Computer Use in Human Services.* New York: Human Science Press, 1982.
A good general review of the use of computers in the human services.

Wienbach, Robert W., and Richard M. Grinnell, Jr. *Statistics for Social Workers.* New York: Longman, 1987.
A presentation of basic statistical techniques with the focus on uses in social work. This book is highly readable and is recommended for anyone in the human services.

Zeisel, Hans. *Say It With Figures,* 6th ed. New York: Harper & Row, 1984.
A classic analysis of how to present data with statistics. It is very useful for policymakers who wish to improve their under-

standing of the statistics presented to them.

☰ Exercises for Class Discussion

Assume that you have just completed the data collection on a needs assessment on the need for a volunteer visitation program for the elderly in your community. You have a random sample of 500 questionnaires completed by people 55 and older that must now be analyzed. If you decide to implement the program, it will cost about $45,000 a year to pay for the coordinator's salary and administrative and advertising costs. Variables included in the survey are sex, age, annual income, proximity to family members, a scale score on perception of neighbors' capacity to help, and a scale indicating desirability of a visitation program. Finally, the question was asked, "If this program were implemented, would you use it?" The question could be answered yes or no.

14.1 Describe the general process you would follow in analyzing the data by listing the main steps to be completed.

14.2 Develop a hypothetical coding scheme for the following variables: age, sex, income, and desirability scale score (assume the scale scores can range from 0 to 30).

14.3 What descriptive statistics would be appropriate for each of the variables included in this study?

14.4 In terms of bivariate relationships, using the final question as the dependent variable, indicate what indicators would be appropriate for each of the independent variables. What if the dependent variable is the scale score?

14.5 What inferential statistical techniques might be used with the yes–no response as the dependent variable? What about the scale score?

14.6 What level of significance do you think would be appropriate for this study? Support your answer.

15

Writing for Research:
Grant Proposals and Report Writing

This chapter focuses on two very important elements of applied research that are often neglected in introductory research methods texts: the role of grants in research and the importance of good writing. The term "grant" refers to the provision of money or other resources to be used for either research or service delivery purposes. Grants are an important funding source for both social research and the provision of human services. In fact, the amount of grant monies awarded each year is truly staggering. For example, at the federal level, the National Science Foundation (NSF), a major provider of grants for research, distributed more than 1.5 billion dollars in 1988 (*National Science Foundation Budget Summary*, 1988). The National Institutes of Health, which provides grants for both research and action programs, served up over six billion dollars in 1988 (*Chronicle of Higher Education*, 1988). Private foundations gave out grants worth more than 5.2 billion dollars in 1985, the last year for which data are available (*The Foundation Directory*, 1987). It should be clear from these figures that vast sums are dispersed through the system of grants. Given the large role grants play in funding research and some activities of nonprofit human service organizations, it is highly likely that you will be directly involved in a grant-funded project as a professional human service worker.

Despite the pervasiveness of grants, a person might properly feel shell-shocked if given the task of preparing a grant proposal without previous experience. Grant writing is sometimes perceived of as a mystical process with strange jargon and convoluted procedures where only seasoned professionals with an inside track are successful in receiving funds. The neophyte would understandably have many questions. What do I do first? Whom do I contact? What do they want to know? In the following discussions we endeavor to answer these questions and many others for the novice grant seeker. Although the prospect of one's first grant proposal can be a daunting one, it is our contention that preparing a fundable proposal involves many of the principles of sound practice and research that are part of professional education. We also hope to demonstrate that, if approached systematically, writing grant proposals can be an interesting challenge rather than something to be feared.

In the space available to us we cannot explore all aspects of grantsmanship nor go into much detail. We will also be focusing on obtaining grants for agency functions, including both service delivery and research purposes. In fact, grants for service delivery typically include a call for needs assessment data and an evaluation of the service delivery, so many grants focus on a combination of practice and research activities. Depending on the demands of the funding source, there may

430

be minor differences between preparing a proposal for a research project, service delivery, or a combination of the two. Those serious about seeking grants are advised to consult one or more of the listings in "For Further Reading." We will conclude this chapter with a more general discussion of the writing process—to assist in writing grant proposals as well as research reports.

The Grant-Funding Process

Sources of grant money fall into three general categories: government agencies, private foundations, and corporations (Smith and McLean, 1988). Of these, government agencies are by far the largest source of grant monies. They are also about the only sources for large grants of more than a few thousand dollars. Even in the case of smaller grants, it often pays to start with government sources first as many of the private foundations refuse funding automatically unless you can prove that efforts to obtain government funding have failed. Among government agencies, branches of the federal government are the largest source for grant money, so we will discuss these first.

Federal Government Funding Sources

Project or Categorical Grants Project or categorical grants (the two terms are synonymous) are narrowly focused on some specific need or problem as defined by some agency of the federal government. Grant-seekers design approaches, within specified guidelines provided by the government agency, to meet the need or ameliorate the problem specified by the government agency. The agencies make their requests for programs or research opportunities known through what is called a Request For Proposals (RFP), which is a formal request for people or agencies to submit proposals on how they would conduct some research or establish and run some program. Agencies or researchers then submit proposals in a competition to obtain the grant money. Grants are then awarded to those submitting the best proposals within the guidelines established by the granting agency. Although less popular than they once were, there is still considerable activity with this type of grant.

Formula Grants Formula grants are part of large-scale, nationwide federal programs and serve as a mechanism for allocating the funds for the programs. For example, at a time of high unemployment, it is common for the federal government to sponsor various "job-creating" activities through formula grants. Because unemployment is experienced in varying levels of severity in various places in the country, the money would be allocated by a "formula" (hence their name) that provides most of the funds to those areas hardest hit by the problem and prorates the remainder of the funds to other areas as needed. Normally, formula grants are channeled through state and local governments until they reach the agency level. This allows each state and locality to tailor their approach to the problem such that it better fits their particular situation. For example, unemployment in one locale may be concentrated among displaced factory workers, while in another it is concentrated among minority teenagers. The most effective approach in the first locale may be retraining programs, but the second locale may benefit more from having its teenagers taught basic job skills such as showing up regularly and on time for work. So, unlike the categorical grants, formula grants allow the applicant more freedom in designing the research project or program as long as it serves the general goals of the grant monies.

Block Grants Block grants are similar to formula grants in that they are a transfer of funds from the federal government to the states, which then do the final allocating to state agencies and on through to nonprofit service providers. Block grants are different in that they cover much broader areas, such as maternal and child health or elementary and secondary education, and are ongoing year after year. In fact, there are only nine categories of block grants, but they represent the largest transfer of funds from the federal government to the states.

Federal Contracts Though not strictly grants, federal government contracts can be an important source of funds. In contracts, it is the government that decides precisely what it wants and how it wants it done. There is very little flexibility left to the researcher or service provider. What the government is looking for is agencies that can perform the desired tasks at the lowest price. Sources of information about contracts and the rules under which they are awarded are different from grants. Also, the number and variety of contracts is vast, so that considerable research may be needed to get involved with the contract side of the federal government. However, despite the obstacles, nonprofit agencies are moving into contracts as a new way to fund research and services. To describe where to begin in dealing with contracts would take a whole book; our purpose in mentioning contracts is to alert you that here is a resource that is not currently being fully exploited by agencies.

State Government Grants

Although states have always dispersed some of their own tax revenue through the granting process, the rise of Federal Block Grants and the occasional Formula Grant have greatly expanded the dispersal of funds at the state level. Since each state disperses these monies differently, we cannot make any blanket statements about how successfully to bid for these funds. Regarding Block Grants, one thing that is consistent across all states is a federally mandated series of open meetings to discuss how the grant money should be used. Although showing up and speaking at these meetings will not ensure that you will get a grant, it will help to assure that some money is allocated for the area of your greatest concern. Another way to increase your chances of getting state grant monies is to keep in contact with the state departments and agencies that oversee and fund research and services related to the human services, such as the department of corrections, the department of mental health, and the department of social services. These state agencies may also publish RFPs as a way of soliciting grant proposals.

Private Funding Sources

Foundations A foundation is a nonprofit, legally incorporated entity organized for the purpose of dispersing funds to projects that meet the guidelines of its charter. The number of private foundations is staggering. Krathwohl (1988) puts the number at approximately 24,000. However, you probably won't need to search through all of these to find one to support your project. First, not all foundations are created equal. The largest 20 percent of foundations control 97 percent of foundation assets, so this narrows the number of likely prospects considerably (Krathwohl, 1988). Second, most foundations award only small grants. According to Bauer (1988), only about 500 foundations typically give grants in excess of $5,000 each. Submitting a proposal, no matter how noble the purpose or how well prepared the paperwork, that calls for a grant of, say, $20,000 to a foundation that has never awarded more than $5,000 in any one grant is probably a waste of time. For the person looking for a small grant, you must then begin looking at some of the other characteristics of foundations to sort through all of the possibilities and find those few most likely to fund your proposal. In general, however, private funding sources are good places to seek grants for agency activities or applied research, since they prefer to fund action programs that produce immediate results rather than research projects that, at best, have some long-term payoff. Also, the complexity of proposal preparation and submission is much less than that encountered with federal agencies.

Types of Foundations There are five distinct types of foundations. *Community foundations* exist to serve the immediate local area in which they are based. Thus, if a project is modest in scale and serves some local need, a community foundation may be a good choice. *General purpose foundations* are often large, such as the Ford Foundation, and operate nationwide. If a project is large in scope, with the potential of having an impact broader than the local community, these large foundations may be ideal. They particularly like innovative demonstration projects that may show the way for other communities to solve various problems. *Special purpose foundations*

carve out a particular area of interest and award grants only to projects that deal directly with that area of specialization. Successful funding from these sources requires some research into which foundations fund what kinds of projects. Fortunately, large foundations typically publish annual reports, much as corporations do, outlining recently funded projects (Krathwohl, 1988). From these lists, one can tell the sorts of issues and projects that various foundations are interested in and willing to support.

Family foundations are the most difficult to categorize because there are so many of them—over 20,000 according to Bauer (1988)—and there is so much variability among them. Some are large and have the resources to award fairly substantial grants, whereas others have a cap on grant size of a few thousand dollars. Some are quite general in the projects they fund, whereas others have very narrow interests. For example, some may fund only projects that benefit a particular religious or ethnic group while others fund only projects that address a particular problem, like alcoholism or child abuse.

Corporate foundations are used by some corporations as the conduit for corporate philanthrophy. Other corporations engage in philanthropy but do not use the foundation mechanism. In either case, nonprofit agencies are common recipients of corporate giving. To maximize your chances of sharing some of this corporate wealth, you must understand a few things about corporate giving. As investor-owned, profit-making enterprises, corporations are giving away the stockholder's money. As such, the directors who make the philanthropic decisions are cautious to fund only those activities that can be justified to the stockholders. This tends to mean that the corporation or its employees must stand to benefit in some way from funded projects. For example, a nonprofit child-care facility used by many corporate employees might receive a corporate grant or other corporate support. Also, because of this need to benefit, corporate giving is concentrated largely in areas where the corporations have their offices, headquarters, or manufacturing facilities.

Computers in Research: Learning About Funding Opportunities

Given all the separate agencies and organizations that disperse grants, how do you find specific funding opportunities? There are publications and computer data bases available that can help in this. The *Catalog of Federal Domestic Assistance* (CFDA), for example, describes all federal government programs. Figure 15.1 provides an illustration from the catalog of a program run by the Department of Health and Human Services. As you can see, the catalog supplies information valuable to the grant-seeker. It tells what the objectives of the program are, the steps in the application process, examples of funded projects, and criteria for selecting proposals. To make the search of the catalog quick and effective, an online computerized system called the Federal Assistance Program Retrieval System (FAPRS) has been developed. The FAPRS allows you to use certain key words to match your proposed project with federal agencies that would be the most likely funding source. This system is similar to some you may have used to conduct library searches. For information on how to obtain a FAPRS search, write to the Federal Program Assistance Center Staff, General Services Administration, Washington, DC 20407.

Grant seekers can use their personal computers to search for funding opportunities through the use of the *Grants Database* prepared by Oryx Press. This on-line service, available from either Orbit or Dialog (two on-line service providers), is the most comprehensive source of current information on grants offered by government, corporate, and private funding sources. In addition to its convenience, the data base has the advantage of being updated monthly, unlike conventional publications that may become dated. Any agency that depends on grants as a routine source of funding should investigate subscribing to the *Grants Database.*

Another useful publication is the *Federal Register.* This daily, magazine-size volume reports on the activities of the federal government. Although it includes a lot of information that is of little use to the grant-seeker, new programs are announced first in it; so it is a good way to keep up with the ever-changing opportunities for obtaining federal funding. Guidelines for obtaining funding under the new programs are also first provided in the *Federal Register.* Eventually, this information gets into the CFDA, but because that is only published annually, many months could pass before a new program gets listed in the latest edition. The *Federal Register* is also available through several computer search services.

Many funding agencies publish periodic newsletters or bulletins describing their latest activities and programs. It is easy to get on mailing lists for these. They often contain RFPs and searching the RFPs, you may find an opportunity for your organization.

A special guide to corporate foundations, *Corporate Foundations Profiles,* is offered by the Foundation Center. This useful volume presents detailed descriptions of the largest 250 corporate foundations and less detailed information on 470 more. This directory, among other things, allows you to determine which corporations have operations in your area and might therefore be likely prospects for funding.

Also published by the Foundation Center is *The Foundation Directory*. It contains a list of foundations of all types, organized by the state in which they are incorporated. While at first this may seem strange, remember that except for the very large nationwide organizations, foundations tend to limit their funding geographically. As illustrated in Figures 15.2 and 15.3 the directory supplies a considerable amount of information about each foundation—information that is useful in the sorting-out process. For example, the financial information gives some idea of the size of grants that a foundation typically makes. It also provides information on "purpose and activities," "types of support," and "limitations" to further screen potential funders. Also, procedures for making application are described and memberships of boards of directors are provided. For those in the business of seeking grants, the *Foundation Directory* is an essential tool. Another publication from the Foundation Center, *Foundation Fundamentals: A Guide for Grant-seekers* (Read, 1986), is particularly useful for the beginner. It outlines the services of the Center along with information on locating foundations, preparing proposals, and submitting proposals to private foundations.

The Foundation Center also provides a computerized search service called COMSEARCH. Several different types of searches can be made. For example, foundations can be selected by type of topic area that they fund, geographical region they focus on, or the dollar amount of grants typically made. These searches quickly and easily narrow the range of foundations down to the most likely prospects.

For more information on locating funding opportunities, see Krathwohl (1988) or Smith and McLean (1988).

Grant Proposal Planning

The grant-funding process involves two players: the funding sources, who sift through proposals seeking worthy projects in which to invest, and the agencies with project ideas that deserve funding. Getting the two together is the heart of the granting enterprise. Having described the funding sources, we now turn our attention to the second process, namely, the development of a fundable proposal.

Proposal Development as a Process

Let us explode, at the very beginning, one myth about obtaining grants: Successful proposals are not started and finished in short order. Rather, they are developed and carefully honed over time. The preparation of grant proposals should be considered an ongoing, continuing function within an agency, rather than a sporadic event. The reasons for this will become clear as we proceed through the grant preparation process, but all too often grants are begun in haste and rushed to partial completion to meet some fast-approaching deadline. The result, too often, is a rejection.

When conceptualized as a process instead of a single event, grant development has many principles in common with the research process introduced in Chapter 1. When the grant is for the purpose of conducting a research project, the connection with the research process is rollment of the Head Start Program. The program expects to serve over 450,000 children in fiscal years 1988 and 1989.

REGULATIONS, GUIDELINES, AND LITERATURE: Chapter XIII of Title 45 Code of Federal Regulations, including 45 CFR parts 1301, 1302, 1303, 1304, 1305. These are available on request at no charge.

INFORMATION CONTACTS:

Regional or Local Office: Regional Program Director, Children, Youth and Families, Office of Human Development Services, HHS Regional Offices (see Appendix IV of the Catalog for list of addresses of Regional Offices).

Headquarters Office: Administration for Children, Youth and Families/Head Start, Office of Human Development Services, Department of Health and Human Services, P.O. Box 1182, Washington, DC 20013. Telephone: (202) 755-7782.

RELATED PROGRAMS: 10.550, Food Distribution.

EXAMPLES OF FUNDED PROJECTS: (1) Full-Year and Full-Day Head Start Programs; (2) Full-Year and Part-Day Head Start Programs; and (3) Parent and Child Center Programs.

CRITERIA FOR SELECTING PROPOSALS: (1) The degree to which the proposed project will meet the Head Start Program Performance Standards or other program objectives as specified in a program announcement; (2) reasonableness of cost; (3) qualification of staff; and (4) other criteria, which are detailed in every program announcement.

13.608 ADMINISTRATION FOR CHILDREN, YOUTH AND FAMILIES—CHILD WELFARE RESEARCH AND DEMONSTRATION

FEDERAL AGENCY: OFFICE OF HUMAN DEVELOPMENT SERVICES, DEPARTMENT OF HEALTH AND HUMAN SERVICES

AUTHORIZATION: Social Security Act, as amended; Title IV, Part B, Section 426, Public Law 86-778; Public Law 96-248, 42 U.S.C. 626.

OBJECTIVES: To provide financial support for research and demonstration projects in the area of child and family development and welfare.

TYPES OF ASSISTANCE: Project Grants.

USES AND USE RESTRICTIONS: Grants are for: (1) special research and demonstration projects in the field of child welfare which are of regional or national significance; (2) special projects for the demonstration of new methods which show promise of substantial contribution to the advancement of child welfare; and (3) projects for the demonstration of the use of research in the field of child welfare. Contracts are for the conduct of research, evaluation, or demonstration projects.

ELIGIBILITY REQUIREMENTS:

Applicant Eligibility: Grants: State and local governments or other nonprofit institutions of higher learning, and other nonprofit agencies or organizations engaged in research or child welfare activities. Contracts: any public or private organizations.

Beneficiary Eligibility: Children and families.

Credentials/Documentation: Nonprofit organizations which have not previously received OHDs program support must submit proof of nonprofit status. Applicable costs and administrative procedures will be determined in accordance with Parts 74 and 92 of Title 45 of the Code of Federal Regulations, which implement the requirements of applicable OMB Circulars No. A-87, No. A-21, and No. A-122.

APPLICATION AND AWARD PROCESS:

Preapplication Coordination: Limited consultation available at Headquarters Office. The standard application forms, as furnished by DHHS and required by OMB Circular No. A-102, must be used for this program. This program is excluded from coverage under E.O. 12372.

Application Procedure: Application form, including budget request and narrative description of project proposal to be submitted to the headquarters Office. This program is subject to the provisions of OMB Circular No. A-110 and No. A-102.

Award Procedure: Review by at least three nonfederal professionals. Final decision by Commissioner, Administration for Children, Youth and Families.

Deadlines: Determined annually for new projects. Application for continuation grants must be received 90 days prior to the start of the new budget period.

Range of Approval/Disapproval Time: From 90 to 180 days.

Appeals: None.

Renewals: Renewals and extensions available through formal submission of progress reports and continuation application.

ASSISTANCE CONSIDERATIONS:

Formula and Matching Requirements There is no statutory formula. Grantees are required to provide at least 5 percent of total direct costs. Amount of matching required is specified in all announcements of availability of grants. This may be either cash or in kind, fairly evaluated.

Length and Time Phasing of Assistance: Grant may be for 1 to 3 years; average duration is 17 months.

POST ASSISTANCE REQUIREMENTS:

Reports: Financial and progress report quarterly; final report and final expenditure report at completion of study.

Audits: In accordance with the provisions of OMB Circular No. A-128, "Audits of State and Local Governments," State and local governments that receive financial assistance of $100,000 or more within the State's fiscal year shall have an audit made for that year. State and local governments that receive between $25,000 and $100,000 within the State's fiscal year shall have an audit made in accordance with Circular No. A-128, or in accordance with Federal laws and regulations governing the programs in which they participate. All other grantees are required to have institutional audits every 2 years in accordance with 45 CFR 74.62.

Records: All financial records are to be maintained 3 years after termination of study, or until audit is completed, whichever occurs first.

FINANCIAL INFORMATION:

Account Identification: 75-1636-0-1-506.

Obligations: (Grants and Contracts) FY 87 $7,786,000; FY 88 est $8,457,000; and FY 89 est $13,244,000. (NOTE: The funds in this program are also available for program contracts. The amounts which can be used for such contracts cannot be predetermined.)

Range and Average of Financial Assistance: $10,000 to $250,000; $100,000.

PROGRAM ACCOMPLISHMENTS: (1) Supported efforts to design models to improve service system response to the needs of emancipated or nearly-emancipated youth; (2) developed coordinated approaches between child welfare, developmental disabilities, and mental retardation agencies to maximize available resources at service at the State and local level; (3) provided public social service agencies, State and local juvenile and family court judges with guidelines or criteria for determining what constitutes "reasonable efforts" to avoid out-of-home placement for children, including an analysis of the factors contributing to the failure of Family Based Child Welfare Services; (4) assisted States in implementing effective Child Welfare licensing policies and procedures; (5) implemented or improved delivery of preplacement preventive services, particularly through the provision of these services by non-profit organizations; (6) developed effective techniques for the intervention and provision of emergency services to depressed and suicidal youth; (7) disseminated and documented the use of information concerning positive characteristics that produce strong families and responsible family guidance in matters such as health, education, career preparation, and the social and emotional growth of children and youth.

REGULATIONS, GUIDELINES, AND LITERATURE: No regulations specific to this program. Annual Priority Statements, applications and submission deadline information are available at no charge.

INFORMATION CONTACTS:

Regional or Local Office: Not applicable. All requests should be directed to Headquarters Office.

Figure 15.1 Illustration from the *Catalog of Federal Domestic Assistance*

Headquarters Office: Chief Discretionary Program Branch, Administration for Children, Youth and Families, Office of Human Development Services, OS, P.O. Box 1182, Washington, DC 20013. Telephone: (202) 755-7420.

RELATED PROGRAMS: 13.623, Administration for Children, Youth and Families—Runaway and Homeless Youth; 13.652, Administration for Children, Youth and Families— Adoption Opportunities; 13.670, Administration for Children, Youth and Families— Child Abuse and Neglect Discretionary Activities; 13.766, Health Care Financing Research, Demonstrations and Evaluations.

EXAMPLES OF FUNDED PROJECTS: (1) Achieving Economic Self-Sufficiency; (2) A Unique Partnership to Promote a New Method of Funding Child Care; (3) Defining Reasonable Efforts; (4) Illinois Child Welfare Licensing Initiative; (5) Comprehensive Child Care Benefits Package; (6) A Knowledge Transfer Project for Strengthening Families; and (7) Demonstration of the Utilization of the Minority Volunteer Network for Child Welfare.

CRITERIA FOR SELECTING PROPOSALS: An assessment is made of the degree to which a proposal promises to meet the specific program objectives defined in the program announcement, considering reasonableness of cost, qualifications of staff and adequacy of methodology.

13.612 NATIVE AMERICAN PROGRAMS— FINANCIAL ASSISTANCE GRANTS

FEDERAL AGENCY: OFFICE OF HUMAN DEVELOPMENT SERVICES, DEPARTMENT OF HEALTH AND HUMAN SERVICES

AUTHORIZATION: Native American Programs Act of 1974, Section 803, Public Law 93-644, 42 U.S.C. 2991 et seq., as amended.

OBJECTIVE: To provide financial assistance to public and private nonprofit organizations including Indian Tribes, urban Indian centers, Native Alaskan villages, Native Hawaiian organizations, rural off-reservation groups, and other Native American organizations for the development and implementation of social and economic development strategies that promote self-sufficiency. These projects are expected to result in improved social and economic conditions of Native Americans within their communities and to increase the effectiveness of Indian Tribes and Native American organizations in meeting their economic and social goals.

TYPES OF ASSISTANCE: Project Grants (Contracts).

USES AND USE RESTRICTIONS: Grants may be used for such purposes as, but not limited to: (1) Governance Projects, to promote self-governance of programs formerly operated by Federal employees; (2) Economic Development Projects, to promote business starts for Indian-owned businesses in manufacturing, trade, retail, and agriculture; improve Indian housing management; and to develop a Tribal health care system; and, (3) Social Development Projects to assume local control of planning and delivering social services in Native American communities. In addition, funding is now available for a revolving loan fund for Native Hawaiian organizations.

ELIGIBILITY REQUIREMENTS:

Applicant Eligibility: Public and private nonprofit agencies, including but not limited to, governing bodies of Indian tribes on Federal and State reservations, Alaskan Native villages and regional corporations established by the Alaska Native Claims Settlement Act, and such public and nonprofit private agencies serving Hawaiian Natives, and Indian organizations in urban or rural nonreservation areas.

Beneficiary Eligibility: American Indians, Native Alaskans, and Native Hawaiians.

Credentials/Documentation: Nonprofit organizations which have not previously received OHDS program support must submit proof of nonprofit status. Applicable costs and administrative procedures will be determined in accordance with Parts 74 and 92 of the Code of Federal Regulations, which implement the requirements of applicable OMB Circulars Nos. A-87, A-21, and A-122.

APPLICATION AND AWARD PROCESS:

Preapplication Coordianation: The provisions of OMB Circular No. A-102 apply to grantees which are State and local governments. The standard application forms, as furnished by DHHS and required by OMB Circular No. A-102, must be used for this program. This program is excluded from coverage under E.O. 12372.

Application Procedure: Information regarding the availability of grant funds will be published from time to time in the Federal Register as Program Announcements, which will provide details on program objectives for which applications are being solicited and other application requirements. The Administratin for Native Americans will provide each applicant agency with the appropriate forms for the application for Federal Assistance and instructions for applying for grants from OHDS programs. Applications should be submitted to OHDS Grants Management Branch, Department of Health and Human Services, Room 345-F, 200 Independence Avenue, SW., Washington, DC 20201. This program is subject to the provisions of OMB Circulars No. A-110 and No. A-102.

Award Procedure: All funds are awarded directly to the grantees.

Deadlines: Program Announcement 13612-881, Competitive Financial Assistance for Projects to promote Social and Economic self-sufficiency for Native Americans has a closing date for receipt of applications on May 20, 1988.

Range of Approval/Disapproval Time: Applicants will receive notice of approval/disapproval approximately 90 days after receipt of application.

Appeals: Appeals procedures are published in 45 CFR 1336.52.

Renewals: Not applicable.

ASSISTANCE CONSIDERATIONS:

Formula and Matching Requirements: This program has no statutory formula for distribution of funds. A matching share of 20 percent is required unless waived in accordance with criteria which are also published in 45 CFR 1336.50. This program has maintenance of effort requirements; and waiver requirements are contained in 1336.50. See funding agency for further details.

Length and Time Phasing of Assistance: Grantees may apply for competitive continuation support within a project period of 1 to 3 years.

POST ASSISTANCE REQUIREMENTS:

Reports: Quarterly Financial Status Reports, Report of Federal Cash Transactions, and Project Progress Reports are required.

Audits: In accordance with the provisions of OMB Circular No. A-128, "Audits of State and Local Governments," State and local governments that receive financial assistance of $100,000 or more within the State's fiscal year shall have an audit made for that year. State and local governments that receive between $25,000 and $100,000 within the State's fiscal year shall have an audit made in accordance with Circular No. A-128, or in accordance with Federal laws and regulations governing the programs in which they participate. All other grantees are required to have institutional audits every 2 years in accordance with 45 CFR 74.62.

Records: Financial records, supporting documents and all other related records pertinent to ANA grants must be maintained for a period of 3 years. If an audit is not completed by the end of the 3-year period, or if audit findings have not been resolved, records shall be retained until resolution of the audit findings.

FINANCIAL INFORMATION:

Account Identifications: 75-1636-0-1-506.

Obligations: (Grants) FY 87 $27,300,000; FY 88 est $28,257,000; and FY 89 est $27,979,000. (NOTE: The funds in this program are also available for program contracts. The amounts which can be used for such contracts cannot be predetermined.)

Range and Average of Financial Assistance: (Tribal Grants) $20,000 to $860,000; $125,000 (Urban Grants) $30,000 to $210,000; $100,000.

PROGRAM ACCOMPLISHMENTS: The program currently serves approximately 968,000 out of an estimated 1.6 million Native Americans. Financial assistance is provided for Native American community projects, research evaluation, technical assistance and

2048—Fisher—MICHIGAN

Officers and Trustee: Max M. Fisher, Pres.; Marjorie S. Fisher, V.P.; Jane Ellen Fisher Sherman, V.P.; Miles Jaffe, Treas.; Julie Cummings, Phillip Fisher, Jason Honigman.
Employer Identification Number: 381784340

2049
Fleischman (Edward I.) Foundation ¤
30350 Hunters Dr.
Farmington Hills 48018

Established in 1952 in MI.
Financial data (yr. ended 12/31/84): Assets, $1,058,446 (M); expenditures, $155,990, including $153,750 for 6 grants (high: $100,000; low: $100)
Purpose and activities: Giving primarily for Jewish welfare.
Officers: Freda Fleischman, Pres.; Marvin Fleischman, V.P.; Steven Robinson, Secy.; Fannie Robinson, Treas.
Employer Identification Number: 386091812

2050
Flint Public Trust, The
902-3 Citizen's Banking Center South
Flint 48502   (313) 232-7241

Community foundation incorporated in 1950 in MI.
Financial data (yr. ended 12/31/86): Assets, $2,725,308 (M); gifts received, $493,799; expenditures, $266,594, including $182,359 for 31 grants (high: $10,000; low: $350; average: $500–$5,000).
Purpose and activities: Giving for conservation and the environment, arts and culture, education, health, and human services.
Types of support: Seed money, matching funds, special projects.
Limitations: Giving limited to Genesee County, MI. No support for sectarian religious purposes. No grants to individuals, or for operating budgets, continuing support, annual campaigns, emergency funds, consulting services, building funds, equipment and materials, land acquisition, endowments, deficit financing, technical assistance, program-related investments, research, publications, conferences, or seminars; no loans.
Publications: Annual report, program policy statement, application guidelines.
Application information: Application form required.
   Initial approach: Letter
   Copies of proposal: 12
   1*Deadline(s):* Last Monday in Dec., Mar., June, and Sept.
   Board meeting date(s): 2nd Thursday in Jan., Apr., July, and Oct.
   Final notification: 1 month after board meeting
   Write: H. Halladay Flynn, Exec. Dir.
Officers and Trustees: C. Rees Dean, Chair.; Helen Philpott, Vice-Chair.; Margaret Stewart, Secy.; Dana A. Czmer, Treas.; William Crick, David Doherty, Raymond Finley, Helen Harris, Al R. Hobson, Jr., John D. Logan, Webb Martin.
Number of staff: 1 full-time professional; 2 part-time support.
Employer Identification Number: 386052394

2051
Ford (Benson and Edith) Fund ¤
100 Renaissance Center, 34th Fl.
Detroit 48243

Incorporated in 1943 in MI as the Hotchkiss Fund.
Donor(s): Benson Ford.†
Financial data (yr. ended 12/31/84): Assets, $4,638,667 (M); gifts received, $240,051; expenditures, $417,556, including $408,500 for 36 grants (high: $100,000; low: $1,000).
Purpose and activities: Giving for education, hospitals, community funds, and the arts, including museums; grants also for church support, child welfare, and youth agencies.
Limitations: No grants to individuals.
Application information: Funds currently committed.
Officers and Trustees: Lyunn F. Alandt,* Pres.; Pierre V. Heftler,* Secy.; Richard M. Cundiff, Treas.
Employer Indentification Number: 386066333

2052
Ford (Eleanor and Edsel) Fund ▼
100 Renaissance Center, 34th Fl.
Detroit 48243

Incorporated in 1944 in MI.
Donor(s): Eleanor Clay Ford.†
Financial data (yr. ended 12/31/85): Assets, $9,132,831 (M); gifts received, $27,228; expenditures, $621,864, including $605,000 for 7 grants (high: $170,000; low: $10,000; average: $10,000–$170,000).
Purpose and activities: Giving for higher and secondary education, the arts, including museums and an orchestra, and a hospital.
Types of support: Building funds, scholarship funds, general purposes.
Limitations: Giving primarily in MI, with emphasis on Detroit. No grants to individuals.
Application Information: Funds presently committed. Applications not accepted.
   Board meeting date(s): Oct. or Nov.
   Write: Pierre V. Heftler, Secy.
Officers: William Clay Ford,* Pres.; Pierre V. Heftler,* Secy.; Richard M. Cundiff, Treas.
Trustees:* Henry Ford II, Josephine F. Ford.
Number of staff: None.
Employer Identification Number: 386066331

2053
Ford (The Henry) II Fund ▼ ¤
100 Renaissance Center, 34th Fl.
Detroit 48243

Incorporated in 1953 in MI
Donor(s): Henry Ford II.
Financial data (yr. ended 12/31/85): Assets, $6,986,601 (M); gifts received, $673,579; expenditures, $995,799, including $979,932 for 49 grants (high: $120,000; low: $100; average: $500–$25,000).
Purpose and activities: Grants to cultural programs, education, a community fund, youth and social services, a Jewish welfare fund, civic and public affairs, and hospitals.
Limitations: No grants to individuals.

Application information: Funds presently committed.
Officers and Trustees: Henry Ford II, Pres.; Pierre V. Heftler, Secy.; Richard M. Cundiff, Treas.
Number of staff: None
Employer Identification Number: 386066332

2054
Ford Motor Company Fund ▼
The American Rd.
Dearborn 48121   (313) 845-8711

Incorporated in 1949 in MI.
Donor(s): Ford Motor Co.
Financial data (yr. ended 12/31/86): Assets, $124,109,118 (L); gifts received, $70,009,875; expenditures, $12,393,349, including $10,535,927 for 965 grants (high: $1,145,000; low: $50; average: $11,500) and $1,759,745 for 6,981 employee matching gifts.
Purpose and activities: Support for education, including matching gifts for colleges and universities and basic research grants; community funds and urban affairs; hospitals; and civic and cultural programs.
Types of support: Matching funds, research, annual campaigns, equipment, general purposes, publications, conferences and seminars, employee matching gifts, continuing support.
Limitations: Giving primarily in areas of company operations nation-wide, with special emphasis on Detroit and the rest of MI. No grants to individuals, or for building or endowment funds, scholarships, or fellowships.
Publications: Annual report, application guidelines, informational brochure.
Application information:
   Initial approach: Letter
   copies of proposal: 1
   Deadline(s): None
   Board meeting date(s): Jan., Apr., June, and Oct.
   Final notification: 6 months
   Write: Leo J. Brennan, Jr., Exec. Dir.
Officers: Donald E. Petersen,* Pres.; Robert A. Taub, V.P.; S.A. Seneker, Treas.
Trustees:* William Clay Ford, A.D. Gilmour, David N. McCammon, Henry R. Nolte, Jr., Peter J. Pestillo, Harold Poling, David Scott
Number of staff: 5
Employer Identification Number: 381459376

2055
Ford (Walter and Josephine) Fund ¤
100 Renaissance Center, 34th Fl.
Detroit 48243

Incorporated in 1951 in MI.
Donor(s): Josephine F. Ford.
Finacial data (yr. ended 12/31/84): Assets, $2,636,114 (M); gifts received, $38,161; expenditures, $365,563, including $352,733 for 105 grants (high: $55,000; low: $50).
Purpose and activities: Giving for education, community funds, the arts, including museums, and hospitals; grants also for Protestant church support, medical research, and youth and social agencies.

Figure 15.2 Sample Pages from *The Foundation Directory*

Limitations: Giving primarily in MI. No grants to individuals.
Application information: Funds currently committed.
Officers and Trustees:* Walter B. Ford II,* Pres.; Josephine F. Ford,* V.P.; Pierre V. Heftler,* Secy.; Richard M. Cundiff, Treas.
Employer Identification Number: 386066334

2056
Ford (William and Martha) Fund ¤
100 Renaissance Center, 34th Fl.
Detroit 48243   (313) 259-7777

Incorporated in 1953 in MI.
Donor(s): William Clay Ford, Martha F. Ford.
Financial data (yr. ended 12/31/85): Assets, $2,936,790 (M); gifts received, $188,080; expenditures, $560,731, including $554,964 for 50 grants (high: $100,000; low: $50).
Purpose and activities: Giving primarily for higher and other education, and hospitals and medical research; support also for community funds, child welfare, church support, the arts, and youth and social service agencies.
Limitations: No grants to individuals.
Applications information: Awards generally limited to organizations known to the donors.
  Initial approach: Letter
  Deadline(s): None
  Write: Pierre V. Heftler, Secy.
Officers: William Clay Ford,* Pres.; Pierre V. Heftler,* Secy.; Richard M. Cundiff, Treas.
Trustees:* Martha F. Ford.
Employer Identification Number: 386066335

2057
Fremont Area Foundation, The ▼
108 South Stewart
Fremont 49412   (616) 924-5350

Community foundation incorporated in 1951 in MI.
Financial data (yr. ended 12/31/86): Assets, $25,343,174 (M); gifts received, $1,493,253; expenditures, $1,231,272, including $941,408 for 67 grants (high: $276,034; low: $175) and $40,075 for 82 grants to individuals.
Purpose and activities: Support for health, education, social welfare, civic responsibilities, arts and culture, character building, and rehabilitation.
Types of support: Operating budgets, seed money, emergency funds, student aid, matching funds, consulting services, equipment, general purposes, renovation projects, special projects.
Limitations: Giving primarily in Newaygo County, MI. No grants to individuals (except for scholarships initiated by the foundation), or for building or endowment funds, or research; no loans.
Publications: Annual report, application guidelines, informational brochure.
Application information:
  Initial approach: Letter or telephone to arrange interview
  Copies of proposal: 8
  Deadline(s): Submit proposal preferably by Oct. 15

Board meeting date(s): Usually in Feb., Apr., July, and Nov.
  Final notification: 3 months
  Write: Bertram W. Vermeulen, Exec. Dir.
Officers: Kenneth B. Peirce,* Pres.; Maynard DeKryger,* V.P.; Bertram W. Vermeulen, Secy. and Exec. Dir.; Virginia Gerber,* Treas.
Trustees:* Gay G. Cummings, Richard Hogancamp, Douglas M. Jeannero, Mary Kendall, L. Max Lee, Gerald E. Martin, Dean H. Morehouse, Dennis C. Nelson, William A. Rottman, Ross G. Scott, Philip T. Smith, Robert A. Stewart.
Number of staff: 3 full-time professional; 1 part-time support.
Employer Identification Number: 381443367

2058
Frey Foundation ¤
200 Ottawa Ave.
Grand Rapids 49503   (616) 451-7212

Established in 1974 in MI.
Donor(s): Edward J. Frey, Sr.
Financial data (yr. ended 12/31/85): Assets, $93,113 (M); gifts received, $220,000; expenditures, $141,462, including $139,435 for 49 grants (high: $25,000; low: $10)
Purpose and activities: Giving primarily for the arts, Protestant religion, and social services.
Types of support: General purposes.
Application information:
  Deadline(s): None.
  Write: Edward J. Frey, Sr., Pres.
Officers and Directors: Edward J. Frey, Sr., Pres.; Frances T. Frey, V.P.; David G. Frey, Secy.-Treas.; Edward J. Frey, Jr., John M. Frey, Mary Frey Rottschafer.
Employer Identification Number: 237094777

2059
Fruehauf Foundation, The
100 Maple Park Blvd., Suite 106
St. Clair Shores 48081-2254   (313) 774-5130

Incorporated in 1968 in MI.
Donor(s): Angela Fruehauf, and others.
Financial data (yr. ended 12/31/85): Assets, $1,570,467 (M); expenditures, $161,379, including $151,775 for 95 grants (high: $18,750; low: $100).
Purpose and activities: Grants primarily for educational institutions, cultural programs, hospitals, health agencies, welfare, including youth agencies, economic research, and churches and religious programs.
Limitations: Giving primarily in MI.
Application information:
  Initial approach: Letter
  Deadline(s): None; applications reviewed monthly
  Board meeting date(s): As required
  Write: Elizabeth J. Woods, Asst. Secy.
Officers and Trustees: Harvey C. Fruehauf, Jr., Pres.; Ann F. Bowman, V.P. and Treas.; Barbara F. Bristol, V.P.; Frederick R. Keydel, Secy.
Employer Identification Number: 237015744

2060
Gabooney Foundation ¤
c/o Michael D. Gibson
2100 Detroit Bank & Trust Bldg.
Detroit 48226

Established in 1981 in MI.
Donor(s): David L. Gamble.
Financial data (yr. ended 3/31/85): Assets, $66,957 (M); gifts received, $115,000; expenditures, $160,675, including $158,134 for 45 grants (high: $5,000; low: $500).
Purpose and activities: Giving primarily for hospitals, social services, and education.
Officers and Trustees: David L. Gamble, Pres.; Michael D. Gibson, Secy. and Mgr.; Robert B. Deans, Jr., Christopher I. Gamble, David B. Gamble, Kimberly N. Gamble, Richard J. Temkow.
Employer Identification Number: 382382126

2061
Garb Foundation, The ¤
c/o E. James Gamble
400 Renaissance Center, 35th Fl.
Detroit 48243

Established in 1983 in MI.
Donor(s): Melvin Garb.
Financial data (yr. ended 1/31/86): Assets, $50,009 (M); gifts received, $15,366; expenditures, $115,000, including $115,000 for 6 grants (high: $55,000; low: $10,000).
Purpose and activities: Giving primarily for Jewish welfare funds and other Jewish associations.
Types of support: General purposes.
Application information:
  Deadline(s): None.
Officers and Trustees: Melvin Garb, Pres.; Harrison Levin, Secy.; Genesse G. Levin, Treas.
Employer Identification Number: 382450840

2062
General Motors Cancer Research Foundation Inc.
13-145 General Motors Bldg.
3044 West Grand Blvd.
Detroit 48202   (313) 556-4260

Established about 1978 in MI.
Donor(s): General Motors Corp.
Financial data (yr. ended 12/31/85): Assets, $3,837,956 (M); gifts received, $2,249,745; expenditures, $1,392,489, including $390,000 for 3 grants to individuals.
Purpose and activities: Awards to individuals for "contributions to the prevention, detection, or treatment of cancer in order to stimulate further research in this field." Candidates for prizes must be nominated by invited proposers.
Types of support: Grants to individuals.
Limitations: No grants for scholarships or fellowships; no loans.
Publications: Application guidelines.
Application information:
  Deadline(s): Oct., for prize nominations
  Board meeting date(s): Apr. or May
  Final notification: June
  Write: J.J. Nowicki, Mgr.

Source: Reprinted with permission from *The Foundation Directory,* 17th ed., the Foundation Center, New York, NY, 1987.

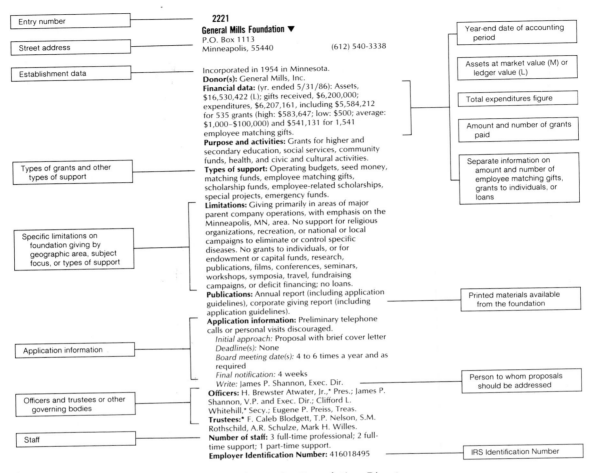

Figure 15.3 Explanation of Sample Entry from *The Foundation Directory*

Source: Reprinted with permission from *The Foundation Directory*, 17th ed., the Foundation Center, New York, NY, 1987.

obvious, but a sound understanding of research principles is also directly applicable to grants for service delivery. In seeking funds, the prospective grantee must identify a problem, hone this into a well-defined and manageable topic, develop objectives for the project, search the literature to devise a method of intervention, and plan an evaluation strategy. Furthermore, just as one research study leads to new questions for study, lessons learned in one grant-funded project lead to new ideas for further projects.

What we will describe in this section is a number of key elements of the grant-funding process. They are not a series of sequential steps but rather a number of separate and interconnected elements that can be accomplished in different orders at different times. Some are ongoing activities of agencies while others are specific things that must be done at a particular point. Together, they culminate in and make possible the actual writing of the grant proposal, which we discuss in the next section. As a way of promoting the concept of the generation of grant proposals as an ongoing part of agency activities, the use of a *Proposal Development Workbook* (PDW) is recommended (Bauer, 1988). This looseleaf binder becomes the mortar that holds the building blocks of a proposal together. As the proposal develops from a vague idea to a full-blown project complete with demonstration of need, evidence of community support, funding source possibilities, and much more, the PDW is used to organize all of the things that go into a successful proposal. As the various components of the proposal are obtained or completed, they are placed conveniently in the PDW. Agency staff should be encouraged to be watchful for items to contribute. For example, favorable news stories about the proposed project are effective demonstrations of community support that help to influence funding decision makers. Some of the materials in the PDW for one project might also be useful for a later project.

Identifying the Topic

Before we can begin filling our PDW, of course, we have to have an idea that can be developed into a fundable proposal. Problems that need to be solved exist in abundance, and many sources of research problems are discussed in Chapter 4. What tends to be in short supply, however, are innovative ways of attacking them. One approach is to organize "brainstorming" sessions (Bauer, 1988). Members of the staff are broken up into small groups and told to develop as many possible solutions or approaches to the selected problem as they can. All of these proposed solutions are recorded for fur-

ther consideration. The goal here is to generate ideas, not come to a consensus as to which solution is "best." In fact, it is desirable to maintain alternative approaches to the problem. One or another may be more palatable politically to a particular funding source, and the chances of obtaining a grant can be significantly enhanced by choosing a solution favored by a funding source.

Once ideas are produced in the brainstorming sessions, they need to be evaluated. Thanks to group dynamics, wildly impractical or just plain stupid ideas usually never make it out of the group. Realistically, however, some of the ideas will be better than others. We want to sort out the best few to save for building into a proposal. One important part of this evaluation is to work out cost–benefit or cost-effectiveness analyses (see Chapter 12). The cost–benefit analyses will tell us if the suggested solutions to the problem are economically viable. With any luck one or more of the considered approaches will show benefits outweighing costs. The cost–benefit analyses of the chosen approach will also be important later as it becomes one of the arguments for funding the proposal. Cost-effectiveness analyses, of course, allow us to select the approaches that produce the greatest effect for the least cost. Being able to argue that the project for which you are seeking funding was the most cost effective of the several considered can only be looked on favorably by the decision makers at the funding source.

Needs Assessment

One of the most important components of a successful grant application is establishing the existence of some problem or need that requires amelioration. All funding sources must operate within their annual budgets, so there is fierce competition for available funds. If you can make the case that the problem or need you wish to address is most pressing, you will have greatly increased your chances of being funded. There are a variety of ways of making a case for your proposal, and successful ones include information from more than one source. The core of the evidence supporting the existence of need will likely come from a *needs-assessment survey.* With a properly drawn sample, it is possible to make quite accurate estimates concerning the extent of some need within a given population. Additional supporting evidence can come from *key informants,* or people who are particularly close to and knowledgeable about the problem at issue. *Community forums* can be held to gather testimony about the problem. Examples of individuals suffering from the problem can be used as *case studies,* which illustrate the problem in more human terms than abstract statistics. Finally, data from *public records* may be used as additional evidence of need. Bauer (1988) makes the useful analogy between the grant-seeker and a lawyer preparing a case for trial. Each wishes to prepare as persuasive a case as possible to influence a set of decision makers (jury or review panel) to reach the desired conclusion. In the case of obtaining grants, documenting need is a crucial part of making your case. Just as it is not enough for a defendant to be innocent of the crime for which he is charged to be found not guilty by a jury, it is not enough for a need to exist in order to convince a funding source to fund a proposal that deals with it. In both situations, evidence must be gathered and the case presented to the decision makers with great care in order to generate a successful verdict.

In some cases, it may be possible to obtain a grant to conduct needs-assess-

ment research. Recall that needs assessment is one of the focal areas considered in this text. Especially with problems about which we know little, funding agencies might be willing to fund a survey to obtain more information. In other cases, a funding agency may require that a needs-assessment survey be included as part of a larger funding proposal which may include a service delivery program that affects the problem. In any event, needs assessment often plays an important part in the grant-funding process.

Specifying the Organization's Mission

Not only must you document that there is a need for services or research, but you must also convince the funding source that your organization is the proper site for a program to address that problem. This entails demonstrating to the funding source that the problem described in the needs assessment is within your organization's domain or mission. Many organizations such as universities have formal mission statements that appear in official publications. However, such statements are often global in nature and may not be adequate for your purpose. At a minimum, the mission statement should include how and why the organization was started and its primary goals. Generally, funding sources look more favorably on organizations with a history and a track record of accomplishment related to the project to be funded. A new organization might have to work hard to prove its viability. The mission statement should also address current activities of the agency, because organizations change with the changing needs of society. Therefore, an organization that originated for one purpose may be doing very different things today. Lastly, the mission statement should include future plans. Funding sources like organizations that appear to be serious and well managed. One way of demonstrating this is by showing that your group plans its future moves carefully.

Another way to convince a funding source that your agency is best suited for a particular project is to focus on the "uniqueness" of your agency. The goal here is to set your agency apart from others that might be similar. There is a tendency to think that one agency is not that much different from others that provide similar services. But with some thought (and perhaps another brainstorming session) you should be able to come up with some things about your agency that make it special in some way. Perhaps it is your geographical location, such as in a particularly remote area or in proximity to a large minority population. Possibly, there is something unusual about your clientele or staff. Or maybe your problem-solving approach is different and uniquely successful. With a little careful consideration, you should be able to develop ways to portray your agency as uniquely qualified to address the need you have documented.

Developing a Program

The most crucial component of any proposal is the research or service project itself. Having established a need, it is necessary to translate that need into specific outcomes for the project and to develop a plan by which those objectives can be achieved. In the case of a research grant, such as a proposal to evaluate the effectiveness of a client advocacy program in a state department of mental health, the task is fundamentally one of preparing a detailed blueprint of the stages of the research process presented in the first chapter. Hypotheses must be developed and a method of testing these hypotheses devised. Issues of subject selection, study design, and data collection and analysis must be taken into account. A service delivery grant requires specification of exactly what will be done to address the need. Direct connections between the goals of the project and the program content must be explicated. Even though service delivery may be the primary emphasis of the proposal, most grants require an evaluation component; so a strategy for monitoring the program and securing data for evaluation purposes must be included.

An important consideration is the time-sequencing of the project. Before subjects can be interviewed, interviewers must be trained and instruments need to be selected or developed. How long will each of these steps take? Must certain staff be hired before the activities can take place? Accounting for all these details requires developing a work plan. The work plan shows the flow of procedures from beginning to end of the project and identifies how the various activities fit together into a coordinated plan. Although a simple time schedule with beginning and ending dates for various phases may suffice for some projects, the use of graphic representation such as a flowchart is often preferred. Such charts can clearly portray the relationships among elements of the project, when each element begins and ends, and which elements overlap. Planning the steps of the project and determining the amount of time for each requires a great deal of effort, but it is effort well spent. For one thing, it forces the agency to analyze how the various parts of the program do fit together. It also serves to uncover difficulties before the proposal is written and approved, avoiding, for example, the discovery midway through the project that some significant and expensive component was overlooked. Finally, when it comes time actually to develop a budget and ask for dollars, the plan serves as justification for the resources.

A number of tools have been developed to aid in developing the work plan. Two of the most common tools are PERT (Program Evaluation Review Technique) and CPM (Critical Path Method). In using the techniques, a collection of tasks is specified that, when completed, results in a final outcome, which in this case would be a completed project. Circles, rectangles, and arrows are used to graphically illustrate the progression of events. The technical details of PERT and CPM are beyond the scope of this text. Computer programs are also available that employ these program-planning principles. For IBM and compatibles there are *Super-Project* from SORCIM/IUS and *Microsoft Project* from Micro Software. Apple has a similar program for its Macintosh line called MacProject. A major advantage of these programs is that you can readily see the budgetary impact of changing situations by manipulating the variables that effect the budget. For example, you could readily determine how much an extra full- or part-time employee would cost over the life of the program by inputting a single different number. Likewise, all other costs can be easily evaluated and a final budget prepared far more accurately than without this useful technology.

Targeting a Funding Source

By this point, you will have amassed the raw material of a proposal, including a clear idea of the problem, data on the need, the preferred program alternative, and cost estimates for the components of that alternative. Before one can organize it into a final proposal, though, consideration must be given to potential funding sources. As a first step, the most appropriate organizations should be identified from among the myriad government agencies and private foundations. However, sending out numerous duplicate proposals to whichever funding sources appear most receptive probably won't work. Proposals must be tuned specifically for each funding source to which they are submitted because each one has different rules and needs. This means some research is required into the nature of the various funding sources—what are their rules of submission, what project areas have they funded in the past, and do they have a particular political viewpoint. Basic issues of locating a funding source were discussed in the first part of this chapter. Once you have a list of possible funding agencies, there are a few ways to narrow the list. One is whether your organization has any advocates who are associated with the funding agency or can make contact with the agency.

By *advocates*, we are referring to individuals who can not only speak on your behalf to funding sources but also offer guidance and advice throughout the funding process. Previously, we described the grant seeker preparing a proposal as analogous to a lawyer preparing a case for trial. That analogy applies once again in the area of using advocates to help make your case for the grant. The lawyer uses witnesses to help convince a jury. Advocates are the grant seekers witnesses, and they supply testimony favorable to your proposal to funding sources. Like the attorney, grant seekers need to envision how advocates might be viewed and select those who can make the most favorable impression because advocates can play a key role in the final out-come.

The best advocates are people who are favorably disposed toward your agency and the proposed project and who have some influence on the funding source. In this respect securing grant funding is a political process, requiring strategies similar to those used by prac-titioners in community practice. The range of people who could help influence a funding source is so vast as to be diffi-cult to discuss in general terms, but some possibilities include people with member-ship on both your agency's and a funding source's governing boards, members of your staff (don't forget spouses) with spe-cial contacts at funding sources, politi-cians at all levels who support your ef-forts, and agency volunteers who may have useful contacts.

Once you have identified your advo-cates and which funding sources they can help you with, it is time to put them to use. Advocates can be helpful in a va-riety of ways. At the initial stage, they can help put you in contact with repre-sentatives of the funding sources for the purpose of establishing a working rela-tionship. They can set up appointments for you with funding sources, they may even accompany you while visiting a funding source, and they may know someone at the funding source who can help ensure that your proposal receives a fair and complete review. When you ac-tually write the proposal, advocates can provide letters of support for you. All of these efforts are intended to increase the likelihood that a proposal will receive at-tention. Funding agencies have limited resources, and they receive many more proposals than they can possibly fund. No matter how numerous or powerful, no collection of advocates will substitute for a worthy project and a well-prepared pro-posal. In all of this we are assuming that those two conditions are met. Advocates are important because a meritorious pro-posal is in competition with other deserv-ing ones. It is when decision-makers are forced to choose from among numerous worthy proposals that advocates come into play.

Contacting and Visiting Funding Sources

Once you have identified a particular agency or foundation as a likely funding source, you should contact them since this can substantially increase the chances of funding (Krathwohl, 1988). If there is an effective advocate available, they could make the first contact. Other-wise, it should be done by letter. Figure 15.4 contains a sample letter with sug-gested content. Note that it is simple and to the point, but it informs the agency of your intent, and it will obtain for you some much needed forms and other in-formation. Assuming that the agency's initial response is not negative, such as "there are no funds available," it is then time to arrange for a personal visit. Call the agency and request an appointment. Before the meeting, though, you have some homework to do.

Note that the letter in Figure 15.4 re-quests a list of last year's grant re-cipients. Before visiting the agency, you will want to contact one or more of these successful organizations. The range of useful information they can supply is vast. They have experience with the agency, and there is no substitute for that in learning the ins and outs of successful grantsmanship with that particular agency. Each agency develops its own particular style of operating as well as a perspective on problems and ways to solve them. It is these bureaucratic idio-

Date:

Name
Title
Address

Dear _____ :

    Our organization is interested in carrying out a project
under your program title _____ . The project will
deal with meeting the needs in the area of _____ .

    Please add me to your mailing list to receive the necessary
application forms, program guidelines and any existing
priorities statements or information that you feel would be
helpful to me. Please include a list of last year's grant
recipients under this program.

    If my project is ineligible under your current guidelines or
there are no funds available, could you please refer me to a
more appropriate agency?

    I have enclosed a self-addressed stamped envelope for your
convenience in returning the list of successful grantees. Thank
you for your cooperation and assistance in this matter.

                Sincerely,

                Name
                Title
                Phone Number

Figure 15.4 Sample Letter to a Federal Agency for Mailing Lists and Past
Grantees

Source: David G. Bauer, *The "How To" Grants Manual*, p. 107. Copyright ©
1988 by American Council on Education/Macmillan Publishing Co. Reprinted by
permission.

syncracies that you want to learn about from the past grant recipients so that you can tailor your proposal to best fit what the agency is looking for.

With your homework now complete, it is time to make the actual visit to the agency. This visit is to accomplish three general purposes. First, it will confirm or

TABLE 15.1   Suggested Questions for Visit to Agency

Do you agree that the need addressed by our project is important?

Your average award in this area last year was X dollars; do you expect that to change?

How will successful grantees from last year affect people putting in new or first applications? Will last year's grantees be in competition with me or have funds been set aside? If so, how much is left for new awards?

Are there any unannounced programs or unsolicited proposal funds in your agency to fund an important project like ours?

What is the most common mistake or flaw in proposals you receive?

Are there any areas you would like to see addressed in a proposal that may have been overlooked by the other grantees or applicants?

We have developed several approaches to this needs area. You may know whether or not one of our approaches has been tried. Could you review our concept paper and give us guidance?

Would you review or critique our proposal if we got it to you early?

Would you recommend a previously funded proposal for us to read for format and style?

What changes do you expect in types or number of awards this year (fewer new awards versus continuing awards, etc.)?

Is there a relationship between the type of grant programs and awards?

The guidelines call for X copies of the proposal. Could you use more? If I provided all copies, may I bind them in an inexpensive binder? What type do you prefer?

Will I create any problems by using tabs or dividers in my proposal?

Source   Bauer, David G., *The "How To" Grants Manual*, pp. 120–122. Copyright 1988 by the American Council on Education/Macmillan Publishing Co. Reprinted by permission.

reject the selection of this agency as a likely funding source. With large federal agencies that offer funding under numerous special programs, information gained during your visit assures that you are applying to the agency most appropriate for your project (Krathwohl, 1988). For example, a research proposal would likely be rejected if submitted to a program designed to fund action-oriented projects even though it might have been funded under some other program controlled by the same agency. Although agency personnel will sometimes route a misdi-

rected proposal to the proper program, such cannot be assumed. It is always better to be sure you have submitted your proposal to the most fitting program in the most appropriate agency. Depending on their reaction, you should leave the agency with a pretty good sense of the chances of receiving funding from them. Second, the visit supplies you with additional information on how best to tailor the proposal to the agency's special needs, thus increasing the chances for funding (Table 15.1 contains some suggested questions). Krathwohl (1988) suggests that agency personnel may be enthusiastically helpful for some proposals because funding successful projects reflects positively on the agency and its employees. He urges seeking out and obtaining as much assistance as agency staff are willing to provide. Third, the visit provides a personal touch for your proposal when it is submitted. Instead of representing a faceless organization, the proposal will be from people who are known personally and who made an impressive presentation of a serious need and their plans to fill it.

At some point during your visit, you will have the opportunity to discuss your plans with one or more agency executives. This, quite obviously, is a very important part of the visit and should be prepared for carefully. The most important part of this presentation is the demonstration of need, so present all of the evidence you can marshal. Even if the agency has reservations about either your organization or your plans to satisfy the need, if you have convinced them of a genuine need, they are more likely to work with you to modify your plans rather than give you an outright rejection. Be sure to use whatever video aids are appropriate since a visual impact can be effective and helps to demonstrate thorough preparation.

Writing the Grant Proposal

Having identified a topic, collected supporting documentation that confirms the need for action or research, formulated a method for addressing the problem, and targeted a funding source, you have completed the groundwork. Actually writing the proposal now, with the information gleaned from these earlier steps, should be a relatively straightforward endeavor but one that requires a great deal of care.

In a number of places in this book, we have emphasized the point that a very important part of both research and practice is to communicate to others what you plan to do and what you have accomplished. Such communication can occur at a number of different points in the research process, of which we will emphasize two in this chapter: preparing a grant proposal and writing a research report. If you cannot prepare a comprehendible and convincing grant proposal, you will not gain the financial support needed to complete a research project. If you cannot write a clear and thorough research report, your research findings—no matter how important—will not be translated into policies and practices by practitioners. We will not pretend that we can make you an accomplished writer by reading this chapter, but we hope to offer some useful suggestions and point you in the direction of useful resources.

Appearance and Writing Style

The old adage that you cannot judge a book by its cover may be true, but people routinely make such superficial judgments anyway. Because of this, both outward appearance and style of presentation in a grant proposal are crucial to success. Because demand for grant monies is great, funding agencies may look for any excuse to reject proposals in order to reduce the number that have to be given full review. Failure to follow any guideline may be seized on as a reason not to consider your proposal further. So, to begin with, follow the guidelines to the letter, even if they appear senseless to you. In particular, be careful about length restrictions. Submitting an overly long proposal, no matter how worthy, will result in certain rejection.

Reviewers have a limited amount of time to review many proposals, so you want to make your proposal attractive and capable of being "skimmed" easily. Using uncomplicated sentences and short paragraphs works toward this end. Underlining key phrases or the use of "bullets" (solid dots used to set off a series of points in a text) for highlighting purposes helps too. Using different type styles, boldface headings, and variable margins and spacing further contribute to overall appearance and readability. Don't forget to include charts and graphs. They enhance visual impact and can convey much information in a far more abbreviated form than text. For example, a graph depicting the increasing incidence of some problem is far more effective at making the point than a simple reference to that fact in the text. The graph is also less likely to be unintentionally passed over by busy reviewers.

Not too long ago, great effort and a professional printer were required to produce a proposal with these desirable features. The advent of word processing and computerized desktop publishing systems, however, has placed the ability to produce high-quality documents in the hands of most agencies. Such systems are strongly recommended for producing your grant proposals. You can bet that at least some of the grant applicants you will be competing against will produce a slick and attractive grant request on a computer. If your agency does not have this kind of technical support available, it may be worth contracting with another organization that can assist you in preparing a polished document. While it is unlikely that you could secure funding strictly to purchase such equipment, you may be able to incorporate acquisition of desktop publishing equipment into a future grant request.

Beyond appearance, the style of the text is important. A dull, lifeless proposal, regardless of merit, will have less chance of being funded than one that exudes interest and excitement. Use action words and express emotions wherever appropriate. You want to interest the reviewers in the problem and your innovative approach to it. If you can reach the reviewers at an emotional level, it may positively influence your chances of being funded. Citing dialogue is one effective approach: Presenting possible future clients describing their problems in their *own words* is likely to be better received than some third-party description. As a general rule, try to maintain a fairly "light," readable style.

As in all writing, a sense of one's audience is crucial to preparing a successful grant proposal. Of particular importance is the fact that review panels, for both federal agencies and private foundations, may contain at least some nonspecialists (Krathwohl, 1988). This means that you must be careful to communicate your intentions in language that will be clear to someone who is not a professional in your field. More specifically, jargon should be avoided or, if unavoidable, explained. Beyond that, no assumptions can be made regarding such things as prior knowledge of the problem, its importance, previous approaches, measurement devices, or analytical techniques. Everything must be explained in detail and in terms the typical layperson can understand. Doing so and at the same time not boring the specialists requires a difficult balancing act in your writing.

The writing of the proposal requires such extreme care because the proposal represents you and your agency to the funding source. It will be seen as an indicator of the quality of your personnel and of their work. A great idea presented in a sloppy proposal will not get the funding it deserves. If you develop a worthy idea, it deserves to be properly presented so that funding can be obtained to implement it. The ultimate goal, after all, is not just to get grant money but to finance programs that accomplish some good.

Once a draft of the proposal is completed and before it is submitted, it is a good idea to have several members of your agency who were not directly involved in its production proofread it. The reason for having people unfamiliar with the proposal do this is that they will approach it much as a reviewer will, with no prior knowledge of its content. The proposal will have to stand on its own just as it will during review by the funding source. In addition to looking for the usual typographical errors and other grammatical failings, the proofreaders should be assessing the total package for content and presentation. Is all of the needed information included? Is the problem adequately documented by the needs assessment? Does the proposed project logically address the problem identified in the needs assessment? Is the budget adequately detailed to justify the requested funds? These and many other questions regarding the content of the proposal should be addressed at this final proofreading stage.

All of these suggestions regarding the appearance, style, and presentation of a proposal should not distract from the central importance of the proposed project itself. No amount of fancy wrappings will make up for an ill-conceived idea. The importance of these matters is to separate your deserving proposal from all of the other deserving proposals to the point that yours gets funded.

Components of the Proposal

A typical proposal to a government agency or major foundation will contain most or all of the components shown in Table 15.2, probably in the order listed.

TABLE 15.2 Typical Proposal Contents and Sequence

1. Cover letter	6. Methods
2. Title page	7. Evaluation
3. Summary	8. Future funding
4. Problem/Need	9. Dissemination
5. Objectives	10. Budget
11. Attachments	

The precise components will depend on the requirements of the specific agency or organization and on whether the proposal is to fund research, service delivery, or both. Notice that the order in Table 15.2 is quite different from the grant development sequence that we have presented. This is because the proposal is organized according to the needs of the reader and not necessarily according to the order in which one prepares the parts.

The Cover Letter The cover letter is probably the last item to be completed, but because it is the first thing read by those who will evaluate your proposal, it is crucial. One very important function of the cover letter is to remind agency personnel of who you are and that you bothered to visit the agency and take into account their suggestions when designing the proposal. The idea is to show that you have done everything right (according to the agency's views) so that, now, your proposal deserves careful consideration.

Title Page The title page is often a standard form supplied by the granting organization. Table 15.3 illustrates the common elements of a title page. A good title is one that describes the project and communicates the anticipated results. Thus, the title, "Reducing Homicide in Family Disputes," is preferable to, "Applying Mental Health Crisis Intervention Techniques to Family Violence," because the first title indicates what the project

TABLE 15.3   Title Page Specifications

1. Title of project
2. Program being applied to
3. Grant Program contact person
4. Name, position, and institutional affiliation of principal investigator
5. Have you applied for funding for this project from any other source? If yes, name source
6. Proposed start-up date and anticipated completion date

plans to achieve with the funds while the second merely describes a service. Beyond serving as a label for your proposal, the title page is used to route your application to the various officials who must process it. The page should clearly identify the applicant's name and address as well as the specific program being applied for and the granting organization contact person.

Summary   Most granting agencies request a brief summary of the proposal so that agency administrators can quickly assess who should receive a copy. This should be no more than a paragraph and should briefly mention all elements of the proposal: research problem or service to be delivered, methods used, and anticipated results.

The Problem or Needs Statement   This is where you really begin to make your case. What should go here has already been discussed in the previous section while analyzing the needs assessment and mission of the organization. What must be done in the proposal is put clearly and coherently into prose what the problem is and why your agency can help solve it.

Objectives   This is where you state very clearly and precisely what it is your proposal will achieve—exactly what re-

search will be done or what service will be delivered. These need to be very concrete and achievable. No funding agency will be impressed if your objective is to discover the "real" truth about spouse abuse. A more concrete objective would be to learn about the role of economic independence in the ability of women to avoid abuse. List all the objectives with no more than a sentence or two devoted to each. They should be presented in the order of their potential importance and contribution, with the most important listed first. In a research proposal, this section would contain theoretical considerations and the development of hypotheses.

Methods   The proposal should include a complete description of how you plan to conduct research or provide a service. In a research proposal, this section would contain all the mechanics of carrying out the research: sample size, sampling technique, research design, and statistical procedures to be used in analyzing the data.

Evaluation   Federal funding sources in particular place great emphasis on evaluation. It is politically (as well as practically) important to gather evidence that shows that the funded activities are achieving the objectives claimed for them. For this reason, virtually all proposals must contain adequate methods for assessing whether and how well your program is achieving its goals. In the case of a service delivery grant, this typically involves conducting research to assess whether the program resulted in the improvements or changes that were intended. A review of Chapter 12 along with some of the suggested readings should be helpful in preparing this part of the proposal.

Future Funding A grant, by its very nature, is a one-time dispersal of funds. Human service organizations, on the other hand, typically support ongoing programs that require continuous funding. The disjunction between the one-time grant and the on-going needs of the program should be addressed in the proposal. When the grant money ends, what then? The agency will want to see that you have thought through this problem and laid plans to deal with it. Plans for local funding, other grants, fund raisers, telethons, whatever, should be included. Agencies like to see lasting and successful programs develop out of their "seed" money. Inclusion of money in the budget for future fund-raising efforts is perfectly appropriate.

Dissemination Dissemination refers to spreading the word about your research, service delivery program, the grant, the funding source, and hopefully, your successes. Inclusion of comments regarding dissemination of results is looked on as an indicator of confidence. Agencies like positive publicity about the "good" that they do and tend to look favorably on opportunities to obtain it. This is a small thing and alone it will not get you a grant, but successful grantsmanship is ultimately a result of doing a lot of little things right and better than the competition.

Budget A carefully detailed budget is an important part of any grant proposal because granting agencies are punctilious in their accounting demands of grant recipients. Essentially, every dollar you request must be accounted for. The methods section of your proposal, where you spell out precisely what the program will do, provides the guide for developing the budget. All costs that will be incurred must be identified and included. Novice grant seekers often underestimate costs or leave out expenses. Because the developers of the project are usually researchers or practitioners and not financial officers, it is important to seek consultation in determining costs. Your organization may have standard formulas for fixing fringe benefit costs, travel, and overhead and may require bidding procedures for purchasing equipment. Be realistic. Promising the moon on a shoestring budget will not endear your proposal to an agency. It will merely be seen as the amateurish effort it is. If costs are reasonable and well justified, it may be possible to negotiate reductions if the total amount is too high.

Attachments The attachments section provides important supporting evidence for claims made elsewhere in the proposal. Bauer (1988) suggests the following as appropriate for inclusion in the attachments section: needs assessment and other supporting research, resumes of key personnel, minutes of advisory committee meetings, names of board members, auditor's financial statement, letters of support from advocates, a copy of your tax-exempt status from the Internal Revenue Service, any pictures or diagrams, and copies of any organization publications.

Documentation of community support is also very important. Some funding sources demand a demonstration that the community is behind a project, but it should be provided even for those who do not require it. Evidence of community support generally comes from two sources: advisory board minutes and newspaper articles. Many agencies of the type we are discussing here have advisory boards that oversee their operations. These boards, composed primarily of other professional service providers, former consumers of the agency's services, and people whose expertise lies in the area of fund-raising, hold regular meetings to discuss the activities of the agencies they oversee. Minutes from meetings when the project for which you are seeking funding was discussed can be used as evidence of community support. Newspaper articles reflecting positively on the project form the other major source of evidence of community support. You can actively seek publicity for the agency and the project you are trying to get funded.

Submitting the Proposal

Public funding sources have quite rigid guidelines, not to mention firm deadlines, that govern the submission process. You, of course, will have obtained these along with all the other information from the funding agency. Because deadlines are involved, the proposal should be submitted either in person or by registered mail. In either case, it is a good idea to telephone the funding source a bit later and check to see that they received the proposal.

With many of the private foundations, it is difficult to generalize about submission procedures, as each foundation has its own peculiar way of doing things. This places an added burden on the grant seeker. In some cases, private foundations do not require the lengthy and detailed proposals that we have described. They do not have the resources in the form of reviewers to evaluate such complex documents. Instead, they rely on what is called the *letter proposal*. As the name suggests, the letter proposal outlines the need, your plans to meet that need, and your grant request all in a fairly brief letter of no more than a few pages in length. Even something as important as the budget is abbreviated. Usually only the estimated total cost is all that is required. Rather than the voluminous detail characteristic of a federal proposal, each important issue in the letter proposal must fit into a paragraph. Brevity and clarity are the watchwords of a letter proposal.

Because you have done your homework, there is a good chance that the grant will be approved, but what if it is not? Understandable disappointment aside, rejection is an opportunity to learn. Contact the funding source and inquire about what was wrong (and right) about your proposal. Learn from them how to do a better job the next time. And remember, the only grant seekers never turned down are those who never submit a proposal. It is the nature of the game.

Grantsmanship is an exciting and increasingly essential element of human service research and practice. We hope that this chapter has made the prospect of preparing a grant proposal a less daunting one. Remember, however, that we have been able to present only a limited amount of material on obtaining grants. We strongly recommend that you read carefully a complete book devoted to grantsmanship such as one of those listed in "For Further Reading" at the end of this chapter.

Writing a Research Report

One of the strengths of the scientific method is the public character of scientific results. Publicizing scientific findings accomplishes several important functions. First, unless research findings are made public, they accomplish little social good. How can others learn from the findings of research if those findings are withheld? Clearly publication of research findings is necessary in order to apply those findings in developing programs and policies.

Second, publication allows the process of replication to ferret out errors, frauds, and falsehoods that inevitably creep into the products of human endeavor. The self-correcting nature of science that has contributed so much to its success depends on the wide dissemination of research results.

Third, publication of research findings makes attempted suppression of those findings more difficult. Recall that in Chapter 12 we noted that historically this had been a problem for evaluation research reports. A few copies were supplied to a sponsor who then had complete control over what was (or was not) done with the results. Broader publicity concerning research findings makes it more likely that they will come to the attention of someone who will use them.

Finally, the publication of research findings, like any written publication, is an effort at persuasion. It is an attempt to influence the readers to accept your ideas or conclusions. In Chapter 3 we discussed the idea of advocacy in research and concluded that human service researchers are especially likely to advocate some particular use of their research findings. To be effective, advocates must communicate positions to others, and one major mode of communication is through the written word. An interesting, well-written, and smooth presentation is more likely to be persuasive.

Given the central role communication of research results plays in the whole scientific enterprise, the proper preparation of the research report is vital. In this section we will assume that you have learned appropriate English grammar and usage. The complexity of the English language being what it is, we strongly recommend that you consult one or more of the style manuals listed in "For Further Reading." No matter how well you think you write, your writing will benefit from a regular perusal of a style manual.

Consideration of the Audience

An important consideration before beginning any writing assignment is the likely audience. For the writing to be most effective, it must be tailored to the intended audience. Although it is possible to identify several distinct audiences for research reports, the most significant distinction is between a *professional* audience and a *lay* audience. Within these two broad categories there are, of course, several more specific audiences that may require special consideration. Not all professionals are created equal. Even in the social sciences and human services, those pursuing research careers will develop a different expertise and professional jargon than those following a more practice-oriented career. Likewise, those concentrating on clinical practice will have a different expertise from those in administration or community practice. They may all be "professionals" within the same discipline, but they do not share the same knowledge. It is important to keep these distinctions in mind when writing reports.

When a report is aimed at an audience of other professionals, certain assumptions can be made, such as familiarity with basic concepts of the discipline and knowledge of common statistical terms. While these assumptions make writing for other professionals easier, such an audience is likely to be more critical of such things as following a proper format, elements of style, and substantive content.

If the intended audience is the lay

public, or others less familiar with research and the human services, the assumptions noted above cannot be made. We would attempt to minimize the use of professional jargon, which is likely to be meaningless or possibly misleading to such an audience. Occasionally, jargon cannot be avoided. Social science disciplines do not make up jargon for its own sake but rather to enhance precision or to describe phenomena that our everyday language does not have words for. When used, professional jargon should be carefully explained to the lay reader. Presentation of data to a lay audience must also be simplified. They probably won't know what a probability coefficient is and may even have difficulty grasping the import of a percentage table. Use the visual impact of graphs and charts to help get your message across. Also, explain fully what each statistic used accomplishes, and what the result means. Professionals who do not work routinely with statistics and data analysis may also need some of this sort of assistance. If you believe in the importance of your research and want it to be useful, careful attention to one's audience will further that goal immensely.

Organization of the Report

While there is some variation, depending on the audience, research reports usually include most or all of the following elements.

Title   The title is an important part of a report and the first thing a reader will see. The major function of the title is to give prospective readers an idea of what the study is about so they can decide whether they are interested in reading further. Therefore, a good title will inform the reader about the major indepen-

dent and dependent variables and, possibly, the major findings. A second reason to develop a good title is that the computerized library searches discussed in Appendix A use key words in titles as one means of selecting articles. Thus, a report with a misleading or poor title may be lost from these searches. The following examples are from a recent issue of the journal *Social Work Research and Abstracts:*

Socialization and the Belief Systems of Traditional-Age and Nontraditional-Age Social Work Students

The Korean Protestant Church: The Role in Service Delivery for Korean Immigrants

The Effect of Short-Term Family Therapy on the Social Functioning of the Chronic Schizophrenic and His Family

Note that each of these titles provides sufficient information for a reader to decide whether to pursue the article further and for a computer retrieval system to identify key words.

Abstract   In most scientific journals and reports, there is an abstract, which is a terse summary of the study that allows the reader to learn enough to decide whether to read the whole thing. (Some examples of this type of abstract were presented in Chapter 4.) Abstracts are also often collected and published in reference volumes, some of which are discussed in Appendix A. In these collections the abstracts allow the reader to decide whether to locate the complete articles. Because of their importance and brevity (125–175 words), abstracts must be carefully written. The first sentence

338. CAPUTO, R. K. Managing domestic violence in two urban police districts. Social Casework, 69(8): 498–504, Oct. 1988.

Goldman-Lazarus Center for the Study of Social Work Practice, Univ. of Pennsylvania, Philadelphia 19104

1 { A study discusses findings of a study of police referrals to and interviews with clients of a practice/research demonstration project in the area of family violence. Self-report, in person interviews with 10 clients of the program addressed four major } 2

3 { concerns: (1) the nature of the incident that resulted in police action, (2) the time it took police to respond, (3) the actions taken by the police, and (4) the levels of victim satisfaction with regard to the actions and response time of the police. The sex, age, and race of victims and batterers were compared with census data in each of two police districts from which referrals were made; also explored were the marital status and living arrangements of referred batterers and victims in each of the two districts studied.

The results revealed that most violent incidents took place at home and involved hitting or pushing, pulling or dragging. The majority of respondents described police as attempting to calm the individuals involved and as having made a report; 48 percent noted that police explained their rights to file charges, and 44 percent signed complaints. Thirty-nine percent said police arrested the batterer. Dissatisfaction with police response time was highly correlated with the actual amount of time it took police to respond. In a follow-up survey of 34 battering victims who went to court, 55 percent felt that sufficient services were not available to victims of domestic violence; however, 80 percent admitted that they did not know much about the services that were available. } 4

Figure 15.5 Example of an Abstract, with Its Component Parts Identified: 1. Statement of problem. 2. Sample selection. 3. Method of study. 4. Results.

Source: Social Work Research and Abstracts, 25:1; Fall 1987, pp. 68–69. Reprinted by permission of the author and publisher.

should contain a clear statement of the problem that was investigated by the study. The research methodology and sampling techniques are then indicated. A brief summary of findings and conclusions completes the abstract. Figure 15.5 shows an abstract with its component parts identified.

Introduction and Problem Statement
The first part of the body of the report will state the research problem and its importance. This should include a literature review of the history of the problem in previous research and theory. This material serves to indicate how the current study flows from that which has gone before. Presentation of the theoretical material sets the stage for presenting the hypotheses that were tested in the study. Of necessity this section must be kept relatively brief. For example, the literature

review typically consists of numerous citations of previous work on the topic area, with only the most relevant aspects of each study commented on. This emphasis on brevity should not be overdone, however. Clarity of presentation in this section is a must because without it, the remainder of the report loses its meaning.

Methods The methods section describes the sample that was studied and the research techniques employed. It also shows how concepts are operationalized and what measurement devices, such as scales, were used. This section is very important because it provides the basis on which the validity and generalizability of conclusions will be judged. It is also the basis for any future replication efforts. As such, this section must be written with sufficient detail so that it can perform both of these functions. Readers must be able to tell precisely what was done in the study and who participated.

Results This section is a straightforward presentation of the findings of the study, devoid of any editorializing or comment as to the meaning of the results. That comes later. Typically, the presentation of results involves the use of tables, graphs, and statistics. The one exception to this would be results from a participant observation study where there is likely to be little quantitative data. As noted previously, you should consider your audience and fashion your presentation so that the data can be readily understood.

Discussion This is the section where conclusions are drawn regarding the implications of the data presented in the results section. Each tested hypothesis should be related to relevant data and a conclusion stated about the degree of support, or nonsupport, the data provide for it. Beyond that, any broader implications of the findings for either research, practice, or social policy should be noted. Any limitations or weaknesses of any of the results should be honestly noted as well. Often, research results raise new questions as they answer others. It is common practice, therefore, to identify those opportunities for future research.

References A listing of all works cited in the report is presented, usually as the last element of the report. There are a variety of formats that can be used, but the one known as the *Harvard method* is the most common in the social sciences, and in a somewhat modified form it is the format used in this book. As sources are cited in the body of the text, the author's last name and date of publication are placed in parentheses at the end of the sentence. The references are then listed in alphabetical order by author's last name, with the publication date prominently displayed on the line below. Any common journal such as the *American Sociological Review, Social Problems,* or the *American Journal of Sociology* may be consulted for examples of this format.

An alternative format is called the *serial method* in which the citations are indicated numerically in the body of the text. The references are then presented in the reference section in the same order as cited. This method is an older style than the Harvard method and is generally less used by researchers because it is more complicated to prepare and not justified except for long research reports with extensive references. Others, however, prefer it because there is less intrusion in the text. The journals *Social*

Work and *Social Work Research and Abstracts* use this format.

The Process of Writing

It is not possible, of course, to cover in a brief chapter all of the elements involved in writing. This is done in writing courses and through practice at writing. However, there are a few points of special importance that we have learned from our own experience as writers and from teaching students how to write.

First, writing is a process rather than a product. You never finish writing, although you may finish a paper or a report because it has to be submitted by a deadline. However, this doesn't mean that you couldn't write and revise further. Writing involves the expression and communication of thoughts. It is difficult to write because, in some respects, language is a poor mechanism for communicating the subjective reality of our thoughts. If you tell someone about the car that almost hit you on the way to school this morning, words like "car" and "hit" seem straightforward and comprehensible. But do those words encompass the reality that you experienced? It was a bright red car, and it was speeding, and the driver seemed not to notice you, and . . . . How much detail do you provide to communicate your experience? You tell the person you were frightened by the close call, and then realizing he might not understand the wrenching terror that shot through you, you repeat that you were "really" frightened, using qualifiers, emphasis, and inflection to make your point. The words may seem inadequate to communicating your experience, but this is precisely the challenge that any writer confronts: using words to describe a very complex and confusing reality. Research-

ers face the challenge of using words to describe a very complex theoretical and methodological reality to various audiences.

A second point, which really flows from the first, is that rewriting and revision are an inherent part of the writing process. Very few writers are capable of making their first draft the final draft. Most writers, including professional writers, must rewrite their material several times before it can be considered clear, comprehensible, and smooth. (The term "smooth" in this context simply means that there are no errors or awkwardnesses that might distract the reader from the content.) One of the keys to revision is to be able to read your prose through the eyes of the intended audience. Would they understand a particular word, phrase, or sentence? Can they follow the sequential organization in the report? Do they grasp the transitions that move the reader from one sentence to another, from one paragraph to another? What is perfectly clear from the writer's perspective may be muddled and unclear from the reader's. The writer's talent is to perceive his or her writing from that other perspective.

Rewriting is an essential, if sometimes tedious, task, and it is also creative. As with other creative efforts, the energy and attention needed to create is greater at some times than at others. This means that the best writing is usually not produced in one sitting. Most writers find it useful to approach revision after they have been away from a paper for some time. This enables them to approach it with fresh insight and attention. For this reason, things that are written at the last minute, with a deadline rapidly approaching, may not be the best.

The task of writing and rewriting, of

course, is made easier by modern computers and word-processing software. As writers who have spanned both the pre-word-processing and word-processing eras, we can attest that the latter is far preferable to the former. However, word processors do not write. There is still the need for a writer to tap words onto the screen. Writing still takes creativity, perception, persistence, and hard work.

☰ Main Points

• Grants have become a very important source of funding for both social research and human services. If they are to successfully gain funding, grant proposals must be written well.

• Sources of grant money fall into three categories: government agencies, private foundations, and corporations, with government being the largest source.

• Government funds come in a number of different forms: project (categorical) grants, formula grants, block grants, federal contracts, and state government grants.

• Although there are many foundations that fund grants, most fund only small projects and some fund research on only limited subject areas. Corporations tend to fund grants that can be justified to the stockholders, such as for services or improvements from which the corporation or its employees stand to benefit.

• Many funding sources can be located through on-line computerized search services.

• The preparation of grant proposals should be considered an on-going, continuing function of a human service agency. The steps in the grant development process are analogous to the steps in the research process.

• The first step in grant development is to identify a fundable topic; this can be assisted by conducting a needs assessment.

• Once the project has been identified, you need to target a funding source that will be interested in your project; this might call for visits to potential funding sources to assess their interest.

• To be successful, grant proposals must be written well, and this requires paying attention to the appearance and to the writing style. Proposals must be neat, interesting to read, and addressed to the audience that will read them.

• A grant proposal should contain all the components necessary to provide a funding source with adequate information to assess it.

• Research reports should also be well written since the communication and publication of scientific results accomplishes important functions for science.

• A research report should be written at the level of the audience for whom it is intended. These might be researchers conversant with the jargon of research and statistics, practitioners unfamiliar with such jargon, or the lay public.

• Most research reports include the following elements: a title, an abstract, an introduction and statement of the problem, a description of methods and results, a discussion of the implications of the findings, and a list of references.

☰ For Further Reading

American Psychological Association's Guide to Research Support. 3d ed. Hyattsville, Md.: American Psychological Association.

A complete guide for social scientists looking for support for their research. It includes information on funding sources—including names, addresses, and telephone numbers—application procedures, and submission deadlines.

Becker, Howard S. *Writing for Social Scientists: How to Start and Finish Your Thesis, Book, or Article.* Chicago: The University of Chicago Press, 1986.

A prolific researcher and writer, Howard Becker shares what he has learned with others. This book goes beyond the basics of style and grammar and offers practical suggestions for such things as overcoming writer's block, how to rewrite and revise, and how to develop a lucid style of prose.

Chicago Guide to Preparing Electronic Manuscripts. Chicago: The University of Chicago Press, 1987.

With virtually everyone using computers or word processors to prepare manuscripts these days, this work, prepared by the editorial staff of the University of Chicago Press, tells you how to get the most from these electronic marvels. It also covers how to submit manuscripts for publication on disk rather than the old-fashioned way.

Chicago Manual of Style, 13th ed. Chicago: The University of Chicago Press, 1982.

Prepared by the editorial staff of the University of Chicago Press, the Chicago Manual has long been considered the definitive writing reference work. If you take your writing seriously, you should have a copy.

Hall, Donald. *Writing Well,* 6th ed. Glenview, Ill.: Scott, Foresman, 1988.

The author of dozens of books brings his experience and expertise to a book that can help anyone improve his or her writing. Unlike many such books that present the rules in a rather stiff and direct fashion, Hall makes learning to write well interesting.

Locke, Lawrence F., Waneen Spirduso, and Stephen J. Silverman. *Proposals That Work: A Guide for Planning Dissertations and Grant Proposals,* 2d ed. Newberry Park, Calif.: Sage, 1987.

This book provides a basic guide for the preparation of grant proposals. A unique feature is its presentation of actual proposals followed by critiques of each which illustrate points made earlier in the book—an effective learning device.

Shertzer, Margaret. *The Elements of Grammar.* New York: Macmillan, 1986.

This little book is a companion to Strunk and White, and covers all aspects of correct English usage. It draws upon hundreds of examples from the greatest contemporary authors for illustrations.

Strunk Jr., William, and E. B. White. *The Elements of Style,* 3d ed. New York: Macmillan, 1979.

Another classic reference work on writing that covers the basics of style. Much shorter and handier than the *Chicago Manual,* this little book should be owned by every college student and anyone else who does much writing.

☰ Exercises for Class Discussion

15.1 Portage Bay is a resort-oriented, medium-size city of about 40,000 persons. Recently, the city council has been receiving numerous complaints from downtown merchants about vagrants and homeless people taking over the parks and public areas along the waterfront mall. A large mental institution is located near the city, and deinstitutionalized patients are accused of driving tourists away and hurting sales. Representatives of several organizations such as the Community Mental Health Center and Community Action Agency counter that the mentally ill are also residents and are being unfairly blamed for the problem. The advocates for the patients contend that there are inadequate services to meet the needs of the homeless in the community. A task force is formed to study the problem and develop a plan that will hopefully resolve the conflict with the merchants and at the same time meet the community's desire to be compassionate and meet the needs of the homeless. It becomes immediately clear that outside funding will be necessary to do a comprehensive study and to implement a plan of action.

a. Make a list of source materials to which the task force might turn to locate funding sources. Do you think government grants or foundation grants would be more appropriate?

b. By using the Catalog of Federal Domestic Assistance and/or the Monthly Catalog for Government Documents, identify a list of several potential grant sources related to the problem faced by the city of Portage Bay.

15.2 Request sample grant application forms from organizations in your state that fund human service research projects. Your college or university probably has an office of research and development that can provide the guidelines, or you might contact agencies such as the state departments of mental health, social services, or corrections.

a. Compare the grant applications in terms of the kind and detail of information that each requires.

b. For each application, determine the problems for which the granting organization will dispense funding. What special priorities, if any, does the granting organization specify? Who is eligible to apply for the grant?

15.3 Select a human-service-related research article from a recent professional publication and review it from the standpoint of the criteria presented in the discussion of writing a research report.

a. To what audience does the article appear to be addressed (e.g., professional social workers, researchers, or the general public)?

b. Is the title effective?

c. Is there an abstract? If so, does it communicate the necessary information?

d. Examine the organization of the study to determine if it contains the basic components described in the text. How are the problem statement, methods description, results, and discussion handled by the author(s)?

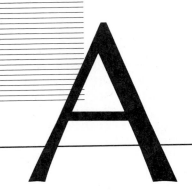

Appendix:
A Guide to the Library

A library is a repository of information in many forms on countless topics. Some human service research projects can be completed in the library if the necessary information or data can be found there. More commonly, the library is used as a means of reviewing existing literature to see what has been done on a particular topic, gain help in developing a research design, locate existing scales, and the like. However, because of the proliferation of materials stored in libraries these days, finding what you want can be a daunting task for those unfamiliar with the organization of the library. To make effective use of the library you must, first, define precisely what it is you need to know; second, determine the best strategy for locating that information; and third, evaluate the information that you do find. This appendix will focus primarily on the second step by providing a basic introduction to the organization of the library. In addition, we will point to some specific resources in the library that would be useful to practitioners in the human services.

Organization of the Library

There are two key elements in the organization of a library that you need to understand to use the library effectively. First, the library contains certain *depart-ments* that perform special functions in the search for information. Second, the library contains a number of important mechanisms for *accessing* information.

Library Departments

One of the most valuable departments in the library for students seeking materials is the *reference department*. In most libraries, the reference department contains the basic tools for searching for information: encyclopedias, indexes, abstracts, dictionaries, handbooks, yearbooks, government documents that summarize statistical data, and an array of other resources. Familiarity with this department is critical for efficient use of the library. In addition to the materials in the reference department, the reference librarians are another valuable asset to the researcher. Highly trained and knowledgeable about how to locate library materials, librarians have as one of their major duties helping library patrons. By working closely with a reference librarian, you will not only locate a specific item, but you can also learn the techniques of thorough and efficient searching for materials in the library. Although you should probably try to locate materials yourself first, do not hesitate to consult the reference librarian if you have difficulties. One rule of thumb is to spend 30 minutes searching on your own before seeking help (Lolley, 1974).

Unless you have access to a very large library, such as the New York Public Library or the Library of Congress, you will undoubtedly find that some books or resource materials that you need are not available in your library. To overcome the problem of unavailable materials, you need to make use of the *interlibrary loan department.* Most libraries participate in a local or regional interlibrary loan program that permits them to borrow books from other libraries. Libraries first attempt to secure materials from libraries within their own region; if this is not possible, they will use computers to locate materials in libraries nationwide. All participating libraries benefit because they can provide a greater range of materials and services to patrons than their own budgets allow. Books are usually sent by mail from one library to another, with the borrower sometimes asked to pay postage and insurance (usually not a large fee because the books are mailed at a very inexpensive "book rate"). In addition, lending libraries sometimes require that books they lend be used only in the borrowing library, in which case the borrowing library will not allow the books to be taken out. Many libraries, as a part of their interlibrary loan service, also participate in a periodical reprint service through which you can request a duplicated copy of an article from a periodical.

All libraries provide some *copying services* that enable you to photocopy certain library materials. In most cases, this will consist of a photocopy machine on which you can copy pages from books or journals at a small charge per copy. Most libraries also have machines that will make copies from microfilm or microfiche because much valuable library material, including old journals and newspapers, is put on microfilm or microfiche

to save library space. Effective use of the library's copying services is important because it gives you a permanent copy of those materials that cannot be removed from the library. In using these services, however, you should be familiar with the federal copyright laws to ensure that you do not violate them. Normally, reproducing one copy for your private use is permissible.

The *documents division* of the library houses government publications, magazines, pamphlets, and sometimes collections of special books. Many government documents are now issued on microfiche. In a small library, the documents division might be integrated with the reference department.

The *stacks* are the part of the library where most books and periodicals are stored. At large universities, there is usually more than one library, so all the books and journals will not necessarily be in the same building. Some libraries permit anyone to roam the stacks whereas others are very restrictive, distributing "stack passes" to a limited number of people such as university faculty, graduate students, or other serious researchers. You should gain as much access to the stacks as possible because browsing in the stacks is a valuable adjunct to the other ways of finding appropriate resource materials. In the stacks, you can review the table of contents and the index of a book, which provide more information about how useful it will be to you than does the brief description of the book found in the public catalog. In addition, because books on similar topics are normally placed near one another in the stacks, you can browse for books that might be useful once you find the right area in the stacks. Furthermore, if a book is misshelved slightly, you may accidentally find it if the library staff sent to retrieve it was unable to do so.

Computers in Research: The Library

The usefulness of modern computers in the research process extends into the library. To cope with the proliferation of materials, libraries over the past few decades have made extensive use of computerization to make library searches faster and more effective. For example, many libraries now have a computerized on-line public access catalog (OPAC) of all the books, periodicals, and other materials in the library. Library patrons can search for materials by author, title, subject, or by the use of keywords. We will describe this in the next section. In addition, many abstracts, indexes, and government documents described later in this appendix are now available on compact disc, commonly referred to as CD-ROM or Compact Disc-Read Only Memory, and readily accessible by microcomputers. There is also a variety of computerized information-retrieval systems that can provide a list of citations to books, articles, and government publications on particular topics. In most cases, the user provides a list of keywords that relate to the topic of interest. The computer then searches through abstracts, indexes, and other materials in its files for citations that are filed under those keywords or contain a keyword or words in the title of the book or article. Keyword searches work like this. If one were interested in child abuse, then keywords such as "child abuse," "discipline," "cruelty to children," "battered children," and "parent–child relationship" could be entered into the computer. It is also possible to narrow the search by cross-referencing a number of keywords.

For example, we could request only materials that are listed under *all* the following keywords: battered children—Native American—male—aged 1 to 4—Michigan. It is also possible to limit the search to works published between specified dates, sponsored by certain organizations, or qualified by any number of other criteria, depending on the search service and the data base searched. Obviously, the more encompassing terms ("parent–child relationship") will result in the retrieval of a longer list of articles than narrower terms ("battered children") or terms that are cross-referenced. This is something to take into consideration if there is a charge for this search service based in part on the number of references provided. Also, the longer list will include many sources not directly relevant to your concerns and could waste your valuable time. The librarians operating the computer search service can give you advice on whether a computer search is appropriate to your topic (sometimes a manual search is better) and also suggestions on useful keywords to maximize your search. Many search services provide a dictionary of terms that are used in the data base. One such data base, for example, is ERIC, or Educational Resources Information Center. If your library has this data base, then it will also have a volume titled *Thesaurus of ERIC Descriptors* that contains all of the subject terms used in the ERIC data base.

Today, many of the computerized services available to library patrons are operated by the patrons themselves. There are easy-to-follow directions, and for many of these services there is no cost to the user. You should join a tour of your library to determine precisely what is available to you.

Accessing Library Materials

Having a library available with ample materials is of little use unless you know how to *access* the materials you want. Students can be easily overwhelmed by the library because there seem to be so many crannies in which relevant resources can hide. There are, however, three basic strategies for locating material. Following these strategies can unlock the secrets of the library. First, you must know how to use the *public catalog system*. Second, you can use *abstracts* and *indexes*. And third, to use government publications, you turn to the *Monthly Catalog of U.S. Government Publications*. Thus, to do a thorough search that locates the most up-to-date sources, you must be familiar with all three strategies for retrieving publications.

Books

The Classification System

Small, local libraries might contain a few thousand books. Small- to medium-size universities have libraries with hundreds of thousands of volumes. Large university and public libraries contain millions of books. Despite the tremendous variation in size of libraries, the systems to classify books in them are so flexible that the system used in the smallest library can also be used in the largest, and, despite their tremendous size, a person in the largest library can easily retrieve a book if he or she knows how the book is classified. Classification systems arrange books according to *subject matter*. First, books are classified into very general categories, such as history, science, or social sciences. Then, within each general cat-

egory, they are further arranged into more precise subcategories. The category of social sciences, for example, is further divided into economics, sociology, and so on. In this fashion, the subject matter of a book is further narrowed until it fits into a fairly specific category. Then each book is given a unique *call number*, which contains all the necessary information from the classification system to identify that particular book.

There are primarily two classification systems used in the United States: the *Library of Congress system* and the *Dewey decimal system*. The Library of Congress system uses a combination of letters and numbers to classify books (see Table A.1). The first letter in the top row of the call number is one of 21 letters of the alphabet used to classify books into the most general categories. The letter *H*, for example, indicates the general category of the social sciences. The second letter in the top row (if there is a second letter) further narrows the subject matter within the social sciences. The letter *Q*, for example, indicates that the book falls in the more specific social science subject matter of "Family, Marriage, Women" whereas *V* refers to the subject of "Social Pathology." The second row of the call number is a number that further narrows the subject matter. Within the classification *HV*, for example, numbers between 701 and 1420 refer to works on the topic of protection, assistance, and relief of children whereas the numbers 5001–5840 refer to books on alcoholism. The third row of the Libary of Congress call number begins with a letter that is the first letter of the last name of the author of the book. This is followed by a number that further identifies the author. These three rows of the call number provide an identification that is unique to this book: No other book has exactly the same call

TABLE A.1 Library of Congress Classification System

A   General Works
B   Philosophy and Religion
C   History (General—Civilization, Genealogy)
D   History—Old World
E   American History and General U.S. History
F   American History (Local) and Latin America
G   Geography, Anthropology, Folklore, Sports, and Other
H   Social Sciences
    HA   Statistics
    HB-HD Economics
    HF   Commerce
    HG–HJ Finance
    HM   Sociology
    HQ   Family, Marriage, Women
    HV   Social Pathology
J   Political Science
K   Law
L   Education
M   Music
N   Fine Arts
P   Language and Literature
Q   Science
R   Medicine
S   Agriculture, Forestry, Animal Culture, Fish Culture, Hunting
T   Technology
U   Military Science
V   Naval Science
Z   Bibliography and Library Science

Example: HV
             875
             F6

number. Books are placed on the shelves in the order of their call numbers. All the *H*'s are placed together, and within the *H*'s all the *HM*'s go together. Within the *HM*'s, books are arranged according to the numbers on the second line, and so on.

The Dewey decimal system arranges books into ten general categories based on a three-digit number on the top row of its call number (see Table A.2). Numbers in the 300 range comprise the social science category. The second and third digit of this top row further narrow the classification within the social sciences. For example, the 360s deal with "welfare and association."

The three-digit number is followed by a decimal point and then by numbers that indicate narrower classifications. In the second row of the Dewey call number is a letter, which is again the first letter of the last name of the author of the book, followed by a number that further identifies the author. This may be followed by a lowercase letter that is the first letter in the first word of the title of the book (excluding "a," "an," and "the"). The Dewey system also provides each book with its own unique call number.

TABLE A.2 Dewey Decimal Classification System

Broad subject areas or classes:

000 Generalities
100 Philosophy and Related Disciplines
200 Religion
300 The Social Sciences
400 Language
500 Pure Sciences
600 Technology (Applied Sciences)
700 The Arts
800 Literature and Rhetoric
900 General Geography and History, and the like

Each class can be subdivided into smaller classes or subclasses:

300 The Social Sciences
310 Statistical Method and Statistics
320 Political Science
330 Economics
340 Law
350 Public Administration
360 Welfare and Association
370 Education
380 Commerce
390 Customs and Folklore

Example: 362.7
          N34

The Public Catalog

With knowledge of the classification system in use at your library, you can locate any book. To do so, you need to find the *public catalog*, which is a listing of all the holdings in the library. In many libraries today, the public catalog is an online computerized catalog of holdings. In some cases, these computer files can tell you not only whether a library owns a particular item but also its status: whether it is checked out, at the bindery, lost, and so on. Some libraries are involved in regional networks with other libraries and their computerized public catalogs will list which libraries in the network own a particular book or other

holding. So, if a book is not available at your library, you can see where it can be found.

Some libraries still retain what used to be called the "card catalog," now known as the "public catalog," where each holding is listed on a card. Whether libraries use cards or computer or both, they catalog books three ways: by author, by title, and by subject matter. For example, Figure A.1 presents a card that is cataloged by subject. The card also indicates that the book is listed under a number of subject headings. If you know the author or title of a book, you simply look it up in the card catalog, jot down the call number, and locate it in the stacks. (Remember that books with similar call

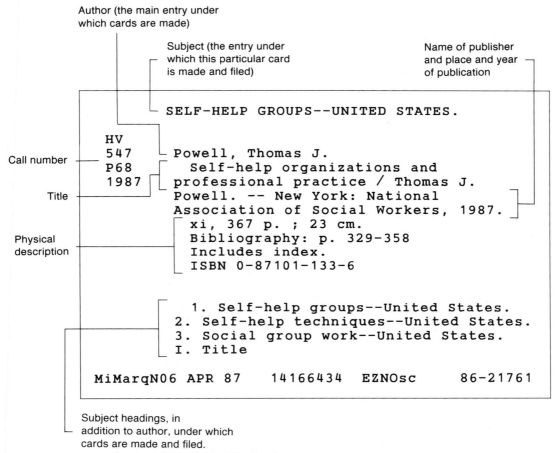

Author (the main entry under which cards are made)

Subject (the entry under which this particular card is made and filed)

Name of publisher and place and year of publication

SELF-HELP GROUPS--UNITED STATES.

Call number

HV
547
P68
1987

Title

Powell, Thomas J.
    Self-help organizations and
professional practice / Thomas J.
Powell. -- New York: National
Association of Social Workers, 1987.

Physical description

    xi, 367 p. ; 23 cm.
    Bibliography: p. 329-358
    Includes index.
    ISBN 0-87101-133-6

    1. Self-help groups--United States.
    2. Self-help techniques--United States.
    3. Social group work--United States.
    I. Title

MiMarqN06 APR 87   14166434   EZNOsc   86-21761

Subject headings, in addition to author, under which cards are made and filed.

Figure A.1 A Sample Card from the Public Catalog

numbers will be about similar topics, so it is a good practice to browse through them.) Typically, there will be a combined author and title catalog and a separate subject catalog. The former is rather straightforward to use, involving an alphabetical listing of all materials by author and by title of book. The subject catalog, however, can be a little more problematic because library patrons sometimes have difficulties finding useful subject headings for their topic. To assist in this task, a volume titled *Library of Congress Subject Headings* can be used. It lists headings acceptable for use in a public catalog, cross-referencing a number of different topics. This volume is usually located somewhere near the public catalog itself. If you use the public catalog to locate books, you will have to determine from the title of the book and the brief descriptions of the contents contained in the listing whether a book will be useful to you. When you do this, it is better to err on the side of jotting down too many call numbers rather than too few.

Once the organizational key to the library is unlocked, it is easy to locate the information stored in books. There are, however, other repositories of information in the library, one of the most important of which is periodicals.

Periodicals

One of the most valuable and heavily used resources of the library, in addition to books, is *periodicals*. Periodicals are published periodically, such as weekly or monthly (hence, the name "periodicals"), and they often contain articles by a number of different authors on a variety of topics. Periodicals come in two basic types although some are a blend of both. *Magazines* are directed at the general public, are written in a light and popular style, and are often commercial ventures. *Journals* are professional periodicals that publish articles primarily intended for members of a particular profession. The *American Sociological Review*, the *Journal of Social Service Research*, and the *Journal of the American Medical Association* are examples. We will focus primarily on journals, but both magazines and journals can be very helpful in researching a problem because, first, periodicals tend to be more current than books, especially in reporting research findings. This is so, in part, because the production process for books is longer than for periodicals. In addition, in many scientific fields, including the human services, much research is reported first in journals. In fact, many books contain primarily summaries or assessments of research that has already appeared in journals. Second, the articles in periodicals are brief and specific, enabling you to gather more information about a particular topic in a shorter period of time.

Periodicals, like books, can be given a call number although not all libraries classify their periodicals according to call number. When periodicals are given a call number, they can be housed in the library in two ways: along with the books in the library by call number or separately from books by call number. When this procedure is used, you will need to look in the public catalog or other location to find the call number of the periodical you wish. The advantage of classifying periodicals by call number is that periodicals on a similar topic will be near one another. Some libraries, however, do not use the periodical call number, arranging periodicals separately from books in alphabetical order by the title of the journal (excluding the first "the" or "a" in the title). Once you locate where the periodicals are stored in your library, any particular periodical can then easily be found because no two periodicals have the same title or call number. Each issue of a journal is further identified by a volume number, the year of its publication, and an issue number indicating its place in the sequence of issues making up a particular volume. Some journals also identify their issues with the month or season (for example, Summer) in which it was published. To locate an issue of a journal, then, you need the following information: the call number or name of the journal, year of issue, volume number, and issue number (or month or season of publication).

There are usually three locations for periodicals in the library. First, most libraries store the *current* periodicals or most recent issues in a separate place where users can browse through them. Typically, the most recent one or two years are kept there. Second, *bound* periodicals contain several issues that have been bound together in one hardcover volume for extended storage. Each bound volume normally contains one year's worth of issues. Most of a library's periodical holdings are in this form. Third, old volumes are often put on *microfilm* or some other space-saving device for long-term storage. These are usually kept in large cabinets located near the machines that magnify them for viewing. There is a problem that can arise when accessing periodicals that, though minor, is irksome to both patrons and librarians. The problem is that the separate issues that make up a volume of a journal must be bound together. This is done by sending the volume to a bindery, which means that the issues in that volume are temporarily unavailable to library patrons. The period is usually brief, but the periodicals are also usually recent ones because the binding is done within the first few years of publication. Students need to be aware that this problem can occur, and it is one reason to begin library research early because some recent journals you are looking for may be available now but sent to the bindery a month from now.

Journals Important to the Human Services

There are literally hundreds of journals in the library that contain materials of use to human service researchers and practitioners. Although no one can be expected to read all of these journals, awareness and occasional perusal of them can uncover much valuable source material. One way to spend some free time is to browse through some of these journals in the current periodicals section of the library. Numerous journals are published primarily for human service professionals. Among the more important are these:

Administration in Social Work
British Journal of Social Work
Child Welfare

Clinical Social Work Journal
Current Contents—Social and Behavioral Sciences
Exceptional Children
Federal Probation
Health & Social Work
International Child Welfare Review
International Journal of the Addictions
International Journal of Aging and Human Development
International Social Work
Journal of Education for Social Work
Journal of Social Service Research
Journal of Social Welfare
Journal of Sociology and Social Welfare
Public Welfare
School Social Work Journal
Smith College Studies in Social Work
Social Casework
Social Security Bulletin
Social Service Review
Social Work
Social Work in Education
Social Work in Health Care
Social Work Research & Abstracts
Social Work with Groups

Because the human service professions use knowledge developed by many of the behavioral sciences, many journals not published directly for human service providers can be of great value, nonetheless. Among the more useful of these are the following:

Administration in Mental Health
American Journal of Orthopsychiatry
American Journal of Public Health
American Journal of Sociology
American Sociological Review
Archives of General Psychiatry
Behavior Therapy
Child Development
Child Psychiatry and Human Development
Community Mental Health Journal
Crime and Delinquency

Criminology
Family and Child Mental Health Journal
Gerontologist
International Journal of Group Psychotherapy
Journal of Abnormal Psychology
Journal of Applied Behavioral Science
Journal of Clinical Psychology
Journal of Consulting and Clinical Psychology.
Journal of Counseling Psychology
Journal of Criminal Law and Criminology
Journal of Drug Issues
Journal of General Psychology
Journal of Gerontology
Journal of Health and Social Behavior
Journal of Marital and Family Therapy
Journal of Marriage and the Family
Journal of Personality and Social Psychology
Journal of Research in Crime and Delinquency
Journal of Studies on Alcohol
Merrill-Palmer Quarterly
Psychological Bulletin
The Public Interest
Social Forces
Social Policy
Social Problems
Social Psychology Quarterly
Sociological Quarterly

Given this diversity of periodicals, how does one find those articles that relate to a particular topic? Two types of reference publications, called "abstracts" and "indexes," are the major keys to accessing the information contained in periodicals.

Abstracts and Indexes

Some periodicals provide an *abstracting* service for library patrons. An *abstract* is a brief description, usually no more than a paragraph, of the contents of a book or article. A good abstract will provide a complete summary of the work, including the thesis of the author, a description of any data collected, the conclusions drawn, and limitations of the study. Abstracts help you locate relevant research and decide whether it is sufficiently useful to read the entire work. Abstracting services provide a list of the journals whose articles are abstracted, usually in the first few pages of the volume of abstracts. Likewise, some journals list in each issue the abstracting and indexing services in which they are included. Some of the abstracts and indexes we will discuss are available on CD-ROM.

Using an abstract is relatively simple. Suppose you are interested in problems surrounding adoption. First, you need to find a topic heading in the subject index of the abstract that will point you toward relevant articles (*see* Figure A.2). Obviously, "adoptive families" would be such a topic heading and should be consulted. Because that heading is very specific, however, it might not be used by an abstracting service. A more general topic heading would be "families." Locating this heading, you glance over the subtopics listed under it for one directly related to your interests. When you find the relevant subheading, there will be one or more numbers following it, each referring to a separate abstract. The abstracts are listed in the volume in numerical order. Abstracting services also provide an author index should you be searching for works by a particular author.

In addition to the summary description, the abstract provides the complete reference so that you can locate the work. In our illustration, the information presented in the reference, in the order it is presented, is this: authors' names, title of article, name of journal, volume of journal, issue in volume, pages of that article

Author Index

Eggers, P. W., 702
Elbow, M., 638
Elliot, C., 719
Elpers, J. R., 738
Elston, R. R., 1068
Encel, S., 782
Endres, T., 1120
Engle, D., 767
English, J. T., 1031
Enos, D. M. 681
Epstein, I., 1006
Esses, L. M., 905
Evans, J. H., 911
Evans, R. C., 639
Evenson, M. L., 682
Evenson, T. L., 682
Eyman, R. K., 1067

F

Fabiszewski, K. J., 548
Falke, R. L., 1089
Fall, M., 683
Faller, K. C., 640
Fanshel, D., 813
Farrington, D. P., 601

Abstract

638. Elbow, M., & Knight, M. Adoption disruption: losses, transitions, and tasks. Social Casework, 68(9): 546–52, Nov. 1987.

400 W. 119th St., New York, NY 10027

When an adoptive placement disrupts, social workers tend to focus on the needs of the child and often overlook their own and the family's sense of loss. A study describes disruption in terms of the losses experienced by the adoption system, which is made up of the child, the adoptive family, the agency, and, in open adoptions, the child's biological family. Examined are the process of disruption, the needs of the child and family, and how the family functions after a child is removed. The instrumental and affective tasks involved are discussed, and a model of intervention to facilitate task mastery is presented. (Author abstract, edited)

639. Evans, R. C., Burlew, A. K., & Oler, C. H. Children with sickle-cell anemia: parental relations, parent-child relations, and child behavior. Social Work, 33(2): 127–30, March/April 1988.

School of Social Work, Aurora Univ., Aurora, IL 60506

The influence of a child with sickle-cell anemia on parental affiliation, parent-child relationships, and the parents' perception of their child's behavior was investigated. A survey questionnaire was administered to 78 parents of children aged 2 to 5 and a control group of 72 parents of healthy children. All subjects were black. The study results revealed that the presence of a child with sickle-cell anemia may create interpersonal difficulties for the parents. For example, parents of a child with sickle-cell anemia reported less positive affect in their relationship with each other than parents without children with sickle-cell anemia.

Subject Index

Extended family: effect of industrialization on prevalence of, in Taiwan, 1110

F

Families (Family): adoptive, effect of adoption disruption on, 638; depression and self-esteem in, of maltreated adolescents, 669; deviant communication in, of schizophrenics demonstrated with Family Rorschach technique, 1016; effect of child's hospitalization on, 643; enrichment programs for, with disabled members, 682; environment of and adjustment of children in, of Holocaust survivors, 1050; family climate and anxiety in, with learning disabled boys, 773; intact and divorced, nutritional status of preschool children from, 714; low-income black single-parent, social network and demographic variables in stress in, 751; multiproblem, mother-infant interactions in, 679; nuclear, reintegration of, with kinship systems as response to adolescent crises, 645; poor, lessons for family therapists from, 822; relation of perceived conflict in, and parental marital status to adjustment in white adolescents, 681; relationship of , and loyalty conflicts of latency-age boys in joint and maternal custody, 693; resistant multiproblem, practice strategies for work with, 847; rigid or chaotic patterns of living time in, 626; role of social workers as educators of, or chronically mentally ill, 762; satisfaction of, with psychiatric evaluations, 1026; single-parent homeless, evaluation of services in emergency shelter for, 660; stable middle-class family violence in, 667; structured mediation for conflicts and courses in, 650; suburban, network groups for, 883; variant of Munchausen by proxy in, with ill child, 708; West Indian, culture-specfic problems and service needs of, 670. **See also** Stepparents
Family Beliefs Inventory (FBI): development and validation of, as measure of unrealistic beliefs among parents and adolescents, 689
Family crisis intervention: structured mediation use as, 650
Family interaction: patterns of, in families of agoraphobics, 1036
Family perspective: influence of, on undergraduate psychology textbook, 892

Figure A.2 Use of an Abstract

Source: Copyright © 1988, National Association of Social Workers, Inc. Reprinted with permission from *Social Work Research & Abstracts*, Vol. 24, No. 2 (Summer 1988).

in the journal, year journal was published, and place of employment of authors. If an abstract suggests that an article will be useful to you, the complete reference should be written down.

The following are some of the major abstracting services that are useful for topics in the human services:

Child Development Abstracts
Criminal Justice Abstracts (formerly *Crime and Delinquency Abstracts*)
Current Literature on Aging
Dissertation Abstracts International
Exceptional Child Education Resources (ECER, formerly *Exceptional Child Education Abstracts*)
Human Resources Abstracts (formerly *Poverty and Human Resources Abstracts*)
Psychological Abstracts
Social Work Research and Abstracts (formerly *Abstracts for Social Workers*)
Sociological Abstracts
Women's Studies Abstracts

Although these are some of the more important abstracts relevant to the human services, there are others. You should consult your reference librarian and become familiar with all the abstracts in your library relevant to the human services. If you make a list of them, you will have a quick reference for any research you need to do while in college or on the job.

In addition to abstracting services, there are other publications that provide indexing services. An *index* is an alphabetical arrangement of materials based on some element of the materials, usually the author's last name, the title of the work, or the subject matter. (This text, for example, has separate name and subject indexes at the end.) Indexing publications usually provide an author index,

which lists all the articles published by a particular author, and a subject index listing all articles on a given subject. An index will also present a list of the journals it indexes. Indexes have both advantages and disadvantages in comparison with abstracts. One advantage is that, because they take less time to prepare, they tend to be more current. Some abstracts are not published until more than a year after the articles covered have appeared. One disadvantage of indexes is that the user must rely on the title of the article to determine whether it is sufficiently relevant to spend the time seeking out the actual work itself. Anyone who has used indexes will attest to the many wild-goose chases where a seemingly useful article turned out to be irrelevant to a particular topic. Likewise, there are undoubtedly useful articles that are ignored because their titles do not seem sufficiently relevant.

There are numerous indexes that can be of value to human service professionals. A list follows.

Criminal Justice Periodical Index
Index to U.S. Government Periodicals
New York Times Index
Nursing and Allied Health Index
Public Affairs Information Service Bulletin (PAIS)
Readers' Guide to Periodical Literature
Social Science Citation Index
Social Sciences Index

As with abstracts, you should make a list of all the indexes relevant to the human service field.

Reference Books for the Human Services

One group of highly useful books that are, unfortunately, often overlooked are general reference books. Within this rather broad category are included encyclopedias, directories, and bibliographies. Although such works will not substitute for a thorough library search, they can save you time, as well as efficiently answer many routine questions. The following is only a partial listing of common reference works:

Alcoholism Subject Bibliography
Child Abuse and Neglect Subject Bibliography
Children and Youth Subject Bibliography
Drug Education Subject Bibliography
Encyclopedia of Aging
Encyclopedia of Alcoholism
Encyclopedia of Drug Abuse
Encyclopedia of Social Work
Juvenile Delinquency Subject Bibliography
National Directory of State Agencies
Public Welfare Directory
Social Service Organizations and Agencies Directory
Social Welfare and Services Subject Bibliography

Government Documents

The United States government is one of the largest publishing houses in the world, pouring forth mountains of books, bulletins, circulars, reports, and the like. Practitioners and researchers in the human service field will find government documents especially important because much of the research done in this area is sponsored by the government. Demonstration projects, program evaluations, and needs assessments, for example, are commonly funded by the government, and the resulting research reports are

published by the government. Government documents also include information on model programs, funding sources, and bibliographies of topics of interest to human service professionals.

The Monthly Catalog

Locating government publications of use to you may at first seem a bewildering endeavor. With the aid of a few basic tools, however, the task can be done quickly, thoroughly, and with relatively little pain. The first thing to learn is whether your library is a "depository library," a designation made by the superintendent of documents at the U.S. Government Printing Office. A "regional depository" library, of which there can be up to two in any state, receives everything published by the printing office. "Selective depositories" receive only some government publications, a listing of which can be found in *List of Classes of U.S. Government Publications Available for Selection by Depository Libraries.* Nondepository libraries will have some government documents, depending on which they choose to purchase.

The next thing you need to determine is which government documents are relevant to your particular topic of interest. The primary source for information on government documents is the *Monthly Catalog of U.S. Government Publications,* which has been published since 1895 and is now available on CD-ROM and accessible by computers. This publication includes a listing of most government publications along with the information necessary to locate them in the library or to purchase them from the office of the superintendent of documents.

Every government document submitted to the office of the superintendent of documents is given a monthly catalog

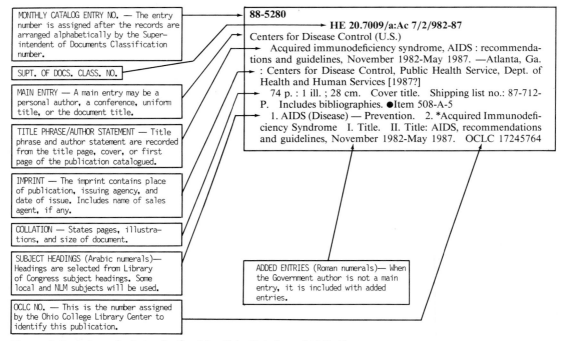

Figure A.3 A Sample Entry in the *Monthly Catalog of U.S. Government Publications*

entry number (see Figure A.3), and documents are listed in the *Monthly Catalog* in order of this number. This number has two components. The first two digits indicate the year the document was published (1988 in the illustration). The second group of digits locates the record in the *Monthly Catalog.* This second number is derived from sequencing the publications alphanumerically according to the classification number of the superintendent of documents or SUDOCS number. The SUDOCS number is like the call number in the public catalog for locating books because the government documents are housed in the library according to this number. Thus, the *Monthly Catalog* entry number helps you locate the document in the *Monthly Catalog,* and the SUDOCS number enables you to locate where the document is shelved in the library.

Simply looking through the *Monthly Catalog* is an inefficient way of finding publications on the exact topic you want. There are several aids that can make your search both quicker and more thorough. These are the subject index, the author index, the title index, and the title keyword index (see Figure A.4). Thus, if you actually know the author or title of a publication, you can simply look these up in the appropriate index. The index will give the *Monthly Catalog* entry number (and since 1987, the SUDOCS number). If you know neither the exact title nor the author, the subject index will provide a listing of documents according to subject matter and again will provide the title and *Monthly Catalog* entry number (and

Author Index

Center of Military History.

The Annapolis Convention., 88-3726

Armies, corps, divisions, and separate brigades /, 88-4957

The Army historian: a publication of the United States Army Center of Military History., 88-664

The Army Medical Department, 1818-1865 /, 88-3731

Army museum newsletter., 88-663

David Brearly., 88-3727

Dissertation year fellowships /, 88-7892

The German campaigns in the Balkans (spring, 1941)., 88-1990

German tank maintenance in World War II., 88-7894

Jonathan Dayton., 88-3728

The medics' war /, 88-1987

Moscow to Stalingrad : decision in the east /, 88-6529

The profession of arms : the 1962 Lees Knowles lectures given at Trinity College, Cambridge /, 88-1988

The staff ride /, 88-1989

Thomas Fitzsimons., 88-3729

U.S. Army mobilization and logistics in the Korean War : a research approach /, 88-7893

Warfare in the far north., 88-7895

William Jackson., 88-3730

Centers for Disease Control (U.S.)

Acquired immunodeficiency syndrome, AIDS : recommendations and guidelines, November 1982-May 1987. (88-5280)

The agents of non-A, non-B viral hepatitis /, 88-2364

AIDS in Africa : an epidemiologic paradigm /, 88-2361

Title Index

Acid rain. (I 19.114:R 13), 88-5751

Acoustic emission/flaw relationship for in-service monitoring of nuclear pressure vessels : progress report / Hutton, P. H. (Y 3.N 88:25/4300/v.4, no.1), 88-6126

Acoustic emission monitoring of fracture development / Anderson, Sterling J. (I 28.23:9077), 88-8443

Acoustic-televiewer and acoustic-waveform logs used to characterize deeply buried basalt flows, Hanford Site, Benton County, Washington [microform] / Paillet, F. L. (I 19.76:85-419), 88-9555

Acquiescence rulings United States. Social Security Administration. (HE 3.44:(date)), 88-844

Acquired Immune Deficiency Syndrome (AIDS) and the Veterans' Administration : hearing before the Subcommittee on Hospitals and Health Care of the Committee on Veterans' Affairs, House of Representatives, One hundredth Congress, first session, June 17, 1987. United States. Congress. House. Committee on Veterans' Affairs. Subcommittee on Hospitals and Health Care. (Y 4.V 64/3:100-19), 88-6304

Acquired immunodeficiency syndrome (AIDS) : fifteenth update, July 1987 through September 1987, 845 citations / Abrams, Estelle J. (HE 20.3614/2:87-13), 88-5261

Acquired immunodeficiency syndrome, AIDS : recommendations and guidelines, November 1982-May 1987. Centers for Disease Control (U.S.) (HE 20.7009/a:Ac 7/2/982-87), (88-5280)

Acquired immunodeficiency syndrome (AIDS) : sixteenth update, October 1987 through December 1987, 1028 citations,

Keyword Index

January — June 1988

.. to families with dependent children (AFDC) pro 88-2233
.. to students., Financial 88-2219

AIDS /, Foreign policy implications of 88-9914
.. / , Progress on the treatment of 88-5246
.. : facts about the disease : how to protect yo 88-4098
.. :, need for immediate OSHA regulations to pro 88-3409
.. : Opportunities for international scientific 88-10204
.. : recommendations and guidelines, November 19 (88-5280)
.. & hepatitis B., Worker exposure to 88-9857
.. and teenagers : 88-8795
.. and the education of our children : a guide f 88-3754
.. and the education of our children : a guide f 88-7933
.. and the law enforcement officer / 88-9805
.. and the Veterans' Administration : 88-10232
.. crisis as related to the federal budget: 88-7526
.. drug development program at NCI. 88-8121
.. for health services research /, Selected bibl 88-9485
.. for policymakers /, An Annotated bibliography 88-6830
.. in Africa : an epidemiologic paradigm / 88-2361
.. knowledge and attitudes for September 1987 / 88-6869
.. knowledge and attitudes : provisional data fr 88-6868
.. patients /, New drug therapy developed for pn 88-6852
.. prevention program operations, Guidelines fo 88-2367
.. published in the Morbidity and Morality Week 88-4101
.. research : 88-4776
.. research and medical care within the Veterans 88-4794
.. research and medical care within the Veterans 88-8971
.. research program /, NCI's 88-5245
.. to navigation bulletin 88-1451
.. vaccine /, Research on development of an 88-5244
.. a public health challenge : state issues, po 88-5227
..), CDC reports on acquired immunodeficiency s 88-2344
..) : fifteenth update, July 1987 through Septem 88-5261
.. Informe del jefe del Servicio de Salud Pub 88-8826
.. Public Health Service guidelines for counse 88-5283
..) : sixteenth update, October 1987 through Dec 88-9474
.. Straight facts about 88-2265
.. , Tips on avoiding 88-6861
..) : twelfth update, October 1986 through Decem 88-2298
.. , Viruses in cancer and 88-8125

Subject Index

Agriculture — United States.

Country-of-origin labeling on imported perishable agricultural commodities : hearing before the Subcommittee on Domestic Marketing, Consumer Relations, and Nutrition of the Committee on Agriculture, House of Representatives, One hundredth Congress, first session, on H.R. 692, H.R. 1176, and H.R. 1246, March 30, 1987. United States. Congress. House. Committee on Agriculture. Subcommittee on Domestic Marketing, Consumer Relations, and Nutrition. (Y 4.Ag 8/1:100-14), 88-6150

Agriculture — United States — Periodicals.

Semiannual report to Congress. United States. Dept. of Agriculture. Office of the Inspector General. (A 1.1/3:987), 88-4801

AIDS (Disease) — Bibliography.

Acquired immunodeficiency syndrome (AIDS) : fifteenth update, July 1987 through September 1987, 845 citations / Abrams, Estelle J. (HE 20.3614/2:87-13) 88-5261

AIDS (Disease) — Prevention.

Acquired immunodeficiency syndrome, AIDS : recommendations and guidelines, November 1982-May 1987. Centers for Disease Control (U.S.) (HE 20.7009/a:Ac 7/2/982-87) (88-5280)

Human T-lymphotropic virus type III/ lymphadenopathy-associated virus : agent summary statement (HE 20.7009/a:H 88/6), 88-5282

Public Health Service guidelines for counseling and antibody testing to prevent HIV infection and AIDS. (HE 20.7009/a:H 88/7), 88-5283

Recommendations for prevention of HIV transmission in health-care settings. (HE 20.7009/a:H 88/8), 88-5284

Summary : recommendations for preventing transmission of infection with human T-lymphotropic virus type III/ lymphadenopathy-associated virus in the workplace. (HE 20.7009/a:H 88/2), 88-5281

Figure A.4 Four Indexes Useful in Locating Documents in the *Monthly Catalog of U.S. Government Publications*

since 1987, the SUDOCS number). If you know a keyword associated with the title, the title keyword index will similarly direct you to the *Monthly Catalog* number. Armed with this number, you simply go to the correct volume of the *Monthly Catalog* according to the entry number. The *Monthly Catalog* provides a variety of details about the publications (see Figure A.3). Generally, in addition to the SUDOCS number that allows you to locate the document, the entry will give the author, title, publication information, price, and subject headings. This is useful for determining whether or not that particular document is of further interest to you.

To summarize, then, the steps followed in finding government documents are these: first, consult an appropriate index and obtain *Monthly Catalog* entry numbers and SUDOCS numbers; second, consult the *Monthly Catalog* for more information about the document, a complete reference, and the classification number of the superintendent of documents; and third, locate the document itself.

In addition to the *Monthly Catalog of U.S. Government Publications,* the following agencies publish separate catalogs of their own publications: the Bureau of the Census, the Commerce and Labor departments, and the Civil Rights Commission.

Subject Bibliographies and State Government Documents

The government also provides useful bibliographies of government documents on a wide range of topics. If one or more of these topics coincides with your interest, the subject bibliographies can provide access to many publications in your topic area. These bibliographies are indexed in the same way as the *Monthly Catalog.*

For example, social welfare is subject no. 30. Turning to bibliography no. 30, one finds a listing of publications on the general topic of social welfare. The entries provide title, author, the SUDOCS number, and the stock number for ordering.

The Library of Congress also publishes a *Monthly Checklist of State Publications.* Although not a complete list of all state publications, it provides information on the data published by state governments. If your library does not receive the state publications, you can probably order them for a small fee.

Sources of Data in the Library

In Chapter 8, we discussed research using available data—data collected by someone else but available to others for analysis. The library is a repository rich in such available data. Some of it can serve as a useful beginning for a research project, and in some cases it can also be used for hypothesis testing and evaluation of programs. In either event, you should be familiar with the major sources of such data in your library.

Government Sources

The United States Government is a major source of data available in libraries. Many of the government documents discussed previously report research findings, describe programs, or analyze social policy. These are not, strictly speaking, sources of raw data to be analyzed but rather are interpretations, assessments, or summaries of data. There are other government publications, however, that present raw data on health, crime, poverty, and many other topics relevant to the human service professions, often without any accompanying interpretation or assessment. We will discuss such publications as are produced by two government agencies, the Bureau of the Census and the Department of Labor.

The U.S. Bureau of the Census publishes a vast array of statistical data that are of use to behavioral scientists and human service workers.

Bulletin of Criminal Justice Statistics. This publication, from the Department of Justice, contains valuable data on prisons, prison populations, and the criminal justice system in general.

Census of Population. The nationwide census is conducted once every decade and provides data on employment, income, race, occupation, poverty, and much more.

County and City Data Book. This is a supplement to the *Statistical Abstract,* reporting data on a local or regional basis. This book is only published every five years.

Current Population Reports. These are a series of annual publications that report on many of the same issues that the census does but are based on a probability sample of the population. There are series on income, household and family characteristics, marital status, living arrangements, and geographic mobility. These are useful publications for keeping current on changing social trends and problems.

Historical Statistics of the U.S.: Colonial Times to 1970. This volume provides historical data to supplement the *Statistical Abstract,* which often includes data from only the past decade or less.

Statistical Abstract of the U.S. This is an annual summary of statistical information about the United States. It contains data on population, birth and death rates, marriage and divorce

rates, crime, health, education, and social services. This is probably the single most useful statistical summary.

The Bureau of Labor Statistics of the Department of Labor publishes many volumes relating to the labor force, employment, and earnings in the United States.

Employment and Earnings of the Monthly Labor Force. Published monthly.

Employment and Earnings Statistics for States and Areas. An annual summary of state and regional trends.

Employment and Earnings Statistics for the United States. An annual summary.

Monthly Labor Review. A journal that presents both statistical and analytical articles relating to work and the labor force.

The Women's Bureau of the Department of Labor also publishes a number of periodicals focusing specifically on women workers, their earnings, their educational attainment, and legislation that affects them.

Nongovernment Sources

Amassing vast amounts of data as the government does each year is, of course, beyond the resources of most nongovernment organizations, such as businesses or nonprofit agencies. Many of them, however, do collect limited amounts of data that can be useful to researchers. Some journals are now published that can help locate sources of data relevant to a variety of topics.

The Review of Public Data Use. Published by DUALabs in Arlington, Virginia, it publishes articles relating to data sets that are accessible to the public. It also covers computer programs for public data use and legislation relating to such use.

S S *Data.* This is a newsletter of the Social Science Archival Acquisitions Laboratory for Political Research at the University of Iowa. It communicates information about acquisitions of data sets by various social science archives.

Although libraries do not normally purchase data sets from such nongovernmental sources as research centers, they do sometimes purchase "code books" that indicate the data available in a particular data set. Especially if some other arm of the university, such as the computer center or one of the behavioral science departments, has purchased the data set, the library may purchase such code books.

Using the Library

A library is a veritable cornucopia of information, and we have tried to provide you with basic information on how to access that information. However, the best way to learn about your library is to *use*

it. Roam around the stacks, browse through the public catalog, delve into government documents. We have emphasized the ways in which you can systematically access information in the library. However, you can also find much useful material in random and casual rovings through the library. Above all, consult with the reference librarians who are there primarily to assist you.

This guide to the library has emphasized its utility to human service practitioners. However, a library is not meant solely to help you write a term paper or complete a research project. A library is a repository of cultural knowledge. It houses research reports on alcoholics along with the epic myths of Homer and the ancient and sacred literature of Hinduism, the Vedas. Literature, philosophy, and theology accompany engineering and celestial mechanics. And you can read the daily newspaper there. The point is that a library is, in a sense, the storehouse of a culture, and we hope that you use it to its fullest extent throughout your life as a source of enrichment and fulfillment.

For Further Reading

Beasley, David. *How to Use a Research Library.* New York: Oxford University Press, 1988.
This book covers almost everything you need to know about using the modern library, including computer data bases and online computer searches. It would be useful to the beginner as well as to the professional researcher.

Horowitz, Lois. *Knowing Where to Look: The Ultimate Guide to Research.* Cincinnati, Ohio: Writer's Digest Books, 1984.

Although this book is not limited to library research, most of its suggestions involve using the library. The book tells you how to find just about any bit of information you might want to know.

Mann, Thomas. *A Guide to Library Research Methods.* New York: Oxford University Press, 1987.
This is another good general guide for how to use the library.

McMillan, Patricia, and James R. Kennedy, Jr. *Library Research Guide to Sociology.* Ann Arbor, Mich.: Pierian Press, 1981.
Of more general utility than its name im-

plies, this volume focuses on using the library to prepare a social research project. It is particularly strong at illustrating the use of common library reference works.

Reed, Jeffrey G., and Pam M. Baxter. *Library Use: A Handbook for Psychology.* Washington, D.C.: American Psychological Association, 1983.

Focused as it is on psychology, this book is nonetheless a valuable guide to the library for someone preparing to conduct a social research project. Among other things, it covers using abstracting services, doing computer searches, and locating various scales and measurement devices.

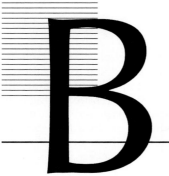
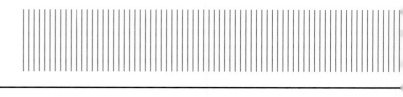

Appendix: Generating Random Numbers

Random numbers are used for many purposes in social research. They are often used, for example, in constructing a probability sample in which elements are selected from a population and placed in the sample on a random basis. In some cases, this is done with a table of random numbers. Tables of random numbers can be found in many places, such as textbooks in statistics. There are even a few volumes that contain nothing but random numbers. Table B.2 at the end of this appendix is a brief table of random numbers. In Chapter 6, while discussing simple random samples, we described in detail how to use such a table, and we need not repeat that discussion here.

It is also possible to generate a list of random numbers of a given sample size through a simple program that can even be used on microcomputers. This relieves researchers of the repetitive chore of selecting numbers from a table.

The following illustration presents a simple program routine, written in BASIC for the Apple IIe, which generates 15 random numbers between 1 and 1000. By modifying the program slightly, one can generate samples of whatever size is required (see Table B.1). Line 10 of the program determines the sample size. To increase the sample size to, say, 250, simply change line 10 to read: 10 for N = 1 TO 250. The second line may look a bit strange to those unfamiliar with pro-

gramming, but the purpose of this statement is fairly straightforward. The RND(1) segment of line 20 generates a random number. However, the random numbers that are generated by the computer are decimals between 0 and 1. Because this is not very useful for our purposes, the INT command is included to tell the computer that we want integers. The "+ 1" sets the minimum number we

TABLE B.1 BASIC Program for Generating Random Numbers

```
]
]
]
]LIST
10 for N = 1 to 15
20 PRINT INT (1000 * RND (1)) + 1
30 NEXT N
40 END
]
]
]RUN
271
140
691
142
153
691
361
629
582
769
724
302
608
248
783
```

483

want at 1 and the 1000 sets the maxi-mum at 1000. All put together, the line says, "Generate a random number be-tween 1 and 1000." Line 30 tells the com-puter to go back and do it again until the desired sample size is reached. With this routine, it is possible to generate the same number more than once, but this is easily solved by generating some extra numbers.

TABLE B.2   A List of Random Numbers

894	920	220	614	090	805	668	331	745	136	071	056	205
493	974	737	304	049	109	097	660	275	036	819	132	807
768	450	669	873	510	712	613	059	924	377	090	315	507
482	379	669	549	746	814	424	217	883	969	246	777	454
621	422	255	762	718	431	883	645	341	148	212	527	557
488	005	671	472	511	746	446	425	889	766	248	860	956
472	782	194	854	272	001	465	118	514	892	258	367	599
554	576	110	002	045	940	724	975	533	401	603	047	221
333	797	019	563	344	349	210	261	204	225	739	730	872
653	346	789	798	616	377	724	625	760	845	430	239	647
018	792	713	967	411	189	654	392	789	308	733	343	168
446	165	992	185	650	158	738	758	284	900	822	217	809
733	098	756	628	982	258	875	694	463	772	162	788	537
324	338	369	374	975	389	657	310	552	951	242	626	135
800	408	564	050	120	844	656	122	270	638	712	442	293
994	349	174	326	424	016	645	595	383	578	393	114	426
776	410	150	051	532	844	219	710	207	763	085	314	858
835	234	461	844	543	475	105	274	191	122	549	991	696
408	051	655	449	318	302	574	581	586	466	123	866	301
356	581	735	113	285	188	235	863	096	585	783	817	030
336	130	491	288	437	351	650	325	673	807	311	844	363
935	737	202	656	201	553	387	933	546	203	930	201	322
975	455	421	422	173	767	163	860	167	939	304	318	227
484	564	624	002	801	589	140	125	059	875	848	345	944
848	669	356	665	029	902	247	804	133	374	407	316	773
836	906	596	608	598	956	481	982	742	757	635	746	967
425	895	530	807	924	685	325	894	571	925	705	559	532
122	251	638	926	678	852	779	707	320	649	809	203	333
034	451	574	656	354	387	913	663	375	079	743	503	635
145	849	295	003	709	118	762	068	784	616	147	959	292
428	232	529	095	487	039	387	957	546	864	107	120	661
755	154	664	651	508	033	915	809	328	137	452	291	539
826	104	222	160	209	051	502	331	146	686	883	400	246
776	604	739	131	166	298	637	123	561	890	701	131	288
407	824	285	927	235	029	020	693	109	638	896	498	486
618	200	842	317	347	457	092	399	155	282	524	001	843
471	229	629	918	141	025	058	833	729	715	300	293	346
820	378	250	979	367	537	907	692	685	185	282	276	351
466	615	866	805	239	138	372	292	787	350	852	026	586
694	817	184	101	428	277	646	584	674	582	545	348	245
378	839	626	595	447	107	403	426	421	177	414	308	652
126	857	405	000	284	823	588	927	228	559	376	230	786
728	088	417	036	171	603	988	692	995	285	056	823	211
719	148	527	527	334	371	726	435	651	414	908	170	684

Source   This table of random numbers was generated by the Computer Center at Northern Mich-igan University with the assistance of John Limback.

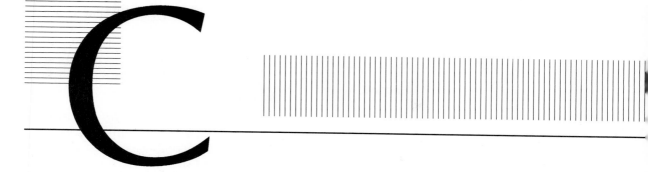

Appendix:
Professional Codes of
Ethics

American Sociological Association

National Association of Social Workers

American Sociological Association

I. SOCIOLOGICAL RESEARCH AND PRACTICE

Objectivity and Integrity

Sociologists should strive to maintain objectivity and integrity in the conduct of sociological research and practice.

1. Sociologists should adhere to the highest possible technical standards in their research. When findings may have direct implications for public policy or for the well-being of subjects, research should not be undertaken unless the requisite skills and resources are available to accomplish the research adequately.

2. Since individual sociologists vary in their research modes, skills and experience, sociologists should always set forth *ex ante* the disciplinary and personal limitations that condition whether or not a research project can be successfully completed and condition the validity of findings.

3. Regardless of work settings, sociologists are obligated to report findings fully and without omission of significant data. Sociologists should also disclose details of their theories, methods and research designs that might bear upon interpretation of research findings.

4. Sociologists must report fully all sources of financial support in their publications and must note any special relations to any sponsor.

5. Sociologists should not make any guarantees to subjects—individuals, groups or organizations—unless there is full intention and ability to honor such commitments. All such guarantees, once made, must be honored unless there is a clear, compelling and overriding reason not to do so.

6. Consistent with the spirit of full disclosure of method and analysis, sociologists should make their data available to other qualified social scientists, at reasonable cost, after they have completed their own analyses, except in cases where confidentiality or the claims of a fieldworker to the privacy of personal notes necessarily would be violated in doing so. The timeliness of this obligation is especially critical where the research is perceived to have policy implications.

7. Sociologists must not accept grants, contracts or research assignments that appear likely to require violation of the principles above, and should dissociate themselves from research when they discover a violation and are unable to achieve its correction.

8. When financial support for a project has been accepted, sociologists must make every reasonable effort to complete the proposed work, including reports to the funding source.

9. When several sociologists, including students, are involved in joint projects, there should be mutually accepted explicit agreements, preferably written, at the outset with respect to division of work, compensation, access to data, rights of authorship, and other rights and

responsibilities. Of course, such agreements may need to be modified as the project evolves.

10. When it is likely that research findings will bear on public policy or debate, sociologists should take particular care to state all significant qualifications on the findings and interpretations of their researches.

Respect for the Rights of Research Populations

1. Individuals, families, households, kin and friendship groups that are subjects of research are entitled to rights of biographical anonymity. Organizations, large collectivities such as neighborhoods, ethnic groups, or religious denominations, corporations, governments, public agencies, public officials, persons in the public eye, are not entitled automatically to privacy and need not be extended routinely guarantees of privacy and confidentiality. However, if any guarantees are made, they must be honored unless there are clear and compelling reasons not to do so.

2. Information about persons obtained from records that are open to public scrutiny cannot be protected by guarantees of privacy or confidentiality.

3. The process of conducting sociological research must not expose subjects to *substantial* risk or personal harm. Where modest risk or harm is anticipated, informed consent must be obtained.

4. To the extent possible in a given study, researchers should anticipate potential threats to confidentiality. Such means as the removal of identifiers, the use of randomized responses, and other statistical solutions to problems of privacy should be used where appropriate.

5. Confidential information provided by research participants must be treated as such by sociologists even when this information enjoys no legal protection or privilege and legal force is applied. The obligation to respect confidentiality also applies to members of research organizations (interviewers, coders, clerical staff, etc.) who have access to the information. It is the responsibility of the chief investigator to instruct staff members on this point.

Source *ASA Footnotes* 10 (March 1982), 9–10. Reprinted by permission of the American Sociological Association.

National Association of Social Workers

I. THE SOCIAL WORKER'S CONDUCT AND COMPORTMENT AS A SOCIAL WORKER

A. Propriety
The social worker should maintain high standards of personal conduct in the capacity or identity as social worker.

1. The private conduct of the social worker is a personal matter to the same degree as is any other person's, except when such conduct

(Continued on next page)

compromises the fulfillment of professional responsibilities.

2. The social worker should not participate in, condone, or be associated with dishonesty, fraud, deceit, or misrepresentation.
3. The social worker should distinguish clearly between statements and actions made as a private individual and as a representative of the social work profession or an organization or group.

B. Competence and Professional Development

The social worker should strive to become and remain proficient in professional practice and the performance of professional functions.

1. The social worker should accept responsibility or employment only on the basis of existing competence or the intention to acquire the necessary competence.
2. The social worker should not misrepresent professional qualifications, education, experience, or affiliations.

C. Service

The social worker should regard as primary the service obligation of the social work profession.

1. The social worker should retain ultimate responsibility for the quality and extent of the service that individual assumes, assigns, or performs.
2. The social worker should act to prevent practices that are inhumane or discriminatory against any person or group of persons.

D. Integrity

The social worker should act in accordance with the highest standards of professional integrity and impartiality.

1. The social worker should be alert to and resist the influences and pressures that interfere with the exercise of professional discretion and impartial judgement required for the performance of professional functions.
2. The social worker should not exploit professional relationships for personal gain.

E. Scholarship and Research

The social worker engaged in study and research should be guided by the conventions of scholarly inquiry.

1. The social worker engaged in research should consider carefully its possible consequences for human beings.
2. The social worker engaged in research should ascertain that the consent of participants in the research is voluntary and informed, without any implied deprivation or penalty for refusal to participate, and with due regard for participants' privacy and dignity.
3. The social worker engaged in research should protect participants from unwarranted physical or mental discomfort, distress, harm, danger, or deprivation.
4. The social worker who engages in the evaluation of services or cases should discuss them only for the professional purposes and only with persons directly and professionally concerned with them.
5. Information obtained about participants in research should be treated as confidential.
6. The social worker should take credit only for work actually done in connection with scholarly and research endeavors and credit contributions made by others.

II. THE SOCIAL WORKER'S ETHICAL RESPONSIBILITY TO CLIENTS

F. Primacy of Clients' Interests

The social worker's primary responsibility is to clients.

1. The social worker should serve clients with devotion, loyalty, determination, and the maximum application of professional skill and competence.
2. The social worker should not exploit relationships with clients for personal advantage, or solicit the clients of one's agency for private practice.
3. The social worker should not practice, condone, facilitate or collaborate with any form of discrimination on the basis of race, color, sex, sexual orientation, age, religion, national origin, marital status, political belief, mental or physical handicap, or any other preference or personal characteristic, condition or status.
4. The social worker should avoid relationships or commitments that conflict with the interests of clients.

Source Reprinted with permission, from *Code of Ethics of the National Association of Social Workers* as adopted by the 1979 NASW Delegate Assembly, effective July 1, 1980.

Glossary

Accidental Samples: samples composed of those elements that are readily available or convenient to the researcher.

Anonymity: a situation in which no one, including the researcher, can link individuals' identities to their responses or behaviors that serve as research data.

Applied Research: research designed with a practical outcome in mind and with the assumption that some group or society as a whole will gain specific benefits from the research.

Area Sampling: a multistage sampling technique that involves moving from larger clusters of units to smaller and smaller ones until the unit of analysis, such as household or individual, is reached.

Available Data: observations collected by someone other than the investigator for purposes that differ from the investigator's but that are available to be analyzed.

Availability Samples: samples composed of those elements that are readily available or convenient to the researcher.

Baseline: a series of measurements of a client's condition prior to treatment that is used as a basis for comparison with the client's condition after treatment is implemented.

Basic Research: research conducted for the purpose of advancing our knowledge about human behavior with little concern for any immediate or practical benefits that might result.

Bivariate Statistics: statistics that describe the relationship between two variables.

Blocking: a two-stage system of assigning subjects to experimental and control groups whereby subjects are first aggregated into blocks according to one or more key variables; members of each block are then randomly assigned to experimental and control conditions.

Causality: the situation where an independent variable is the factor—or one of several factors—that produces variation in a dependent variable.

Clinical-Research Model: the merger of clinical practice and research through the use of single-subject designs.

Closed-Ended Questions: questions that provide respondents with a fixed set of alternatives from which they are to choose.

Cluster Sampling: a multistage sampling technique that involves moving from larger clusters of units to smaller and smaller ones until the unit of analysis, such as household or individual, is reached.

Coding: the categorizing of behavior into a limited number of categories.

Common Sense: practical judgments based on the experiences, wisdom, and prejudices of a people.

Concepts: mental constructs or images developed to symbolize ideas, persons, things, or events.

Concurrent Validity: a type of criterion validity where the results of a newly developed measure are correlated with results of an existing measure.

Confidentiality: ensuring that information or responses will not be publicly linked to specific individuals who participate in research.

Construct Validity: a complex approach to establishing the validity of measures involving relating the measure to a complete theoretical framework including all the concepts and propositions that comprise the theory.

Content Analysis: a method of transforming the contents of documents from a qualitative, unsystematic form to a quantitative, systematic form.

Content Validity: an approach to establishing the validity of measures involving assessing the logical relationship between the proposed measure and the theoretical definition of the variable.

Continuous Variables: variables that theoretically have an infinite number of values.

Control Condition: the condition in an experiment that does not receive the experimental stimulus.

Control Group: the subjects in an experiment who are not exposed to the experimental stimulus.

Control Variables: variables whose value is held constant in all conditions of an experiment.

Convenience Samples: samples composed of those elements that are readily available or convenient to the researcher.

Cost–Benefit Analysis: an approach to program evaluation wherein program costs are related to program benefits expressed in dollars.

Cost-Effective Analysis: an approach to program evaluation wherein program costs are related to program effects, with effects measured in whatever units they naturally occur.

Cover Letter: a letter that accompanies a mailed questionnaire and serves to introduce and explain it to the recipient.

Criterion Validity: a technique for establishing the validity of measures that involves demonstrating a correlation between the measure and some other standard.

Cross-Sectional Research: research based on data collected at one point in time.

Data Analysis: the process of placing observations in numerical form and manipulating them according to their arithmetic properties to derive meaning from them.

Data Archives: a national system of data libraries that lend sets of data much as ordinary libraries lend books.

Deductive Reasoning: inferring a conclusion from more abstract premises or propositions.

Dependent Variable: the passive variable in a relationship or the one that is affected by an independent variable.

Descriptive Research: research that attempts to discover facts or describe reality.

Descriptive Statistics: procedures that assist in organizing, summarizing, and interpreting the sample data we have at hand.

Dimensional Sampling: a sampling technique designed to enhance the representativeness of small samples by specifying all important variables and choosing a sample that contains at least one case to represent all possible combinations of variables.

Direct Costs: a proposed program budget or actual program expenditures.

Direct Replication: the repeated application of the same treatment by the same clinician to clients suffering from the same basic problem.

Discrete Variables: variables with a finite number of distinct and separate values.

Discriminatory Power Score: a value calculated during construction of a Likert scale that indicates the degree to which each item discriminates between high scorers and low scorers on the entire scale.

Double-Blind Experiment: an experiment conducted in such a way that neither the subjects nor the experimenters know which groups are in the experimental and which are in the control condition.

Ecological Fallacy: inferring something about individuals from data collected about groups.

Ethics: the responsibilities that researchers bear toward those who participate in research, those who sponsor research, and those who are potential beneficiaries of research.

Evaluability Assessment: a preliminary investigation into a program prior to its evaluation to determine those aspects of the program that are evaluable.

Evaluation Research: the use of scientific research methods to plan intervention programs, to monitor the implementation of new programs and the operation of existing programs, and to determine how effectively programs or clinical practices achieve their goals.

Experiential Knowledge: knowledge gained through firsthand observation of events and based on the assumption that truth can be achieved through personal experience.

Experimental Condition: the condition in an experiment that receives the experimental stimulus.

Experimental Group: those subjects who are exposed to the experimental stimulus.

Experimental Stimulus: the independent variable in an experiment that is manipulated by the experimenter to assess its effect on behavior.

Experimental variability: variation in a dependent variable produced by an independent variable.

Experimentation: a controlled method of observation in which the value of one or more independent variables is changed in order to assess its causal effect on one or more dependent variables.

Explanatory Research: research whose goal is to determine why or how something occurs.

External Validity: the extent to which causal inferences made in an experiment can be generalized to other times, settings, or people.

Extraneous Variability: variation in a dependent variable from any source other than an experimental stimulus.

Face Validity: another name for content validity. *See* **Content Validity.**

Field Experiments: experiments conducted in naturally occurring settings as people go about their everyday affairs.

Field Notes: detailed, descriptive accounts of observations made in a given setting.

Formative Evaluation Research: evaluation research that focuses on the planning, development, and implementation of a program.

Guttman Scale: a measurement scale in which the items have a fixed progressive order and that has the characteristic of reproducibility.

Human Services: professions whose primary goal is enhancing the relationship between people and societal institutions so that people may maximize their potential.

Hypotheses: testable statements of presumed relationships between two or more concepts.

Independent Variable: the presumed active or causal variable in a relationship.

Index: a measurement technique that combines a number of items into a composite score.

Indicator: an observation that is assumed to be evidence of the attributes or properties of some phenomenon.

Inductive Reasoning: inferring something about a whole group or class of objects from knowledge of one or a few members of that group or class.

Inferential Statistics: procedures that allow us to make generalizations from sample data to the populations from which the samples were drawn.

Informed Consent: telling potential research participants about all aspects of the research that might reasonably influence their decision to participate.

Internal Validity: an issue in experimentation concerning whether the independent variable actually produces the effect it appears to have on the dependent variable.

Interval Measures: measures that classify observations into mutually exclusive categories with an inherent order and equal spacing between the categories.

Interview: a technique in which an interviewer reads questions to respondents and records their verbal responses.

Interview Schedule: a document, used in interviewing, similar to a questionnaire, that contains instructions for the interviewer, specific questions in a fixed order, and transition phrases for the interviewer.

Item: a single indicator of a variable, such as an answer to a question or an observation of some behavior or characteristic.

Judgmental Sampling: a nonprobability sampling technique in which investigators use their judgment and prior knowledge to choose people for the sample who would best serve the purposes of the study.

Laboratory Experiments: experiments conducted in artificial settings constructed in such a way that selected elements of the natural environment are simulated and features of the investigation are controlled.

Levels of Measurement: rules that define permissible mathematical operations on a given set of numbers produced by a measure.

Likert Scale: a measurement scale consisting of a series of statements followed by five response alternatives, typically: strongly agree, agree, no opinion, disagree, or strongly disagree.

Longitudinal Research: research based on data gathered over an extended time period.

Matching: a process of assigning subjects to experimental and control groups in which each subject is paired with a similar subject in the other group.

Measurement: the process of describing abstract concepts in terms of specific indicators by the assignment of numbers or other symbols to these indicants in accordance with rules.

Measurement Scale: a measurement device in which responses to a number of items are combined to form a composite score on a variable.

Measures of Association: statistics that describe the strength of relationships between variables.

Measures of Central Tendency: statistics, also known as averages, that summarize distributions of data by locating the "typical" or "average" value.

Measures of Dispersion: statistics that indicate how dispersed or spread out the values of a distribution are.

Missing Data: incomplete data found in available data sets.

Multidimensional Scaling: a scaling technique designed to measure complex variables composed of more than one dimension.

Multistage Sampling: a multiple-tiered sampling technique that involves moving from larger clusters of units to smaller and smaller ones until the unit of analysis, such as the household or individual, is reached.

Multitrait-Multimethod Approach to Validity: a particularly complex form of construct validity involving the simultaneous assessment of numerous measures and numerous concepts through the computation of inter-correlations.

Multivariate Statistics: statistics that describe the relationships among three or more variables.

Nominal Definitions: verbal definitions in which one set of words or symbols is used to stand for another set of words or symbols.

Nominal Measures: measures that classify observations into mutually exclusive categories but with no ordering to the categories.

Nonprobability Samples: samples in which the probability of each population element being included in the sample is unknown.

Nonreactive Observation: observation where those under study are not aware that they are being studied and the investigator does not change their behavior by his or her presence.

Observational Techniques: the collection of data through direct visual or auditory experience of behavior.

Open-Ended Questions: questions without a fixed set of alternatives, thus leaving respondents completely free to formulate their own responses.

Operational Definitions: definitions that indicate the precise procedures or operations to be followed in measuring a concept.

Opportunity Costs: the value of forgone opportunities incurred by funding one program as opposed to some other program.

Ordinal Measures: measures that classify observations into mutually exclusive categories that have an inherent order to them.

Panel Study: research in which data are gathered from the same people at different times.

Participant Observation: a method in which the researcher is a part of, and participates in, the activities of the people, group, or situation that is being studied.

Physical Traces: objects or evidence that results from people's activities that can be used as data to test hypotheses.

Pilot Study: a trial run on a small scale of all procedures planned for a research project.

Population: all possible cases of what we are interested in studying.

Positivism: the perspective that human behavior should be studied only in terms of behavior that can be observed and recorded by means of some objective technique.

Predictive Research: research that attempts to make projections about what will occur in the future or in other settings.

Predictive Validity: a type of criterion validity wherein scores on a measure are used to predict some future state of affairs.

Preexperimental Designs: crude experimental designs that lack the necessary controls of the threats to internal validity.

Pretest: a preliminary application of the data-gathering technique to assess the adequacy of the technique.

Privacy: the ability to control when and under what conditions others will have access to your beliefs, values, or behavior.

Probability Samples: samples in which each element in the population has a known chance of being selected into the sample.

Probes: follow-up questions used during an interview to elicit clearer and more complete responses.

Propositions: statements about the relationship between elements in a theory.

Pure Research: research conducted for the purpose of advancing our knowledge about human behavior with little concern for any immediate or practical benefits that might result.

Purposive Sampling: a nonprobability sampling technique where investigators use their judgment and prior knowledge to choose people for the sample who would best serve the purposes of the study.

Quasi-Experimental Designs: designs that approximate experimental control in nonexperimental settings.

Questionnaire: a set of written questions that people respond to directly on the form itself without the aid of an interviewer.

Quota Sampling: a type of nonprobability sampling that involves dividing the population into various categories and determining the number of elements to be selected from each category.

Random Assignment: a process for assigning subjects to experimental and control groups that relies on probability theory to equalize the groups.

Random Errors: measurement errors that are neither consistent nor patterned.

Ratio Measures: measures that classify observations into mutually exclusive categories with an inherent order, equal spacing between the categories, and an absolute zero point.

Reactivity: the degree to which the presence of a researcher influences the behavior being observed.

Reliability: the ability of a measure to yield consistent results each time it is applied.

Representative Sample: a sample that accurately reflects the distribution of relevant variables in the target population.

Research Design: a detailed plan outlining how a research project will be conducted.

Response Bias: responses to questions that are shaped by factors other than the person's true feelings, intentions, and beliefs.

Response Rate: the percentage of a sample that completes and returns a questionnaire or agrees to be interviewed.

Sample: one or more elements selected from a population.

Sampling Error: the extent to which the values of a sample differ from those of the population from which it was drawn.

Sampling Frame: a listing of all the elements in a population.

Scale: a measurement technique, similar to an index, that combines a number of items into a composite score.

Science: a method of obtaining objective knowledge about the world through systematic observation.

Secondary Analysis: the reanalysis of data collected for some other research project.

Semantic Differential: a scaling technique that involves respondents rating a concept on a scale between a series of polar opposite adjectives.

Simple Random Sampling: a sampling technique wherein the target population is treated as a unitary whole and each element has an equal probability of being selected for the sample.

Single-Subject Designs: quasi-experimental designs featuring continuous or nearly continuous measurement of the dependent variable on a single research subject over a time interval that is divided into a baseline phase and one or more additional phases during which the independent variable is manipulated; experimental effects are inferred by comparisons of the subject's responses across baseline and intervention phases.

Snowball Sampling: a type of nonprobability sampling where a few cases of the type we wish to study lead to more cases, who, in turn, lead to still more cases until a sufficient sample is built up.

Social Research: a systematic examination (or reexamination) of empirical data collected by someone at firsthand, concerning the social or psychological forces operating in a situation.

Statistics: procedures for assembling, classifying, and tabulating numerical data so that some meaning or information is derived.

Stratified Sampling: a sampling technique wherein the population is subdivided into strata with separate subsamples drawn from each strata.

Summated Rating Scales: scales in which a respondent's score is determined by summing the numbers of questions answered.

Summative Evaluation Research: evaluation research that assesses the effectiveness and efficiency of programs and the extent to which program effects are generalizable to other settings and populations.

Survey: a data collection technique in which information is gathered from individuals, called respondents, by having them respond to questions.

Systematic Errors: measurement errors that are consistent and patterned.

Systematic Replication: an attempt to

extend a treatment to different settings, practitioners, or client disorders or any combination of these conditions.

Systematic Sampling: a type of simple random sampling wherein every *k*th element of the sampling frame is selected for the sample.

Theory: a set of interrelated propositions or statements, organized into a deductive system, that offers an explanation of some phenomenon.

Thurstone Scale: a measurement scale consisting of a series of items with a predetermined scale value to which respondents indicate their agreement or disagreement.

Time Sampling: a sampling technique used in observational research where observations are made only during certain preselected times.

Traditional Knowledge: knowledge based on custom, habit, and repetition.

Trend Study: research in which data are gathered from different people at different points in time.

True Experimental Designs: experimental designs that utilize randomization, control groups, and other techniques to control threats to internal validity.

Unidimensional Scale: a multiple-item scale that measures one, and only one, variable.

Units of Analysis: the specific objects or elements whose characteristics we wish to describe or explain and about which data are collected.

Univariate Statistics: statistics that describe the distribution of a single variable.

Unobtrusive Observation: observation where those under study are not aware that they are being studied and the investigator does not change their behavior by his or her presence.

Validity: the degree to which a measure accurately reflects the theoretical meaning of a variable.

Variables: operationally defined concepts that can take on more than one value.

Verification: The process of subjecting hypotheses to empirical tests to see if a theory is supported or refuted.

Verstehen: the effort to view and understand a situation from the perspective of the people actually in that situation.

References

Achen, C. H. *The Statistical Analysis of Quasi-Experiments.* Berkeley, Calif.: University of California Press, 1986.

Adair, J. G., Terrance W. Dushenko, and R. C. L. Lindsay. Ethical Regulations and Their Impact on Research Practice. *American Psychologist,* 40 (January 1985), 59–72.

Adams, S., and M. Orgel. *Through the Mental Health Maze: A Consumer's Guide to Finding a Psychotherapist.* Washington, D.C.: Health Research Group, Public Citizen, 1975.

Adler, P. A. *Wheeling and Dealing: An Ethnography of an Upper-Level Drug Dealing and Smuggling Community.* New York: Columbia University Press, 1985.

Allen, G. J. Case Study: Implementation of Behavior Modification Techniques in Summer Camp Settings. *Behavior Therapy,* 4 (1973), 570–575.

Allen-Meares, P. Content Analysis: It Does Have a Place in Social Work Research. *Journal of Social Service Research,* 7 (Summer 1984), 51–68.

Amato, P. R. Family Processes in One-Parent, Stepparent, and Intact Families: The Child's Point of View. *Journal of Marriage and the Family,* 49 (May 1987), 327–337.

Annis, R. C., and B. Corenblum. Effect of Test Language and Experimenter Race on Canadian Indian Children's Racial and Self-Identity. *Journal of Social Psychology,* 126 (December 1986), 761–773.

Archer, D., B. Iritiani, D. D. Kimes, and M. Barrios. Face-ism: Five Studies of Sex Differences in Facial Prominence. *Journal of Personality and Social Psychology,* 45 (1983), 725–735.

Armstrong, J. S., and E. J. Luck. Return Postage in Mail Surveys: A Meta-Analysis. *Public Opinion Quarterly,* 51 (Summer 1987), 233–248.

Arnold, D. O. Dimensional Sampling: An Approach for Studying a Small Number of Cases. *The American Sociologist,* 5 (1970), 147–150.

Arrests of Wife-Beaters Rise in New Policy in Minneapolis. *New York Times,* July 24, 1984, 10.

Ashcraft, N., and A. E. Scheflen. *People Space: The Making and Breaking of Human Boundaries.* New York: Doubleday, 1976.

Babbie, E. R. *The Practice of Social Research.* 4th ed. Belmont, Calif.: Wadsworth, 1986.

————. *The Practice of Social Research.* 5th ed. Belmont, Calif.: Wadsworth, 1989.

Bachman, J. G., and P. M. O'Malley. Yea-Saying, Nay-Saying, and Going to Extremes: Black-White Differences in Response Styles. *Public Opinion Quarterly,* 48 (1984), 491–501.

Backstrom, C. H., and G. D. Hursh. *Survey Research.* 2d ed. New York: Macmillan, 1981.

Bailey, K. *Methods of Social Research.* 3d ed. New York: The Free Press, 1987.

Baker, T., and W. W. Vosburgh. Workers, Cases, and Errors: The Effect of Workload on Errors in Public Assistance Eligibility Determinations. *Administration in Social Work,* 1 (1977), 161–170.

Bales, R. F. *Interaction Process Analysis.* Cambridge, Mass.: Addison-Wesley, 1950.

————. Some Uniformities of Behavior in Small Social Systems. In G. E. Swanson, T. M. Newcomb, and E. L. Hartley, eds., *Readings in Social Psychology,* rev. ed. New York: Henry Holt and Company, 1952, 146–159.

Barlow, D. H., S. C. Hayes, and R. O. Nelson. *The Scientist Researcher: Research and Accountability in Clinical and Educational Settings.* New York: Pergamon Press, 1984.

————, and M. Hersen. *Single Case Experimental Designs: Strategies for Studying Behavior Change,* 2d ed. New York: Pergamon Press, 1984.

————, and M. Hersen. Single-Case Experimental Designs: Uses in Applied Clinical Research. *Archives of General Psychiatry,* 29 (1973), 319–325.

Barth, R. P. Education for Practice-Research: Toward a Reorientation. *Journal of Education for Social Work,* 17 (1981), 19–25.

Barth, S. The Men Who Hit Women. *Coastlines,* 15 (October/November 1984), 4–7.

Bassuk, E. L. The Homelessness Problem. *Scientific American,* 251 (July 1984), 40–45.

Bauer, D. G. *The "How To" Grants Manual: Successful Grantseeking Techniques for Obtaining Public and Private Funds.* New York: American Council on Education/Macmillan Publishing Co., 1988.

Baumrind, D. Research Using Intentional Deception. *American Psychologist,* 40:2 (February 1985), 165–174.

Bean, G. J., Jr., M. E. Stefl, and S. R. Howe. Mental Health and Homelessness: Issues and Findings. *Social Work,* 32 (September/October 1987), 411–416.

Beauchamp, T. L., R. R. Faden, R. J. Wallace, Jr., and L. Walters, eds. *Ethical Issues in Social Science Research.* Baltimore, Md.: The Johns Hopkins University Press, 1982.

Becerra, R. M., and R. E. Zambrana. Methodological Approaches to Research on Hispanics. *Social Work Research and Abstracts,* 21 (Summer 1985), 42–49.

Becker, H. S. Becoming a Marijuana User. *American Journal of Sociology,* 59 (1953), 235–242.

————. Whose Side Are We On? *Social Problems,* 14 (1967), 239–247.

Bedell, J. R., J. C. Ward, Jr., R. P. Archer, and M. K. Stokes. An Empirical Evaluation of a Model of Knowledge Utilization. *Evaluation Review,* (9 April 1985), 109–126.

Bell, A. P., and M. S. Weinberg. *Homosexualities: A Study of Diversity Among Men and Women,* New York: Simon & Schuster, 1978.

Bell, W. *Contemporary Social Welfare,* 2d ed. New York: MacMillan, 1987.

Berk, R. A., and D. Rauma. Capitalizing on Nonrandom Assignment to Treatments: A Regression Discontinuity Evaluation of a Crime-Control Program. *Journal of the American Statistical Association,* 78 (1983), 21.

————, et al. Social Policy Experimentation: A Position Paper. *Evaluation Review,* 9 (August 1985), 387–430.

Berman, P., and E. Pauly. *Federal Programs Supporting Educational Change.* Vol. 2: *Factors Affecting Change Agent Projects.* Santa Monica, Calif.: Rand, 1975.

Berry, S. H., and D. E. Kanouse. Physican Response to a Mailed Survey: An Experiment in Timing of Payment. *Public Opinion Quarterly*, 51 (Spring 1987), 102–114.

Biklen, D. P. Behavior Modification in a State Mental Hospital: A Participant Observer's Critique. *American Journal of Orthopsychiatry*, 46 (1976), 53–61.

Billups, J. O., and M. C. Julia. Changing Profile of Social Work Practice. *Social Work Research and Abstracts*, 23 (Winter 1987), 17–22.

Binder, A., G. Geis, and D. Bruce. *Juvenile Delinquency: Historical, Cultural, and Legal Perspectives*. New York: Macmillan, 1988.

Blatterbauer, S., M. J. Kupst, and J. L. Schulman. Enhancing the Relationship Between Physician and Patient. *Health and Social Work*, 1 (1976), 489–506.

Blenkner, M. Obstacles to Evaluative Research in Casework, Part I. *Social Casework*, 31 (1950), 54–60.

Bloom, M. Challenges to the Helping Professions and the Response of Scientific Practice. *Social Service Review*, 52 (1978), 584–595.

————, and J. Fischer. *Evaluating Practice: Guidelines for the Accountable Professional*. Englewood Cliffs, N.J.: Prentice-Hall, 1982.

Bodemann, M. Y. A Problem of Sociological Praxis: The Case For Interventive Observation in Field Work. *Theory and Society*, 5 (1978), 387–420.

Boffey, P. M. Spread of AIDS Abating, But Deaths Will Still Soar. *New York Times*, February 14, 1988, 1.

Bogdan, R., and S. J. Taylor. *Introduction to Qualitative Research Methods*. New York: Wiley, 1975.

Bonjean, C. M., R. J. Hill, and S. D. McLemore. *Sociological Measurement: An Inventory of Scales and Indices*. San Francisco, Calif.: Chandler, 1967.

Bradburn, N. M., and S. Sudman. *Improving Interview Method and Questionnaire Design*. San Francisco, Calif.: Jossey-Bass, 1979.

Bradford, J. D., and B. S. Stein. *The Ideal Problem Solver: A Guide for Improving Thinking, Learning, and Creativity*. New York: Freeman, 1984.

Briar, S. Incorporating Research into Education for Clinical Practice in Social Work: Toward a Clinical Science in Social Work. In A. Rubin and A. Rosenblatt, eds., *Sourcebook on Research Utilization*. New York: Council on Social Work Education, 1979.

Bridge, R. G. *Nonresponse Bias in Mail Surveys*. Defense Advanced Research Projects Agency R-1501. Santa Monica, Calif.: Rand, 1974.

Bronowski, J. *The Origins of Knowledge and Imagination*. New Haven, Conn.: Yale University Press, 1978.

Bronson, D. E., and B. J. Blythe. Computer Support for Single-Case Evaluation of Practice. *Social Work Research and Abstracts*, 23 (1987), 10–13.

Brown, J. S., and B. G. Gilmartin. Sociology Today: Lacunae, Emphases, and Surfeits. *The American Sociologist*, 4 (1969), 283–291.

Brown, S. V. The Commitment and Concerns of Black Adolescent Parents. *Social Work Research and Abstracts*, 19 (1983), 27–34.

Brunner, G. A., and S. J. Carroll. Effect of Prior Telephone Appointments on Completion Rates and Response Content. *Public Opinion Quarterly*, 31 (1967), 652–654.

Brunswick-Heineman, M. The Obsolete Scientific Imperative in Social Work Research. *Social Service Review*, 55 (1981), 371–397.

Buckhout, R. Eyewitness Testimony. *Scientific American*, 231 (1974), 23–31.

Burch, G., and V. Mohr. Evaluating a Child Abuse Intervention Program. *Social Casework*, 61 (1980), 90–99.

Burgess, R. G. *In the Field: An Introduction to Field Research*. London: George Allen and Unwin, 1984.

Burgess, R. L., and R. D. Conger. Family Interaction in Abusive, Neglectful, and Normal Families. *Child Development*, 49 (1978), 1163–1173.

Burnam, M. A., and P. Koegel. Methodology for Obtaining a Representative Sample of Homeless Persons: The Los Angeles Skid Row Study. *Evaluation Review*, 12 (April 1988), 117–152.

Campbell, D. T., and D. W. Fiske. Convergent and Discriminant Validity by the Multitrait-Multimethod Matrix. *Psychological Bulletin*, 56 (1959), 81–105.

————, and H. L. Ross. The Connecticut Crack-down on Speeding: Time Series Data in Quasi-Experimental Analysis. *Law and Society Review*, 3 (1968), 33–53.

————, and J. C. Stanley. *Experimental and Quasi-Experimental Designs for Research.* Chicago: Rand McNally, 1963.

Campbell, J. A. Client Acceptance of Single-System Evaluation Procedures. *Social Work Research and Abstracts*, 24 (1988), 21–22.

Cannell, C. F., and R. L. Kahn. Interviewing. In G. Lindzey and E. Aronson, eds. *The Handbook of Social Psychology.* 2d ed. Vol. 2. Reading, Mass.: Addison-Wesley, 1968.

Carley, M. *Social Measurement and Social Indicators: Issues of Policy and Theory.* Boston: Allen and Unwin, 1983.

Carlock, C. J., and P. Y. Martin. Sex Composition and the Intensive Group Experience. *Social Work*, 22 (1977), 27–32.

Carpenter, E. H. The Evolving Statistics and Research Process Using Microcomputer Statistical Software. *Social Science Microcomputer Review*, 5 (Winter 1987), 529–545.

Carpenter, J., D. Deloria, and D. Morganstein. Statistical Software for Microcomputers. *Byte*, (April 1984), 234–264.

Carroll, L. *Through the Looking Glass.* New York: Random House, 1946.

Cartwright, A., and W. Tucker. An Attempt to Reduce the Number of Calls on an Interview Inquiry. *Public Opinion Quarterly*, 31 (1967), 299–302.

Catlin, G., and S. Ingram. The Effects of CATI on Costs and Data Quality: A Comparison of CATI and Paper Methods. In Centralized Interviewing in R. G. Groves, et al., eds. *Telephone Survey Methodology.* New York: Wiley, 1988.

Cavan, S. *Liquor License.* Chicago: Aldine, 1966.

Ceci, S. J., D. Peters, and J. Plotkin. Human Subjects Review, Personal Values, and the Regulation of Social Science Research. *American Psychologist*, 40 (September 1985), 994–1002.

Chaiken, M. R., and J. M. Chaiken. Offender Types and Public Policy. *Crime and Delinquency*, 30 (April 1984), 195–226.

Chalfant, H. P., and R. A. Kurtz. Factors Affecting Social Workers' Judgments of Alcoholics. *Journal of Health and Social Behavior*, 13 (1972), 331–336.

Champion, D. J. *Basic Statistics for Social Research.* 2d ed. Scranton, Pa.: Chandler, 1981.

Chen, H., and P. H. Rossi. The Multi-Goal, Theory-Driven Approach to Evaluation: A Model Linking Basic and Applied Social Science. *Social Forces*, 59 (1980), 106–122.

Christie, R., and F. L. Geis. *Studies in Machiavellianism.* New York: Academic Press, 1970.

Chronicle of Higher Education, June 22, 1988, A–22.

Chun, K., S. Cobb, and J. French. *Measures for Psychological Assessment.* Ann Arbor, Mich.: Institute for Social Research, University of Michigan, 1975.

Coehlo, R. J. *An Experimental Investigation of Two Multi-Component Approaches on Smoking Cessation.* Unpublished doctoral dissertation, Michigan State University, East Lansing, Mich., 1983.

Cohen, J. *Statistical Power Analysis for the Behavioral Sciences*, rev. ed. New York: Academic Press, 1977.

Cohen, L. E. *Delinquency Dispositions: Analytic Report 9.* U.S. Department of Justice, Law Enforcement Assistance Administration, National Criminal Justice Information and Statistics Service. Washington, D.C.: U.S. Government Printing Office, 1975.

Cohen, M. R., and E. Nagel. *An Introduction to Logic and Scientific Method.* New York: Harcourt, 1934.

Colby, D., and D. Baker. Socioeconomic and Psychological Determinants of Welfare Policy Attitudes: Path Models. *Journal of Social Service Research,* 1 (1978), 345–356.

Committee on the Status of Women in Sociology. *The Treatment of Gender in Research.* Washington, D.C.: American Sociological Association, 1986.

Connaway, R. S., and M. E. Gentry. *Social Work Practice.* Englewood Cliffs, N.J.: Prentice Hall, 1988.

Cook, T. D., and D. T. Campbell. *Quasi-Experimentation: Design and Analysis Issues for Field Settings.* Chicago: Rand McNally, 1979.

—————, F. L. Cook, and M. M. Mark. Randomized and Quasi-Experimental Designs in Evaluation Research: An Introduction. In L. Rutman, ed. *Evaluation Research Methods.* Beverly Hills, Calif.: Sage, 1977.

Corcoran, K., and J. Fischer. *Measures For Clinical Practice: A Sourcebook.* New York: Free Press, 1987.

Corry, J. Children's TV Found Dominated by White Men. *New York Times,* July 15, 1982, p. 14.

Cotter, P. R., J. Cohen, and P. B. Coulter. Race-Of-Interviewer Effects in Telephone Interviews. *Public Opinion Quarterly,* 46 (1982), 278–284.

Coulton, C. J. Developing an Instrument to Measure Person-Environment Fit. *Journal of Social Service Research,* 3 (1979), 159–174.

Council on Social Work Education. *Handbook of Accreditation Standards and Procedures.* Washington, D.C., 1987

Cox, D. E., and C. N. Sipprelle. Coercion in Participation as a Research Subject. *American Psychologist,* 26 (1971), 726–728.

Crime Records in Police Management: New York City. Institute of Public Administration, 1952. In M. Wolfgang, L. Savitz, and N. Johnston, eds. *The Sociology of Crime and Delinquency.* 2d ed. New York: Wiley, 1970, 114–116.

Cronbach, L. J. Coefficient Alpha and the Internal Structure of Tests. *Psychometrica,* 16 (1951), 197–334.

—————, and P. Meehl. Construct Validity in Psychological Tests. *Psychological Bulletin,* 52 (1955), 281–302.

Crosby, F., S. Bromley, and L. Saxe. Recent Unobtrusive Studies of Black and White Discrimination and Prejudice. *Psychological Bulletin,* 87 (1980), 546–563.

Croxton, T. A. The Therapeutic Contract in Social Treatment. In P. Glasser, R. Sarri, and R. Vinter, eds. *Individual Change Through Small Groups.* New York: Free Press, 1974.

Datesman, S. K., and F. R. Scarpitti. Female Delinquency and Broken Homes: A Reassessment. *Criminology,* 13 (1975), 33–55.

Davis, A. J. Sex-Differentiated Behaviors in Nonsexist Picture Books. *Sex Roles,* 11 (July 1984), 1–16.

Davis, L. V. Beliefs of Social Service Providers About Abused Women and Abusing Men. *Social Work,* 29 (May/June 1984), 243–250.

—————. A Feminist Approach to Social Work Research. *Affilia,* (Spring 1986), 32–47.

Dawson, J. A., and J. J. D'Amico, Involving Program Staff in Evaluation Studies: A Strategy for Increasing Information Use and Enriching the Data Base. *Evaluation Review,* 9 (April 1985), 173–188.

Dean, J. P. Participant Observation and Interviewing. In J. T. Doby, ed. *Introduction to Social Research,* Harrisburg, Pa.: Stackpole, 1954.

—————, R. L. Eichhorn, and L. R. Dean. Establishing Field Relations. In G. J. McCall and J. L. Simmons, eds. *Issues in Participant Observation.* Reading, Mass.: Addison-Wesley, 1969.

DeMaio, T. J. Social Desirability and Survey Measurement: A Review. In C. F. Turner and E. Martin, eds. *Surveying Subjective*

Phenomena, 2. New York: Russell Sage Foundation, 1984.

Denzin, N. K. *The Research Act*. Chicago: Aldine, 1970.

————. *The Research Act*, 2d ed. New York: McGraw-Hill, 1978.

Deutch, S. J., and F. B. Alt. The Effect of Massachusetts' Gun Control Law on Gun-Related Crimes in the City of Boston. *Evaluation Quarterly*, 1 (1977), 543–567.

DiVista, F. J. A Developmental Study of the Semantic Structure of Children. *Journal of Verbal Learning and Verbal Behavior*, 5 (1966), 249–259.

Dotson, L. E., and G. F. Summers. Elaboration of Guttman Scaling Techniques. In G. F. Summers, ed. *Attitude Measurement*. Chicago: Rand McNally, 1970.

Dougherty, S. A. Single Adoptive Mothers and Their Children. *Social Work*, 23 (1978), 311–314.

Dougherty, W. H., and R. E. Engel. An 80's Look for Sex Equality in Caldecott Winners and Honors Books. *Reading Teacher*, 40 (January 1987), 394–398.

Dressel, P. L., and D. M. Petersen. Becoming a Male Stripper: Recruitment, Socialization, and Ideological Development. *Work and Occupations*, 9 (August 1982), 387–406.

Duehn, W. D., and E. K. Proctor. Initial Clinical Interaction and Premature Discontinuance in Treatment. *American Journal of Orthopsychiatry*, 47 (1977), 284–290.

Dutton, D. G. *The Domestic Assault of Women*. Boston: Allyn and Bacon, 1988.

Edlesen, J. L. Rapid Assessment Instruments for Evaluating Practice with Children and Youth. *Journal of Social Service Research*, 8 (1985), 17–31.

Edwards, A. L. *Techniques of Attitude Scale Construction*. New York: Appleton-Century-Crofts, 1957.

————. *Statistical Methods*. 2d ed. New York: Holt, Rinehart and Winston, 1967.

————, and F. P. Kilpatrick. A Technique for the Construction of Attitude Scales. *Journal of Applied Psychology*, 32 (1948), 374–384.

Eichler, M. *Nonsexist Research Methods: A Practical Guide*. Boston: Allen and Unwin, 1988.

Elliott, D. S., and D. Huizinga. Social Class and Delinquent Behavior in a National Youth Panel: 1976–1980. *Criminology*, 21 (1983), 149–177.

Elms, A. C. Keeping Deception Honest: Justifying Conditions for Social Scientific Research Strategies. In T. L. Beauchamp, R. R. Faden, R. J. Wallace, Jr., and L. Walters, eds. *Ethical Issues in Social Science Research*. Baltimore, Md.: The Johns Hopkins University Press, 1982.

Engler, R. L., et al. Misrepresentation and Responsibility in Medical Research. *New England Journal of Medicine*, 17 (November 26, 1987), 1383–1389.

Epstein, I., and T. Tripodi. *Research Techniques for Program Planning, Monitoring, and Evaluation*. New York: Columbia University Press, 1977.

Erikson, K. T. A Comment on Disguised Observation in Sociology. *Social Problems*, 14 (1967), 366–373.

Estroff, S. E. Making It Crazy: Some Paradoxes of Psychiatric Patienthood in an American Community and a Research/Discovery Process to Encounter Them. Paper presented at the Annual Meeting of the American Anthropological Association, Los Angeles, Calif., 1978.

Fanshel, D. *Foster Parenthood*. Minneapolis, Minn.: University of Minnesota Press, 1966.

————. Status Differentials: Men and Women in Social Work. *Social Work*, 21 (1976), 448–454.

Farley, Reynolds. *Blacks and Whites: Narrowing the Gap*. Cambridge, Mass.: Harvard University Press, 1984.

Federal Bureau of Investigation. *Uniform Crime Reports: Crime in the United States, 1986*. Washington, D. C.: U.S. Government Printing Office, 1987.

Feldman, R. A., and T. E. Caplinger. Social Work Experience and Client Behavioral Change: A Multivariate Analysis of Process and Outcome. *Journal of Social Service Research*, 1 (1977), 5–33.

Festinger, L., H. Riecken, and S. Schachter. *When Prophecy Fails.* New York: Harper & Row, 1956.

Fischer, J. Is Casework Effective? A Review. *Social Work*, 18 (1973), 5–20.

————. *Effective Casework Practice: An Eclectic Approach.* New York: McGraw-Hill, 1978.

————. The Social Work Revolution. *Social Work*, 26 (1981). 199–207.

Fisher, E. Children's Books: The Second Sex, Junior Division. In Judith Stacey, et al., eds. *And Jill Came Tumbling After: Sexism in American Education.* New York: Dell, 1974.

Fortune, A. E. Communication in Task-Centered Treatment. *Social Work*, 24 (1979), 390–397.

Foundation Directory, 11th ed. New York: The Foundation Center, 1987.

Frankel, F., and V. Graham. Systematic Observation of Classroom Behavior of Retarded and Autistic Preschool Children. *American Journal of Mental Deficiency*, 81 (1976), 73–84.

Franklin, D. L. Differential Clinical Assessments: The Influence of Class and Race. *Social Service Review*, 59 (March 1985), 44–61.

Frey, J. H. An Experiment with a Confidentiality Reminder in a Telephone Survey. *Public Opinion Quarterly*, 50 (Summer 1986), 267–269.

Fridlund, A. J. Statistics Software. *Infoworld*, (September 1, 1986), 31–39.

Frisch, M. B., and R. L. Higgins. Instructional Demand Effects and the Correspondence Among Role-Play, Self-Report, and Naturalistic Measures of Social Skill. *Behavioral Assessment*, 8 (Summer 1986), 221–236.

Gallagher, B. J., III. *The Sociology of Mental Illness*, 2d ed. Englewood Cliffs, N.J.: Prentice Hall, 1987.

Galtung, J. *Theory and Methods of Social Research.* New York: Columbia University Press, 1967.

Gardner, J. E. Behavior Therapy Treatment Approach to a Psychogenic Seizure Case. *Journal of Consulting Psychology*, 31 (1967), 209–212.

Garner, J. H., and C. A. Visher. Policy Experiments Come of Age. *National Institute of Justice Reports*, 211 (September/October 1988), 2–7.

Gelles, R. J. What to Learn From Cross-Cultural and Historical Research on Child Abuse and Neglect: An Overview. In R. J. Gelles, and J. B. Lancaster, eds. *Child Abuse and Neglect: Biosocial Dimensions.* New York: Aldine de Gruyter, 1987.

————. Methods for Studying Sensitive Family Topics. *American Journal of Orthopsychiatry*, 48 (1978), 408–424.

Gentry, M. E., R. S. Connaway, and M. Morelock. Research Activities of Social Workers in Agencies. *Social Work Research and Abstracts*, 20 (Winter 1984), 3–5.

Gettinger, S., and K. Krajick. The Demise of Prison Medical Research. *Corrections Magazine*, (December 1979), 5–15.

Gibbs, L. E. Evaluation Researcher: Scientist or Advocate? *Journal of Social Service Research*, 7 (Fall 1983), 81–92.

Gilligan, C. *In a Different Voice: Psychological Theory and Women's Development.* Cambridge, Mass.: Harvard University Press, 1982.

Gold, R. L. Roles in Sociological Field Observations. *Social Forces*, 36 (1958), 217–223.

Goldberg, G. S., R. Kantrow, E. Kremen, and L. Lauter. Spouseless, Childless Elderly Women and Their Social Supports. *Social Work*, 31 (March/April 1986), 104–112.

Goode, W. J., and P. K. Hatt. *Methods in Social Research.* New York: McGraw-Hill, 1952.

Gorden, R. L. *Interviewing: Strategies, Techniques and Tactics.* 4th ed. Chicago, Ill.: Dorsey Press, 1987.

Gordon, M. M. *The Scope of Sociology.* New York: Oxford University Press, 1988.

Gordon, R. A. Issues in the Ecological Study of

Delinquency. *American Sociological Review*, 32 (1967), 927–944.

Gordon, W. E. Knowledge and Value: Their Distinction and Relationship in Clarifying Social Work Practice. In B. R. Compton and B. Galaway, eds. *Social Work Processes*, rev. ed. Homewood, Ill.: Dorsey Press, 1979.

Gottman, J. M. *Time-Series Analysis: A Comprehensive Introduction for Social Scientists*. New York: Cambridge University Press, 1981.

—————. Observational Measures of Behavior Therapy Outcome: A Reply to Jacobson. *Behavioral Assessment*, 7 (Fall 1985), 317–321.

Gouldner, A. W. Anti-Minotaur: The Myth of a Value-Free Sociology. *Social Problems*, 9 (1962), 199–213.

Gove, W. R., and M. Geerken. Response Bias in Surveys of Mental Health: An Empirical Investigation. *American Journal of Sociology*, 82 (1977), 1289–1317.

—————, and R. D. Crutchfield. The Family and Juvenile Delinquency. *The Sociological Quarterly*, 23 (1982), 301–319.

Goyder, J. Face-to-Face Interviews and Mailed Questionnaries: The Net Difference in Response Rate. *Public Opinion Quarterly*, 49 (Summer 1985), 234–252.

Graham, K., L. LaRocque, R. Yetman, T. J. Ross, and E. Guistra. Aggression and Barroom Environments. *Journal of Studies on Alcohol*, 41 (1980), 277–292.

Graham, K. R. *Psychological Research: Controlled Interpersonal Research*. Monterey, Calif.: Brooks/Cole, 1977.

Gray, B. H. The Regulatory Context of Social and Behavioral Research. In T. L. Beauchamp, R. R. Faden, R. J. Wallace, Jr., and L. Walters, eds. *Ethical Issues in Social Science Research*. Baltimore, Md.: The Johns Hopkins University Press, 1982.

Greenberg, D. S. Probers Charge Top Psychologist Faked Research Results. *Science and Government Report*. 17 (March 15, 1987a), 1–5.

—————. Researcher Sounds Fraud Alarm—and Loses NIMH Grant. *Science and Government Report*, 17 (April 1, 1987b), 1–3.

Greene, J. G. Stakeholder Participation and Utilization of Program Evaluation. *Evaluation Review*, 12 (April 1988), 91–116.

Greenley, J. R., and R. A. Schoenherr. Organization Effects on Client Satisfaction with Humaneness of Service. *Journal of Health and Social Behavior*, 22 (1981), 2–18.

Grichting, W. L. Do Laws Make a Difference? *Journal of Social Service Research*, 2 (1979), 245–265.

Groves, R. M., P. B. Blemer, L. E. Lyberg, J. T. Massey, W. L. Nicholls, and J. Waksberg, eds. *Telephone Survey Methodology*. Somerset, N.J.: J. Wiley, 1988.

Guttman, L. A Basis for Scaling Qualitative Data. *American Sociological Review*, 9 (1944), 139–150.

—————. The Cornell Technique for Scale and Intensity Analysis. *Educational and Psychological Measurement*, 7 (1947), 247–280.

—————. The Basis for Scalogram Analysis. In S. A. Stouffer, et al., eds. *Measurement and Prediction*. Princeton, N.J.: Princeton University Press, 1950.

Hakim, C. *Secondary Analysis in Social Research: A Guide to Data Sources and Methods with Examples*. London: George Allen and Unwin, 1982.

Hall, J. A. Development and Evaluation of a Social Work Practice Model: Communication Training for Parents of Adolescents. Doctoral Dissertation, University of Wisconsin-Madison, 1980. Dissertation Abstracts International, 42, 858A, 1981.

Hall, V. R. *Managing Behavior: Behavior Modification in School and Home*. Lawrence, Kans.: H & H Enterprises, 1971.

Harris, F. N., and W. R. Jenson. Comparisons of Multiple-Baseline Across Persons Designs and *AB* Designs with Replication: Issues and Confusions. *Behavioral Assessment*, 7 (Spring 1985), 121–127.

Harrison, W. D. Role Strain and Burnout in Child-Protective Service Workers. *Social Service Review*, 54 (1980), 31–44.

Hawkins, J. D., and B. R. Salisbury. Delinquency Prevention Programs for Minorities of Color. *Social Work Research and Abstracts,* 19 (1983), 5–12.

Hayden, M. F. Group Work: Efficacy of a Multicomponent Social Skills Program for Children in an Interracially Mixed and Mainstreamed Middle School. Doctoral dissertation, University of Wisconsin-Madison, 1988. Dissertation Abstracts International, in press.

Heberlein, T. A., and R. Baumgartner. Factors Affecting Response Rates to Mailed Questionnaires: A Quantitative Analysis of the Published Literature. *American Sociological Review,* 43 (1978), 447–462.

Heineman, M. B. The Obsolete Scientific Imperative in Social Work Research. *Social Service Review,* 55 (September 1981), 371–397.

Heise, D. R. The Semantic Differential and Attitude Research. In G. F. Summers, ed. *Attitude Measurement.* Chicago: Rand McNally, 1970.

Hepler, J. Evaluation of a Multi-Component Group Approach for Improving The Social Skills of Elementary School Children. Doctoral Dissertation, University of Wisconsin-Madison, 1986. Dissertation Abstracts International, 47, 3188A, 1987.

Hepworth, D. H., and J. A. Larsen. *Direct Social Work Practice: Theory and Skills.* Homewood, Ill.: Dorsey Press, 1982.

Higgins, P. C., and J. M. Johnson. *Personal Sociology.* New York: Praeger, 1988.

Holmes, D. S. Debriefing After Psychological Experiments: Effectiveness of Postexperimental Desensitizing. *American Psychologist,* 31 (1976), 858–875.

Holsti, O. R. *Content Analysis for the Social Sciences and Humanities.* Reading, Mass.: Addison-Wesley, 1969.

Homans, G. C. Contemporary Theory in Sociology. In R. E. L. Faris, ed. *Handbook of Modern Sociology.* Chicago: Rand McNally, 1964.

Honey, M. *Creating Rosie the Riveter: Class, Gender, and Propaganda.* Amherst, Mass.: The University of Massachussetts Press, 1984.

Hooker, E. The Adjustment of the Male Overt Homosexual. *Journal of Projective Techniques,* 21 (1957), 18–31.

Hornung, C. A., B. C. McCullough, and T. Sugimoto. Status Relationships in Marriage: Risk Factors in Spouse Abuse. *Journal of Marriage and the Family,* 43 (1981), 675–692.

Horowitz. R. Community Tolerance of Gang Violence. *Social Problems,* 34 (December 1987), 437–450.

Hoshino, G., and M. M. Lynch. Secondary Analysis of Existing Data. In R. M. Grinnell, Jr., ed. *Social Work Research and Evaluation.* Itasca, Ill.: F. E. Peacock, 1981.

Huber, B. New Human Subjects Policies Announced; Exemptions Outlined. *ASA Footnotes,* 9 (1981), 1.

Hudson, W. W. *The Clinical Measurement Package: A Field Manual.* Homewood, Ill.: Dorsey Press, 1982.

————. *CAS: The Clinical Assessment System.* Tallahassee, Fla.: WALMYR Publishing Co., 1988.

————, and K. L. Hudson, *SPPC: A Statistical Package for the Personal Computer,* Version 4.0. Tallahassee, Fla.: WALMYR, 1988.

————, and P. Nurius: *Computer-Assisted Practice: Theory, Methods, and Software.* Belmont, Calif.: Wadsworth Publishing Company (in press).

Humphreys, L. *Tearoom Trade: Impersonal Sex in Public Places.* Chicago: Aldine-Atherton, 1970.

Hyman, H. *Interviewing in Social Research.* Chicago: University of Chicago Press, 1954.

Irwin, D. M., and M. M. Bushnell. *Observational Strategies for Child Study.* New York: Holt, Rinehart and Winston, 1980.

Ivanoff, A., E. A. R. Robinson, and B. J. Blythe. Empirical Clinical Practice from a Feminist Perspective. *Social Work,* (September/October, 1987), 417–423.

Jackson, B. O., and L. B. Mohr. Rent Subsidies: An Impact Evaluation and an Application of the Random-Comparison-Group Design. *Evaluation Review,* 10 (August 1986), 483–517.

Jacobson, N. S. Problem Solving and Contingency Contracting in the Treatment of Marital Discord. *Journal of Consulting and Clinical Psychology*, 45 (1977), 92–100.

Jayaratne, S. Single-Subject and Group Designs in Treatment Evaluation. *Social Work Research and Abstracts*, 13 (1977), 35–42.

—————. Analytic Procedures for Single-Subject Designs. *Social Work Research and Abstracts*, 14 (Fall 1978), 30–40.

—————, and R. Levy. *Empirical Clinical Practice*. New York: Columbia University Press, 1979.

Jeger, A. M., and R. S. Slotnick. Community Mental Health: Toward a Behavioral-Ecological Perspective. In A. M. Jeger and R. S. Slotnick, eds. *Community Mental Health and Behavioral Ecology*. New York: Plenum Press, 1982.

Jendrek, M. P. *Through the Maze: Statistics with Computer Applications*. Belmont, Calif.: Wadsworth, 1985.

Johnson, F. C. Practice Versus Research: Issues in Teaching of Single-Subject Research Skills. *Journal of Education for Social Work*, 17 (1981), 62–68.

Johnson, J. M. *Doing Field Research*. New York: Free Press, 1975.

Johnson, S. M., and O. D. Bolstad. Methodological Issues in Naturalistic Observation: Some Problems and Solutions for Field Research. In L. A. Hamerlynck, L. C. Handy, and E. J. Mash, eds. *Behavior Change*. Champaign, Ill.: Research Press, 1973.

—————, and G. White. Self-Observation as an Agent of Behavioral Change. *Behavioral Therapy*, 2 (1971), 488–497.

Jones, J. H. *Bad Blood: The Tuskegee Syphilis Experiment*. New York: Free Press, 1982.

Jones, M. A., Reducing Foster Care Through Services to Families. *Children Today*, 5 (1976), 7–10.

Kadushin, A. *The Social Work Interview*. New York: Columbia University Press, 1972.

Kamerman, J. B., *Death in the Midst of Life:*

Social and Cultural Influences on Death, Grief and Mourning. Englewood Cliffs, N.J.: Prentice Hall, 1988.

Kassebaum, G., D. Ward, and D. Wilner. *Prison Treatment and Parole Survival*. New York: Wiley, 1971.

Katz, J. *Experimentation with Human Beings*. New York: Russell Sage Foundation, 1972.

Kazdin, A. E. *Single-Case Research Designs*. New York: Oxford University Press, 1982.

—————. Selection of Target Behaviors: The Relationship of the Treatment Focus to Clinical Dysfunction. *Behavioral Assessment*, 7 (Winter 1985), 33–47.

Kelly, J. R., and J. E. McGrath. *On Time and Method*. Beverly Hills, Calif.: Sage, 1988.

Kemeny, J. G. *A Philosopher Looks at Science*. Princeton, N.J.: D. Van Nostrand Co., 1959.

Kemper, P., D. Long, and C. Thornton. *The Supported Work Evaluation: Final Benefit-Cost Analysis*. New York: Manpower Demonstration Research Corporation, 1981.

Kenny, G. K. The Metric Properties of Rating Scales Employed in Evaluation of Research: An Empirical Examination. *Evaluation Review*, 10 (June 1986), 397–408.

Kershaw, D. N., and J. C. Small. Data Confidentiality and Privacy: Lessons from the New Jersey Negative Income Tax Experiment. *Public Policy*, 20 (1972), 257–280.

Kiecolt, K. J., and L. E. Nathan. *Secondary Analysis of Survey Data*. Beverly Hills, Calif.: Sage, 1985.

Kinsey, A. C., W. B. Pomeroy, C. E. Martin and P. H. Gebhard. *Sexual Behavior in the Human Female*. Philadelphia: Saunders, 1953.

Kirk, J., and M. L. Miller. *Reliability and Validity in Qualitative Research*. Beverly Hills, Calif.: Sage, 1986.

Kirk, K. A., and J. Karbon. Environmental Content Analysis in Children's Books. *Education Digest*, 52 (December 1986), 28–30.

Kirk, R. E. *Experimental Design: Procedures for the Behavioral Sciences*, 2d ed. Belmont, Calif.: Brooks/Cole, 1982.

Kirkham, G. L. *Signal Zero*. Philadelphia: Lippincott, 1976.

Kish, L. *Survey Sampling*. New York: Wiley, 1965.

Kline, D. The Power of the Placebo. *Hippocrates: The Magazine of Health and Medicine*, 2 (May/June 1988), 24–26.

Knudsen, D. D., H. Pope, and D. P. Irish. Response Differences to Questions on Sexual Standards: An Interview-Questionnaire Comparison. *Public Opinion Quarterly*, 31 (1967), 290–297.

Kogan, L. S. Principles of Measurement. In N. A. Polansky, ed. *Social Work Research*. Chicago: University of Chicago Press, 1975.

Korbin, J. E. Child Maltreatment in Cross-Cultural Perspective: Vulnerable Children and Circumstances. In R. J. Gelles, and J. B. Lancaster, eds. *Child Abuse and Neglect: Biosocial Dimensions*, New York: Aldine de Gruyter, 1987.

Kraemer, H. C., and S. Thiemann. *How Many Subjects? Statistical Power Analysis in Research*. Newbury Park, Calif.: Sage, 1987.

Krajick, K., and F. J. Moriarty. LIfe in the Lab: Safer than the Cell Blocks? *Corrections Magazine*, (December 1979), 15–20.

Krasnick, J. A., and D. F. Alwin. An Evaluation of a Cognitive Theory of Response-Order Effects in Survey Measurement. *Public Opinion Quarterly*, 51 (Summer 1987): 201–219.

Krathwohl, D. R. *How to Prepare a Research Proposal: Guidelines for Funding and Dissertations in the Social and Behavioral Sciences*, 3d ed. New York: Distributed by Syracuse University Press, 1988.

Krippendorff, K. *Content Analysis: An Introduction to Its Methodology*. Beverly Hills, Calif.: Sage, 1980.

Kuhn, M. H., and T. McPartland. An Empirical Investigation of Self-Attitudes. *American Sociological Review*, 19 (1954), 68–76.

Kuo, W. H., and Y. Tsai. Social Networking,

Hardiness and Immigrant's Mental Health. *Journal of Health and Social Behavior*, 27 (June 1986), 133–149.

Kutchins, H., and S. A. Kirk. The Reliability of DSM-III: A Critical Review. *Social Work Research and Abstracts*, 22 (Winter 1986), 3–12.

Lake, D. G., M. B. Miles, and R. B. Earle, eds. *Measuring Human Behavior: Tools for the Assessment of Social Functioning*. New York: Teachers College Press, 1973.

Lally, J. J. Social Determinants of Differential Allocation of Resources to Disease Research: A Comparative Analysis of Crib Death and Cancer Research. *Journal of Health and Social Behavior*, 18 (1977), 125–138.

Lander, B. *Towards an Understanding of Juvenile Delinquency*. New York: Columbia University Press, 1954.

Landrine, H. Race and Class Stereotypes of Women. *Sex Roles*, 13 (July 1985), 65–75.

Lantz, H. R., R. Schmitt, M. Britton, and E. C. Snyder. Pre-Industrial Patterns in the Colonial Family in America: A Content Analysis of Colonial Magazines. *American Sociological Review*, 33 (1968), 413–426.

Lavrakas, P. J. *Telephone Survey Methods: Sampling, Selection, and Supervision*. Beverly Hills, Calif.: Sage, 1987.

Leading Researcher Indicted On Charges of Falsifying Data for U.S. Grant. *New York Times*, April 17, 1988, 18.

Lehman, R. Statistics on the Macintosh. *Byte*, (July 1987), 207–214.

Lenihan, K. *Unlocking the Second Gate*. Department of Labor R & D Monograph 45. Washington, D.C.: U.S. Government Printing Office, 1977.

Levin, J., and J. L. Spates. Hippie Values: An Analysis of the Underground Press. *Youth and Society*, 2 (1970), 59–73.

Levitt, J. L., and W. J. Reid, Rapid-assessment Instruments for Practice. *Social Work Research and Abstracts*, 17 (1981), 13–19.

Levy, R. L., and D. G. Olson. The Single-Subject Methodology in Clinical Practice: An

Overview. *Journal of Social Service Research*, 3 (1979), 25–49.

Lewis, K. G. Children of Lesbians: Their Point of View. *Social Work*, 25 (1980), 198–203.

Liebow, E. *Talley's Corner*. Boston: Little, Brown, 1967.

Likert, R. A Technique for the Measurement of Attitudes. *Archives of Psychology*, 21, no. 140 (1932).

Linsk, N., M. W. Howe, and E. M. Pinkston. Behavioral Group Work in a Home for the Aged. *Social Work*, 20 (1975), 454–463.

Lockhart, L. L. Methodological Issues in Comparative Racial Analyses: The Case of Wife Abuse. *Social Work Research and Abstracts*, 21 (Summer 1985), 35–41.

Lofland, J. *Analyzing Social Settings*. Belmont, Calif.: Wadsworth, 1971.

————, and L. H. Lofland. *Analyzing Social Settings*, 2d ed. Belmont, Calif.: Wadsworth, 1984.

Lolley, J. L. *Your Library—What's in It for You?* New York: Wiley, 1974.

Lyons, J. A., and K. A. Serbin. Observer Bias in Scoring Boys' and Girls' Aggression. *Sex Roles*, 14 (March 1986), 301–314.

Magnet, M. Behind the Bad-News Census. *Fortune*, 103 (1981), 88–93.

Magura, S., and B. S. Moses, *Outcome Measures for Child Welfare Services: Theory and Applications*. Washington, D.C.: Child Welfare League of America, Inc., 1986.

Manning, P. K. Review of Signal Zero by George L. Kirkham. *Criminology*, 16 (1978), 133–136.

Manson, S. M. Recent Advances in American Indian Mental Health Research: Implications for Clinical Research and Training. In M. R. Miranda, and H. H. L. Kitano, eds. *Mental Health Research and Practice in Minority Communities: Development of Culturally Sensitive Training Programs*. Rockville, Md.: U.S. Department of Health and Human Services, DHHS Publication No. (ADM) 86-1466, 1986.

Marascuilo, L., and P. L. Busk. Combining Statistics for Multiple-Baseline *AB* and Replicated *ABAB* Designs Across Subjects. *Behavioral Assessment*, 10 (No. 1, 1988), 1–28.

Martin, R. M. Using Nazi Scientific Data. *Dialogue*, 25 (Autumn 1986), 403–411.

Marx, K. *Selected Writings in Sociology and Philosophy*. Edited by T. B. Bottomore and M. Rubel. Baltimore, Md.: Penguin, 1964. (originally published 1848).

Maslach, C. Burned-Out. In J. R. Folta and E. S. Deck, eds. *A Sociological Framework for Patient Care*. 2d ed. New York: Wiley, 1979.

Matarazzo, J. Interviewer Mm-Humm and Interviewee Speech Duration. *Psychotherapy: Therapy, Research and Practice*, 1 (1964), 109–114.

Mayo, J. K., R. C. Hornick, and E. G. McAnany. *Educational Reform with Television: The El Salvador Experience*. Palo Alto, Calif.: Stanford University Press, 1976.

McCaghy, C. H., and S. A. Cernovich. *Crime in American Society*. New York: Macmillan, 1987.

McCord, J. A Thirty-Year Follow-Up of Treatment Effects. *American Psychologist*, 33 (1978), 284–289.

McCord, W., and J. McCord. *Origins of Crime*. New York: Columbia University Press, 1959.

McCoy, E. Children of Single Parents. *New York Times*, May 6, 1982, 19.

McFall, R. M. Effects of Self-monitoring on Normal Smoking Behavior. *Journal of Consulting and Clinical Psychology*, 35 (1970), 135–142.

McGranahan, D. V., and I. Wayne. German and American Traits Reflected in Popular Drama. *Human Relations*, 1 (1948), 429–455.

McKillip, J. *Need Analysis: Tools for Human Services and Education*. Beverly Hills, Calif.: Sage, 1987.

McNair, R. *Assessment of Social Functioning: A Client Instrument For Practitioners*, 6, Human Services Series. Athens, Ga.: Institute of Community and Area Development, University of Georgia, 1981.

————, and E. McKinney. *Assessment of Child and Adolescent Functioning: A Practitioner's Instrument for Assessing Clients.* Athens, Ga.: Institute of Community and Area Development, University of Georgia, 1983.

McNeely, R. L., and G. Robinson-Simpson. The Truth About Domestic Violence: A Falsely Framed Issue. *Social Work,* 32 (November/December, 1987), 485–490.

Meade, A. C. The Labeling Approach to Delinquency: State of the Theory as a Function of Method. *Social Forces,* 53 (1974), 83–91.

Mechanic, D. *Medical Sociology,* 2d ed. New York: Free Press, 1978.

Melbin, M. Behavior Rhythms in Mental Hospitals. *American Journal of Sociology,* 74 (1969), 650–665.

Mendes, H. A. Single Fatherhood. *Social Work,* 21 (1976), 308–312.

Michigan Women's Commission. *Sex Discrimination in an Elementary Reading Program.* Lansing, Michigan, 1974.

Miller, D. C. *Handbook of Research Design and Social Measurement.* 3d ed. New York: McKay, 1977.

————. *Handbook of Research Design and Social Measurement,* 4th ed. New York: Longmans, 1983.

Miller, L. P. The Application of Research to Practice: A Critique. *American Behavioral Scientist,* 30 (September/October 1987), 70–80.

Mitchell, J. V. *The Ninth Mental Measurements Yearbook.* Lincoln: University of Nebraska Press, 1985.

Mitsos, S. B. Personal Constructs and the Semantic Differential. *Journal of Abnormal and Social Psychology,* 62 (1961), 433–434.

Moe, K. Should the Nazi Research Data Be Cited? *The Hastings Center Report,* 14 (December 1984), 5–7.

Moody, E. J. Urban Witches. In J. E. Nash and J. P. Spradley, eds. *Sociology: A Descriptive Approach.* Chicago: Rand McNally, 1976.

Morash, M., and J. R. Greene. Evaluating Women on Patrol: A Critique of Contemporary Wisdom. *Evaluation Review,* 10 (April 1986), 230–255.

Moser, C. A., and G. Kalton. *Survey Methods in Social Investigation.* 2d ed. New York: Basic Books, 1972.

Mueller, D. J. *Measuring Social Attitudes; A Handbook for Researchers and Practitioners.* New York: Teachers College Press, 1986.

Murray, L., R. Donovan, B. L. Kail, and L. J. Medvene. Protecting Human Subjects During Social Work Research: Researchers' Opinions. *Social Work Research and Abstracts,* 16 (1980), 25–30.

Nachmias, D., and C. Nachmias. *Research Methods in The Social Sciences.* 3d ed. New York: St. Martin's Press, 1987.

National Science Foundation Budget Summary—Fiscal 1988. Washington D.C.: U.S. Government Printing Office, 1988.

Needleman, C. Discrepant Assumptions in Empirical Research: The Case of Juvenile Court Screening. *Social Problems.* 28 (1981), 247–262.

Nelsen, J. C. Issues in Single-Subject Research for Nonbehaviorists. *Social Work Research and Abstracts,* 17 (1981), 31–37.

Nelson, M. K. Providing Family Day Care: An Analysis of Home-Based Work. *Social Problems,* 35 (February 1988), 78–94.

Newman, E., and J. Turem. The Crisis of Accountability. *Social Work,* 19 (1974), 5–16.

News and Notes. *Social Science Microcomputer Review,* 5 (1987), 576–577.

New York Office of Mental Health. *Who Are the Homeless? A Study of Randomly Selected Men Who Use the New York City Shelters.* Albany: New York Office of Mental Health, May 1982.

Nielson, J. M., ed. *Feminist Research Methods.* Boulder, Colo.: Westview Press, 1989.

Nigro, G. N., et al. Changes in the Facial Prominence of Women and Men Over the Last Decade. *Psychology of Women Quarterly,* 12 (June 1988), 225–235.

Norland, S. E., J. R. Hepburn, and D. R. Monette. Labeling Positive Differentiation: Effects on the Construction of Deviance. *Sociology and Social Research*, 61 (1976), 83–95.

Nurius, P., N. Hooyman, and A. E. Nicoll. The Changing Face of Computer Utilization in Social Work Settings. *Journal of Social Work Education*, 24 (Spring/Summer 1988), 186–197.

Ogilvie, D. M., P. J. Stone, and E. S. Shneidman. Some Characteristics of Genuine Versus Simulated Suicide Notes. In P. J. Stone, D. C. Dunphy, M. S. Smith, and D. M. Ogilvie, eds. *The General Inquirer: A Computer Approach to Content Analysis in the Behavioral Sciences*. Cambridge, Mass.: M.I.T. Press, 1966.

Oksenberg, L., A. Vinokur, and C. Cannell. The Effects of Commitment to Being a Good Respondent on Interview Performance. In C. Cannell, L. Oksenberg, and C. Converse, eds. *Experiments in Interviewing Techniques*. Ann Arbor, Mich.: University of Michigan, Institute for Social Research, 1979.

————, L. Coleman, and C. F. Cannell. Interviewer's Voices and Refusal Rates in Telephone Surveys. *Public Opinion Quarterly*, 50 (Spring 1986), 97–111.

Orme, J. G., and T. D. Combs-Orme. Statistical Power and Type II Errors in Social Work Research. *Social Work Research and Abstracts*, 22 (1986), 3–10.

————, and R. M. Tolman. The Statistical Power of a Decade of Social Work Education Research. *Social Service Review*, 60 (1986), 619–632.

Orne, M. T. On the Social Psychology of the Psychological Experiment: With Particular Reference to Demand Characteristics and Their Implications. *American Psychologist*, 17 (1962), 776–783.

Orshansky, M. Counting the Poor: Another Look at the Poverty Profile. *Social Security Bulletin*, 28 (1965), 3–29.

Osgood, C. E., G. J. Suci, and P. H. Tannenbaum. *The Measurement of Meaning*. Urbana, Ill.: University of Illinois Press, 1957.

Parker, M. W., G. H. Chynoweth, D. Blankinship, E. R. Zaldo, and M. J. Matthews. A Case for Computer Applications in Social Work. *Journal of Social Work Education*, 23 (Spring/Summer 1987), 57–68.

Peterson, J. L., and N. Zill. Marital Disruption, Parent-Child Relationships, and Behavior Problems in Children. *Journal of Marriage and the Family*, 48 (May 1986), 295–307.

Peterson, R. D. The Anatomy of Cost-Effectiveness Analysis. *Evaluation Research*, 10 (February 1986), 29–44.

Peyrot, M. Coerced Voluntarism: The Micropolitics of Drug Treatment. *Urban Life*, 13 (January 1985), 343–365.

Phillips, D. P. The Impact of Mass Media Violence on U.S. Homicides. *American Sociological Review*, 48 (August 1983), 560–568.

Phillips, J. L., Jr. *The Origins of Intellect: Piaget's Theory*. San Francisco: Freeman, 1969.

Piliavin, I., and S. Briar. Police Encounters with Juveniles. *American Journal of Sociology*, 70 (1964), 206–214.

————, S. Masters, and T. Corbett. Factors Influencing Errors in AFDC Payments. *Social Work Research and Abstracts*, 15 (1977), 3–17.

Pincus, A., and A. Minahan. *Social Work Practice: Model and Method*. Itasca, Ill.: Peacock, 1973.

Pollard, W. E. Decision Making and the Use of Evaluation Research. *American Behavioral Scientist*, 30 (July/August 1987), 661–676.

Polsky, N. *Hustlers, Beats and Others*. Chicago: Aldine, 1967.

Pressman, J., and A. Wildavsky. *Implementation: Or How Great Expectations in Washington Are Dashed in Oakland*. Berkeley, Calif.: University of California Press, 1973.

Prothro, J. W. Verbal Shifts in the American Presidency: A Content Analysis. *American Political Science Review*, 50 (1956), 726–739.

Punch, M. *The Politics and Ethics of Fieldwork*. Beverly Hills, Calif.: Sage, 1986.

Radbill, S. X. Children in a World of Violence: A History of Child Abuse. In C. H. Kempe and R. Helfer, eds. *The Battered Child*. 3d ed. Chicago: University of Chicago Press, 1980.

Rainwater, L., and D. J. Pittman. Ethical Problems in Studying a Politically Sensitive and Deviant Community. *Social Problems*, 14 (1967), 357–366.

Rank, M. R. Exiting from Welfare: A Life-Table Analysis. *Social Service Review*, 59 (September 1985), 358–376.

Rankin, J. H. The Family Context of Delinquency. *Social Problems*, 30 (1983), 466–479.

Rathje, W. L., and M. McCarthy. Regularity and Variability in Contemporary Garbage. In S. South, ed. *Research Strategies in Historical Archeology*. New York: Academic Press, 1977.

Ratzan, R. M. The Experiment That Wasn't: A Case Report in Clinical Geriatric Research. *The Gerontologist*, 21 (1981), 297–302.

Read, P. E., ed. *Foundation Fundamentals: A Research Guide for Grant Seekers*. 3d ed. New York: Foundation Center, 1986.

Reese, H. W., and W. J. Fremouw. Normal and Normative Ethics in Behavioral Science. *American Psychologist*, 39 (1984), 863–876.

Reid, P. N., and J. H. Gundlach. A Scale for the Measurement of Consumer Satisfaction with Social Services. *Journal of Social Service Research*, 7 (1983), 37–54.

Reid, W. The Social Agency as a Research Machine. *Journal of Social Service Research*, 2 (1978), 11–23.

————, and P. Hanrahan. Recent Evaluations of Social Work: Grounds for Optimism. *Social Work*, 27 (1982), 328–340.

Rein, M. Social Service Crisis, *Social Policy*. New York: Random House, 1970.

Reinherz, H., M. C. Grob, and B. Berkman. Health Agencies and a School of Social Work: Practice and Research in Partnership. *Health and Social Work*, 8 (1983), 40–47.

Reiss, A. K., and L. Rhodes. An Empirical Test of Differential Association Theory. *Journal of Research in Crime and Delinquency*, 4 (1967), 28–42.

Reynolds, P. D. *Ethical Dilemmas and Social Science Research*. San Francisco: Jossey-Bass, 1979.

Richmond-Abbott, M. *Masculine and Feminine: Sex Roles Over the Life Cycle*. Reading, Mass.: Addison-Wesley, 1983.

Ring, K., K. Wallston, and M. Corey. Mode of Debriefing as a Factor Affecting Subjective Reaction to a Milgram-Type Obedience Experiment. *Representative Research in Social Psychology*, 1 (1970), 67–88.

Robinson, J. P., and P. R. Shaver. *Measures of Social Psychological Attitudes*. Ann Arbor, Mich.: University of Michigan, Institute for Social Research, 1973.

Robinson, W. S. Ecological Correlations and the Behavior of Individuals. *American Sociological Review*, 15 (1950), 351–357.

Rose, S. D. Use of Data in Identifying and Resolving Group Problems in Goal-Oriented Treatment Groups. *Social Work with Groups*, 7 (1984), 23–36.

————. Practice Experiments for Doctoral Dissertations: Research Training and Knowledge Building. *Journal of Social Work Education*, 24 (1988), 115–122.

————, and R. Tolman. Evaluation of Client Outcomes in Groups. In M. Sundel, P. Glasser, R. Sarri, and R. Vinter, eds. *Individual Change Through Small Groups*, 2d ed. New York: Free Press, 1985.

Rosenberg, M. *The Logic of Survey Analysis*. New York: Basic Books, 1969.

Rosenhan, D. L. On Being Sane in Insane Places. *Science*, 179 (1973), 250–258.

Rosenthal, R. Covert Communication in the Psychological Experiment. *Psychological Bulletin*, 67 (1967), 356–367.

————, and R. Rosnow. *The Volunteer Subject*. New York: Wiley, 1975.

Rossi, P. H., R. A. Berk, and K. J. Lenihan. *Money, Work, and Crime: Experimental*

Evidence. New York: Academic Press, 1980.

————, and H. E. Freeman. *Evaluation: A Systematic Approach.* 3d ed. Beverly Hills, Calif.: Sage, 1985.

————, J. D. Wright, G. A. Fisher, and G. Willis. The Urban Homeless: Estimating Composition and Size. *Science,* 235 (March 13, 1987), 1336–1341.

Roth, D., J. Bean, N. Lust, and T. Saveanu. *Homelessness in Ohio: A Study of People in Need.* Columbus: Ohio Department of Mental Health, Office of Program Evaluation and Research, February 1985.

Runcie, J. F. *Experiencing Social Research.* rev. ed. Homewood, Ill.: Dorsey Press, 1980.

Russell, B. On the Notion of Cause, with Applications to the Free-Will Problem. In H. Feigel and M. Brodbeck, eds. *Readings in the Philosophy of Science.* New York: Appleton-Century-Crofts, 1953.

Rutman, L. Introduction. In L. Rutman, ed. *Evaluation Research Methods,* 2d ed. Beverly Hills, Calif.: Sage, 1984.

SAS User's Guide, 1979 edition. Cary, N.C.: SAS Institute, Inc., 1979.

Saunders, D. G. Other 'Truths' About Domestic Violence: A Reply to McNeely and Robinson-Simpson. *Social Work,* (March/April 1988), 179–183.

Saxe, L., and M. Fine. *Social Experiments: Methods for Design and Evaluation.* Beverly Hills, Calif.: Sage, 1981.

Schaeffer, N. C. Evaluating Race-Of-Interviewer Effects in a National Survey. *Sociological Methods and Research,* 8 (1980), 400–419.

Schafer, A. On Using Nazi Data: The Case Against. *Dialogue,* 25 (Autumn 1986), 413–419.

Scheaffer, R. L., W. Mendenhall, and L. Ott. *Elementary Survey Sampling,* 2d ed. Boston: Duxbury Press, 1986.

Schinke, S. P. Behavioral Assertion Training in Groups: A Comparative Clinical Study. Doctoral Dissertation, University of Wisconsin-Madison, 1976. Dissertation Abstracts International, 36, 5554A, 1976.

Schuman, H., and S. Presser. The Open and Closed Question. *American Sociological Review,* 44 (1979), 692–712.

Scott, C. Research on Mail Surveys. *Journal of The Royal Statistical Society,* Series A, 124 (1961), 143–195.

Scott, R. A. The Selection of Clients by Social Welfare Agencies: The Case of the Blind. In Y. Hasenfeld and R. A. English, eds. *Human Service Organizations.* Ann Arbor, Mich.: University of Michigan Press, 1975.

Sechrest, L., and J. Belew. Nonreactive Measures of Social Attitudes. *Applied Social Psychology Annual,* 4. Beverly Hills, Calif.: Sage, 1983.

Segal, S. P. Research on the Outcome of Social Work Therapeutic Intervention: A Review of the Literature. *Journal of Health and Social Behavior,* 13 (1972), 3–17.

Seibert, S. M., and N. V. Ramanaiah. On the Convergent and Discriminant Validity of Selected Measures of Aggression in Children. *Child Development,* 49 (1978), 1274–1276.

Seiler, L. H., and R. L. Hough. Empirical Comparisons of the Thurstone and Likert Techniques. In G. F. Summers, ed. *Attitude Measurement.* Chicago: Rand McNally, 1970.

Sellitz, C., L. S. Wrightsman, and S. W. Cook. *Research Methods in Social Relations.* 3d ed. New York: Holt, Reinhart and Winston, 1976.

Sheafor, B. W., C. R. Horejsi, and G. A. Horejsi. *Techniques and Guidelines for Social Work Practice.* Boston: Allyn and Bacon, 1988.

Shearing, C. D. How to Make Theories Untestable: A Guide to Theorists. *The American Sociologist,* 8 (1973), 33–37.

Sheley, J. F. A Study in Self-Defeat: The Public Health Venereal Disease Clinic. *Journal of Sociology and Social Welfare,* 4 (1976), 114–124.

Shepard, R. N., A. K. Romney, and S. Nerlove eds. *Multidimensional Scaling: Theory and Applications in the Behavioral Sciences.* New York: Academic Press, 1971.

Sherman, L. W., and R. A. Berk. The Specific Deterrent Effects of Arrest for Domestic Assault. *American Sociological Review*, 49 (1984), 261–271.

Shilts, R. *And the Band Played On: Politics, People, and the AIDS Epidemic*. New York: St. Martin's Press, 1987.

Shireman, J. F., and P. R. Johnson. A Longitudinal Study of Black Adoptions: Single Parent, Transracial, and Traditional. *Social Work*, 31 (May/June, 1986), 172–176.

Shulman, L. A Study of Practice Skills. *Social Work*, 23 (1978), 274–280.

Shupe, A. D., Jr., and D. G. Bromley. Walking a Tightrope: Dilemmas of Participant Observation of Groups in Conflict. *Qualitative Sociology*, 2 (1980), 3–21.

Sibley, E. Scientific Sociology at Bay? *The American Sociologist*, 6 (1971), 13–17.

Sidman, M. *Tactics of Scientific Research*. New York: Basic Books, 1960.

Siegel, K., and P. Tuckel. The Utilization of Evaluation Research: A Case Analysis. *Evaluation Review*, 9 (June 1985), 307–328.

Singer, E. Informed Consent: Consequences for Response Rate and Response Quality in Social Surveys. *American Sociological Review*, 43 (1978), 144–161.

Siporin, M. *Introduction to Social Work Practice*. New York: Macmillan, 1975.

Skinner, H. A. Benefits of Sequential Assessment. *Social Work Research and Abstracts*, 17 (1981), 21–28.

Skipper, J. K. Stripteasers: A Six Year History of Public Reaction to a Study. In L. Cargan and J. Ballantine, eds. *Sociological Footprints*. Boston: Houghton Mifflin, 1979.

Smith, A. W. Problems and Progress in the Measurement of Black Public Opinion. American Behavioral Scientist, 30 (March/April 1987), 441–455.

Smith, A. Another Look at Content Analysis: An Essay Review. *Social Work Research and Abstracts*, 18 (Winter 1982), 5–10.

Smith, H. W. *Strategies of Social Research*. 2d ed. Englewood Cliffs, N.J.: Prentice-Hall, 1981.

Smith, S. H., and D. D. McLean. *ABC's of Grantsmanship*. Reston, Va.: American Alliance for Health, Physical Education, Recreation, and Dance, 1988.

Smith, S. S., and D. Richardson. Amelioration of Deception and Harm in Psychological Research: The Important Role of Debriefing. *Journal of Personality and Social Psychology*. 44:5 (1983), 1075–1082.

Smith, T. W. That Which We Call Welfare by Any Other Name Would Smell Sweeter: An Analysis of the Impact of Question Wording on Response Patterns. *Public Opinion Quarterly*, 51 (Spring 1987), 75–83.

Socolar, M. J. *Greater Use of Exemplary Education Programs Could Improve Education for Disadvantaged Children*. GAO Report to Congress. Washington, D.C.: U.S. Government Printing Office, 1981.

Spitzer, R. L., J. Endicott, and J. Cohen. The Psychiatric Status Schedule: A Technique for Evaluating Psychopathology and Impairment in Role Functioning. *Archives of General Psychiatry*, 23 (1970), 41–55.

SPSS^X: User's Guide. New York: McGraw-Hill, 1983.

Stein, J. *Fiddler on the Roof*. New York: Crown, 1964.

Straus, M. A. Leveling, Civility, and Violence in the Family. *Journal of Marriage and the Family*, 36 (1974), 13–29.

————, and R. J. Gelles. Societal Change and Change in Family Violence from 1975 to 1985 as Revealed by Two National Surveys. *Journal of Marriage and the Family*, 48 (August 1986), 465–479.

Street, D., R. D. Vinter, and C. Perrow. *Organizations for Treatment: A Comparative Study of Institutions for Delinquents*. New York: Free Press of Glencoe, 1966.

Strickland, S. P. *Politics, Science and Dread Disease*. Cambridge, Mass.: Harvard University Press, 1972.

Sudman, S. Time Allocation on Survey Interviews and Other Field Occupations. *Public Opinion Quarterly*, 29 (1965), 638–648.

————. *Applied Sampling*. New York: Academic Press, 1976.

————. Mail Surveys of Reluctant Professionals. *Evaluation Research*, 9 (June 1985), 349–360.

————, and N. M. Bradburn. *Asking Questions*. San Francisco, Calif.: Jossey-Bass, 1982.

Suen, H. K., and D. Ary, Poisson Cumulative Probabilities of Systematic Errors in Single-Subject and Multiple-Subject Time Sampling. *Behavioral Assessment*, 8 (Spring 1986), 155–169.

Sullivan, G. L., and P. J. O'Connor. Women's Role Portrayals in Magazine Advertising: 1958–1983. *Sex Roles*, 18 (February 1988), 181–188.

Sullivan, T. J., and K. S. Thompson. *Introduction to Social Problems*. New York: Macmillan, 1988.

Sutherland, E. *Criminology*. Philadelphia: Lippincott, 1939.

Taber, M., and I. Shapiro. Social Work and Its Knowledge Base: A Content Analysis of the Periodical Literature. *Social Work*, 10 (October 1965), 100–107.

Taeuber, R. C., and R. C. Rockwell. National Social Data Series: A Compendium of Brief Descriptions. *Review of Public Data Use*. 10 (1982), 23–111.

Tallant, S. H. Evaluation of a Multi-Method Group Treatment Approach for the Management of Stress. Doctoral dissertation, University of Wisconsin-Madison, 1985. Dissertation Abstracts International, 46, 3863A, 1986.

Tate, C. N. Microcomputer Data-base Programs in Social Research. *Evaluation Review*, 10 (1986), 682–693.

Taylor, J. B. *Using Microcomputers in Social Agencies*. Beverly Hills, Calif.: Sage, 1981.

Terry, R. M. The Screening of Juvenile Offenders. *Journal of Research in Crime and Delinquency*, 4 (1967), 218–230.

Thomas, C. W., and C. M. Sieverdes. Juvenile Court Intake; An Analysis of Discretionary Decision Making. *Criminology*, 12 (1975), 413–432.

Thomas, E. J. The BESDAS Model for Effective Practice. *Social Work Research and Abstracts*, 13 (1977), 12–16.

Thurstone, L. L., and E. J. Chave. *The Measurement of Attitudes*. Chicago: The University of Chicago Press, 1929.

Timms, N., and J. Mayer. *The Client Speaks*. London: Routledge and Paul, 1971.

Tolman, R. M. The Effectiveness of Group Multi-Modal Coping Skills Training in Reducing Stress. Doctoral Dissertation, University of Wisconsin-Madison, 1984. Dissertation Abstracts International, 46, 1092A, 1985.

Toseland, R. W., and W. J. Reid. Using Rapid Assessment Instruments in a Family Service Agency. *Social Casework*, 66 (1985), 547–555.

Treas, J., and A. VanHilst. Marriage and Remarriage Rates Among Older Americans. *The Gerontologist*, 16 (1976), 132–140.

Tripodi, T. *Uses and Abuses of Social Research in Social Work*. New York: Columbia University Press, 1974.

————, and I. Epstein. The Use of Content Analysis to Monitor Social Work Performance. In *Research Techniques for Clinical Social Workers*. New York: Columbia University Press, 1980.

Trochim, W. M. K., and J. E. Davis. Computer Simulation for Program Evaluaton. *Evaluation Review*, 10 (1986), 609–634.

U.S. Bureau of the Census. *Statistical Abstract of the United States: 1988*, 108th ed. Washington, D.C.: U.S. Government Printing Office, 1987.

Vander Zanden, J. W. *Human Development*, 3d ed. New York: Knopf, 1985.

Vannicelli, M., and G. Hamilton. Sex-Role Values and Bias in Alcohol Treatment Personnel. *Advances in Alcohol and Substance Abuse*, 4 (1984), 57–68.

Vinokur, A., L. Oksenberg, and C. Cannell. Effects of Feedback and Reinforcement on the Report of Health Information. In C. Cannell, L. Oksenberg, and C. Converse, eds. *Experiments in Interviewing Tech-*

niques. Ann Arbor, Mich.: University of Michigan, Institute for Social Research, 1979.

Wagenaar, A. C., and M. B. T. Wiviott. Effects of Mandating Seatbelt Use: A Series of Surveys on Compliance in Michigan. *Public Health Reports*, 101 (September/October 1986), 505–512.

Wallace, D. A. Case For—and Against—Mail Questionnaires. *Public Opinion Quarterly*, 18 (1954), 40–52.

Ward, D. A., and G. G. Kassebaum. On Biting the Hand That Feeds: Some Implications of Sociological Evaluations of Correctional Effectiveness. In C. H. Weiss, ed. *Evaluating Social Programs: Readings in Social Action and Education*. Boston: Allyn & Bacon, 1972.

Warwick, D. P., and C. Lininger. *The Sample Survey: Theory and Practice*. New York: McGraw-Hill, 1975.

Wax, R. H. Reciprocity as a Field Technique. *Human Organization*, 11 (1952), 34–37.

Webb, E. J., D. T. Campbell, R. D. Schwartz, L. Sechrest, and J. B. Grove. *Nonreactive Measures in the Social Sciences*. Boston: Houghton Mifflin Co., 1981.

Weber, M. Science as a Vocation. In H. H. Gerth and C. W. Mills, eds. From *Max Weber: Essays in Sociology*. New York: Free Press, 1946 (originally published in 1922).

———. *The Theory of Social and Economic Organization*. Trans. by A. M. Henderson and T. Parsons. New York: Free Press. 1957 (originally published in 1925).

Weber, R. P. Computer-Aided Content Analysis: A Short Primer. *Qualitative Sociology*, 1/2 (1984), 126–147.

———. *Basic Content Analysis*. Beverly Hills, Calif.: Sage, 1985.

Weeks, M. Call Scheduling with CATI: Current Capabilities and Methods. In R. G. Groves, et al., eds. *Telephone Survey Methodology*. New York: Wiley, 1988.

Weinbach, R. W., and R. M. Grinnell, Jr. *Statistics for Social Workers*. New York: Longman, 1987.

———, and A. Rubin, eds. *Teaching Social Work Research: Alternative Programs and Strategies*. New York: Council on Social Work Education, 1980.

Weinberg, M. Sexual Modesty, Social Meanings and the Nudist Camp in M. Truzzi, ed. *Sociology and Everyday Life*. Englewood Cliffs, N.J.: Prentice-Hall, 1968.

Weiss, C. *Evalution Research: Methods for Assessing Program Effectiveness*. Englewood Cliffs, N.J.: Prentice-Hall, 1972.

Weiss, R. L., and P. E. Frohman. Behavioral Observation as Outcome Measures: Not Through a Glass Darkly. *Behavioral Assessment*, 7 (Fall 1985), 309–315.

Weitzman, S., D. Eifler, E. Hokada, and C. Ross. Sex Role Socialization in Picturebooks for Preschool Children. *American Journal of Sociology*, 72 (1972), 1125–1150.

Wells, W. D., and G. Smith. Four Semantic Rating Scales Compared. *Journal of Applied Psychology*, 44 (1960), 393–397.

Westhues, K. The Drop-In Center: A Study in Conflicting Realities. *Social Casework*, 53 (1972), 361–368.

Whyte, W. F. *Street Corner Society*. 2d ed. Chicago: University of Chicago Press, 1955.

———. Freedom and Responsibility in Research: The Springdale Case. *Human Organization*, 17 (1958), 1–2.

Wingard, D. Trends and Characteristics of California Adoptions: 1964–1982. *Child Welfare*, 66 (July/August, 1987), 303–314.

Witkin, B. R. *Assessing Needs in Educational and Social Programs*. San Francisco, Calif.: Jossey-Bass, 1984.

Wolfe, V. V., et al. Negative Affectivity in Children: A Multitrait-Multimethod Investigation. *Journal of Consulting and Clinical Psychology*, 55 (April 1987), 245–250.

Wolfgang, M. E. Confidentiality in Criminological Research and Other Ethical Issues. *Journal of Criminal Law and Criminology*, 72 (1981), 345–361.

Wollins, M. Group Care: Friend or Foe? *Social Work*, 14 (1969), 35–53.

Wright, B. *A Semantic Differential and How to Use It.* Chicago: Social Research, Inc., 1958.

Wuebben, P. L., B. C. Straits, and G. I. Schulman. *The Experiment as a Social Occa-sion.* Berkeley, Calif.: Glendessary Press, 1974.

Yates, B. T. Cost-Effectiveness Analysis and Cost-Benefit Analysis: An Introduction. *Behavioral Assessment*, 7 (Summer 1985), 207–234.

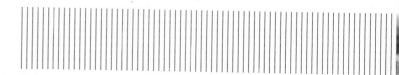

Name Index

A

Achen, C. H., 285, 316, 318, 350
Adair, J., 58, 300
Adams, S., 3
Adler, P. A., 237
Alkin, M. C., 362
Allen, G. J., 321, 328
Allen-Meares, P., 212, 218
Alt, F. B., 350
Amato, P. R., 26
Anderson, A., 200
Annis, R. C., 190
Archer, D. B., 226
Archer, R. P., 360
Armstrong, J. S., 177
Arnold, D. O., 155
Ary, D., 255
Ashcraft, N., 64

B

Babbie, E. R., 48, 138, 179
Bachman, J. G., 189
Backstrom, C. H., 147, 150
Bailey, K., 18, 65, 146, 154, 240, 258
Baker, T., 206
Bales, R. F., 212, 245, 246, 247
Barlow, D. H., 3, 18, 27, 304, 305, 308, 313, 314, 316, 317, 320, 326, 328, 330
Barth, R. P., 285
Bassuk, E. L., 156

Bauer, D. G., 433, 441, 442, 446, 447, 452
Baumgartner, R., 175, 177
Baumrind, D., 55, 58
Baxter, P. M., 481
Bean, G. J., 158
Bean, J., 157
Beasley, D., 480
Beauchamp, T. L., 74
Becerra, R. M., 120, 159
Becker, H. S., 70, 237, 460
Bedell, J. R., 360
Belew, J., 142
Bell, A. P., 136
Bell, W., 36
Bennett, C. A., 362
Bensman, J., 59
Berk, R. A., 283, 284, 340, 347, 349, 352, 353
Berkman, B., 2
Berman, P., 341
Bermant, G., 74
Berry, S. H., 177
Besag, F., 427
Besag, P., 427
Biklen, D. P., 238, 239
Billups, J., 221
Binder, A., 122
Blalock, H. M., 427
Blenkner, M., 338
Bloom, M., 306, 333
Blumer, M., 74
Blythe, B. J., 93, 331
Bodemann, M. Y., 70
Boffey, B. M., 84

Bogdan, R., 254, 264
Bolstad, O. D., 258
Bonjean, C. M., 114, 392
Bracht, N. F., 127
Bradburn, N. M., 170, 186, 189
Bransford, J. D., 99
Breuning, S. E., 66, 67
Briar, S., 4, 257
Bridge, R. G., 174
Britton, M., 215, 223
Broad, W., 75
Bromley, D. G., 236, 259, 260, 261
Bronowski, J., 25, 27
Bronson, D. E., 331, 332
Brown, J. S., 167
Brown, S. V., 83
Brunner, G. A., 185
Brunswick-Heinemann, M., 70
Buckhout, R., 256
Burch, G., 281
Burgess, G., 128
Burgess, R. G., 233
Burgess, R. L., 252, 253
Burnam, M. A., 157, 158
Bushnell, M. M., 255, 264
Busk, P. L., 317

C

Campbell, D. T., 4, 115, 223, 229, 242, 258, 275, 281, 286, 288, 289, 290, 294
Campbell, J. A., 117

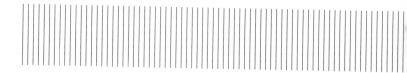

Subject Index